Handbook of Research on the Psyc
Mathematics Education
Past, Present and Future

Handbook of Research on the Psychology of Mathematics Education
Past, Present and Future

Edited by

Angel Gutiérrez

Universidad de Valencia (Valencia, Spain)

Paolo Boero

Università di Genova (Genova, Italy)

SENSE PUBLISHERS
ROTTERDAM / TAIPEI

A C.I.P. record for this book is available from the Library of Congress.

ISBN 90-77874-19-4

Published by:
Sense Publishers,
P.O. Box 21858,
3001 AW Rotterdam,
The Netherlands

Printed on acid-free paper

Printed in the UK.

To E. Fischbein, H. Freudenthal, R. Skemp,
and the other 81 colleagues who began this adventure
thirty years ago.

CONTENTS

RINA HERSHKOWITZ AND CHRIS BREEN

FOREWORD – EXPANSION AND DILEMMAS

There is nothing like a vision which turns into a reality. This volume was first conceived of in Rina's period of office as President in 2002 and has reached fruition during Chris's tenure in 2006 as we celebrate 30 years of PME. We both offer our sincere appreciation for all the cooperative work, insight and dedication that has been put into the project by the IC members who were the pioneers in processing the volume idea, the volume editors, authors and reviewers of the various chapters. Congratulations are due to all concerned!

This volume is intended to provide a window through which researchers in the mathematics education community as a whole, as well as researchers and students in other educational communities, can join with the insiders –PME members and their students– to gain an understanding of the scope and contribution of some of the various areas of PME research.

This volume also represents a milestone for the PME community as it celebrates 30 years of existence. The organization has grown considerably in numbers since its formation in 1976 and it is appropriate for PME to mark the occasion by presenting a consolidated report on important PME research interests, questions and methodologies, findings and conclusions, as well as some hints of possible future activity in the field.

Although neither of us had the opportunity to be one of the lucky few who were present at the start of PME, we are able to access some of the history through the introductory chapter of a previous PME milestone publication consisting of 7 chapters which was edited by Perla Nesher and Jeremy Kilpatrick in 1990. In the introductory chapter to that book the founder of PME and first PME President, Professor Efraim Fischbein, described the history of PME and how it came to be established. He then went on to analyze the similarities and differences between mathematics and psychology and why the two fields should communicate and cooperate for the sake of improving mathematics education (Fischbein, 1990).

A reading of both milestone PME books shows that we moved beyond debating this issue some time ago. It is clear that the learning and teaching of mathematics lies at the core of PME research, and that cognitive psychology generally forms the basis of the theoretical framework as well as most of the methodological tools, the data analyses as well as their interpretation and conclusions. In addition, this new PME30 volume showcases some new trends and tools, which interweave with the existing trends in the accumulation of the body of PME research work. We both believe that this ability to adjust to changing conditions and priorities clearly

A. Gutiérrez, P. Boero (eds.), Handbook of Research on the Psychology of Mathematics Education: Past, Present and Future, ix–xii.

demonstrates the strength and openness of both the organization and its strong research focus.

In the last chapter of the 1990 research book, Nicolas Balacheff wrote on some "Future perspectives for research on psychology of mathematics education" (Balacheff, 1990, p. 138), and sketched each of them carefully and briefly. In this present PME30 research volume, it is noticeable that each of these named future perspectives has become a main topic of research and has been addressed in several chapters of the PME30 volume.

As we have said earlier, we believe that the way in which new trends and foci of attention have evolved and developed in parallel with well established fields over the years is one of the very positive characteristics of PME as a scientific group. We would like to highlight three examples of such trends.

Socio-cultural research trends, in its broadest meaning *(At least 3 explicit chapters in this volume)*

The start of this trend at PME was clearly announced in the middle of the eighties with the lecture of Bishop (1985), and this emphasis on the impact of socio-cultural influences, including socio and/or cultural influences on learning and teaching of mathematics has accelerated in the ensuing years as contextual influences on learning becoming better understood. Through this research the focus of attention has moved from the investigation of the subjects' constructing of mathematical knowledge in laboratory conditions to their own natural conditions. Some of this research has expanded beyond a focus on the immediate context of the group and classroom to include some of the broader influences of culture and society on the teaching and learning of mathematics.

Sub-trends of this socio-cultural research trend can be identified, such as:

- Classroom research. The focus has been on the very many interactions that the student has with other students in the classroom, with the teacher, with the mathematical tasks and with learning tools such as the computer.
- Research in which factors of equity and justice have become more pronounced.
- The effects of affective elements on learning and teaching mathematics.

This growing socio-cultural trend also touches on two other important trends, which have both becoming increasingly evident as a PME field of research in the past two decades:

Teaching, teachers and teacher education *(At least three explicit chapters in this volume)*

Research in this area has often been driven from a teacher-centered approach where the focus is on a need to know more about teaching styles, teacher beliefs, teacher decision-making, and different possibilities for improving mathematics teacher education. In this area, there are also an increasing number of reports of collaborative research undertaken by researchers with teachers as well as an interest in the way in which teachers might develop valid ways of researching their own practice. A second aspect of this research trend overlaps with classroom research where the teacher is seen as a partner of the learning/teaching process and interacts with students to influence the way in which they construct knowledge.

Computer tools in mathematics learning and teaching *(At least two explicit chapters in this volume)*

The source of this trend was influenced by the development and increased availability of computers and computerized tools as cultural artifacts. Research has focused on the introduction and potential contribution to the learning of mathematics of both "general" computerized tools such as Excel, as well as those, which were created especially for their use in learning mathematics. Researchers have been interested in the effects on the mathematics learning/teaching processes and on mathematics as a learning subject. Do computerized tools broaden or lessen the potential scope of the mathematical topic being investigated, or does this depend on the special context? The voice of this debate is still being heard. Another issue in this field that has been the focus of recent observation and analysis has been the processes by which students use computerized tools in learning mathematics in computerized environment, and the extent to which these tools can become assimilated as part of the students' inner instruments.

This brief summary of three recent trends in PME research highlights the way in which the field of research inevitably changes over a period of thirty years. We have previously commended the way in which PME as an organization has been able to naturally grow in size and expand its focus of attention over its thirty years of existence. As we celebrate the publication of this volume which commemorates these thirty years we would like to draw attention to the degree to which these three trends draw on different paradigms, theories and research methodologies from those which dominated past studies. As a research organization we have to consider the dilemmas that this raises for the community. We have to consider questions such as:

- What are the inner relationships between research paradigms and research methodologies? Do they fit together? (Schoenfeld, 1994). Do such methodologies exist? For example: Which methodologies are appropriate for a research domain such as classroom research?
- How do we ensure that we maintain an appropriate balance between the unifying trend of using established and familiar research methodological tools and applications of scientific language while, at the same time, embracing the insights that are emerging from new ideas and paradigms?
- How do we try to ensure that the unifying pressures of globalization of knowledge and internationally comparative research findings do not prevent us from ensuring that the critical voices of difference as regards research priorities, agenda and methodologies that have been silenced in a variety of ways across the world can still be heard at our annual conference?

We are both convinced that PME has an important and crucial role to play in addressing these questions. The strength of PME lies in the varied and textured nature of its research and in the way that it provides a dynamic forum for international mathematics educators to meet on an annual basis to exchange ideas and perspectives in a tolerant and open-minded conversational space. The annual meeting provides the seed for this international exchange of ideas through its various options of plenary presentations, research reports, research fora, and oral and poster presentations and particularly throught he Discussion Groups and Working Sessions. Many cutting edge developments in the field have resulted from these interactions and the way in which PME members have been prepared to engage with issues and dilemmas in constructive ways over the period of thirty years.

This volume provides a very welcome opportunity for us to take stock and acknowledge the rich and diverse spread of PME research and the significant contribution that this research makes to mathematics education across the world. We are both proud to be associated with its publication.

REFERENCES

Balacheff, N. (1990). Future perspectives for research in the psychology of mathematics education. In P. Nesher & J. Kilpatrick (Eds.), *Mathematics and cognition: A research synthesis by the International Group for the Psychology of Mathematics Education* (pp. 135–148). Cambridge, UK: Cambridge University Press.

Bishop, A. J. (1985). The social psychology of mathematics education. In L. Streefland (Ed.), *Proceedings of the 9th PME International Conference, 2*, 1–13.

Fischbein, E. (1990). Introduction. In P. Nesher & J. Kilpatrick (Eds.), *Mathematics and cognition: A research synthesis by the International Group for the Psychology of Mathematics Education* (pp. 1–13). Cambridge, UK: Cambridge University Press.

Nesher, P., & Kilpatrick, J. (Eds.). (1990). *Mathematics and cognition: A research synthesis by the International Group for the Psychology of Mathematics Education.* Cambridge, UK: Cambridge University Press.

Schoenfeld, A. H. (1994). Some notes on the enterprise. In E. Dubinsky, A. H. Schoenfeld, & J. Kaput (Eds.), *Research in collegiate mathematics education* (Vol. IV, pp. 1–20). Providence: American Mathematical Society.

Rina Hershkowitz (PME President 2001 - 2004[1])
Science Teaching Department
The Weizmann Institute of Science
Rehovot 76100 (Israel)
rina.hershkovitz@weizmann.ac.il

Chris Breen (PME President 2004 - 2007)
School of Education
University of Cape Town, Private Bag
Rondebosch, 7701 (South Africa)
cb@humanities.uct.ac.za;
http://www.chrisbreen.net

[1] Peter Gates was Acting President of PME for the last year of Rina's term of office.

ANGEL GUTIERREZ AND PAOLO BOERO

INTRODUCTION

The *International Group for the Psychology of Mathematics Education* (PME Group)[1] was founded in 1976 in Karlsruhe (Germany), during the ICME-3 Congress. The first meeting of the PME Group took place in Utrecht (The Netherlands) in 1977, organized by Hans Freudenthal. Since then, every year the PME Group has met somewhere in one of the five Continents. From the very beginning, the PME Group developed as one of the most interesting and successful examples of international co-operation in the field of educational research (not only in mathematics education!). Nowadays such development still continues –not exempt of tensions sometimes–, as a result of a continuous effort of the PME Group to evolve, to develop new ways of looking into mathematics teaching and learning, and to integrate new ideas coming from other scientific research fields. As a consequence, we believe, the PME Group is the most influential forum of research in mathematics education, and the proceedings of the PME conferences are a primary source of information for any researcher in mathematics education, since they summarize the state of the art at that time in the field (all the proceedings are available in ERIC; A list can be found at the end of this Introduction).

There are several reasons that can explain the success of that initiative: The human and scientific quality of the founding members; The fact that the growth of "PME" –as the Group is familiarly named– happened during the full development of mathematics education as a research domain, contributing to that development, but also profiting from it; The diversity of research traditions and developments in mathematics education, from all over the world, that converged and merged in the PME community, which motivated and fostered co-operation between different countries and research orientations; The intrinsic interest and fascination of a systematic co-operation between mathematics educators, psychologists and mathematicians engaged in the improvement of the teaching and learning of mathematics.

The aim of this volume is to account for the quantity and quality of the research work performed and enhanced within the PME Group since its origins, 30 years ago, with an eye to future developments. Such an enterprise was started by the PME International Committee, and designed according to the following steps:

– choice of the target public,

---

[1] Detailed information about the activities of the PME Group can be found in its web page http://igpme.org

A. Gutiérrez, P. Boero (eds.), Handbook of Research on the Psychology of Mathematics Education: Past, Present and Future, 1–10.

– choice of criteria for organizing the surveys,
– choice of areas for the different chapters, and
– choice of authors and reviewers.

This volume is willing to act as a point of reference for future research in mathematics education. It should be useful mainly to both researchers in mathematics education and mathematics teachers' trainers with any level of expertise in the field. However, particular attention was paid to the needs of people approaching the task of research in mathematics education –particularly PhD students– and to persons having difficulties in keeping regular contacts with research in mathematics education at the international level.

Having as a core aim of this volume to give an overview of the research made by the PME community, a decision was necessary respect to a question inherent to the scope of the synthesis to be made: The chapters could survey research contributions produced strictly within the PME Group (ignoring external developments or influences from the exterior), or could survey the whole field of research in mathematics education (within and out of the PME Group). An intermediate position was adopted, and the authors were requested to make an effort to focus mainly on the contributions presented at the PME conferences, but keeping also into account their possible origin out of the PME environment and their further developments in other media different from the proceedings of the PME conferences (articles on international journals, books, etc.).

This choice did not exclude relevant research orientations or research areas in mathematics education from the volume. Indeed, if we consider this volume and compare its contents with other survey volumes (handbooks) of research in mathematics education recently published, we must recognize that most research in mathematics education is well represented in the PME Group, and that many research contributions produced within the PME Group have been very influential in orienting research in several areas of mathematics education.

In concordance to the above mentioned core aim of this volume, the chapters were organized to provide a wide unbiased account of that research in specific areas. The structure of the chapters was planned to avoid two opposite styles of surveying: The "list style", resulting in a mere flat description of contributions, and the "unilateral reconstruction style", according to which an author interprets the evolution of research in a given area of mathematics education from his/her personal research interests and orientation. The guidelines given to the authors of the chapters reflected the decision to meet the challenge of writing personal surveys of a field that try to account for the variety of paradigms, positions and contributions apparent within the PME Group, to summarize key issues, to contrast or compare perspectives, to show the inner evolution of PME research in the given field, and also to include indications of possible potential developments for future research in the field. And this is what the authors have done!

The choice of areas for the different chapters was a delicate issue (even more delicate than the previous ones). Indeed it was not possible neither to consider only the present PME classification of research domains (which reflects the present status of our research), nor to create an abstract set of areas, trying to take into account "old" ones and "new" ones. The base for the choice of the areas of the different chapters was the present situation of the research in PME, but an effort was made through the choice of the authors and formal and informal contacts with them in order to ensure that they would keep into account both the present main orientations of research and their roots (this is evident particularly for those chapters dealing with areas that emerged as relevant areas in the last two decades, or even in the last decade).

On the other side, we have not tried to include in the volume a chapter for "every" research area present in the PME proceedings, but we have selected those research areas having a consolidated research agenda in the PME Group, more than just a set of unconnected reports. In some cases, the chapters evidence the characteristics of consolidated research areas, with research agendas smoothly evolving along the time. In other cases, the chapters well represent tensions that are inherent in the PME Group as a permanently "young" community, tensions inherent in the evolution of the cultural and scientific policy of the PME Group, and concerning the leading scientific orientations for the future.

The choice of authors was not intended to "give a prize" to someone, or to recognize a leading personality in a given field of research. Besides a high scientific quality and great expertise in the area of a chapter, the facts of being within the PME research community for a long time, having had responsibilities in promoting working groups, discussion groups, or having been a member of the International Committee, were considered as qualities that could ensure the authors would have necessaries knowledge of the PME activity, experience, capability, and equilibrium and distance from personal research orientations to ensure that they would write top quality chapters. With them, some young but knowledgeable researchers have collaborated in the writing of some chapters.

On the other side, an effort was also made to represent the variety of regions and cultural orientations present within the PME Group. Here we must recognize that it was not easy to get a final group of authors as representative as we intended, mainly due to the barrier of native languages –a delicate issue in an international organization like the PME Group. This caused the set of authors to be more biased in favour of the English-speaking countries than the present distribution of PME people is[2].

A strategy we could use for some chapters was to form teams of researchers from different countries and research traditions (or scientific orientations) to cooperate in writing the same chapter. We must say that we were very lucky in having joined those groups of authors; It would have been very difficult to make better teams.

As concerns the reviewing process, it was decided that each chapter had to be reviewed by two PME members, both having great expertise in the area of the paper, one of them near to the scientific orientation of the authors, and the other far from it. A main difficulty was to get people who, fitting the scientific requirements,

---

2 60% of the authors, against an average of almost 44% of PME members in 2000-2005, are native English speakers. On the other side, 37% of the reviewers are native English speakers.

could accept the difficult task of reviewing a survey chapter, in some cases in a narrow time.

The volume includes 15 chapters, organized into five sections, devoted to the main research domains of interest to the PME Group. The first section summarizes cognitively oriented research on learning and teaching specific mathematics content areas –algebra, geometry and measurement, and numbers. The second section has the same orientation as the first one, but it focuses on mathematical transversal areas –young children's development, advanced mathematical thinking, deductive reasoning, and visualization.

The third section presents the PME research centred on the teaching and learning of mathematics in technologically rich environments; Most research on computer based environments by the PME Group was centred on algebra, calculus, and geometry, so the chapters of this section summarize the research on those mathematics contents.

The fourth section is devoted to the research on social aspects of mathematics education like affect, gender, equity, constructivism, and other socio-cultural elements influencing the teaching and learning of mathematics.

Finally, the fifth section includes two chapters summarizing the PME research on teachers training and professional life of mathematics teachers.

Coming to the end of this Introduction, we want to acknowledge the enormous effort of the authors, who unselfishly have devoted a great part of their time to write the top quality chapters in this volume, and the reviewers, who have also devoted many time to make constructive comments on the chapters to raise still more their quality -the names of the reviewers can be found at the end of this Introduction. We must also acknowledge that the task of co-ordinating the production of this volume was made easier by some circumstances: The commitment of the International Committee, particularly our President, in giving us advice in several crucial moments of the production; The collaborative style of work of authors and reviewers, who have made their best to ensure the quality of the chapters; The help of the PME executive secretary and other PME members, who provided the authors or the editors with first hand information about the early years of the PME Group.

Lastly, we want to use these pages to render a tribute to all people who have collaborated in making so successful the project, initiated 30 years ago, of creating a place, the PME Group, where any person concerned with the mathematics education could meet other persons with similar interests and share their research activity:

- Thanks to the thousands of (more or less) anonymous mathematics researchers who have felt the need to communicate with their colleagues and have found in the PME meetings an adequate place. The PME Group is alive thanks to all them.
- Thanks to those persons who volunteered as members of the International Committee. They assumed the responsibility of driving the PME Group and taking decisions affecting its scientific orientation. In particular, special thanks to the Presidents of the PME Group.

- Thanks to Joop van Dormolen, for many years the executive secretary of the PME Group. He has been a tireless worker in the shadow, taking care of every administrative aspect of the Group and making easier others' work.
- Thanks to all those anonymous persons, from undergraduate students to senior researchers, who, year after year, accepted the responsibility of collaborating in the organization of a PME conference. Those having had such experience know that, for a year, their main endeavour was to work to have everything ready to ensure the success of the next conference.

Angel Gutiérrez
Departamento de Didáctica de la Matemática
Universidad de Valencia
Apartado 22045
46071 Valencia (Spain)
angel.gutierrez@uv.es
http://www.uv.es/Angel.Gutierrez

Paolo Boero
Dipartimento di Matematica
Università di Genova
Via Dodecaneso, 35
16146 Genova (Italy)
boero@dima.unige.it

REVIEWERS OF THE CHAPTERS IN THIS VOLUME

The following persons collaborated with the editors of this volume by reviewing one of its chapters:

Janet Ainley (UK)
Abraham Arcavi (Israel)
Nicolas Balacheff (France)
Mariolina Bartolini Bussi (Italy)
José Carrillo (Spain)
Paul Cobb (USA)
Martin Downs (Greece)
Jeff Evans (UK)
Athanasios Gagatsis (Greece)
Nuria Gorgorió (Spain)
Markku Hannula (Finland)
Lulu Healy (Brazil)
Barbara Jaworski (UK)
Keith Jones (UK)
Jean-Baptiste Lagrange (France)
Carolyn Maher (USA)
Nicolina Malara (Italy)
Joanna Mamona-Downs (Greece)
John Monaghan (UK)
Pearla Nesher (Israel)
Bernard Parzysz (France)
Erkki Pehkonen (Finland)
Demetra Pitta (Cyprus)
David Reid (Canada)
Adalira Sáenz-Ludlow (Colombia/USA)
Judith Sowder (USA)
David Tall (UK)

PRESIDENTS OF THE INTERNATIONAL GROUP FOR THE PSYCHOLOGY OF MATHEMATICS EDUCATION

The following persons acted as Presidents of the PME Group:

Efraim Fischbein (Israel)	1977 - 1980
Richard R. Skemp (UK)	1980 - 1982
Gérard Vergnaud (France)	1982 - 1984
Kevin F. Collis (Australia)	1984 - 1986
Pearla Nesher (Israel)	1986 - 1988
Nicolas Balacheff (France)	1988 - 1990
Kathleen M. Hart (UK)	1990 - 1992
Carolyn Kieran (Canada)	1992 - 1995
Stephen Lerman (UK)	1995 - 1998
Gilah C. Leder (Australia)	1998 - 2001
Rina Hershkowitz (Israel)	2001 - 2004
Chris Breen (South Africa)	2004 - 2007

LOCAL ORGANIZERS OF THE PME INTERNATIONAL CONFERENCES

The following persons acted as Chairs of the local organizing committees of the PME International Conferences:

No.	Year	Chair	Place
PME 1	1977	Hans Freudenthal	Utrecht (Holland)
PME 2	1978	Elmar Cohors-Fresenborg	Osnabrück (Germany)
PME 3	1979	David Tall	Warwick (UK)
PME 4	1980	Robert Karplus	Berkeley (USA)
PME 5	1981	Claude Comiti	Grenoble (France)
PME 6	1982	Alfred Vermandel	Antwerpen (Belgium)
PME 7	1983	Rina Hershkowitz	Shoresh (Israel)
PME 8	1984	Beth Southwell	Sidney (Australia)
PME 9	1985	Leen Streefland	Noordwijkerhout (Holland)
PME 10	1986	Leone Burton and Celia Hoyles	London (UK)
PME 11	1987	Jacques C. Bergeron	Montreal (Canada)
PME 12	1988	Andrea Borbás	Veszprem (Hungary)
PME 13	1989	Gérard Vergnaud	Paris (France)
PME 14	1990	Teresa Navarro de Mendicuti	Oaxtepex (Mexico)
PME 15	1991	Paolo Boero	Assisi (Italy)
PME 16	1992	William E. Geeslin	Durham (USA)
PME 17	1993	Nobuhiko Nohda	Tsukuba (Japan)
PME 18	1994	João Pedro da Ponte	Lisbon (Portugal)
PME 19	1995	Luciano Meira	Recife (Brazil)
PME 20	1996	Angel Gutiérrez	Valencia (Spain)
PME 21	1997	Erkki Pehkonen	Lahti (Finland)
PME 22	1998	Alwyn Olivier	Stellenbosch (South Africa)
PME 23	1999	Orit Zaslavsky	Haifa (Israel)
PME 24	2000	Tadao Nakahara	Hiroshima (Japan)
PME 25	2001	Marja van den Heuvel-Panhuizen	Utrecht (Holland)
PME 26	2002	Anne D. Cockburn	Norwich (UK)
PME 27	2003	A. J. (Sandy) Dawson	Honolulu (USA)
PME 28	2004	Marit J. Høines	Bergen (Norway)
PME 29	2005	Helen L. Chick	Melbourne (Australia)
PME 30	2006	Jarmila Novotná	Prague (Czech Republic)

PROCEEDINGS OF THE PME CONFERENCES

The table below indicates the ERIC ED numbers for the proceedings of the PME International Conferences. Many PME proceedings can also be freely retrieved from the ERIC web page http://www.eric.ed.gov/.

PME INTERNATIONAL GROUP CONFERENCES

No.	Year	Place	ERIC number
1	1977	Utrecht, The Netherlands	Not available
2	1978	Osnabrück, Germany	ED226945
3	1979	Warwick, United Kingdom	ED226956
4	1980	Berkeley, USA	ED250186
5	1981	Grenoble, France	ED225809
6	1982	Antwerp, Belgium	ED226943
7	1983	Shoresh, Israel	ED241295
8	1984	Sydney, Australia	ED306127
9	1985	Noordwijkerhout, The Netherlands	ED411130 (v. 1), ED411131 (v. 2)
10	1986	London, United Kingdom	ED287715
11	1987	Montréal, Canada	ED383532
12	1988	Veszprém, Hungary	ED411128 (v. 1), ED411129 (v. 2)
13	1989	Paris, France	ED411140 (v. 1), ED411141 (v. 2), ED411142 (v. 3)
14	1990	Oaxtepex, Mexico	ED411137 (v. 1), ED411138 (v. 2), ED411139 (v. 3)
15	1991	Assisi, Italy	ED413162 (v. 1), ED413163 (v. 2), ED413164 (v. 3)
16	1992	Durham, USA	ED383538
17	1993	Tsukuba, Japan	ED383536
18	1994	Lisbon, Portugal	ED383537
19	1995	Recife, Brazil	ED411134 (v. 1), ED411135 (v. 2), ED411136 (v. 3)
20	1996	Valencia, Spain	ED453070 (v. 1), ED453071 (v. 2), ED453072 (v. 3), ED453073 (v. 4), ED453074 (addenda)
21	1997	Lahti, Finland	ED416082 (v. 1), ED416083 (v. 2), ED416084 (v. 3), ED416085 (v. 4)
22	1998	Stellenbosch, South Africa	ED427969 (v. 1), ED427970 (v. 2), ED427971 (v. 3), ED427972 (v. 4)
23	1999	Haifa, Israel	ED436403
24	2000	Hiroshima, Japan	ED452301 (v. 1), ED452302 (v. 2), ED452303 (v. 3), ED452304 (v. 4)
25	2001	Utrecht, The Netherlands	ED466950
26	2002	Norwich, United Kingdom	ED476065

No.	Year	Place	ERIC number
27	2003	Hawai'i, USA	Being processed. Also available in http://onlinedb.terc.edu.
28	2004	Bergen, Norway	Being processed.
29	2005	Melbourne, Australia	Being processed.

PME NORTH AMERICAN CHAPTER (PME-NA) CONFERENCES

The table below indicates the ERIC ED numbers for the proceedings of PME-NA Conferences published separately from the procedings of PME International Conferences. Many PME-NA proceedings can also be freely retrieved from the ERIC web page http://www.eric.ed.gov/.

No.	Year	Place	ERIC number
3	1981	Minnesota, USA	ED223449
4	1982	Georgia, USA	ED226957
5	1983	Montreal, Canada	ED289688
6	1984	Wisconsin, USA	ED253432
7	1985	Ohio, USA	ED411127
8	1986	Michigan, USA	ED301443
10	1988	Illinois, USA	ED411126
11	1989	New Jersey, USA	ED411132 (v. 1), ED411133 (v. 2)
13	1991	Virginia, USA	ED352274
15	1993	Califomia, USA	ED372917
16	1994	Louisiana, USA	ED383533 (v. 1), ED383534 (v. 2)
17	1995	Ohio, USA	ED389534
18	1996	Florida, USA	ED400178
19	1997	Illinois, USA	ED420494 (v. 1), ED420495 (v. 2)
20	1998	North Carolina, USA	ED430775 (v. 1), ED430776 (v. 2)
21	1999	Cuernavaca, Mexico	ED433998
22	2000	Arizona, USA	ED446945
23	2001	Utah, USA	ED476613
24	2002	Georgia, USA	ED471747
26	2004	Toronto, Canada	Being processed.
27	2005	Virginia, USA	Being processed.

CAROLYN KIERAN

RESEARCH ON THE LEARNING AND TEACHING OF ALGEBRA

A Broadening of Sources of Meaning

The learning and teaching of algebra has always been a fundamental and vibrant stream of the research carried out within the PME community – from the 1st PME conference in 1977 to the 29th in 2005 when 33 algebra research reports were presented. While the themes of the past are still to be found in the algebra research of the present, there have been some major shifts. Earlier research tended to focus on algebraic concepts and procedures, algebra word problem solving, and students' difficulties in making the transition from arithmetic to algebra. The letter-symbolic was the primary algebraic mode that was investigated and theoretical frameworks for analyzing research data rarely went beyond the Piagetian. However, over time, PME algebra research broadened to encompass other representations, the use of technological tools, different perspectives on the content of algebra, and a wide variety of theoretical frameworks for thinking about algebra learning/teaching and for analyzing data. Each new phase of the research, in fact, embedded ongoing themes as it expanded its scope in an attempt to more fully explain algebra learning and teaching. This process, the highlights of which are the subject of this chapter, is one of ever-increasing complexity as researchers continue to develop theoretical and empirical foundations for their descriptions of algebra teaching and for the meaning making, and its myriad paths, engaged in by students of algebra.

Examples have been drawn from the body of algebra research over the 30-year history of PME. They reflect the main themes of interest of PME algebra researchers over the years. Some date back to the first years and continue to today; others are more recent. In order to capture the newer interests as they came into existence, the main highlights are presented more or less chronologically according to themes – in fact, three theme-groups, which emerged over the 30-year history of PME algebra research (see Table 1). The first theme-group, which points to the interests of PME algebra researchers from the start of PME in 1977, includes a focus on the transition from arithmetic to algebra, on variables and unknowns, equations and equation solving, and algebra word problems. During approximately the mid-1980s, the field of PME algebra research witnessed the growth of themes that reflected an interest in algebra as generalization, and a focus on multiple representations and the use of new technological learning tools. Then, during the mid-1990s, PME algebra research began to encompass themes related to algebraic

A. Gutiérrez, P. Boero (eds.), Handbook of Research on the Psychology of Mathematics Education: Past, Present and Future, 11–49.

thinking among elementary school students, a focus on the algebra teacher and algebra teaching, as well as on the learning of algebra within dynamic environments that included the dynamic modeling of physical situations.

Table 1. Major themes that have emerged over the 30-year history of PME algebra research from 1977 to 2006.

Time Period	*Theme-Groups that emerged*
1977 to 2006	1. Transition from arithmetic to algebra, variables and unknowns, equations and equation solving, and algebra word problems.
Mid-1980s to 2006	2. Use of technological tools and a focus on multiple representations and generalization.
Mid-1990s to 2006	3. Algebraic thinking among elementary school students, a focus on the algebra teacher/teaching, and dynamic modeling of physical situations and other dynamic algebra environments.

However, the new themes that arose during these time periods did not simply "join" the existing research. Changing theoretical and methodological frameworks over the years altered the ways in which even the earliest themes came to be researched. Thus, the story to be recounted in this chapter, while it deals primarily with the main theme-groups of the research conducted by members of the PME community, also attempts to suggest the ways in which the process of conducting this research changed as theoretical and methodological frames shifted. The first three sections of this chapter treat the three main theme-groups with their accompanying theoretical and methodological considerations. The fourth and final section of the chapter integrates these themes within a discussion of sources of meaning in algebra learning, and demonstrates that research on the ways in which students derive meaning in algebra has widened considerably in perspective over the years.

The body of literature that forms the foundation for this review chapter is obviously the PME Proceedings during the past 30 years. However, when a PME research report was further elaborated and subsequently published in a journal article or book, it is the journal article or book that will generally be cited. As well, for PME research that has been situated within a broader field of research, a reference to this broader field will often be provided. It is also noted that additional PME algebra resources exist –resources that more fully discuss some of the ideas referred to in this chapter– for example, the chapter, "Cognitive Processes Involved in Learning School Algebra," in the PME monograph, *Mathematics and Cognition* (Nesher & Kilpatrick, 1990), and the volume, *Perspectives on School Algebra* (Sutherland, Rojano, Bell & Lins, 2001), which was the culmination of the 1990s activity of the PME Working Group on Algebraic Processes and Structure. Other sources in the literature to which members of the PME community of algebra researchers have contributed include: Wagner & Kieran (1989), Grouws (1992), Bednarz, Kieran & Lee (1996), Bishop, Clements, Keitel, Kilpatrick & Laborde (1996), Chick, Stacey, Vincent & Vincent (2001), Kieran, Forman & Sfard (2001), English (2002), Mason & Sutherland (2002) and Stacey, Chick & Kendal (2004).

THEME-GROUP ONE: THE ORIGINAL STRANDS WITH THEIR FOCUS ON THE TRANSITION FROM ARITHMETIC TO ALGEBRA, ON VARIABLES AND UNKNOWNS, EQUATIONS AND EQUATION SOLVING, AND ALGEBRA WORD PROBLEMS

In its early years, the PME community of algebra researchers generally considered the algebra curriculum as a given, focusing attention primarily on students' thinking and methods as they encountered the symbols and procedures that were the standard algebra fare in the beginning years of high school (Kieran, 1979, 1990). The historical development of algebra as a symbol system served both as a backdrop for researchers' thinking about the evolution in students' usage of symbolism (see, e.g., Harper, 1981, 1987) as well as a theoretical framework for more broadly interpreting empirical data of algebra learning research (e.g., Filloy, 1990). An additional perspective that was current in those early years was the view of algebra as generalized arithmetic (Booth, 1981, 1984). Meaning for algebra was to be derived from its numerical foundations, but as well it was expected that students would learn to see structural similarities and equivalences in the expressions and equations they transformed. However, the fact that the signs and symbols in algebra were to be interpreted differently from the ways in which they were interpreted in arithmetic created discontinuities for students beginning algebra.

Interpreting algebraic signs, unknowns, and variables

While arithmetic and algebra share many of the same signs and symbols, such as the equal sign, addition and subtraction signs, even the use of letters (e.g., Area (A) = Length (L) x Width (W)), many conceptual adjustments are required of the beginning algebra student as these signs and symbols shift in meaning from those commonly held in arithmetic. Early research on the ways in which students interpret algebraic symbols tended to focus on cognitive levels (Küchemann, 1981), prior arithmetic experience and methods of thinking (Booth, 1984), and difficulty with notation such as the equal sign with its multiple meanings (Kieran, 1981; Vergnaud, 1984) and the use of brackets (Kieran, 1979). Included in this strand of research were teaching experiments aimed at, for example, extending students' meaning for the equal sign from the "do-something signal" (Behr, Erlwanger & Nichols, 1976) prevalent in elementary school arithmetic reasoning to a consideration of the symmetric and transitive character of equality (Vergnaud, 1988) and its use in algebraic equations (e.g., Herscovics & Kieran, 1980).

In coming to make sense of algebra, students' prior arithmetical usage of letters in formulas and as labels has to make room for letters as unknowns and as variables, and later as parameters. Early research on students' thinking about the literal symbols of algebra disclosed a host of undeveloped interpretations (see Collis, 1974; Küchemann, 1981; Wagner, 1981; Clement, 1982). In a teaching experiment designed specifically to encourage the acquisition of the notion of letter as generalized number, Booth (1982, 1983) found strong resistance on the part of students to the assimilation of this idea. Among the large number of PME studies that have continued to be devoted to researching students' difficulties in understanding various aspects of the concept of variable is the work of Ursini and her colleagues (e.g., Ursini, 1990; Ursini & Trigueros, 1997; Trigueros & Ursini, 1999), Fujii (1993) and Bills (1997, 2001). Also included in this body of work is the research of Stacey and MacGregor (1997) on the presence of multiple referents and shifts in the meaning of the unknown, and that of Vlassis (2004) on the polysemy of the minus sign in algebraic expressions and equations. In studies involving older students, Furinghetti and Paola (1994) have found that only a small minority could adequately describe differences among parameters, unknowns, and variables (see also Bloedy-Vinner, 1994, 2001, on parameters, and Kopelman, 2002, on free and bound variables).

Some of the recent work within this theme group has focused on additional factors that impinge on students' interpretation of algebraic notation: For example, what one is able to perceive and prepared to notice (Sfard & Linchevski, 1994) and the nature of the instructional activity (Wilson, Ainley & Bills, 2003). These latter studies suggest some of the changes in perspective present in current research that nevertheless continues the study of a conceptual area that has been of research interest since PME's first days.

Working with expressions, equations, and equation solving

Early PME research involving algebraic forms disclosed students' difficulties in interpreting expressions such as $a + b$ as both *process* and *name/object* (an obstacle related to the findings of Davis, 1975, and to the notion of *acceptance of lack of closure*, developed by Collis, 1974). Teaching experiments intended to help students construct meaning for expressions by means of, for example, rectangular area models (Chalouh & Herscovics, 1988) and for equations by means of arithmetic identities (Herscovics & Kieran, 1980) suggested that students could more easily construct meaning for equations than for expressions. This was borne out by the results of the research of Wagner, Rachlin and Jensen (1984) who noted that students tried to add "= 0" to any expression they were asked to simplify.

A significant number of early studies focused on the equation-solving procedures of beginning algebra students: (i) Intuitive approaches, which included the use of number facts, counting techniques, and cover-up methods (Bell, O'Brien & Shiu, 1980; Booth, 1983); (ii) Trial-and-error substitution (Kieran, 1985); and (iii) Formal methods (Whitman, 1976; Kieran, 1983, 1988). Equation-solving errors of students have also been of research interest: For example, ignoring the minus sign preceding a pair of numbers to be combined (Herscovics & Linchevski, 1994); reduction errors (Carry, Lewis & Bernard, 1980); and erroneous checking behavior (Perrenet & Wolters, 1994; Pawley, 1999). More recent research has also begun to inquire into the methods used by students to solve inequalities (e.g., Tsamir & Bazzini, 2002), noting that students intuitively use the balance model to do the same thing to both sides of an inequality, and continue to draw on equation-related analogies when dividing both sides by a not-necessarily positive value. Systems of equations have, of late, also attracted research attention. Filloy, Rojano and Solares (2003, 2004), who observed students working with problems that can be solved by systems of equations, found that these students, who had already been introduced to the solving of one-unknown linear equations, tended to make more sense of comparison-based than substitution-based solving methods.

Solving algebra word problems

Another of the discontinuities faced by beginning algebra students is the introduction of formal representations and methods to solve problems that, up to this stage in their schooling, have been handled intuitively. Because arithmetic is largely procedural, students are used to thinking about the operations they use to solve a problem rather than the operations that they should use to represent the relations of the problem situation. Not only does setting up an equation require a different way of thinking about the problem, the beginning algebra student must also learn to solve the equation with procedures that yield successive equivalent equations until the solution is found. Filloy and Rojano (1989) have pointed out that a *didactical cut* occurs between equations of the type $ax + b = c$ that can be solved by arithmetic methods, and equations of the type $ax + b = cx + d$ which necessitate formal algebraic methods. They explored the use of various concrete models (both the balance and geometric area models) in the teaching of formal equation-solving methods and found that these models did not significantly increase most students' abilities to operate formally with equations having two occurrences of the unknown.

Additional research on the use of concrete models and manipulatives in equation solving includes a study by Boulton-Lewis, Cooper, Atweh, Pillay, Wilss and Mutch (1997). They reported that the 8th graders (approximately 14 years of age) of their study did not use the concrete manipulatives (cups, counters, and sticks) that were made available for solving linear equations, and suggested that the concrete representations increased processing load. In contrast, advocates of such models (e.g., Linchevski & Williams, 1996; Radford & Grenier, 1996) argue that the balance scale facilitates the understanding of the operation of eliminating the same term from both sides of an equation. In particular, Vlassis (2002) found that, for the two classes of 8th graders whom she observed over a period of 16 lessons, the balance model was an effective tool in conveying the principles of transformation. However, according to Vlassis, if students have not already extended their numerical range to encompass the negative integers, cancellation errors will be inevitable (for further research on negative numbers, see Gallardo, 2002).

Continuing research on representing the relationships within typical word problems has produced evidence of students' preference for arithmetic reasoning and difficulties with the use of equations to solve word problems (e.g., Bednarz & Janvier, 1996; Cortés, 1998). Stacey and MacGregor (1999) have observed that, at every stage of the process of solving problems by algebra, students were deflected from the algebraic path by reverting to thinking grounded in arithmetic problem-solving methods. Another study (Van Amerom, 2003) dealing with the setting up of equations within the activity of word-problem-solving has reported that, for 6th

and 7th graders (about 12 to 13 years of age), reasoning and symbolizing appear to develop as independent capabilities; that is, students could write equations to represent problems, but did not use these equations to find the solution, preferring instead to use more informal methods. However, as is suggested by the examples of student work that are presented by Van Amerom, the students did use the equations they had generated as a basis for their reasoning about the problems and for finding their solutions. Similarly, Malara (1999) has observed students successfully using numerical substitution within problem representations in order to arrive at solutions. Kutscher and Linchevski (1997) have also noted the beneficial effect of numerical instantiations as mediators in solving word problems. De Bock, Verschaffel, Janssens and Claes (2000), who have explored the influence of authentic and realistic contexts and of self-made drawings on the illusion of linearity in length and area problems, found no beneficial effect of the authenticity factor, nor of the drawing activity, on pupils' performance. Furthermore, the researchers suggest that realistic problems may, in fact, steer pupils away from the underlying mathematical structure of a problem.

Noticing structure

Some of the early research on equation solving also addressed the issue of students' awareness of the structure of algebraic equations and expressions (e.g., Kieran, 1989). For instance, Wagner, Rachlin and Jensen (1984) found that algebra students have difficulty dealing with multi-term expressions as a single unit and do not perceive that the structure of, for example, $4(2r+1) + 7 = 35$ is the same as $4x + 7 = 35$. According to Kieran (1984), students also find it demanding to judge, without actually solving, whether equations such as $x + 37 = 150$ and $x + 37 - 10 = 150 + 10$ are equivalent, that is, whether they have the same solution. More recently, Linchevski and Livneh (1999) found that 12-year-old students' difficulties with interpreting equations containing several numerical terms and an unknown were a reflection of the same difficulties that they experienced in purely numerical contexts. The researchers suggested that algebra instruction be designed to foster the development of structure sense by providing experience with equivalent structures of expressions and with their decomposition and recomposition. In a study of 11th graders (approximately 17 years of age), Hoch and Dreyfus (2004) found that very few students used structure sense and those who did so were not consistent. The presence of brackets seemed to help students see structure, focusing their attention on like terms and breaking up long strings of symbols. However, as noted by Demby (1997), students are poor at identifying structure, in particular, the properties they use when they transform algebraic expressions. As well, Hoch and Dreyfus (2005) have reported the difficulties that students experience with seeing that expressions such as $(x-3)^4 - (x+3)^4$ can be treated as a difference of squares.

The kinds of errors that students tend to make in algebraic manipulative activity have suggested to some researchers (e.g., Kirshner, 1989) that it is not an absence of theoretical/structural control that is the issue but rather a misperception of form.

In a study that extended Kirshner's earlier work on the visual syntax of algebra, Kirshner and Awtry (2004) reported on research aimed at investigating the role of *visual salience*[1] in the initial learning of algebra. They found that students did indeed engage with the visual characteristics of the symbol system in their initial learning of algebra rules: The percentage-correct scores for recognition tasks were significantly higher for visually salient rules than for non-visually-salient rules. Similarly, Hewitt (2003), in a study of 40 teachers and a class of 11- to 12-year-olds, found that the inherent mathematical structure, and the visual impact of the notation itself, had an effect on the way in which an equation was manipulated. (Before concluding this section, it is noted that a review of the PME studies on the learning of abstract algebra –e.g., Leron, Hazzan & Zazkis, 1994; Chin & Tall, 2000; Iannone & Nardi, 2002– and of linear algebra –e.g., Rogalski, 1996; Sierpinska, Trgalová, Hillel & Dreyfus, 1999; Maracci, 2003– is beyond the scope of this chapter.)

Additional remarks

The research reviewed in this first section has focused primarily on the themes initially seen during the early years of PME; nevertheless, as has been seen, research on those strands has continued to the present day. However, more recent work in this theme-group has reflected the theoretical and methodological shifts that have been occurring over the last two and a half decades. The theoretical framework of constructivism blossomed in the 1980s (see the plenary papers by Kilpatrick, Sinclair, Vergnaud & Wheeler in the 1987 PME Proceedings), attracting PME researchers with its notion that knowledge is actively constructed by the cognizing subject, not passively received from the environment (in this regard, see also Cobb & Steffe, 1983; Confrey, 1987). This theoretical perspective led algebra researchers to move their attention from, for example, the errors made by students to the ways in which they craft their understandings of algebraic concepts and procedures. While the focus was still cognitive, it tended to be much broader than that suggested by the research analyses carried out during PME's first few years.

During the 1990s, an additional change occurred. The socio-cultural theoretical perspective, which had developed outside the PME community, began to emerge within PME (see John-Steiner's, 1995, plenary paper presented at the PME19 conference in Brazil). The earlier constructivist/cognitive orientation shifted, for a large number of PME algebra researchers, toward analyses of social factors affecting algebra learning, with an accompanying interest in the mediating role of cultural tools (see, e.g., Meira, 1995, 1998; see also Cobb, 1994; Cobb & Yackel, 1995). This shift also led to an increase in classroom-based studies with a focus on teacher-student and student-student discourse (e.g., Bartolini Bussi, 1995; Sfard, 2001).

---

[1] According to the researchers, "visually salient rules have a visual coherence that makes the left- and right-hand sides of the equations appear naturally related to one another" (p. 229). While $(x^y)^z = x^{yz}$ is considered a visually-salient rule, $x^2 - y^2 = (x - y)\ (x + y)$ is not.

The impact of the advent of technology in the mid-1980s, in combination with first one and then the other of the above two theoretical perspectives, will be noted in the next section, where the use of technological tools in algebra learning will be one of the principal foci of discussion.

THEME-GROUP TWO: THE USE OF TECHNOLOGICAL TOOLS IN ALGEBRA LEARNING AND A FOCUS ON MULTIPLE REPRESENTATIONS AND GENERALIZATION

During the 1980s, the primarily letter-symbolic emphasis of algebra research began to experience some movement. While the study of functions had been considered a separate domain of study in the years prior, the two began to merge in algebra research. Functions, with their graphical, tabular, and symbolic representations, came to be seen as *bona fide* algebraic objects (Schwartz & Yerushalmy, 1992). Graphical representations, in particular, began to be viewed as tools for infusing letter-symbolic representations with meaning (Romberg, Fennema & Carpenter, 1993). Some mathematicians and mathematics educators (e.g., Fey, 1984) argued that computing technology could have significant effects on the content and emphases of school-level and university-level mathematics. Early visionaries promoted the idea that computing technology could be harnessed to more fully integrate the multiple representations of mathematical objects in mathematics teaching. Soon a functional perspective could be seen throughout algebraic activity, but especially in the solution of "real world" problems by methods other than by-hand symbol manipulation, such as technology-supported methods (Fey & Good, 1985). This functional perspective has been summarized by Heid (1996) as follows: "The functional approach to the emergence of algebraic thinking ... suggests a study of algebra that centers on developing experiences with functions and families of functions through encounters with real world situations whose quantitative relationships can be described by those models" (p. 239).

Research on functions and multiple representations, without technological tools

Even before the use of technological tools to support the learning of multiple representations began to be studied by researchers, the difficulties experienced by students with graphical representations had been a theme of interest at PME (e.g., Kerslake, 1977; Janvier, 1981; Clement, 1985; Ponte, 1985). Kerslake (1977), for example, showed that in reading graphs representing the time taken to traverse mountain roads of various steepness, students confused the graph with the shape of the road itself. In a study of students' work with diverse representations, Dreyfus and Eisenberg (1981) found that high-ability students preferred graphical representations, while low-ability students preferred the tabular.

For many researchers, understanding the connections between equations and graphs is considered fundamental to developing meaning for various algebraic representations and continues to be central to PME research. Drawing on studies by Moschkovich, Schoenfeld and Arcavi (1993), Knuth (2000) examined 9th to 12th

grade students' understanding of the concept that the coordinates of any point on a line will satisfy the equation of the line, within the context of problems that require the use of this knowledge. Knuth found an overwhelming reliance on letter-symbolic representations, even on tasks for which a graphical representation seemed more appropriate. The findings also indicated that for familiar routine problems many students had mastered the connections between the letter-symbolic and graphical representations; however, such mastery appeared to be superficial at best.

Zaslavsky, Sela and Leron (2002) have found evidence of much confusion regarding the connections between algebraic and geometric aspects of slope, scale and angle. Responses to a simple but non-standard task concerning the behavior of slope under a non-homogeneous change of scale revealed two main approaches – analytic and visual– as well as combinations of the two. The researchers recommended that instruction on slope distinguish between the erroneous conception of 'visual slope' –the slope of a line (for which the angle is a relevant feature)– and the 'analytic slope' –the rate of change of a function.

Algebra as generalization activity

"Algebra as generalization" is a perspective that has its PME roots in the use of algebraic notation as a tool for expressing proofs (e.g., Bell, 1976; Fischbein & Kedem, 1982; Mason & Pimm, 1984). The position that generalization is also a route to algebra was developed by Mason, Graham, Pimm and Gowar (1985; see also Mason, Graham & Johnston-Wilder, 2005). In some of the pioneering PME research on the use of algebraic notation as a tool for expressing general and figural patterns, and for justifying equivalent forms of these patterning relations, Lee (1987) and Lee & Wheeler (1987) found that few students use algebra or appreciate its role in justifying a general statement about numbers. Similar findings have been reported by MacGregor and Stacey (1993), who observed that an additional difficulty lies in students' inability to articulate clearly the structure of a pattern or relationship using ordinary language.

Healy and Hoyles (1999) have pointed out that the visual approaches generated in tasks involving generalization of matchstick patterns can provide strong support for the algebraic representation of sequences and the development of a conceptual framework for functions, but emphasized that there is a need to work hard to connect the observed number patterns to symbolic form. Ainley, Wilson and Bills (2003), in a report that compared *generalization of the context* with *generalization of the calculation*, found that generalizing the context did not seem to be sufficient to support pupils in moving to a symbolic version of the rule. However, Radford (2000), who has studied the transition from the particular to the general, has argued that such processes take time.

In a study that focused on the role of tabular representations, Sasman, Olivier and Linchevski (1999) presented 8th graders (14-year-olds) with generalization activities in which they varied the representation along several dimensions, namely the type of function, the nature of the numbers, the format of tables, and the structure of pictures. Results showed that varying these dimensions had little effect on students' thinking. According to Mason (1996), a scrutiny of established school practice involving generalizing in algebra reveals that often, starting from geometric figures or numeric sequences, the emphasis is on the construction of tables of values from which a closed-form formula is extracted and checked with one or two examples. This approach in effect short-circuits all the richness of the process of generalization. In fact, it has been suggested by other researchers (e.g., Moss, 2005) that tabular representations may actually get in the way of students' coming to see the general relationships underlying patterns and representing them algebraically. Mason suggests several possible investigative approaches that can lead to students' construction of algebraic formulas, including visualization and manipulation of the figure on which the generalizing process is based.

Related to the research on generalization and justification is the body of PME work on elementary number-theoretic activity. For example, Garuti, Boero and Lemut (1998), in a study involving problems of the type, "Prove that the sum of two consecutive odd numbers is a multiple of 4," found that students needed to gradually learn how to explore and transform the given statement in order to construct a proof. Additional difficulties centered on students' not seeing how to connect their proving work to algebraic notation. Zazkis and Campbell (1996), who studied participants' understanding of the property that "every n^{th} number is divisible by n" found that such properties are not among those that the majority of students are familiar with. Some strategies for helping students become aware of such number-theoretic properties have been described by Mason (2002) and by Guzmán and Kieran (2002). (See also the report of the 2002 PME Research Forum on number theory.)

In research involving older students, Arzarello, Bazzini and Chiappini (1994) observed a link between expressing the relations of number-theoretic problems in suitable algebraic code and success in determining the solution to such problems. According to the researchers, appropriate naming is linked to the anticipatory aspects of solving and allows students to orient the solution process toward the aims of the problem. They also pointed out that some students, who could express the elements of a problem by using natural language, were unable to express them using the algebraic language. In contrast, Douek (1999) found that non-standard representations of number-theoretic problems did not prevent students from producing valid proofs and problem solutions. However, Alcock and Weber (2005) have reported, based on their research involving proof-related tasks, that students use both referential (involving some instantiation) and syntactic approaches (involving manipulation); and that students who use referential approaches may have a more meaningful understanding of their proofs but may not be able to complete them.

Early research on the use of technological tools in algebra learning

While the growth in interest in multiple representations was fed by the advent of technology, some of the early PME algebra research involving technology focused rather on programming. For example, a study by Soloway, Lochhead and Clement (1982) showed that students could better cope with translating a word problem into an "equation" when the equation was in the form of a short computer program specifying how to compute the value of one variable based on another –findings supported by Sfard's (1987) results regarding the overwhelming predominance of operational/process conceptions of functions among algebra students. Additional PME research on the role of programming and other related environments in algebra learning includes the studies with Logo (e.g., Hoyles, Sutherland & Evans, 1985), with BASIC (e.g., Thomas & Tall, 1986), with software for exploring structured equivalent expressions (Thompson & Thompson, 1987), and with the CARAPACE environment featuring process-oriented approaches to algebra problem solving (Kieran, Boileau & Garançon, 1989). Despite the positive results of these early programming-oriented studies, many of the environments did not include the making of explicit connections with conventional algebraic concepts and notation.

Spreadsheets: A technological tool for bridging to algebraic forms and methods

Among the studies that have explored the use of spreadsheets as a means to introduce students to algebra are those conducted by Ainley (1996), where 11-year-olds used both the numerical-tabular and graphical facilities to model various problem situations. Building on their earlier research with spreadsheets (e.g., Sutherland & Rojano, 1993), Filloy, Rojano and Rubio (2001) have found that the spreadsheet serves as a bridging tool to algebra because it helps students both to create conceptual meaning for algebraic objects and operations and to move from focusing on a specific example to describing general relationships. For Dettori, Garuti and Lemut (2001), the functional orientation of spreadsheets allows for their effective use in the investigation of variation, but can cause difficulties later when solving equations or inequalities. When these researchers investigated 13- and 14-year-olds working on algebraic problems with spreadsheets, Dettori and colleagues were led to conclude that, "spreadsheets can start the journey of learning algebra, but do not have the tools to complete it" (p. 206). Balacheff (2001) has voiced similar concerns regarding the so-called algebra-like notation of spreadsheet environments. As well, Hershkowitz, Dreyfus, Ben-Zvi, Friedlander, Hadas, Resnick, Tabach and Schwarz (2002) have described how students tend, in the spreadsheet (tabular) environment, to generalize recursively rather than explicitly, which makes it more difficult for them to generate closed-form algebraic rules for patterns.

Graphing calculators and other related technological tools

Schwarz and Hershkowitz (1999) have investigated 9th graders' learning of the concept of mathematical function in an environment that included problem situations, graphing calculators and multi-representational software tools, and where students were encouraged to make their own decisions about which representations to use, when and how to link the representations, and in which medium to work. A questionnaire was presented that included questions on the interpretation of graphical representations, the generation of graphical representations, and the relation of certain graphs to algebraic representations. The researchers found that the students: (a) Often used the prototypical linear and quadratic functions, but did not consider them as exclusive (for persistence of linear models in students' reasoning, see De Bock, Verschaffel & Janssens, 2002, as well as findings from earlier research on functional thinking, e.g., Markovits, Eylon & Bruckheimer, 1986), (b) Used prototypes as levers to handle a variety of other examples, (c) Articulated justifications often accounting for context, and (d) Understood functions' attributes. Schwarz and Hershkowitz suggest that the numerous manipulative experiences that were afforded by the graphing calculators and multi-representational software influenced positively students' understanding of the functions' attributes.

In contrast, Cavanagh and Mitchelmore (2000) have noted the presence of several misconceptions among their interviewees as they carried out various graphical tasks: A tendency to accept the graphical image uncritically, without attempting to relate it to other symbolic or numerical information; a poor understanding of the concept of scale; and an inadequate grasp of accuracy and approximation. Furthermore, in research reported by Hershkowitz and Kieran (2001) involving 16-year-olds working on a function-based problem situation integrating the graphing calculator as a tool, students were found to go from entering lists to a graphical representation by means of the regression tool, without ever seeing or having to examine the algebraic representation of the situation –a phenomenon that, according to the researchers, may suggest some caution in the way in which algebra instruction that integrates the use of graphing calculators is orchestrated. Despite what appear to be mixed results emerging from the above studies regarding students' understanding of graphical representations, a large majority of the research investigating the impact of graphing technology tools have reported significant benefits with respect to students' conceptualizing of functions, especially when these tools are used over long periods of time (e.g., Streun, Harskamp & Suhre, 2000).

Word problems and multiple representations

Much of the algebra research involving technological tools has focused on the solving of word problems by means of multiple representations. For example, Huntley, Rasmussen, Villarubi, Sangtong and Fey (2000) have found that, when students were able to use context clues and had graphing calculators available, those who were not strong in symbol-manipulation skills could outperform symbolically-capable students when the tasks required formulation and interpretation of situations. The impact of the availability of a range of representations on students' solving of complex contextual problems has also been demonstrated by Molyneux-Hodgson, Rojano, Sutherland and Ursini (1999). In this cross-national study, the multiple representations supported algebra learning within the cultures of the schools in different ways: Mexican students learned to appreciate and use graphical and numerical representations; and English students, to make more sense of letter-symbolic representations.

The long-term impact of a problem-based, functional approach to the teaching of algebra, one that was supported by intensive use of multi-representation technology, was studied by Yerushalmy (2000). By means of classroom observations and clinical interviews with students over their three years of following such a course, Yerushalmy found that the representation of problem situations evolved as follows: From numbers as the only means of modeling, to intensive work with graphs and tables, to the use of more symbolic representations. Students also moved from analyzing patterns of numbers by watching the behavior of increments to more explicit, closed-form, formulations of functional relationships involving pairs of numbers. Yerushalmy noted as well that students took a rather long time to appreciate algebraic symbols, and that they continued to prefer to use the situation as the source for their answers.

Further research (Yerushalmy & Shternberg, 2001), as well as the long-term observations of Chazan (2000), has led Yerushalmy (2000) to argue that, "a curricular sequence of algebra based on functions might have to address more subtleties and transitions than initially expected ... and that the complexity of helping students to value algebraic symbols may require more than bridging between representations" (p. 145). The results from a follow-up study suggested to Gilead and Yerushalmy (2001) that graphical tools may be useful as an exploratory support only for canonical problems (i.e., where y-intercept and slope are both given).

Computer algebra systems and other structured symbol manipulation environments

Recent research in the French *didactique* tradition (e.g., Guin & Trouche, 1999; Artigue 2002; Lagrange, 2003) has shown that technological tools, such as Computer Algebra Systems (CAS), can promote both conceptual and technical growth in mathematics, as long as the technical aspects are not ignored. More specifically, Lagrange (2000), adapting a framework developed by Chevallard (1999), has elaborated the notion that technique is the bridge between task and theory. In other words, as students develop techniques in response to certain tasks, they engage in a process of theory building. Instrumentation theory, which articulates the relation between tool use and conceptual development (Trouche, 2000), has begun to be applied to the learning of algebra (e.g., Drijvers, 2003).

The introduction of CAS use in high school algebra classes has been accompanied by research interest in students' conceptions of equivalence. Ball, Pierce and Stacey (2003) have recently reported that recognizing equivalence, even in simple cases, is a significant obstacle for students. According to the researchers, "The ability to recognize equivalent algebraic expressions quickly and confidently is important for doing mathematics in an intelligent partnership with computer algebra; it is also a key aspect of algebraic expectation, the algebraic skill that parallels numeric expectation" (p. 4-16). They add that attention to equivalence is likely to take on new importance in future curricula (in this regard, see also Kieran & Saldanha, 2005). Despite its being a core idea in algebra, only a few of the earlier studies explicitly addressed students' notions of equivalence (e.g., Kieran, 1984; Linchevski & Vinner, 1990; Steinberg, Sleeman & Ktorza, 1990).

Another example of some of the most recent research in this area is the work of Cerulli and Mariotti (2001). These researchers have reported on a teaching experiment that involved 9th grade classes (15-year-olds) and the algebra microworld, *l'Algebrista*, created by Cerulli (2004). Their aim was to develop in students a theoretical perspective on algebraic manipulation, by basing activity on proving and the concept of equivalence relation. The written justifications that students provided of their equivalence transformations, as seen in the iconography of the axiom buttons that were mediating their thinking, suggested to the researchers that a "proving" approach to equivalence was yielding positive results with respect to students' learning to solve equations and produce equivalent expressions.

Additional remarks

The research reviewed in this section has focused on the strands of work that first began to be seen in PME research from about the mid-1980s and that have continued to the present day. As was noted, one of the main influences on the research of this period has been the advent of technological tools that could be applied to the learning of algebra. Not only did this phenomenon encourage the movement of the study of functions with their multiple representations toward the domain of school algebra, it also succeeded in broadening the sources of meaning making that algebra students might invoke. Algebra became more than the study of equations and equation solving; it grew to encompass functions (and their representations) and the study of change, as well as include real world situations that could be modeled by these functions. In addition to the several research studies carried out on these themes, generalization also became a focus of research attention.

As was mentioned in the concluding remarks of the previous section, a socio-cultural theoretical perspective had begun to permeate PME research in the 1990s. The combination of digital tools being used in algebra learning, and the socio-cultural lens being applied to both the design of learning studies and the analysis of the resulting data, led to new questions about the nature of learning with these tools and the roles of the different participants in the classroom. Kaput (1992) pointed out: "[With these tools] the locus of social authority becomes more diffuse; provision must be made for students to generate, refine, and prove conjectures; the teacher must routinely negotiate between student-generated mathematics and the teacher's curricular agenda" (p. 548). Moreover, as emphasized by Hoyles (2002): "Tools can no longer be regarded as neutral players in the process of meaning making" (p. 275). There is no question but that the face of PME research in algebra was being indelibly altered by these forces. Not only was the content of algebra being widened by functional and generalization-based approaches, but also the theoretical and technological lenses that were being used to design and interpret research served to complexify analyses of the sources from which students might derive meaning in algebra. Additional contributing factors are discussed in the upcoming section.

THEME-GROUP THREE: ALGEBRAIC THINKING AMONG ELEMENTARY SCHOOL STUDENTS, A FOCUS ON THE ALGEBRA TEACHER/TEACHING, AND DYNAMIC MODELING OF PHYSICAL SITUATIONS AND OTHER DYNAMIC ALGEBRA ENVIRONMENTS

With the extension of equation-based algebra to include functions and the modeling of real world situations by various functional representations, the notion that algebra could be made accessible to more students (Chazan, 1996), even elementary school students (Kaput, 1995), was soon elaborated. Research on the development of algebraic thinking at the elementary school level began to be presented at PME during the mid-1990s. At about the same time, there was a significant increase in the amount of research involving the teacher of algebra. The learner has tended to be the main focus of attention of algebra researchers throughout the years of PME's existence; nevertheless, a large number of studies devoted to the algebra teacher and to the practice of algebra teaching have, of late, also been carried out.

As well, further developments in technology-related algebra research were seen in the mid-1990s in studies involving the integration of dynamic environments in algebra learning and the exploration and modeling of physical situations with technological tools. New theoretical perspectives soon evolved in an attempt to more adequately take into account the diverse dimensions of algebra learning that were being studied, in particular the roles being played by gestures, bodily movement, and language.

Algebraic thinking among elementary school students

The emerging body of research on an area that has come to be known as *Early Algebra* was reflected in the holding of a Research Forum on Early Algebra at the 2001 PME (Ainley, 2001). While the question of whether the study of algebra should be spread over all of grades 2 to 12 has been debated since the 1960s according to Davis (1985), the research focus on the algebraic thinking of the elementary age student is quite new.

As had been suggested by the algebra research findings emanating from the previous two decades of PME studies carried out with pupils beginning high school algebra, students operating in an arithmetic frame of reference tend not to see the relational aspects of operations; their focus is on calculating. Thus, considerable adjustment is required in learning, for example, to compare expressions for equivalence and to view the equal sign as other than a signal to compute an answer. The many research studies that centered on the difficulties involved in moving from an arithmetic to an algebraic form of reasoning (e.g., Kieran, 1979; Booth, 1981, 1984; Lee & Wheeler, 1989; Wagner & Kieran, 1989; Herscovics &

Linchevski, 1991, 1994; Kieran, 1992; Linchevski, 1995) have, by extension, provided both the motivation for thinking about beginning algebraic explorations in elementary school and the foundation for some of the recent research on the emergence of algebraic thinking among elementary school students.

Some of the principal Early Algebra themes that have been developed in the research by members of the PME community include: Relational thinking about numeric equalities, symbolizing relationships among quantities, working with equations, developing functional thinking, and fostering an understanding of mathematical properties. Among the studies focusing on the emergence of relational views of numeric equalities is the research of Fujii (2003), who has introduced young children to algebraic thinking through generalizable numerical expressions, using numbers as *quasi-variables* (e.g., number sentences such as 78 – 49 + 49 = 78, which are true whatever number is taken away and then added back). A related study by Ishida and Sanjii (2002) has found that the understanding of structure increases from grades 4 to 6 (from age 10 to age 12), which suggested to the researchers that as students grow older they come to understand the role of a mathematical expression from the point of view of both structure and generality. The multi-year research program of Zack (1995, 1997, 2002) has provided evidence of the ways in which 10- and 11-year-olds learn to reason about, prove, and represent symbolically the complex generalizations underlying the structure of problems such as "squares on a chessboard" or "ferret tunnels / handshakes / polygon diagonals."

Another strand in Early Algebra research has been the symbolizing of relationships among quantities. According to the approach developed by Davydov and his colleagues (see Schmittau & Morris, 2004), it is not experience with number that serves as the basis for learning algebra; rather its foundation rests on relationships between quantities that children search out across contextualized situations. Dougherty and Slovin (2004), who integrated Davydov's approach within their *Measure Up* project, have reported that 3rd graders can learn to use algebraic symbols and diagrams meaningfully by working with measurement situations.

The research findings of Schliemann, Carraher, Brizuela, Earnest, Goodrow, Lara-Roth and Peled (2003) have led these researchers to argue that students as young as 9 and 10 years of age are able to develop an enlarged sense of the equality sign, represent unknown quantities with a letter, represent relations with variables, work with unknowns, write equations, and even solve letter-symbolic linear equations. Warren (2003) has, however, noted that 8- and 9-year-olds can experience difficulty in handling problems with unknowns. Nevertheless, Da Rocha Falcão, Brito Lima, De Araújo, Lins Lessa and Oliveira Osório (2000) have also reported that activity involving symbolic representation, manipulation of relations of difference and equality, and manipulation of unknowns is feasible with 10- to 12-year-olds, provided that the passage from known to unknown quantities is handled carefully and with adequate preparatory activities that include verbalization.

Although pattern finding in single-variable situations is now fairly common in elementary curricula according to Blanton and Kaput (2004), they argue that elementary school programs should also include functional thinking within algebraic reasoning activities. They base this argument on their findings that students as young as those in kindergarten can engage in covariational thinking, that 1st graders can describe how quantities correspond, and that 3rd graders can use letters as variables (see also Warren, 2005).

While certain proponents of algebraic thinking in elementary school support the early introduction of the letter-symbolic (e.g., Schliemann et al., 2003); others hold the opposite position (e.g., Fujii, 2003). Thus, definitions of algebraic thinking in the early grades rarely take both perspectives into consideration. Kieran (1996) has characterized the activities of school algebra according to three types: Generational, transformational, and global/meta-level. While this characterization was initially designed with the secondary school student in mind, the global/meta-level activities of algebra, which provide context and a sense of purpose for letter-symbolic work in algebra, afford a basis for delineating algebraic thinking that is broad enough to include the various positions regarding the introduction of symbolic work at the elementary school level:

> *Algebraic thinking in the early grades* involves the development of ways of thinking within activities for which letter-symbolic algebra can be used as a tool, but which are not exclusive to algebra, and which could be engaged in without using any letter-symbolic algebra at all, such as, analyzing relationships between quantities, noticing structure, studying change, generalizing, problem solving, modeling, justifying, proving, and predicting. (Kieran, 2004, p. 149)

A potential advantage of appropriating this definition of algebraic thinking for Early Algebra is the bridge building it affords between research in algebra learning involving the elementary school student and that of the older student at the secondary level. In addition, this characterization captures the main thrust of the algebra research to date at the elementary school level, research that has focused on the analysis of relationships between quantities (e.g., Dougherty, 2003), the noticing of structure within activity on numerical properties (e.g., Carpenter, Franke & Levi, 2003), the study of change (e.g., Noble, Nemirovsky, Wright & Tierney, 2001), generalizing (e.g., Fujii, 2003), and the solving of problems with a focus on relations (e.g., Zack, 2002).

Algebra teaching and the algebra teacher

While it could be argued that all research on algebra learning implicitly involves teaching, it was not until the 1990s that algebra teaching and the algebra teacher became a focus of analysis by PME researchers. In 1987, Shaughnessy (1987) remarked in his reaction to the then-current PME research on teachers and teaching that most of this research remained quite general and had yet to feature the teaching of specific mathematical content. Coincidentally, the following year, Even

(1988) presented a research report at PME on pre-service teachers' conceptions of the relationships between functions and equations. That these prospective teachers held a limited view of functions as equations only, was not so surprising, given the rather recent integration of functions into the domain of school algebra. What was remarkable about this research report was that it signaled the gradual emergence, during the ensuing years, of PME research on algebra teaching and the algebra teacher (e.g., Even, 1990; Robinson, Even & Tirosh, 1992; Pence, 1994) and the beginnings of the growth of theoretical frames of reference suitable for analyzing data on the algebra teacher and teaching (see the following research reports for some of these theoretical frameworks: Solomon & Nemirovsky, 1999; Coles, 2001; Boaler, 2003; Doerr, 2003; English & Doerr, 2003; Simmt, Davis, Gordon & Towers, 2003).

The research that foregrounds the teacher of algebra and/or the teaching of algebra can be grouped into the following three categories: Studies dealing with the practicing teacher in the algebra classroom, those conducted within professional development or in-service training programs, and those involving the preservice teacher of algebra. The research on algebra teaching and the practicing algebra teacher has produced studies related to teachers' knowledge of students' ways of thinking (e.g., Hadjidemetriou & Williams, 2002), as well as the various influences on teachers' practice (e.g., Doerr & Zangor, 2000; Guin & Trouche, 2000).

Teachers' knowledge of students' ways of thinking in the context of algebra has been the focus of research by Tirosh, Even and Robinson (1998). Their research has led them to argue for more of the following kind of study: "While one can use the mathematics education literature in order to raise teachers' sensitivity to students' ways of thinking, ... this literature does not offer enough information and discussion regarding the impact of various approaches and teaching methods related to this conception; ... it is important for teachers to be acquainted with various teaching methods and to be aware of their pros and cons in different contexts with different teaching aims, and with different students" (pp. 62-63).

From her analyses of traditional and reform-oriented classroom teaching, Boaler (2003) has found that, contrary to the common perception that reform-oriented classrooms are less teacher-centered, teachers actually spend more time questioning the whole class in reform classes. However, it is not just the amount of time that is different, it is the nature of the teacher talk. According to Boaler, "the teachers in the traditional classes *gave* students a lot of information, while the teachers of the reform classes chose to *draw* information out of students, by presenting problems and asking students questions" (p. 1-4).

The research that has been conducted within the context of professional development or in-service training of algebra teachers has focused on two areas in particular, the algebra content knowledge and beliefs of teachers (e.g., Barkai, Tsamir, Tirosh & Dreyfus, 2002), as well as the integration of new curricula, teaching approaches, and technological environments into the algebra classroom (e.g., Stacey, Kendal & Pierce, 2002; Cedillo & Kieran, 2003; Zehavi, 2004; Thomas & Hong, 2005). An example is drawn from the ArAl project (Malara, 2003), an in-service teacher education project devoted to the renewal of the teaching of arithmetic and algebra in the 6th to 8th grades. The research explicitly included the classroom teacher as a researcher and emphasized knowledge of pedagogical content, the teacher's role in the teaching of mathematics, the impact of his/her personality, as well as social issues within the class group. A second example is provided by the research of Ruthven and Hennessy (2002), who interviewed groups of teachers from the mathematics departments of seven secondary schools in England –teachers involved in a project on integrating new technologies into their teaching. The researchers found that the teachers tended to embrace a broad use of computing tools in the teaching of mathematics at these grade levels, including spreadsheets, graphical software, and Logo programming, in addition to courseware that had been designed to teach or test a particular mathematical topic.

Research involving the preservice teacher of algebra has inquired into, for instance, the role of beliefs and attitudes (e.g., Vermeulen, 2000), as well as the nature of the content knowledge of the preservice trainee (e.g., Zazkis & Liljedahl, 2002; Presmeg & Nenduradu, 2005). For example, Van Dooren, Verschaffel and Onghena (2002, 2003), who have studied preservice teachers' preferential strategies for solving arithmetic and algebra word problems, found evidence that future secondary school mathematics teachers tend to use algebraic methods for solving even very easy problems that could have been handled more appropriately with arithmetic methods. Half of the primary school preservice teachers in the study could switch flexibly between arithmetic and algebraic methods, while the other half had difficulty with algebraic methods. It was also found that the methods the teachers used as individuals were strongly correlated with that which they would expect their future students to use and by which they would evaluate student work. Similar results have been reported by Schmidt and Bednarz (1997).

Dynamic modeling of physical situations and other dynamic algebra environments

Another rather recent strand in PME algebra research involves modeling activity that includes actual physical artifacts and/or technological modeling tools. The phenomena that students have been observed modeling within various research studies include cars moving along tracks (Schnepp & Nemirovsky, 2001) and devices with gears of different sizes (Bartolini Bussi, 1995; Meira, 1998). For instance, Schnepp and Nemirovsky (2001) have reported on an environment where a computer is linked to miniature cars on parallel linear tracks (or to a miniature stationary bike) and where the user can construct a graph on a computer, which in turn communicates with a motor that moves the mechanical device according to the graphical specifications. In this example, it is noted that the activity involves the inverse of modeling, that is, the direct control of a mathematical model in order to manipulate a physical object (see related examples in Kaput & Roschelle, 1997).

Arzarello and Robutti (2001) have described a study introducing 9th graders to algebra and involving the interpretation of body-motion graphs with a symbolic-graphing calculator connected to a motion sensor (a calculator-based ranger – CBR). Initially students were encouraged to try various running patterns in order to create different graphs. The continuous nature of the CBR graphing allowed students to test conjectures in a direct manner, controllable by their own physical movement. Arzarello and Robutti observed that, "students' cognitive activity passes through a complex evolution, which starts in their bodily experience (namely, running in the corridor), goes on with the evocation of the just lived experience through gestures and words, continues connecting it with the data representation, and culminates with the use of algebraic language to write down the relationships between the quantities involved in the experiment" (p. 39).

Other such environments offering *dynamic control*, that is, "the direct manipulation of an object or a representation of a mathematical object –the manipulation being of a continuous nature, or discrete" (Kieran & Yerushalmy, 2004, p. 120), include those where direct manipulation is achieved by means of slidergraphs (Zbiek & Heid, 2001), sliders (Schwartz & Yerushalmy, 1996), dragging facilities (Borba, 1993), and so on. The research being conducted in these environments has led to the development of new theoretical perspectives where bodily experience and other factors that could be said to be exterior to the mathematics are considered to play vital roles in the creation of meaning for algebraic objects.

Remarks on the recent emergence of new theoretical perspectives

An indication of the growth of research interest in this new source of meaning in algebra learning was the holding of the first Research Forum on the role of perceptuo-motor activity in mathematical learning, organized by Nemirovsky (2003), at the 2003 PME conference. The research findings presented at that forum suggested a complex relationship between gestures and words that allows students to make sense of algebraic expressions (Radford, Demers, Guzmán & Cerulli, 2003) and illustrated how motion experiences contribute to students' meaning making in algebra (Robutti & Arzarello, 2003). As well, Ferrara (2003), using a framework based on the theory of Lakoff and Núñez (2000), described how metaphors can serve as vehicles of algebraic knowledge and means of sharing knowledge (see also Sfard, 1994; Boero, Bazzini & Garuti, 2001). While these viewpoints with their emphases on discourse and activity clearly intersect with discursive frames of reference (e.g., Kieran, Forman & Sfard, 2001) and the construct of "situated abstraction" (Noss & Hoyles, 1996), they also add a perspective previously unseen in PME algebra learning research with their attention to gestures, bodily experience, and metaphors as a source of meaning making in algebra.

TRAVERSING THE VARIOUS THEME-GROUPS THAT HAVE EMERGED IN PME ALGEBRA RESEARCH: A BROADENING OF SOURCES OF MEANING

The question of meaning lies at the heart of PME research in algebra. The various shifts in emphasis over the years from the letter-symbolic through multiple representations to algebra learning in dynamic environments hint at the evolution that has occurred with respect to sources of meaning in algebra learning research. Researchers of the PME community have long been and continue to be interested in issues of meaning making in mathematics, in general, and algebra, in particular (e.g., Kaput, 1989; Sackur, Drouhard, Maurel & Pécal, 1997; Arzarello, Bazzini & Chiappini, 2001; Filloy, Rojano & Rubio, 2001; Lins, 2001). For example, Kaput (1989) has described four sources of meaning in mathematics, which he divides into two complementary categories: *Referential extension*, which consists of translations between mathematical representation systems and translations between mathematical and nonmathematical systems; and *consolidation*, which consists of pattern and syntax learning through transforming and operating within a representation system and building conceptual entities through reifying actions and procedures. Clearly related to this latter category, consolidation, are the various theoretical process-object distinctions that have been developed with respect to the construction of meaning in mathematics (e.g., Dubinsky, 1991; Sfard, 1991; Gray & Tall, 1994), as well as the recent models of abstraction (e.g., Hershkowitz, Schwarz & Dreyfus, 2001; Schwarz, Hershkowitz & Dreyfus, 2002).

Another framework for thinking about meaning, which has been used in several algebra studies, is that of Frege's semiotic triangle (e.g., Sackur et al., 1997; Arzarello et al., 2001; Bazzini, Boero & Garuti, 2001; Drouhard & Teppo, 2004), in particular his distinction between sense and denotation[2]. For example, in their theoretical analyses of the meaning of symbolic expressions in algebra, Arzarello et al. (2001) explain that, "All possible senses of an expression constitute its so called intensional aspects, while its denotation within a universe represents its so called extensional aspect. ... The official semantics used in mathematics, and particularly in algebra, cuts off all intensional aspects, insofar as it is based on the assumption of the extensionality axiom (two sets are equal if they contain the same elements, independently from the way they are described or produced)" (p. 64). However, as they and others (e.g., Sfard & Linchevki, 1994) have pointed out, intensional aspects are crucial to algebra learning because of the difficulties students experience in mastering the invariance of denotation with respect to sense.

Yet another perspective is that of Kirshner (2001), who has characterized the approaches to meaning making in elementary algebra in terms of the structural and the referential. According to Kirshner, "the structural approach builds meaning internally from the connections generated within a syntactically constructed system, while the referential approach imports meaning into the symbol system from external domains of reference" (p. 84).

More recently, the various ways of thinking about meaning making in algebra have been reconceptualized to suggest a threefold approach. For Radford (2004), meaning in school algebra is produced in the "crossroads of diverse semiotic mathematical and non-mathematical systems" (p. 1-163) and is, according to Radford, deemed to come from three primary sources: (i) The algebraic "structure" itself, (ii) The problem context, and (iii) The exterior of the problem context (e.g.,

---

2 Within the Fregean theoretical framework involving sense and denotation, the expressions $4x + 2$ and $2(2x + 1)$ have different senses, but denote the same functional object.

linguistic activity, gestures and bodily language, metaphors, lived experience, image building, etc.).

A comparison of Radford's threefold classification with the more general, triple perspective on "meaning in mathematics education" offered by Noss and Hoyles (1996) –*meanings from mathematical objects*, *meanings from problem solving*, and *meanings constructed by the individual learner*– as well as a consideration of the existing body of algebra research findings, suggests that Radford's first source of meaning, the "algebraic structure itself," could usefully be expanded further to take into account the meaning building that is derived from other mathematical objects, such as graphical forms. This leads to my following adaptation of Radford's schema for algebraic meaning and its sources (see Figure 1). A limited elaboration of these four sources of meaning will ensue in the upcoming paragraphs, with brief connections drawn to the themes that have emerged in PME algebra research over the past 30 years.

Figure 1: Sources of meaning in algebra (adapted from Radford, 2004).

```
1. Meaning from within mathematics:
     1(a). Meaning from the algebraic structure itself,
           involving the letter-symbolic form.
     1(b). Meaning from multiple representations.

2. Meaning from the problem context.

3. Meaning derived from that which is exterior to the
   mathematics/problem context (e.g., linguistic
   activity, gestures and bodily language, metaphors,
   lived experience, image building, etc.).
```

Meaning from the algebraic structure itself, involving the letter-symbolic form

Booth (1989) has argued that, "our ability to manipulate algebraic symbols successfully requires that we first understand the structural properties of mathematical operations and relations which distinguish allowable transformations from those that are not. These structural properties constitute the *semantic* aspects of algebra. ... The essential feature of algebraic representation and symbol manipulation, then, is that it should *proceed from* an understanding of the semantics or referential meanings that underlie it." (pp. 57-58). In other words, "the sense of meaningfulness comes with the ability of 'seeing' abstract ideas hidden behind the symbols" (Sfard & Linchevski, 1994, p. 224), that is, the symbols become transparent. This aspect of algebra is sometimes referred to as its internal semantics.

This structural source of meaning not only links letter-symbolic representations to their numerical foundations but also interweaves the forms of algebra, its equivalences, and its property-based transformational activity (as noted, for example, in the research of Cerulli and Mariotti, 2001, where "the use of axioms becomes the only way to state the equivalence between two expressions, whilst numerical verification becomes the main way to prove that two expressions are not equivalent", p. 184). While "grasping the structure of expressions" –a phrase often used in research dealing with the structural source of meaning in algebra– is rarely spelled out in detail, researchers have nevertheless offered definitions for related phrases, for example, *structure* (Hoch & Dreyfus, 2004), *structure sense* (Linchevski & Livneh, 1999), *symbol awareness* (MacGregor & Price, 1999; see also the framework for *algebraic expectation* by Pierce & Stacey, 2001), and *symbol sense* (Arcavi, 1994). Even though the nature of the meaning that students draw from algebraic structure can be elusive (e.g., Demby, 1997), this source of meaning is considered by many mathematics educators and researchers to be fundamental to algebra learning.

Meaning from multiple representations

Kaput (1989) has argued that the problem of student learning in algebra is compounded by (a) the inherent difficulties in dealing with the highly concise and implicit syntax of formal algebraic symbols and (b) the lack of linkages to other representations that might provide feedback on the appropriate actions taken. As a consequence, he has promoted the kind of mathematical meaning building that has its source in *translations between mathematical representations systems*. While tables, graphs, and equations can all be used to display binary relations, a critical difference, according to Kaput, between tables and graphs is that, "a graph engages our gestalt-producing ability, which allows us to consolidate a binary (and especially a functional) quantitative relationship into a single graphical entity –a curve or line" (Kaput, 1989, p. 172, parentheses in the original).

Multi-representational sources of meaning and functional approaches to the teaching of algebra clearly go hand-in-hand. It is noted that various representations are generally seen as mediators between certain characteristics of the representing notation and features of the world being modeled –a source of meaning to be treated in the next subsection. However, in the context of within-mathematical sources of meaning, it is the interrelationships among the various mathematical representations themselves that are considered to support meaning building in algebra. The opportunity to coordinate objects and actions within two different representations, such as the graphical and the letter-symbolic, has been found to be helpful in creating meaning in algebra (e.g., Fey, 1989; Romberg, Fennema & Carpenter, 1993; Yerushalmy & Schwartz, 1993), Nevertheless, inferring from visualization of graphs has also been shown to be potentially misleading (e.g., Goldenberg, 1988). Difficulties arise as well from the need to be flexible and competent in translating back and forth between visual and analytic reasoning based on the various representations (e.g., Arcavi, 2003; Amit & Fried, 2005).

Researchers whose studies have integrated computers and calculators involving symbolic manipulation, with graphical and tabular representations (e.g., Guin & Trouche, 1999; Artigue, 2002; Lagrange, 2003), have argued that the emergence of meaning for both symbolic forms and graphical representations, and the relation between the two, cannot be achieved without the simultaneous development of techniques that are both mathematical and technological. However, as has been pointed out by Yerushalmy and Chazan (2002), multiple representation technology brings with it not only access to representations that are different from the letter-symbolic, but also added complexity due to the potential functional interpretations of the algebraic objects being represented. The question of the meaning given to processes such as equation solving, when the meaning for the equation being manipulated is related to a functional graphical representation, is one where further research is indeed needed.

Meaning from the problem context

In contrast to the internal semantics of algebra as a site for meaning making, as argued by Booth (1989), the external semantics of a problem permit the algebra learner to fuse symbols and notations with events and situations, thereby creating an external meaning for certain objects and processes of algebra. A large body of research in algebra learning holds that problem-solving contexts are foundational to the emergence and evolution of algebraic reasoning (e.g., Bednarz & Janvier, 1996; Bell, 1996). This stance is based to a certain extent on historical grounds whereby problem solving made a major contribution to the development of algebra, as well as on the gradual growth in the status of algebra as a privileged tool for expressing general methods for solving whole classes of problems. Additional arguments are based on relevance and purpose. Despite these positions in favor of the role of problem solving as a source of meaning building in algebra, it has also been emphasized (e.g., Pirie & Martin, 1997; Balacheff, 2001) that there are significant epistemological issues associated with the whole idea of using word problems for creating algebraic meaning making. However, a broader perspective on problem solving has been advanced by Bell (1996):

> For introducing and developing algebra, I understand problem solving to refer to the solving of problems by the forming and solving of equations; this is the narrow sense of the term. But the essential mathematical activity is that of exploring problems in an open way, extending and developing them in the search for more results and more general ones. Hence [all algebraic learning] ... is based on problem explorations. This is the broad sense of the term. (p. 167)

Included within this source of algebra meaning making are "real problems," that is, those that involve the modeling of situations with some mathematical representation, applying mathematical techniques to solve them, and translating the results back to the original situation. Much of the current modeling activity that occurs in algebra classes uses actual physical artifacts and/or technological modeling tools as an integral part of the activity. In these cases, the contextual aspect of the situation is very much intertwined with gestures and body language in the process of constructing a mathematical model; this combines two sources of meaning, one derived from the problem context and the other which is exterior to the context and which is discussed directly below.

Meaning derived from that which is exterior to the mathematics/problem context

As pointed out in earlier theoretical remarks related to the research directions that began to emerge in PME during the mid-1990s, a recent approach by algebra researchers to thinking about meaning making concerns the sources of meaning that are exterior to both the mathematics and the problem situation. (It is noted that much of this meaning building that is "exterior" to both the mathematics and the problem situation is related to that which is uniquely human, and thus is clearly "interior" in a very real sense.) Research with an eye to students' processes of meaning production in terms of the way diverse resources such as gestures, bodily movement, words, and artifacts become interwoven during mathematical activity has attracted much interest (e.g., Arzarello & Robutti, 2001; Boero, Bazzini & Garuti, 2001; Nemirovsky, 2003; Radford et al., 2003; Robutti & Arzarello, 2003; Radford, Bardini, Sabena, Diallo & Simbagoye, 2005). Past studies of students' ways of thinking in algebra had always suggested that they brought more to bear on their learning of algebra than were accounted for by the theories available at the time; thus, the explicit focus in recent algebra research on bodily activity, language, and past lived experience as a source of meaning is a natural evolution and one that merits further theoretical and empirical attention.

Based on his seminal studies of students' production of (oral and written) signs and the meanings they ascribe to them as they engage in the construction of expressions of mathematical generality, Radford (2000) has observed that:

> Students, at the very beginning, tend to have recourse to other experiential aspects more accessible to them than the structural one. ... Novice students bring meanings from other domains (not necessarily mathematical domains) into the realm of algebra. Hence it seems to us, one of the didactic questions with which to deal is ... that of the understanding of how those non-algebraic meanings are progressively transformed by the students up to the point to attain the standards of the complex algebraic meanings of contemporary school mathematics. (p. 240)

With the broadening of sources of meaning in algebra to include that which is derived from the exterior of the mathematics/problem context, Radford's question is an obvious one for future research and one with which to bring this chapter to a close, that is, how do students come to integrate and transform the meanings they derive from the various sources, both mathematical and non-mathematical, so as to "attain the standards of the complex algebraic meanings of contemporary school mathematics." This fundamental question, within the intricacy of a multiple-sources-of-meaning perspective, offers a rich springboard for future PME research in algebra.

ACKNOWLEDGMENTS

I am grateful to the two reviewers, Janet Ainley and Nicolina Malara, whose insightful suggestions proved most helpful in the preparation of a revised version of this chapter.

REFERENCES

Ainley, J. (1996). Purposeful contexts for formal notation in a spreadsheet environment. *Journal of Mathematical Behavior, 15*, 405–422.

Ainley, J. (Coord.). (2001). Research Forum: Early algebra. In M. van den Heuvel-Panhuizen (Ed.), *Proceedings of the 25th PME International Conference, 1*, 129–159.

Ainley, J., Wilson, K., & Bills, L. (2003). Generalising the context and generalising the calculation. In N. A. Pateman, B. J. Dougherty, & J. T. Zilliox (Eds.), *Proceedings of the 27th PME International Conference, 2*, 9–16.

Alcock, L., & Weber, K. (2005). Referential and syntactic approaches to proof: Case studies from a transition course. In H. L. Chick & J. L. Vincent (Eds.), *Proceedings of the 29th PME International Conference, 2*, 33–40.

Amit, M., & Fried, M. N. (2005). Multiple representations in 8th grade algebra lessons: Are learners really getting it? In H. L. Chick & J. L. Vincent (Eds.), *Proceedings of the 29th PME International Conference, 2*, 57–64.

Arcavi, A. (1994). Symbol sense: Informal sense-making in formal mathematics. *For the Learning of Mathematics, 14*(3), 24–35.

Arcavi, A. (2003). The role of visual representations in the learning of mathematics. *Educational Studies in Mathematics, 52*, 215–241.

Artigue, M. (2002). Learning mathematics in a CAS environment: The genesis of a reflection about instrumentation and the dialectics between technical and conceptual work. *International Journal of Computers for Mathematical Learning, 7*, 245–274.

Arzarello, F., Bazzini, L., & Chiappini, G. (1994). The process of naming in algebraic thinking. In J. P. Ponte & J. F. Matos (Eds.), *Proceedings of the 18th PME International Conference, 2*, 40–47.

Arzarello, F., Bazzini, L., & Chiappini, G. (2001). A model for analysing algebraic processes of thinking. In R. Sutherland, T. Rojano, A. Bell, & R. Lins (Eds.), *Perspectives on school algebra* (pp. 61–82). Dordrecht, The Netherlands: Kluwer.

Arzarello, F., & Robutti, O. (2001). From body motion to algebra through graphing. In H. Chick, K. Stacey, J. Vincent, & J. Vincent. (Eds.), *Proceedings of the 12th ICMI Study Conference: The Future of the Teaching and Learning of Algebra* (pp. 33–40). Melbourne, Australia: The University of Melbourne.

Balacheff, N. (2001). Symbolic arithmetic vs. algebra: The core of a didactical dilemma. In R. Sutherland, T. Rojano, A. Bell, & R. Lins (Eds.), *Perspectives on school algebra* (pp. 249–260). Dordrecht, The Netherlands: Kluwer.

Ball, L., Pierce, R., & Stacey, K. (2003). Recognising equivalent algebraic expressions: An important component of algebraic expectation for working with CAS. In N. A. Pateman, B. J. Dougherty, & J. T. Zilliox (Eds.), *Proceedings of the 27th PME International Conference, 4*, 15–22.

Barkai, R., Tsamir, P., Tirosh, D., & Dreyfus, T. (2002). Proving or refuting arithmetic claims: The case of elementary school teachers. In A. D. Cockburn & E. Nardi (Eds.), *Proceedings of the 26th PME International Conference, 2*, 57–64.

Bartolini Bussi, M. G. (1995). Analysis of classroom interaction discourse from a Vygotskian perspective. In L. Meira & D. Carraher (Eds.), *Proceedings of the 19th PME International Conference, 1*, 95–101.

Bazzini, L., Boero, P., & Garuti, R. (2001). Moving symbols around or developing understanding: The case of algebraic expressions. In M. van den Heuvel-Panhuizen (Ed.), *Proceedings of the 25th PME International Conference, 2*, 121–128.

Bednarz, N., & Janvier, B. (1996). Emergence and development of algebra as a problem-solving tool: Continuities and discontinuities with arithmetic. In N. Bednarz, C. Kieran & L. Lee (Eds.), *Approaches to algebra: Perspectives for research and teaching* (pp. 115–136). Dordrecht, The Netherlands: Kluwer.

Bednarz, N., Kieran, C., & Lee, L. (Eds.). (1996). *Approaches to algebra: Perspectives for research and teaching*. Dordrecht, The Netherlands: Kluwer.

Behr, M., Erlwanger, S., & Nichols, E. (1976). *How children view equality sentences* (PMDC Technical Report No. 3). Tallahassee: Florida State University. (ERIC ED144802)

Bell, A. (1976). A study of pupils' proof-explanations in mathematical situations. *Educational Studies in Mathematics, 7*, 23–40.

Bell, A. (1996). Problem-solving approaches to algebra: Two aspects. In N. Bednarz, C. Kieran & L. Lee (Eds.), *Approaches to algebra: Perspectives for research and teaching* (pp. 167–185). Dordrecht, The Netherlands: Kluwer.

Bell, A., O'Brien, D., & Shiu, C. (1980). Designing teaching in the light of research on understanding. In R. Karplus (Ed.), *Proceedings of the 4th PME International Conference, 1*, 119–125.

Bills, L. (1997). Stereotypes of literal symbol use in senior school algebra. In E. Pehkonen (Ed.), *Proceedings of the 21st PME International Conference, 2*, 73–80.

Bills, L. (2001). Shifts in the meanings of literal symbols. In M. van den Heuvel-Panhuizen (Ed.), *Proceedings of the 25th PME International Conference, 2*, 161–168.

Bishop, A. J., Clements, K., Keitel, C., Kilpatrick, J., & Laborde, C. (Eds.). (1996). *International handbook of mathematics education*. Dordrecht, The Netherlands: Kluwer.

Blanton, M. L., & Kaput, J. J. (2004). Elementary students' capacity for functional thinking. In M. J. Høines & A. B. Fuglestad (Eds.), *Proceedings of the 28th PME International Conference, 2*, 135–142.

Bloedy-Vinner, H. (1994). The analgebraic mode of thinking: The case of parameter. In J. P. Ponte & J. F. Matos (Eds.), *Proceedings of the 18th PME International Conference, 2*, 88–95.

Bloedy-Vinner, H. (2001). Beyond unknowns and variables – parameters and dummy variables in high school algebra. In R. Sutherland, T. Rojano, A. Bell, & R. Lins (Eds.), *Perspectives on school algebra* (pp. 177–189). Dordrecht, The Netherlands: Kluwer.

Boaler, J. (2003). Studying and capturing the complexity of practice: The case of the dance of agency. In N. A. Pateman, B. J. Dougherty, & J. T. Zilliox (Eds.), *Proceedings of the 27th PME International Conference, 1*, 3–16.

Boero, P., Bazzini, L., & Garuti, R. (2001). Metaphors in teaching and learning mathematics: A case study concerning inequalities. In M. van den Heuvel-Panhuizen (Ed.), *Proceedings of the 25th PME International Conference, 2*, 185–192.

Booth, L. R. (1981). Strategies and errors in generalized arithmetic. In Equipe de Recherche Pédagogique (Eds.), *Proceedings of the 5th PME International Conference, 1*, 140–146.

Booth, L. R. (1982). Developing a teaching module in beginning algebra. In A. Vermandel (Ed.), *Proceedings of the 6th PME International Conference, 1*, 280–285.

Booth, L. R. (1983). A diagnostic teaching programme in elementary algebra: Results and implications. In R. Hershkowitz (Ed.), *Proceedings of the 7th PME International Conference, 1*, 307–312.

Booth, L. R. (1984). *Algebra: Children's strategies and errors*. Windsor, UK: NFER-Nelson.

Booth, L. R. (1989). A question of structure. In S. Wagner & C. Kieran (Eds.), *Research issues in the learning and teaching of algebra* (Volume 4 of *Research agenda for mathematics education*, pp. 57–59). Reston, USA: NCTM.

Borba, M. (1993). *Students' understanding of transformations of functions using multi-representational software.* Unpublished PhD dissertation, Cornell University, Ithaca, USA.

Boulton-Lewis, G., Cooper, T., Atweh, B., Pillay, H., Wilss, L., & Mutch, S. (1997). Processing load and the use of concrete representations and strategies for solving linear equations. *Journal of Mathematical Behavior, 16*, 379–397.

Carpenter, T. P., Franke, M. L., & Levi, L. (2003). *Thinking mathematically: Integrating arithmetic and algebra in elementary school.* Portsmouth, USA: Heinemann.

Carry, L. R., Lewis, C., & Bernard, J. (1980). *Psychology of equation solving: An information processing study* (Final Technical Report). Austin, USA: University of Texas at Austin, Department of Curriculum and Instruction.

Cavanagh, M., & Mitchelmore, M. (2000). Student misconceptions in interpreting basic calculator displays. In T. Nakahara & M. Koyama (Eds.), *Proceedings of the 24th PME International Conference, 2*, 161–168.

Cedillo, T., & Kieran, C. (2003). Initiating students into algebra with symbol-manipulating calculators. In J. T. Fey (Ed.), *Computer algebra systems in secondary school mathematics education* (pp. 219–239). Reston, USA: NCTM.

Cerulli, M. (2004). *Introducing pupils to algebra as a theory: L'Algebrista as an instrument of semiotic mediation.* Unpublished PhD dissertation, Università degli Studi di Pisa, Italy. Retrieved from http://www-studenti.dm.unipi.it/~cerulli/tesi/.

Cerulli, M., & Mariotti, M. A. (2001). L'Algebrista: A microworld for symbolic manipulation. In H. Chick, K. Stacey, J. Vincent, & J. Vincent (Eds.), *Proceedings of the 12th ICMI Study Conference: The Future of the Teaching and Learning of Algebra* (pp. 179–186). Melbourne, Australia: The University of Melbourne.

Chalouh, L., & Herscovics, N. (1988). Teaching algebraic expressions in a meaningful way. In A. Coxford (Ed.), *The ideas of algebra, K-12* (Yearbook of the NCTM, pp. 33–42). Reston, USA: NCTM.

Chazan, D. (1996). Algebra for all students?. *Journal of Mathematical Behavior, 15*, 455–477.

Chazan, D. (2000). *Beyond formulas in mathematics and teaching: Dynamics of the high school algebra classroom.* New York: Teachers College Press.

Chevallard, Y. (1999). L'analyse des pratiques enseignantes en théorie anthropologique du didactique. *Recherches en Didactique des Mathématiques, 19*, 221–266.

Chick, H., Stacey, K., Vincent, J., & Vincent, J. (Eds.). (2001). *Proceedings of the 12th ICMI Study Conference: The Future of the Teaching and Learning of Algebra.* Melbourne, Australia: The University of Melbourne.

Chin, E.-T., & Tall, D. (2000). Making, having and compressing formal mathematical concepts. In T. Nakahara & M. Koyama (Eds.), *Proceedings of the 24th PME International Conference, 2*, 177–184.

Clement, J. (1982). Algebra word problem solutions: Thought processes underlying a common misconception. *Journal for Research in Mathematics Education, 13*, 16–30.

Clement, J. (1985). Misconceptions in graphing. In L. Streefland (Ed.), *Proceedings of the 9th PME International Conference, 1*, 369–375.

Cobb, P. (1994). Where is mind? Constructivist and sociocultural perspectives on mathematical development. *Educational Researcher, 23*(7), 13–20.

Cobb, P., & Steffe, L. P. (1983). The constructivist researcher as teacher and model builder. *Journal for Research in Mathematics Education, 14*, 83–94.

Cobb, P., & Yackel, E. (1995). Constructivist, emergent, and sociocultural perspectives in the context of developmental research. In D. T. Owens, M. K. Reed, & G. M. Millsaps (Eds.), *Proceedings of the 17th PME–NA Annual Meeting, 1*, 3–29.

Coles, A. (2001). Listening: A case study of teacher change. In M. van den Heuvel-Panhuizen (Ed.), *Proceedings of the 25th PME International Conference,* 2, 281–288.

Collis, K. F. (1974). *Cognitive development and mathematics learning.* Paper presented at the Psychology of Mathematics Workshop, Centre for Science Education, Chelsea College, London, UK.

Confrey, J. (1987). The constructivist. In J. C. Bergeron, N. Herscovics, & C. Kieran (Eds.), *Proceedings of the 11th PME International Conference, 3*, 307–317.

Cortés, A. (1998). Implicit cognitive work in putting word problems into equation form. In A. Olivier & K. Newstead (Eds.), *Proceedings of the 22nd PME International Conference, 2*, 208–216.

Da Rocha Falcão, J. T., Brito Lima, A. P., De Araújo, C. R., Lins Lessa, M. M., & Oliveira Osório, M. (2000). A didactic sequence for the introduction of algebraic activity in early elementary school. In T. Nakahara & M. Koyama (Eds.), *Proceedings of the 24th PME International Conference, 2*, 209–216.

Davis, R. B. (1975). Cognitive processes involved in solving simple algebraic equations. *Journal of Children's Mathematical Behavior, 1*(3), 7–35.

Davis, R. B. (1985). ICME-5 report: Algebraic thinking in the early grades. *Journal of Mathematical Behavior, 4*, 195–208.

De Bock, D., Verschaffel, L., & Janssens, D. (2002). The effects of different problem presentations and formulations on the illusion of linearity in secondary school students. *Mathematical Thinking and Learning, 4*, 65-89.

De Bock, D., Verschaffel, L., Janssens, D., & Claes, K. (2000). Involving pupils in an authentic context: Does it help them to overcome the "illusion of linearity"? In T. Nakahara & M. Koyama (Eds.), *Proceedings of the 24th PME International Conference, 2*, 233–240.

Demby, A. (1997). Algebraic procedures used by 13- to 15-year-olds. *Educational Studies in Mathematics, 33*, 45–70.

Dettori, G., Garuti, R., & Lemut, E. (2001). From arithmetic to algebraic thinking by using a spreadsheet. In R. Sutherland, T. Rojano, A. Bell, & R. Lins (Eds.), *Perspectives on school algebra* (pp. 191–207). Dordrecht, The Netherlands: Kluwer.

Doerr, H. M. (2003). Using students' ways of thinking to re-cast the tasks of teaching about functions. In N. A. Pateman, B. J. Dougherty, & J. T. Zilliox (Eds.), *Proceedings of the 27th PME International Conference, 2*, 333–340.

Doerr, H. M., & Zangor, R. (2000). Creating meaning for and with the graphing calculator. *Educational Studies in Mathematics, 41*, 143–163.

Douek, N. (1999). Argumentative aspects of proving: Analysis of some undergraduate mathematics students' performances. In O. Zaslavsky (Ed.), *Proceedings of the 23rd PME International Conference, 2*, 273–280.

Dougherty, B. J. (2003). Voyaging from theory to practice in learning: Measure Up. In N. A. Pateman, B. J. Dougherty, & J. T. Zilliox (Eds.), *Proceedings of the 27th PME International Conference, 1*, 17–23.

Dougherty, B. J., & Slovin, H. (2004). Generalized diagrams as a tool for young children's problem solving. In M. J. Høines & A. B. Fuglestad (Eds.), *Proceedings of the 28th PME International Conference, 2*, 295–302.

Dreyfus, T., & Eisenberg, T. (1981). Function concepts: Intuitive baseline. In Equipe de Recherche Pédagogique (Eds.), *Proceedings of the 5th PME International Conference, 1*, 183–188.

Drijvers, P. (2003). Algebra on screen, on paper, and in the mind. In J. T. Fey (Ed.), *Computer algebra systems in secondary school mathematics education* (pp. 241–267). Reston, USA: NCTM.

Drouhard, J.-Ph., & Teppo, A. R. (2004). Symbols and language. In K. Stacey, H. Chick, & M. Kendal (Eds.), *The future of the teaching and learning of algebra: The 12th ICMI Study* (pp. 227–264). Dordrecht, The Netherlands: Kluwer.

Dubinsky, E. (1991). Reflective abstraction in advanced mathematical thinking. In D. Tall (Ed.), *Advanced mathematical thinking* (pp. 95–123). Dordrecht, The Netherlands: Kluwer.

English, L. D. (Ed.). (2002). *Handbook of international research in mathematics education.* Mahwah, USA: Lawrence Erlbaum.

English, L. D., & Doerr, H. M. (2003). Perspective-taking in middle-school mathematical modelling: A teacher case study. In N. A. Pateman, B. J. Dougherty, & J. T. Zilliox (Eds.), *Proceedings of the 27th PME International Conference, 2*, 357–364.

Even, R. (1988). Pre-service teachers' conceptions of the relationships between functions and equations. In A. Borbás (Ed.), *Proceedings of the 12th PME International Conference, 1*, 304–311.

Even, R. (1990). The two faces of the inverse function: Prospective teachers' use of undoing. In G. Booker, P. Cobb, & T. N. Mendicuti (Eds.), *Proceedings of the 14th PME International Conference, 1*, 37–44.

Ferrara, F. (2003). Metaphors as vehicles of knowledge: An exploratory analysis. In N. A. Pateman, B. J. Dougherty, & J. T. Zilliox (Eds.), *Proceedings of the 27th PME International Conference, 2*, 373–380.

Fey, J. T. (Ed.). (1984). *Computing and mathematics: The impact on secondary school curricula.* Reston, USA: NCTM.

Fey, J. T. (1989). School algebra for the year 2000. In S. Wagner, & C. Kieran (Eds.), *Research issues in the learning and teaching of algebra* (Volume 4 of *Research agenda for mathematics education*, pp. 199–213). Reston, VA: NCTM.

Fey, J. T., & Good, R. A. (1985). Rethinking the sequence and priorities of high school mathematics curricula. In C. R. Hirsch, & M. J. Zweng (Eds.), *The secondary school mathematics curriculum* (Yearbook of the NCTM, pp. 43–52). Reston, USA: NCTM.

Filloy, E. (1990). PME algebra research: A working perspective. In G. Booker, P. Cobb, & T. N. Mendicuti (Eds.), *Proceedings of the 14th PME International Conference, 1*, PII 1–33.

Filloy, E., Rojano, T. (1989). Solving equations: The transition from arithmetic to algebra. *For the Learning of Mathematics, 9*(2), 19-25.

Filloy, E., Rojano, T., & Rubio, G. (2001). Propositions concerning the resolution of arithmetical-algebraic problems. In R. Sutherland, T. Rojano, A. Bell, & R. Lins (Eds.), *Perspectives on school algebra* (pp. 155–176). Dordrecht, The Netherlands: Kluwer.

Filloy, E., Rojano, T., & Solares, A. (2003). Two meanings of the "equal" sign and senses of comparison and substitution methods. In N. A. Pateman, B. J. Dougherty, & J. T. Zilliox (Eds.), *Proceedings of the 27th PME International Conference, 4*, 223–229.

Filloy, E., Rojano, T., & Solares, A. (2004). Arithmetic/algebraic problem solving and the representation of two unknown quantities. In M. J. Høines & A. B. Fuglestad (Eds.), *Proceedings of the 28th PME International Conference, 2*, 391–398.

Fischbein, E., & Kedem, I. (1982). Proof and certitude in the development of mathematical thinking. In A. Vermandel (Ed.), *Proceedings of the 6th PME International Conference, 1*, 128–131.

Fujii, T. (1993). A clinical interview on children's understanding and misconceptions of literal symbols in school mathematics. In I. Hirabayashi, N. Nohda, K. Shigematsu, & F.-L. Lin (Eds.), *Proceedings of the 17th PME International Conference, 1*, 173–180.

Fujii, T. (2003). Probing students' understanding of variables through cognitive conflict problems: Is the concept of variable so difficult for students to understand? In N. A. Pateman, B. J. Dougherty, & J. T. Zilliox (Eds.), *Proceedings of the 27th PME International Conference, 1*, 49–65.

Furinghetti, F., & Paola, D. (1994). Parameters, unknowns and variables: A little difference? In J. P. Ponte & J. F. Matos (Eds.), *Proceedings of the 18th PME International Conference, 2*, 368–375.

Gallardo, A. (2002). The extension of the natural-number domain to the integers in the transition from arithmetic to algebra. *Educational Studies in Mathematics, 49*, 171–192.

Garuti, R., Boero, P., & Lemut, E. (1998). Cognitive unity of theorems and difficulty of proof. In A. Olivier & K. Newstead (Eds.), *Proceedings of the 22nd PME International Conference, 2*, 345–352.

Gilead, S., & Yerushalmy, M. (2001). Deep structures of algebra word problems: Is it approach (in)dependent? In M. van den Heuvel-Panhuizen (Ed.), *Proceedings of the 25th PME International Conference, 3*, 41–48.

Goldenberg, E. P. (1988). Mathematics, metaphors, and human factors: Mathematical, technical and pedagogical challenges in the educational use of graphical representations of functions. *Journal of Mathematical Behavior, 7*, 135–173.

Gray, E., & Tall, D. (1994). Duality, ambiguity, and flexibility: A "proceptual" view of simple arithmetic. *Journal for Research in Mathematics Education, 25*, 116–140.
Grouws, D. A. (Ed.). (1992). *Handbook of research on mathematics teaching and learning*. New York, USA: Macmillan.
Guin, D., & Trouche, L. (1999). The complex process of converting tools into mathematical instruments: The case of calculators. *International Journal of Computers for Mathematical Learning, 3*, 195–227.
Guin, D., & Trouche, L. (2000). Thinking of new devices to make viable symbolic calculators in the classroom. In T. Nakahara & M. Koyama (Eds.), *Proceedings of the 24th PME International Conference, 3*, 9–16.
Guzmán, J., & Kieran, C. (2002). The role of calculators in instrumental genesis: The case of Nicolas and factors and divisors. In A. D. Cockburn & E. Nardi (Eds.), *Proceedings of the 26th PME International Conference, 3*, 41–48.
Hadjidemetriou, C., & Williams, J. (2002). Teachers' pedagogical content knowledge: Graphs from a cognitivist to a situated perspective. In A. D. Cockburn & E. Nardi (Eds.), *Proceedings of the 26th PME International Conference, 3*, 57–64.
Harper, E. W. (1981). Psychological changes attending a transition from arithmetical to algebraic thought. In Equipe de Recherche Pédagogique (Eds.), *Proceedings of the 5th PME International Conference, 1*, 171–176.
Harper, E. W. (1987). Ghosts of Diophantus. *Educational Studies in Mathematics, 18*, 75–90.
Healy, L., & Hoyles, C. (1999). Visual and symbolic reasoning in mathematics: Making connections with computers? *Mathematical Thinking and Learning, 1*, 59–84.
Heid, M. K. (1996). A technology-intensive functional approach to the emergence of algebraic thinking. In N. Bednarz, C. Kieran, & L. Lee (Eds.), *Approaches to algebra: Perspectives for research and teaching* (pp. 239–255). Dordrecht, The Netherlands: Kluwer.
Herscovics, N., & Kieran, C. (1980). Constructing meaning for the concept of equation. *The Mathematics Teacher, 73*, 572–580.
Herscovics, N., & Linchevski, L. (1991). Pre-algebraic thinking: Range of equations and informal solution processes used by seventh graders prior to any instruction. In F. Furinghetti (Ed.), *Proceedings of the 15th PME International Conference, 2*, 173–180.
Herscovics, N., & Linchevski, L. (1994). A cognitive gap between arithmetic and algebra. *Educational Studies in Mathematics, 27*, 59–78.
Hershkowitz, R., Dreyfus, T., Ben-Zvi, D., Friedlander, A., Hadas, N., Resnick, T., Tabach, M., & Schwarz, B. (2002). Mathematics curriculum development for computerized environments: A designer-researcher-teacher-learner activity. In L. D. English (Ed.), *Handbook of international research in mathematics education* (pp. 657–694). Mahwah, USA: Lawrence Erlbaum.
Hershkowitz, R., & Kieran, C. (2001). Algorithmic and meaningful ways of joining together representatives within the same mathematical activity: An experience with graphing calculators. In M. van den Heuvel-Panhuizen (Ed.), *Proceedings of the 25th PME International Conference, 1*, 96–107.
Hershkowitz, R., Schwarz, B. B., & Dreyfus, T. (2001). Abstraction in context: Epistemic actions. *Journal for Research in Mathematics Education, 32*, 195–222.
Hewitt, D. (2003). Notation issues: Visual effects and ordering operations. In N. A. Pateman, B. J. Dougherty, & J. T. Zilliox (Eds.), *Proceedings of the 27th PME International Conference, 3*, 63–69.
Hoch, M., & Dreyfus, T. (2004). Structure sense in high school algebra: The effects of brackets. In M. J. Høines & A. B. Fuglestad (Eds.), *Proceedings of the 28th PME International Conference, 3*, 49–56.
Hoch, M., & Dreyfus, T. (2005). Students' difficulties with applying a familiar formula in an unfamiliar context. In H. L. Chick & J. L. Vincent (Eds.), *Proceedings of the 29th PME International Conference, 3*, 145–152.
Hoyles, C. (2002). From describing to designing mathematical activity: The next step in developing a social approach to research in mathematics education? In C. Kieran, E. Forman, & A. Sfard (Eds.),

Learning discourse: Discursive approaches to research in mathematics education (pp. 273–286). Dordrecht, The Netherlands: Kluwer.

Hoyles, C., Sutherland, R., & Evans, J. (1985). *The Logo Maths Project: A preliminary investigation of the pupil-centred approach to the learning of Logo in the secondary mathematics classroom, 1983–84.* London, UK: University of London, Institute of Education.

Huntley, M. A., Rasmussen, C. L., Villarubi, R. S., Sangtong, J., & Fey, J. T. (2000). Effects of standards-based mathematics education: A study of the Core-Plus Mathematics Project Algebra and Functions Strand. *Journal for Research in Mathematics Education, 31*, 328–361.

Iannone, P., & Nardi, E. (2002). A group as a 'special set'? Implications of ignoring the role of the binary operation in the definition of a group. In A. D. Cockburn & E. Nardi (Eds.), *Proceedings of the 26th PME International Conference, 3*, 121–128.

Ishida, J., & Sanjii, A. (2002). Can poor students identify the good features of a demonstrated problem solving method and use it to solve a generalization problem? In A. D. Cockburn & E. Nardi (Eds.), *Proceedings of the 26th PME International Conference, 3*, 137–144.

Janvier, C. (1981). Difficulties related to the concept of variable presented graphically. In Equipe de Recherche Pédagogique (Eds.), *Proceedings of the 5th PME International Conference, 1*, 189–192.

John-Steiner, V. (1995): Spontaneous and scientific concepts in mathematics: A Vygotskian approach. In L. Meira & D. Carraher (Eds.), *Proceedings of the 19th PME International Conference, 1*, 30-44.

Kaput, J. J. (1989). Linking representations in the symbol systems of algebra. In S. Wagner, & C. Kieran (Eds.), Research issues in the learning and teaching of algebra (Volume 4 of Research agenda for mathematics education, pp. 167–194). Reston, USA: NCTM.

Kaput, J. J. (1992). Technology and mathematics education. In D. A. Grouws (Ed.), *Handbook of research on mathematics teaching and learning* (pp. 515–556). New York, USA: Macmillan.

Kaput, J. J. (1995). A research base supporting long term algebra reform? In D. T. Owens, M. K. Reed, & G. M. Millsaps (Eds.), *Proceedings of the 7th PME–NA Annual Meeting, 1*, 71–94. (ERIC ED 389539)

Kaput, J. J., & Roschelle, J. (1997). Developing the impact of technology beyond assistance with traditional formalisms in order to democratize access to ideas underlying calculus. In E. Pehkonen (Ed.), *Proceedings of the 21st PME International Conference, 1*, 105–112.

Kerslake, D. (1977). The understanding of graphs. *Mathematics in School, 6*(2), 22–25.

Kieran, C. (1979). Children's operational thinking within the context of bracketing and the order of operations. In D. Tall (Ed.), *Proceedings of the 3rd PME International Conference, 1*, 128–133.

Kieran, C. (1981). Concepts associated with the equality symbol. *Educational Studies in Mathematics, 12*, 317–326.

Kieran, C. (1983). Relationships between novices' views of algebraic letters and their use of symmetric and asymmetric equation-solving procedures. In J. C. Bergeron, & N. Herscovics (Eds.), *Proceedings of the 5th PME–NA Annual Meeting, 1*, 161–168.

Kieran, C. (1984). A comparison between novice and more-expert algebra students on tasks dealing with the equivalence of equations. In J. M. Moser (Ed.), *Proceedings of the 6th PME–NA Annual Meeting, 1*, 83–91.

Kieran, C. (1985). Use of substitution procedure in learning algebraic equation solving. In S. K. Damarin, & M. Shelton (Eds.), *Proceedings of the 7th PME–NA Annual Meeting, 1*, 145–152.

Kieran, C. (1988). Two different approaches among algebra learners. In A. F. Coxford (Ed.), *The ideas of algebra, K-12* (Yearbook of the NCTM, pp. 91–96). Reston, USA: NCTM.

Kieran, C. (1989). The early learning of algebra: A structural perspective. In S. Wagner, & C. Kieran (Eds.), *Research issues in the learning and teaching of algebra* (Volume 4 of *Research agenda for mathematics education*, pp. 33–56). Reston, USA: NCTM.

Kieran, C. (1990). Cognitive processes involved in learning school algebra. In P. Nesher, & J. Kilpatrick (Eds.), *Mathematics and cognition: A research synthesis by the International Group for the Psychology of Mathematics Education* (pp. 96–112). Cambridge, UK: Cambridge University Press.

Kieran, C. (1992). The learning and teaching of school algebra. In D. A. Grouws (Ed.), *Handbook of research on mathematics teaching and learning* (pp. 390–419). New York, USA: Macmillan.

Kieran, C. (1996). The changing face of school algebra. In C. Alsina, J. Alvarez, B. Hodgson, C. Laborde, & A. Pérez (Eds.), *8th International Congress on Mathematical Education: Selected lectures* (pp. 271–290). Seville, Spain: S.A.E.M. Thales.

Kieran, C. (2004). Algebraic thinking in the early grades: What is it? *The Mathematics Educator, 8*(1), 139–151.

Kieran, C., Boileau, A., & Garançon, M. (1989). Processes of mathematization in algebra problem solving within a computer environment: A functional approach. In C. A. Maher, G. A. Goldin, & R. B. Davis (Eds.), *Proceedings of the 11th PME–NA Annual Meeting, 1*, 26–34.

Kieran, C., Forman, E., & Sfard, A. (Eds.). (2001). Bridging the individual and the social: Discursive approaches to research in mathematics education [special issue]. *Educational Studies in Mathematics, 46*(1–3).

Kieran, C., & Saldanha, L. (2005). Computer algebra systems (CAS) as a tool for coaxing the emergence of reasoning about equivalence of algebraic expressions. In H. L. Chick & J. L. Vincent (Eds.), *Proceedings of the 29th PME International Conference, 3*, 193–200.

Kieran, C., & Yerushalmy, M. (2004). Research on the role of technological environments in algebra learning and teaching. In K. Stacey, H. Chick, & M. Kendal (Eds.), *The future of the teaching and learning of algebra: The 12th ICMI Study* (pp. 99–152). Dordrecht, The Netherlands: Kluwer.

Kirshner, D. (1989). The visual syntax of algebra. *Journal for Research in Mathematics Education, 20*, 274–287.

Kirshner, D. (2001). The structural algebra option revisited. In R. Sutherland, T. Rojano, A. Bell, & R. Lins (Eds.), *Perspectives on school algebra* (pp. 83–98). Dordrecht, The Netherlands: Kluwer.

Kirshner, D., & Awtry, T. (2004). Visual salience of algebraic transformations. *Journal for Research in Mathematics Education, 35*, 224–257.

Knuth, E. J. (2000). Student understanding of the Cartesian connection: An exploratory study. *Journal for Research in Mathematics Education, 31*, 500–508.

Kopelman, E. (2002). Misunderstanding of variables by students in an advanced course. In A. D. Cockburn & E. Nardi (Eds.), *Proceedings of the 26th PME International Conference, 3*, 225–232.

Küchemann, D. (1981). Algebra. In K. Hart (Ed.), *Children's understanding of mathematics: 11–16* (pp. 102–119). London, UK: John Murray.

Kutscher, B., & Linchevski, L. (1997). Number instantiations as mediators in solving word problems. In E. Pehkonen (Ed.), *Proceedings of the 21st PME International Conference, 3*, 168–175.

Lagrange, J.-B. (2000). L'intégration d'instruments informatiques dans l'enseignement: une approche par les techniques. *Educational Studies in Mathematics, 43*, 1–30.

Lagrange, J.-B. (2003). Learning techniques and concepts using CAS: A practical and theoretical reflection. In J. T. Fey (Ed.), *Computer Algebra Systems in secondary school mathematics education* (pp. 269–283). Reston, USA: NCTM.

Lakoff, G., & Núñez, R. (2000). *Where mathematics comes from: How the embodied mind brings mathematics into being*. New York, USA: Basic Books.

Lee, L. (1987). The status and understanding of generalised algebraic statements by high school students. In J. C. Bergeron, N. Herscovics, & C. Kieran (Eds.), *Proceedings of the 11th PME International Conference, 1*, 316–323.

Lee, L., & Wheeler, D. (1987). *Algebraic thinking in high school students: Their conceptions of generalisation and justification* (Research Report). Montreal, Canada: Concordia University, Mathematics Department.

Lee, L., & Wheeler, D. (1989). The arithmetic connection. *Educational Studies in Mathematics, 20*, 41–54.

Leron, U., Hazzan, O., & Zazkis, R. (1994). Students' constructions of group isomorphism. In J. P. Ponte & J. F. Matos (Eds.), *Proceedings of the 18th PME International Conference, 3*, 152–159.

Linchevski, L. (1995). Algebra with numbers and arithmetic with letters: A definition of pre-algebra. *Journal of Mathematical Behavior, 14*, 113–120.

Linchevski, L., & Livneh, D. (1999). Structure sense: The relationship between algebraic and numerical contexts. *Educational Studies in Mathematics, 40*, 173–196.

Linchevski, L., & Vinner, S. (1990). Embedded figures and structures of algebraic expressions. In G. Booker, P. Cobb, & T. N. Mendicuti (Eds.), *Proceedings of the 14th PME International Conference, 2*, 85–92.

Linchevski, L., & Williams, J. (1996). Situated intuitions, concrete manipulations and the construction of mathematical concepts: The case of integers. In L. Puig & A. Gutiérrez (Eds.), *Proceedings of the 20th PME International Conference, 3*, 265–272.

Lins, R. C. (2001). The production of meaning for algebra: A perspective based on a theoretical model of semantic fields. In R. Sutherland, T. Rojano, A. Bell, & R. Lins (Eds.), *Perspectives on school algebra* (pp. 37–60). Dordrecht, The Netherlands: Kluwer.

MacGregor, M., & Price, E. (1999). An exploration of aspects of language proficiency and algebraic learning. *Journal for Research in Mathematics Education, 30*, 449–467.

MacGregor, M., & Stacey, K. (1993). Seeing a pattern and writing a rule. In I. Hirabayashi, N. Nohda, K. Shigematsu, & F.-L. Lin (Eds.), *Proceedings of the 17th PME International Conference, 1*, 181–188.

Malara, N. (1999). An aspect of a long-term research on algebra: The solution of verbal problems. In O. Zaslavsky (Ed.), *Proceedings of the 23rd PME International Conference, 3*, 257–264.

Malara, N. (2003). The dialectics between theory and practice: Theoretical issues and practice aspects from an early algebra project. In N. A. Pateman, B. J. Dougherty, & J. T. Zilliox (Eds.), *Proceedings of the 27th PME International Conference, 1*, 31–48.

Maracci, M. (2003). Difficulties in vector space theory: A compared analysis in terms of conceptions and tacit models. In N. A. Pateman, B. J. Dougherty, & J. T. Zilliox (Eds.), *Proceedings of the 27th PME International Conference, 3*, 229–236.

Markovits, Z., Eylon, B., & Bruckheimer, M. (1986). Functions today and yesterday. *For the Learning of Mathematics, 6*(2), 18–24, 28.

Mason, J. (1996). Expressing generality and roots of algebra. In N. Bednarz, C. Kieran, & L. Lee (Eds.), *Approaches to algebra: Perspectives for research and teaching* (pp. 65–86). Dordrecht, The Netherlands: Kluwer.

Mason, J. (2002). What makes an example exemplary? Pedagogical and research issues in transitions from numbers to number theory. In A. D. Cockburn & E. Nardi (Eds.), *Proceedings of the 26th PME International Conference, 1*, 224–229.

Mason, J., Graham, A., & Johnston-Wilder, S. (2005). *Developing thinking in algebra.* London, UK: Sage.

Mason, J., Graham, A., Pimm, D., & Gowar, N. (1985). *Routes to roots of algebra.* Milton Keynes, UK: Open University Press.

Mason, J., & Pimm, D. (1984). Generic examples: Seeing the general in the particular. *Educational Studies in Mathematics, 15*, 277–289.

Mason, J., & Sutherland, R. (2002). *Key aspects of teaching algebra in schools* (Report prepared for the Qualifications and Curriculum Authority). London, UK: QCA.

Meira, L. (1995). Mediation by tools in the mathematics classroom. In L. Meira & D. Carraher (Eds.), *Proceedings of the 19th PME International Conference, 1*, 102–111.

Meira, L. (1998). Making sense of instructional devices: The emergence of transparency in mathematical activity. *Journal for Research in Mathematics Education, 29*, 121–142.

Molyneux-Hodgson, S., Rojano, T., Sutherland, R., & Ursini, S. (1999). Mathematical modeling: The interaction of culture and practice. *Educational Studies in Mathematics, 39*, 167–183.

Moschkovich, J., Schoenfeld, A. H., & Arcavi, A. (1993). Aspects of understanding: On multiple perspectives and representations of linear relations and connections among them. In T. A. Romberg, E. Fennema, & T. P. Carpenter. *Integrating research on the graphical representation of function* (pp. 69–100). Hillsdale, USA: Lawrence Erlbaum.

Moss, J. (2005). *Integrating numeric and geometric patterns: A developmental approach to young students' learning of patterns and functions.* Paper presented at Annual Meeting of the Canadian Mathematics Education Study Group, Ottawa, Canada.

Nemirovsky, R. (Coord.). (2003). Research Forum: Perceptuo-motor activity in mathematics learning. In N. A. Pateman, B. J. Dougherty, & J. T. Zilliox (Eds.), *Proceedings of the 27th PME International Conference, 1,* 103–135.

Nesher, P., & Kilpatrick, J. (Eds.). (1990). *Mathematics and cognition: A research synthesis by the International Group for the Psychology of Mathematics Education.* Cambridge, UK: Cambridge University Press.

Noble, T., Nemirovsky, R., Wright, T., & Tierney, C. (2001). Experiencing change: The mathematics of change in multiple environments. *Journal for Research in Mathematics Education, 32,* 85–108.

Noss, R., & Hoyles, C. (1996). *Windows on mathematical meanings.* Dordrecht, The Netherlands: Kluwer.

Pawley, D. (1999). To check or not to check? Does teaching a checking method reduce the incidence of the multiplicative reversal error? In O. Zaslavsky (Ed.), *Proceedings of the 23rd PME International Conference, 4,* 17–24.

Pence, B. (1994). Teachers' perceptions of algebra. In J. P. Ponte & J. F. Matos (Eds.), *Proceedings of the 18th PME International Conference, 4,* 17–24.

Perrenet, J. C., & Wolters, M. A. (1994). The art of checking: A case study of students' erroneous checking behavior in introductory algebra. *Journal of Mathematical Behavior, 13,* 335–358.

Pierce, R., & Stacey, K. (2001). A framework for Algebraic Insight. In J. Bobis, B. Perry, & M. Mitchelmore (Eds.), *Proceedings of the 24th MERGA Conference, 2,* 418–425.

Pirie, S. E. B., & Martin, L. (1997). The equation, the whole equation and nothing but the equation! One approach to the teaching of linear equations. *Educational Studies in Mathematics, 34,* 159–181.

Ponte, J. (1985). Geometric and numerical strategies in students' functional reasoning. In L. Streefland (Ed.), *Proceedings of the 9th PME International Conference, 1,* 413–418.

Presmeg, N., & Nenduradu, R. (2005). An investigation of a preservice teacher's use of representations in solving algebraic problems involving exponential relationships. In H. L. Chick & J. L. Vincent (Eds.), *Proceedings of the 29th PME International Conference, 4,* 105–112.

Radford, L. (2000). Signs and meanings in students' emergent algebraic thinking: A semiotic analysis. *Educational Studies in Mathematics, 42,* 237–268.

Radford, L. (2004). Syntax and meaning. In M. J. Høines & A. B. Fuglestad (Eds.), *Proceedings of the 28th PME International Conference, 1,* 161–166.

Radford, L., Bardini, C., Sabena, C., Diallo, P., & Simbagoye, A. (2005). On embodiment, artifacts, and signs: A semiotic-cultural perspective on mathematical thinking. In H. L. Chick & J. L. Vincent (Eds.), *Proceedings of the 29th PME International Conference, 4,* 113–120.

Radford, L., Demers, S., Guzmán, J., & Cerulli, M. (2003). Calculators, graphs, gestures and the production of meaning. In N. A. Pateman, B. J. Dougherty, & J. T. Zilliox (Eds.), *Proceedings of the 27th PME International Conference, 4,* 55–62.

Radford, L., & Grenier, M. (1996). Les apprentissages mathématiques en situation. *Revue des Sciences de l'Éducation, XXII,* 253–275.

Robinson, N., Even, R., & Tirosh, D. (1992). Connectedness in teaching algebra: A novice-expert contrast. In W. Geeslin & K. Graham (Eds.), *Proceedings of the 16th PME International Conference, 2,* 258–265.

Robutti, O., & Arzarello, F. (2003). Approaching algebra through motion experiences. In N. A. Pateman, B. J. Dougherty, & J. T. Zilliox (Eds.), *Proceedings of the 27th PME International Conference, 1,* 111–115.

Rogalski, M. (1996). Teaching linear algebra: Role and nature of knowledges in logic and set theory which deal with some linear problems. In L. Puig & A. Gutiérrez (Eds.), *Proceedings of the 20th PME International Conference, 4,* 211–218.

Romberg, T. A., Fennema, E., & Carpenter, T. P. (Eds.). (1993). *Integrating research on the graphical representation of function.* Hillsdale, USA: Lawrence Erlbaum.

Ruthven, K., & Hennessy, S. (2002). A practitioner model of the use of computer-based tools and resources to support mathematics teaching and learning. *Educational Studies in Mathematics, 49*, 47–88.

Sackur, C., Drouhard, J.-Ph., Maurel, M., & Pécal, M. (1997). Comment recueillir des connaissances cachées en algèbre et qu'en faire? *Repères – IREM, 28*, 37–68.

Sasman, M. C., Olivier, A., & Linchevski, L. (1999). Factors influencing students' generalisation thinking processes. In O. Zaslavsky (Ed.), *Proceedings of the 23rd PME International Conference, 4*, 161–168.

Schliemann, A., Carraher, D. W., Brizuela, B. M., Earnest, D., Goodrow, A., Lara-Roth, S., & Peled, I. (2003). Algebra in elementary school. In N. A. Pateman, B. J. Dougherty, & J. T. Zilliox (Eds.), *Proceedings of the 27th PME International Conference, 4*, 127–134.

Schmidt, S., & Bednarz, N. (1997). Raisonnements arithmétiques et algébriques dans un contexte de résolution de problèmes: Difficultés rencontrées par les futurs enseignants. *Educational Studies in Mathematics, 32*, 127–155.

Schmittau, J., & Morris, A. (2004). The development of algebra in the elementary mathematics curriculum of V. V. Davydov. *The Mathematics Educator, 8*, 60–87.

Schnepp, M., & Nemirovsky, R. (2001). Constructing a foundation for the fundamental theorem of calculus. In A. A. Cuoco, & F. R. Curcio (Eds.), *The roles of representation in school mathematics* (Yearbook of the NCTM, pp. 90–102). Reston, USA: NCTM.

Schwartz, J., & Yerushalmy, M. (1992). Getting students to function in and with algebra. In E. Dubinsky, & G. Harel (Eds.), *The concept of function: Aspects of epistemology and pedagogy* (MAA Notes, 25, pp. 261–289). Washington, DC, USA: Mathematical Association of America.

Schwartz, J., & Yerushalmy, M. (1996). *Calculus unlimited* [Computer software]. Tel-Aviv, Israel: Center for Educational Technology.

Schwarz, B. B., & Hershkowitz, R. (1999). Prototypes: Brakes or levers in learning the function concept? The role of computer tools. *Journal for Research in Mathematics Education, 30*, 362–389.

Schwarz, B. B., Hershkowitz, R., & Dreyfus, T. (2002). Abstraction in context: Construction and consolidation of knowledge structures. In A. D. Cockburn & E. Nardi (Eds.), *Proceedings of the 26th PME International Conference, 1*, 120–125.

Sfard, A. (1987). Two conceptions of mathematical notions: Operational and structural. In J. C. Bergeron, N. Herscovics, & C. Kieran (Eds.), *Proceedings of the 11th PME International Conference, 3*, 162–169.

Sfard, A. (1991). On the dual nature of mathematical conceptions: Reflections on processes and objects as different sides of the same coin. *Educational Studies in Mathematics, 22*, 1–36.

Sfard, A. (1994). Reification as the birth of a metaphor. *For the Learning of Mathematics, 14*, 44–55.

Sfard, A. (2001). There is more to discourse than meets the ears: Looking at thinking as communication to learn more about mathematical thinking. *Educational Studies in Mathematics, 46*, 13–57.

Sfard, A., & Linchevski, L. (1994). The gains and the pitfalls of reification – the case of algebra. *Educational Studies in Mathematics, 26*, 191–228.

Shaughnessy, M. (1987). Research reports on projects with in-service teachers: A reaction. In J. C. Bergeron, N. Herscovics, & C. Kieran (Eds.), *Proceedings of the 11th PME International Conference, 2*, 149–162.

Sierpinska, A., Trgalová, J., Hillel, J., & Dreyfus, T. (1999). Teaching and learning linear algebra with Cabri. In O. Zaslavsky (Ed.), *Proceedings of the 23rd PME International Conference, 1*, 119–134.

Simmt, E., Davis, B., Gordon, L., & Towers, J. (2003). Teachers' mathematics: Curious obligations. In N. A. Pateman, B. J. Dougherty, & J. T. Zilliox (Eds.), *Proceedings of the 27th PME International Conference, 4*, 175–182.

Solomon, J., & Nemirovsky, R. (1999). "This is crazy, differences of differences!" On the flow of ideas in a mathematical conversation. In O. Zaslavsky (Ed.), *Proceedings of the 23rd PME International Conference, 4*, 217–224.

Soloway, E., Lochhead, J., & Clement, J. (1982). Does computer programming enhance problem solving ability? Some positive evidence on algebra word problems. In R. J. Seidel, R. E. Anderson, & B. Hunter (Eds.), *Computer literacy* (pp. 171–185). New York, USA: Academic Press.

Stacey, K., Chick, H., & Kendal, M. (Eds.). (2004). *The future of the teaching and learning of algebra: The 12th ICMI Study*. Dordrecht, The Netherlands: Kluwer.

Stacey, K., Kendal, M., & Pierce, R. (2002). Teaching with CAS in a time of transition. *The International Journal of Computer Algebra in Mathematics Education, 9*, 113–127.

Stacey, K., & MacGregor, M. (1997). Multiple referents and shifting meanings of unknowns in students' use of algebra. In E. Pehkonen (Ed.), *Proceedings of the 21st PME International Conference, 4*, 190–197.

Stacey, K., & MacGregor, M. (1999). Learning the algebraic method of solving problems. *Journal of Mathematical Behavior, 18*, 149–167.

Steinberg, R. M., Sleeman, D. H., & Ktorza, D. (1990). Algebra students' knowledge of equivalence of equations. *Journal for Research in Mathematics Education, 22*, 112–121.

Streun, A. V., Harskamp, E., & Suhre, C. (2000). The effect of the graphic calculator on students' solution approaches: A secondary analysis. *Hiroshima Journal of Mathematics Education, 8*, 27–40.

Sutherland, R., & Rojano, T. (1993). A spreadsheet approach to solving algebra problems. *Journal of Mathematical Behavior, 12*, 353–383.

Sutherland, R., Rojano, T., Bell, A., & Lins, R. (Eds.). (2001). *Perspectives on school algebra.* Dordrecht, The Netherlands: Kluwer.

Thomas, M. O. J., & Hong, Y. Y. (2005). Teacher factors in integration of graphic calculators into mathematics learning. In H. L. Chick & J. L. Vincent (Eds.), *Proceedings of the 29th PME International Conference, 4*, 257–264.

Thomas, M. O. J., & Tall, D. (1986). The value of the computer in learning algebra concepts. In Univ. of London Institute of Education (Eds.), *Proceedings of the 10th PME International Conference, 1*, 313–318.

Thompson, P. W., & Thompson, A. G. (1987). Computer presentations of structure in algebra. In J. C. Bergeron, N. Herscovics, & C. Kieran (Eds.), *Proceedings of the 11th PME International Conference, 1*, 248–254.

Tirosh, D., Even, R., & Robinson, N. (1998). Simplifying algebraic expressions: Teacher awareness and teaching approaches. *Educational Studies in Mathematics, 35*, 51–64.

Trigueros, M., & Ursini, S. (1999). Does the understanding of variable evolve through schooling? In O. Zaslavsky (Ed.), *Proceedings of the 23rd PME International Conference, 4*, 273–280.

Trouche, L. (2000). La parabole du gaucher et de la casserole à bec verseur: Étude des processus d'apprentissage dans un environnement de calculatrices symboliques. *Educational Studies in Mathematics, 41*, 239–264.

Tsamir, P., & Bazzini, L. (2002). Algorithmic models: Italian and Israeli students' solutions to algebraic inequalities. In A. D. Cockburn & E. Nardi (Eds.), *Proceedings of the 26th PME International Conference, 4*, 289–296.

Ursini, S. (1990). Generalization processes in elementary algebra: Interpretation and symbolization. In G. Booker, P. Cobb, & T. N. Mendicuti (Eds.), *Proceedings of the 21st PME International Conference, 2*, 149–156.

Ursini, S., & Trigueros, M. (1997). Understanding of different uses of variable: A study with starting college students. In E. Pehkonen (Ed.), *Proceedings of the 14th PME International Conference, 4*, 254–261.

Van Amerom, B. A. (2003). Focusing on informal strategies when linking arithmetic to early algebra. *Educational Studies in Mathematics, 54*, 63–75.

Van Dooren, W., Verschaffel, L., & Onghena, P. (2002). The impact of preservice teachers' content knowledge on their evaluation of students' strategies for solving arithmetic and algebra word problems. *Journal for Research in Mathematics Education, 33*, 319–351.

Van Dooren, W., Verschaffel, L., & Onghena, P. (2003) Pre-service teachers' preferred strategies for solving arithmetic and algebra word problems. *Journal of Mathematics Teacher Education, 6*, 27–52.

Vergnaud, G. (1984). Understanding mathematics at the secondary-school level. In A. Bell, B. Low, & J. Kilpatrick (Eds.), *Theory, research and practice in mathematical education* (Report of ICME5 Working Group on Research in Mathematics Education, pp. 27–35). Nottingham, UK: Shell Centre for Mathematical Education.

Vergnaud, G. (1988). Long terme et court terme dans l'apprentissage de l'algèbre. In C. Laborde (Ed.), *Actes du Premier Colloque Franco-Allemand de Didactique des Mathématiques et de l'Informatique* (pp. 189–199). Grenoble, France: La Pensée Sauvage.

Vermeulen, N. (2000). Student teachers' concept images of algebraic expressions. In T. Nakahara & M. Koyama (Eds.), *Proceedings of the 24th PME International Conference, 4*, 257–264.

Vlassis, J. (2002). The balance model: Hindrance or support for the solving of linear equations with one unknown. *Educational Studies in Mathematics, 49*, 341–359.

Vlassis, J. (2004). *Sens et symboles en mathématiques: Étude de l'utilisation du signe «moins» dans les réductions polynomiales et la résolution d'équations du premier degré à une inconnue* (doctoral dissertation). Liège, Belgium: Université de Liège, Faculté de Psychologie et des Sciences de l'Éducation.

Wagner, S. (1981). Conservation of equation and function under transformation of variable. *Journal for Research in Mathematics Education, 12*, 107–118.

Wagner, S., & Kieran, C. (Eds.). (1989). *Research issues in the learning and teaching of algebra* (Volume 4 of *Research agenda for mathematics education*). Reston: NCTM.

Wagner, S., Rachlin, S. L., & Jensen, R. J. (1984). *Algebra Learning Project: Final report*. Athens, USA: University of Georgia, Department of Mathematics Education.

Warren, E. (2003). Young children's understanding of equals: A longitudinal study. In N. A. Pateman, B. J. Dougherty, & J. T. Zilliox (Eds.), *Proceedings of the 27th PME International Conference, 4*, 379–386.

Warren, E. (2005). Young children's ability to generalise the pattern rule for growing patterns. In H. L. Chick & J. L. Vincent (Eds.), *Proceedings of the 29th PME International Conference, 4*, 305–312.

Whitman, B. S. (1976). *Intuitive equation solving skills and the effects on them of formal techniques of equation solving.* PhD dissertation, Florida State University, USA. (*Dissertation Abstracts International, 36*, 5180A. University Microfilms No. 76-2720)

Wilson, K., Ainley, J., & Bills, L. (2003). Comparing competence in transformational and generational algebraic activities. In N. A. Pateman, B. J. Dougherty, & J. T. Zilliox (Eds.), *Proceedings of the 27th PME International Conference, 4*, 427–434.

Yerushalmy, M. (2000). Problem solving strategies and mathematical resources: A longitudinal view on problem solving in a function-based approach to algebra. *Educational Studies in Mathematics, 43*, 125–147.

Yerushalmy, M., & Chazan, D. (2002). Flux in school algebra: Curricular change, graphing, technology, and research on student learning and teacher knowledge. In L. English (Ed.), *Handbook of international research in mathematics education* (pp. 725–755). Mahwah, USA: Lawrence Erlbaum.

Yerushalmy, M., & Schwartz, J. L. (1993). Seizing the opportunity to make algebra mathematically and pedagogically interesting. In T. A. Romberg, E. Fennema, & T. P. Carpenter (Eds.), *Integrating research on the graphical representation of function* (pp. 41–68). Hillsdale, USA: Lawrence Erlbaum.

Yerushalmy, M., & Shternberg, B. (2001). Charting a visual course to the concept of function. In A. A. Cuoco, & F. R. Curcio (Eds.), *The roles of representation in school mathematics* (Yearbook of the NCTM, pp. 251–268). Reston, USA: NCTM.

Zack, V. (1995). Algebraic thinking in the upper elementary school: The role of collaboration in making meaning of 'generalization'. In L. Meira & D. Carraher (Eds.), *Proceedings of the 19th PME International Conference, 2*, 106–113.

Zack, V. (1997). You have to prove me wrong: Proof at the elementary school level. In E. Pehkonen (Ed.), *Proceedings of the 21st PME International Conference, 4*, 291–298.

Zack, V. (2002). Learning from learners: Robust counterarguments of fifth graders' talk about reasoning and proving. In A. D. Cockburn & E. Nardi (Eds.), *Proceedings of the 26th PME International Conference, 4*, 434–441.

Zaslavsky, O., Sela, H., & Leron, U. (2002). Being sloppy about slope: The effect of changing the scale. *Educational Studies in Mathematics, 49*, 119–140.

Zazkis, R., & Campbell, S. (1996). Divisibility and multiplicative structure of natural numbers: Preservice teachers' understanding. *Journal for Research in Mathematics Education, 27*, 540–563.

Zazkis, R., & Liljedahl, P. (2002). Generalization of patterns: The tension between algebraic thinking and algebraic notation. *Educational Studies in Mathematics, 49*, 379–402.

Zbiek, R. M., & Heid, M. K. (2001). Dynamic aspects of function representations. In H. Chick, K. Stacey, J. Vincent, & J. Vincent (Eds.), *Proceedings of the 12th ICMI Study Conference: The future of the teaching and learning of algebra* (pp. 682–689). Melbourne, Australia: The University of Melbourne.

Zehavi, N. (2004). Symbol sense with a symbolic-graphical system: A story in three rounds. *Journal of Mathematical Behavior, 23*, 183–203.

AFFILIATION

Carolyn Kieran
Département de Mathématiques
Université du Québec à Montréal
C.P. 8888, succ. Centre-Ville
Montréal, QC, H3C 3P8 (Canada)
kieran.carolyn@uqam.ca

LIEVEN VERSCHAFFEL, BRIAN GREER, AND JOKE TORBEYNS

NUMERICAL THINKING [1]

1. INTRODUCTION

In their chapter in the precursor to this volume, on the (psychological aspects of) early arithmetic, Bergeron and Herscovics (1990) raised some of the major issues on which research in early arithmetic had focused during the previous 15 years. Most of their chapter is about learning about natural numbers (i.e. the positive whole numbers), the number word sequence, and counting. By means of a systematic review of that literature and references to their own work, they argued that two separate theoretical and methodological approaches that had dominated research on natural number concepts up to that point are not opposed but, rather, complementary within a broader theoretical perspective. These two approaches are: Piagetian theory, that takes logical reasoning as the basis for the construction of natural number concepts, and the counting-based approach, that contends that numerical concepts evolve from counting skills acquired through the quantification process. Having discussed, at length, research about the child's acquisition of basic knowledge about natural numbers, the authors considered the early stages of development of the conceptual field of additive structures (Vergnaud, 1996), describing the procedures employed by younger children as they attempt to solve one-step word problems involving addition and subtraction of natural numbers. These procedures have been categorized into three main types: direct modeling (with physical objects), verbal counting, and mental strategies involving direct recall of some basic addition or subtraction fact. Finally, they reviewed the literature on the semantic aspects of children's elementary additive word problem solving. Major conclusions were that additive problems can be divided according to their main semantic structural characteristics, that these semantic categories can help to explain the level of difficulty, the solution strategies, and the errors on these word problems, and that the growth of the child's ability to solve these word problems can be seen as part of a global cognitive development within which the child's schemes are changing, enabling him/her to comprehend and solve more

[1] The production of this chapter was supported in part by a grant for a Senior Fellowship of the Research Fund K.U. Leuven for Brian Greer, by a post-doctoral grant from the Fund for Scientific Research-Flanders for Joke Torbeyns, and by the Concerted Research Action GOA/2006/01 of the Research Fund K.U. Leuven.

A. Gutiérrez, P. Boero (eds.), Handbook of Research on the Psychology of Mathematics Education: Past, Present and Future, 51–82.

complicated situations. Finally, follow-up studies were reviewed showing that some non-semantic variables also contribute to the child's level of performance, such as the presence of particular lexical items (e.g., "more" or "both"), the order of the different information elements, and the clarity with which the semantic elements and relations are stated in the text.

In their review, Bergeron and Herscovics (1990) emphasized that "the philosophy that is being brought out here is very much that of constructivism" (p. 51). Indeed, looking back at the chapter, it is, first of all, striking how prototypical it is, at a higher paradigmatic level, for a (classical) constructivist view that analyzes, mainly on the basis of one-on-one interviews, individual children's mathematical development in terms of stage-like changes in abstract conceptual schemes. A second striking characteristic of the research, acknowledged by the authors, is that the cognitive structures described "are of a local nature, that is, relative to the specific aspect of number or addition and subtraction (e.g., the different number-word skills, the different modeling procedures in addition)" and do not address the issue of "how these local cognitive structures interact with each other to create what might be termed global structures, one encompassing all the aspects of the number scheme, another encompassing all the aspects of addition and subtraction" (Bergeron & Herscovics, 1990, p. 51). (It is noteworthy that here, as in much of the literature generally, "number" means exclusively the natural numbers). Third, the review is mostly, if not exclusively, restricted to ascertaining studies assessing children's existing knowledge, mainly using Piagetian clinical interviews. Therefore, it is not surprising that the authors made a plea for undertaking research of a more pedagogical character in order to explore and assess the cognitive effects of various types of instructional interventions, especially interventions wherein children are put in problem situations that confront them with the need to resolve a cognitive conflict created by contradictions within their own reasoning or between their own reasoning, on the one hand, and contradictory information from outside, on the other hand (Bergeron & Herscovics, 1990, p. 52).

In the rest of this chapter, it is shown how PME research in the domain of number and arithmetic has developed since Bergeron and Herscovics' (1990) review. We do this by listing evolving and emerging trends, illustrated mainly by means of research reported in the PME proceedings from the last fifteen years. In the next section we review research on natural numbers and on operations with these numbers, with a focus on the elementary school years (for the numerical understanding that develops before formal schooling, see the chapter by Mulligan and Vergnaud in this volume). The following section deals with research on aspects of number that go beyond the natural numbers. Then we review studies that focus on the appreciation and exploitation of structure, including approaches to teaching/learning arithmetic that anticipate the later learning of formal algebra. In the final section, we summarize overarching trends and make some recommendations. Space restrictions prevented us from touching on the relations between numerical thinking and geometry and measurement, probability and data handling. However, we consider algebra so intimately related with arithmetic that it must be included.

2. NATURAL NUMBERS

2.1 Computational strategies

The characteristics and the development of the strategies that elementary school children use to operate on natural numbers have attracted a lot of research attention within the PME community. One important line of research, starting already before the 1990s (see above), focuses on the cognitive/rationalist analysis of individual children's existing strategies in the domain of elementary arithmetic. Since the 1990s, a second line of research has clearly emerged. Inspired by new theoretical frameworks such as socio-constructivism, ethnomathematics, and situated cognition, an ever-growing number of studies within the PME community aim at unraveling and enhancing children's acquisition of mathematical knowledge and skills in particular and diverse socio-cultural contexts -of which school is one (obviously of special importance). The major trends and issues within the first and second line of research are discussed in sections 2.1.1 and 2.1.2, respectively.

2.1.1 Cognitive analysis of computational strategies. During the last decade, scholars within the PME community have significantly refined and elaborated our understanding of the developmental changes in children's strategies in the domain of elementary arithmetic by examining several themes that were left largely unexplored until the 1990s. (Note that in this section we cover only the results of ascertaining studies, conducted without instructional intervention. We discuss the results of teaching experiments aiming at enhancing children's operations with natural numbers within designed environments in section 2.1.2).

A first theme addresses the characteristics and development of children's strategies in the domain of single-digit multiplication and division (e.g., Mitchelmore & Mulligan, 1996; Mulligan & Wright, 2000). As for the domain of addition and subtraction, most studies in the domain of multiplication and division have documented a large variability in strategies that children use to solve these calculations, including direct counting, repeated addition and subtraction, and the application of derived and known facts, with gradual progress from the frequent application of direct counting strategies to the frequent use of efficient derived and known facts.

A second topic that has attracted increasing research attention since the 1990s is that of children's operations with multi-digit numbers (e.g., Cooper, Heirdsfield & Irons, 1996; Heirdsfield, 2005; Heirdsfield, Cooper, Mulligan & Irons, 1999). Studies in the domain of multi-digit addition and subtraction (Cooper et al., 1996) revealed that children flexibly apply three different types of mental calculation strategies, namely decomposition (or "split" or "separation") strategies, sequential (or "jump" or "aggregation") strategies, and varying strategies. Before (conventional) instruction in the addition and subtraction algorithm, children spontaneously use one or more of these types of strategies. Once the algorithm has been introduced, the frequency of decomposition strategies, and more specifically decomposition strategies in which the units are handled first, increases significantly, while the frequency of the other types of strategies decreases (Cooper et al., 1996). Similarly, studies in the domain of multi-digit multiplication and division demonstrated that children use diverse mental computation strategies, including direct modeling, complete number, partitioning number, and compensation strategies, before they are taught the traditional paper-and-pencil algorithms. However, after the introduction of the written algorithms in the (conventional) classroom, children tend to rely ever less frequently on flexible mental computation strategies, and apply the standard algorithms ever more frequently, even in cases where mental arithmetic would have been more efficient (Heirdsfield et al., 1999).

A third noteworthy new research theme has to do with low achievers' acquisition of simple arithmetic strategies. Gray and his colleagues conducted detailed analyses of the strategies that mathematically weak children and children with mathematical difficulties (MD) apply on single-digit additions and subtractions (e.g., Gray, Pitta & Tall, 1997; see also Gervasoni, 2005; Hopkins & Lawson, 2004; Ostad, 1998; Torbeyns, Verschaffel & Ghesquière, 2004). These analyses revealed that low achievers and children with MD use the same types of strategies as their normally achieving peers, but rely more often on immature counting strategies and less often on more efficient mental strategies than the latter. According to Gray et al. (1997), these differences in the strategy development of low achievers/children with MD and normally achieving children might be due to differences in their perception of numbers. Whereas the former interpret numbers as concrete entities to be manipulated through a counting process ("procedural thinkers"), the latter are able to flexibly use numbers either as a trigger for carrying out a procedure or as a representation of a mental object that may be decomposed, recomposed, and manipulated at a higher level ("proceptual thinkers").

2.1.2 Developing arithmetic competence in diverse contexts. Besides the continuation of cognitive/rationalist research on the variety and development of individual children's computational strategies and skills (see section 2.1.1), another perspective has come to the fore in what Lerman (2000) called "the social turn in mathematics education research", which emphasizes the social and cultural nature of learning mathematics within situated practices. In particular, from this perspective the learning of arithmetic at school is characterized as part of a process through which the learner develops a mathematical disposition (involving the integrated mastery of different categories and knowledge, skills and attitudes) and becomes a skilful participant within a mathematical discourse community. However, school is not the only environment in which mathematical activities take place, and making connections between school mathematics and diverse forms of out-of-school mathematical practices has become a major concern. Here, we focus on three major issues within the broad line of research inspired by this perspective, namely: (a) The design, implementation and evaluation of powerful instructional environments that embrace the dispositional view of mathematical expertise and view of mathematics learning as the active and joint construction of meaning in sociocultural contexts; (b) The role of teachers' knowledge, beliefs and actions in such learning environments; and (c) The acquisition and use of arithmetical knowledge and skills in out-of-school contexts and its potential connections with, and enhancement of, school mathematics. While all of these aspects, clearly, are important in the learning of domains of mathematics other than arithmetic, much of the pioneering and most significant work in this tradition has been in the domain of arithmetic, so it is appropriate to deal with it fully in this chapter.

With respect to the first major issue, the studies of, for instance, Anghileri (2001, 2004), Cobb (1994), Gravemeijer, McClain & Stephan (1998), Kutscher, Linchevski & Eisenman (2002), Murray, Olivier & Human (1994, 1998), Steinberg, Carpenter & Fennema (1994), Whitenack, Cobb & McClain (1995) and Wittmann (2001) have unraveled several key characteristics of learning environments that have been shown to enhance children's early development of a mathematical disposition. The following set of five design principles, developed by the Realistic Mathematics Education (RME) approach in The Netherlands, provides a rather good summary of the key characteristics of these environments: (a) Learning mathematics is a constructive activity, which means that children gather, discover, and create their own mathematical knowledge and skills in the course of some social activity that has a purpose; (b) The use of meaningful or realistic context problems as anchoring points for the children to develop (or re-invent) their own mathematical knowledge and skills, and to prevent mathematics becoming separated from reality; (c) Progressing towards higher levels of abstraction and formalization, using carefully chosen mathematical models and tools as scaffolds to bridge the gap between, on the one hand, children's intuitive notions and informal strategies and, on the other hand, the concepts and procedures of formal mathematics; (d) Learning through social interaction and cooperation, which are considered as essential tools to mobilize children to reflect on their own constructions and (thus) to enhance their progressive development towards higher level concepts and strategies; and (e) Interconnecting the various learning strands within mathematics teaching (e.g. procedural and declarative knowledge, strategies for different arithmetic operations, etc.) to allow the construction of a coherent and well-organized knowledge base (Gravemeijer & Kindt, 2001). For instance, the design experiments of Murray et al. (1994, 1998) indicated that children who received instruction based on these RME design principles were able to (re)invent efficient computational strategies to solve complex multiplications and divisions, and apply these strategies meaningfully and flexibly on diverse types of problems. More recently, studies by Anghileri (2001, 2004) showed that Dutch children, who had been taught division according to the RME design principles, could correctly answer complex division problems by means of the insightful application of one of their self-invented strategies, whereas their English and American peers, who had received conventional instruction in the division algorithm, experienced serious problems with the solution of complex division tasks as they tried to solve such sums by using an incorrect version of the ill-understood paper-and-pencil algorithm. In a series of design studies developed in line with the above-mentioned RME principles and realized in the first grades of the elementary school, Cobb, Yackel, and their colleagues demonstrated the importance of the classroom micro-culture in the successful realization of such reform-based interventions (Cobb, 1994; McClain & Cobb, 1999; Yackel, 1998, 2001; see also Herbst, 1997; Krummheuer, 2000; Steinbring, 2000, 2001). More particularly, they revealed the importance of the establishment (by the teacher) of appropriate socio-mathematical norms, already from a very early age, that regulate the classroom discourse and influence the learning opportunities. Typical examples of such socio-mathematical norms include what counts as an appropriate mathematical problem, a different, a (more) sophisticated, or a (more) efficient mathematical solution, or good argumentation within mathematical discourse. For instance, after a child has explained his or her solution strategy to solve a mathematical problem, the teacher might ask the other children if they solved the problem in a different or more efficient way. In such situations, the teacher and the children renegotiate what counts as a different or more efficient mathematical solution strategy as they respond to contributions that are proposed as being different or being more efficient.

Studies related to the second theme provided empirical evidence for the claim that teachers' content knowledge (CK) and pedagogical content knowledge (PCK), as well as their mathematics-related beliefs, strongly influence children's mathematics learning (e.g., Askew, Brown, Rhodes, Wiliam & Johnson, 1997; Brown, Askew, Rhodes, Wiliam & Johnson, 1997; Chick & Baker, 2005; Lamb & Booker, 2004; McClain & Bowers, 2000; Selter, 2001). In an early report on what is one of the most systematic and sustained programs aimed at helping teachers improve their teaching by exploiting research-based knowledge, Carpenter and Fennema (1989) reported on initial results from the Cognitively Guided Instruction approach (since considerably expanded). Generally, teachers who value children's self-invented procedures, who emphasize the establishment of connections within children's mathematical knowledge and skills, and who have a full, deep, and connected understanding of our number system, prove more effective teachers than teachers who view mathematics as a collection of separate routines and procedures and/or who have a limited understanding of our number system. The former provide their pupils more opportunities to relate different mathematical ideas and different representations of these ideas than the latter, resulting in clearly visible differences in their children's mathematical knowledge and skills (Askew et al., 1997; Brown et al., 1997). Moreover, several researchers have attempted to actively alter teachers' mathematics-related conceptions and beliefs as a means to enhance children's mathematical development (Lamb & Booker, 2004; Selter, 2001). The study of Lamb and Booker (2004), for instance, demonstrated that the improvement of teachers' understanding of the division algorithm resulted in similar increases in the insightful use of this algorithm by their pupils.

Concerning the third theme, the studies of Schliemann and colleagues (e.g., Nunes, Schliemann & Carraher, 1993; Schliemann, 1995; Schliemann, Araujo, Cassundé, Macedo & Nicéas, 1994) revealed a contrast between, on the one hand, children's mathematical achievements at school ("school mathematics") and, on the other hand, their mathematical knowledge and skills in practical, out of school contexts ("everyday mathematics"). Confronted with mathematical problems at school, children tend to solve these problems by applying the explicitly taught standard algorithms in a rather inefficient and meaningless way, suggesting a limited understanding of the required mathematical concepts and procedures. In contrast, when offered the same type of problems in out-of-school contexts, children are able to efficiently answer these problems using diverse self-invented mental computation strategies that are strongly connected to meaningful situational referents, indicating a deep understanding of the properties of our decimal number system (Nunes et al., 1993; Schliemann, 1995). Unfortunately, while the strong connection to meaningful situational referents in the latter type of strategies allows children to preserve the meaning of the operations performed throughout the series of computational steps until a final answer is reached, it also constrains children's further exploration of the mathematical properties of the number system and the operations (see Section 4). As illustrated by Schliemann et al. (1994), street children's use of repeated addition strategies to solve multiplication problems in everyday contexts tends to postpone their understanding of multiplication as a commutative operation. Therefore, school instruction should attempt to bridge the gap between children's everyday mathematical knowledge and skills, on the one hand, and the mathematical content offered at school, on the other, by stimulating children to reflect on mathematical relations that are embedded in meaningful, socially relevant situations where mathematics is used as a tool to achieve relevant goals. These situations should not be restricted to those that take place in out-of-school environments, but rather allow for a wider variety of concepts that are not usually involved in everyday situations (Schliemann, 1995).

The complex relationship between relating mathematics to children's experience and developing powerful and general mathematical tools is illustrated by the work of Sethole (2005), describing the problematic attempts of two 8th grade teachers to systematically and purposefully draw on socio-culturally very rich and relevant everyday world experiences in their teaching of mathematics and mathematical problem solving. More specifically, he documents the teachers' difficulties in finding a proper balance between "embracing the everyday" in its full richness and complexity, on the one hand, and "using the everyday as a see-through towards the mathematics", resulting in different forms of "inauthenticating" of the real world contexts under investigation (Sethole, 2005, p. 175; see also Verschaffel, 2002).

2.2 Arithmetical operations as models for situations

Whereas the previous section focused on PME research on the variety and the development of children's strategies for doing whole-number arithmetic, we now turn to the linkage between these arithmetic procedures and meaningful situations to which they relate. Four research themes will be very briefly reviewed: (a) Conceptual structures (schemes) for representing and solving word problems; (b) Word problems viewed from a problem-solving perspective; (c) A sociocultural analysis of performance on arithmetic word problems; and (d) The emergent modeling approach.

2.2.1 Analyzing and teaching basic schemes. (Computer) modeling of the conceptual structures (schemes) for understanding and solving elementary arithmetic word problems continued to elicit the attention of cognitive psychologists in the 1990s. However, math educators became more and more critical about the internal and ecological validity of these (purely) cognitive/rationalist models, which had played such a central role in the word problem solving research throughout the 1980s. In particular, we would point to the implicit assumption in these models, generally, that the students' cognition develops universally, independent of their social, cultural, and, especially, instructional experience. Nevertheless, the topic continued to attract some research interest within the PME community.

First, based on the above literature, several authors continued to develop, implement, and test schema-based approaches for measuring and teaching word problem solving. These approaches make extensive use of graphical representations of problems as a means to measure or enhance the required conceptual knowledge structures in pupils, and, in some cases, encouraging indications for the effectiveness of this approach were found (e.g., Kyriakides, Philippou & Charalambous, 2002; Philippou & Christou, 1999).

Second, until the early nineties, the theoretical models and empirical findings were much more elaborated for problems schematically related to changes in quantities ("change" problems) and combination/decomposition of sets ("combine" problems) than for the most difficult problems, those involving comparison. Therefore, it is no surprise that in the last decade many researchers have taken a closer look, typically by means of interviews, at how children understand and solve compare problems (Mekhmandarov, Meron & Peled, 1996; Schliemann, Lara-Roth & Epstein, 2000). Even more than for other problem types, these studies have revealed that a correct answer to the question in a compare problem does not guarantee that the child fully understands the relationship involved in it.

Third, while the developers of (computer) models had always claimed that their models of one-step word problem solving were, in principle, (easily) extensible to more complex problems, little or no attempts towards such extensions have been made. However, during the nineties, several ascertaining studies and design experiments were carried out whereby the cognitive scheme approach was elaborated in the direction of two-step arithmetic word problems (see e.g., Hershkowitz & Nesher, 1991; Rico, 1994).

2.2.2 Analyzing and teaching problem-solving strategies. Another line of research on arithmetic word problem solving, which has also been well represented in the PME community during the past 15 years, takes a general problem-solving perspective. Rather than trying to account for differences between children in terms of the availability of conceptual knowledge structures (schemas) needed to understand and solve particular types of word problems, these investigations, which rely mainly on the seminal work of Polya (1945) and Schoenfeld (1992), view children's growing competence in solving word problems basically in terms of the availability and active use of efficient heuristic and/or metacognitive skills.

A first series of studies examined the role of particular heuristic strategies, such as making a picture or a diagram of the problem, thinking of an analogous problem, and making an organized list, in successful (non-routine) problem solving (De Bock, Verschaffel & Janssens, 1996; Pantziara, Gagatsis & Pitta-Pantazi, 2004; Shimizu, 2000). These studies confirm that many pupils do not spontaneously apply these valuable cognitive strategies when solving word problems. Other studies have revealed that in many pupils' solution attempts to solve word problems, moments of metacognitive awareness or self-regulatory activities such as analyzing the problem, monitoring the solution process, and evaluating the outcome are absent too (e.g., Shigematsu & Yoshio, 2000). Over the past two decades, the PME research community has also shown increased interest in the relationship between these cognitive and metacognitive (or self-regulatory) strategies, on the one hand, and different types of interrelated affects, emotions and beliefs, on the other hand, in the context of mathematical (word) problem solving (see e.g. Marcou & Philippou, 2005; Op 't Eynde, 2004). For instance, based on an analysis of the data from a large group of 5th and 6th graders, using a self-report questionnaire designed to measure children's motivational beliefs and self-regulated learning and a paper-and-pencil test consisting of several non-routine word problems, Marcou and Philippou (2005) found not only a significant relation between children's motivational beliefs and their self-regulatory skills, but also between these motivational beliefs and self-regulatory skills, on the one hand, and their performance in mathematical word problem solving, on the other hand.

Starting from these findings from ascertaining studies, several scholars within the PME community have started to design, implement, and evaluate instructional programs aimed at the development of heuristic and/or metacognitive skills for word problem solving. A pioneering study was done by Lester and Kroll (1990). While in some of these studies (see e.g. Teong, Threlfall & Monaghan, 2000) the computer is used to enhance the power of the (meta)cognitive training, in most the metacognitive instruction was deployed in cooperative settings in which small groups of students worked together (see e.g., Kramarski & Mevarech, 2001). The results of most of these intervention studies suggest that providing heuristic and metacognitive training has a significant but moderate impact on students' mathematical performance.

A special line of research that has been quite prominent in the PME research community is the so-called open-ended approach, developed especially by Japanese mathematics educators, wherein problems are used that do not have only one answer or one approach to finding the answer that is either correct or incorrect (for an overview of this work see Nohda, 2000).

Finally, the nineties also witnessed the emergence of attempts to use problem posing as a vehicle to study, and to promote, problem solving. Seminal work in this respect has been done by English (1997).

2.2.3 Realistic mathematical modeling. A general limitation of the studies described above is that this work has been almost entirely confined to word problems that can be "unproblematically" modeled by operations with small, positive, whole numbers given in the problem statement. This leads to the question whether these psychological models and instructional programs, that strongly reflect the presuppositions of the cognitive/rationalist approach, have succeeded in capturing the quintessence of mathematizing situations presented verbally (or otherwise). Influenced by insights coming from sociocultural theory, ethnomathematics, and situated cognition, as well as by a few famous and spectacular examples of pupils' lack of sense making while doing word problem solving, several researchers, including within the PME community, began to look in a more systematic way at children's solutions of arithmetic word problems not from a (purely) cognitive or metacognitive perspective, but from a perspective wherein social and cultural and affective factors are as much part of students' thinking and behavior as are these (meta)cognitive factors (Verschaffel, 2002). These additional factors might include, for example, the need to make sense of the situation and to adapt to the "didactical contract" (Brousseau, 1997) or to socio-mathematical classroom norms and practices (Yackel & Cobb, 1996).

By analyzing pupils' reactions to so-called "problematic" items, wherein the appropriate mathematical model or solution is neither obvious nor indisputable (at least if one seriously takes into account the realities of the context evoked by the problem statement), several researchers have provided strong empirical evidence that most elementary school children perceive school word problems as artificial, routine-based tasks that are unrelated to the real world, and, accordingly, approach these problems with superficial coping strategies that have little to do with authentic mathematical modeling reflecting the real world outside the school (cf. Asman & Markovits, 2001; Boaler, 1998; Nesher & Hershkovitz, 1997; Peled & Bassan-Cincinatus, 2005; Ruwisch, 1999; Van Dooren, De Bock, Janssens & Verschaffel, 2005; Verschaffel, 2002). According to these authors, this apparent "suspension of sense-making" among children can be construed as sense-making of a different sort. As Schoenfeld (1991) expresses it:

> ... such behavior is sense-making of the deepest kind. In the context of schooling, such behavior represents the construction of a set of behaviors that results in praise for good performance, minimal conflict, fitting in socially etc. What could be more sensible than that? (p. 340)

Moreover, it has been claimed that students' tendency to neglect real world knowledge results from being immersed in the culture and practice of the mathematics classroom (Verschaffel, 2002). Some support for this claim comes from a study by Verschaffel, De Corte and Borghart (1996), the results of which indicated that future teachers share, though in a less extreme form, students' tendency to suspend sense making.

In line with the above criticisms on the traditional practice surrounding word problems in schools, researchers have set up design studies to develop, implement, and evaluate experimental programs aimed at the enhancement of strategies for, and attitudes about, (authentic) mathematical modeling and problem solving, beginning as early as elementary school. Characteristics common to these experimental programs include: (a) The use of more realistic and challenging tasks than traditional textbook problems; (b) A variety of teaching methods and learner activities, including expert modeling of the strategic aspects of the competent solution process, small-group work, and whole-class discussions; (c) The creation of a classroom climate that is conducive to the development in pupils of an elaborated view of mathematical modeling, and of the accompanying beliefs and attitudes. Positive outcomes have been obtained in terms of both outcomes and underlying processes (see e.g., English & Watters, 2004; 2005; Shorr & Amit, 2005; Verschaffel & De Corte, 1995). For instance, English and Watters (2005) report on the mathematical modeling of four classes of 4th grade children as they worked on a modeling problem involving the selection of an Australian swimming team for the 2004 Olympics. The problem was implemented during the second year of the children's participation in a 3-year longitudinal program of modeling experiences that comprised the three above-mentioned instructional pillars. During this second year the children completed several comprehensive modeling problems, one of which was the Olympics problem. From a careful qualitative analysis of the children's transcripts as they worked (in small groups) on the modeling problems and reported to their peers, English and Watters (2005) concluded that the children displayed several modeling cycles as they worked through these problems and adopted different approaches to model construction.

2.2.4 Emergent mathematical modeling. Especially among researchers and designers working at the elementary level, the term mathematical modeling is used to refer not only to a process whereby a situation has to be problematized and understood, translated into mathematics, worked out mathematically, translated back into the original (real world) situation, evaluated and communicated (as the term was used in section 2.2.3). Besides this type of modeling, which requires that the student has already at his disposal at least some mathematical tools for mathematizing, there is another kind of modeling, wherein model-eliciting activities are used as a vehicle for the development (rather than the application) of mathematical concepts. This idea was initially put forward by Freudenthal (1983), but Gravemeijer (2002) has developed it further into a design heuristic, called "emergent modeling". The emergent modeling heuristic assigns a role to models that differs greatly from, and constitutes even a sharp criticism towards, the traditional didactical role of models in the sense of manipulatives, visual displays, etc., namely to concretize abstract mathematical knowledge, presented by an external authority. Instead, what is aimed for is that the model which emerges from the students' informal activity with respect to realistic problems ("model of") gradually develops into a "model for" more formal mathematical reasoning. This "emergent modeling approach" to models has become the dominant view within PME research on how to design and use different kinds of real world contexts, models, manipulatives, visual displays, virtual materials, etc., to enhance the development of children's elementary arithmetic concepts (e.g., Nemirovsky, Kaput & Roschelle, 1998; Whitenack et al., 1995). In this respect, it is interesting to refer again to the design experiment of English and Watters (2005), who observed not only improved modeling skills among the 9-year old children from the experimental classes (see above), but also that the models that these children developed of this realistic problem revealed informal understandings of important mathematical contents, such as variation, aggregation and ranking of numerical data, inverse proportion, and weighting of variables, which could gradually develop into models for more formal reasoning about these mathematical contents.

3. BEYOND THE NATURAL NUMBERS

The historical and cultural diversity of the complex of constructions that mathematicians (and other people) have agreed to label "number" reflects a combination of responses to real problems (e.g. fractions for sharing and measuring, negative numbers for financial transactions), applications (e.g. ratio in the theory of music), and motivations from within mathematics for systemic completeness through the resolution of various forms of disequilibrium/lack of closure (notably rational numbers and negative numbers). Pedagogical challenges and psychological complexity occur throughout this development, particularly at the points where radical conceptual restructuring is necessary. Here we reflect the beginnings of a shift within the PME community towards a more balanced view of number as a research area, with a considerable amount of research on the rational numbers and on negative numbers, and some work on more advanced conceptions, notably the structure and properties of the real numbers.

3.1. Rational number

3.1.1. Interpretations and representations of fractions. As stated by Charalambous and Pitta-Pantazi (2005, p. 233) "there is consensus among researchers that one of the predominant factors contributing to the complexities of teaching and learning fractions lies in the fact that fractions comprise a multifaceted construct". Behr, Harel, Post and Silver (1983) proposed an influential model (reproduced in Charalambous & Pitta-Pantazi, 2005) in which part-whole/partitioning is posited as a fundamental subconstruct underlying four further subconstructs, namely ratio, operator, quotient, and measure. These in turn are differentially implicated in problems involving equivalence (linked to ratio), multiplication (operator), and addition (measure) of fractions, and collectively in problem solving with fractions. Charalambous and Pitta-Pantazi (2005) tested this model empirically using structural equation modeling. They report that the study supported the fundamental role of the part-whole subconstruct and suggest that this justifies the traditional role of this subconstruct in introducing fractions. However, while they found it strongly linked to ratio and operator subconstructs, it was weakly linked to the measure and quotient subconstructs. Accordingly (p. 239), they "underline the need for emphasizing the other subconstructs of fractions" and recommend further research to cross-validate the model derived from their data. Mamede, Nunes, and Bryant (2005) concentrated on two subconstructs, namely part-whole and quotient, and examined their differential relationships to problems involving equivalence, ordering, and representation of fractions. They report that children performed better in problems presented in quotient situations and that the strategies used differed in the two situations.

The very structure of the symbol $^3/_4$ reflects its duality as process (division of 3 by 4) and product (the result of dividing 3 by 4). Herman, Ilucova, Kremsova, Pribyl, Ruppeldtova, Simpson et al. (2004) asked Czech children in grades 6-9 to respond to fractions presented: (a) In isolation, and (b) Within the context of an addition. They suggest that the representations children used in the former case (an example of "fractions as processes") were not readily adapted for the second case (an example of "fractions in processes") (though it is not clear what representations they would have considered appropriate for the additions). Pitta-Pantazi, Gray and Christou (2004) directly elicited students' responses to verbal and visual cues (e.g. "Talk for 30 seconds about what comes in your mind when you hear the word ... fraction, half, three quarters" (cf. Goldin & Passantino, 1996; Pirie, Martin & Kieren, 1994). They classified responses into a number of categories ranging from those relying on reference to surface or episodic features to generic and proceptual, and concluded that high-achieving students' responses generally showed higher levels of abstraction.

The multiplicity of interpretations and applications of fractions is generally not reflected in a corresponding variety of representations used and problems presented within the designed environments of schools. The dominant representations are regularly shaped regions divided into equal parts of which some are distinguished, and the number line. Hannula (2003) found that, for Finnish students in 5th and 7th grades, the number line was more problematic and postulated that their earlier experience led them to look for something divided into 4 parts of which they could take 3, but without having a clear idea of what the appropriate "whole" would be. This finding neatly exemplifies the complexity of teaching/learning fractions with a view to being aware of, and ultimately synthesizing, their multiple interpretations and representations.

As with the work on natural numbers reviewed in the first section, much of the work that has been done, often working with teachers, is aimed, in general terms, at sense making as opposed to rule following (e.g. see Strang, 1990, whose results show limited understanding of fractions of Finnish comprehensive school Grades 3-6 students which is attributed to a reliance on mechanical learning of rules in textbooks and instruction). Many students indiscriminately identify a presentation of m indicated out of n parts of a region as a representation of $^m/_n$. Such a limited "expertise" is manifest in widely documented behaviors such as accepting a representation of m out of n unequal parts (Newstead & Olivier, 1999), not accepting that m out of n equal parts can also represent any equivalent fraction (Carraher & Schliemann, 1991), failure to grasp the interpretation of fractions as numbers (Amato, 2005), and confusion over the unit, e.g. between $^m/_n$ meters and $^m/_n$ of k meters (Hasekawa, 2000).

Some reports from studies in South Africa are broadly representative of approaches towards the teaching of fractions, with attention to, for example, young children's informal knowledge of fractions (Murray, Olivier & Human, 1996), both positive and negative effects of linking to everyday knowledge and intuitions (Newstead & Murray, 1998), the difficulty of reteaching older students fractions for understanding (Murray, Olivier & De Beer, 1999). Newstead and Olivier (1999) report results showing limited success with a carefully designed instructional environment for students in Grades 6-7 based on previous ascertaining research (Newstead & Murray, 1998) and emphasizing: the use of sharing situations; exposure to a wide variety of fractions and of meanings of fractions "not only the fraction as part-of-a-whole where the whole is a single discrete object, but also for example the fraction as part of a collection of objects, the fraction as a ratio, and the fraction as an operator" (Newstead & Olivier, 1999, p. 329); encouragement to construct their own representations; delayed introduction of conventional symbols; grounding in contexts; sociomathematical norms emphasizing problem solving, discussion, and challenge (cf. the RME principles, Section 2.1.2).

As just exemplified, it is noticeable that the bulk of the work surveyed is framed in terms of social constructivism and sense making rather than classical constructivism. An exception is the work of Olive and Steffe (Olive, 2002, 4-1, and see Tzur, 1996, for similar work). Pairs of children worked with a teacher/researcher using specially designed computer tools that allow flexible simulated actions such as breaking, joining, partitioning, iterating to be performed on line segments ("sticks"). With interesting echoes to historical Greek conceptions of rational numbers, students are reported to have become adept at constructing "commensurate fractions". This work raises certain fundamental questions that, arguably, have contributed to the retreat from the Piagetian epistemologically framed research and theory-building remarked upon in the introduction, notably: (a) What is the ontological nature of the various schemes (e.g. "commensurate fractional scheme") the "having" of which is ascribed to the students with alarming certitude? (b) Accepting that it exists, how transferable is this schematic knowledge to contexts other than that in which it was constructed? These studies are certainly interesting in suggesting the potential of representations of fractions using the new representational power offered by computers. (In general, we found a noticeable scarcity of references to software for teaching arithmetic).

3.1.2. Decimals. Most of the work on rational numbers represented as decimals is framed in terms of misconceptions, many of which are attributed to students attempting to assimilate decimal fractions to their existing natural number knowledge (appropriate in many cases, but not in others) and also, to some extent, fraction knowledge (at the syntactic level). (Note that, in referring to "misconceptions" we are following the terminology used in the papers cited). One form that this attempted assimilation takes is to treat a decimal number as a pair of whole numbers (Brekke, 1996, reporting on the testing of a diagnostic instrument). (Hannula, 2003 points out that the tendency may be exacerbated in countries where the separator is a comma rather than a full stop). A widely documented manifestation is to rank as greater decimals with more digits after the decimal point (e.g. 3.521 is judged greater 3.75 on the grounds, presumably, that 521 > 75). Fuglestad (1996) reported similar findings, also with Norwegian students. The complexity of such misconceptions is clearly shown by the work of Steinle and Stacey (2003, 2004) focusing simply on the issue of comparing two decimals through the use of a 30-item Decimal Comparison Test.

The second major way in which natural number knowledge may be extended reflects the structural relationship whereby decimals constitute an extension of the decimal place-value-based representational system for natural numbers. Understanding this extension can be undermined both by the conception of a decimal as two whole numbers and by weak understanding of place-value and the principles underlying the decimal system. Ingenious items using sequences such as 0.3, 0.6, 0.9, ..., ... were used diagnostically by Fuglestad (1996) who developed spreadsheet exercises for working with such sequences as a means of addressing the misconception. She, and also Brekke (1996, p. 141), used items designed to test place-value understanding such as:

Add 0.1 and write the answer. (a) 4,256 (b) 3,9 (c) 6,98 (d) 5,4 (e) 7,03

There is a natural linkage between decimals and units of measurement based on the decimal system, which may often be represented as a number line (with a particularly close relationship when the quantity being measured is length). Teaching approaches based on these relationships were presented by Basso, Bonotto & Sorzio (1998) and by Boufi & Skaftourou (2002). Basso's use of a ruler exemplifies a social constructivist approach, characterized thus:

> Effective learning environments support the participants in their moving from 'primitive doing' of mathematical actions through the use of tools, towards progressively sophisticated abstractions ... In such environments, the learners do not construct their representations of mathematical symbols in a vacuum, but have manifold opportunities to ground their construction of mathematical meanings in 'situation-specific imagery', as elaborated in practice through the use of cultural forms. (p. 72)

3.1.3. Extending the operations. Within PME, we can assume a strong consensus that students should understand not just the computations for the arithmetical operations but also how these operations model aspects of the real world (see Section 2.2.3). However, relatively little work appears in PME proceedings about the extension of the four basic operations beyond the natural numbers. One important line of research follows the influential theory of primitive intuitive models proposed by Fischbein, Deri, Nello and Marino (1985), concentrating on multiplication and division. They proposed that the intuitive model for multiplication is repeated addition (which is how multiplication was defined by Euclid). The implications are that a situation in which the multiplier is not a whole number is more difficult to construe as being modeled by multiplication. In the case of a number greater than 1, Fischbein et al. (1985) postulated that the fractional part would be "absorbed" into the whole-number part. The repeated addition model also implies that the result of a multiplication will be larger than the multiplicand, a constraint broken when the multiplier is less than 1. For division, two intuitive models are proposed, depending on the situation described. Partitive division is based on the idea of equal sharing, which requires the divisor to be a whole number and smaller than the dividend. Quotitive division relates to now many times the divisor goes into the dividend, and implies that the dividend be larger than the divisor.

Harel, Behr, Post and Lesh (1989) tested and extended the theory with preservice teachers. Their results supported the general form of the theory while suggesting refinements. The findings suggested, for example, that the constraint for partitive division that the divisor be smaller than the dividend is relatively weak. They also showed that the "absorbtion effect" apparently does not apply to the divisor in partitive division problems. Another notable aspect of their findings was that, in general, they considered the results as very discouraging insofar as preservice and inservice teachers showed serious misconceptions similar to those found in students.

To further test the theory of intuitive models, De Corte and Verschaffel (1994) used a contrasting methodology, namely presenting students with number sentences (number sentences giving a multiplication or division of two numbers, together with the result) and asking them to generate word problems for which those calculations are appropriate. Many (but not all) of the findings supported Fischbein's model. In particular, the results reinforced the conclusion by Harel et al. (1989) that the constraint for partititive division that the divisor be smaller than the dividend is much weaker. They concluded that "it is necessary to aim at the design of a more comprehensive theory which takes into account that solving problems with a multiplicative structure is influenced by a large variety of factors interacting in multiple and complex ways" (pp. 262-263).

A suggested line of research for the future is to build on these ascertaining studies to design curriculum to help students through the complex conceptual restructuring involved in extending multiplication and division beyond the natural numbers (Greer, 1994).

3.2. Negative numbers

As pointed out by Linchevski and Williams (1996), there is a continuing debate about whether negative numbers should be introduced through models and/or concrete representations or as formal abstractions, as argued by Fischbein (1987), for example. Most of the work reported in PME takes the former approach, and almost all deals with addition and subtraction, stopping short of multiplication and division -it is with multiplication and division by negative numbers that the limitations of real world models become acute. The most usual approach in extending numbers and operations on them into the domain of negative numbers is from natural numbers to integers, though Bruno and Martinón (1996) suggest instead establishing the positive real numbers first and then extending to negative real numbers.

Attempts to introduce negative numbers in relation to either concrete models/representations or real world situations (or some combination) take a number of standard forms, which reappear frequently with variations. Among these we may identify, in particular: (a) Abstract games (De Souza, Mometti, Scavazza & Baldino, 1995); (b) The number line (Peled, Mukhopadhyay & Resnick, 1989); (c) The "matter/antimatter" model (limited to addition and subtraction) (Lyttle, 1994); (d) Contexts such as debt, distance above and below sea-level, and so on. Linchevski and Williams (1996) constructed an elaborate scenario involving a disco with several gates, at each of which a child records people coming in and out. Mukhopadhyay, Resnick and Schauble (1990) presented young children with a 5-page story about a character's financial vicissitudes in order to tap their intuitive understandings of changing debts and assets. They found that the children performed better on problems posed in the context of the story than on similar problems presented purely symbolically; this effect was particularly strong with unschooled children from India, who were very familiar with the social and practical elements of the story.

3.3. Beyond the rational numbers

There are, of course, many further extensions of the number concept. Here we concentrate (as do the PME papers) on understanding of the real number system. Fischbein, Jehaim and Cohen (1994) studied epistemological obstacles to the understanding of irrational numbers, with students in Grades 9 and 10, and college students. Specifically they tested the assumption, based on historical and psychological grounds, that students' intuitions would lead them to believe that: (a) Any two lengths are commensurable, that is to say it is possible to find a unit in which each can be measured exactly (this of course is the assumption that caused an intellectual crisis among the Pythagoreans) and (b) Although the rational numbers are everywhere dense on any interval, they do not cover all the points. In fact, neither hypothesis was supported. Fischbein et al. (1994) suggested that the postulated intuitions are secondary intuitions that depend on a level of mathematical sophistication mainly lacking in the students tested.

Romero and Rico (1996) report a teaching experiment on introducing the real numbers to 14-15-year-olds in Spain, and on the conceptual difficulties experienced by students. By way of example, some students evinced a conflict between $\sqrt{3}$ as a finite length and its expression as an infinite decimal. Romero and Rico suggest that a shift is needed from thinking of an infinite decimal expression as a process to its acceptance as an object (a full awareness of which Lee (1994) found lacking in a group of future secondary teachers in China).

One salient respect in which the real numbers differ from the natural numbers is that they are dense (i.e. within any interval on the number line, there are an infinite number of real numbers -also an infinite number of rational numbers). In studying this aspect in particular, Merenluoto (2003) found that most of the Finnish students beginning calculus that she studied "were still far from a radical conceptual change in their number concept, namely changing their frame of reference of numbers from natural numbers to real numbers" (p. 291).

3.4. Teachers' knowledge and beliefs

As illustrated earlier with respect to work on natural number (Section 2.1.2) it is noteworthy that future and practicing teachers have become the object of much research. These studies may be categorized into three types. In the first type of study, teachers' content knowledge (CK) is tested, often revealing alarming weaknesses. For example, Philippou and Christou (1994) found that future teachers' understanding of fractions was limited to computational competence, while Zazkis and Sirotic (2004) elegantly demonstrated the fragility of teachers' CK about rational numbers relative to their representations. Pinto and Tall (1996) documented subtle misconceptions about rational numbers exhibited by students studying to be teachers. In particular, they commented how "the definition of the rational numbers is rarely used to test whether specific numbers are rational other than those explicitly given as a ratio of integers, illustrating a wider problem with the use of formal definitions in mathematics" (p. 139).

The second group of studies is aimed at teachers' pedagogical content knowledge (PCK) -here we refer to two studies as exemplary of this type. Leu (1999) studied elementary teachers' understanding of students' cognition relating to fractions, for example, using both paper-and-pencil test and interviews. For the teachers interviewed, only 18% were classified as excellent, in the sense that they were able to explain why students make certain assumptions and to posit reasons for students' difficulties with equivalent fractions. The author finishes the paper by spelling out the likely consequences if teachers do not fully understand their students' learning of fractions. Klein, Barkai, Tirosh and Tsamir (1998) examined awareness of students' conceptions of operations with rational numbers. One of their findings, that is of major significance if it holds generally, was that practicing teachers did not perform much better than inservice teachers, suggesting that teaching mathematics, per se, does not necessarily enhance understanding of students' thinking. They found that PCK in this domain could be improved by participation in a specially designed course, but point out that it remains to be tested if this improved PCK translates into better teaching and learning.

Less attention has been paid to intervention studies documenting the effects on students of enhancing teachers' CK and PCK (as opposed to teaching experiments, per se, several of which have been mentioned). One example is a report by Baturo (2004) showing how the results achieved by the students of an experienced and capable teacher improved markedly when that teacher received carefully designed instruction about fractions.

4. STRUCTURE IN ARITHMETIC

As stated by Blanton and Kaput (2002):

> Traditionally, the focus of elementary mathematics has been deeply oriented to arithmetic and computation, with little attention given to the relationships and structure underlying simple arithmetic tasks. (p. 105)

Much of the recent work on arithmetic focuses, in one way or another, on the structural properties of number systems and operations. In this section we argue for, and selectively illustrate, (a) The inherently algebraic nature of arithmetic, and (b) The scope of early arithmetic for laying foundations for processes of conjecture and proof. Accordingly, the reader may find an overlap with the chapters in this volume by Kieran on algebra and by Mariotti on proof.

One manifestation of this shift in emphasis is the change from a primarily sequential view whereby arithmetic comes first, followed by a transition to algebra. This shift is reflected to differing degrees in terminology such as "pre-algebra", "emergent algebra" (Ainley, 1999), "incipient algebraic thinking" (Friedlander, Hershkowitz & Arcavi, 1989), and the principle that an algebraic strand should be integrated with arithmetic from the earliest years (Freiman & Lee, 2004). From this perspective, the need for formal algebraic tools emerges from intrinsically algebraic processes such as finding and extending patterns, generalization, and (informal) proof (Blanton & Kaput, 2002).

A standard form of activity that embodies this integration exploits patterned geometrical sequences (e.g. Radford 2001, Warren, 2005), with a series of tasks including:

- Continue the pattern by generating the next elements in the sequence.
- Determine an element further ahead in the sequence without generating the intermediate terms.
- Describe how to continue the sequence and how to determine the general term culminating in:
- Represent the general term symbolically.

4.1. Properties of arithmetic operations

Booth (1989) was an early proponent of the argument for laying the foundations of algebra within elementary arithmetic, specifically on the grounds that "students' difficulties in algebra are in part due to their lack of understanding of various structural notions in arithmetic" (p. 141). Using arithmetical statements to probe students' implicit understand of properties of inversion, associativity, and commutativity, she concluded that many Grade 8 students in Australia had weak grasp of allowable transformations of numerical expressions involving addition and subtraction. Banerjee and Subramaniam (2005) present a teaching approach based on creating strong understanding of arithmetic expressions as foundational for algebra.

A number of studies have investigated children's ability flexibly to use strategies such as compensation (e.g. Warren, 2002). In the context of the drive for numeracy in British elementary schools, Brown, Askew, Rhodes, Denvir, Ranson and Wiliam (2002) cite data using items whereby students are stimulated to use the result 86 + 57 = 143 to quickly work out related results such as 87 + 57, 86 + 86 + 57 + 57, 860 + 570. The related research on students' strategies for multidigit computations was reviewed in Section 2.1.1.

Children exploiting the structure of arithmetical operations are demonstrating what Vergnaud (1996) termed "theorems-in-action". This notion was invoked by Vermeulen, Olivier and Human (1996) in studying students' awareness of the distribution property (which is, as they point out, inherent –but generally hidden– in the standard algorithm for multiplying multidigit whole numbers). They posited a 5-level model spanning the range from "theorem-in-action" (implicit) to "theorem, in action" (explicit): spontaneous utilization, recognition, intentional utilization, generalization, explanation. They carried out a teaching experiment based on this analysis, with moderately successful results.

A particular aspect of the structure of arithmetical processes that has recently received much attention in the literature within and beyond PME is the understanding of the equals sign (Freiman & Lee, 2004). The key point here is that exposing children to usage of this symbol exclusively preceded by an arithmetical expression and followed by a single number –with the implicit meaning "results in"– leads to problems later in algebra where the meaning of "equals" as an equivalence relation is central (not to mention many other meanings). A minimal intervention is to introduce early arithmetical statements such as 8 = 3 + 5, 4 + 12 = 5 + 11. Jones and Pratt (2005) describe how (p. 185) "the nature of the meaning [of equals] constructed is highly dependent on specifics of the task design and the tools available" and report that the use of a microworld promoted adoption of the equivalence meaning.

In general, this body of work is a prime example illustrating why long-term curricular planning is essential and how harmful the effects of not implementing such thinking ahead can be.

4.2. Structure of the natural numbers

Rico, Castro and Romero (1996) made the point that "the dynamic character of the natural numerical system gets blocked by the inertia of the common decimal representation" (p. 93). Sequences of point configurations (which have historical basis, of course) offer one way in which to investigate numerical structures. For example, the structure of a sequence of rectangular point arrays, 1 x 2, 2 x 3, 3 x 4,... can be expressed in many equivalent ways, such as: 2, 3 + 3, 4 + 4 + 4 ... or $1^2 + 1$, $2^2 + 2$, $3^2 + 3$, ... An essential element here is leaving the arithmetical expressions uncomputed, a move that will often help in establishing algebraic ways of thinking prior to formal algebraic symbolization.

Recently, Zazkis and Campbell (2002) have been making the case for number theory on the grounds that it provides "natural avenues for developing mathematical thinking, for developing enriched appreciation and understanding of numerical structure, especially with respect to identifying and formulating conjectures, and establishing their truth" (p. 207).

Mathe 2000 is a major curricular project that, as pointed out by Verschaffel (2001, p. 218) takes seriously the conception of mathematics as "the science of patterns". The emphasis on classrooms "in which mathematical structure latent in an artifact is actively (re)-constructed by learners with assistance from their tutor" (Ruthven, 2001, p. 216) is very much aligned with the principles of RME (see Section 2.1.2). An example of such a "substantial learning environment" based on "arithmogons" is described by Wittmann (2001).

4.3. Generalization, argumentation, and proof

One response to quite widespread concern about older students' understanding of, and creativity in, proof has been to recognize the structure of the natural numbers and operations on them as a rich domain for generalization and proof, in the informal sense of more or less convincing general arguments (Mason, Burton & Stacey, 1985). A standard approach to the introduction of algebraic notation has for long been the generalization of patterns, often represented spatially -such as the classic handshakes problem and variants thereof (e.g. Blanton & Kaput, 2002; Zack, 1995). Blanton and Kaput characterize this problem as an example of one that can be "algebrafied" by asking for a general solution (as opposed to the tradition in elementary school mathematics to ask for "the answer"). They also pointed out the beneficial effect of leaving expressions (e.g. 1 + 2 + 3 + 4 + 5 + 6) uncomputed (see comment above).

Many puzzle-like or apparently magical manifestations of structure can be used as motivating starting-points for experimentation, conjecture, generalization, and possibly proof (Mason et al., 1985). For example, Reggiani (1994) used a traditional "think of a number" puzzle:

> Think of a number, double it, add 5, subtract the number you thought of, add 2, now subtract the number you thought of again and then multiple the total by 3. (p. 100)

A particularly rich example (Zack, 1997) of argumentation by 5th grade Canadian students is based on the traditional puzzle "How many squares are there on a chessboard?" (meaning not just 1 x 1, but also 2 x 2, 3 x 3 ... squares). The students demonstrate defense of their discovered pattern through conjecture, refutation, and generalization, and the teacher promotes the position that, in mathematics, finding a pattern is not enough, we need to understand why it works.

5. DISCUSSION

Taking Bergeron and Herscovics' (1990) review of the PME work on early number and arithmetic up to the early nineties as our starting point, we have tried to outline in this chapter some major (new) trends in the last 15 years of PME research on number and operations on numbers.

First of all, this review has revealed that the focus on what should be learnt in order to acquire numerical competence has moved further away from a view that emphasizes the mastery of particular concepts, procedures and their skilled application, towards a dispositional view of *mathematical competence* involving the integrated availability and flexible application of different components. This notion of disposition involves, besides availability of conceptual schemes and strategies, notions of inclination and sensitivity, as nicely reflected in the increasingly popular construct of "number sense" (or "numeracy").

Accordingly, researchers' views of *mathematics learning* have more and more evolved –to use Sfard's (2003) terminology– from an "acquisitionist" perspective, as reflected in traditional cognitivist/rationalist approaches that explain learning in terms of changes in cognitive schemes, tacit models, and (mis)conceptions, towards a "participationist" framework wherein learning is viewed as a construction of meaning and reorganization of activity accompanying the integration of an individual learner within a community of practice. This latter view of learning has profited greatly from the substantial amount of research carried out since the mid-eighties (a) On the influence of cultural and situational factors on mathematics learning in communities of practice outside school settings (classified under the heading of "ethnomathematics and everyday mathematical cognition"), as well as (b) On how the social interaction and negotiation of meaning in the microculture of the mathematics class influence the kind of mathematical competencies that pupils develop ("school mathematics characterized as a form of situated practice").

With respect to *instruction*, research within the PME community has witnessed a continuously increasing interest in the role and the problems teachers face when attempting to teach their students mathematics according to the reform-based ideas that emphasize understanding and flexibility. Moreover, our review of recent research revealed a major development to complement ascertaining studies, predominantly carried out with individual children and about specific curricular topics, with extended classroom-based action research and design studies wherein researchers work with teachers, students, and administrators to construct powerful learning environments that reflect the above-mentioned reform-based dispositional view on mathematical expertise and on learning as the co-construction of meaning within a community of practice.

An aspect to which we have not given much attention, and which should receive more in the future, is cultural diversity, in a world in which, for example, Arabic, Vietnamese, and Italian children are learning arithmetic in Australian schools (Clarkson, 1996), and Somali children in London schools (Jones, 1996). Apart from the obvious need to be aware of linguistic and symbolic variation, and diversity of forms of thinking, studying and learner/teacher interactions, there is another point to be considered, namely that if more attention is given to linking in-school mathematics and the out-of-school mathematics of children's lived experience (for example, through more emphasis on modeling aspects of that experience (Verschaffel, 2002)) then we are bound to take account of variation in that experience not only between cultures, but also within (Zilliox, 2003).

Much of the work that we have reviewed can be seen as implying that, rather than concentrating on computational competence alone, arithmetic should be seen as affording an opportunity to establish foundations of a sound mathematic disposition through intellectual activities that are key to mathematical practices – understanding through simple examples the relationships between mathematical statements and the situations they model (or do not model), wanting to know the reason why a pattern appears, learning the arts of conjecture, argumentation, and (more or less informal) proof (e.g. in the realm of number theory)– even, ideally, becoming aware of the nature of radical conceptual restructuring as the meaning of "number" is progressively extended.

There is also a growing awareness of the need to take a longer-term curricular view with correspondingly integrative theoretical tools. Two aspects within the domain of arithmetic are central in this respect. One is the development of all those mathematical objects to which we attach the name "number" and how to tackle the successive epistemological obstacles that historically lay along that path and face every student. The more sophisticated the conception of number, the less research, so that, for example, work on complex numbers is virtually non-existent (Tirosh & Almog, 1989). In particular, as pointed out by Romero and Rico (1996) there is lack of research with a curricular orientation on students' understanding of real numbers. Thus, there is a need for more research on the more advanced aspects of number. For example, "Have you ever thought why (I mean really why) the multiplication of two negative numbers yields a positive one?" (Núñez, 2000, p. 3). The second fundamental aspect, which we elaborated in Section 4, is the careful orchestration of the relationship between arithmetic and algebra.

As implied by Bergeron and Herscovics (1990) in referring to "local" cognitive structures (see introduction), radical improvement in mathematics education will depend on a coherent, comprehensive theoretical framework. From this perspective, it is essential to develop integrative theoretical structures. Fischbein's (1987) theory of intuition, in particular the theory of intuitive models, is one such framework. Another is Vergnaud's (1996) theory of conceptual fields (a major advance on the use of terms such as "the concept of number" which is essentially meaningless in the absence of clarification). Another unifying construct, which has appeared in several variants, relates to the relationship between mathematical processes and objects, which spans from simple operations on natural numbers to conceptualizing infinity as potential or actual (Arzarello, Bartolini Bussi & Robutti, 2004). One recent ambitious attempt at a unifying theory is that of Lakoff and Núñez (2000) (and see Núñez, 2000) who propose a comprehensive explanation of how it has been possible to extend what is meant by "number" from the natural numbers (so-called for good reasons) to abstractions such as $e^{i\pi} + 1 = 0$.

REFERENCES

Ainley, J. (1999). Doing algebra type stuff: Emergent algebra in the primary school. In O. Zaslavsky (Ed.), *Proceedings of the 23 PME International Conference, 2*, 916.

Amato, S. A. (2005). Developing students' understanding of the concept of fractions as numbers. In H. L. Chick & J. L. Vincent (Eds.), *Proceedings of the 29th PME International Conference, 2*, 49–56.

Anghileri, J. (2001). What are we trying to achieve in teaching standard calculating procedures? In M. van den Heuvel-Panhuizen (Ed.), *Proceedings of the 25th PME International Conference, 2*, 41–48.

Anghileri, J. (2004). Disciplined calculators or flexible problem solvers? In M. J. Høines & A. B. Fuglestad (Eds.), *Proceedings of the 28th PME International Conference, 1*, 41–46.

Arzarello, F., Bartolini Bussi, M. G., & Robutti, O. (2004). Infinity as a multi-faceted concept in history and in the mathematics classroom. In M. J. Høines & A. B. Fuglestad (Eds.), *Proceedings of the 28th PME International Conference, 4*, 89–96.

Askew, M., Brown, M., Rhodes, V., Wiliam, D., & Johnson, D. (1997). Effective teachers of numeracy in UK primary schools: Teachers' beliefs, practices and pupils' learning. In E. Pehkonen (Ed.), *Proceedings of the 21st PME International Conference, 2*, 25–32.

Asman, D., & Markovits, Z. (2001). The use of real world knowledge in solving mathematical problems. In M. van den Heuvel-Panhuizen (Ed.), *Proceedings of the 25th PME International Conference, 2*, 65–72.

Banerjee, R., & Subramaniam, K. (2005). Developing procedure and structure sense of arithmetic expressions. In H. L. Chick & J. L. Vincent (Eds.), *Proceedings of the 29th PME International Conference, 2*, 121–128.

Basso, M., Bonotto, C., & Sorzio, P. (1998). Children's understanding of the decimal numbers through the use of the ruler. In A. Olivier & K. Newstead (Eds.), *Proceedings of the 22nd PME International Conference, 2*, 72–79.

Baturo, A. R. (2004). Empowering Andrea to help year 5 students construct fraction understanding. In M. J. Høines & A. B. Fuglestad (Eds.), *Proceedings of the 28th PME International Conference, 2*, 95–102.

Behr, M., Harel, G., Post, T., & Silver, E. (1983). Rational number concepts. In R. Lesh & M. Landau (Eds.), *Acquisition of mathematics concepts and processes* (pp. 91–125). New York, USA: Academic Press.

Bergeron, J. C., & Herscovics, N. (1999). Psychological aspects of learning early arithmetic. In P. Nesher & J. Kilpatrick (Eds.), *Mathematics and cognition. A research synthesis by the International Group for the Psychology of Mathematics Education* (pp. 31–52). Cambridge, UK: Cambridge University Press.

Blanton, M. L., & Kaput, J. J. (2002). Design principles for tasks that support algebraic thinking in elementary school classrooms. In A. D. Cockburn & E. Nardi (Eds.), *Proceedings of the 26th PME International Conference, 2*, 105–112.

Boaler, J. (1998). Beyond street mathematics. The challenge of situated cognition. In A. Olivier & K. Newstead (Eds.), *Proceedings of the 22nd PME International Conference, 2*, 212–219.

Booth, L. R. (1989). Grade 8 students' understanding of structural properties in mathematics. In G. Vergnaud, J. Rogalski, & M. Artigue (Eds.), *Proceedings of the 13th PME International Conference, 1*, 141–148.

Boufi, A., & Skaftourou, F. (2002). Supporting students reasoning with decimal numbers: A study of a classroom's mathematical development. In A. D. Cockburn & E. Nardi (Eds.), *Proceedings of the 26th PME International Conference, 2*, 153–160.

Brekke, G. (1996). A decimal number is a pair of whole numbers. In L. Puig & A. Gutiérrez (Eds.), *Proceedings of the 20th PME International Conference, 2*, 137–144.

Brousseau, G. (1997). *Theory of didactical situations in mathematics*. Dordrecht, The Netherlands: Kluwer.

Brown, M., Askew, M., Rhodes, V., Denvir, H., Ranson, E., & Wiliam, D. (2002). Measuring progress in numeracy learning. In A. D. Cockburn & E. Nardi (Eds.), *Proceedings of the 26th PME International Conference, 1*, 175–180.

Brown, M., Askew, M., Rhodes, V., Wiliam, D., & Johnson, D. (1997). Effective teachers of numeracy in UK primary schools: Teachers' content knowledge and pupils' learning. In E. Pehkonen (Ed.), *Proceedings of the 21st PME International Conference, 2*, 121–128.

Bruno, A., & Martinón, A. (1996). Beginning learning negative numbers. In L. Puig & A. Gutiérrez (Eds.), *Proceedings of the 20th PME International Conference, 2*, 161–168.

Carpenter, T. P., & Fennema, E. (1989). Building on the knowledge of students and teachers. In G. Vergnaud, J. Rogalski, & M. Artigue (Eds.), *Proceedings of the 13th PME International Conference, 1*, 34–45.

Carraher, D. W., & Schliemann, A. D. (1991). Children's understanding of fractions as expressions of relative magnitude. In F. Furinghetti (Ed.), *Proceedings of the 15th PME International Conference, 1*, 184–191.

Charalambous, C. Y., & Pitta-Pantazi, D. (2005). Revisiting a theoretical model on fractions: Implications for teaching and research. In H. L. Chick & J. L. Vincent (Eds.), *Proceedings of the 29th PME International Conference, 2*, 233–240.

Chick, H. L., & Baker, M. K. (2005). Investigating teachers' responses to student misconceptions. In H. L. Chick & J. L. Vincent (Eds.), *Proceedings of the 29th PME International Conference, 2*, 249–256.

Clarkson, P. C. (1996). NESB migrant students studying mathematics: Vietnamese and Italian students in Melbourne. In L. Puig & A. Gutiérrez (Eds.), *Proceedings of the 20th PME International Conference, 2*, 225–232.

Cobb, P. (1994). A summary of four case studies of mathematical learning and small group interaction. In J. P. Ponte & J. F. Matos (Eds.), *Proceedings of the 18th PME International Conference, 2*, 201–208.

Cooper, T. J., Heirdsfield, A. M., & Irons, C. J. (1996). Years 2 and 3 children's correct-response mental strategies for addition and subtraction word problems and algorithmic exercises. In L. Puig & A. Gutiérrez (Eds.), *Proceedings of the 20th PME International Conference, 2*, 241–248.

De Bock, D., Verschaffel, L., & Janssens, D. (1996). The illusion of linearity: A persistent obstacle in students' thinking about problems involving length and area of similar plane figures. In L. Puig & A. Gutiérrez (Eds.), *Proceedings of the 20th PME International Conference, 2*, 273–280.

De Corte, E., & Verschaffel, L. (1994). Using student-generated word problems to further unravel the difficulty of multiplicative structures. In J. P. Ponte & J. F. Matos (Eds.), *Proceedings of the 18th PME International Conference, 2*, 256–263.

De Souza, A. C. C., Mometti, A. L., Scavazza, H. A., & Baldino, R. R. (1995). Games for integers: Conceptual or semantic fields? In L. Meira & D. Carraher (Eds.), *Proceedings of the 19th PME International Conference, 2*, 232–239.

English, L. D. (1997). Development of seventh-grade students' problem posing. In E. Pehkonen (Ed.), *Proceedings of the 21st PME International Conference, 2*, 241–248.

English, L. D., & Watters, J. J. (2004). Mathematical modeling with young children. In M. J. Høines & A. B. Fuglestad (Eds.), *Proceedings of the 28th PME International Conference, 2*, 335–342.

English, L. D., & Watters, J. J. (2005). Mathematical modeling with 9-year-olds. In H. L. Chick & J. L. Vincent (Eds.), *Proceedings of the 29th PME International Conference, 2*, 297–304.

Fischbein, E. (1987). *Intuition in science and mathematics: An educational approach*. Dordrecht, The Netherlands: Reidel.

Fischbein, E., Deri, M., Nello, M. S., & Marino, M. S. (1985). The role of implicit models in solving verbal problems in multiplication and division. *Journal for Research in Mathematics Education, 16*, 3–17.

Fischbein, E., Jehaim, R., & Cohen, D. (1994). The irrational numbers and the corresponding epistemological obstacles. In J. P. Ponte & J. F. Matos (Eds.), *Proceedings of the 18th PME International Conference, 2*, 352–359.

Freiman, V., & Lee, L. (2004). Tracking primary students' understanding of the equality sign. In M. J. Høines & A. B. Fuglestad (Eds.), *Proceedings of the 28th PME International Conference, 2*, 415–422.

Freudenthal, H. (1983). *Didactical phenomenology of mathematical structures*. Dordrecht, The Netherlands: Kluwer.

Friedlander, A., Hershkowitz, R., & Arcavi, A. (1989). Incipient "algebraic" thinking in pre-algebra students. In G. Vergnaud, J. Rogalski, & M. Artigue (Eds.), *Proceedings of the 13th PME International Conference, 1*, 283–290.

Fuglestad, A. B. (1996). Students' misconceptions with decimal numbers – Preliminary results from a study of computer based teaching. In L. Puig & A. Gutiérrez (Eds.), *Proceedings of the 20th PME International Conference, 2*, 369–376.

Gervasoni, A. (2005). The diverse learning needs of young children who were selected for an intervention program. In H. L. Chick & J. L. Vincent (Eds.), *Proceedings of the 29th PME International Conference, 3*, 33–40.

Goldin, G. A., & Passantino, C. B. (1996). A longitudinal study of children's fraction representations and problem-solving behavior. In L. Puig & A. Gutiérrez (Eds.), *Proceedings of the 20th PME International Conference, 3*, 3–10.

Gravemeijer, K. (2002). Building new mathematical reality, or how emergent modeling may foster abstraction. In A. D. Cockburn & E. Nardi (Eds.), *Proceedings of the 26th PME International Conference, 1*, 125–128.

Gravemeijer, K., & Kindt, M. (2001). "Polder mathematics". Mathematics education in The Netherlands. In M. van den Heuvel-Panhuizen (Ed.), *Proceedings of the 25th PME International Conference, 1*, 89–91.

Gravemeijer, K., McClain, K., & Stephan, M. (1998). Supporting students' construction of increasingly sophisticated ways of reasoning through problem solving. In A. Olivier & K. Newstead (Eds.), *Proceedings of the 22nd PME International Conference, 1*, 194–209.

Gray, E. M., Pitta, D., & Tall, D. O. (1997). The nature of the object as an integral component of numerical processes. In E. Pehkonen (Ed.), *Proceedings of the 21st PME International Conference, 1*, 115–130.

Greer, B. (1994). Extending the meaning of multiplication and division. In G. Harel & J. Confrey (Eds.), *The development of multiplicative reasoning in the learning of mathematics* (pp. 61–85). Albany, NY, USA: SUNY Press.

Hannula, M. S. (2003). Locating fraction on a number line. In N. A. Pateman, B. J. Dougherty, & J. T. Zilliox (Eds.), *Proceedings of the 27th PME International Conference, 3*, 17–24.

Harel, G., Behr, M., Post, T., & Lesh, R. (1989). Fischbein's theory: A further consideration. In G. Vergnaud, J. Rogalski, & M. Artigue (Eds.), *Proceedings of the 13th PME International Conference, 2*, 52–59.

Hasegawa, J. (2000). Classroom discussion on the representation of quantity by fractions: Stability of misconception and implications to practice. In T. Nakahara & M. Koyama (Eds.), *Proceedings of the 24th PME International Conference, 3*, 41–48.

Heirdsfield, A. M. (2005). One teacher's role in promoting understanding in mental computation. In H. L. Chick & J. L. Vincent (Eds.), *Proceedings of the 29th PME International Conference, 3*, 113–120.

Heirdsfield, A. M., Cooper, T. J., Mulligan, J., & Irons, C. J. (1999). Children's mental multiplication and division strategies. In O. Zaslavsky (Ed.), *Proceedings of the 23rd PME International Conference, 3*, 89–96.

Herbst, P. G. (1997). Effectiveness of a strategy as a sociomathematical norm. In E. Pehkonen (Ed.), *Proceedings of the 21st PME International Conference, 3*, 57–64.

Herman, J., Ilucova, L., Kremsova, V., Pribyl, J., Ruppeldtova, J., Simpson, A., et al. (2004). Images of fractions as processess and images of fractions in processes. In M. J. Høines & A. B. Fuglestad (Eds.), *Proceedings of the 28th PME International Conference, 4*, 249–256.

Hershkowitz, S., & Nesher, P. (1991). Two step problems. The scheme approach. In F. Furinghetti (Ed.), *Proceedings of the 15th PME International Conference, 2*, 189–196.

Hopkins, S., & Lawson, M. (2004). Explaining variability in retrieval times for addition produced by students with mathematical learning difficulties. In M. J. Høines & A. B. Fuglestad (Eds.), *Proceedings of the 28th PME International Conference, 3*, 57–64.

Jones, I., & Pratt, D. (2005). Three utilities for the equals sign. In H. L. Chick & J. L. Vincent (Eds.), *Proceedings of the 29th PME International Conference, 3*, 185–192.

Jones, L. (1996). Somali children learning mathematics in Britain: A conflict of cultures. In L. Puig & A. Gutiérrez (Eds.), *Proceedings of the 20th PME International Conference, 3*, 153–160.

Klein, R., Barkai, R., Tirosh, D., & Tsamir, P. (1998). Increasing teachers awareness of students' conceptions of operations with rational numbers. In A. Olivier & K. Newstead (Eds.), *Proceedings of the 22nd PME International Conference, 3*, 120–127.

Kramarski, B., & Mevarech, Z. (2001). Structuring group interaction in mathematics cooperative classrooms. The effect of metacognitive instruction vs worked out examples. In M. van den Heuvel-Panhuizen (Ed.), *Proceedings of the 25th PME International Conference, 1*, 330.

Krummheuer, G. (2000). Narrative elements in mathematical argumentations in primary education. In T. Nakahara & M. Koyama (Eds.), *Proceedings of the 24th PME International Conference, 3*, 175–182.

Kutscher, B., Linchevski, L., & Eisenman, T. (2002). From the Lotto game to subtracting two-digit numbers in first-graders. In A. D. Cockburn & E. Nardi (Eds.), *Proceedings of the 26th PME International Conference, 3*, 249–256.

Kyriakides, L., Philippou, G., & Charalambous, C. (2002). Testing a developmental model of measuring problem solving skills based on schema theory. In A. D. Cockburn & E. Nardi (Eds.), *Proceedings of the 26th PME International Conference, 3*, 257–265.

Lakoff, G., & Núñez, R. (2000). *Where mathematics comes from: How the embodied mind brings mathematics into being*. New York, USA: Basic Books.

Lamb, J., & Booker, G. (2004). The impact of developing teacher conceptual knowledge on students' knowledge of division. In M. J. Høines & A. B. Fuglestad (Eds.), *Proceedings of the 28th PME International Conference, 3*, 177–192.

Lee, B. (1994). Prospective secondary mathematics teachers' beliefs about "0.999...=1". In J. P. Ponte & J. F. Matos (Eds.), *Proceedings of the 18th PME International Conference, 3*, 128–135.

Lerman, S. (2000). The social turn in mathematics education research. In J. Boaler (Ed.), *Multiple perspectives on mathematics teaching and learning* (pp. 19–44). Westport, CT, USA: Ablex.

Lester, F. K., & Kroll, D. L. (1990). Teaching students to be reflective: A study of two grade-seven classes. In G. Booker, P. Cobb, & T. N. Mendicuti (Eds.), *Proceedings of the 14th PME International Conference, 1*, 151–158.

Leu, Y.-C. (1999). Elementary school teachers' understanding of knowledge of students' cognition in fractions. In O. Zaslavsky (Ed.), *Proceedings of the 23rd PME International Conference, 3*, 225–232.

Linchevski, L., & Willams, J. (1996). Situated intuitions, concrete manipulations and the construction of mathematical concepts: The case of integers. In L. Puig & A. Gutiérrez (Eds.), *Proceedings of the 20th PME International Conference, 3*, 265–272.

Lytle, P. A. (1994). Investigation of a model based on the neutralization of opposites to teach integer addition and subtraction. In J. P. Ponte & J. F. Matos (Eds.), *Proceedings of the 18th PME International Conference, 3*, 192–199.

Mamede, E., Nunes, T., & Bryant, P. (2005). The equivalence and ordering of fractions in part-whole and quotient situations. In H. L. Chick & J. L. Vincent (Eds.), *Proceedings of the 29th PME International Conference, 3*, 281–288.

Marcou, A., & Philippou, G. (2005). Motivational beliefs, self-regulated learning, and mathematical problem solving. In H. L. Chick & J. L. Vincent (Eds.), *Proceedings of the 29th PME International Conference, 3*, 297–304.

Mason, J., Burton, L., & Stacey, K. (1985). *Thinking mathematically*. Wokingham, UK: Addison-Wesley.

McClain, K., & Cobb, P. (1997). An analysis of the teacher's role in guiding the evolution of sociomathematical norms. In E. Pehkonen (Ed.), *Proceedings of the 21st PME International Conference, 3*, 224–231.

Mekhmandarov, I., Meron, R., & Peled, I. (1996). Performing and understanding: A closer look at comparison word problems. In L. Puig & A. Gutiérrez (Eds.), *Proceedings of the 20th PME International Conference, 3*, 285–390.

Merenluoto, K. (2003). Abstracting the density of numbers on the number line – A quasi-experimental study. In N. A. Pateman, B. J. Dougherty, & J. T. Zilliox (Eds.), *Proceedings of the 27th PME International Conference, 3*, 285–292.

Mitchelmore, M. C., & Mulligan, J. T. (1996). Children's developing multiplication and division strategies. In L. Puig & A. Gutiérrez (Eds.), *Proceedings of the 20th PME International Conference, 3*, 407–414.

Mukhopadhyay, S., Resnick, L. B., & Schauble, L. (1990). Social sense-making in mathematics: Children's ideas of negative numbers. In G. Booker, P. Cobb, & T. N. Mendicuti (Eds.), *Proceedings of the 14th PME International Conference, 3*, 281–288.

Mulligan, J. T., & Wright, R. (2000). Interview-based assessment of early multiplication and division. In T. Nakahara & M. Koyama (Eds.), *Proceedings of the 24th PME International Conference, 4*, 17–24.

Murray, H., Olivier, A., & De Beer, T. (1999). Reteaching fractions for understanding. In O. Zaslavsky (Ed.), *Proceedings of the 23rd PME International Conference, 3*, 305–312.

Murray, H., Olivier, A., & Human, P. (1994). Fifth graders' multi-digit multiplication and division strategies after five years problem-centered learning. In J. P. Ponte & J. F. Matos (Eds.), *Proceedings of the 18th PME International Conference, 3*, 399–406.

Murray, H., Olivier, A., & Human, P. (1996). Young students' informal knowledge of fractions. In L. Puig & A. Gutiérrez (Eds.), *Proceedings of the 20th PME International Conference, 4*, 43–50.

Murray, H., Olivier, A., & Human, P. (1998). Learning through problem solving. In A. Olivier & K. Newstead (Eds.), *Proceedings of the 22nd PME International Conference, 1*, 169–185.

Nemirovsky, R., Kaput, J., & Roschelle, J. (1998). Enlarging mathematical activity from modeling phenomena to generating phenomena. In A. Olivier & K. Newstead (Eds.), *Proceedings of the 22nd PME International Conference, 3*, 287–294.

Nesher, P., & Hershkovitz, S. (1997). Real world knowledge and mathematical knowledge. In E. Pehkonen (Ed.), *Proceedings of the 21st PME International Conference, 3*, 280–287.

Newstead, K., & Murray, H. (1998). Young students' constructions of fractions. In A. Olivier & K. Newstead (Eds.), *Proceedings of the 22nd PME International Conference, 3*, 295–302.

Newstead, K., & Olivier, A. (1999). Addressing students' conceptions of common fractions. In O. Zaslavsky (Ed.), *Proceedings of the 23rd PME International Conference, 3*, 329–336.

Nohda, N. (2000). Teaching by open-approach method in Japanese mathematics classrooms. In T. Nakahara & M. Koyama (Eds.), *Proceedings of the 24th PME International Conference, 1*, 39–54.

Nunes, T., Schliemann, A. D., & Carraher, D. W. (1993). *Street mathematics and school mathematics*. New York, USA: Cambridge University Press.

Núñez, R. E. (2000). Mathematical idea analysis: What embodied cognitive science can say about the human nature of mathematics. In T. Nakahara & M. Koyama (Eds.), *Proceedings of the 24th PME International Conference, 1*, 3–22.

Olive, J. (2002). The construction of commensurate fractions. In A. D. Cockburn & E. Nardi (Eds.), *Proceedings of the 26th PME International Conference, 4*, 1–8.

Op 't Eynde, P. (2004). A socio-constructivist perspective on the study of affect in mathematics education. In M. J. Høines & A. B. Fuglestad (Eds.), *Proceedings of the 28th PME International Conference, 1*, 118–122.

Ostad, S. A. (1998). Subtraction strategies in developmental perspective: A comparison of mathematically normal and mathematically disabled children. In A. Olivier & K. Newstead (Eds.), *Proceedings of the 22nd PME International Conference, 3*, 311–318.

Pantziara, M., Gagatsis, A., & Pitta-Pantazi, D. (2004). The use of diagrams in solving non-routine problems. In M. J. Høines & A. B. Fuglestad (Eds.), *Proceedings of the 28th PME International Conference, 3*, 489–496.

Peled, I., & Bassan-Cincinatus, R. (2005). Degrees of freedom in modeling: Taking certainty out of proportion. In H. L. Chick & J. L. Vincent (Eds.), *Proceedings of the 29th PME International Conference, 4*, 57–64.

Peled, I., Mukhopadhyay, S., & Resnick, L. B. (1989). Formal and informal sources of mental models for negative numbers. In G. Vergnaud, J. Rogalski, & M. Artigue (Eds.), *Proceedings of the 13th PME International Conference, 3*, 106–110.

Philippou, G., & Christou, C. (1994). Prospective elementary teachers' conceptual and procedural knowledge of fractions. In J. P. Ponte & J. F. Matos (Eds.), *Proceedings of the 18th PME International Conference, 4*, 33–40.

Philippou, G., & Christou, C. (1999). A schema-based model for teaching problem solving. In O. Zaslavsky (Ed.), *Proceedings of the 23rd PME International Conference, 4*, 57–64.

Pinto, M., & Tall, D. (1996). Student teachers' conceptions of the rational numbers. In L. Puig, & A Gutierrez (Eds.), *Proceedings of the 20th PME International Conference, 4*, 139–146.

Pirie, S. E. B., Martin, L., & Kieren, T. E. (1994). Mathematical images for fractions: Help or hindrance? In J. P. Ponte & J. F. Matos (Eds.), *Proceedings of the 18th[th] PME International Conference, 3*, 247–254.

Pitta-Pantazi, D., Gray, E. M., & Christou, C. (2004). Elementary school students' mental representations of fractions. In M. J. Høines & A. B. Fuglestad (Eds.), *Proceedings of the 28th PME International Conference, 4*, 41–48.

Polya, G. (1945). *How to solve it.* Princeton, NJ, USA: Princeton University Press.

Radford, L. (2001). Factual, contextual and symbolic generalizations in algebra. In M. van den Heuvel-Panhuizen (Ed.), *Proceedings of the 25th PME International Conference, 4*, 81–88.

Reggiani, M. (1994). Generalization as a basis for algebraic thinking: Observations with 11–12 year old pupils. In J. P. Ponte & J. F. Matos (Eds.), *Proceedings of the 18th[th] PME International Conference, 4*, 97–104.

Rico, L. (1994). Two-step addition problems with duplicated structure. In J. P. Ponte & J. F. Matos (Eds.), *Proceedings of the 18th PME International Conference, 4*, 121–129.

Rico, L., Castro, E., & Romero, I. (1996). The role of representation systems in the learning of numerical structures. In L. Puig & A. Gutiérrez (Eds.), *Proceedings of the 20th PME International Conference, 1*, 87–102.

Romero, I., & Rico, L. (1996). On the introduction of real numbers in secondary school. An action-research experience. In L. Puig & A. Gutiérrez (Eds.), *Proceedings of the 20th PME International Conference, 4*, 227–234.

Ruthven, K. (2001). Reaction 1: Between psychologising and mathematising. In M. van den Heuvel-Panhuizen (Ed.), *Proceedings of the 25th PME International Conference, 1*, 216–217.

Ruwisch, S. (1999). Division with remainder strategies in real-world contexts. In O. Zaslavsky (Ed.), *Proceedings of the 23rd PME International Conference, 4*, 137–144.

Schliemann, A. D. (1995). Some concerns about bringing everyday mathematics to mathematics education. In L. Meira & D. Carraher (Eds.), *Proceedings of the 19th PME International Conference, 1*, 45–60.

Schliemann, A. D., Araujo, C., Cassundé, M. A., Macedo, S., & Nicéas, L. (1994). School children versus street sellers' use of the commutative law for solving multiplication problems. In J. P. Ponte & J. F. Matos (Eds.), *Proceedings of the 18th PME International Conference, 4*, 209–216.

Schliemann, A. D., Lara-Roth, S., & Epstein, J. (2000). Understanding how children solve compare problems. In T. Nakahara & M. Koyama (Eds.), *Proceedings of the 24th PME International Conference, 1*, 184.

Schoenfeld, A. H. (1991). On mathematics as sense-making: An informal attack on the unfortunate divorce of formal and informal mathematics. In J. F. Voss, D. N. Perkins, & J. W. Segal (Eds.), *Informal reasoning and education* (pp. 311–343). Hillsdale, NJ, USA: Lawrence Erlbaum.

Schoenfeld, A. H. (1992). Learning to think mathematically. Problem solving, metacognition and sense-maing in mathematics. In D. A. Grouws (Ed.), *Handbook of research on mathematics teaching and learning* (pp. 334–370). New York, USA: MacMillan.

Schorr, R. Y., & Amit, M. (2005). Analyzing student modeling cycles in the context of a 'real world' problem. In H. L. Chick & J. L. Vincent (Eds.), *Proceedings of the 29th PME International Conference, 4*, 137–144.

Selter, C. (2001). Understanding – the underlying goal of teacher education. In M. van den Heuvel-Panhuizen (Ed.), *Proceedings of the 25th PME International Conference, 1*, 198–202.

Sethole, G. (2005). From the everyday, through the inauthentic, to mathematics: Reflection on the process of teaching from contexts. In H. L. Chick & J. L. Vincent (Eds.), *Proceedings of the 29th PME International Conference, 4*, 169–176.

Sfard, A. (2003). Balancing the unbalanceable: The NCTM Standards in light of theories of mathematics. In J. Kilpatrick, W. G. Martin, & D. Schifter (Eds.), *A research companion to Principles and Standards for School Mathematics* (pp. 353–392). Reston, VA, USA: NCTM.

Shigematsu, K., & Yoshio, K. (2000). Metacognition: The role of the "inner teacher". In T. Nakahara & M. Koyama (Eds.), *Proceedings of the 24th PME International Conference, 4*, 137–144.

Shimizu, N. (2000). An analysis of "make an organized list" strategy in problem solving process. In T. Nakahara & M. Koyama (Eds.), *Proceedings of the 24th PME International Conference, 4*, 145–152.

Steinberg, R., Carpenter, T. C., & Fennema, E. (1994). Children's invented strategies and algorithms in division. In J. P. Ponte & J. F. Matos (Eds.), *Proceedings of the 18th PME International Conference, 4*, 305–312.

Steinbring, H. (2000). The genesis of new mathematical knowledge as a social construction. In T. Nakahara & M. Koyama (Eds.), *Proceedings of the 24th PME International Conference, 4*, 177–184.

Steinbring, H. (2001). Analysis of mathematical interaction in teaching processes. In M. van den Heuvel-Panhuizen (Ed.), *Proceedings of the 25th PME International Conference, 1*, 211–215.

Steinle, V., & Stacey, K. (2003). Grade-related trends in the prevalence and persistence of decimal misconceptions. In N. A. Pateman, B. J. Dougherty, & J. T. Zilliox (Eds.), *Proceedings of the 27th PME International Conference, 4*, 259–266.

Steinle, V., & Stacey, K. (2004). Persistence of decimal misconceptions and readiness to move to expertise. In M. J. Høines & A. B. Fuglestad (Eds.), *Proceedings of the 28th PME International Conference, 4*, 225–232.

Strang, T. (1990). The fraction-concept in comprehensive school at grade-levels 3–6 in Finland. In G. Booker, P. Cobb, & T. N. Mendicuti (Eds.), *Proceedings of the 14th PME International Conference, 3*, 75–80.

Teong, S.-K., Threlfall, J., & Monaghan, J. (2000). The effects of metacognitive training in mathematical word problem solving in a computer environment. In T. Nakahara & M. Koyama (Eds.), *Proceedings of the 24th PME International Conference, 4*, 193–200.

Tirosh, D., & Almog, N. (1989). Conceptual adjustments in progressing from real to complex numbers. In G. Vergnaud, J. Rogalski, & M. Artigue (Eds.), *Proceedings of the 13th PME International Conference, 3*, 221–227.

Torbeyns, J., Verschaffel, L., & Ghesquière, P. (2004). Efficiency and adaptiveness of multiple school-taught strategies in the domain of simple addition. In M. J. Høines & A. B. Fuglestad (Eds.), *Proceedings of the 28th PME International Conference, 4*, 321–328.

Tzur, R. (1996). Children's interaction and fraction learning in a computer microworld: Construction of the iterative fraction scheme. In L. Puig & A. Gutiérrez (Eds.), *Proceedings of the 20th PME International Conference, 4*, 355–362.

Van Dooren, W., De Bock, D., Janssens, D., & Verschaffel, L. (2005). Students' overreliance on linearity: An effect of school-like word problems? In H. L. Chick & J. L. Vincent (Eds.), *Proceedings of the 29th PME International Conference, 4*, 265–272.

Vergnaud, G. (1996). The theory of conceptual fields. In L. P. Steffe, P. Nesher, P. Cobb, G. A. Goldin, & B. Greer (Eds.), *Theories of mathematical learning* (pp. 219–239). Hillsdale, NJ, USA: Lawrence Erlbaum.

Vermeulen, N., Olivier, A., & Human, P. (1996). Students' awareness of the distributive property. In L. Puig & A. Gutiérrez (Eds.), *Proceedings of the 20th PME International Conference, 4*, 379–386.

Verschaffel, L. (2001). Reaction 2: Design and use of substantial learning environments in mathe 2000. In M. van den Heuvel-Panhuizen (Ed.), *Proceedings of the 25th PME International Conference, 1*, 218–219.

Verschaffel, L. (2002). Taking the modeling perspective seriously at the elementary school level: Promises and pitfalls. In A. D. Cockburn & E. Nardi (Eds.), *Proceedings of the 26th PME International Conference, 1*, 64–80.

Verschaffel, L., & De Corte, E. (1995). Teaching realistic mathematics modeling in the elementary school. A teaching experiment with fifth graders. In L. Meira & D. Carraher (Eds.), *Proceedings of the 19th PME International Conference, 1*, 105–112.

Verschaffel, L., De Corte, E., & Borghart, I. (1996). Pre-service teachers' conceptions and beliefs about the role of real-world knowledge in arithmetic word problem solving. In L. Puig & A. Gutiérrez (Eds.), *Proceedings of the 20th PME International Conference, 4*, 387–394.

Warren, E. (2002). Unknowns, arithmetic to algebra: Two exemplars. In A. D. Cockburn & E. Nardi (Eds.), *Proceedings of the 26th PME International Conference, 4*, 362–369.

Warren, E. (2005). Young children's ability to generalize the pattern rule for growing patterns. In H. L. Chick & J. L. Vincent (Eds.), *Proceedings of the 29th PME International Conference, 4*, 305–312.

Whitenack, J. W., Cobb, P., & McClain, K. (1995). A preliminary report of a first-grade teaching experiment: Mathematizing, modeling and mathematical learning in the classroom microculture. In L. Meira & D. Carraher (Eds.), *Proceedings of the 19th PME International Conference, 3*, 256–263.

Wittmann, E. C. (2001). Designing, researching and implementing mathematical learning environments – the research group "Mathe 2000". In M. van den Heuvel-Panhuizen (Ed.), *Proceedings of the 25th PME International Conference, 1*, 189–220.

Yackel, E. (1998). A study of argumentation in a second-grade mathematics classroom. In A. Olivier & K. Newstead (Eds.), *Proceedings of the 22nd PME International Conference, 4*, 209–216.

Yackel, E. (2001). Explanation, justification and argumentation in mathematics classrooms. In M. van den Heuvel-Panhuizen (Ed.), *Proceedings of the 25th PME International Conference, 1*, 9–24.

Yackel, E., & Cobb, P. (1996). Sociomathematical norms, argumentations, and autonomy in mathematics. *Journal for Research in Mathematics Education, 27*, 458–477.

Zack, V. (1995). Algebraic thinking in the upper elementary school: The role of collaboration in making meaning of 'generalisation'. In L. Meira & D. Carraher (Eds.), *Proceedings of the 19th PME International Conference, 2*, 106–113.

Zack, V. (1997). "You have to prove us wrong": Proof at the elementary school level. In E. Pehkonen (Ed.), *Proceedings of the 21st PME International Conference, 4*, 291–298.

Zazkis, R., & Campbell, S. R. (2002). Making a case for number theory. In A. D. Cockburn & E. Nardi (Eds.), *Proceedings of the 26th PME International Conference, 1*, 206–207.

Zazkis, R., & Sirotic, N. (2004). Making sense of irrational numbers: Focusing on representation. In M. J. Høines & A. B. Fuglestad (Eds.), *Proceedings of the 28th PME International Conference, 4*, 497–504.

Zilliox, J. (2003). Voyaging from theory to practice in learning: Teacher professional development. In N. A. Pateman, B. J. Dougherty, & J. T. Zilliox (Eds.), *Proceedings of the 27th PME International Conference, 1*, 25–31.

AFFILIATIONS

Lieven Verschaffel
Center for Instructional Psychology and Technology
University of Leuven
Vesaliusstraat 2
B-3000 Leuven (Belgium)
lieven.verschaffel@ped.kuleuven.be
http://www.psy.kuleuven.ac.be/cipt/

Brian Greer
Portland State University
Department of Educational Policy, Foundations, and Administrative Studies
2632 NE 7th Ave
Portland OR 97212 (USA)
brian1060ne@yahoo.com

Joke Torbeyns
Center for Instructional Psychology and Technology
University of Leuven
Vesaliusstraat 2
B-3000 Leuven (Belgium)
joke.torbeyns@ped.kuleuven.be
http://www.psy.kuleuven.ac.be/cipt/

KAY OWENS AND LYNNE OUTHRED

THE COMPLEXITY OF LEARNING GEOMETRY AND MEASUREMENT

This chapter gives an overview of some of the research on geometry and measurement. Other relevant material may be found in chapters on visualisation, problem solving, proof, technology in mathematics education and teacher education.

The research in geometry and spatial thinking has evolved from studies in psychology. Initially problem solving was a focus of these studies and it has continued as an area of research over the 30 years. In the 1970s, some researchers were interested in the relationship of spatial abilities to mathematical learning and problem solving but others continued to build on Piaget's theory that children's thinking becomes more sophisticated over time (Lesh, 1978). There was also a shift away from factor analytic studies towards understanding the development of students' constructions of geometric concepts and the role of visual imagery. This shift resulted in the development of theoretical perspectives on visualisation, concept development and problem solving in geometry.

The emphasis on cognition and structural theories has been supplemented by more recent studies on the context of learning. There is a continuing tension between research studies that emphasise visual and contextual aspects of conception and those that interpret learning in terms of developmental theories, for example, the Van Hieles' theory (Gutiérrez, 1996; Tall, 2004). The Van Hieles' theory has strongly influenced work on early conceptions of geometrical ideas and the processes by which children move from initial knowledge and visual skills to geometric concepts and their definitions. There has been an increasing emphasis on students' perceptions of two-dimensional shapes, particularly their prototypical images and representations. However, there have been fewer studies on three-dimensional shapes partly because of the dominance of research on structuralist developmental theories and the complexity of visualisation (Gutiérrez, 1996).

In the late 1970s, an understanding of proof in Euclidean theorems was found to be assisted by experiences of transformational geometry and the movement of shapes. From then on, many studies focussed on the use of computer technologies, including Logo and more recently dynamic geometry software. An overview of the research on technology and proof may be found in the chapters on these topics.

A. Gutiérrez, P. Boero (eds.), Handbook of Research on the Psychology of Mathematics Education: Past, Present and Future, 83–115.

PROBLEM SOLVING – INITIAL AND LATER RESEARCH

Research in space and geometry was influenced by a trend towards problem solving as a way of learning (Lesh, 1978). In a summary of research Lesh (1979) noted that good problem solvers make early assessments of the problem, view the problem from different angles, persevere, apply a stock of conceptual models and structural metaphors, and assess relevant information.

During problem solving, students may focus on limited aspects of the problem or misinterpret the problem because of preconceived biases and self-oriented perspectives (Lesh, 1979). For example, 7th grade students viewed the direction of right from their position rather than from a line on the paper (Krainer, 1991) and confused everyday usage and mathematical terminology (Krainer, 1991; Lopez-Real, 1991). Such limited interpretations may be reduced by working in groups because of the socialising effect of group work (cf. theory by Vygotsky, 1978). Groups provide the opportunity for imitation, satisfaction, and self-esteem as well as the realisation that a problem may be solved in different ways (Lesh, 1979). For example, Malara and Gherpelli (1994) found that secondary students could pose geometry problems when working in groups but not individually and when problems were ambiguous, group discussion sometimes assisted them to clarify the text.

Spatial problem solving strategies have been described by Gorgorió (1996) as (a) Structuring strategies to relate past experience or to simplify the problem, (b) Processing strategies (visual or verbal), and (c) Approaching strategies (global or partial). She found some gender differences in the use of structuring strategies. Metacognitive knowledge of strategies was found to be important for older students who were asked to solve a problem involving construction of a quadrilateral but such performance monitoring was not so effective for younger (grade 3) students (Yamaguchi, 1993). Yamaguchi's findings have been supported by Owens (1996b) who found that year 2 students made perceptual checks but lacked confidence in, or were not aware of, their strategies. For upper secondary school students, metacognition was also found to be important (Reiss, Klieme & Heinze, 2001). These researchers reported that the variables which correlated with scores on geometric questions (TIMSS items) were spatial ability assessed by spatial reasoning tasks, the metacognition evident in solving these tasks, declarative knowledge of geometric concepts, and knowledge of procedures for generating proof.

Students use a variety of discourse and drawing strategies when problem solving (Robotti, 2001). Transcripts showed how students formed lists of information from a diagram based on observation or from known concepts. Students reduced long lists by focussing on the purpose of the task (meta-discourse). The meta-discourse moved the problem solving onto a new strategy, clearer purpose, or deduction.

PIAGET'S LEGACY

Developmental psychologists like Piaget have influenced research about change in thinking (Bishop, 1979). The key change is in "progression from a state of relative globality and lack of differentiation to a state of increasing differentiation, articulation and hierarchic integration" (Werner, 1964, as cited in Bishop, 1979, p. 22). A key element in effecting change is intuition, about which Piaget commented: "although effective at all stages and remaining fundamental from the point of view of invention, the cognitive role of intuition diminishes (in a relative sense) during development. ... Formalisation ... progressively limits the field of intuition (in the sense of non-formalised operational thought)" (Beth & Piaget, 1966, p. 225).

Studies of very young children found that intuitive symmetry and pattern making were evident in their paintings (Booth, 1984). She outlined stages of spontaneous painting linked to aspects of logico-mathematics. The stages are the scribble stage, the topology stage and the geometric pattern stage with the last category showing patterns arising from a systematic repetition of an element, or division of the plane resulting in translation, reflection or even rotational patterns. By naming the pattern, she postulated that intuitive thought becomes conscious and the pattern takes on symbolic significance.

Similarly, studies of children's drawings show that by the age of two, children may produce different kinds of scribbles, and many may represent a circle and a line when presented with a series of diagrams to copy. At age 3 most can form two separate circles or crossing horizontal and vertical lines and at age 4, squares, oblique crossing lines, and intersecting circles are drawn. As figures become more complex, the age at which children can reproduce the figures varies considerably (Noelting, 1979). Nevertheless, the order of difficulty is fairly consistent, especially the complexity of lines, use of oblique lines and intersecting figures. Students gradually master perspective through coordination of part-whole relations and direction (Noelting, 1979; Mitchelmore, 1983).

Knowledge developed through incidental learning experiences may provide the backdrop for intuition (Van Hiele, 1986) and may explain why children could recognise right-angled triangles in the standard position with the shorter sides in the horizontal and vertical position but not in various oblique positions, even after training (Cooper & Krainer, 1990). The effect of prior knowledge was found to affect students' development of simple geometrical concepts, especially reflection in a line (Schmidt, 1980). Students did not attend to the important features of the diagram and had difficulty producing symmetrical pictures.

Later research showed that intuition is not limited to early childhood. For example, tertiary students lacked connection of intuitive processes and mental images with the analytical and graphic representations of the stationary state in heat equations (Farfán & Hitt, 1990). Intuition based on prior experience was called the "geometric eye" by Fujita and Jones (2002) who believed it developed from practical exercises prior to looking at theoretical theorems. The Van Hieles also provided practical experiences before moving on to deductive proof (Van Hiele, 1986). This "primitive knowing" and "image making" have been postulated as the basis of learning (Kieren & Pirie, 1992).

THE VAN HIELE MODEL OF GEOMETRICAL THINKING

The Van Hieles proposed a model of geometric thinking which comprises five levels of reasoning –recognition (perception is visual only); analysis (a figure is identified by properties); classification or informal deduction (the significance of the properties is realised); formal deduction (geometric proofs are constructed); and rigour (an aspect later shown to be difficult to operationalise and differentiate from the previous level). Thinking develops from a gestalt-like visual level, through increasingly sophisticated levels involving description, analysis, abstraction and proof. The Van Hieles believed that the instruction should match the students' levels of thought and proposed a model of teaching and learning that suggested how to move students from one level of thinking to the next (Hoffer, 1983). In the Van Hiele model the levels were considered to be hierarchical and discontinuous, with each level dependent on mastery of the previous level (Afonso, Camacho & Socas, 1999; Clements & Battista, 1991; Lawrie, 1998). However, Burger and Shaughnessy (1986) proposed that the levels were dynamic and continuous, rather than static and discrete.

Clements and Battista (1991) considered that the levels appear to describe students' geometric development. However, they found that students may be difficult to classify, especially in the transition from Level 2 to Level 3 and that there is also some evidence for a more basic level than the Van Hiele's Level 1 (visual thinking). They reported that "research consistently indicates that the levels are hierarchical, although here too there are exceptions" (p. 224). Level 5 has been found to be different from the other levels, which may explain why Van Hiele also proposed a three-level model collapsing Levels 3-5 into one because of the difficulties of assessing these levels. Assignment to levels is not strictly related to age, and development through the hierarchy is a function of teaching and learning. Nakahara (1995) found that the concepts of basic quadrilaterals develop in accordance with the Van Hiele model but that the level a student is assigned may vary depending on the geometrical figure involved.

The transition between levels has been the focus of a number of studies. Significant aspects of the transition from Level 1 (recognition based on global perspective of a figure) to Level 2 (analysis of the properties of figures) were (a) A realisation that aspects of a figure are important (identification of features), (b) An attempt to document more than one feature, and, (c) Grouping figures based on a single property (Pegg & Baker, 1999). As mentioned, the transition from Level 2 to Level 3 has been identified as problematic (Clements & Battista, 1991). A distinguishing feature of Level 3 is class inclusion —the interrelation between two sets when all members of the first are members of the second, (for example, squares as a subset of rectangles). A lack of recognition of this relationship indicated that many 8th grade students are at Level 2 (Matsuo, 1993; Currie & Pegg, 1998). Matsuo (1993) suggested students' classification of a square as a rectangle seemed to depend on the property that they focussed on. If their concept definition of a rectangle was four right angles or parallel sides, they were likely to consider a square as belonging to the class of rectangles. However, if they focussed on rectangles as having two long sides and two shorter sides, the square was classified as a separate case.

De Villiers (1998) argued that formal definitions may only develop at Level 3 since at this level students begin to notice interrelationships between the properties of a figure. He discussed allowing visual, uneconomic and economic definitions at Levels 1 to 3 respectively, and also considered hierarchical and partitional definitions. Hierarchical definitions define concepts in such a way that the more particular classes form subclasses of the more general concepts, while in partitional definitions the various subclasses of concepts are considered disjoint from one another, for example, squares are excluded from the class of rectangles (Heinze, 2002). De Villiers found that many students preferred a partitional definition, rather than a hierarchical one, and concluded that students should be actively involved in formulating and evaluating definitions. Students who engaged in argumentation and justification about different features of a mathematical definition were found to change their opinion as a result of interactions and discussions with peers, as well as realising that textbook definitions were not inviolable, and that alternative definitions were possible (Shir & Zaslavsky, 2002). Definitions that required analysis (e.g., three angles of 90° and two neighbouring sides of the same length) encouraged students to think about necessary and sufficient conditions at Van Hiele's Level 3 (Heinze, 2002).

Shir and Zaslavsky (2001, 2002) comment that there is disagreement among researchers about whether a definition of a shape should be minimal in information. They classified arguments used by the students as: (a) Mathematical (correct, equivalent to a known definition, useful or minimal), (b) Receptive (e.g. clear, based on basic concepts, short, familiar) or (c) Figurative (based on properties). An activity designed to highlight different definitions was regarded as valuable in engaging students in argumentation and justification and in realising that mathematics is "a humanistic discipline in which there is room for various opinions" (Shir & Zaslavsky, 2002, p. 208). Procedural (construction-oriented) definitions seemed to dominate 10th grade students' work when using Cabri (Furinghetti & Paola, 2002).

Individual interviews indicated that quasi-empirical arguments were satisfying to students in Grades 6-10 (De Villiers, 1991). Thus, folding an isosceles triangle along the line of symmetry was sufficient to explain that base angles are equal. Repeating an experiment with different examples was also convincing. However, in one class group, De Villiers found that some students needed an explanation that was logico-deductive. Patronis (1994) argued that such "pragmatic arguments" are not just descriptions of specific experiences but they provide interpretations of mathematical activity and social construction of concepts. For example, a class of 16 year olds took adjacent angles whose sum was a straight angle and showed that the bisectors of the angles were perpendicular, relying on angle measurements for "proof". Laborde and Capponi (1995) have shown that students continuously move from what they call "spatio-graphic geometry" to "theoretical geometry". When elaborating a proof, the student alternately uses the figure to make conjectures or to control results, then shifts to using definitions and theorems, then goes back to the figure and so on. Recent research by Lin (2005) on proof showed that students could learn effective practices like refutation and conjecturing in geometry.

Much of the Van Hiele research has involved students' recognition of geometric figures and their properties. By contrast, Callingham (2004) investigated tessellations. The progression of students' knowledge of tessellations is not well understood, with the exception of an array of square units (Outhred & Mitchelmore, 2004). Callingham used the Van Hiele levels as a way of describing students' understanding of tessellations. Most students could describe an array of squares at Level 1 or 2 (name shapes and either informally or technically, describe the transformation) but for other shapes students were at the visualisation level and could only recognise and name shapes.

Assessment of the Van Hiele levels

A number of researchers have proposed and evaluated different ways of assessing the Van Hiele levels. Gutiérrez and Jaime (1987) administered tests on polygons, measurement and solids to preservice elementary teachers and showed a hierarchy for Van Hiele Levels 1 to 4 but the authors suggested Level 5 (rigour) would warrant further investigation. A student's level for one topic did not necessarily predict their level for another topic (Gutiérrez, Jaime & Fortuny, 1991). They found that student progression through the levels may not be strictly linear, as students may be developing in several levels simultaneously. Subsequently, Gutiérrez, Jaime, Shaughnessy and Burger (1991) compared two different ways of assessing the levels, clinical interview versus paper-and pencil test, and two different interpretations of level acquisition, one assuming discrete levels, the other that levels were continuous. The authors felt that degrees of acquisition of each level gave a better assessment compared to assignment to a single level.

A framework for designing tests to assess the Van Hiele model was proposed by Jaime and Gutiérrez (1994). They identify four processes characterising the first four Van Hiele levels; identification, definition, classification and proof and assessed each process that they considered to be fundamental to reasoning at that level. The results of their test on polygons and related concepts showed that very few secondary students had an intermediate or better understanding of Levels 3 or 4 (Gutiérrez & Jaime, 1995). The authors suggested that a contributing factor may be an emphasis on formal proof when students are only reasoning at Level 1 or 2.

Lawrie (1998, 1999) compared two methods for assessing the Van Hiele levels. She suggested that Gutiérrez, Jaime and Fortuny's (1991) method, which assumed the levels are continuous and that a response may show thinking at more than one level, was more appropriate for assessing than Mayberry's test which assumed the levels were discontinuous and so each item was designed to test a specific level. Lawrie (1999) also found that not all questions in the Mayberry test assessed the level for which they were designed. Her results supported the hierarchy of the Van Hiele levels and showed that the higher the level, the lower the degree of acquisition. Nevertheless, high-performing students misinterpreted some Level 1 questions, while the generalised phrasing of some Level 3 questions contributed to difficulties, and assessing the highest level was problematic. The assessment of the three highest levels had been identified as problematic in earlier research (Fuys, Geddes & Tischler, 1988).

The pre-service teacher education students in Lawrie's study showed only Level 1 and 2 reasoning and her findings for student teachers are supported by Afonso, Camacho and Socas (1999) whose in-depth study of six teachers showed only two had attained Level 3. The authors concluded that not only geometrical knowledge, but also approaches to teaching would prevent teachers' implementation of a geometry curriculum based on Van Hiele theory.

The Van Hiele model explains development of student learning about two-dimensional shapes in geometry but Guillén (1996) proposed a characterisation of Levels 1 to 3 for three-dimensional solids. Based on the Van Hiele levels, a test incorporating Del Grande's (1987) spatial perception categories was designed to measure three-dimensional geometric understanding by Saads and Davis (1997).

CHANGING THEORETICAL VIEWS

In the 1970s psychologists were interested in how spatial abilities were related to mathematics learning (Schonberger, 1979). Spatial ability items were analysed in terms of testing factors. Typically, these factors involved orientation, recognition of either two-dimensional or three-dimensional shapes in different orientations, and spatial relations, recognition of a piece in a design or the folding of a net to form a three-dimensional shape (Schonberger, 1979; Tartre, 1990).

Although there is a long history of interest in the relationship between spatial ability and mathematical knowledge (Bishop, 1980, 1989), the move from large factor analytic studies to clinical interviews provided the stimulus for recognition of individual differences in the way children solved problems and spatial tasks. Such studies allow educators to study the effects of culture and training on spatial and mathematical ability, although the results of such studies may not be consistent (Bishop, 1979). For example, training has been found effective in several studies (Ben-Haim, 1983; Bishop, 1979; Kwon, Kim & Kim, 2001; Owens, 1992) but less effective in others (Malara & Iaseros, 1997). Home background and context were evident in a number of studies. For example, Mitchelmore (1984) suggested the home industries of the students' families gave students an exceptional symmetry understanding, Boero (2002) suggested rural experience affected sunshadow problems, and Masingila (1992) found carpet layers and estimators estimated, visualised spatial arrangements and used informal measurement. Techniques for dividing up rectangles and making right angles were embedded in practices that used non-geometric tools (Fioriti & Gorgorió, 2001; Masingila, 1992). Berthelot (1994) and Bishop (1979) also emphasised the impact of three kinds of space: (a) Micro-space (toys, drawing, models), (b) Meso-space (rooms) and (c) Macro-space (outside spaces) as there is a different point of view for each. Each of these studies could be said to be considering spatial sense.

Researchers started to think of spatial abilities and spatial sense in terms of imagery (Brown & Presmeg, 1993). Spatial abilities and imagery involve functional processes and strategies. Bellin (1980) attempted to integrate stage-structuralist theory approaches (such as Piaget's and Van Hiele's) and process-oriented functional (strategy) approaches to geometric development. He studied six year olds undertaking transformation (flips, slides, turns) activities and found successful patterns of strategy use. Bellin concluded that strategy use, rather than presumed cognitive structure, explained the results.

The link between spatial abilities and the learning of geometric concepts was strengthened by the visual approaches to learning geometry introduced by Logo programming. Logo is an open-ended computer environment that may provide an alternative approach to learning geometric concepts. In Hillel's (1986) study, students intuitively divided up a figure into parts. These parts were not necessarily the shapes for which students had procedures, but may have been primary parts, such as lines. He suggested that lack of conceptual knowledge may have restricted progress and not just the ability to establish the direction of turn or to calculate its size. Edwards (1990) detailed changes in concept knowledge and students' abilities to develop a symbolic representation of geometric transformation to demonstrate the advantage of immediate feedback with a Logo-based Microworld. Her data for three students making transformations showed that they needed help with rotation about a point, reflection in a line away from the shape and in undoing the transformation (Edwards, 1994). The ease with which a shape could be copied assisted secondary students' symmetry knowledge because students not only had fun but could observe what was happening, ask questions and investigate (Haddas, 1990).

VISUAL REASONING

In an attempt to draw together the various psychological perspectives on visualisation with structured development, Gutiérrez (1996) summarised much of the discussion on visualisation. He noted that visual processes were involved in interpreting: (a) External representations to form mental images and (b) The mental image in order to generate information. Both interpretations were assisted by visualisation abilities such as figure-ground perception (embedding/disembedding), mental rotation, perception of spatial position, perception of spatial relationships and the ability to focus on the property despite other features (e.g. colour, orientation or size) of the image. These visual processes (interpretation and visualisation abilities) form visual reasoning.

Visual reasoning was categorised as either local or global by Hershkowitz, Friedlander and Dreyfus (1991). They analysed responses of grade 9-10 students to an item requiring them to identify drawings of loci satisfying a given condition after experience with a software package, LOCI that illustrated geometric loci visually. Some students reasoned systematically in all or most cases but others changed their reasoning from case to case. The problem context also affected the level of reasoning used by students. Gutiérrez and Jaime (1993) recommended that students experience a variety of both concrete and computer objects representing shapes in different orientations to promote the students' strategies such as analysis and rotation of images and visual reasoning.

Several researchers (Brown & Wheatley, 1989; Reynolds & Wheatley, 1991; Presmeg, 1986a, 1986b) found that students use imagery to construct mathematical meaning and hypothesised that imagery in mathematics classes may assist development of meaningful, relational mathematics (Brown & Presmeg, 1993). Following Presmeg's earlier work on types of imagery, Brown and Presmeg (1993) found 5th and 11th grade students showed many common types of imagery although there were also large individual differences between students in type and facility of imagery used. Students with greater relational understanding tended to use more abstract forms of imagery such as dynamic and pattern imagery. Owens (1992, 1996b) showed a similar range of imagery forms during spatial problem solving by younger students. She clustered these into the following five groups (Owens, 1999): (a) Preliminary or emerging strategies; (b) Perceptual strategies (materials needed to be used); (c) Static pictorial imagery strategies; (d) Pattern and dynamic imagery; and (e) Efficient strategies (explained using both visual and verbal knowledge).

Visual imagery is one of a number of cognitive processes that may assist in spatial problem solving (Owens, 1996b). Other cognitive processes were selectively attending, perceiving, listening, looking, intuitive thinking, conceptualising, and heuristics such as establishing the meaning of the problem, developing tactics, self-monitoring and checking, together with affective processes such as success, confidence, interest, and tolerance of open-ended situations. The importance of her research was that it was classroom based, and may indicate greater divergence in spatio-visual thinking than might have previously been expected (Gray, 1999).

The importance of what students attend to when solving spatial problems has been extensively researched (e.g. Battista & Clements, 1992; Latner & Movshovitz-Hadar, 1999; Kieren & Pirie, 1992; Leung, 2003; Mason, 1992; Owens & Clements, 1998). Kieren and Pirie (1992) illustrated learning as nested circles with the innermost circle being primitive knowing. They conjectured that students learn through "image making", "image having", "property noticing", "formalising", "observing", "structuring" and "inventising". When necessary students fold back to an earlier level before progressing.

The computer program, Logo, was also shown to assist attention and extend visual reasoning. Students who used Logo to develop geometric concepts such as square, rectangle and quadrilateral outperformed control students (Battista & Clements, 1992). Case studies illustrated the strength of the visual reasoning developed by the use of Logo. For example, students talked about equal turns to make a square and tilted squares. Logo encouraged more sophisticated visual thinking by younger students but also allowed students in higher grades to notice properties. Older students recognised that squares had specific rectangular properties and gradually developed a structured relationship between rectangles and squares. They noted "appropriate use of Logo helps students begin to make the transition from Van Hiele's visual to the descriptive/analytic level of thought" (p. 57).

Technology assisted with shape classification by focussing student attention on similarity for classification according to Ruiz, Lupiañez and Valdemoros (2002). Their study showed that some tasks involving computer software were effective in elementary school but others were more suitable for establishing notions of ratio and proportion in early secondary school. The tasks themselves were engaging and encompassed several mathematical areas. Initially intuitive judgements were made followed by comparisons in which the objects (screen shapes) were superimposed over each other, followed by quantitative comparisons. For example, in elementary school a range of rectangles were superimposed and compared. Visual perception of similarity was followed by measurement to confirm the perception.

Theoretical papers dealing with images, concepts and processes were reviewed by Meissner (2001). He referred to (a) The work of Tall and his colleagues in terms of the symbol signifying both process and product; (b) Sfard's theory on interiorisation of the process, condensation through diverse examples, and reification with a concept image, and (c) Dubinsky's theory of actions, processes, object and schema. Meissner's contribution to this area was to provide diagrams which he called symbols to provide the flexible thinking associated with procepts —preliminary concept formations for specific concepts. He illustrated how diagrams of nets and other diagrams could, like other symbols, develop as a set of procedures with rules (transformations), act as both a process and an object, be extended, varied and manipulated.

To examine the interplay of image and concept, and the role of prototypical images and procepts, we may look at the concept of angle. Angles have numerous meanings associated with images, metaphors and metonymic structures, which are constructed by students out of their experiences and condensed as cognitive models (Matos, 1994). Many concepts are embedded in bodily experiences (e.g. the model of a turning body or of a trajectory). Other notions are angles as points, as a source, as a path, as two connecting lines, as a meeting point, as an interior corner, and as an opening. Each notion is associated with an image, metaphor and metonymic structure. However, students initially perceive an angle as static, rather than as dynamic turning (Mitchelmore & White, 1996). These authors suggested that students first understand angles in a particular context, prior to abstracting a general concept of angle. They showed that children in grades 2, 4, and 6 encountered angles in a range of different contexts, some of which were dynamic, as in opening and closing doors and scissors, while others were static such as an angle on a shape (Mitchelmore & White, 1998). They found the following development in recognition of the angle similarity: (a) Contexts of walls, road junctions, and tiles, (b) Scissors, (c) Fan and sloping signpost, (d) Door opening and hill slope, and (e) Wheel turning. The scissors, fan and door were all openings, the hill slope and sloping signpost were similar while the wheel was most difficult because no arms of the angle were visible.

An alternative context for learning about angles has been Logo computer software. Results of an earlier study by Kieran (1986) could be explained by the difficulties that Mitchelmore and White have articulated. Angle as an amount of turn formed by the moving turtle on the screen continued to confuse students after experience (Kieran, 1986). Even an attempt to highlight the turning of the line by laser lines did not enable students to see the size of turn, instead of the finished static angle between two lines. The concept of an angle and ability to recognise equal angles when arm length and orientation were changed was not much greater for students in the laser than in the non-laser group. "Most children are not going to acquire the powerful mathematical ideas underlying Logo without a good nudge now and then" (Kieran, 1986, p. 104). She found that fourth graders, after one year of Logo, seemed to keep static "angles" and their measurement in one mental compartment, and dynamic turns and their input in another, as well as relying on "perceptual cues" rather than "known knowledge". Sixth graders seemed more able to integrate static and dynamic imagery. Mitchelmore and White (1998) refer to this development as the abstraction of the angle concept.

Noss (1986), however, found using Logo had a significant effect on comparing unequal angles in different orientations and in identifying the smallest angle in a set. The results of Scally's (1987) investigation indicated that Logo may have assisted students to develop angle concepts but almost all students were at Van Hiele Levels 1 and 2 for both pre- and post-test assessments.

Students need to learn to reason systematically and visually and to be aware of prototypical images. Stylianou, Leilin and Silver (1999) explored students' solution strategies in solving spatial visualisation problems involving nets. About half the eighth grade students used a mental mode to devise nets while the other half used concrete methods. In both modes, some students worked systematically while others used trial and error methods. Students using concrete materials might cut off a face and systematically place it in various positions to form new nets. Students who switched between two- and three-dimensions generally had more trials and repeated nets. Similar systematic approaches for making pentominoes were evident in Owens' (1992) study. The difficulties inherent in mentally unfolding three-dimensional solids were shown when students were asked to unfold a tetrahedron, parallelepiped and cube mentally (Mariotti, 1991, 1993). She found the mental image of the tetrahedron was affected by past experiences of standard figures of nets of the square pyramid (a prototypical image). Students who successfully analysed three-dimensional shapes using mental objects were not necessarily able to keep track of features on a physical model.

Students' answers to specific spatial questions were the same whether they used a model or a diagram (Kopelman & Vinner, 1994). The researchers noted that improvements with age indicated the societal basis of spatial concepts. Prior experiences and concepts influenced adults' recognition of equal angles in complex diagrams (Owens, 1999) but did not seem to assist experienced learners to extend their understanding of parallel lines or angles between lines that were not co-planar (Kopelman, 1996).

Students face other visual difficulties when solving problems. Perpendicularity and parallelism have an impact on making and interpreting drawings and on concept formation. Initial research (Mitchelmore, 1983) showed that an acceptable representation of a regular three-dimensional figure required young children to recognise parallel lines on the solid, to realise that parallel lines are significant cues, and to represent parallels appropriately. Later Mitchelmore (1992) showed students' conceptions of perpendiculars were not perceptually primitive, as were parallels. Some students thought all intersecting lines were at right angles or did not recognise them in rectangles and even better students did not recognise right angles without horizontal and vertical sides (e.g. embedded in hexagons) or when they had to be imagined for the non-adjacent sides of the rectangular octagon. Students have also been found to have difficulty disembedding the angle from the configuration (Owens, 1996a) and the context when abstracting the angle concept (Mitchelmore & White, 1998). Experiences with acting out the directions of angles and making a simple protractor, accompanied by reflection on the experience, were found to be beneficial in learning about the angle concept (Krainer, 1991).

Intuition was established in the initial sections of this chapter as an important notion for understanding students' learning of geometry. This section has illustrated that prototypical images (Hershkowitz & Vinner, 1983) continue to be important aspects of intuition and extend the research to show how prototypical images may also lead to difficulties in learning. However, visual perception is not the only process that may limit students' conceptual development. Tactile perception may also present difficulties related to experience of objects, initial gestalt decisions or lack of connection between short-term memory and long-term memory as far as recognising parts of solids (Jirotková & Littler, 2002). The task of tactilely exploring a solid placed in a bag and then feeling the same solid in another bag resulted in a wider than expected range of solution paths.

Interpreting and using diagrammatic representations

Interpreting two-dimensional representations of three-dimensional shapes is influenced by cultural experiences and classroom experiences (Bishop, 1983). Students need to learn conventions for diagrams as this knowledge affects their performance on problems as well as to recognise critical and non-critical features of an image (Hershkowitz, 1989; Lopez-Real & Veloo, 1993; Harada, Gallou-Dumiel & Nohda, 2000; Dvora & Dreyfus, 2004). Representations may have a double status: "(a) a 'finiteness' in the sense of a finite and varied form in its spatio-temporality; (b) a geometrical form in its 'ideal objectiveness', detached from the material constraints linked to external representation" (Mesquita, 1994, p. 271). Representations constructed using geometrical relationships have the characteristics of objects (representations of mental schema) whereas topological or projective diagrams have the characteristics of illustrations. When working on an illustration developed from a context (rather than mathematics lesson), students readily encode and use control procedures which assist them "to understand geometry and rules of its reasoning" (Mesquita, 1994, p. 277). Students appeared more likely to attend to the diagram, rather than the verbal description of a problem (Mesquita, 1996) and in addition, changes to a diagram during problem solving may assist perception of new relationships and recognition of redundant information (Nunokawa, 1994). Wu and Ma (2005) showed that certain differences between shapes were apprehended more readily than others, especially those between curved and straight-sided figures and those with obtuse angles.

Diagrams help students pay attention to key features. When preservice teachers were asked to provide a description of a solid made from cubes using "words and/or diagrams", the majority made a drawing with many words (Burton, Cooper & Leder, 1986). Most students who rebuilt the solid successfully from the description worked initially from the diagram. When students produced coded orthogonal plans for a variety of polycubical shapes their strategies ranged from one- to three-dimensional systems of reference (Noelting, Gaulin & Puchalska, 1986). After instruction on these coded systems of representation, boys shifted from verbal to graphic representation and girls to mixed mode —81% were successful regardless of grade level and sex (Ben-Chaim, 1986).

Critical and non-critical attributes of a diagram have an impact on geometrical concepts (Vinner & Hershkowitz, 1980, 1983; Vinner, 1981). Initial images, that is prototypical images, are particularly important in being either a starting point or a limitation on concept formation. These authors have shown that the order of acceptance for quadrilaterals in terms of four-sided figures was first, the convex quadrilateral with all sides unequal in length, second, the concave quadrilateral, and third, the square; a few students also selected the bitrian (two triangles having a common vertex). Hershkowitz and Vinner (1984) showed the levels of difficulty of specific diagrams in the different tasks were the same for teachers as for students, although teachers generally made fewer errors. Nevertheless, about 30% of teachers found the complex diagrams difficult. Orientation of the figure or a distracting (unusual) feature influenced teachers who did not seem to use given definitions, either because they were unaware of their lack of knowledge or unable to analyse the diagram sufficiently to apply the definition.

Levels for drawing three-dimensional shapes were proposed by Hazama and Akai (1993). The levels were: (a) Inaccurate faces, joined at a point or partially; (b) One or two orthogonal face representations; (c) Faces joined but presented to form straight lines; (d) An idea of perspective with sloping faces; and (e) Adequate perspective drawings. The authors also noted that students focused on certain features, for example, the position of the face on the solid (e.g. front), the names of the face, or the viewpoint of the picture. First and second graders tended to use key features, 3rd and 4th grades supplemented their drawings with words, and 5th and 6th graders added dotted lines for hidden edges and measures relevant to the spatial properties. Some students from all grades attempted to give a three-dimensional perspective with older students achieving better results and often moving to a higher level.

The reluctance to draw diagrams may result from student expectations that school mathematical knowledge is sequential and not diagrammatic (Dreyfus & Eisenberg, 1990) and be limited by writing sentences in which each element is linked only to the two elements before and after it, whereas diagrammatic information presents information as a group in which each element may connect to many elements, thus requiring a higher order of thinking to evaluate the intent of the diagram. Duval (2000) also suggested that semiotic information may be socially constructed but needs to be coordinated with the individual's subjective imagery for mathematical learning.

THE VALUE OF PHYSICAL REPRESENTATIONS

Young children showed a range of strategies for solving spatial problems with shapes represented by cardboard cut outs. For example a square could be covered by two right-angled isosceles triangles or two rectangles (Mansfield & Scott, 1990). An inefficient strategy used by some 4-6 children was to pick up and discard pieces without rotating them. Translations were commonly used but only high-performing students used rotations and flips. In general, older children solved more problems than younger children, mainly as a result of persistence, rather than use of more efficient or varied strategies. Children who succeeded on the tasks seemed to recognise shapes which would not lead to a solution, and would re-position pieces. A similar study showed some students at lower levels were likely to select a large shape with a similar length to cover a square, rather than manipulate given shapes to cover it (Wheatley & Cobb, 1990).

The naming of coordinate points on geo-boards assisted young students to focus on analysing the translations and symmetry of shapes. Difficulties, such as the reversal of coordinates for a point, were especially productive during the exchange of messages because students discussed the legitimacy of reversing the coordinates as well as the effect on coordinates of the translation or symmetry (Lowenthal & Marco, 1981).

Vincent and McCrae (1991) had students build models from geostrips, then draw the model and consider the various aspects of the model in order to verify how it worked. One problem required a solution built on angles of the triangle but some students failed to visualise a triangle, one side of which was not part of the physical model representation. The use of a pantograph of four linked straight, rigid sides and an elastic triangle illustrated how transformations may be made to physical materials in order for students to develop their concept images (Hasegawa, 1993). Rotating an image of a quadrilateral, counting vertices, counting sides, using a transformation, and generalising (illustrated by the physical transformations of the linked edges and the elastic sides of a triangle) were all ways of deciding how to classify a shape. Dynamic three-dimensional models assist students to build relationships between geometrical solids and their properties and between the solids themselves (Markopoulos & Potari, 1999). Teachers were able to use students' self-developed changes to cubes to discuss the variant and invariant properties of three-dimensional solids (Markopoulos & Potari, 2000).

Other researchers have used models to obtain young children's conceptions (Elia, Gagatsis & Kyriakides, 2003; Hoyos, 2003; Mitchelmore & White, 1998). These conceptions may then be further developed. For example, spatial strategies, assignment of meaning, focus on influencing factors, measurement, planning and evaluation methods were elicited when students made boxes to fit given objects

(Lampen & Murray, 2001). Similarly, when young students composed and decomposed two-dimensional figures, they worked from parts to whole or from whole to parts at different levels of complexity and success. Students' results could be classified into the following levels: (a) Combined shapes into pictures, (b) Synthesised combinations of shapes into composite shapes and (c) Eventually operated on and iterated those composite shapes (Clements, Sarama & Wilson, 2001).

THE EFFECTS OF CLASSROOM CONTEXT

The classroom context —the set problem, the classroom expectations, the materials, the teacher and other students— may influence the solution process. Students selectively attend to aspects of this environment as they mentally work with their perceptions and link these to their existing memories. Student-student and student-teacher interaction in the classroom context may influence what students notice and their affective and heuristic responses (Owens, 1996b).

Aspects of communication are important in developing argument and proof. First the teacher might pose an interesting problem in order to generate substantive communication about the topic between students and with the teacher (Owens, 2005). For example, Mariotti, Bartolini Bussi, Boero, Ferri and Garuti (1997) selected three quite different contexts: (a) Drawing a table from a specific perspective, (b) A discussion of sun shadows and (c) The geometrical constructions in the Cabri environment. The researchers wished to show a progression from student discussion of empirical observations, to argumentation in the sense that defined rules were met, prior to communication of proof or validation. Students' explanations about the length of sun shadows were later classified in terms of their causal, conditional and descriptive nature (Boero, 2002). A reasonable understanding of the physical phenomenon would seem to be important if students are to draw the sun shadow diagram as a right-angled triangle with the sunray as hypotenuse and shadow as the horizontal base. Douek (1998) described the use of sun shadows in detail, showing how students gradually constructed the shadow schema, the meaning of direction and inclination, and the plane representation of the sun and shadow moving in a three-dimensional field. Year 5 students' sun shadow diagrams and attempts to draw the fan diagram are described as a process of geometric modelling and production by Mariotti (1996) who remarked that the teacher's request for a diagram brought the conflict to the fore and the necessity of finding a means of communicating the mathematical phenomenon consistently. Teachers' interventions may be important in moving students' knowledge forward. For example, in Mariotti's (1994) study teachers' intervention helped students see similarity, whereas students' perceptions emphasised differences between models.

Teacher's intervention may be provocative (pointing students towards the solution) or invocative in which case the intervention encourages students to recognise the need to fold back into an inner level of mathematical understanding (Kieren & Pirie, 1992). Intervention encourages the student to validate by representing mathematical action verbally, symbolically or figuratively. The impact of each type of intervention on students' responses was illustrated by examples of 14 year olds comparing pattern block pieces. Koyama (1996) used a two-axis model with one axis showing the learning stages of intuition, reflection and analysis while the other shows levels of understanding. The combination of set tasks involving geometric paths between two points and students' reflective practices were used to validate the three learning stages. Intuitions were modified by reflection, especially during the whole class discussion. Koyama (1996) illustrated how students reflected at different levels of understanding —higher level students realised the mathematical structure of the problem whereas less competent students worked on calculations. In a second lesson students' intuitions were influenced by the experiences of the first lesson and were more akin to logico-mathematics.

For several years, a number of researchers have focussed on dynamic geometry technology, especially the research group in Grenoble, France. Laborde (2001) summarises the prospective uses of dynamic geometry software in four ways: (a) To facilitate drawing with results similar to that made with paper-and-pencil; (b) To facilitate the mathematical task which involves conjecturing and drawing many examples in order to reach a solution; (c) To change a task requiring the use of properties rather than perception to solve the problem; and (d) New tasks that may only be achieved in dynamic geometric software environments. Only recent papers illustrating how the software provides a context for learning are discussed in this chapter.

The concrete objects (or drawings) help students to establish the abstract generalisation of a set of drawings (or figures) (Giraldo, Belfort & Carvalho, 2004). For this reason, Cabri may assist the development of definitions, for example, of quadrilaterals (Pratt & Davison, 2003). Nevertheless, teachers need skill in using dynamic geometry technology. Teachers may use dynamic geometry technology for direct instruction but it is more effectively used to engage students in a challenge linked to a mathematical concept (Guimaraes & Belfort, 2004). Classroom context also influences learning with dynamic geometry (Gardiner, Hudson & Povey, 1999) and interaction, often generated by conflict between students, may occur (Giraldo, Belfort & Carvalho, 2004). The strengths of Cabri include the availability of numerical and figural cues and the ability to produce and refine objects to find a solution (Love, 1996; Hazzan & Goldenberg, 1997) but the lack of image accuracy may be a drawback (Sinclair, 2003). Another strength is that Cabri extends drawing tools for straight lines and circles to include the parabola (Love, 1996).

The teacher's intervention in pointing out dependency in Cabri was needed for students to progress when they could not drag a point of intersection because of its dependency on other objects (Jones, 1996). Students extended their idea of dependency to realise a circle's size depends on its radius and deleting an object deletes all dependent objects. Students related the idea of dependency to a function showing a relationship between objects.

However, teacher's personal naïve definitions (e.g., "similar figures are the same but different sizes") may lead to inadequate activities and interventions for students (Zaslavsky, 1991; Linchevsky, Vinner & Karsenty, 1992). Similarly, teachers' skills in using Logo need to improve if an improvement in figure classification and recognising similarities in figures is to occur as a result of Logo experiences (Olive & Lakenau, 1987). Furthermore, Lemerise (1990) pointed out that Logo (incorporated into Microworlds) provided an alternative to the traditional geometry approach but use of Logo is likely to be rejected because it is not linked to curricula. The approach to geometry in the curriculum is too different for teaching to incorporate Logo readily. A similar concern was expressed by Love (1996) about dynamic geometry software.

MEASUREMENT

In the first years of PME, measurement, as a topic in its own right, is not evident. The first paper that was primarily about measurement focussed on methods used to teach conversions, none of which involved practical length measurement (Eisenberg, Goldstein & Gorodetsky, 1982). Not until 1987, was there a section designated as "Measurement" in the Table of Contents of a PME proceedings and only in 2003 was there a plenary that involved measurement concepts (Dougherty & Zilliox, 2003). In recent years, there have been papers that have focussed on the structure of measurement concepts and teaching programs.

Programs for teaching measurement

The *Measure Up* (MU) program (Dougherty & Zilliox, 2003) mentioned in the plenary is based on the notion that measurement may provide a cohesive foundation across all mathematics (Davydov, Gorbov, Mukulina, Savelyeva & Tabachnikova, 1999, cited in Dougherty & Zilliox, 2003). In the MU program young children start by describing and defining physical attributes of objects that may be compared and measured by units which may be counted. First graders realize that to count, they have to first identify what unit they are using in order to make sense of both process and result. Use of continuous quantities allows students to readily develop the notions surrounding the properties of commutativity, associativity, and inverseness. Students simultaneously link physical, diagrammatic, and symbolic representations. The MU research indicated that Grade 3 students may use algebraic symbols and abstract, generalized diagrams to solve problems (Dougherty & Slovin, 2004).

Another measurement program for elementary schools (Department of Education and Training, 2003, 2004; Outhred & McPhail, 2000; Outhred, Mitchelmore, McPhail & Gould, 2003) is based on a conceptual framework and includes knowledge and strategies teachers should assess, combined with lesson ideas and plans linked to the framework. The program focuses on general principles of measurement, developed through practical, open-ended activities, with an emphasis on recording and discussion. Teacher assessments of students indicated improved measurement concepts.

STUDENT UNDERSTANDING OF SPATIALLY-ORGANISED QUANTITIES

For length, area and volume the spatial organisation of the units, in one, two or three dimensions respectively, is fundamental to an understanding of measurement of the quantity. By contrast, spatial structure is not important for mass, temperature and time, except in terms of reading a scale. The following sections present the research for each of the spatially-organised quantities. Almost no research related to students' conceptions of mass, temperature and time was found in the PME proceedings.

Length

Studies of children working with Logo prompted research on children's understanding of number and unit for continuous quantities. Students using Logo achieved nearly as well as students 1 to 3 years older on length conservation and length combination items in a study by Hoyles and Noss (1987) but the researchers noted that many learning experiences were needed before students were able to connect symbolic relationships and the visual outcome satisfactorily. Campbell, Fein and Schwartz (1987) investigated young children's knowledge of the inverse relationship between unit size and number of units. These authors considered that the Logo environment allowed children to control transformations of unit size and number, without the dexterity required in practical measuring tasks. The researchers found that children understood that distance could be traversed by iterating a unit of measure but when the unit size was halved or the distance increased, estimation of length became more difficult. The measurement tasks showed a direct link to counting schema rather than length schema. This finding was supported by Cannon's (1991) study of middle school students. Cannon (1991) gave a task in which students represented equivalent length in centimetres on a ruler marked in "flugs" (1 flug = 2 cm), an aggregate unit task (this line is 4 units, draw a line 12 units long) and a task involving partitioning a line into a given number of units. Students were more likely to represent units as discrete points in the partitioning task, because they thought the number of points determines the number of units. Initially, discrete units counting predominated, but many students redefined their representations as line segments. Stephan and Cobb (1998) also found that young students' explanations of pacing activities concerned the number of paces rather than an amount of space.

An emphasis on discrete points (or marks) on a ruler was evident in a study of length measurement (Bragg & Outhred, 2000). They presented students with items that were procedural (the technique of using a ruler) and conceptual (an understanding of the construction of a scale). By age 10, most students could use a ruler accurately to measure and construct lines. Almost all errors involved problems with zero (measuring from one or the end of the ruler). However, only about half the students could successfully complete tasks, such as measuring with a "broken" ruler, which required knowledge of scale. These authors (Bragg & Outhred, 2001) also showed that there was a gulf between students' use of informal units to measure and their understanding of a formal linear unit (the centimetre).

Although students could measure using informal units and use a ruler, many of the students could not indicate the centimetre units on a ruler. They focussed on marks, or where the line ended; many of them also appeared to have a two-dimensional concept of a centimetre. A subsequent study of older students showed that many of them still did not seem to have a conceptual knowledge of a scale but considered the marks as units (Bragg & Outhred, 2004). The results indicated that an emphasis on counting might obscure the linear nature of the units, and that most students did not understand the relationship between linear units and a formal scale.

Nuhrenborger's (2001) analysis of children's structural connections between linear units and numbers in the children's representations of a ruler found that at the beginning of grade 2, few students knew that a ruler comprises different, but related units. Young children do not understand how units are structured and coordinated and that dealing with three-dimensional, informal units obscures the linear nature of the measurement unit. Problems involving scale are difficult. Maranhãa and Campos (2000) investigated whether knowledge of non-conventional instruments and informal units could assist students who could already measure with conventional metric instruments to solve problems of scale and concluded such procedures were beneficial.

In a study of the sophistication of students' thinking about length, Battista (2003) examined how students reasoned about the lengths of a variety of straight and non-straight paths. Battista documented both non-measurement and measurement levels of reasoning. His three levels of non-measurement reasoning included using visual, transformation-based, or geometric strategies to compare lengths. The measurement levels included iteration of a unit length to an abstracted a concept of length when students may use rulers meaningfully and reason about length without iterating units.

Area

The move from one-dimensional units involves additional complexity, so not surprisingly, research indicates that students have poor understanding of units of area and their spatial characteristics. Héraud (1987) interviewed students who had not been taught about area, and found that their choice of a measuring unit was strongly influenced by the shape of the figure to be covered. He felt students need experiences with a variety of units before they realise that a square unit is a rational choice.

Information that students gain in school depends on the knowledge their teachers bring to the topic. Tierney, Boyd and Davis (1990) found that many prospective primary teachers thought of area only as length by width; generalised the formula for finding the area of a rectangle to plane figures other than rectangles; used the formula but recorded linear, rather than square units; confused area and perimeter; and used whatever numbers were visible or counted something, e.g. squares on the perimeter. The student teachers might compute area as length times width, but that the choice of multiplication is often the result of procedural, rather than conceptual thinking. In another study of student teachers, Simon and

Blume (1992) found no one in the class seemed to connect a visual sense of area as an amount of surface with an abstract concept of multiplication. Students seemed to focus on two quantities, the number of rectangles along the length and width, without reconstituting these quantities as the number of rectangles in a row and the number of rows.

Students' understanding of area as a quantification of surface was investigated by Outhred and Mitchelmore (1992, 1996) who found that few young students used multiplication to enumerate the number of elements in an array. Half the students counted individual elements, while 38% used repeated addition. These results were replicated with a larger sample in Outhred and Mitchelmore (2000, 2004). The way the students drew squares to cover a rectangle and their enumeration strategies seemed to be related. Students who represented the structure of an array in terms of rows and columns tended to count by groups (rows or columns) or used multiplication. These authors recommended that linking counting to the structure of arrays could be a powerful technique to develop both multiplication and area concepts.

An analysis of students' understanding of area before being formally taught showed that knowledge of array structure provided the basis for working out the number of unit squares needed to cover a rectangle (Outhred & Mitchelmore, 1996). In particular, students' realisation, that the number of units in each row and column may determine the lengths of the sides of the rectangle, was a fundamental principle of area measurement. Drawing an array of units using two sets of parallel lines was found to be more difficult than expected, suggesting that the structure of a square tessellation is not obvious to students, but must be learned (Outhred & Michelmore, 2000). Only a quarter of Callingham's (2004) middle school sample could describe a square tessellation at an abstract level.

In teaching measurement practical activities using informal units are often recommended because they may be used to show principles of measurement. However, students do not always link the practical activities with the formalisation and ways of bridging the gap between practical materials and the formalisation were proposed by Hart (1993). Students' success in solving problems may be determined by the symbolic system used, the tools that are available and the problem situation. In a study by Nunes, Light, Mason and Allerton (1994) students had access to one of two different tools, rulers and bricks. The students who had access to bricks, although insufficient to cover the area, were more successful than those using the ruler on both post-test and delayed post-test (one month later). The authors suggest that the formula which students are taught does not fit well with the patterns that students develop themselves. However, bricks also structure the tessellation, whereas to use a ruler, students must be able to visualise the partitioned area. Doig, Cheeseman and Lindsay (1995) also found students who used wooden tiles to cover a surface were twice as successful as those who used paper squares because the wooden tiles fitted together, structuring the tessellation.

The size and shape of the unit may affect calculation of area. A study of fourth-grade students who were faced with comparing two areas, one rectangular and one irregular figure which could be visualised as rectangles of different sizes, found that some students explained rectangular area as "length x width" while others explained it as a multiple of an area unit (Fujita & Yamamoto, 1993). These authors suggest that students need to understand the need for a universal unit of area and the process of using different-sized units to measure. The unit's shape may also affect students' visualisation of the tessellation. In a large study, elementary students had to determine (by visualising or drawing) how many units (square, equilateral and right-angled triangles, and rectangles) would be needed to cover regular and irregular shapes (Owens & Outhred, 1997). Students had more difficulty visualising a tessellation of triangular units.

The findings of a study by Furinghetti and Paola (1999) indicated that the secondary students' had many images and definitions associated with area but did not have a mathematically acceptable definition that was coordinated, consistent and clear. Seventh grade students' writing gave evidence of the confusion between area and perimeter and the belief that there is a direct relationship between area and perimeter. This latter belief seemed more resistant to change than the confusion between area and perimeter (Moreira & Contente, 1997). Kidman and Cooper (1997) found the perception that area is the sum of a rectangle's dimensions was common across grades 4, 6 and 8. About half the students appeared to be using an additive integration rule (area = length + width) while many other students' rules were inconsistent. The additive rule persisted when a semi-circular piece was removed from the rectangular area but not when a rectangular piece was removed. Eighth grade students who undertook preliminary work with irregular figures, before being taught formulae for perimeter and area of common figures showed an improvement although students could not always identify relevant dimensions to use in calculation (Comiti & Moreira, 1997). The role of this intuitive or tacit knowledge has been further explored by Frade (2005). She found that when a student lacks explicit knowledge of formulae then tacit knowledge assists in communicating with others on the topic.

Enlargement and reduction

Area has also been studied in terms of developing the theory of intuitive rules. Tsamir and Mandel (2000) postulated that when the two sides of a square were enlarged by a given factor, and concomitantly, the other two sides were reduced by the same factor, students would argue that the perimeter and area would be unchanged. Secondary students were given two tasks in which responses were consistent with the intuitive rule (same A-same B rule) and two in which responses ran counter to the intuitive rule. For the tasks where the intuitive rule was not applicable, about a third gave incorrect responses for area (addition and subtraction of a constant) and about a quarter for perimeter (multiplication and division by a constant). Incorrect arguments were more prevalent for younger and less competent students.

De Bock, Verschaffel and Janssens (1996) provide an explanation of why area and perimeter are so complex for students, especially in situations when figures are enlarged or reduced. Secondary students were given problems involving proportional and non-proportional reasoning for three types of figures (squares, circles and irregular figures). Students used a linear model to solve, not only the proportional items, but also the non-proportional items resulting in only 2% giving correct responses on the latter items. Similar results were found (De Bock, Van Dooren, Verschaffel & Janssens, 2001; Modestou, Gagatsis & Pitta-Pantazi, 2004) for area and volume enlargement problems. De Bock et al. (2001) presented two forms of cognitive conflict; in one, alternative answers were shown and in the other, a fictitious peer gave the correct reasoning. Even when told the correct reasoning, only 25% of the sample changed their response; the others justified their original answer. Students appeared to approach such problems in a superficial way, without making realistic representations of problems. Research on proportional and non-proportional reasoning related to area and volume tasks indicate how powerful an impact the linear model has on student reasoning.

Volume

Research on volume shows a similar trend to area studies on students' lack of structure of units in measuring. Knowledge of the numerical operations is not sufficient; students also need to visualise or construct the array structure. Students' structuring of volume concepts was assessed for a range of two-dimensional (pictorial) and three-dimensional tasks using the SOLO taxonomy (Collis & Campbell, 1987). These authors postulated that the way "children organised individual cubes for counting would reflect successive steps in their ability to conceptualise and integrate the three dimensions" (p. 292). Children at a lower level in the Solo taxonomy (unistructural) primarily counted visible cubes in the pictured constructions and did not have an organised strategy for invisible cubes. By contrast, children at the next level (multistructural) began to organise their counting by rows, columns or layers. They also found that children "who did not include invisible cubes when counting the total construction, can focus on them when asked about a particular part of the construction." However, they found these children could not organise the visible and invisible parts sequentially to provide a construction of the whole when they were asked to recount the cubes. A large proportion of students in grades 4 to 6 did not use multiplication to solve the cube items, yet obtained correct answers on most multiplication items. The authors concluded that the cube tasks required two separate sets of skills, mastery of the relevant numerical operations and an understanding of the internal structure of the solid.

Student understanding of volume was studied by Saiz (2003) who found that student teachers in her sample considered that volume-measurable objects are those for which three lengths may be obtained. Thin objects were perceived as surfaces and so were not considered to have a measurable volume. Teachers considered some everyday objects did not have volume because of their irregular shape. The dominant meaning that students had for volume was of a number obtained by multiplying the length, width and height of an object.

CONCLUSION

This chapter highlights the diversity of studies on the learning of space and geometry and indicates the complexity of the task confronting researchers and teachers –how to synthesise the research into a coherent view of teaching and learning geometry and measurement. In geometry, initially studies focussed on understanding and improving spatial abilities but clinical interviews showed the range of individual differences in spatial learning. Problem solving was shown to be a key in students attending to key features of shapes and working towards understanding the relationship between shapes. This development was frequently described in terms of Van Hiele levels. These levels were shown to be continuous rather than discrete and studies showed a range of issues in assessing students in accordance with this theory. Nevertheless, experiences that influence preliminary intuitive approaches and more complex visual imagery are important in students' geometry education.

Studies which have explored the role of materials, context, computer programs and the teacher in extending geometric thinking have found that semiotic, social representations or individual visual representations of mathematics may be made and used by students but they need mental coordination (Duval, 2000). Heinze (2002) summarised much of the research in space and geometry by saying that the notion of a personal image of a concept (Vinner, 1991) should be extended to a concept-understanding scheme, which contains the concept definition, the concept image and the concept usage (Moore, 1994).

Studies in measurement also focussed on development of concepts, in particular the importance of students recognising the structure of units when measuring the spatially-organised attributes of length, area and volume. There has been considerable research about students' interpretations of length and area units and the use of tools to measure but little research about students' development of volume concepts, which are far more complex, because of the three-dimensional nature of the quantity and because both liquid and cubic units must be considered.

Research indicates that student teachers have many of the same misconceptions about geometric and measurement concepts as the students whom they will eventually teach. The challenge for researchers is to take the diversity of research and consolidate it to show the implications and applications for teachers, so that students' understanding of geometry and measurement is built on a firm foundation.

REFERENCES

Afonso, M. C., Camacho, M., & Socas, M. M. (1999). Teacher profile in the geometry curriculum based on the Van Hiele theory. In O. Zaslavsky (Ed.), *Proceedings of the 23rd PME International Conference, 2*, 1–8.

Battista, M. T. (2003). Levels of sophistication in elementary students reasoning about length. In N. A. Pateman, B. J. Dougherty, & J. T. Zilliox (Eds.), *Proceedings of the 27th PME International Conference, 2*, 73–80.

Battista, M. T., & Clements, D. H. (1992). Students' cognitive construction of squares and rectangles in Logo Geometry. In W. Geeslin & K. Graham (Eds.), *Proceedings of the 16th PME International Conference, 1*, 57–64.

Bellin, H. (1980). Geometry structures and processing strategies in young children. In R. Karplus (Ed.), *Proceedings of the 4th PME International Conference,* 279–285.

Ben-Chaim, D. (1986). Adolescent girls' and boys' ability to communicate a description of a 3-dimensional building. In Univ. of London Institute of Education (Eds.), *Proceedings of the 10th PME International Conference, 1*, 75–80.

Ben-Haim, D. (1983). Spatial visualization – Sex and grade level differences in grade five through eight. In R. Hershkowitz (Ed.), *Proceedings of the 7th PME International Conference,* 235–240.

Berthelot, R. (1994). Common spatial representations, and their effects upon teaching and learning of space and geometry. In J. P. Ponte & J. F. Matos (Eds.), *Proceedings of the 18th PME International Conference, 2*, 72–79.

Beth, E., & Piaget, J. (1966). *Mathematical epistemology and psychology*. Dordrecht, The Netherlands: Reidel.

Bishop, A. (1979). Visual abilities and mathematics learning, In D. Tall (Ed.), *Proceedings of the 3rd PME International Conference, 1*, 21–26.

Bishop, A. (1980). Spatial abilities and mathematics education. A review. *Educational Studies in Mathematics, 11*, 257–269.

Bishop, A. (1983). Space and geometry. In R. Lesh & M. Landau (Eds.), *Acquisition of mathematics concepts and processes* (pp. 176–204). New York, USA: Academic Press.

Bishop, A. (1988). A review of research on visualisation in mathematics education. In A. Vermandel (Ed.), *Proceedings of the 6th PME International Conference, 1*, 170–176.

Bishop, A. (1989). Review of research on visualization in mathematics education. *Focus on Learning Problems in Mathematics, 11*, 7–16.

Boero, P. (2002). Geometric signs and students' verbal reports: The case of the geometric model of sun shadows. In A. D. Cockburn & E. Nardi (Eds.), *Proceedings of the 26th PME International Conference, 2*, 129–136.

Booth, D. (1984). Aspects of logico-mathematical intuition in the development of young children's spontaneous pattern painting. In B. Southwell, R. Eyland, M. Cooper, J. Conroy, & K. Collis (Eds.), *Proceedings of the 8th PME International Conference,* 225–237.

Bragg, P., & Outhred, L. (2000). Students' knowledge of length units: Do they know more than rules about rulers? In T. Nakahara & M. Koyama (Eds.), *Proceedings of the 24th PME International Conference, 2*, 97–104.

Bragg, P., & Outhred, L. (2001). So that's what a centimetre looks like: Students' understanding of linear units. In M. van den Heuvel-Panhuizen (Ed.), *Proceedings of the 25th PME International Conference, 2*, 209–216.

Bragg, P., & Outhred, L. (2004). A measure of rulers – The importance of units in a measure. In M. J. Høines & A. B. Fuglestad (Eds.), *Proceedings of the 28th PME International Conference, 2*, 159–165.

Brown, D. L., & Presmeg, N. (1993). Types of imagery used by elementary and secondary school students in mathematical reasoning. In I. Hirabayashi, N. Nohda, K. Shigematsu, & F.-L. Lin (Eds.), *Proceedings of the 17th PME International Conference, 2*, 137–145.

Brown, D., & Wheatley, G. (1989). Relationship between spatial ability and mathematics knowledge. In C. A. Maher, G. A. Goldin, & R. B. Davis (Eds.), *Proceedings of the 11th PME–NA Annual Meeting,* 143–148.

Burger, W., & Shaughnessy, J. (1986). Characterising the Van Hiele levels of development in geometry. *Journal for Research in Mathematics Education, 17*, 31–48.

Burton L., Cooper M., & Leder G. (1986). Representations of three-dimensional figures by mathematics teachers-in-training. In Univ. of London Institute of Education (Eds.), *Proceedings of the 10th PME International Conference, 1*, 81–86.

Callingham, R. (2004). Primary students' understanding of tessellation: An initial exploration. In M. J. Høines & A. B. Fuglestad (Eds.), *Proceedings of the 28th PME International Conference, 2*, 183–190.

Campbell, P. F., Fein, G. G., & Schwartz, S. S. (1987). Young children's understanding of number and unit in a continuous domain. In J. G. Bergeron, N. Herscovics, & C. Kieran (Eds.), *Proceedings of the 11th PME International Conference, 2*, 85–291.

Cannon, P. L. (1992). Middle grade students' representations of linear units. In W. Geeslin & K. Graham (Eds.), *Proceedings of the 16th PME International Conference, 1*, 105–112.

Clements, D. H., & Battista, M. T. (1991). Van Hiele levels of learning geometry. In F. Furinghetti (Ed.), *Proceedings of the 15th PME International Conference, 1*, 223–230.

Clements, D. H., Sarama, J., & Wilson, D. C. (2001). Composition of geometric figures. In M. van den Heuvel-Panhuizen (Ed.), *Proceedings of the 25th PME International Conference, 2*, 273–280.

Collis, K. F., & Campbell, K. J. (1987). Mechanisms of transition in the calculation of volume during the concrete symbolic mode. In J. G. Bergeron, N. Herscovics, & C. Kieran (Eds.), *Proceedings of the 11th PME International Conference, 3*, 292–298.

Comiti, C., & Moreira, B. P. (1997). Learning process for the concept of area of planar regions in 12–13 year olds. In E. Pehkonen (Ed.), *Proceedings of the 21st PME International Conference, 3*, 264–271.

Cooper, M., & Krainer, K. (1990). Children's recognition of right angled triangles in unlearned positions. In G. Booker, P. Cobb, & T. N. Mendicuti (Eds.), *Proceedings of the 14th PME International Conference, 2*, 227–234.

Currie, P., & Pegg, J. (1998). "Three sides equal means it is not isosceles". In A. Olivier & K. Newstead (Eds.), *Proceedings of the 22nd PME International Conference, 2*, 216–223.

Davydov, V. V., Gorbov, S., Mukulina, T., Savelyeva, M., & Tabachnikova, N. (1999). *Mathematics*. Moscow, Russia: Moscow Press.

De Bock, D., Van Dooren, W., Verschaffel, L., & Janssens, D. (2001). Secondary school pupils' improper proportional reasoning: An in-depth study of the nature and persistence of pupils' errors. In M. van den Heuvel-Panhuizen (Ed.), *Proceedings of the 25th PME International Conference, 2*, 313–320.

De Bock, D., Verschaffel, L., & Janssens, D. (1996). The illusion of linearity: A persistent obstacle in pupils' thinking about problems involving length and area of similar plane figures. In L. Puig & A. Gutiérrez (Eds.), *Proceedings of the 20th PME International Conference, 2*, 273–280.

De Villiers, M. (1991). Pupils' needs for conviction and explanation within the context of geometry. In F. Furinghetti (Ed.), *Proceedings of the 15th PME International Conference, 1*, 255–262.

De Villiers, M. (1998). To teach definitions in geometry or teach to define? In A. Olivier & K. Newstead (Eds.), *Proceedings of the 22nd PME International Conference, 2*, 248–255.

Del Grande, J. (1987). Spatial perception and primary geometry. In M. Lindquist (Ed.), *Learning and teaching geometry, K-12* (pp. 127–135). Reston, VA, USA: NCTM.

Department of Education and Training (2003). *Teaching Measurement: Early Stage 1 and Stage 1*. Sydney, Australia: NSWDET.

Department of Education and Training (2004). *Teaching Measurement: Stage 2 and Stage 3*. Sydney, Australia: NSWDET.

Doig, B., Cheeseman, J., & Lindsey, J. (1995). The medium is the message: Measuring area with different media. In B. Atweh & S. Flavel (Eds.), *Galtha* (Proceedings of 18th Annual Conference of MERGA (pp. 229–234). Darwin, Australia: MERGA.

Douek, N. (1998). Analysis of a long term construction of the angle concept in the field of experience of sunshadows. In A. Olivier & K. Newstead (Eds.), *Proceedings of the 22nd PME International Conference, 2*, 264–271.

Dougherty, B., & Slovin, H. (2004). Generalised diagrams as a tool for young children's problem solving. In M. J. Høines & A. B. Fuglestad (Eds.), *Proceedings of the 28th PME International Conference, 2*, 295–302.

Dougherty, B., & Zilliox, J. (2003). Voyaging from theory to practice in teaching and learning. In N. A. Pateman, B. J. Dougherty, & J. T. Zilliox (Eds.), *Proceedings of the 27th PME International Conference, 1*, 17–31.

Dreyfus, T., & Eisenberg, T. (1990). On difficulties with diagrams: Theoretical issues. In G. Booker, P. Cobb, & T. N. Mendicuti (Eds.), *Proceedings of the 14th PME International Conference, 1*, 27–36.

Duval, R. (2000). Basic issues for research in mathematics education. In T. Nakahara & M. Koyama (Eds.), *Proceedings of the 24th PME International Conference, 1*, 55–69.

Dvora, T., & Dreyfus, T. (2004). Unjustified assumptions based on diagrams in geometry. In M. J. Høines & A. B. Fuglestad (Eds.), *Proceedings of the 28th PME International Conference, 2*, 311–318,

Edwards, L. D. (1990). The role of microworlds in the construction of conceptual entities. In G. Booker, P. Cobb, & T. N. Mendicuti (Eds.), *Proceedings of the 14th PME International Conference, 2*, 235–249.

Edwards, L. (1994). Making sense of a mathematical microworld: A pilot study from a Logo project in Costa Rica. In J. P. Ponte & J. F. Matos (Eds.), *Proceedings of the 18th PME International Conference, 2*, 296–303.

Elia, I., Gagatsis, A., & Kyriakides, L. (2003). Young children's understanding of geometric shapes: The role of geometric models. In N. A. Pateman, B. J. Dougherty, & J. T. Zilliox (Eds.), *Proceedings of the 27th PME International Conference, 2*, 349–355.

Eisenberg, T., Goldstein, E., & Gorodetsky, M. (1982). On teaching the comparison of metric measurements in a vocational school. In A. Vermandel (Ed.), *Proceedings of the 6th PME International Conference*, 218–222.

Farfán, R. M., & Hitt, F. (1990). Intuitive processes, mental image, and analytical and graphic representations of the stationary state. In G. Booker, P. Cobb, & T. N. Mendicuti (Eds.), *Proceedings of the 14th PME International Conference, 1*, 45–52.

Fioriti, G., & Gorgorió, N. (2001). Geometry at work (or Pythagoras will never fail you!). In M. van den Heuvel-Panhuizen (Ed.), *Proceedings of the 25th PME International Conference, 2*, 425–432.

Frade, C. (2005). The tacit-explicit nature of students' knowledge: A case study on area measurement. In H. L. Chick & J. L. Vincent (Eds.), *Proceedings of the 29th PME International Conference, 2*, 281–288.

Fujita, T., & Jones, K. (2002). The bridge between practical and deductive geometry: Developing the 'geometrical eye'. In A. D. Cockburn & E. Nardi (Eds.), *Proceedings of the 26th PME International Conference, 2*, 384–391.

Fujita, H., & Yamamoto, S. (1993) The study of understanding in arithmetic education: Understanding phase and learning process model – in case of area-learning fourth graders. In I. Hirabayashi, N. Nohda, K. Shigematsu, & F.-L. Lin (Eds.), *Proceedings of the 17th PME International Conference, 1*, 236–243.

Furinghetti, F., & Paola, D. (1999). Exploring students' images and definitions of area. In O. Zaslavsky (Ed.), *Proceedings of the 23rd PME International Conference, 2*, 345–352.

Furinghetti, F., & Paola, D. (2002). Defining within a dynamic geometry environment: Notes from the classroom. In A. D. Cockburn & E. Nardi (Eds.), *Proceedings of the 26th PME International Conference, 2*, 392–399.

Fuys, D., Geddes, D., & Tischler, R. (1988). *The Van Hiele model of thinking in geometry among adolescents* (JRME Monograph No. 3). Reston, USA: NCTM.

Gardiner, J., Hudson, B., & Povey, H. (1999). "What Can We All Say?" – Dynamic geometry in a whole-class zone of proximal development. In O. Zaslavsky (Ed.), *Proceedings of the 23rd PME International Conference, 3*, 1–8.

Giraldo, V., Belfort, E., & Carvalho, L. M. (2004). Descriptions and conflicts in dynamic geometry. In M. J. Høines & A. B. Fuglestad (Eds.), *Proceedings of the 28th PME International Conference, 2*, 455–462.

Gorgorió, N. (1996). Choosing a visual strategy: The influence of gender on the solution process of rotation problems. In L. Puig & A. Gutiérrez (Eds.), *Proceedings of the 20th PME International Conference, 3*, 19–26.

Gray, E. (1999). Spatial strategies and visualization. In O. Zaslavsky (Ed.), *Proceedings of the 23rd PME International Conference, 1*, 235–242.

Guillén, G. (1996). Identification of Van Hiele levels of reasoning in three-dimensional geometry. In L. Puig & A. Gutiérrez (Eds.), *Proceedings of the 20th PME International Conference, 3*, 43–50.

Guimaraes, L. C., & Belfort, E. (2004). Teacher's practices and dynamic geometry. In M. J. Høines & A. B. Fuglestad (Eds.), *Proceedings of the 28th PME International Conference, 2*, 503–510.

Gutiérrez, A. (1996). Visualization in 3-dimensional geometry: In search of a framework. In L. Puig & A. Gutiérrez (Eds.), *Proceedings of the 20th PME International Conference, 1*, 3–20.

Gutiérrez, A., & Jaime, A. (1987). Estudio de las caracteristicas de los niveles de Van Hiele. In J. G. Bergeron, N. Herscovics, & C. Kieran (Eds.), *Proceedings of the 11th PME International Conference, 3*, 131–137.

Gutiérrez, A., & Jaime, A. (1993). An analysis of the students' use of mental images when making or imagining movements of polyhedra. In I. Hirabayashi, N. Nohda, K. Shigematsu, & F.-L. Lin (Eds.), *Proceedings of the 17th PME International Conference, 2*, 153–160.

Gutiérrez, A., & Jaime, A. (1995). Towards the design of a standard test for the assessment of students' reasoning in geometry. In L. Meira & D. Carraher (Eds.), *Proceedings of 19th PME International Conference, 3*, 11–18.

Gutiérrez, A., Jaime, A., & Fortuny, J. (1991). An alternative paradigm to evaluate the acquisition of the Van Hiele levels. *Journal for Research in Mathematics Education, 22*, 237–251.

Gutiérrez, A., Jaime, A., Shaughnessy, J. M., & Burger, W. F. (1991). A comparative analysis of two ways of assessing the Van Hiele levels of thinking. In F. Furinghetti (Ed.), *Proceedings of the 15th PME International Conference, 2*, 109–116.

Haddas, R. (1990). The cognitive challenge involved in Escher's potato stamps microworld. In G. Booker, P. Cobb, & T. N. Mendicuti (Eds.), *Proceedings of the 14th PME International Conference, 2*, 243–258.

Harada, K., Gallou-Dumiel, E., & Nohda, N. (2000). The role of figures in geometrical proof-problem solving – students' cognitions of geometrical figures in France and Japan. In T. Nakahara & M. Koyama (Eds.), *Proceedings of the 24th PME International Conference, 3*, 25–32.

Hart, K. (1993). Confidence in success. In I. Hirabayashi, N. Nohda, K. Shigematsu, & F.-L. Lin (Eds.), *Proceedings of the 17th PME International Conference, 1*, 17–31.

Hasegawa, J. (1993). The concept formation of triangle and quadrilateral in the 2nd grade. In I. Hirabayashi, N. Nohda, K. Shigematsu, & F.-L. Lin (Eds.), *Proceedings of the 17th PME International Conference, 2*, 105–112.

Hazama, S., & Akai, T. (1993). Pupil's development of graphical representations of 3-dimensional figures: On technical difficulties, conflicts or dilemmas, and controls in drawing process. In I. Hirabayashi, N. Nohda, K. Shigematsu, & F.-L. Lin (Eds.), *Proceedings of the 17th PME International Conference, 2*, 161–168.

Hazzan, O., & Goldenberg, P. (1997). An expression of the idea of successive refinement in dynamic geometry environments. In E. Pehkonen (Ed.), *Proceedings of the 21st PME International Conference, 3*, 49–56.

Heinze, A. (2002). "... because a square is not a rectangle" – Students' knowledge of simple geometrical concepts when starting to learn proof. In A. D. Cockburn & E. Nardi (Eds.), *Proceedings of the 26th PME International Conference, 3*, 81–88.

Héraud, B. (1987). Conceptions of area units by 8–9 year old children. In J. G. Bergeron, N. Herscovics, & C. Kieran (Eds.), *Proceedings of the 11th PME International Conference, 3*, 299–304.

Hershkowitz, R. (1989). Visualization in geometry – two sides of the coin. *Focus on Learning Problems in Mathematics, 11*(1), 61–76.

Hershkowitz, R., Friedlander, A., & Dreyfus, T. (1991). LOCI and visual thinking. In F. Furinghetti (Ed.), *Proceedings of the 15th PME International Conference, 2*, 181–188.

Hershkowitz, R., & Vinner, S. (1983). The role of critical and non-critical attributes in the concept image of geometrical concepts. In R. Hershkowitz (Ed.), *Proceedings of the 7th PME International Conference,* 223–228.

Hershkowitz, R., & Vinner, S. (1984). Children's concepts in elementary geometry. A reflection of teachers' concepts? In B. Southwell, R. Eyland, M. Cooper, J. Conroy, & K. Collis (Eds.), *Proceedings of the 8th PME International Conference,* 63–70.

Hillel, J. (1986). Procedural thinking by children aged 8–12 using turtle geometry. In Univ. of London Institute of Education (Eds.), *Proceedings of the 10th PME International Conference, 1,* 433–438.

Hoffer, A. (1983). Van Hiele based research. In R. Lesh & M. Landau (Eds.), *Acquisition of mathematics concepts and processes* (pp. 205–227). New York, USA: Academic Press.

Hoyles, C., & Noss, R. (1987). Seeing what matters: Developing an understanding of the concept of parallelogram through a logo microworld. In J. Bergeron, N. Herscovics, & C. Kieran (Eds.), *Proceedings of the 11th PME International Conference, 2,* 17–23.

Hoyos, V. (2003). Mental functioning of instruments in the learning of geometrical transformations. In N. A. Pateman, B. J. Dougherty, & J. T. Zilliox (Eds.), *Proceedings of the 27th PME International Conference, 3,* 95–102.

Jaime, A., & Gutiérrez, A. (1994). A model of test design to assess the Van Hiele levels. In J. P. Ponte & J. F. Matos (Eds.), *Proceedings of the 18th PME International Conference, 3,* 41–48.

Jirotkova, D., & Littler, G. H. (2002). Investigating cognitive and communicative processes through children's handling of solids. In A. D. Cockburn & E. Nardi (Eds.), *Proceedings of the 26th PME International Conference, 3,* 145–152.

Jones, K. (1996). Coming to know about "dependency" within a dynamic geometry environment. In L. Puig & A. Gutiérrez (Eds.), *Proceedings of the 20th PME International Conference, 3,* 145–153.

Kidman, G., & Cooper, T. J. (1997). Area integration rules for grade, 4, 6 and 8 students. In E. Pehkonen (Ed.), *Proceedings of the 21st PME International Conference, 3,* 136–143.

Kieran, C. (1986). LOGO and the notion of angle among fourth and sixth grade children. In Univ. of London Institute of Education (Eds.), *Proceedings of the 10th PME International Conference, 1,* 99–104.

Kieren, T., & Pirie, S. (1992). The answer determines the question. Interventions and growth of mathematical understanding. In W. Geeslin & K. Graham (Eds.), *Proceedings of the 16th PME International Conference, 2,* 1–8.

Kopelman, E. (1996). Invisible angles and visible parallels which bring deconstruction to geometry. In L. Puig & A. Gutiérrez (Eds.), *Proceedings of the 20th PME International Conference, 3,* 185–192.

Kopelman, E., & Vinner, S. (1994). Visualisation and reasoning about lines in space: School and beyond. In J. P. Ponte & J. F. Matos (Eds.), *Proceedings of the 18th PME International Conference, 3,* 97–103.

Koyama, M. (1996). Research on the complementarity of intuition and logical thinking in the process of understanding mathematics: An examination of the two-axes process model by analysing an elementary school mathematics class. In L. Puig & A. Gutiérrez (Eds.), *Proceedings of the 20th PME International Conference, 3,* 193–200.

Krainer, K. (1991). Consequences of a low level of acting and reflecting in geometry learning – Findings of interviews on the concept of angle. In F. Furinghetti (Ed.), *Proceedings of the 15th PME International Conference, 2,* 254–261.

Kwon, O. N., Kim, S. H., & Kim, Y. (2001). Enhancing spatial visualization through virtual reality on the web: Software design and impact analysis. In M. van den Heuvel-Panhuizen (Ed.), *Proceedings of the 25th PME International Conference, 3,* 265–272.

Laborde, C. (2001). Integration of new technology in the design of geometry tasks with Cabri-Geometry. *International Journal of Computers for Mathematical Learning, 6,* 283–317.

Laborde, C., & Capponi, B. (1995). Modelisation a double sens. *Actes de la 8e Ecole d'Eté de Didactique des Mathématiques.* France: IREM de Clermont-Ferrand.

Lampen, E., & Murray, H. (2001). Children's intuitive knowledge of the shape and structure of three dimensional containers. In M. van den Heuvel-Panhuizen (Ed.), *Proceedings of the 25th PME International Conference, 3*, 273–280.

Latner, L., & Movshovitz-Hadar, N. (1999). Storing a 3-D image in the working memory. In O. Zaslavsky (Ed.), *Proceedings of the 23rd PME International Conference, 3*, 201–208.

Lawrie, C. (1998). An alternative assessment: The Gutiérrez, Jaime and Fortuny technique. In A. Olivier & K. Newstead (Eds.), *Proceedings of the 22nd PME International Conference, 3*, 175–182.

Lawrie, C. (1999). Exploring Van Hiele levels of understanding using a Rasch analysis. In O. Zaslavsky (Ed.), *Proceedings of the 23rd PME International Conference, 3*, 209–216.

Lemerise, T. (1990). Integrating Logo in the regular mathematics curriculum. A developmental risk or opportunity? In G. Booker, P. Cobb, & T. N. Mendicuti (Eds.), *Proceedings of the 14th PME International Conference, 2*, 267–273.

Lesh, R. (1978). Some trends in research and the acquisition and use of space and geometry concepts. In E. Cohors-Fresenborg & I. Wachsmuth (Eds.), *Proceedings of the 2nd PME International Conference*, 193–213.

Lesh, R. (1979). Social/affective factors influencing problem solving capabilities. In D. Tall (Ed.), *Proceedings of the 3rd PME International Conference*, 142–147.

Leung, A. (2003). Dynamic geometry and the theory of variation. In N. A. Pateman, B. J. Dougherty, & J. T. Zilliox (Eds.), *Proceedings of the 27th PME International Conference, 3*, 197–204.

Lin, F.-L. (2005). Modelling students' learning in argumentation and mathematics proof. In H. Chick & J. Vincent (Eds.), *Proceedings of the 29th PME International Conference, 1*, 3–18.

Linchevsky, L., Vinner, S., & Karsenty, R. (1992). To be or not to be minimal? Student teachers' views about definitions in geometry. In W. Geeslin & K. Graham (Eds.), *Proceedings of the 16th PME International Conference, 2*, 48–55.

Lopez-Real, F. (1991). Describing geometric diagrams as a stimulus for group discussions. In F. Furinghetti (Ed.), *Proceedings of the 15th PME International Conference, 2*, 342–349.

Lopez-Real, F., & Veloo, P. (1993). Children's use of diagrams as a problem-solving strategy. In I. Hirabayashi, N. Nohda, K. Shigematsu, & F.-L. Lin (Eds.), *Proceedings of the 17th PME International Conference, 2*, 169–176.

Love, E. (1996). Letting go: An approach to geometric problem solving. In L. Puig & A. Gutiérrez (Eds.), *Proceedings of the 20th PME International Conference, 3*, 281–288.

Lowenthal, F., & Marco, J. (1981). Logic, auxiliary formalism and geometry by telephone call. In Equipe de Recherche Pédagogique (Eds.), *Proceedings of the 5th PME International Conference, 1*, 265–270.

Malara, N. A., & Gherpelli, L. (1994). Problem posing and hypothetical reasoning in geometrical realm. In J. P. Ponte & J. F. Matos (Eds.), *Proceedings of the 18th PME International Conference*, 3, 216–223.

Malara, N. A., & Iaserosa, R. (1997). On the difficulties met by students in learning direct plane isometries. In E. Pehkonen (Ed.), *Proceedings of the 21st PME International Conference, 3*, 208–215.

Mansfield, H., & Scott, J. (1990). Young children solving spatial problems. In G. Booker, P. Cobb, & T. N. Mendicuti (Eds.), *Proceedings of the 14th PME International Conference, 2*, 275–282.

Maranhãa, C., & Campos, T. (2000). Length measurement: Conventional units articulated with arbitrary ones. In T. Nakahara & M. Koyama (Eds.), *Proceedings of the 24th PME International Conference, 3*, 255–262.

Mariotti, M. A. (1991). Age variant and invariant elements in the solution of unfolding problems. In F. Furinghetti (Ed.), *Proceedings of the 15th PME International Conference, 2*, 389–396.

Mariotti, M. A. (1993). The influence of standard images in geometrical reasoning. In In I. Hirabayashi, N. Nohda, K. Shigematsu, & F.-L. Lin (Eds.), *Proceedings of the 17th PME International Conference, 2*, 177–182.

Mariotti, M. A. (1994). Figural and conceptual aspects in a defining process. In J. P. Ponte & J. F. Matos (Eds.), *Proceedings of the 18th PME International Conference, 3*, 232–238.

Mariotti, M. A. (1996), Reasoning geometrically through the drawing activity. In L. Puig & A. Gutiérrez (Eds.), *Proceedings of the 20th PME International Conference, 3*, 329–336.

Mariotti, M. A., Bartolini Bussi, M. G., Boero, P., Ferri, F., & Garuti, R. (1997). Approaching geometry theorems in contexts: From history and epistemology to cognition. In E. Pehkonen (Ed.), *Proceedings of the 21st PME International Conference, 1*, 180–195.

Markopoulos, C., & Potari, D. (1999). Forming relationships in three-dimensional geometry through dynamic environments. In O. Zaslavsky (Ed.), *Proceedings of the 23rd PME International Conference, 3*, 273–280.

Markopoulos, C., & Potari, D. (2000). Dynamic transformations of solids in the mathematics classroom. In T. Nakahara & M. Koyama (Eds.), *Proceedings of the 24th PME International Conference, 3*, 263–270.

Masingila, J. (1992). Mathematics practice in carpet laying. In W. Geeslin & K. Graham (Eds.), *Proceedings of the 16th PME International Conference, 2*, 80–87.

Mason, J. (1992). Doing and construing mathematics in screenspace. In B. Southwell, K. Owens, & B. Perry (Eds.), *Proceedings of the 15th MERGA Conference, 1*, 1–17.

Mason, J. (1994). The role of symbols in structuring reasoning: Studies about the concept of area. In J. P. Ponte & J. F. Matos (Eds.), *Proceedings of the 18th PME International Conference, 3*, 255–262.

Matos, J. M. (1994). Cognitive models of the concept of angle. In J. P. Ponte & J. F. Matos (Eds.), *Proceedings of the 18th PME International Conference, 3*, 263–270.

Matsuo, N. (1993). Students' understanding of geometrical figures in transition from Van Hiele level 1 to 2. In I. Hirabayashi, N. Nohda, K. Shigematsu, & F.-L. Lin (Eds.), *Proceedings of the 17th PME International Conference, 2*, 113–120.

Meissner, H. (2001). Encapsulation of a process in geometry. In M. van den Heuvel-Panhuizen (Ed.), *Proceedings of the 25th PME International Conference, 3*, 359–366.

Mesquita, A. L. (1994). On the utilization of non-standard representations in geometrical problems. In J. P. Ponte & J. F. Matos (Eds.), *Proceedings of the 18th PME International Conference, 3*, 271–278.

Mesquita, A. L. (1996). On the utilization of encoding procedures on the treatment of geometrical problems. In L. Puig & A. Gutiérrez (Eds.), *Proceedings of the 20th PME International Conference, 3*, 399–406.

Mitchelmore, M. (1983). 3D drawings and parallel concept. In R. Hershkowitz (Ed.), *Proceedings of the 7th PME International Conference*, additional papers (pp. 40–56).

Mitchelmore, M. (1984). Spatial abilities and geometry teaching. *Unesco Studies in Mathematics Education, 3,* 135–143.

Mitchelmore, M. (1992). Children's concepts of perpendiculars. In W. Geeslin & K. Graham (Eds.), *Proceedings of the 16th PME International Conference, 2*, 120–127.

Mitchelmore, M., & White, P. (1996). Children's concepts of turning: Dynamic or static? In L. Puig & A. Gutiérrez (Eds.), *Proceedings of the 20th PME International Conference, 3*, 415–421.

Mitchelmore, M., & White, P. (1998). Recognition of angular similarities between familiar physical situations. In A. Olivier & K. Newstead (Eds.), *Proceedings of the 22nd PME International Conference, 3*, 271–278.

Modestou, M., Gagatsis, A., & Pitta-Pantazi, D. (2004). Students' improper proportional reasoning: The case of area and volume of rectangular figures. In M. J. Høines & A. B. Fuglestad (Eds.), *Proceedings of the 28th PME International Conference, 3*, 345–352.

Moore, R. (1994). Making transition to formal proof. *Educational Studies in Mathematics, 27*, 249–266.

Moreira, C. Q., & Contente, M. do R. (1997). The role of writing to foster pupils' learning about area. In E. Pehkonen (Ed.), *Proceedings of the 21st PME International Conference, 3*, 256–263.

Nakahara, T. (1995). Children's construction process of the concepts of basic quadrilaterals in Japan. In L. Meira & D. Carraher (Eds.), *Proceedings of the 19th PME International Conference, 3*, 27–34.

Noelting, G. (1979). Hierarchy and process in the construction of the geometrical figure in the child and adolescent, *Proceedings of the 3rd PME International Conference, 1*, 163–169.

Noelting, G., Gaulin, C., & Puchalska, E. (1986). Structures and processes in the ability to communicate spatial information by means of coded orthogonal views. In Univ. of London Institute of Education (Eds.), *Proceedings of the 10th PME International Conference, 1*, 111–116.

Noss, R. (1986). What mathematics do children take away from LOGO? In Univ. of London Institute of Education (Eds.), *Proceedings of the 10th PME International Conference, 1*, 277–282.

Nuhrenborger, M. (2001). Insights into children's ruler concepts – grade-2-students' conceptions and knowledge of length measurement and paths of development. In M. van den Heuvel-Panhuizen (Ed.), *Proceedings of the 25th PME International Conference, 3*, 447–454.

Nunes, T., Light, P., Mason, J., & Allerton, M. (1994). The role of symbols in structuring reasoning: Studies about the concept of area. In J. P. Ponte & J. F. Matos (Eds.), *Proceedings of the 18th PME International Conference, 3*, 255–262.

Nunokawa, K. (1994). Naturally generated elements and giving them senses: A usage of diagrams in problem solving. In J. P. Ponte & J. F. Matos (Eds.), *Proceedings of the 18th PME International Conference, 3*, 376–383.

Olive, J., & Lankenau, C. (1987). The effects of Logo-based learning experiences on students' non-verbal cognitive abilities. In J. Bergeron, N. Herscovics, & C. Kieran (Eds.), *Proceedings of the 11th PME International Conference, 2*, 24–30.

Outhred, L., & McPhail, D (2000). A framework for teaching early measurement. In J. Bana & A. Chapman (Eds.), *Proceedings of the 23rd MERGA Conference*, 487–494.

Outhred, L., & Mitchelmore, M. (1992). Representation of area: A pictorial perspective. In W. Geeslin & K. Graham (Eds.), *Proceedings of the 16th PME International Conference, 2*, 194–201.

Outhred, L., & Mitchelmore, M. (1996). Children's intuitive understanding of area measurement. In L. Puig & A. Gutiérrez (Eds.), *Proceedings of the 20th PME International Conference, 4*, 91–98.

Outhred, L., & Mitchelmore, M. (2000). Young children's intuitive understanding of area measurement. *Journal for Research in Mathematics Education, 31*(2), 144–167.

Outhred, L., & Mitchelmore, M. (2004). Students' structuring of rectangular arrays. In M. J. Høines & A. B. Fuglestad (Eds.), *Proceedings of the 28th PME International Conference, 3*, 465–472.

Outhred, L., Mitchelmore, M., McPhail, D., & Gould, P. (2003). Count Me Into Measurement: A program for the early elementary school. In G. Bright, & D. Clements (Eds.), *Measurement (2003 Yearbook)*. Reston, VA, USA: NCTM.

Owens, K. (1992). Spatial thinking takes shape through primary-school experiences. In W. Geeslin & K. Graham (Eds.), *Proceedings of the 16th PME International Conference, 2*, 202–209.

Owens, K. (1996a). Recent research and a critique of theories of early geometry learning: The case of the angle concept. *Nordisk Matematikk Didaktikk – Nordic Studies in Mathematics Education, 4*(2/3), 85–106.

Owens, K. (1996b). Responsiveness: A key aspect of spatial problem solving. In L. Puig & A. Gutiérrez (Eds.), *Proceedings of the 20th PME International Conference, 4*, 99–106,

Owens, K. (1999). The role of visualization in young students' learning. In O. Zaslavsky (Ed.), *Proceedings of the 23rd PME International Conference, 1*, 220–234.

Owens, K. (2005). Substantive communication in space mathematics in upper primary school. In H. Chick & J. Vincent (Eds.), *Proceedings of the 29th PME International Conference, 4*, 33–40.

Owens, K., & Clements, M. A. (1998). Representations used in spatial problem solving in the classroom. *Journal of Mathematical Behavior, 17*(2), 197–218.

Owens, K., & Outhred L. (1997). Early representations of tiling areas. In E. Pehkonen (Ed.), *Proceedings of the 21st PME International Conference, 3*, 312–319.

Patronis, T. (1994). On students' conceptions of axioms in school geometry. In J. P. Ponte & J. F. Matos (Eds.), *Proceedings of the 18th PME International Conference, 4*, 9–16.

Pegg, J., & Baker, P. (1999). An exploration of the interface between Van Hiele's levels 1 and 2: Initial findings. In O. Zaslavsky (Ed.), *Proceedings of the 23rd PME International Conference, 4*, 25–32.

Pratt, D., & Davison, I. (2003). Interactive whiteboards and the construction of definitions for the kite. In N. A. Pateman, B. J. Dougherty, & J. T. Zilliox (Eds.), *Proceedings of the 27th PME International Conference, 4*, 31–38.

Presmeg, N. (1986a). Visualization in high school mathematics. *For the Learning of Mathematics, 6*(3), 42–46.

Presmeg, N. (1986b). Visualization and mathematical giftedness. *Educational Studies in Mathematics, 17*, 297–311.

Reiss, K., Klieme, E., & Heinze, A. (2001). Prerequisites for the understanding of proofs in the geometry classroom. In M. van den Heuvel-Panhuizen (Ed.), *Proceedings of the 25th PME International Conference, 4*, 97–104.

Reynolds, A., & Wheatley, G. (1991). The elaboration of images in the process of mathematics meaning making. In W. Geeslin & K. Graham (Eds.), *Proceedings of the 16th PME International Conference, 2*, 242–249.

Robotti, E. (2001). Verbalisation as a mediator between figural and theoretical aspects. In M. van den Heuvel-Panhuizen (Ed.), *Proceedings of the 25th PME International Conference, 4*, 105–112.

Ruiz, E. F., Lupiañez, J. L., & Valdemoros, M. (2002). Didactical reflections on proportionality in the Cabri environment based on previous experience with basic education students. In A. D. Cockburn & E. Nardi (Eds.), *Proceedings of the 26th PME International Conference, 4*, 153–160.

Saads, S., & Davis, G. (2000). Spatial abilities, Van Hiele levels and language use in three dimensional geometry. In E. Pehkonen (Ed.), *Proceedings of the 21st International Conference, 4*, 104–111.

Saiz, M. (2003). Primary teachers' conceptions about the concept of volume: The case of volume-measurable objects. In N. A. Pateman, B. J. Dougherty, & J. T. Zilliox (Eds.), *Proceedings of the 27th PME International Conference, 4*, 95–102.

Scally, S. (1987). The effects of learning Logo on ninth-grade students' understanding of geometric relations. In J. C. Bergeron, N. Herscovics, & C. Kieran (Eds.), *Proceedings of the 11th PME International Conference, 3*, 46–52.

Schmidt, V. G. (1980). The effects of previous knowledge on learning geometry. Concept images and common cognitive paths in the development of some simple geometrical concepts. In R. Karplus (Ed.), *Proceedings of the 4th PME International Conference,* 185–192.

Schonberger, A. K. (1979). The relationship between visual spatial abilities and mathematical problem solving are there sex-related differences? In D. Tall (Ed.), *Proceedings of the 3rd PME International Conference,* 1, 179–185.

Shir, K., & Zaslavsky, O. (2001). What constitutes a (good) definition? The case of a square. In M. van den Heuvel-Panhuizen (Ed.), *Proceedings of the 25th PME International Conference, 4*, 161–168.

Shir, K., & Zaslavsky, O. (2002). Students' conception of an acceptable geometric definition. In A. D. Cockburn & E. Nardi (Eds.), *Proceedings of the 26th PME International Conference,* 4, 201–208.

Simon, M., & Blume, G. (1992). Understanding multiplicative structures: A study of prospective elementary teachers. In W. Geeslin & K. Graham (Eds.), *Proceedings of the 16th PME International Conference, 3*, 11–19.

Sinclair, M. P. (2003). The provision of accurate images with dynamic geometry. In N. A. Pateman, B. J. Dougherty, & J. T. Zilliox (Eds.), *Proceedings of the 27th PME International Conference, 4*, 191–198.

Stephan, M., & Cobb, P. (1998). The evolution of mathematical practices: How one first-grade classroom learned to measure. In A. Olivier & K. Newstead (Eds.), *Proceedings of the 22nd PME International Conference, 4*, 97–104.

Stylianou, D. A., Leikin, R., & Silver, E. A. (1999). Exploring students' solution strategies in solving a spatial visualization problem involving nets. In O. Zaslavsky (Ed.), *Proceedings of the 23rd PME International Conference, 4*, 241–248.

Tall, D. (2004). Thinking through three worlds of mathematics. In M. J. Høines & A. B. Fuglestad (Eds.), *Proceedings of the 28th PME International Conference, 4*, 281–288.

Tartre, L. (1990). Spatial skills, gender, and mathematics. In E. Fennema & G. C. Leder (Eds.), *Mathematics and gender*. New York, USA: Teachers College Press.

Tierney, C., Boyd, C., & Davis, D. (1990). Prospective primary teachers' conceptions of area. In G. Booker, P. Cobb, & T. N. Mendicuti (Eds.), *Proceedings of the 14th PME International Conference, 2*, 307–315.

Tsamir, P., & Mandel, N. (2000). The intuitive rule same A-same B: The case of area and perimeter. In T. Nakahara & M. Koyama (Eds.), *Proceedings of the 24th PME International Conference, 4*, 225–232.

Van Hiele, P. M. (1986). *Structure and insight: A theory of mathematics education.* New York, USA: Academic Press.

Vincent, J., & McCrae, B. (2001). Mechanical linkages and the need for proof in secondary school geometry. In M. van den Heuvel-Panhuizen (Ed.), *Proceedings of the 25th PME International Conference, 4*, 367–374.

Vinner, S. (1981). The nature of geometrical objects as conceived by teachers and prospective teachers. In Equipe de Recherche Pédagogique (Eds.), *Proceedings of the 5th PME International Conference, 1*, 375–380.

Vinner, S. (1991). The role of definitions in teaching and learning of mathematics. In D. Tall (Ed.), *Advanced mathematical thinking* (pp. 65–81). Dordrecht, The Netherlands: Kluwer.

Vinner, S., & Hershkowitz, R. (1980). Concept images and common cognitive paths in the development of some simple geometrical concepts. In R. Karplus (Ed.), *Proceedings of the 4th PME International Conference,* 177–184.

Vinner, S., & Hershkowitz, R. (1983). On concept formation in geometry. *Zentralblatt fur Didaktik der Mathematik, 83*(1), 20-25.

Vygotsky, L. (1978). *Mind in society: The development of higher psychological processes.* Cambridge, USA: Harvard Press.

Wheatley, G., & Cobb, P. (1990). Analysis of young children's spatial constructions. In L. P. Steffe & T. Wood (Eds.), *Transforming children's mathematics education* (pp. 161–173). Hillsdale, NJ, USA: Lawrence Erlbaum.

Wu, D., & Ma, H. (2005). A study of the geometric concepts of the elementary school students who are assigned to the Van Hiele level one. In H. Chick & J. Vincent (Eds.), *Proceedings of the 29th PME International Conference, 4*, 329–336.

Yamaguchi, T. (1993). A study of metacognition in mathematical problem solving: The roles of metacognition on solving a construction problem. In I. Hirabayashi, N. Nohda, K. Shigematsu, & F.-L. Lin (Eds.), *Proceedings of the 17th PME International Conference, 3*, 89–96.

Zaslavsky, O. (1991). In what ways are similar figures similar? In F. Furinghetti (Ed.), *Proceedings of the 15th PME International Conference, 3*, 378–385.

AFFILIATIONS

Kay Owens
Faculty of Education
Charles Sturt University
Locked Bag 49
Dubbo 2830 (Australia)
kowens@csu.edu.au

Lynne Outhred
School of Education
Australian Centre for Educational Studies
Macquarie University
North Ryde NSW 2109 (Australia)
lynne.outhred@mq.edu.au

JOANNE MULLIGAN AND GERARD VERGNAUD

RESEARCH ON CHILDREN'S EARLY MATHEMATICAL DEVELOPMENT

Towards Integrated Perspectives

The study of young children's mathematical development represents a strong, integral part of the research work of the PME community from its inception to the present time. Theoretical bases of the early work of many PME researchers, particularly those with cognitive psychological perspectives, were explicated largely through research with young children. This fuelled initiative for further research on the early development of mathematical concepts and processes that flourished in next decades. While there are some variations in research themes over the years, several areas have sustained research attention, such as counting and arithmetic. These were considered almost exclusive to the study of young children's mathematics, but were viewed more broadly, theoretically. Over time, mathematical content domains that were primarily the focus of research with older students were expanded to include younger subjects, such as the study of multiplicative reasoning, algebra, data exploration and mathematical modeling.

During the first two decades of PME, there was much more research concentration at the primary school level and in the area of arithmetical learning than during the last decade. This included the identification of units in counting, the emergence of concepts of cardinality, the progressive understanding of additive and multiplicative structures, initial fraction concepts, and some study of geometrical figures. In comparison, research reported at PME conferences over the past decade or so has been limited compared with that focused on middle and secondary school students, as interest shifted to older students and much broader research issues. For example, studies encompassing early mathematical development from the preschool to Grade 3 level reported at PME conferences from 1995-2005 comprised on average, less than 10% of the total number of contributions (this excludes studies focused on professional development and teacher change).

Although there have been some shifts in research agendas and fewer studies conducted, this latter period is characterized by research that shows both a broadening of mathematical content and processes, and a wider scope of enquiry such as in cross-sectional and longitudinal studies. Research paradigms have become more dynamic where they are no longer restricted by the study of single content domains, but by the study of the child's mathematical development within

A. Gutiérrez, P. Boero (eds.), Handbook of Research on the Psychology of Mathematics Education: Past, Present and Future, 117–146.

classroom practice. Studies focused on specific mathematical concepts have analyzed teaching and learning through classroom studies such as constructivist teaching experiments or design studies followed by individual interviews. Other groups of researchers have shifted perspectives from analyses of children's levels and strategies to the development of instructional and learning environments (e.g. Anghileri, 2001; Van den Heuvel-Panhuizen, 2002). Some recent contributions have been derived from large-scale government numeracy projects, which have developed frameworks based on the work of PME researchers (e.g. Askew, Brown and colleagues; Clarke, McDonough & Sullivan, 2002; Gravemeijer and colleagues; Wright & Gould, 2002). To some extent, there has been a shift to research on teaching early numeracy, rather than examining solely the psychological bases of mathematical development.

Several chapters in this volume expound different mathematical content areas and complement the present discussion, so readers are advised to refer to them for a full account of research on a particular domain. We aim to extend the previous review of early arithmetic (Bergeron & Herscovics, 1990) and complement the chapter by Verschaffel, Greer and Torbeyns in this volume. Although we have restricted the content of this chapter to early number and arithmetic we intend that this research should not be viewed in isolation; rather we argue for the need to take a more integrated view of research in early mathematical thinking. We will also limit our discussion to research pertaining to young children from the preschool to middle primary years, approximately 4 to 9 years of age. We aim to capture the most significant and consistent strands of this research particularly those of the past decade, without diminishing the importance of smaller isolated studies. One thread of our review will highlight conferences that focused on particular theoretical views, or specific content domains. For instance, early counting schemes and symbolization (PME8), elementary numerical thinking (PME21), mathematics in the preschool (PME26) and early algebra (PME28).

With these features in mind, we have structured the chapter under three broad areas:

- Theoretical perspectives on the study of young children's mathematical development.
- Key areas of research interest: Mathematical content domains.
- Possible directions for future research.

THEORETICAL PERSPECTIVES: RESEARCH ON CHILDREN'S MATHEMATICAL DEVELOPMENT DURING THE FIRST DECADE OF PME

We provide first, some reflection on theoretical approaches developed during the early years of PME. Many of these ideas were directly connected with the study of young children's learning and development from various psychological perspectives. Some important examples of these contributions follow: 'Intuitive models' (Fischbein); the 'structure of learning outcomes' (Collis); 'fields of experience' (Boero) and 'conceptual fields' (Vergnaud); 'early counting' and 'reflective abstraction' (Steffe); the impact of constructivism; 'cognitive structural development' (Goldin); a 'proceptual' view (Gray, Pitta & Tall) and social constructivist (Yackel) and interactionist persepctives (Hershikowitz).

Intuitive models

Fischbein's (1978) theory of intuitive models provided a strong foundation for PME researchers and mathematics education research generally. Fischbein claimed that primitive, implicit models impact on the child's development of concepts and problem-solving behaviour and these models continue to exert influence when learning more complex mathematics (Fischbein, 1983). His research on multiplication and division problems and probabilistic thinking contributed significantly to understanding mathematical thinking and difficulties experienced by middle and secondary school students. The psychological bases of his theory are apparent in many studies concerning children's intuitive development that emerged through the PME group.

Structure of observed learning outcomes

Many of the early theoretical contributions reflected a strong tradition in developmental psychology to identify stages of cognitive development, and to characterize them in logical terms. On the basis of Piagetian theory, Collis & Romberg (1981) and Collis & Watson (1985) presented several papers elucidating his cognitive model of the Structure of Observed Learning Outcomes (SOLO) based on modes of functioning and levels of structure in students' responses: *Prestructural, unistructural, multistructural, relational,* and *extended abstract.* Although this general model advanced our understanding of the development of cognitive structure there were some limitations in applying it explicitly to the learning of school mathematics, particularly for young children, and a lack of didactical recommendations. The same limitations associated with Collis' model could be argued for other proposed descriptions of developmental levels, more or less influenced by the Piagetian theory of stages, such as the one proposed by Harrison, Bye and Schroeder (1985): Pre-operational, early concrete operational, late concrete, early formal, and formal operations. In other words, the PME community progressively felt the need to address more directly, the content of school mathematics.

Fields of experience and conceptual fields

In the mid 1980s PME researchers developed broader perspectives about learning mathematics that viewed children's knowledge as developing mainly by their facing situations in and out of school. The early work of the Brazilian school (Nunes & Schliemann, 1987) was highlighted at several PME meetings, offering robust examples of the mathematics that children (and adolescents and adults) could use in selling fruit or lotteries on the street, when they would fail on classroom problems requiring the same arithmetical operations. They convinced the whole PME community that it was essential to study informal mathematical knowledge, and to understand how that knowledge could be used in school. An important didactical question was how much everyday experience one should introduce into classroom mathematics. A systematic reflection and analysis of this problem was advanced by Boero (1989) at PME13. Lesh (1985) and others also contributed to this question. However, other PME members asserted that the reference to experience was not necessarily self-sufficient from an epistemological point of view, as it did not lead directly to strong mathematical concepts of number, space, algebra and geometry.

Accordingly, the idea of *conceptual field* offered a connection between experience and conventional mathematics by identifying the main relationships and concepts that may be taken as mathematical objects and studied. The situations met in experience were not considered organized in a systematic manner. Therefore it was useful to reflect on situations from a conceptual point of view and attempt to organize them in a structured set-of-situations. For that purpose, Vergnaud (1981) introduced the concept of *conceptual field* (additive structures, multiplicative structures, elementary algebra, and elementary geometry), which directed much of the work on arithmetical word problems that followed (Vergnaud, 1983, 1990). Vergnaud coined the terms 'additive' and 'multiplicative' structures to describe this new field of work based on conceptual structures.

Research on counting

It is in the proceedings of PME10 held in Grenoble in 1981, that one finds many seminal contributions on the notion of counting units (e.g. papers by Comiti and Bessot; Fischer; Richards; Schmidt; Steffe; Van den Brink; and Von Glasersfeld). Steffe, Von Glasersfeld and Richards each discuss the role of counting in children's first conceptions of number (Richards, 1981; Steffe, 1981; Von Glasersfeld, 1981). They questioned whether a counting unit is concrete or abstract: What is the element to be counted? This depended on its position in the overall sequence of counting actions, and on the problem to be solved. It was understood that there was a tacit integration of the counting sequence in the goal to be reached: Find the cardinal number of a set, find the result of joining two sets, and find how many elements are hidden. The seminal work of Steffe provided an innovative approach to what is now known as screening by hiding the first elements of a set, informing the child that there were, for example, eight elements in all (when only five of them were visible), and asking how many were hidden. This problem could be solved either by subtracting 5 from 8 (which young children could not do), by counting forwards the number of steps from 5 to 8, or by counting backwards. Counting forwards was not that easy, but counting backwards was considerably more difficult. Counting backwards implied bi-directionality and was difficult for many children; as well, when the perceptual identification of a unit was not possible, counting required the child to *imagine abstract units*, related to both the hidden elements and the sequence of counting actions.

It was generally understood that there were two important mathematical concepts underlying the scheme of counting a set: (1) The concept of one to one correspondence between four different kinds of sets: The objects to be counted, the gestures of the arm and finger, the gestures of the eyes, the gestures of the voice (one, two, three ...); and (2) The concept of cardinal, that gives the child not only the capability to answer the question "How many?" but also supports the meaning of addition; it is possible to add cardinals, not positions. Comiti and Bessot (1981) analyzed different mathematical axioms that are necessary to articulate numbers as cardinals and numbers as ordered positions. For instance, in a race involving n participants, if a runner gives up, what will be the position of the runner that arrives last? The right answer, $n - 1$ (the 29th position where $n = 30$) is not easily given before Grade 2. Fischer (1981) replicated the findings of Gelman and Gallistel to show that the principles they identified depended on the size of the set to be counted and on the age of the subjects employed. Schmidt (1981) examined different aspects grasped by 5-6 year olds, not studied by other researchers, such as magnitude, operator, and scale. Similarly, Van den Brink (1981) introduced the ideas of acoustic counting and counting movements (instead of objects). He observed children when the interviewer skipped over an element (or several), and explained that, if they counted movements, children would not be sensitive to the problem of skipping, and therefore miss the one-to-one correspondence principle.

Hall, Fuson and Willis (1985) possibly provided the most detailed study of the gestures children make when counting, whether they count on (a certain number of steps for addition), whether they count down (subtraction), or count up to a certain number to find how many steps there are between two numbers (subtraction again). The fact that these gestures may involve one hand or both hands, an inside movement of the fingers or an outside one, is essentially cultural, but also depends on the individual child. Consequently, a variety of counting schemes emerged but they cannot be considered merely as cultural stereotypes.

Early bases of research on additive structures

As early as 1978, several research groups proposed classifications of cognitive tasks involved in addition and subtraction problems. There are some differences between those classifications, but also strong similitudes. For instance at PME3, Vergnaud (1978) on one hand, and at PME6, Nesher and Greeno (1981) on the other hand identified three main relationships that children would have to deal with: Combination of two parts into a whole, transformation of an initial state into a final state, and comparison of two quantities. Carpenter and Moser (1979) had also worked at this problem of classification, and arrived at similar categories, adding the case of equalizing two quantities. Vergnaud considered more complex relationships like the combination of transformations, the combination of relationships and the transformation of a relationship. The advantage was that it extended the classification to problems involving directed numbers, including subtraction of numbers of different signs, a case that raises long lasting obstacles, even for 15 year olds and adults. The main contribution of the research on these classifications is that they made it possible to study systematically the comparative difficulty of different cognitive tasks involved. These classifications also made it possible to introduce the framework of conceptual fields and the concepts of scheme, concept-in-action and theorem-in-action (Vergnaud, 1982, 1984).

The growth of research across multiplicative structures and fractions

The conceptual field of multiplicative structures provided another major contribution to the study of children's arithmetical processes. Vergnaud illustrated the prototype of multiplicative structure as the four-term relationship of proportion, which is often overlooked in simple multiplication and division problems because one of the terms is the number 1. He described four prototypical cases: Multiplication, quotition, partition, and find-the-fourth-term (for an account of these structures see Vergnaud, 1984). Many studies were presented at PME meetings in the first decades on multiplication and division problems (partition and quotition) and on find-the-fourth-term situations. If one considers a fraction as a concept associated with division and multiplication in the conceptual field of multiplicative structures, it is probably the domain most consistently represented over the early years of PME (there are five to six reports each year). For example, Behr, Bell, Figueras, Fischbein, Greer, Hunting, Karplus, Lesh, Nohda, Post, Reiss, Seeger, Southwell, Streefland, Vinner, Wachsmuth, and many others contributed to the field. Most contributions concerned both primary and secondary school, as problems of proportion were not considered mastered by children until the end of primary school. The striking fact is that, in spite of the large number of research works reported at PME, insufficient work has been done on the relationship of fractions with proportional reasoning, even though a fraction is first understood as a scalar relationship between two quantities or two magnitudes of the same kind.

Symbolic representations: Numeration

A number of contributions at early PME meetings throughout the 1980s were concerned with children's understanding of symbols and their use in teaching. There were several contexts where symbolic systems deserved consideration, because they were useful but caused children difficulties: Tables and graphs, algebraic symbols, and fractions. But the primary system investigated was the place value representation of whole numbers and decimals. The place value notation for numbers is so essential but the fact that the underlying structure is polynomial, and therefore implies some understanding of powers, makes it a fragile system for children: Some of them tend to stick to the meaning of the figures placed side by side. The introduction of decimals makes the situation more complex as many children tend to consider that a decimal is composed of two whole numbers, one on each side of the dot. Janvier and Bednarz (1989) diagnosed errors persisting through primary school (for example, children could not recognize the equivalence of 40 tens and 400). Nunes (1989) also showed difficulties met by Brazilians in out-of-school situations.

The impact of constructivist theories

One could hardly find a behaviorist or a defender of dogmatic teaching among the first PME participants. Most of them would refer to a constructivist approach, according to which children not only are taught mathematics, but also develop their mathematical competencies and ideas by facing situations, interpreting them, and generating processes and behaviors on the spot. Advocates of this approach did not claim that culture and society were not important, or that the social background of students and the quality of the teacher were negligible conditions. Generally, it meant that the student was an active constructor of knowledge, and that no one else could really understand the student's ideas.

To make this point clear, let us return to Piaget (who was probably the most important constructivist), and to his findings concerning conservation of discrete quantities: Having placed seven eggcups in a visual one-to-one correspondence with seven eggs, one makes larger the egg-cup row and asks the child whether there are now more egg cups, or less, or as many. Around the age of 6 or 7 years, children usually find it obvious that there are as many eggs as egg cups, and they give several reasons for this (compensation of length and density, reversibility, one has not added or subtracted any element); but two years earlier they would have found it obvious the other way around, that there were more egg cups, because the row was longer. They would not be convinced by the reasons they would give later. This conceptual change is the child's *construction*: Whatever conditions teachers or parents may use to help the child use conservation in their answer, they cannot decide in their place.

Going further than the above Piagetian position, Von Glasersfeld and his colleagues (Cobb, Confrey, Richards and Steffe), promoted a radical constructivist approach. According to their approach, it was impossible to represent the real world, and therefore knowledge could not directly correspond with reality, but only in pragmatic and subjective actions. Communication itself would be entirely problematic, as words and symbols could not have unequivocal meanings. According to this view, there would be no room for objectivity, as individual representations all differed from one another. Whereas in the beginning (PME-NA 1983) Von Glasersfeld presented a weaker version of radical constructivism, the theory became rapidly very dogmatic, asserting that not only was knowledge actively constructed by the cognizing subject through an adaptive process that organizes their experience, but also that there was no independent pre-existing world to be discovered.

As one of the most contentious issues in the history of PME, Kilpatrick (1987) argued for a more balanced view, saying it was impossible that "Priestley constructed oxygen" or "Cartier constructed the Saint Laurence River". He claimed that after all, constructivists had not yet been able to develop new methods for the teaching and learning of mathematics. At the same PME session, Sinclair (1987) reported that Piaget had never been a radical constructivist but rather an "interactive constructivist" or even a "dialectical constructivist". For him, knowing outcomes from the transformations the subject, introduces in the knower/known relationship an 'action and reaction'. Vergnaud (1987) also argued that Piaget had devoted great attention to the physical properties of objects, even though he opposed too much the idea of abstraction from action (and mathematics) on one side, and abstraction from objects (and physics) on the other side. Vergnaud cautioned that it would be dangerous to go too far in the critique of constructivism, because some alternative frameworks like information-processing, symbol manipulation, or the long lasting sequels of behaviorism could also be counterproductive for research in mathematics education. The predominant ideology of teachers of the time was still dogmatism (mathematical truth to be exposed and transmitted) and empiricism (science consists of observed regularities). Therefore, constructivism had the potential fecundity to question the learning process and teachers' representations, provided that it took into account specific epistemology of mathematical concepts. Even though most PME researchers supported constructivism as a broad level, the potential danger of the 'radical' version at that time seemed to deny objectivity and science, and underestimated the importance of social interaction and teaching in learning mathematics.

Despite apparent conflict in theoretical positions and the interpretations and disparities offered by research factions, constructivist-based research in early mathematical development flourished throughout the 1980s and well into the 1990s and beyond. The work of Steffe (1984) and his colleagues on early counting and multiplicative schemes from as early as PME8 was instrumental in articulating the process of reflective abstraction and the development of children's arithmetical strategies. The constructivist teaching experiment captured the interplay between researcher as teacher and the individual construction of mathematical understandings and strategies (Cobb & Steffe, 1983). This approach had a very significant impact on the direction of research particularly for the North American PME group.

THEORETICAL PERSPECTIVES: EMERGING PERSPECTIVES ON MATHEMATICS LEARNING

By the late 1980s other researchers turned their attention to the role of representations in the development of mathematical ideas and problem-solving behavior. Goldin's model of problem-solving competency structures (Goldin, 1988) provided a general theoretical construct that informed a range of studies. This distinguished cognitive representational systems internal to problem solvers, a theoretical construct used to describe children's inner cognitive processing, from external systems of representations that can be used to characterize task variables and task structures. Goldin's model was integral to a stream of studies examining the complex processes by which children's internal systems of representation develop and how that development can be inferred from tasks- based interviews (e.g., De Windt-King & Goldin, 1997; Goldin & Passantino, 1996; Thomas, Mulligan & Goldin, 1994, 1996, 2002). One of the key contributions of this work is the explicit description of children's representations of mathematical ideas and the identification of common structural features.

A proceptual view of elementary mathematical thinking

At PME15, Gray and Tall (1991) first proposed an alternative, proceptual theory of the development of mathematical concepts–a view of simple arithmetic where symbols used dually as process and concept, are termed 'procepts'. Later, Gray and Pitta (1996) extended the notion of procepts to different kinds of mental representations. At the PME21 Research Forum on Elementary Numerical Thinking, Gray, Pitta and Tall (1997) built on their theory of procepts: Children's interpretations of arithmetical symbolism and imagery associated with these interpretations were influenced by the ways that children concentrate on different objects, or different aspects of objects, which are integral components of numerical processing. The nature of the object resonates with different cognitive styles and these styles influence the quality of the cognitive shift from concrete to abstract thought.

From their analysis of children's responses to simple addition facts, Gray and colleagues found that low achievers concretize and focus on all the information with imagery strongly associated with procedural aspects of numerical processing. Thus, low achievers may seek the security of counting procedures on objects rather than the development of more flexible arithmetic. The theoretical perspective of Gray, Pitta and Tall was advanced through a stream of contributions at PME meetings, such as the study of images (Pitta & Gray, 1996), an explanatory theory of success and failure in mathematics (Gray & Tall, 2001), and the role of imagery in mental arithmetic (Bills & Gray, 2001). More recent application of their theory has been reflected in studies on fractions (Pitta-Pantazi, Christou & Gray, 2002), and the analysis of pattern and structure (Mulligan, Prescott & Mitchelmore, 2004) in early numeracy.

Social constructivist and interactionist perspectives

By the late 1980s and 1990s there had been a shift to more dynamic research paradigms focused on analysis of teaching and learning within the classroom. Socio-cultural and interactionist views of learning mathematics influenced researchers who sought to better understand the relationship between teaching and learning through classroom practices. The social constructivist perspective moved research beyond viewing the individual as a subject of mathematical development to the development of socially constructed meaning through negotiation and consensus within the community of learners (see the chapter by Verschaffel et al. in this volume). Teaching experiments such as those conducted by Cobb, Yackel, Wood and colleagues, over lengthy periods, typified this developmental and design research in the early years of schooling (Cobb, 1994; McClain & Cobb, 2001). At PME25, Yackel (2001) discussed the importance of developing ways to analyze classrooms that foster meaningful mathematics learning. She described how the constructs of social and socio-mathematical norms, which grew out of taking a symbolic perspectives, provided a means by which to analyze and foster aspects of explanation, justification and argumentation in mathematics classrooms. Yackel drew on examples of teacher/student interactions in the second grade where sophisticated forms of explanation and justification were provided in describing mental strategies for addition. Important ideas emerged from group thinking because it allowed the mathematical reasoning and argumentation to emerge.

It was at PME23 that Hershkowitz (1999) highlighted the complexity of mathematics education research as "multiple interaction learning environments among students, between students and teacher, with the tool or with the tasks, etc." (p. 9). She asserted that while social interaction within the classroom community is being investigated, the role of the individual as the one who uses the constructed knowledge and shares it should not be neglected. Thus, researchers need to take account of the need for different kinds of documentation and for longitudinal evidence where the individual is observed in different contexts. From this view both the individuals' learning and their interactions within their learning environment are observed.

THEORETICAL PERSPECTIVES: RECENT RESEARCH DIRECTIONS FOR THE PRESCHOOL AND THE EARLY YEARS OF SCHOOLING

At PME26 the research community was made more aware of issues concerning mathematics learning in the early years prior to formal schooling. Groves (2002) provided much insight into the work on young children's use of calculators in the Calculator Aware Number Project conducted during the 1990s in Australia. The need to revisit the role of calculators in early mathematics learning was urged as there had been few studies following through the potential impact on the development of early mathematical concepts such as the PRIME Project in the UK.

At the same conference, Hughes (2001) highlighted the differences between the kinds of learning in which children engage at school and outside school and ways that the two can be brought closer together. He urged that greater recognition be paid to mathematical practices already occurring in children's homes and that we needed more radical approaches to link these practices more directly with practices at school. Ginsburg (2002) described the effectiveness of a comprehensive US mathematics curriculum for young children (Big Mathematics for Little Kids). The goal was to help children think mathematically beyond the play situation building on everyday mathematics but incorporating traditional strands of the mathematics curriculum. The process of curriculum implementation highlighted the competencies and potentialities of young children learning mathematics. Ginsburg raised important challenges for further research: We need to investigate the way young children can move beyond the boundaries of what is traditionally expected.

The following year at PME27, a discussion group on *Mathematical Thinking of Young Children Pre Kindergarten-Grade 2* reported the upsurge in interest in the mathematical capabilities of young children following advances in cognitive science, with convincing evidence that young children are more capable learners than current practices reflect, and evidence that good educational experiences in the early years can have a positive impact on school learning (Hunting & Pearn, 2003). Three key issues were raised:

- The need for integrated curriculum and pedagogy to foster children's mathematical thinking.
- The importance of taking into account different forms of children's mathematical reasoning (both individually and within the social context) in the transition from preschool to school.
- The development of frameworks to underpin research for children in the early years.

Several of these issues were taken up at the PME29 Research Forum: *A Progression of Early Number Concepts* (Hart & Gervasoni, 2005). Gervasoni used growth points to describe pathways for young children's number learning while Pearn reported on aspects of *Mathematics Recovery* describing a framework to assist students' construction of arithmetical knowledge. Hart reported on number attainment in Sri Lankan primary schools, followed by international comparison of curriculum scope and sequence for early number.

The first segment of this chapter has aimed to provide some highlights of the diversity of perspectives, whether they be psychological, cognitive or social theories that have shaped the research on early mathematical development over the life of the PME group. The following section will provide a more detailed discussion of some recent research on number concepts and arithmetic processes, mathematical modeling, reasoning, and early algebra.

KEY AREAS OF RESEARCH INTEREST: MATHEMATICAL CONTENT DOMAINS

The work of PME researchers has looked beyond traditional Piagetian notions of classification, counting, and cardinality as essential pre-requisites to further mathematical learning. Earlier research based on Piagetian notions of counting moved to the central idea of collections-based counting (see the chapter by Verschaffel et al. in this volume for a review of this work); these studies occupied much research attention throughout the 1980s and well into the last decade. However, in recent years, fewer but more integrated studies have emerged. For example, much of the constructivist-based recent research on early number and fractions can be traced to the early analysis of Steffe (1984) and colleagues. Wright's analysis of counting strategies developed a progression of arithmetical strategies in five stages: Emergent, perceptual, figurative, counting on and back, and facile. Wright (1998) also drew on the work of Sinclair and colleagues to analyze children's beginning knowledge of numerals and the relationship to their knowledge of number words. This research led to a Mathematics Recovery Program and a Learning Framework in Number (Wright & Gould, 2002). Recent work by Hunting (2003) conducted with preschoolers' explored dynamic part-whole situations found that children's part-whole reasoning and counting were closely related; they were capable of much more than manipulation of perceptual patterns. Children's ability to change focus from counting individual items to counting a group or unit was found to be fundamental to their developing number knowledge.

Gervasoni (2003, 2005) also explored the counting development of low-attaining children participating in an intervention program linked to an *Early Numeracy Research Project* (Clarke et al., 2002). The intervention was found to be effective for children who could not count collections of 20 items and it was more effective for Year 1 than Year 2 children. The effectiveness of the intervention was shown by the transitions that children made across growth points; the transition from counting forwards and backwards by ones was prolonged for many of these children. Several common difficulties mostly related to bridging decades when counting forwards or backwards. From a different perspective, Luwel and colleagues studied children's estimation strategies for numerosity judgement from the perspective of 'strategic change' (Luwel, Verschaffel, Onghena & De Corte, 2001). They investigated the relationship between children's strategies, their accuracy and speed measures in a numerosity judgement task. It was shown that addition and subtraction strategies were relatively accurate whereas an estimation strategy was less accurate.

Other approaches to the study of counting and the number system have also aimed at describing underlying conceptual bases. Based on Goldin's model of representations, Thomas and colleagues (Thomas et al., 1994, 1996, 2002; Thomas, 2004) described how children's internal representational systems for numbers 1-100 change through a period of structural development to become powerful autonomous systems. Structural features in children's external representations comprised notations depicting grouping, regrouping, partitioning and patterning; pictorial and iconic representations primarily displayed few structural features. Thomas's larger study of 132 children from grades K-6 showed that even at Grade 6, few children could generalize the structure of numeration and place value (Thomas, 2004). Grouping strategies were not well linked to the formation of multiunits, and additive rather than multiplicative relations dominated the interpretation of multidigit numbers.

Slovin and Dougherty (2004) presented a controversial approach to counting based on the work of Davydov, as part of the Measure Up (MU) research and development project. Davydov proposed that a general-to-specific approach was much more conducive to student understanding than a spontaneous concept approach. Children in the MU begin their mathematical development from the perspective of measurement and algebraic representations (see the chapters by Kay Owens & Lynne Outhred, and by Carolyn Kieran in this volume). Second graders use multiple bases with skilfulness in counting and representing numbers. However analysis of their responses showed different levels of generalization of method and explanation of underlying ideas. Students who used conceptual reasoning referred to the main unit, how many units were needed to create the supplementary unit as determined by the base or the structure of the measures that comprise a place-value system. Other students gave responses that were indicative of their procedural or specific skills rather than generalizations. This work emphasizes that competence is not always accompanied by conceptual understanding.

Addition and subtraction

One of the most coherent and systematic research themes of the PME group has centred on the operations of addition, subtraction, multiplication and division. Much of this work provides an analysis of children's counting and arithmetical strategies used to solve different classes of word problems and how these strategies developed over time (for review of this research, see Bergeron & Herscovics, 1990; Hiebert & Carpenter, 1992). One general finding of this work is that young children could intuitively model and represent the action or relationship inherent in semantic structures prior to instruction in these processes. Further analyses articulated the development of a rich variety of increasingly sophisticated counting and arithmetical strategies. Since PME24, there have been several studies from different research perspectives that have broadened the scope of research enquiry on addition and subtraction processes. Some recent studies have extended the early work on additive structures, students' representations, and strategy use to a variety of contexts and more varied populations of students (e.g. Draisma, 2000; Gagatsis & Elia, 2004; Kutscher, Linchevski & Eisenman, 2002; Meron & Peled, 2004; Price, 2001; Selva, Da Rocha Falcão, & Nunes, 2005; Thompson, 2003; Torbeyns, Verschaffel & Ghesquière, 2001; Voutsina & Jones, 2001).

Voutsina and Jones (2001) analyzed the micro-development of 5- and 6- year-old children's problem-solving strategies when tackling addition tasks. Children modified initial successful strategies (success-oriented behavior) to a more organized–oriented phase during which they exerted better control over the features of the tasks. The initial success based on procedural knowledge became more explicit, flexible and organized when the children were given the opportunity to build on that knowledge. Another study by Meron and Peled (2004) investigated the flexibility of additive schema in new contexts and unfamiliar semantic structures through an experimental curriculum with first graders. The instruction involved a didactical model combining the context of two stories with a structured part-part-whole schema. In this study the operations were not imposed as a model prior to solving the problems but were expected to emerge through children's operations within situations. Although the part-part-whole schema was introduced in the context of two specific stories, the researchers found that the schema constructed by children was not situated. The combination of using context and structure helped children abstract additive schema.

Torbeyns et al. (2001) investigated second graders' strategy use and task performance for 25 simple addition problems in choice and no-choice conditions. The findings showed that use of multiple strategies, adaptive strategy choices, and ability group differences in strategy choice and strategy execution were in parallel with differences in task performance. When children were given a choice to use their preferred strategy, a rich variety of strategy use was observed (such as counting all, counting up to and use of retrieved facts) and children adapted strategies to increase efficiency. Forcing children to use one strategy such as count up to 10 influenced response time negatively and did not influence their accuracy.

Other studies investigated the role of representation in solving additive problems. For example, in a large recent study of 1447 students from Grades 1 to

3, Gagatsis and Elia (2004) examined the effects of four different modes of representation (verbal text, number line and decorative and informational pictures) on solutions to one-step additive problems. The study showed coherence and similarity in the way students handled representations implying that they overlooked the presence of the number line or picture and gave attention only to the text of the problem. The use of pictures did not enhance understanding of the text and indicated that the cognitive demands of informational pictures in solving mathematical problems differ from other forms of representation. The findings also revealed the existence of possible developmental trends in pupils' problem-solving abilities based on different forms of representation.

In a study focused on the influence of curriculum change, Price (2001) studied the teaching and learning of addition among 4-6 year olds. Children taught through an atomistic approach with a traditional developmental sequence for addition made less progress than those taught through a holistic approach where the focus was on counting and the number system. Another recent report reflected the trend in curriculum reform where Kühne, Van den Heuvel-Panhuizen and Ensor (2005) and colleagues found that teachers' had limited understanding of children's number learning. They support the idea of a learning pathway description to assist with broadening teachers' understanding of learning and teaching early number. A research and development project inspired by the Dutch TAL Learning Trajectory for calculation with whole numbers (Van den Heuvel-Panhuizen, 2002) was initiated which aims to develop and measure the impact of a Learning Pathway for Number (LPN) at the Foundation Phase.

Multiplication and Division

Research interest on addition and subtraction word problems soon spread to the analyses of multiplication and division word problems in the 1990s and beyond (e.g. the work of these researchers and their colleagues: Anghileri, Carpenter, Confrey, De Corte, Verschaffel, Mulligan, and Murray). Some studies with older students (such as Bell, Fischbein, Greer, Brekke, Nesher and colleagues) reflected strong theoretical bases of PME research. To some extent, research with young students integrated the analysis of children's construction of multiplying schemes and the use of composite units (Steffe, 1990) and the use of classifications for multiplicative word problems (Vergnaud, 1984). Studies of multiplication and division processes reported at PME in recent years have to some degree integrated approaches adopted in earlier studies (Anghileri, 2001; Verschaffel & De Corte, 1996; Droukova, 2003; Hino, 2000; Mechmandarov, 2000; Watanabe, 1996).

For example, Fischbein's intuitive models theory inspired several studies by Mulligan and colleagues on children's intuitive models for multiplication and division. Mulligan integrated Vergnaud's classification of multiplicative structures and Steffe's analysis of multiplying schemes to investigate children's informal solutions to multiplication and division word problems prior to and after instruction. This longitudinal study reflected the design used by Carpenter and colleagues, where 70 Grade 2 students were tracked through to Grade 3 and later to

Grade 6. Although semantic structure was found to influence students' strategies, there was stronger evidence indicating that the intuitive model employed to solve a particular problem did not necessarily reflect any specific problem feature but rather the mathematical structure that the student was able to impose on it (Mulligan, 1992; Mitchelmore & Mulligan, 1996; Mulligan & Mitchelmore, 1997). Students acquired increasingly sophisticated strategies based on an equal-groups (composite) structure and their calculation procedures changed to reflect this structure. Many students who had limited development of multiplicative structure in Grade 2 were found to be still reliant on the same models and strategies in Grade 6. In a related teaching experiment third graders used modeling, drawn representations and written explanations to represent the structure of multiplicative situations. Many children were limited to a repeated addition model of multiplication. Further analyses identified levels of structure using the SOLO model first proposed by Collis and Romberg (1981).

One direct application of this research was in the development of a constructivist-based interview schedule and instructional framework for a large scale Australian early numeracy project, *Count Me In Too* (Mulligan & Wright, 2000). Sullivan, Clarke, Cheeseman and Mulligan (2001) extended the work of Mulligan and colleagues in the *Early Numeracy Research Project* (see next section). They developed an assessment schedule and used interview data on the progress of multiplicative learning by 5 to 8 year-olds in order to explore 'growth points'. The 'abstracting growth point' was found to be a significant barrier for many children, suggesting the need for children to develop visualization of multiplicative structures and progressively remove concrete models of multiplicative situations.

Some recent studies reported at PME are now integrating theoretical and methodological approaches to advance the earlier work on multiplicative structures. One such study examined students' use of mathematically based (MB) and practically based (PB) explanations for multiplication. In a study of students in Grades 2-6, Levenson, Tirosh and Tsamir (2004) compared students' explanations for multiplication before and after formal instruction. Results indicated that in every grade, students were more likely to use MB explanations than PB explanations. Young children were able to give explanations that relied solely on mathematical notions so the study raises the question of whether it is more appropriate to encourage MB explanations rather than using a PB approach with concrete materials and real life contexts.

The research on arithmetic word problems and processes has categorized problem types, analyzed underlying conceptual structures and computational skills, and presented models of developmental stages of students' strategies. Some classroom studies have emerged that show the advantages and potentialities of problem-based learning from the first years of schooling such as the Cognitively Guided Instruction studies (Romberg, Carpenter and colleagues) or problem-centred studies by Murray, Olivier and Human (1992). Notwithstanding the enormous impact of this work, there is still much research needed on how children may simultaneously develop additive and multiplicative structures from an informal to formal level. Moreover, this investigation may highlight a much broader problem. Children may not distinguish between additive and multiplicative structures and therefore they persist in using counting and additive strategies for solving problems involving other domains such as measurement, ratio and proportion, and rational number. Further research is needed to ascertain how young children build these conceptual structures, not only within the whole number and rational number domains but also in the development of other mathematical areas such as measurement, probabilistic and algebraic reasoning.

Discussion groups on multiplicative reasoning (e.g. Watanabe, Anghileri & Pesci, 1999) have viewed the development of multiplication and division concepts in a more integrated way by taking account of the role of children's understanding of early measurement, fraction, ratio and proportion concepts. These studies are reflected in a stream of research focused on the role of unitizing across a number of mathematical domains (e.g., Lamon, 1996). There has also been strong sustained interest in children's development of fraction concepts emanating from the early studies by researchers such as Hunting, Davis and colleagues, and ongoing work on children's fraction schemes (e.g. Olive, 2003; Sáenz-Ludlow, 1992; Tzur, 1996). While we have not been able to provide a review of this work here, these studies have provided in-depth analysis of the development of children's fraction knowledge (see the chapter by Verschaffel et al. in this volume). There has also been continued research interest in older students' difficulties with fractions and decimals (e.g. Stacey, 2005) with many PME reports focused on difficulties emerging in the upper elementary school.

Early Numeracy Projects

An emerging emphasis on early numeracy and international comparisons of numeracy standards at primary school level (such as the Third International Mathematics and Science Survey, TIMSS) has stimulated research in countries such as the UK, USA, Canada, Australia and New Zealand through large-scale numeracy projects. For example, the *Luverhulme Numeracy Research Programme* in the UK (Askew, 2003; Brown, 2002), the *Count Me In Too* and the *Early Numeracy Research Project* in Australia (Clarke et al., 2002; Wright & Gould, 2002) and the *British Columbia Early Numeracy Project* (Nicol, Kelleher & Saundry, 2004). For example, the *Count Me In Too* project developed a Learning Framework in Number reflecting Steffe's and Wright's model of counting-based strategies, as well as the design of effective instructional practices and sustained professional development informed by research such as Gravemeijer (1994), McClain & Cobb (2001) and Mulligan & Mitchelmore (1997). Similarly, a Number Framework was developed for the New Zealand Numeracy Development Project. The *Early Numeracy Research Project* (ENRP) also examined early counting and arithmetical development through 'growth points' of children in the first years of schooling (Clarke et al., 2002). One of the issues for further research is how we might track the long term impact of numeracy projects on children's numeracy development and classroom teaching practices. From a wider perspective, there seems to be potential for comparing the theoretical bases of different numeracy frameworks in light of empirical evidence of children's numeracy growth.

CURRENT RESEARCH INITIATIVES ON CHILDREN'S MATHEMATICAL PROCESSES

One of the most important shifts in research attention over the past two decades has been the development of research into children's powerful ideas associated with mathematical processes. These ideas include mathematical modeling and reasoning, representation, and communication of ideas (for full reviews see Jones, Langrall, Thornton & Nisbett, 2002; Perry & Dockett, 2002; Verschaffel, 2002). This body of research reveals strong theoretical bases that can be traced to significant work of the PME community. An emphasis on problem solving and mathematical thinking among older students during the 1980s and 1990s and increased evidence of young children's problem-solving capabilities, inspired researchers to devise investigations of mathematical modeling and reasoning in the early years. This trend in turn provided direction for more recent research on mathematical representations, modelling and reasoning, and early algebraic thinking.

The role of imagery and mathematical representations

Several research groups investigating young children's problem-solving strategies and mathematical reasoning have focused on aspects such as visualisation and imagery (Gray & Pitta, 1999; Pitta-Pantazi, Christou & Gray, 2002). Some investigations have employed longitudinal studies in order to track development such as children's reasoning in fraction learning (Goldin & Passantino, 1996) and structured investigations (Diezmann, Watters & English, 2001; Maher, 2002). Other studies have investigated the use of diagrams in problem solving (Diezmann, 2000). At the same time, research on children's problem-solving processes has integrated the role of patterning and structural development in a variety of studies such as those on counting (Thomas et al., 2002), number patterns using calculators (Groves, 2002), and analogical reasoning (English, 2004).

Some recent studies reported at PME28 and PME29 have integrated the role of imagery in the study of pattern and structure with young children. For example, in a descriptive study of 103 first graders, including 16 longitudinal case studies, Mulligan, Prescott & Mitchelmore (2004) and Mulligan, Mitchelmore & Prescott (2005) found that children's perception and representation of mathematical structure generalized across a range of mathematical domains (counting, partitioning, unitizing, patterning, measurement, space and graphs). They describe how children's mathematical concepts develop through five stages of structural development. Early school mathematics achievement was found related to children's development and perception of mathematical pattern and structure. These findings support what many PME researchers have said about the importance of imagery and structure in mathematical understanding (Gray & Tall, 2001). Several theories espoused by PME researchers support the notion that imagery is a central influence in the structural development of mathematical ideas (for example, the work of Pirie & Kieren, 1994; Presmeg, 1996; Sfard, 1991). However, there have been few studies that examine teaching and learning practices that encourage young children to focus on pattern and structure in early mathematics. This may require researchers to pay more attention to the process of representation and abstraction and to the development of mathematical structure inherent in various situations.

Mathematical modeling and reasoning

Early research interest in mathematical modeling focused largely on children's solving of arithmetic word problems (for a full review see Verschaffel & De Corte, 1996). Some PME researchers have built on this research base to investigate mathematical reasoning and communication processes in more open-ended problem-solving contexts using more dynamic research paradigms. One example of this is the continued work of English and colleagues whom, over the past two decades, have investigated elementary students' development of mathematical modeling, problem solving, problem posing, and mathematical reasoning such as deductive, combinatorial, and analogical reasoning (English, 1996, 1997, 1999, 2004). English (1999) found that children used structural understanding in combinatorial problems presented in various task situations. However, they had difficulties in explaining fully the two-dimensional structure of the combination problems and could rarely identify the cross-multiplication feature of these problems. In a recent longitudinal, cross-cultural study, English (2004) tracked the development of analogical and mathematical reasoning in 4- to 7- year old children. Children who scored higher on analogical and mathematical reasoning tasks were observed to reflect on what they had learned and to apply this knowledge to new situations. English and Watters' (2005) current 3-year longitudinal study engages 8-year-old children in modeling problems where they are involved in problem posing, hypothesizing and mathematizing and where they focus on structural characteristics such as patterns, and relationships among elements rather than superficial features.

Early algebraic reasoning

More recently, there has been a surge of interest in the study of early algebraic thinking (see the chapter by Carolyn Kieran in this volume) represented by the PME Early Algebra Working Group. Studies of children's early algebraic thinking (e.g. Blanton & Kaput, 2002, 2004; Schliemann, Carraher, Brizuela, Earnest, Goodrow, Lara-Roth & Peled, 2003; Tabach & Hershkowitz, 2002; Warren, 2005) are primarily concerned with the early bases of mathematical abstraction and generalization. In particular, recent research on functional thinking (Blanton & Kaput, 2004; Schliemann et al., 2003) focuses attention on an untapped source of algebraic reasoning of young children in the 3-to 8-year age range. In a longitudinal study of early algebra, Schliemann et al. (2003) found that third graders developed a rich understanding of function and were able to represent algebraic thinking using multiple representations. Other researchers have responded to the move away from the almost exclusive focus on arithmetic and computation by studying children's understanding of the algebraic nature of arithmetic (Fujii & Stephens, 2001). Computational efficiency is no longer considered the dominant rationale for the study of arithmetic. Another aspect of the link between algebra and arithmetic is the understanding of equivalence, but there have been few studies examining this area with younger students (Irwin, 1990; Warren, 2003; Womack & Williams, 1998).

FUTURE DIRECTIONS FOR RESEARCH IN EARLY MATHEMATICAL DEVELOPMENT

In raising some possibilities for future research we must question what are the current and emerging problems and challenges we face in understanding more about how young children acquire mathematical concepts, and in developing effective pedagogy and curriculum. Do we need more fine-grained analysis of children's concept development? Do we need to study early mathematical development from different theoretical perspectives using different tools? The work of PME researchers has certainly moved well beyond the investigation of counting and arithmetic. However, there seems too few recent studies focused on the psychological and cognitive processes underlying the development of mathematical concepts to advance substantially, theoretical frameworks and knowledge of specific content domains (English, 2002). Studies of the teaching of early mathematics using socio-cultural approaches are also limited with insufficient cross-cultural and ethnographic studies.

The theoretical bases of research on children's mathematical development developed throughout the early years of PME enabled researchers to follow common research questions and build new theoretical frameworks. Without these theoretical bases there would have been little coherence in the development of much of the work on early number and arithmetic. The advancement of our knowledge about young children's mathematical learning may depend on how well theoretical frameworks are integrated and supported by new evidence of children's mathematical development. We may need to revisit some fundamental theories that provided, in many ways, integrated theoretical frameworks of mathematical processes. For example, Fischbein's theory of intuition has not yet been fully explored particularly in the context of young children's learning or in its practical implications for instructional settings. Similarly Vergnaud's theory of conceptual fields that encompasses additive and multiplicative structures could be integrated in the development of new research frameworks. There has been much research interest in early counting and computational processes. In regard to future research across specific content domains, there seems now to be a need for further integration–research investigating the way young children form conceptual structures and relationships between all four processes would provide more coherence (c.f. the work with older students of Fuson, Wearne, Hiebert, Murray, Olivier, Carpenter & Fennema, 1997). This may be warranted even for those students in Grades 1 or 2 who can already operate with 2 digit numbers and solve additive and multiplicative problems. Studies might also be tackled at the preschool level through investigation in naturalistic settings.

Research directions on early algebraic reasoning

Current research is seeking to identify teaching and learning influences that tend to promote or impede the development of structure and generalization in children's mathematics learning. Yet, despite curriculum reforms and recent research interest in early algebraic thinking there remains a paucity of research on the development of young children's mathematical patterning, and studies of instructional programs promoting patterning (Fox, 2005; Papic, 2005). Perhaps an important advance for research in the early years is the analysis of children's identification and representation of the structure of patterns beyond those using a single variable and simple repetition (Blanton & Kaput, 2004; Warren, 2005).

Investigation of early algebraic functional thinking can further our understanding of how children distinguish between additive and multiplicative relationships. Research on multiplication and division concepts and processes has shown that children in the first years of schooling can solve a range of multiplicative problems including semantic structures of 'factor' or 'times as many', and ratio. However, as researchers we have not really explored this potential in terms of functional thinking. One might regard the research on early mathematical reasoning and mathematical modeling inextricably linked to the study of early algebra. Considering this, it might be advantageous to use research tasks that involve quantitative and spatial patterns, modeling and reasoning within the same study. In this way it might be possible to ascertain links between early number concepts and relationships and the generalization of numerical expressions, or generalizations drawn from numerical and spatial patterns applied to other aspects of mathematics.

Research on the role of technology

Although there has been substantial work by PME members and beyond on older students' use of technology in learning mathematics, there has been limited study of the use and influence of technology in early mathematical development. We have not been able to give this attention in this chapter. We must question, though, what impact a world rapidly influenced by information and communication technologies has on young children's mathematical development prior to, and early on in formal schooling. In order to answer this questions we may need to study young children's development of mathematical concepts linked to use of technology-based toys, software, games, and use of the Internet. Research on the use of technology for instruction has provided new opportunities for integrating technology in classroom practice but teachers are still yet to really embrace technology in elementary and early childhood programs. The implementation of handheld calculators has also been limited despite research evidence of their positive impact in the preschool and elementary school. Another area that seems to be under-represented is the development of elementary concepts of measurement such as time, speed, growth and change, often represented through the use of technology.

Promoting research on quantitative literacy in the early years

Over the past two decades educators have promoted the integration of early numeracy and literacy through media such as shared book reading but there has been scant research on its influence on young children's mathematics learning. Studies of children's reading and use of literature in out-of-school, preschool and classroom environments could provide more insights into the development of mathematical concepts, language and reasoning. This may contribute to furthering our understanding of the social, cultural and psychological bases of early mathematical learning.

Another area of research impetus in quantitative literacy might be the increase in studies that focus on data exploration and data-handling skills. An investigation of young children's representations of simple graphs and tables, including the use of technology, is warranted (Jones et al., 2002). Recent work has provided, for example, analyses of elementary students' performance on graphical languages in mathematics (Lowrie & Diezmann, 2005). Similarly increased research interest in the links between young children's number concepts and graphical representation is emerging (Selva et al., 2005). A related research agenda that explores probabilistic reasoning would provide a more coherent picture of children's development of this domain (e.g. Perry, Putt, Jones, Thornton, Langrall & Mooney, 2000; Spinillo, 1997; Way & Ayres, 2002).

Providing a More Holistic Picture: Integrating Research Perspectives

One of the questions that we can take from this overview is whether we revisit or extend existing research on the early development of mathematical concepts and relationships as separate content domains. Rather, do we need to look more closely at the common underlying features of early mathematical development across a more diverse range of concepts such as early algebra and statistical thinking including the role of technology? The study of mathematical modeling and reasoning, patterning and structural relationships would complement this research. It may be advantageous for PME researchers primarily focused on explicit mathematical content domains such as algebra or measurement to work more closely with colleagues whose research concerns early mathematical learning per se. This would provide opportunities to build on common theoretical bases and analyze the complex interrelationships represented by existing research across mathematical content domains. For example how does the extant work on early number learning assist in formulating new research questions linking arithmetic and early algebraic reasoning? Collaboration between teams of researchers at an international level would encourage cross-cultural studies and a broadening of the research bases of the PME group. Moreover, the integration of PME research with other domains such as science and literacy, may contribute significantly to shaping future studies of young children's learning and development that transgress traditional curriculum boundaries.

At PME26 Brown highlighted the need for research from multiple perspectives in order to have a more holistic view of teaching and learning and avoid simplistic conclusions. A key question is whether to integrate several aspects of research interest and different methodologies to examine the early development of mathematical learning as in multi-focused projects such as the Luverhulme Project, and longitudinal studies such as Maher's study of the development of student reasoning. In the last decade research attention has been placed on the influence of teaching on learning in classroom settings (Boaler, 2003; Wood & McNeal, 2003). In studies such as those focused on teacher knowledge and professional development, the teaching process, or curriculum and assessment, researchers have shifted research attention beyond specific content domains or age groups. Some studies have evaluated the impact of professional development embedded within early numeracy projects, or design studies in the first years of schooling. Other studies have observed social aspects of the learning situation such as the role of the task in learning (Groves & Doig, 2002), children's discourse (Irwin & Ginsburg, 2001) or dialogical interaction between student and teacher (Sáenz-Ludlow, 2003).

Clearly research in the elementary years has shifted from the clinical study of the development of mathematical concepts to the study of teaching practice in classroom and small group settings. Yet there is a paucity of research on how young children construct their mathematical knowledge prior to schooling, and in out-of-school settings. We may not need to necessarily focus on 'instructional' programs for very young children but to examine more closely how children develop mathematics in out-of-school contexts and in the home and community. At the PME28 meeting in Bergen the theme of *Inclusion and Diversity* drew attention to the issue of enabling more effective learning for all students (Hershkowitz, 2004). It is therefore important to consider the potential influence of broader cross-cultural research and in diverse populations of very young children. Perhaps our attention should be drawn to multi-focused research on developing early mathematical learning, as well as professional programs and strategies that can eliminate to some extent, disadvantage.

A review of the contributions of Discussion and Working Groups, and Research Fora at PME conferences over the past decade presents valuable but irregular opportunities for discourse addressing early mathematics learning. So we might question whether we need to bring together, through meta-analyses or study groups, emerging theoretical approaches to the study of early mathematical development. This may enable the PME community to re-formulate research directions, and address gaps and disparities representative of this field of research in the past decade or so. After thirty years of focused research activity we are now developing more complex, multi-focused and integrated approaches to the study of young children's mathematical development. Perhaps we will see a 'blurring of boundaries' that were initially imposed by research concentrations in particular age groups, single content domains, or by preferred theoretical or methodological approaches. This may encourage much needed development of a rich and complex research agenda prioritizing early mathematical learning that forges stronger collaboration within the PME community in the next decades.

REFERENCES

Anghileri, J. (2001). What are we trying to achieve in teaching standard calculating procedures? In M. van den Heuvel-Panhuizen (Ed.), *Proceedings of the 25th PME International Conference, 2*, 41–48.

Askew, M. (2003). Mental calculation: Interpretations and implementation. In N. A. Pateman, B. J. Dougherty, & J. T. Zilliox (Eds.), *Proceedings of the 27th PME International Conference, 1*, 202.

Bergeron, J. C., & Herscovics, N. (1990). Psychological aspects of learning early arithmetic. In P. Nesher & J. Kilpatrick (Eds.), *Mathematics and Cognition: A research synthesis by the International Group for the Psychology of Mathematics Education* (pp. 31–52). Cambridge, UK: Cambridge University Press.

Bills, C., & Gray, E. (2001). The 'particular', 'generic' and 'general' in young children's mental calculations. In M. van den Heuvel-Panhuizen (Ed.), *Proceedings of the 25th PME International Conference, 2*, 153–160.

Blanton, M. L., & Kaput, J. J. (2002). Design principles for tasks that support algebraic thinking in elementary school classrooms. In A. D. Cockburn & E. Nardi (Eds.), *Proceedings of the 26th PME International Conference, 2*, 105–112.

Blanton, M. L., & Kaput, J. J. (2004). Elementary students' capacity for functional thinking. In M. J. Høines & A. B. Fuglestad (Eds.), *Proceedings of the 28th PME International Conference, 2*, 135–142.

Boaler, J. (2003). Studying and capturing the complexity of practice-the case of the dance of agency. In N. A. Pateman, B. J. Dougherty, & J. T. Zilliox (Eds.), *Proceedings of the 27th PME International Conference, 1*, 3–16.

Boero, P. (1989). Mathematical literacy for all experiences and problems. In G. Vergnaud, J. Rogalski, & M. Artigue (Eds.), *Proceedings of the 13th PME International Conference, 1*, 62–76.

Brown, M. (2002). Researching primary numeracy. In A. D. Cockburn & E. Nardi (Eds.), *Proceedings of the 26th PME International Conference, 1*, 15–30.

Carpenter, T. P., & Moser, J. M. (1979). The development of addition and subtraction concepts in young children. In D. Tall (Ed.), *Proceedings of the 3rd PME International Conference, 1*, 40–46.

Clarke, B., McDonough, A., & Sullivan, P. (2002). Measuring and describing learning: The early numeracy research project. In A. D. Cockburn & E. Nardi (Eds.), *Proceedings of the 26th PME International Conference, 1*, 181–185.

Cobb, P. (1994). A summary of four case studies of mathematical learning and small group interaction. In J. P. Ponte & J. F. Matos (Eds.), *Proceedings of the 16thth PME International Conference, 2*, 210–218.

Cobb, P., & Steffe, L. (1983). The constructivist researcher as a teacher and model builder. *Journal for Research in Mathematics Education, 14*, 83–94.

Collis, K. F., & Romberg, T. A. (1981). Cognitive functioning, classroom learning and evaluation: Two projects. In Equipe de Recherche Pédagogique (Eds.), *Proceedings of the 5th PME International Conference, 2*, 64–77.

Collis, K. F., & Watson, J. M. (1985). A SOLO mapping procedure. In G. Vergnaud, J. Rogalski, & M. Artigue (Eds.), *Proceedings of the 13th PME International Conference, 1*, 180–187.

Comiti, C., & Bessot, A. (1981). Etude du fonctionnement de certaines propriétés de la suite des nombres dans le domaine numérique (1–30) chez des élèves de fin de première année de l'école obligatoire en France. In Equipe de Recherche Pédagogique (Eds.), *Proceedings of the 5th PME International Conference, 1*, 31–37.

DeWindt-King, A. M., & Goldin, G. A. (2001). A study of children's visual imagery in solving problems with fractions. In M. van den Heuvel-Panhuizen (Ed.), *Proceedings of the 25th PME International Conference, 2*, 345–352.

Diezmann, C. M. (2000). The difficulties students experience in generating diagrams for novel problems. In T. Nakahara & M. Koyama (Eds.), *Proceedings of the 24th PME International Conference, 2*, 241–248.

Diezmann, C. M., Watters, J. J., & English, L. D. (2001). Difficulties confronting young children undertaking investigations. In M. van den Heuvel-Panhuizen (Ed.), *Proceedings of the 25th PME International Conference, 2*, 353–360.

Draisma, J. (2000). Gesture and oral computation as resources in the early learning of mathematics. In T. Nakahara & M. Koyama (Eds.), *Proceedings of the 24th PME International Conference, 2*, 257–264.

Droukova, M. (2003). The role of metaphors in the development of multiplicative reasoning of a young child. In N. A. Pateman, B. J. Dougherty, & J. T. Zilliox (Eds.), *Proceedings of the 27th PME International Conference, 1*, 213.

English, L. D. (1996). Children's reasoning in solving novel problems of deduction. In L. Puig & A. Gutiérrez (Eds.), *Proceedings of the 20th PME International Conference, 2*, 329–336.

English, L. D. (Ed.), (1997). *Mathematical reasoning: Analogies, metaphors, and images.* Mahwah, New Jersey, USA: Lawrence Erlbaum.

English, L. D. (1999). Assessing for structural understanding in children's combinatorial problem solving. *Focus on Learning Problems in Mathematics, 21*(4), 63–82.

English, L. D. (2002). Priority themes and issues in international mathematics education research. In L. D. English (Ed.), *Handbook of international research in mathematics education* (pp. 3–16). Mahwah, New Jersey, USA: Lawrence Erlbaum.

English, L. D. (2004). Promoting the development of young children's mathematical and analogical reasoning. In L. D. English (Ed.), *Mathematical and analogical reasoning of young learners* (pp. 210–215). Mahwah, NJ, USA: Lawrence Erlbaum.

English, L. D., & Watters, J. J. (2005). Mathematical modelling with 9-year-olds. In H. L. Chick & J. L. Vincent (Eds.), *Proceedings of the 29th PME International Conference, 2*, 297–304.

Fischbein, E. (1978). Intuition and mathematical education. In E. Cohors-Fresenborg & I. Wachsmuth (Eds.), *Proceedings of the 2nd PME International Conference,* 148–176.

Fischbein, E. (1983). Role of implicit models in solving elementary arithmetical problems. In R. Hershkowitz (Ed.), *Proceedings of the 7th PME International Conference*, 2–18.

Fischer, J. P. (1981). L'enfant et le comptage. In Equipe de Recherche Pédagogique (Eds.), *Proceedings of the 5th PME International Conference, 1*, 38–43.

Fox, G. (2005). Child-initiated mathematical patterning in the pre-compulsory years. In H. L. Chick & J. L. Vincent (Eds.), *Proceedings of the 29th PME International Conference, 2*, 313–320.

Fujii, T., & Stephens, M. (2001). Fostering an understanding of algebraic generalization through numerical expressions: The role of quasi-variables. In H. L. Chick, K. Stacey, & J. Vincent (Eds.), *Proceedings of the 12th ICMI study conference: The future of teaching and learning algebra* (pp. 258–264). Melbourne, Australia: University of Melbourne.

Fuson, K. C., Wearne, D., Hiebert, J. C., Murray, H. G., Olivier, A. I., Carpenter, T. P., et al. (1997). Children's conceptual structures for multidigit numbers and methods of multidigit addition and subtraction. *Journal for Research in Mathematics Education, 28*, 130–162.

Gagatsis, A., & Elia, I. (2004). The effects of different modes of representation on mathematical problem solving. In M. J. Høines & A. B. Fuglestad (Eds.), *Proceedings of the 28th PME International Conference*, *2*, 447–455.

Gervasoni, A. (2003). Key transitions in counting development for young children who experience difficulty. In N. A. Pateman, B. J. Dougherty, & J. Zilliox (Eds.), *Proceedings of the 27th PME International Conference, 2*, 421–437.

Gervasoni, A. (2005). The diverse learning needs of young children who were selected for an intervention program. In H. L. Chick & J. L. Vincent (Eds.), *Proceedings of the 29th PME International Conference, 3*, 33–40.

Ginsburg, H. P. (2002). Little children, big mathematics: Learning and teaching in the preschool. In A. D. Cockburn & E. Nardi (Eds.), *Proceedings of the 26th PME International Conference, 1*, 3–14.

Goldin, G. A. (1988). The development of a model for competence in mathematical problem solving. In A. Borbás (Ed.), *Proceedings of the 12th PME International Conference, 2*, 358–368.

Goldin, G. A., & Passantino, C. B. (1996). A longitudinal study of children's fraction representations and problem-solving behavior. In L. Puig & A. Gutiérrez (Eds.), *Proceedings of the 20th PME International Conference, 3*, 3–10.

Gravemeijer, K. (1994). Educational development and development research in mathematics education. *Journal for Research in Mathematics Education, 25*, 443–471.

Gray, E. M., & Pitta, D. (1996). Number processing: Qualitative differences in thinking and the role of imagery. In L. Puig & A. Gutiérrez (Eds.), *Proceedings of the 20th PME International Conference, 3*, 155–162.

Gray, E. M., & Pitta, D. (1999). Images and their frames of reference: A perspective on cognitive development in elementary arithmetic. In O. Zaslavsky (Ed.), *Proceedings of the 23rd PME International Conference, 3*, 49–56.

Gray, E. M., Pitta, D., & Tall, D. O. (1997). The nature of the object as an integral component of numerical processes. In E. Pehkonen (Ed.), *Proceedings of the 21st PME International Conference, 1*,115–130.

Gray, E. M., & Tall, D. O. (1991). Duality, ambiguity and flexibility in successful mathematical thinking. In F. Furinghetti (Ed.), *Proceedings of the 15th PME International Conference, 2*, 72–79.

Gray, E. M., & Tall, D. O. (2001). Relationships between embodied objects and symbolic procepts: An explanatory theory of success and failure in mathematics. In M. van den Heuvel-Panhuizen (Ed.), *Proceedings of the 25th PME International Conference, 3*, 65–72.

Groves, S. (2002). Calculators – The first day. In A. D. Cockburn & E. Nardi (Eds.), *Proceedings of the 26th PME International Conference, 1*, 98–109.

Groves, S., & Doig, B. (2002). Developing conceptual understanding: The role of the task in communities of mathematical inquiry. In A. D. Cockburn & E. Nardi (Eds.), *Proceedings of the 26th PME International Conference, 3*, 25–32.

Hall, J. W., Fuson, K. F., & Willis, G. B. (1985). Teaching counting on for addition and counting up for subtraction. In L. Streefland (Ed.), *Proceedings of the 9th PME International Conference, 1*, 322–327.

Harrison, B., Bye, M. P., & Schroeder, T. L. (1985). Pupil cognitive ability levels compared with curricular demands when six-to-eight-year-olds are taught arithmetic operations. In L. Streefland (Ed.), *Proceedings of the 9th PME International Conference, 1*, 210–215.

Hart, K., & Gervasoni, A. (2005). A progression of early number concepts. In H. L. Chick & J. L. Vincent (Eds.), *Proceedings of the 29th PME International Conference, 1*, 155–165.

Hershkowitz, R. (1999). Where in shared knowledge is the individual knowledge hidden? In O. Zaslavsky (Ed.), *Proceedings of the 23rd PME International Conference, 1*, 9–24.

Hershkowitz, R. (2004). From diversity to inclusion and back: Lenses on learning. In M. J. Høines & A. B. Fuglestad (Eds.), *Proceedings of the 28th PME International Conference, 1*, 55–68.

Hiebert, J., & Carpenter, T. P. (1992). Learning and teaching with understanding. In D. A. Grouws (Ed.), *Handbook of research on mathematics teaching and learning* (pp. 65–97). New York, USA: Macmillan.

Hino, K. (2000). Process of internalizing new use of multiplication through classroom instruction: A case study. In T. Nakahara & M. Koyama (Eds.), *Proceedings of the 24th PME International Conference, 3*, 49–56.

Hughes, M. (2001). Linking home and school mathematics. In M. van den Heuvel-Panhuizen (Ed.), *Proceedings of the 25th PME International Conference, 1*, 5–8.

Hunting, R. (2003). The role of fingers in preschoolers' mathematical problem solving. In N. A. Pateman, B. J. Dougherty, & J. Zilliox (Eds.), *Proceedings of the 27th PME International Conference, 1*, 233.

Hunting, R., & Pearn, C. (2003). The mathematical thinking of young children: Pre-K-2. In N. A. Pateman, B. J. Dougherty, & J. Zilliox (Eds.), *Proceedings of the 27th PME International Conference, 1*, 187.

Irwin, K. (1990). Children's understanding of compensation, addition and subtraction in part-whole relationships. In G. Booker, P. Cobb, & T. N. Mendicuti (Eds.), *Proceedings of the 14th PME International Conference, 3*, 257–264.

Irwin, K. C., & Ginsburg, H. P. (2001). Early mathematical discourse. In M. van den Heuvel-Panhuizen (Ed.), *Proceedings of the 25th PME International Conference, 3*, 185–192.

Janvier, C., & Bednarz, N. (1989). Representation and contextualisation. In G. Vergnaud, J. Rogalski, & M. Artigue (Eds.), *Proceedings of the 13th PME International Conference, 2*, 139–146.

Jones, G. A., Langrall, C. W., Thornton, C. A., & Nisbet, S. (2002). Elementary students' access to powerful mathematical ideas. In L. D. English (Ed.), *Handbook of international research in mathematics education* (pp. 113–141). Mahwah, NJ, USA: Lawrence Erlbaum.

Kilpatrick, J. (1987). What constructivism might be in mathematics education. In J. C. Bergeron, N. Herscovics, & C. Kieran (Eds.), *Proceedings of the 11th PME International Conference, 1*, 3–27.

Kühne, C., Van den Heuvel-Panhuizen, M., & Ensor, P. (2005). Learning and teaching early number: Teachers' perceptions. In H. L. Chick & J. L. Vincent (Eds.), *Proceedings of the 29th PME International Conference, 3*, 209–216.

Kutscher, B., Linchevski, L., & Eisenman, T. (2002). From the Lotto game to subtracting two-digit numbers in first-graders. In A. D. Cockburn & E. Nardi (Eds.), *Proceedings of the 26th PME International Conference, 3*, 249–256.

Lamon, S. J. (1996). Partitioning and unitizing. In L. Puig & A. Gutiérrez (Eds.), *Proceedings of the 20th PME International Conference, 3*, 233–240.

Lesh, R. (1985). Conceptual analyzes of mathematical ideas and problem-solving processes. In L. Streefland (Ed.), *Proceedings of the 9th PME International Conference, 2*, 73–96.

Levenson, E., Tirosh, D., & Tsamir, P. (2004). Elementary school students' use of mathematically-based and practically-based explanations: The case of multiplication. In M. J. Høines & A. B. Fuglestad (Eds.), *Proceedings of the 28th PME International Conference, 3*, 241–248.

Lowrie, T., & Diezmann, C. (2005). Fourth-grade students' performance on graphical languages in mathematics. In H. L. Chick & J. L. Vincent (Eds.), *Proceedings of the 29th PME International Conference, 3*, 265–272.

Luwel, K., Verschaffel, L., Onghena, P., & De Corte, E. (2001). Children's strategies for numerosity judgement in square grids: The relationship between process and product data. In M. van den Heuvel-Panhuizen (Ed.), *Proceedings of the 25th PME International Conference, 3*, 329–334.

Maher, C. (2002). How students structure their own investigations and educate us: What we've learned from a 14-year study. In A. D. Cockburn & E. Nardi (Eds.), *Proceedings of the 26th PME International Conference, 1*, 31–46.

McClain, K., & Cobb, P. (2001). An analysis of development of sociocultural norms in one first grade classroom. *Journal for Research in Mathematics Education, 32*, 236–266.

Mekhmandarov, I. (2000). Analysis and synthesis of the cartesian product by kindergarten children. In T. Nakahara & M. Koyama (Eds.), *Proceedings of the 24th PME International Conference, 3*, 295–302.

Meron, R., & Peled, I. (2004). Situated or abstract: The effect of combining context and structure on constructing an additive (part-part-whole) schema. In M. J. Høines & A. B. Fuglestad (Eds.), *Proceedings of the 28th PME International Conference, 4*, 1–8.

Mitchelmore, M. C., & Mulligan, J. T. (1996). Children's developing multiplication and division strategies. In L. Puig & A. Gutiérrez (Eds.), *Proceedings of the 20th PME International Conference, 3*, 407–414.

Mulligan, J. T. (1992). Children's solutions to multiplication and division word problems: A longitudinal study. In W. Geeslin & K. Graham (Eds.), *Proceedings of the 16th PME International Conference, 2*, 144–152.

Mulligan, J. T., & Mitchelmore, M. C. (1997). Young children's intuitive models of multiplication and division. *Journal for Research in Mathematics Education, 28*(3), 309–331.

Mulligan, J. T., Mitchelmore, M. C., & Prescott, A., (2005). Case studies of children's development of structure in early mathematics: A two-year longitudinal study. In H. L. Chick & J. L. Vincent (Eds.), *Proceedings of the 29th PME International Conference, 4*, 1–8.

Mulligan, J. T., Prescott, A., & Mitchelmore, M. C. (2004). Children's development of structure in early mathematics. In M. J. Høines & A. B. Fuglestad (Eds.), *Proceedings of the 28th PME International Conference, 3*, 393–401.

Mulligan, J. T., & Wright, R. (2000). Interview-based assessment of early multiplication and division. In T. Nakahara & M. Koyama (Eds.), *Proceedings of the 24th PME International Conference, 4*, 17–24.

Murray, H., Olivier, A., & Human, P. (1992). The development of young children's division strategies. In W. Geeslin & K. Graham (Eds.), *Proceedings of the 16th PME International Conference, 2*, 152–160.

Nesher, P., & Greeno, J. G. (1981). Semantic categories of word problems reconsidered. In Equipe de Recherche Pédagogique (Eds.), *Proceedings of the 5th PME International Conference*, 63– 68.

Nicol, C., Kelleher, H., & Saundry, C. (2004). What a simple task can show: Teachers explore the complexity of children's thinking. In M. J. Høines & A. B. Fuglestad (Eds.), *Proceedings of the 28th PME International Conference, 3*, 145–152.

Nunes, T. (1989). Numeracy without schooling. In G. Vergnaud, J. Rogalski, & M. Artigue (Eds.), *Proceedings of the 13th PME International Conference, 1*, 164–171.

Nunes, T., & Schliemann, A. D. (1987). Manipulating equivalences in the market and in mathematics. In J. C. Bergeron, N. Herscovics, & C. Kieran (Eds.), *Proceedings of the 11th PME International Conference, 1*, 289–294.

Olive, J. (2003). Nathan's strategies for simplifying and adding fractions in third grade. In N. A. Pateman, B. J. Dougherty, & J. T. Zilliox (Eds.), *Proceedings of the 27th PME International Conference, 3*, 421–429.

Papic, M. (2005). The development of patterning in early childhood. In H. Chick, & J. Vincent (Eds.), *Proceedings of the 29th PME International Conference, 1*, 269.

Perry, B., & Dockett, S. (2002). Young children's access to powerful mathematical ideas. In L. D. English (Ed.), *Handbook of international research in mathematics education* (pp. 81–111). Mahwah, NJ, USA: Lawrence Erlbaum.

Perry, B., Putt, I. J., Jones, G. A., Thornton, C. A., Langrall, C. W., & Mooney, E. S. (2000). Elementary school students' statistical thinking: An international perspective. In T. Nakahara & M. Koyama (Eds.), *Proceedings of the 24th PME International Conference, 4*, 65–72.

Pirie, S., & Kieren, T. (1994). Growth in mathematical understanding: How can we characterize it and how can we represent it? *Educational Studies in Mathematics, 26*, 165–190.

Pitta-Pantazi, D., Christou, C., & Gray, E., (2002). Mental representations in elementary arithmetic. In A. D. Cockburn & E. Nardi (Eds.), *Proceedings of the 26th PME International Conference, 4*, 65–72.

Presmeg, N. (1996). Visualization in high school mathematics. *For the Learning of Mathematics, 6*(3), 42–46.

Price, A. J. (2001). Atomistic and holistic approaches to the early primary mathematics curriculum for addition. In M. van den Heuvel-Panhuizen (Ed.), *Proceedings of the 25th PME International Conference, 4*, 73–80.

Richards, J. (1981). Pre-numerical counting. In Equipe de Recherche Pédagogique (Eds.), *Proceedings of the 5th PME International Conference, 1*, 25–30.

Sáenz-Ludlow, A. (1992). Ann's strategies to add fractions. In W. Geeslin & K. Graham (Eds.), *Proceedings of the 16th PME International Conference, 2*, 266–273.

Sáenz-Ludlow, A. (2003). An interpreting game in a third grade classroom. In N. A. Pateman, B. J. Dougherty, & J. T. Zilliox (Eds.), *Proceedings of the 27th PME International Conference, 4*, 79–87.

Schliemann, A., Carraher, D. W., Brizuela, B. M., Earnest, D., Goodrow, A., Lara-Roth, S., et al. (2003). Algebra in elementary school. In N. A. Pateman, B. J. Dougherty, & J. T. Zilliox (Eds.), *Proceedings of the 27th PME International Conference, 4*, 127–134.

Schmidt, S. (1981). An inventory of the performance of how kindergarten (5–6 years of age) use the different aspects of natural numbers. In Equipe de Recherche Pédagogique (Eds.), *Proceedings of the 5th PME International Conference, 1*, 44–49.

Selva, A. C. V., Da Rocha Falcão, J. T., & Nunes, T. (2005). Solving additive problems at pre-elementary school level with the support of graphical representation. In H. L. Chick & J. L. Vincent (Eds.), *Proceedings of the 29th PME International Conference, 4*, 161–168.

Sfard, A. (1991). On the dual nature of mathematical conceptions: Reflections on processes and objects as different sides of the same coin. *Educational Studies in Mathematics, 22*, 1–36.

Sinclair, H. (1987): Constructivism and the psychology of mathematics. In J. C. Bergeron, N. Herscovics, & C. Kieran (Eds.), *Proceedings of the 11th PME International Conference, 1*, 28–41.

Slovin, H., & Dougherty, B. (2004). Children's conceptual understanding of counting. In M. J. Høines & A. B. Fuglestad (Eds.), *Proceedings of the 28th PME International Conference, 4*, 209–216.

Spinillo, A. G. (1997). Chance estimates by young children: Strategies used in an ordering chance task. In E. Pehkonen (Ed.), *Proceedings of the 21 st International PME Conference, 4*, 182–189.

Stacey, K. (2005). Traveling the road to expertise: A longitudinal study of learning. In H. L. Chick & J. L. Vincent (Eds.), *Proceedings of the 29th PME International Conference, 1*, 19–36.

Steffe, L. P. (1981). Operational counting and position. In Equipe de Recherche Pédagogique (Eds.), *Proceedings of the 5th PME International Conference, 1*, 12–17.

Steffe, L. P. (1984). Children's prenumerical adding schemes. In B. Southwell, R. Eyland, M. Cooper, J. Conroy, & K. Collis (Eds.), *Proceedings of the 8th PME International Conference*, 313–327.

Steffe, L. P. (1990). A child generated multiplying scheme. In G. Booker, P. Cobb, & T. N. Mendicuti (Eds.), *Proceedings of the 14th PME International Conference, 3*, 329–336.

Sullivan, P., Clarke, D., Cheeseman, J., & Mulligan, J. (2001). Moving beyond physical models in learning multiplicative reasoning. In M. van den Heuvel-Panhuizen (Ed.), *Proceedings of the 25th PME International Conference, 4*, 233–240.

Tabach, M., & Hershkowitz, R. (2002). Construction of knowledge and its consolidation: A case study from the early-algebra classroom. In A. D. Cockburn & E. Nardi (Eds.), *Proceedings of the 26th PME International Conference, 4*, 265–272.

Thomas, N. (2004). The development of structure in the number system. In M. J. Høines & A. B. Fuglestad (Eds.), *Proceedings of the 28th PME International Conference, 4*, 305–312.

Thomas, N., Mulligan, J. T., & Goldin, G. A. (1994). Children's representation of the counting sequence 1–100: Study and theoretical interpretation. In J. P. Ponte & J. F. Matos (Eds.), *Proceedings of the 16th PME International Conference, 3*, 1–8.

Thomas, N., Mulligan, J., & Goldin, G. A. (1996). Children's representation of the counting sequence 1–100: Cognitive structural development. In L. Puig & A. Gutiérrez (Eds.), *Proceedings of the 20th PME International Conference, 4*, 307–314.

Thomas, N., Mulligan, J. T., & Goldin, G. A. (2002). Children's representations and cognitive structural development of the counting sequence 1–100. *Journal of Mathematical Behavior, 21*, 117–133.

Thompson, I. (2003). An investigation of the relationship between young children's understanding of the concept of place value and their competence at mental addition. In N. A. Pateman, B. J. Dougherty, & J. T. Zilliox (Eds.), *Proceedings of the 27th PME International Conference, 1*, 255.

Torbeyns, J., Verschaffel, L., & Ghesquière, P. (2001). Investigating young children's strategy use and task performance in the domain of simple addition, using the "choice/no-choice" method. In M. van den Heuvel-Panhuizen (Ed.), *Proceedings of the 25th PME International Conference, 4*, 273–278.

Tzur, R. (1996). Children's interaction and fraction learning in a computer microworld: Construction of the iterative fraction scheme. In L. Puig & A. Gutiérrez (Eds.), *Proceedings of the 20th PME International Conference*, 4, 355–362.

Van den Brink, J. (1981). Queries around the number concept. In Equipe de Recherche Pédagogique (Eds.), *Proceedings of the 5th PME International Conference, 1*, 56–62.

Van den Heuvel-Panhuizen, M. (2002). From core goals to learning-teaching trajectories as a guide for teaching primary school mathematics in the Netherlands. In A. D. Cockburn & E. Nardi (Eds.), *Proceedings of the 26th PME International Conference, 1*, 191–196.

Vergnaud, G. (1978). The acquisition of arithmetical concepts. In E. Cohors-Fresenborg & I. Wachsmuth (Eds.), *Proceedings of the 2nd PME International Conference,* 344–355.

Vergnaud, G. (1981). Quelques orientations théoriques et méthodologiques des recherches françaises en didactique des mathématiques. In Equipe de Recherche Pédagogique (Eds.), *Proceedings of the 5th PME International Conference, 2*, 7–17.

Vergnaud, G. (1982). A classification of cognitive tasks and operations of thought involved in addition and subtraction problems. In T. P. Carpenter, J. M. Moser, & T. A. Romberg (Eds.), *Addition and Subtraction: A cognitive perspective* (pp. 39–59). Hillsdale NJ, USA: Lawrence Erlbaum.

Vergnaud, G. (1983). Multiplicative structures. In R. Lesh & M. Landau (Eds.), *Acquisition of mathematics concepts and processes* (pp. 127–174). New York, USA: Academic Press.

Vergnaud, G. (1984). Problem solving and symbolism in the development of mathematical concepts. In B. Southwell, R. Eyland, M. Cooper, J. Conroy, & K. Collis (Eds.), *Proceedings of the 8th PME International Conference,* 27–38.

Vergnaud, G. (1987). About constructivism. In J. C. Bergeron, N. Herscovics, & C. Kieran (Eds.), *Proceedings of the 11th PME International Conference, 1*, 42–54.

Vergnaud, G. (l990). Epistemology and psychology of mathematics education. In J. Kilpatrick & P. Nesher (Eds.), *Mathematics and cognition* (pp. 14–30). Cambridge, UK: Cambridge University Press.

Verschaffel, L. (2002). Taking the modeling perspective seriously at the elementary school level: Promises and pitfalls. In A. D. Cockburn & E. Nardi (Eds.), *Proceedings of the 26th PME International Conference, 1*, 64–80.

Verschaffel, L., & De Corte, E. (1996). Number and arithmetic. In A. J. Bishop, K. Clements, C. Keitel, J. Kilpatrick, & C. Laborde (Eds.), *International handbook of mathematics education* (1, pp. 99–137). Dordrecht, The Netherlands: Kluwer.

Von Glasersfeld, E. (1981) Things, plurality and counting. In Equipe de Recherche Pédagogique (Eds.), *Proceedings of the 5th PME International Conference, 1*, 18–24.

Voutsina, C., & Jones, K. (2001). The micro-development of young children's problem solving strategies when tackling addition tasks. In M. van den Heuvel-Panhuizen (Ed.), *Proceedings of the 25th PME International Conference, 4*, 391–398.

Warren, E. (2003). Young children's understanding of equals: A longitudinal study. In N. A. Pateman, B. J. Dougherty, & J. T. Zilliox (Eds.), *Proceedings of the 27th PME International Conference, 4*, 379–386.

Warren, E. (2005). Young children's ability to generalise the pattern rule for growing patterns. In H. L. Chick & J. L. Vincent (Eds.), *Proceedings of the 29th PME International Conference, 4*, 305–312.

Watanabe, T. (1996). Understanding of multiplicative concepts. In L. Puig & A. Gutiérrez (Eds.), *Proceedings of the 20th PME International Conference, 1*, 152.

Watanabe, T., Anghileri, J., & Pesci, A. (1999). Understanding of multiplicative concepts. In O. Zaslavsky (Ed.), *Proceedings of the 23rd PME International Conference, 1*, 257.

Way, J., & Ayres, P. (2002). The instability of young students probability notions. In A. D. Cockburn & E. Nardi (Eds.), *Proceedings of the 26th PME International Conference, 4*, 393–400.

Womack, D., & Williams, J. (1998). Intuitive counting strategies of 5–6 year old children within a transformational arithmetic framework. In A. Olivier & K. Newstead (Eds.), *Proceedings of the 22nd PME International Conference, 4*, 185–192.

Wood, T., & McNeal, B. (2003). Complexity in teaching and children's mathematical thinking. In N. A. Pateman, B. J. Dougherty, & J. T. Zilliox (Eds.), *Proceedings of the 27th PME International Conference, 4*, 435–441.

Wright, B. (1998). Children's beginning knowledge of numerals and its relationship to their knowledge of number works: An exploratory, observational study. In A. Olivier & K. Newstead (Eds.), *Proceedings of the 22nd PME International Conference, 4*, 201–208.

Wright, R., & Gould, P. (2002). Using a learning framework to document students' progress in mathematics in a large school system. In A. D. Cockburn & E. Nardi (Eds.), *Proceedings of the 26th PME International Conference, 1*, 197–202.

Yackel, E. (2001). Explanation, justification and argumentation in mathematics classrooms. In M. van den Heuvel-Panhuizen (Ed.), *Proceedings of the 25th PME International Conference, 1*, 9–24.

AFFILIATIONS

Joanne Mulligan
Centre for Research In Mathematics and Science Education (CRiMSE)
Australian Centre for Educational Studies
Macquarie University
Sydney (Australia)
joanne.mulligan@mq.edu.au

Gerard Vergnaud
Équipe C3U, Laboratoire Paragraphe
Université Paris 8
2, rue de la Liberté
F 93526 Saint Denis cedex (France)
vergnaud@univ-paris8.fr

GUERSHON HAREL, ANNIE SELDEN, AND JOHN SELDEN

ADVANCED MATHEMATICAL THINKING

Some PME Perspectives

1. INTRODUCTION

In the early 1980s, to complement a previous PME emphasis on elementary mathematical thinking, some PME members, chiefly Gontran Ervynck and David Tall, wanted to consider "mathematics in school that led on to university mathematics and linked ... to the thinking of mathematicians" (David Tall, personal communication). The result was the formation of the Advanced Mathematical Thinking (AMT) Working Group[1] that met in 1986 to begin work on a book (Tall, 1991) of the same name. Thus, within PME, it was clear from the beginning that the full range of mathematical thinking from the later years of secondary school through formal axiomatic mathematics based on definition and proof would be included under the term *advanced mathematical thinking* (AMT).

Subsequently in other venues, the meaning of the phrase *advanced mathematical thinking* has been debated –should the term "advanced" refer to the mathematics, or to the thinking, or to both?[2] In fact, as Sternberg (1996) noted in his concluding chapter to a book devoted to the nature of mathematical thinking, there is not even consensus on what *mathematical thinking* is. However, in this chapter, we consider both perspectives, as was the intent of the founders of the PME AMT Working Group.

In our review of research on advanced mathematical thinking, we did not limit ourselves only to major contributions to *PME Proceedings*, such as plenaries, research fora, working groups, and research reports, but also took into account the vast array of short orals and posters. In addition, we considered related work in various journals and books, such as *Advanced Mathematical Thinking* (Tall, 1991).

It is clear that there has been a large PME research output on tertiary students' learning of a diverse array of specific topics. To take only a few examples, these range from calculus (e.g., Bezuidenhout & Olivier, 2000), linear algebra (e.g., Dorier, 1995; Maracci, 2003), and differential equations (e.g., Kwon, Cho, Ju & Shin, 2004; Artigue, 1992) to functions (e.g., DeMarois & Tall, 1999; Harel &

---

1 According to David Tall (personal communication), the idea to form a PME working group focusing on "advanced mathematical thinking" –as opposed to the "elementary mathematical thinking", that had characterized most of the then work of PME– arose from a proposal by Gontran Ervynck.

2 See, for example, Pimm (1995) or Selden and Selden (2005).

A. Gutiérrez, P. Boero (eds.), Handbook of Research on the Psychology of Mathematics Education: Past, Present and Future, 147–172.

Dubinsky, 1992), equivalence relations (e.g., Chin & Tall, 2001), and transfinite numbers (e.g., Penalva, Gaulin & Gutiérrez, 1996). In addition, mathematicians have been observed and interviewed regarding their teaching of various tertiary courses (e.g., Moreno & Azcárate, 1996; Nardi, 1999); university students have been surveyed regarding their views of teaching and learning mathematics (e.g., Forgaz & Leder, 1998); and PhD students' learning experiences have been explored (e.g., Duffin & Simpson, 2002; Moutsios-Rentzos & Simpson, 2005). However, due to space limitations and a desire to present more than the most minimal, telegraphic reviews, we have not attempted to survey the PME community's entire AMT output.

Our main focus will be a number of ideas that have emerged in considerations of advanced mathematical thinking and are widely used, or could be more widely used, in mathematics education research.[3] We begin with several theoretical considerations that were first introduced in the setting of advanced mathematics learning and have been influential in moving the entire field forward. These are: (a) The concept image/concept definition distinction (Section 2); (b) The role of definitions and the act of defining (Section 3); and (c) The process-object and procept views of concept construction/acquisition (Section 4).[4] Next in Section 5, we consider the small, but growing, body of research on the practices of mathematicians. Finally in Section 6, we address future research considerations.

2. CONCEPT IMAGE VERSUS CONCEPT DEFINITION

2.1 Making the Distinction between Concept Image and Concept Definition

It is perhaps surprising, given the acknowledged difference between the rather specialized if-and-only-if definitions of mathematical concepts, such as function or group, and the much more common, descriptive definitions of everyday concepts, such as car or democracy, that purely psychological research on concepts prior to the 1970s emphasized the less common, and somewhat artificial, if-and-only-if concepts. However, beginning with Eleanor Rosch's groundbreaking work suggesting that for every category (or concept), of whatever kind, one has a single representative prototype, alternatives to the classical psychological view have been proposed, including that each person has a schema, or perhaps a set of exemplars, for representing and identifying each concept that he/she knows (Murphy, 2004).

As psychologists were rethinking the nature and development of concepts in the late 1970s and early 1980s, some PME members turned their attention to the distinction between how mathematical concepts are defined and how they are used, especially by students more familiar with everyday concepts. Vinner and Hershkowitz (1980), in reference to geometry, introduced the terms *concept*

[3] For a different perspective on research in, and issues related to, advanced mathematical thinking, see Mamona-Downs and Downs (2002).

[4] While concept acquisition, formal definitions, and proof all have very important roles to play in AMT, except for some questions (Section 6.5), we have left consideration of research on proof largely to the separate chapter on that topic.

definition and *concept image*, in order to distinguish between a concept's formal, public definition, and an individual's corresponding mental structure consisting of all her/his associated examples, nonexamples, facts, and relationships. This distinction was further elaborated by Tall and Vinner (1981) in regard to limits and continuity. According to these authors, the term *concept image* describes an individual's total cognitive structure associated with a concept; this includes all the associated mental pictures, properties, and processes. One's concept image is built up over years through experience, changing as the individual meets new stimuli. The term *concept definition*, on the other hand, refers to a form of words used to specify a concept. A concept definition can be *personal* or *formal*. The latter is a concept definition that has been institutionalized by the mathematics community at large; the epsilon-delta definition of *limit* is an example.

Recently the Tall and Vinner (1981) paper was selected for inclusion in a volume of seventeen "classics" of the mathematics education research literature (Carpenter, Dossey & Koehler, 2004). Indeed, it is now quite common for researchers investigating students' conceptions to frame part of their discussion in terms of the concept image/concept definition distinction (e.g., Biza, Souyoul & Zachariades, 2005) and also to use it when communicating with teachers of tertiary mathematics (e.g., Edwards & Ward, 2004). Also, one normally differentiates between a *concept*, such as function, meaning its formal, public mathematical definition, and an individual's *conception*, meaning that person's private, mental understanding of it.

2.2 Enhancing Concept Images and Making Sense of Formal Concept Definitions

Students' concept images include, and often are based on, their prior knowledge, which they acquire through different experiences, including daily experience. Cornu (1981) calls them spontaneous conceptions. The tendency of many students to evoke (part of) their concept image, instead of the concept definition, when responding to a variety of related mathematical tasks is not necessarily bad; indeed in many situations, it is desirable to have and evoke rich concept images. However, many mathematical concepts, such as that of a uniformly convergent sequence of functions, are introduced to students at tertiary level via formal definitions, and the ability to use such definitions to produce examples and counterexamples is helpful in building one's concept image (Dahlberg & Housman, 1997).

One of the ways instruction attempts to enrich students' concept images is by helping them acquire the ability to visualize mathematical concepts. Dreyfus and Eisenberg (1990) showed that students experience major difficulties dealing with visual information in the form of graphs. Yet, research also shows that visualization can facilitate mathematical understanding (Presmeg, 1994). Further, even students who are mathematically mature and are able to think visually are reluctant to visualize mathematical concepts (Dreyfus & Eisenberg, 1986, 1990; Vinner, 1989). Eisenberg and Dreyfus compare visual processing with analytic processing and suggest several reasons for students' preference for the latter. One of the reasons for this reluctance, Dreyfus and Eisenberg suggest, is that teachers convey to their students –implicitly or explicitly– the belief that visual reasoning is inferior to analytic reasoning. Other scholars have arrived at similar conclusions (Presmeg, 1986; Vinner, 1989). Also, Zazkis, Dubinsky and Dautermann (1996) indicate that "perhaps the most harmful, yet quite common difficulty with visualization is that students have shown a lack of ability to connect a diagram with its symbolic representation", a process they and other scholars consider "an essential companion to visualization."

In constructing proofs, many resources, such as strategic knowledge, are called upon; however, it is usually a precondition that one be able to unpack the definitions of the concepts involved, including their logical structure. Tertiary students often have difficulty with this (Selden & Selden, 1995). Definitions need to become *operable* for an individual, that is, a student should be able to "focus on the properties required to make appropriate logical deductions in proofs" (Bills & Tall, 1998). Referring to their observations of students in a twenty-week Analysis course, they continue,

> We find that the struggle to make definitions operable can mean that some students meet concepts [such as least upper bound, continuity, Riemann integral] at a stage when the cognitive demands are too great for them to succeed, others never have operable definitions, relying on earlier experiences and inoperable concept images, whilst occasionally a concept without an operable definition can be applied in a proof by using imagery that happens to give the necessary information required in the proof. (p. 104)

In another Real Analysis study, students exhibited two distinct modes of handling formal definitions, either by *giving meaning* through consideration of (often visual) examples or by *extracting meaning* through manipulation of and reflection on the definition itself. To be successful with the first mode required ongoing reconstruction of personal ideas to focus on essential properties of the definition and to integrate the formal theory. While the latter mode avoided some pitfalls of the first, students could end up with a formal theory unconnected to informal imagery. Furthermore, students could be successful, or unsuccessful, using either mode (Pinto & Tall, 1999). Similar results of undergraduate students' use of these two approaches, referred to as *referential* and *syntactic*, have been observed in proof construction attempts (Alcock & Weber, 2005).

Some inquiry-based courses in which students are asked to prove most of the main results for themselves seem effective in promoting (accurate) use of definitions (Alcock & Simpson, 1999), but more research needs to be done on how tertiary students cope with formal definitions, on how to help students unpack, understand, and use definitions in proving assertions, and on how to help them distinguish between a definition and its equivalent versions arising from theorems. Students' difficulties in these areas are well documented (see, for example, Robert & Robinet, 1989, in relation to linear algebra, and Selden & Selden, 1987, in relation to abstract algebra).

In addition to the concept image/concept definition distinction, other aspects of definitions and defining have been considered.

3. THE ROLE OF DEFINITIONS AND DEFINING

By constructing and negotiating their own definitions, students can acquire more robust understandings of specific mathematical concepts. We discuss features of defining that rarely make their way into current textbooks. Specifically, we will address: (a) The distinction between mathematical and everyday definitions; (b) The dialectical interplay between defining and proving; and (c) Defining as organizing.

3.1 The Distinction between Mathematical and Everyday Definitions

Many tertiary mathematics students seem unaware of the distinction between dictionary definitions and mathematical definitions.[5] Of eight interviewed mathematics majors in a Real Analysis course, "only one student show evidence of what could be considered a mathematically acceptable understanding of the role of formal definitions" (Edwards, 1999, p. 207).

De Villiers (1998) has argued that students should be actively engaged in defining mathematical concepts. Quoting Freudenthal (1973, p. 458), he distinguishes two types of defining: (1) *Descriptive (a posteriori) defining* "outlines a known object by singling out a few characteristic properties." In this case, a concept has been known for some time and is only defined afterwards. (2) *Constructive (a priori) defining* that "models new objects out of familiar ones." Constructive defining takes place when a "given definition of a concept is changed through the exclusion, generalization, specialization, replacement or addition of properties to the definition so that a new concept is constructed in the process. In other words, a new concept is defined 'into being' " (De Villiers, 1998, p. 250). In a teaching experiment with Grade 10 students on descriptive defining, the aims were to help students realize that alternative definitions for the same concept (in this case, quadrilaterals such as a rhombus) are possible and that economical definitions can lead to shorter, easier proofs, as well as to help students' develop their ability to construct formal, economical definitions. Typically some student definitions were incomplete, but this afforded opportunities to provide counterexamples and discuss the need to provide sufficient information to ensure which geometric figure was being talked about.

Features of mathematical definitions that mathematicians value and that have been described in the mathematics education research literature include that they should be: (1) Existent (i.e., an example should exist); (2) Non-contradictory (i.e., internally consistent); (3) Unambiguous (i.e., define a unique concept); (4) Logically equivalent to other definitions of the same concept; (5) Hierarchical (i.e., depend only on basic or previously defined terms); and (6) Invariant under changes of representation (Shir & Zaslavsky, 2001, 2002). Also, definitions should: (7) Address the purpose for which they were invented; (8) Be well-defined; and (9) Be stated in a usable form (Mamona-Downs & Downs, 2002, p. 180). Other, not uniformly agreed upon, considerations include that definitions should be: (10)

---

[5] Dictionary definitions are also referred to as *descriptive*, *extracted*, or *synthetic*, whereas mathematical definitions are also referred to as *stipulated* or *analytic*.

Minimal (i.e., economical, with no superfluous conditions); (11) Elegant (a hard-to-articulate and subjective criterion); and (12) Easily comprehended by students (a pedagogical consideration).

To see how secondary mathematics teachers and top-level 12th grade students viewed such features of definitions, Shir and Zaslavsky (2001, 2002), as part of a larger study, constructed eight equivalent definitions of a square for their consideration first alone in response to a questionnaire and later in groups. Among the teachers there was little agreement on reasons for accepting or rejecting the proposed definitions, with 21% agreeing that "Of all the rectangles with a fixed perimeter, the square is the rectangle with the maximum area" and 92% agreeing that "A square is a quadrangle in which all sides are equal and all angles are 90°" were definitions. The authors suggest this activity, although designed as a research tool, has the potential of creating a rich learning environment able to facilitate students' discovery of different features of mathematical definitions.

3.2 The Dialectical Interplay between Defining and Proving

According to Lakatos (1961), there can be a dialectical interplay between concept formation, definition construction, and proof. To bring this interplay to students' awareness, one needs to design problem situations whose resolution requires definition construction –something that can be difficult. Following Lakatos (1961), Ouvrier-Buffet (2004) considered: Zero-definitions, tentative or "working definitions" emerging at the start of an investigation; and proof-generated definitions, directly linked to problem situations and attempts at proof.

In order to engage university students in zero-definition construction, Ouvrier-Buffet (2002) selected the mathematical concept of *tree* (giving it a neutral name), partly because there are many equivalent definitions (she lists seven), and in France formal definitions of tree are not presented in secondary school. She first gave several groups of students four examples and two nonexamples of trees, asking them to infer a definition. This was followed by a problem situation, namely, a request to prove: *Let G be a connected graph (i.e., a collection of vertices and edges, so that between any two vertices there is a path, that is, a sequence of vertices each joined to the next by an edge). Prove that G contains a spanning tree (i.e., a tree that is a subgraph and has the same vertex set as G)*, in order to allow students to return to, and possibly reconstruct, their original zero-definitions. Attempting the proof sometimes, but did not always, result in revised proof-generated definitions. In a subsequent zero-definition construction experiment, Ouvrier-Buffet (2004) chose the concept of *discrete straight line* (i.e., the discretization of a straight line, using a set of approximating pixels).

In particular instructional interventions, where justification and proof are expected, students' mathematical activities can lead to both descriptive and constructive definitions. The longitudinal study, now in its seventeenth year, by Maher and associates (see, for example, Maher & Speiser, 1997 or Maher, 2002) is an example. Video episodes from the study over the years –from their elementary school years to senior-high school and early university years– illustrate how in the process of attempting to explain their reasoning to their classmates or the teacher, the students articulated their images and later elaborated and presented them in symbolic expressions.

Many students at the secondary and post-secondary levels judge arguments by empirical or intuitive evidence rather than by strictly logical consideration (see, for example, Healy & Hoyles, 2000). Even first-year university mathematics students generally feel more comfortable when they are allowed to judge arguments empirically or intuitively rather than deductively (Finlow-Bates, Lerman & Morgan, 1993). As it is commonly difficult for students to appreciate the precision and economy of thought afforded by formal proof, it is likely that they experience similar difficulty with mathematical definitions –descriptive or constructive. The lack of such an appreciation may explain students' difficulties in distinguishing among axioms, definitions, and theorems. Vinner (1977) found that only about half of a group of University of California, Berkeley sophomores and juniors in mathematics correctly identified all of three statements about exponents as definitions, as opposed to theorems or laws or axioms. Linchevsky, Vinner and Karsenty (1992) found that only about one-fourth of their university mathematics majors in Israel understood that it is possible to have alternate definitions for concepts.

These studies speak to meta-proof topics. But meta-proof topics cannot be mastered without understanding proof topics themselves. In this case, the topics in question involve the meaning and role of axioms and definitions. These studies suggest a weak, or even absent, axiomatic proof scheme among mathematics majors –an observation that is consistent with findings of Harel and Sowder (1998).

We mentioned earlier Rosch's work suggesting that for every category (or concept) that one knows, one has a single prototype for representing and identifying that concept (Murphy, 2004). Alcock and Simpson (1999) showed that indeed students often seem to argue from particular examples they view as prototypical of a class of objects at hand rather than from the definition of that class. They demonstrated this finding in a study in Real Analysis. Students responded to the task "prove that x^n is convergent" not by showing that x^n satisfies the definition of convergence, but by arguing from particular examples of convergent sequences they seemed to view as prototypical of the set of convergent sequences.

3.3 Defining as Organizing

One can also view defining as a way of organizing concrete or mathematical situations. Asghari (2004), following Freudenthal's (1983) view that definitions "have been invented to organize the phenomena ... from the concrete world as well as from mathematics", conducted a study on definitions. He designed two contextual situations, one based on the standard definition of equivalence relation (involving a mad dictator, ten cities, a law about visiting, and a rectangular grid on which to represent the law), and another based on the definition of partition (involving the mad dictator, too much ink wasted on drawing up the laws, and a decree that officials must provide the least amount of information possible on each grid). For the first task, students, with no previous formal experience with equivalence relations or related concepts, were asked to come up with valid visiting laws and represent them on a rectangular grid of points; for the second task, they were to find the fewest grid examples so that the dictator could deduce the visiting law. In this finite context, several students came up with a new, unexpected, yet equivalent, definition of equivalence relation based on reflexivity and a concept of the students' own devising (the "box concept"). Also, see Asghari & Tall (2005).

In addition to knowledge about concept construction, what students gained from the above two approaches to definition construction (Asghari, 2004; Asghari & Tall, 2005; Ouvrier-Buffet, 2002, 2004), was experience in the mathematical practice of defining.[6] Although here we have concentrated on defining, there are other practices of mathematicians that are often considered advanced –visualizing, representing, generalizing, abstracting, synthesizing, axiomatizing, symbolizing, algorithmatizing, and proving.

At least in the development of geometrical thinking, as described by Van Hiele (1986), defining and organizing may be cognitively interdependent. Functioning at Level 2 (Analysis) involves viewing figures in terms of collections of properties. At this level, a geometric object is described by listing all the properties the student knows without distinguishing between those that are necessary and those that are sufficient. As students transition to Level 3 (Abstraction), sufficient conditions are selected to describe an object; meaningful definitions are created; and with these, logical implications and class inclusions, such as squares being a type of rectangle, are understood. In Level 4 (Formal Deduction), students recognize the difference among undefined terms, definitions, axioms, and theorems and can construct original proofs in Euclidean geometry (Clements & Battista, 1992). The full transition to AMT takes place in going to Level 5 (Rigor), at which students can reason abut relationships between formally defined constructs. (For more information on the Van Hiele levels, see the chapter by Owens and Outhred in this volume).

4. CONCEPT ACQUISITION

In addition to unpacking and understanding formal mathematical definitions and using defining activities, there are other ways of coming to know a concept, namely, through comparing its various equivalent definitions, through converting between its (multiple) representations (see Duval, 1999), through knowing its diverse properties, and through making connections to other concepts. Furthermore, an individual can have an *operational* (*process*) view of a given concept or an *structural* (*object*) view of that concept. By the former is meant a

---

[6] For a discussion of defining, framed in terms horizontal and vertical mathematizing, see Rasmussen, Zandieh, King and Teppo (2005).

more computational and procedural point of view, whereas by the latter is meant a more formal, static, and object-like point of view.[7]

The process-object and operational-structural distinctions have been extensively investigated and elaborated on, especially with respect to the concept of function (Breidenbach, Dubinsky, Hawks & Nichols, 1992; Harel & Kaput, 1991; Sfard, 1991). Both of these perspectives afford complementary ways of working with a concept, and a flexible student uses whichever view is appropriate for a given mathematical situation. The structural (object) view is more abstract and entails an implicit belief about the nature of mathematical entities –they are "objects" (at least metaphorically)– as suggested by the formal definitions of modern mathematics.

Below, we first consider the operational-structural distinction, and then proceed to the action-process-object-schema view of concept acquisition. This is followed by a discussion of procepts, proceptual thinking, and the role of symbols

4.1 Operational and Structural Conceptions

To arrive at the current Dirichlet (correspondence) and Bourbaki (ordered pair) definitions of the elusive concept of function took close to 300 years (Kleiner, 1989). Noting this, and the similar long historical evolution of other mathematical concepts such as number, Sfard (1987, p. 163) concluded that "most mathematical notions had been conceived operationally long before their structural definitions and representations were formulated"[8] and conjectured that "learning processes must follow a similar pattern."

Elaborating on this, Sfard (1991) noted that "the formation of a structural conception is a lengthy, often painfully difficult process" and postulated that it transpires in a hierarchy of three stages: Interiorization, condensation, and reification. At the interiorization stage a learner becomes skilled with computations and procedures (e.g., algebraic manipulations with a variety of specific functions). In the *condensation* phase, the learner becomes more capable of thinking of the process as a whole, without going into details (e.g., seeing a function in terms of input and output). While the first two stages of concept acquisition occur gradually, *reification* requires "an ontological shift –a sudden ability to see something familiar in a totally new light" (e.g., functions become objects, that is, they can be acted upon and transformed).

In this regard, Sfard (1989, 1992) has enunciated two pedagogical principles: (1) New concepts should not be introduced in structural terms. (2) A structural approach should not be adopted as long as the student can do without it. She further observed that "students' [initial] conceptions seem closer to operational

---

[7] In the literature, one can find two uses of the term *structural* – one refers to an object that has a structure on it, while the other refers to an object defined by an axiomatic structure (David Tall, personal communication).

[8] Here Sfard may implicitly be referring to mathematical notions occurring at school level or in early tertiary mathematics courses. Many mathematical concepts introduced to advanced undergraduate and graduate students today have not undergone such a long evolutionary process.

than to structural" and that many students, when introduced to concepts via formal (structural) definitions, may develop pseudostructural conceptions (Sfard, 1992, pp. 70-75). For example, in a curriculum introducing functions as sets of ordered pairs, high school students tended to associate functions with algebraic formulae, viewing them both as computational algorithms and as static relations (Sfard, 1989, p. 155).

While these principles and observations seem reasonable when applied to high school students or tertiary students in beginning or service mathematics courses, most advanced tertiary mathematics students are introduced to new concepts via formal, structural definitions and must somehow learn to cope with them (Alcock & Simpson, 1999). Indeed, a structural approach to concepts is essential to proof construction, and given the pace of most upper-level and graduate mathematics courses, there appears to be inadequate time to introduce most concepts in other than a structural way. Since mathematicians themselves quickly come to understand new structurally defined concepts, it would be interesting to investigate how they developed the ability to do so.

Since explicating the above operational-structural view of concept acquisition, Sfard (1996) has observed that this view is part of a larger theoretical "acquisition metaphor" and has contrasted it to the more recent "participation metaphor", in which discourse, communication, negotiation, and participation in a mathematical community are dominant. As she observed, both can contribute to our understanding of learning and teaching.

4.2 Action, Process, Object, and Schema

Dubinsky and colleagues (Dubinsky, Hawks & Nichols, 1989; Breidenbach et al., 1992; Asiala, Brown, DeVries, Dubinsky, Mathews & Thomas, 1996) have investigated the somewhat similar process-object distinction, expanding it to include four kinds of mental conceptions: Action, process, object, and schema (referred to as APOS). Questions of students' understanding of concepts are set within an extension of the Piagetian theory of reflective abstraction.

Four kinds of mental constructions are subsumed under reflective abstraction: Acts of interiorization, coordination, encapsulation, and generalization. *Interiorization* is the translation of a succession of material or mental actions into a repeatable whole. *Coordination* is construction of a new process from two or more existing processes. *Encapsulation* is the conversion of a dynamic process into a static object and is reminiscent of reification. *Generalization* is the application of an existing schema to a wider collection of phenomena (Dubinsky, 1991).

We again consider the concept of function. An action conception of function is held by students who treat functions as sequences of commands (actions) for them to perform; for example, interpreting $f(x) = x^2 + 1$ as "first square a given number, then add one". A *process* conception of function allows an individual to think of functions as receiving inputs, performing one or more operations on those inputs, and returning outputs. An *object* conception of function results when an individual, reflecting on operations applied to a process, "becomes aware of the process as a totality, realizes that transformations (whether they be actions or processes) can act on it" (Asiala, et al., 1996, p. 11). A *schema* is an individual mental construction connecting related processes and objects, and appears to be somewhat similar to one's concept image (Tall & Vinner, 1981), or to part of it. It should be noted that the notion of "schema" is a theoretical construct that has been used extensively by many PME scholars in offering conceptual models to account for students' mathematical behaviors, both in "elementary mathematics" and "advanced mathematics." One of the early uses of this construct by PME scholars was by Skemp (1985); his *varifocal theory* of cognitive concepts, in which a concept may be conceived as a global whole or at various levels of detail (Skemp, 1979), anticipated later ideas of schema-object construction.

Action conceptions, while extremely limited, "form the crucial beginning of understanding of a concept" and "activities designed to help students construct actions" form an important beginning of the pedagogical approach of Dubinsky et al. (Asiala, et al., 1996, p. 10). To get from an action to a process conception of function, one needs to reflect on and interiorize many repeatable actions, such as evaluating algebraic functions, until one sees a function as a transformation accepting inputs and producing outputs. To get from a process to an object conception, one needs to encapsulate the process into an object, that is, to see it as a "thing" and perform actions on it. Since moving flexibly between process and object conceptions is important, one must also be able to de-encapsulate an object view back to a process view.

The pedagogical approach taken by Dubinsky et al. is based upon the APOS view of concept acquisition. It consists of three components: Activities, class discussion, and exercises, referred to as the ACE Teaching Cycle. The activities, which usually take place in a computer lab, are "to provide students with an experience base." Building on these activities, there are classroom paper-and-pencil tasks done in small groups, followed by inter-group discussions to provide an opportunity for reflection. Finally, relatively traditional exercises are assigned for completion outside of class to reinforce the constructed ideas (Asiala et al., 1996, p. 14).

In addition to function, the APOS framework has been applied by Dubinsky, et al. to concepts ranging from group theory (Dubinsky, 1997) to infinity (Weller, Brown, Dubinsky, McDonald & Stenger, 2004).

4.3 Symbols and Procepts

What binds the operational (process) and structural (object) views together? Tall and colleagues suggest it is largely the mathematical symbolism that allows one to be able to go back and forth flexibly between these two conceptions in a variety of mathematical situations. In considering the duality of process and object, Gray and Tall (1991) observed that both are typically denoted using the same symbolism and conjectured that this ambiguity of notation allows successful mathematical thinkers to move flexibly between the two views. They coined the term *procept* for an amalgam of process and concept (object). Gray and Tall (1991) further noted that a beginning student typically first meets a concept as a process, then a symbolism is introduced for the product of that process, and finally that symbolism takes on the dual meaning of both process and product (object). They illustrated this idea with a range of examples: Going from the process of adding to the concept of sum (with 5+4 evoking both the counting on process and its result 9); to going from the process of tending to a limit to the concept of limit (both represented by the same notation $\lim_{x \to a} f(x)$). They also introduced the notion of the *proceptual divide*, noting (in the context of arithmetic) that all students are "initially given processes to carry out mathematical tasks but success eventually only comes not through being good at those processes, but by encapsulating them as part of a procept which solves the tasks in a more flexible way" (p. 77).

Explicating these ideas further mainly in the context of arithmetic, Gray and Tall (1994, pp. 117-121) distinguished between *process*, designating "the cognitive representation of a mathematical operation" and *procedure*, designating "a specific algorithm for implementing a process." They noted a "fundamental dichotomy between procedures and concepts, between things to do and things to know." They suggested that resolution of the conundrum of how anything can be both a process and an object at the same time "lies in the way professional mathematicians cope with this problem"; namely, "the mathematician simplifies matters by replacing the cognitive complexity of process-concept duality by the notational convenience of process-product ambiguity." Refining their ideas further, they proposed: "An *elementary procept* is an amalgam of three components: A *process* that produces a mathematical *object*, and a *symbol* that represents either the process or the object. ... A *procept* consists of a collection of elementary procepts that have the same object." For an individual, a symbol gradually comes to stand for a rich conceptual structure having both conceptual and procedural links –something referred to as *proceptual encapsulation*. Gray and Tall (1994) termed the associated flexible thinking, in which a vast array of mathematical ideas are compressed under a single symbol, *proceptual thinking*.

Continuing the explication of the role of symbols in proceptual thinking, Tall, Gray, Ali, Crowley, DeMarois, McGowen et al. (2001, pp. 81-85) observed that "mathematical symbols work in a very special and powerful way that involves a compression of knowledge", allowing one "to switch almost effortlessly from *doing* a process to *thinking* about a concept." Furthermore, the notion of procept "has been given increasingly subtle meaning since its first formulation (Gray & Tall, 1991). It is now seen mainly as a *cognitive* construct in which the symbol can act as a *pivot*, switching from a focus on process to compute or manipulate, to a concept that may be *thought* about as a manipulable entity."

Another perspective on mathematical symbols can be found in Dörfler (1991), who regards symbolic icons as concrete carriers that, for each individual suggest, but do not represent, meanings that are inherently unshareable. These meanings are seen as mental structures called *image schemata*, following Johnson (1987) and Lakoff (1987), and closely resemble the mental models of Johnson-Laird (1983). This view provides a non-verbal, non-propositional component of cognition that contrasts with a formal approach to mathematics that calls on verbal, propositional aspects of cognition. We suspect that in doing advanced mathematics these two components of cognition are integrated, with image schemata providing insight and intuition to guide one's verbal, propositional cognition. Mason and Johnston-Wilder (2004) comment that an implication of this position is that "teaching is not a matter of constructing and presenting learners with representations of ideas or ideals, but rather of bringing into their presence connections and images which then contribute to learners' construction of understanding" (pp. 201-202).

Also, a PME Working Group on Symbolic Cognition in Advanced Mathematics has recently been considering how mathematical signs and symbols "help us do mathematics, build intuitions, develop mathematical concepts and construct powerful mathematical ideas" (Hegedus, Tall & Eisenberg, 2004).

4.4 From Procepts to Advanced Mathematical Thinking

Tall et al. (2001, pp. 94-95) see a long route going from arithmetic to algebra to calculus to axiomatic mathematics with its formal definitions and proof.[9] "Different procepts operate in different ways, leading to the need for cognitive reconstruction" at various stages. While the "basic arithmetic symbols all have a dual meaning as process and concept" there are subtle differences. The sum of two whole numbers is another whole number, but division gives rise to an entirely new entity –fractions. Somewhat later, the shift from arithmetic to algebra leads to a new kind of procept, where the expression $2 + 3x$ is an "answer" with only the *potential* process of evaluation. The shift from algebra to calculus poses new problems, with limit symbols, such as $\sum_{n=1}^{\infty} 1/n^2$, indicating *potentially infinite* processes. However, at the formal level, procepts play a minor role. A notion, such as group, is not a procept, but rather a "bigger structure given by a definition that specifies the properties it must have. The processes to construct formal meaning are now *logical* processes, and the concepts are formally constructed. A further discontinuity, this time of major proportions, intervenes, signalling the step from 'elementary mathematics' of calculation and manipulation to 'advanced mathematics' of defining and proving."

Tall et al. (2001, p. 97) elaborated as follows, "The move from elementary to advanced mathematics requires a significant reconstruction in thinking. ... a complete shift in focus from the existence of perceived objects and symbols representing actions on objects to new theories based on specified *properties* of formally defined mathematical structures. ... Imagery is useful, even essential, for suggesting what kinds of definitions will be most useful and what theorems to prove. However the essential quality that makes advanced mathematical thinking different from elementary mathematics is the introduction of formal definitions and proofs."

---

9 Tall et al. (2001) is a summative article combining ideas from a broad range of earlier work, including his PME19 plenary (Tall, 1995) and specific results of many of his Ph.D. students.

A similar perspective was put forth by Edwards, Dubinsky and McDonald (2005, pp. 17-18): "Advanced mathematical thinking is thinking that requires deductive and rigorous reasoning about mathematical notions that are not entirely accessible to us through our five senses. ... [It] resides on a continuum of mathematical thought that seems to transcend, but does not ignore, the procedural experiences or intuitions of elementary mathematical thinking."[10] It would appear that, at least for some, advanced mathematical thinking has to do with the thinking, practices, and products of mathematicians. What do we know about these?

5. THE PRACTICES OF MATHEMATICIANS

Based on "an underlying assumption that a closer look at the practice of research mathematicians can reveal information of potential importance for mathematics education" (Misfeldt, 2003, p. 302), there is a small, but growing, body of research investigating mathematicians' writing, problem solving, and proving.[11] In an interview study of research mathematicians' uses of writing (whether with pencil-and-paper, blackboard, or computer), Misfeldt (2003) distinguished five functions of that writing: (1) Getting and trying out ideas and seeing connections, often written non-linearly using mainly symbolic notation; (2) Investigating more deeply and precisely in a linear fashion to check details, using a combination of natural language and symbolic notation;[12] (3) Saving information and ideas in a linearly ordered document for later access; (4) Communicating more developed ideas with colleagues; and (5) Producing a finished article for publication. While implications for students are unclear, it is possible that students' problem-solving attempts reflect (1) above and they should be encouraged to write, or rewrite, their results in more detail to make sure they are correct and can be read by others.

Burton (1999) undertook an interview study of the practices of seventy research mathematicians (thirty-five women, thirty-five men) with a focus on how they "come to know" mathematics, finding that collaborative research is more common than it previously was. The interviewed mathematicians were looking for connections with other areas of mathematics and spoke in terms of a sense of excitement, personal struggle, and achievement upon finding results, but for the most part, as teachers of tertiary mathematics they were not "giving learners a sense of the fun, excitement, [and] challenge which holds them in the discipline" (p. 139). (For more information, a theoretical model, and implications for learning school mathematics through enquiry, see Burton, 2004).

---

[10] Other perspectives on advanced mathematical thinking (Harel & Sowder, 2005) and advancing mathematical activity (Rasmussen et al., 2005) have been offered.

[11] There is also a growing body of research on mathematicians' teaching practices (e.g., Moreno & Azcárate, 1996; Nardi, 1999).

[12] Written proofs are organized linearly because they should be read, or checked, linearly (except for possible side excursions, such as looking up a definition). Unfortunately, many inexperienced students may believe proofs are also normally constructed linearly, but this is far from the actual practice of mathematicians.

While problem solving has been a concern of mathematics educators at least since Pólya's (1945) description of problem-solving processes, few studies have examined mathematicians' problem-solving behavior until recently. Working with secondary and tertiary students, Schoenfeld (1985) posited a framework for examining what people know and do as they work on mathematical problems of moderate difficulty –ones for which the solver does not have easy access to some procedure for solving the problem, but does have adequate background with which to make progress on it. Schoenfeld's framework considered: (a) Resources (e.g., skills, intuitions, facts, procedures about the problem domain); (b) Heuristics (e.g., drawing figures, introducing notation, reformulating the problem, working backwards); (c) Control (e.g., metacognitive acts such as planning, monitoring, assessing one's progress); and (d) Belief systems (e.g., about oneself, the topic, and mathematics that influence one's behavior). Using this framework to analyze task-based interviews, Schoenfeld (1985) found, for example, that naive problem solvers often "embarked on a series of computations without considering their utility and failed to curtail those explorations when (to the outside observer) it became clear that they were on a wild goose chase" (p. 316).

More recently, building on and extending the problem-solving work of others (e.g., Schoenfeld, 1985; DeBellis & Goldin, 1997; Hannula, 1999), Carlson (2000) and Carlson & Bloom (2005) proposed a multidimensional problem-solving framework based on interviews with twelve mathematicians. Their framework elucidates four phases of problem-solving behavior that may be repeated multiple times: (a) Orienting (e.g., sense making, organizing, constructing a personal representation of the problem); (b) Planning (conjecturing, imagining, evaluating), (c) Executing (e.g., constructing, computing); and (d) Checking (verifying, decision making). They also presented detailed characterizations of how resources, affect, heuristics, and monitoring interact with these four phases and influence the solution path of a solver.

Carlson and Bloom (2005) selected problems from basic geometry, algebra, and proportions that were challenging enough to engage mathematicians, would lead to a variety of solution paths, and were sufficiently complex to lead to dead ends and elicit strong affective responses. The mathematicians rarely solved problems by working through in linear fashion; their well-connected conceptual knowledge influenced all phases of their problem-solving and was helpful in accessing mathematical knowledge at the right moment; and effective management of frustration was an important factor in their persistence. Carlson and Bloom (2005) hope their insights will prove useful in attempts to promote effective problem-solving behavior in students.[13]

In a study of mathematicians' and students' proving, four undergraduates, who had recently completed their second course in abstract algebra, and four mathematicians, who regularly used group-theoretic concepts in their research, were interviewed about isomorphism (Weber & Alcock, 2004). The algebraists thought about groups in terms of group multiplication tables and also in terms of

[13] Within PME, there have also been studies of tertiary students' problem solving (e.g., Ferrari, 1997), but here we concentrated on the problem solving of mathematicians.

generators and relations, as well as having representations that applied to specific groups, such as matrix groups. In contrast, none of the undergraduates could provide a single intuitive description of a group; for them, it was a structure that satisfies a list of axioms. While all four undergraduates could give the formal definition of isomorphic groups, none could provide an intuitive description. To prove or disprove that two groups were isomorphic, these undergraduates said they would first compare the order (i.e., the cardinality) of the two groups. If the groups were of the same order, they would look for bijective maps between them and check whether these maps were isomorphisms –a generally ineffective strategy.

In another study comparing the proving behaviors of four undergraduates who had just completed abstract algebra and four doctoral students, who were writing dissertations on algebraic topics, it was found that the doctoral students, unlike the undergraduates, had knowledge of, and could quickly recall, theorems (e.g., the First Isomorphism Theorem) that are important when considering homomorphisms. When the doctoral students were asked why they used such sophisticated techniques, a typical response was, "Because this is such a fundamental and crucial fact that it's one of the first things you turn to" (Weber, 2001). It may be that undergraduates mainly study completed proofs and focus on their details, rather than noticing the importance of certain results and how they fit together.

It seems likely that further studies of the practices of mathematicians would provide additional insights and information.

6. FUTURE RESEARCH

6.1 Cognitive versus Social and Cultural Considerations

As can seen from the above review, with a few exceptions (see, for example, a recent *Mathematical Thinking and Learning* Special Issue, Selden & Selden, 2005), the theoretical frameworks of AMT studies –at least those reported in *PME Proceedings*– are largely cognitively, rather socially or culturally, oriented. This is rather surprising since "the role played by context has great implications for understanding the cognitive development that takes place within it. Context does not influence but essentially determines the kind of knowledge constructed (Lave, 1988)" (as quoted in Bottino & Chiappini, 2002, p. 764). It would be enlightening to incorporate social and cultural constructs, such as the notion of *field of experience*, offered by PME scholars, into AMT studies. *Field of experience* refers to "a sector of human culture which the teacher and students can recognize and consider unitary and homogeneous" and includes "the student's 'inner context' (experience, mental representations, procedures concerning the field of experience), the teacher's 'inner context' and the 'external context' (signs, objects, objective constraints specific of the field of experience" (Boero, Dapueto, Ferrari, Ferrero, Garuti, Lemut et al., 1995, p. 153). According to Boero, the notion of field of experience can be utilized to analyze the development of advanced mathematical thinking. Of particular importance are analyses of certain developments such as the cognitive and cultural roots of advanced mathematics concepts and skills in everyday experience (the concept of derivative in relation to one's physical experience of rate of change phenomena such as one's experience of "fastness" is an example). Another type of analysis concerns the transition to theories that organize the students' mathematical field of experience.

6.2 The Need for Explanatory Models

The notions of *concept definition* and *concept image* (Section 2) allow the articulation of significant lessons that mathematics educators have learned from experience and research during the last fifty years. For example, experience with the "new mathematics" of the 1960s and subsequent research in mathematics education suggested that many (especially younger) students do not learn mathematics by merely presenting them with clearly stated axioms, definitions, theorems, and formal proofs. Nor can students' mathematical knowledge be assessed merely by *personal concept definition* or by the degree their words match a *formal concept definition*.

These observations highlight an important need for basic research in mathematics education: The need for insightful explanatory models of students' mathematical behaviors (Clement, 2000). In particular, there is a need to address the question: Is a learner's current concept image a consequence of a specific teaching approach or is it an unavoidable construct due to the structure and limitation of the human brain, mind, culture, and social interaction? Núñez (2000) suggests that those limitations play a crucial role in mathematization processes. In particular, Lakoff and Núñez (2000) posit the argument that such cognitive phenomena as mathematical abstraction and logical inference manifest themselves naturally through largely unconscious bodily mental images. At the same time, this work shows that formal concept definitions (for example, the Weierstrass definitions of *limit* and *continuity*) fail to capture salient features of our bodily mental images. This work can potentially shed light on the source of the well-documented difficulties that students experience in constructing adequate concept images for formal concept definitions, especially those in the area of advanced mathematics.

There is another approach one can take here. In addition to investigating students' difficulties in constructing adequate concept images from formal concept definitions, one can note that mathematicians can, and do, independently construct such concept images for themselves, and ask how they developed this ability. Any answer should be helpful with our next question.

6.3 Teaching Practices

How can one help tertiary mathematics students independently learn to develop rich concept images[14] for formally defined concepts, such as group or locally compact space? The importance of this question arises from the large amount of mathematics tertiary students must learn as they near the end of their

[14] Here the work of Dahlberg and Housman (1997) or Watson and Mason (2002) might be helpful.

undergraduate work and the beginning of their graduate studies. It is difficult to see how additional time can be found for explicitly helping them develop concept images.

Can studies of mathematicians' practices (in research, in problem solving, in proving, in learning new mathematics for themselves, in teaching) inform the teaching of tertiary mathematics students? It seems that this sort of investigation might have some of the difficulties of expert-novice studies. We know where the students are,[15] we know where the mathematicians are, but we just don't know how to get tertiary mathematics students from where they are to where we want them to be.

Would the early introduction of appropriate defining activities help students see mathematics as more of a human activity, that is, as an endeavor in which they can participate, rather than as a passively received body of procedures and techniques developed by bright people of the past, such as Euclid or Newton? How do the constraints of the current university culture and practices (e.g., large lectures, an emphasis on research rather than teaching) contribute to: (1) Mathematicians' views of their students as learners of mathematics, and (2) Tertiary students' views of mathematics and their role in knowing/constructing it? Not all tertiary students are going into mathematics; many will be engineers or other professionals who use mathematics. Would it be informative to further study those professionals' uses of mathematics[16] and their views of mathematics?

6.4 The Transition between Secondary Education and Tertiary Education

The transition between secondary education and tertiary education has not been sufficiently examined. Robert and Speer (2001) raise the issue of discontinuities between these two levels. "Many of the differences in teaching (and learning) seem to depend upon whether students are typically asked to work on or with specific functions or mathematical objects, or whether the functions and objects are described generically. Are students asked to explore the properties of a particular function f (say $f(x) = 7x^3 + 5x^2 - 2x + 4$) or the properties of an arbitrary cubic?" Praslon (1999) examined these differences with respect to the concept of derivative and concluded that the experiences that students have in secondary school do not prepare them to deal with the problems posed to them at the tertiary level. (For more information on the secondary/tertiary transition and how universities are attempting to deal with it, see Selden, 2005, pp. 134-137).

Finally, we turn to a research suggestion for examining how to help tertiary students construct proofs.

---

15 For example, Harel and Sowder (1998) have produced a classification of student proof schemes, that is, "what constitutes ascertaining and persuading for that person" (p. 244).

16 For example, Roth (1999) has studied how scientists read and interpret graphs.

6.5 Enhancing Tertiary Students' Ability to Construct Proofs

The ability to construct proofs appears to be intrinsically valued by the mathematics community and also has great survival value for students, because typically students' understanding in upper-division mathematics courses is largely assessed through their construction of original proofs or proof fragments. Why this is so would be an interesting research topic itself, but is not our main concern here. What concerns us is that many tertiary students must construct proofs, but have difficulty doing so, and furthermore, this may be so even when students have some knowledge of logic and are aware that proofs are necessary (Balacheff, 1991).

There is, by now, considerable research on various components of proving that are often problematic for undergraduates (e.g., Weber, 2001), but a more modest literature on whether, which, or especially, how teaching interventions[17] might actually help. Perhaps the first requirement for extending such research is some kind of platform, or setting, in which student proof construction could be observed, but customary (teacher-centered, lecture-driven) upper-division mathematics courses are not really suitable for this.

6.5.1 A "platform" for observing students constructing proofs. One platform allowing better observation could be obtained by dividing a class into small groups and engaging them in in-class proof construction, perhaps with a roving teacher asking Socratic-type questions. The working of several groups could be recorded and analyzed over a number of class meetings. Teaching experiments of this kind[18] would allow observation of interventions, as well as the relationship between students' earlier and subsequent proof constructing attempts.

6.5.2 A need for a theoretical framework. Perhaps the second requirement of such research is a theoretical framework that is richer than the relevant concepts of the customary mathematical register, e.g., proofs by induction, cases, or contradiction, straight forward proofs, subproofs, and holes/gaps. We will suggest a few possible additions, but no doubt more will be found.

It appears that a proof can be divided into two parts that might be called the *formal-rhetorical* part and the *problem-centered* part, the construction of which require very different abilities. By the formal-rhetorical part we mean an extension of the idea of a proof framework (Selden & Selden, 1995) that requires a kind of knowledge somewhere between language and logic. It can also require manipulating formal definitions, but not genuine problem solving ability or a real understanding of the concepts. For example, if what is to be proved starts, "For all real numbers x ...", then in the proof, or subproof, one may write, "Let x be a real number" and x must be clearly independent of any previously mentioned variable. In the statement to be proved, x is a predicate calculus variable and can be thought

---

[17] For one alternative instructional treatment of proof using mathematical induction, see Harel (2002).

[18] Rasmussen, using a somewhat similar technique, captured how some undergraduates reinvented a standard tool (a phase line) in a student-centered differential equations course (Rasmussen et al., 2005, pp. 57-60).

of as a place holder or blank space, while in the proof, it can be though of as a "fixed, but arbitrary" real number.

A considerable portion of a written proof may consist entirely of such formal-rhetorical sentences. After this portion has been dealt with, what remains (if anything) will require real understanding of the concepts and problem solving ability in the sense of Schoenfeld (1985) –that remaining portion is what might be called the problem-centered part. In some proofs that tertiary students are asked to construct, the rhetorical part dominates, e.g., in much of elementary set theory. In other proofs, the problematic part dominates, e.g., in much of Euclidean geometry. In still other proofs, both parts have an important role, and dealing with the rhetorical part first, may serve to expose the "real problem", e.g., in some of real analysis. Also, constructing the formal-rhetorical and problem-centered parts of proofs seems to call for different kinds of knowledge, and hence of teaching.

In observing students constructing proofs, it might also be useful to gauge the hardness of the proofs being constructed. This appears to depend partly on what is in the students' minds and partly on which proofs they are asked to construct. As to what is in the students' minds, one might examine *multi-concept maps*, something like concept maps,[19] except centered on a number of related concepts and theorems (instead of on a single concept) that the teacher knows are related to the theorem (or sequence of theorems) at hand. Regarding the hardness of the proof itself, one might start by looking at levels of subproof or subconstruction.

Additionally, some students believe the order in which various parts of the proof are constructed should be that of the final text, that is, one constructs a proof from top to bottom, as if one were reading it. In attempting to construct some proofs, this belief may present an insurmountable obstacle. This suggests student beliefs[20] about proof construction might also be profitably investigated.

Finally, one might investigate *hidden junctures* (essential to the construction of proofs, but not appearing in the final text) or the use of intuition. Here one might distinguish between visual/spatial and what one might call *relational* intuition, that is, intuition based on familiarity with relevant concepts, definitions, and theorems. An example of the latter sometimes occurs when students can prove trigonometric identities without understanding that the identities are about circular functions.

REFERENCES

Alcock, L., & Simpson, A. (1999). The rigour prefix. In O. Zaslavsky (Ed.), *Proceedings of the 23rd PME International Conference, 2*, 17–24.

Alcock, L., & Weber, K. (2005). Referential and syntactic approaches to proof: Case studies from a transition course. In H. L. Chick & J. L. Vincent (Eds.), *Proceedings of the 29th PME International Conference, 2*, 33–40.

Artigue, M. (1992). Functions from an algebraic and graphic point of view: Cognitive difficulties and teaching practices. In G. Harel & E. Dubinsky (Eds.), *The concept of function: Aspects of*

[19] For example, concept maps were used to investigate tertiary students' cognitive development of the function concept in a developmental Intermediate Algebra course (McGowen & Tall, 1999).

[20] Tertiary students' self-efficacy beliefs about the learning of mathematics (Risnes, 1998) and their views of mathematics and its uses (Patronis, 1999) have been studied.

epistemology and pedagogy. MAA Notes (25, pp. 109–132). Washington, DC, USA: Mathematical Association of America.

Asghari, A. H. (2004). Organizing with a focus on defining: A phenomenographic approach. In M. J. Høines & A. B. Fuglestad (Eds.), *Proceedings of the 28th PME International Conference, 2*, 63–70.

Asghari, A. H., & Tall, D. (2005). Students' experience of equivalence relations: A phenomenographic approach. In H. L. Chick & J. L. Vincent (Eds.), *Proceedings of the 29th PME International Conference, 2*, 81–88.

Asiala, M., Brown, A., DeVries, D. J., Dubinsky, E., Mathews, D., & Thomas, K. (1996). A framework for research and curriculum development in undergraduate mathematics education. In J. Kaput, A. H. Schoenfeld, & E. Dubinsky (Eds.), *Research in Collegiate Mathematics Education, II* (pp. 1–32). Providence, RI, USA: American Mathematical Society.

Balacheff, N. (1991). The benefits and limits of social interaction: The case of mathematical proof. In A. J. Bishop, S. Mellin-Olsen, & J. van Dormolen (Eds.), *Mathematical knowledge: Its growth through teaching* (pp. 175–192). Dordrecht, The Netherlands: Kluwer.

Bezuidenhout, J., & Olivier, A. (2000). Students' conceptions of the integral. In T. Nakahara & M. Koyama (Eds.), *Proceedings of the 24th PME International Conference, 2*, 73–80.

Bills, L., & Tall, D. (1998). Operable definitions in advanced mathematics: The case of the least upper bound. In A. Olivier & K. Newstead (Eds.), *Proceedings of the 22nd PME International Conference, 2*, 104–111.

Biza, I., Souyoul, A., & Zachariades, T. (2005). *Conceptual change in advanced mathematical thinking*. Presentation at the CERME4 Conference, Sant Feliu de Guíxols, Spain. Retrieved from http://cerme4.crm.es/Papers definitius/14/biza.pdf

Boero, P., Dapueto, C., Ferrari, P., Ferrero, E., Garuti, R., Lemut, E., et al. (1995). Aspects of the mathematics-culture relationship in mathematics teaching-learning in compulsory school. In L. Meira & D. Carraher (Eds.), *Proceedings of the 19th PME International Conference, 1*, 151–166.

Bottino, R., & Chiappini, G. (2002). Advanced technology and learning environments: Their relationships within the arithmetic problem-solving domain. In L. D. English (Ed.), *Handbook of international research in mathematics education* (pp. 757–786). Mahwah, NJ, USA: Lawrence Erlbaum.

Breidenbach, D., Dubinsky, E., Hawks, J., & Nichols, D. (1992). Development of the process conception of function. *Educational Studies in Mathematics, 23*, 247–285.

Burton, L. (1999). The practices of mathematicians: What do they tell us about coming to know mathematics? *Educational Studies in Mathematics, 37*, 121–143.

Burton, L. L. (2004). *Mathematicians as enquirers: Learning about learning mathematics*. Berlin, Germany: Springer.

Carlson, M. P. (2000). A study of the mathematical behaviors of mathematicians: The role of metacognition and mathematical intimacy in problem solving. In T. Nakahara & M. Koyama (Eds.), *Proceedings of the 24th International PME Conference, 2*, 137–144.

Carlson, M. P., & Bloom I. (2005). The cyclic nature of problem solving: An emergent multidimensional problem solving framework. *Educational Studies in Mathematics, 58*, 45–76.

Carpenter, T. P., Dossey, J. A., & Koehler, J. L. (Eds.). (2004). *Classics in mathematics education research*. Reston, VA, USA: NCTM.

Chin, E.-T., & Tall, D. (2001). Developing formal mathematical concepts over time. In M. van den Heuvel-Panhuizen (Ed.), *Proceedings of the 25th PME International Conference, 2*, 241–248.

Clement, J. (2000). Analysis of clinical interviews: Foundations and model viability. In A. E. Kelly & R. Lesh (Eds.). *Handbook of research design in mathematics and science education* (pp. 547–590). Mahwah, NJ, USA: Lawrence Erlbaum.

Clements, D. H., & Battista, M. T. (1992). Geometry and spatial reasoning. In D. A. Grouws (Ed.), *Handbook of research on mathematics teaching and learning* (pp. 420–494). New York, USA: Macmillan.

Cornu, B. (1981). Apprentissage de la notion de limite: Modèles spontanés et modèles propres. In Equipe de Recherche Pédagogique (Eds.), *Proceedings of the 5th PME International Conference*, 322–326.

Dahlberg, R. P., & Housman, D. L. (1997). Facilitating learning events through example generation. *Educational Studies in Mathematics*, *33*, 283–299.

DeBellis, V. A., & Goldin, G. A. (1997). The affective domain in mathematical problem-solving. In E. Pehkonen (Ed.), *Proceedings of the 21st PME International Conference*, *2*, 209–216.

DeMarois, P., & Tall, D. (1999). Function: Organizing principle or cognitive root? In O. Zaslavsky, (Ed.), *Proceedings of the 23rd PME International Conference*, *2*, 257–264.

De Villiers, M. (1998). To teach definitions in geometry or to teach to define? In A. Olivier & K. Newstead (Eds.), *Proceedings of the 22nd PME International Conference*, *2*, 248–255.

Dörfler, W. (1991). Meaning: Image schemata and protocols. Plenary Lecture. In F. Furinghetti (Ed.), *Proceedings of the 15th PME International Conference*, *1*, 17–32.

Dorier, J.-L. (1995). Meta level in the teaching of unifying and generalizing concepts in mathematics. *Educational Studies in Mathematics*, *29*, 175–197.

Dreyfus, T., & Eisenberg, T. (1986). On visual versus analytical thinking in mathematics. In Univ. of London Inst. of Educ. (Eds.), *Proceedings of the 10th PME International Conference*, *1*, 152–158.

Dreyfus, T., & Eisenberg, T. (1990). On difficulties with diagrams: Theoretical issues. In G. Booker, P. Cobb, & T. N. Mendicuti (Eds.), *Proceedings of the 14th PME International Conference*, *1*, 27–34.

Dubinsky, E. (1991). Reflective abstraction in advanced mathematical thinking. In D. Tall (Ed.), *Advanced mathematical thinking* (pp. 95–123). Dordrecht, The Netherlands: Kluwer.

Dubinsky, E. (Guest Ed.). (1997). An investigation of students' understanding of abstract algebra (binary operations, groups and subgroups) and the use of abstract structures to build other structures (through cosets, normality and quotient groups) [special issue]. *The Journal of Mathematical Behavior*, *16*(3).

Dubinsky, E., Hawks, J., & Nichols, D. (1989). Development of the process conception of function by pre-service teachers in a discrete mathematics course. In G. Vergnaud, J. Rogalski, & M. Artigue (Eds.), *Proceedings of the 13th PME International Conference*, *1*, 291–298.

Duffin, J., & Simpson, A. (2002). Encounters with independent graduate study: Changes in learning style. In A. D. Cockburn & E. Nardi (Eds.), *Proceedings of the 26th PME International Conference*, *2*, 305–312.

Duval, R. (1999). Representation, vision and visualization: Cognitive functions in mathematical thinking. Basic issues for learning. In F. Hitt & M. Santos (Eds.), *Proceedings of the 21st PME–NA Conference*, *1*, 3–26.

Edwards, B. (1999). Revisiting the notion of concept image/concept definition. In F. Hitt & M. Santos (Eds.), *Proceedings of the 21st PME–NA Conference*, *1*, 205–210.

Edwards, B. S., Dubinsky, E., & McDonald, M. A. (2005). Advanced mathematical thinking. *Mathematical Thinking and Learning*, *7*, 15–25.

Edwards, B. S., & Ward, M. B. (2004). Surprises from mathematics education research: Student (mis)use of mathematical definitions. *American Mathematical Monthly*, *111*(5), 411–424.

Finlow-Bates, K., Lerman, S., & Morgan, C. (1993). A survey of current concepts of proof held by first year mathematics students. In I. Hirabayashi, N. Nohda, K. Shigematsu, & F.-L. Lin (Eds.), *Proceedings of the 17th PME International Conference*, *1*, 252–259.

Ferrari, P. L. (1997). Action-based strategies in advanced algebraic problem solving. In E. Pehkonen (Ed.), *Proceedings of the 21st PME International Conference*, *2*, 257–264.

Forgaz, H. J., & Leder, G. C. (1998). Affective dimensions and tertiary mathematics students. In A. Olivier & K. Newstead (Eds.), *Proceedings of the 22nd PME International Conference*, *2*, 296–303.

Freudenthal, H. (1973). *Mathematics as an educational task*. Dordrecht, The Netherlands: Reidel.

Freudenthal, H. (1983). *Didactical phenomenology of mathematical structures*. Dordrecht, The Netherlands: Reidel.

Gray, E., & Tall, D. (1991). Duality, ambiguity and flexibility in successful mathematical thinking. In F. Furinghetti (Ed.), *Proceedings of the 15th PME International Conference*, *2*, 72–79.

Gray, E., & Tall, D. (1994). Duality, ambiguity, and flexibility: A "proceptual" view of simple arithmetic. *Journal for Research in Mathematics Education, 25*, 116–140.

Hannula, M. (1999). Cognitive emotions in learning and doing mathematics. In G. Philippou (Ed.), *Proceedings of the Eighth European Workshop on Research on Mathematical Beliefs* (pp. 57–66). Nicosia, Cyprus: University of Cyprus.

Harel, G. (2002). The development of mathematical induction as a proof scheme: A model for DNR-based instruction. In S. R. Campbell & R. Zazkis (Eds.), *Learning and teaching number theory: Research in cognition and instruction* (pp. 185–212). Westport, CT, USA: Ablex.

Harel, G., & Dubinsky, E. (Eds.). (1992). *The concept of function: Aspects of epistemology and pedagogy* (MAA Notes, Vol. 25). Washington, DC, USA: Mathematical Association of America.

Harel, G., & Kaput, J. (1991). The role of conceptual entities and their symbols in building advanced mathematical concepts. In D. Tall (Ed.), *Advanced mathematical thinking* (pp. 82–94). Dordrecht, The Netherlands: Kluwer.

Harel, G., & Sowder, L. (1998). Students' proof schemes; Results from exploratory studies. In A. H. Schoenfeld, J. Kaput, & E. Dubinsky (Eds.), *Research in collegiate mathematics education. III* (pp. 234–283). Providence, RI, USA: American Mathematical Society.

Harel, G., & Sowder, L. (2005). Advanced mathematical-thinking at any age: Its nature and its development. *Mathematical Thinking and Learning, 7*, 27–50.

Healy, L., & Hoyles, C. (2000). A study of proof conceptions in algebra. *Journal for Research in Mathematics Education, 31*(4), 396–428.

Hegedus, S. J., Tall, D. O., & Eisenberg, T. (2004). Symbolic cognition in advanced mathematics. In M. J. Høines & A. B. Fuglestad (Eds.), *Proceedings of the 28th PME International Conference, 1*, 274.

Johnson, M. (1987). *The body in the mind.* Chicago, IL, USA: University of Chicago Press.

Johnson-Laird, P. N. (1983). *Mental models.* Cambridge, UK: Cambridge University Press.

Kleiner, I. (1989). Evolution of the function concept: A brief survey. *The College Mathematics Journal, 20*, 282–300.

Kwon, O. N., Cho, K., Ju, M.-K., & Shin, K. (2004). Category of students' justification and its relation to the structure of argumentation: An analysis of discourse in systems of linear differential equation. In M. J. Høines & A. B. Fuglestad (Eds.), *Proceedings of the 28th PME International Conference, 1*, 352.

Lakatos, I. (1961). *Essays in the logic of mathematical discovery.* Unpublished PhD dissertation, Cambridge University, Cambridge, UK.

Lakoff, G. (1987). *Women, fire and dangerous things.* Chicago, IL, USA: University of Chicago Press.

Lakoff, G., & Núñez, R. E. (2000). *Where mathematics comes from: How the embodied mind brings mathematics into being.* New York, USA: Basic Books.

Lave, J. (1988). *Cognition in practice.* Cambridge, UK: Cambridge University Press.

Linchevsky, L., Vinner, S., & Karsenty, R. (1992). To be or not to be minimal? Student teachers' views about definitions in geometry. In W. Geeslin & K. Graham (Eds.), *Proceedings of the 16th PME International Conference, 2*, 48–55.

Maher, C. A. (2002). How students structure their own investigations and educate us: What we've learned from a fourteen year study. In A. D. Cockburn & E. Nardi (Eds.), *Proceedings of the 26th PME International Conference, 1*, 31–46.

Maher, C. A., & Speiser, R. (1997). How far can you go with block towers? In E. Pehkonen (Ed.), *Proceedings of the 21st International PME Conference, 4*, 174–181.

Mamona-Downs, J., & Downs, M. (2002). Advanced mathematical thinking with a special reference to reflection on mathematical structure. In L. D. English (Ed.), *Handbook of international research in mathematics education* (pp. 165–195). Mahwah, NJ, USA: Lawrence Erlbaum.

Maracci, M. (2003). Difficulties in vector space theory: A compared analysis in terms of conceptions and tacit models. In N. A. Pateman, B. J. Dougherty, & J. Zilliox, (Eds.), *Proceedings of the 27th PME International Conference, 3*, 229–236.

Mason, J., & Johnston-Wilder, S. (Eds.). (2004). *Fundamental constructs in mathematics education.* London, UK: Routledge Falmer.

McGowen, M., & Tall, D. (1999). Concept maps & schematic diagrams as devices for documenting the growth of mathematical knowledge. In O. Zaslavsky (Ed.), *Proceedings of the 23rd PME International Conference*, *3*, 281–288.

Misfeldt, M. (2003). Mathematicians' writing. In N. A. Pateman, B. J. Dougherty, & J. Zilliox (Eds.), *Proceedings of the 27th PME International Conference*, *2*, 301–308.

Moreno, M., & Azcárate, C. (1996). Teaching differential equations to chemistry and biology students: An overview on methodology of qualitative research. A case study. In L. Puig & A. Gutiérrez (Eds.), *Proceedings of the 20th PME International Conference*, *4*, 11–18.

Moutsios-Rentzos, A., & Simpson, A. (2005). The transition to postgraduate study in mathematics: A thinking styles perspective. In H. L. Chick & J. L. Vincent (Eds.), *Proceedings of the 29th PME International Conference*, *3*, 329–336.

Murphy, G. L. (2004). *The big book of concepts*. Cambridge, MA, USA: A Bradford Book, The MIT Press.

Nardi, E. (1999). Using semi-structured interviewing to trigger university mathematics tutors' reflections on their teaching practices. In O. Zaslavsky (Ed.), *Proceedings of the 23rd PME International Conference*, *3*, 321–328.

Núñez, R. (2000). Mathematical idea analysis: What embodied cognitive science can say about the human nature of mathematics. In T. Nakahara & M. Koyama (Eds.), *Proceedings of the 24th PME International Conference*, *1*, 3–22.

Ouvrier-Buffet, C. (2002). An activity for constructing a definition. In A. D. Cockburn & E. Nardi (Eds.), *Proceedings of the 26th PME International Conference*, *4*, 25–32.

Ouvrier-Buffet, C. (2004). Construction of mathematical definitions: An epistemological and didactical study. In M. J. Høines & A. B. Fuglestad (Eds.), *Proceedings of the 28th PME International Conference*, *3*, 473–480.

Patronis, T. (1999). An analysis of individual students' views of mathematics and its uses: The influence of academic teaching and other social contexts. In O. Zaslavsky (Ed.), *Proceedings of the 23rd PME International Conference*, *4*, 9–16.

Penalva, C., Gaulin, C., & Gutiérrez, A. (1996). The use of cognitive maps for analyzing the understanding of transfinite numbers. In L. Puig & A. Gutiérrez (Eds.), *Proceedings of the 20th PME International Conference*, *1*, 229.

Pimm, D. (1995). The advance party. *Educational Studies in Mathematics*, *29*, 97–122.

Pinto, M. M. F., & Tall, D. (1999). Student construction of formal theory: Giving and extracting meaning. In O. Zaslavsky (Ed.), *Proceedings of the 23rd PME International Conference*, *4*, 65–72.

Pólya, G. (1945). *How to solve it: A new aspect of mathematical method.* Princeton, NJ, USA: Princeton University Press.

Praslon, F. (1999). Discontinuities regarding the secondary/university transition: The notion of derivative, as a special case. In O. Zaslavsky (Ed.), *Proceedings of the 23rd PME International Conference*, *4*, 73–80.

Presmeg, N. C. (1986). Visualization and mathematical giftedness. *Educational Studies in Mathematics*, *17*, 297–311.

Presmeg, N. C. (1994). The role of visually mediated processes in classroom mathematics. *Zentralblatt für Didaktik der Mathematik*, *26*(4), 114–117.

Rasmussen, C., Zandieh, M., King, K., & Teppo, A. (2005). Advancing mathematical activity: A practice-oriented view of advanced mathematical thinking. *Mathematical Thinking and Learning*, *7*, 51–73.

Risnes, M. (1998). Self-efficacy beliefs as mediators in math learning: A structural model. In A. Olivier & K. Newstead (Eds.), *Proceedings of the 22nd PME International Conference*, *4*, 49–56.

Robert, A., & Robinet, J. (1989). *Quelques résultats sur l'apprentissage de l'alègbre linéaire en première anné de DEUG.* (Cahiers de Didactique des Mathématiques, 52). Paris, France: IREM, Université de Paris 7.

Robert, A., & Speer, N. (2001). Research on the teaching and learning of calculus/elementary analysis. In D. Holton (Ed.), *The teaching and learning of mathematics at university level* (pp. 283–299). Dordrecht, The Netherlands: Kluwer.

Roth, W.-M. (1999). Professionals read graphs (imperfectly?). In F. Hitt & M. Santos (Eds.), *Proceedings of the 21st PME–NA Conference, 1*, 385–391.

Schoenfeld, A. H. (1985). *Mathematical problem solving*. San Diego, CA, USA: Academic Press.

Selden, A. (2005). New developments and trends in tertiary mathematics education: Or, more of the same? *International Journal of Mathematical Education in Science and Technology, 2–3*, 131–147.

Selden, A., & Selden, J. (1987). Errors and misconceptions in college level theorem proving. In J. Novak (Ed.), *Proceedings, Second International Seminar on Misconceptions and Educational Strategies in Science and Mathematics* (3, pp. 456–470). Ithaca, NY, USA: Cornell University

Selden, A., & Selden, J. (Guest Eds.). (2005). Advanced mathematical thinking [special issue]. *Mathematical Thinking and Learning, 7*(1).

Selden, J., & Selden, A. (1995). Unpacking the logic of mathematical statements. *Educational Studies in Mathematics, 29*(2), 123–151.

Sfard, A. (1987). The conceptions of mathematical notions: Operational and structural. In J. C. Bergeron, N. Herscovics, & C. Kieran (Eds.), *Proceedings of the 11th PME International Conference, 3*, 162–169.

Sfard, A. (1989). Transition from operational to structural conception: The notion of function revisited. In G. Vergnaud, J. Rogalski, & M. Artigue (Eds.), *Proceedings of the 13th PME International Conference, 3*, 151–158.

Sfard, A. (1991). On the dual nature of mathematical conceptions, *Educational Studies in Mathematics, 22*, 1–36.

Sfard, A. (1992). Operational origins of mathematical objects and quandary of reification – The case of function. In G. Harel & E. Dubinsky (Eds.), *The concept of function: Aspects of epistemology and pedagogy*. MAA Notes (25, pp. 59–84). Washington, DC, USA: Mathematical Association of America.

Sfard, A. (1996). On acquisition metaphor and participation metaphor for mathematics learning. In C. Alsina, J. M. Alvarez, B. Hodgson, C. Laborde, & A. Pérez (Eds.), *8th International Congress on Mathematical Education. Selected lectures* (pp. 397–411). Sevilla, Spain: S.A.E.M. 'Thales'.

Shir, K., & Zaslavsky, O. (2001). What constitutes a (good) definition? The case of a square. In M. van den Heuvel-Panhuizen (Ed.), *Proceedings of the 25th PME International Conference, 4*, 161–168.

Shir, K., & Zaslavsky, O. (2002). Students' conceptions of an acceptable geometric definition. In A. D. Cockburn & E. Nardi (Eds.), *Proceedings of the 26th PME International Conference, 4*, 201–208.

Skemp, R. R. (1979). *Intelligence, learning, and action*. London, UK: Wiley.

Skemp, R. R. (1985). A progress report. In L. Streefland (Ed.), *Proceedings of the 9th PME International Conference*, 447.

Sternberg, R. J. (1996). What is mathematical thinking? In R. J. Sternberg & T. Ben-Zeev (Eds.), *The nature of mathematical thinking* (pp. 303–318). Mahwah, NJ, USA: Lawrence Erlbaum.

Tall, D. (Ed.). (1991). *Advanced mathematical thinking*. Dordrecht, The Netherlands: Kluwer.

Tall, D. (1995). Cognitive growth in elementary and advanced mathematical thinking. Plenary lecture. In L. Meira & D. Carraher (Eds.), *Proceedings of the 19th PME International Conference, 1*, 61–75.

Tall, D., Gray, E., Ali, M. B., Crowley, L., DeMarois, P., McGowen, M., et al. (2001). Symbols and the bifurcation between procedural and conceptual thinking. *Canadian Journal of Science, Mathematics and Technology Education, 1*(1), 81–104.

Tall, D., & Vinner, S. (1981). Concept image and concept definition with particular reference to limits and continuity. *Educational Studies in Mathematics, 12*, 151–169.

Van Hiele, P. M. (1986). *Structure and insight: A theory of mathematics education*. Orlando, FL, USA: Academic Press.

Vinner, S. (1977). The concept of exponentiation at the undergraduate level and the definitional approach. *Educational Studies in Mathematics, 8*, 17–26.

Vinner, S. (1989). The avoidance of visual considerations in calculus students. *Focus on Learning Problems in Mathematics, 11*(2), 149–156.

Vinner, S., & Hershkowitz, R. (1980). Concept images and common cognitive paths in the development of some simple geometrical concepts. In R. Karplus (Ed.), *Proceedings of the 4th PME International Conference*, 177–184.

Watson, A., & Mason, J. (2002). Extending example spaces as a learning/teaching strategy in mathematics. In A. D. Cockburn & E. Nardi (Eds.), *Proceedings of the 26th PME International Conference, 4*, 378–385.

Weber, K. (2001). Student difficulty in constructing proofs: The need for strategic knowledge. *Educational Studies in Mathematics, 48*, 101–119.

Weber, K., & Alcock, L. (2004). Semantic and syntactic proof productions. *Educational Studies in Mathematics, 56*, 209–234.

Weller, K., Brown, A., Dubinsky, E., McDonald, M., & Stenger, C. (2004). Intimations of infinity. *Notices of the AMS, 51*, 741–750.

Zazkis, R., Dubinsky, E., & Dautermann, J. (1996). Coordinating visual and analytic strategies: A study of students' understanding of the group D4. *Journal for Research in Mathematics Education, 27*, 435–457.

AFFILIATIONS

Guershon Harel
Department of Mathematics - 0112
University of California at San Diego
La Jolla CA 92093-0112 (U.S.A.)
harel@ucsd.edu
http://www.math.ucsd.edu/~harel

Annie Selden
Department of Mathematical Sciences
New Mexico State University
P.O. Box 30001, Dept. 3MB
Las Cruces, NM 88003-8001 (U.S.A.)
aselden@emmy.nmsu.edu

John Selden
Department of Mathematical Sciences
New Mexico State University
P.O. Box 30001, Dept. 3MB
Las Cruces, NM 88003-8001 (U.S.A.)
jselden@emmy.nmsu.edu

MARIA ALESSANDRA MARIOTTI

PROOF AND PROVING IN MATHEMATICS EDUCATION

INTRODUCTION

Nowadays, differently to ten years ago, there seems to be a general consensus on the fact that the development of a sense of proof constitutes an important objective of mathematical education, so that there seems to be a general trend towards including the theme of proof in the curriculum. Take, for instance, the following quotation.

> Reasoning and proof are not special activities reserved for special times or special topics in the curriculum but should be a natural, ongoing part of classroom discussions, no matter what topic is being studied. (NCTM, 2000, p. 342)

I wonder whether these words would have been possible only a few years ago, and still now the idea of "proof for all" claimed in this quotation is not a view that most teachers hold, even in countries where there is a longstanding tradition of including proof in the curriculum. I'm thinking of my country, Italy, but also, as far as I know, France or Japan. In fact, the main difficulties encountered by most students have lead many teachers to abandon this practice and prompted passionate debate amongst math educators, which has produced a great number of studies. Proof has also been a constant theme of discussion in the PME community and at PME conferences, which has given rise to a large number of Research Reports, although not at the same rate every year (the reader can find a useful, although not yet complete, collection of references at the site http://www.lettredelapreuve.it/).

The debate is far from being closed and has generated a number of research questions which have evolved in the decades, also in accordance with an evolution of the general trend of Mathematics education research. A quick overview of PME contributions on the theme of proof –probably not dissimilarly from what happened for other themes– shows a move away from early studies, focussed on students' (and more rarely teachers') conceptions of proof, and generally speaking on difficulties that pupils face in coping with proof and proving, towards more recent studies where researchers present and discuss opinions on whether and how is it possible to overcome such difficulties through appropriate teaching interventions. As a general trend, it is possible to observe a change in the methodology: Reports

A. Gutiérrez, P. Boero (eds.), Handbook of Research on the Psychology of Mathematics Education: Past, Present and Future, 173–204.

on teaching experiments[1] have increased while reports discussing quantitative analysis based on questionnaires have decreased, though questionnaires and quantitative analysis remain the main methods in large scale investigations, when nationwide investigations or cross cultural comparisons are carried out. We will return to this point in later.

An exemplar of earlier studies is the classic research report presented by Fischbein and Kedem (1982). Repeatedly quoted and subsequently re-discussed, this study focused on the crucial tension between the empirical and formal approach to proof.

Exemplars of recent studies centred on teaching experiments can be found among the number of reports concerning the use of Dynamic Geometry Environments: A specific section will be devoted to discussing these.

The variety and the complexity of the PME contributions, differently related to proof, required a drastic selection in order to give a reasonable account in the space of a chapter and within the limits of my capacity: I therefore apologize for the unavoidable incompleteness.

The discussion is organized according to three main streams of research, identified by three main categories of research questions, which I summarize as follows:

Proof at school. What is the status of proof at school? This quite general question is formulated differently in different studies, but the general characteristic aim consists in searching for a global view that captures widespread phenomena and possible correlations between them.

Students' difficulties. The general issue concerns the study of students' difficulties, and it refers to two main questions, roughly corresponding to describing and to interpreting students' behaviours in proving tasks. What are the main difficulties that students face in relation to proof? Which might be the origin of such difficulties?

Teaching interventions. Is it possible to overcome the difficulties that students meet in relation to proof? How can teaching interventions be designed? What general suggestions can be given?

Before starting the discussion I'd like to share with the reader some introductive reflections. As clearly pointed out by Balacheff (2002/04), the epistemological perspective taken by the researcher is not always made explicit, and this can be considered one of the main reasons for the failure of communication: Instead of correctly fuelling the debate, contributions risk becoming blocked in the impasse of misunderstanding.

Epistemological issues are not often directly addressed in the Research Reports presented at PME Conferences. Nonetheless the centrality of these issues in the debate was clearly discussed by Gila Hanna at PME20 Conference (Hanna, 1996) and two papers have explicitly dealt with them in the recent past (Godino & Recio, 1997; Reid, 2001). Both contributions focus, in different ways, on the differences in the meaning of the term proof as it appears in people's use of this word. The first

---

[1] This term is used in a broader, but consistent, sense in respect to Steffe and Thompson (2000) to indicate research projects based on classroom practice.

paper takes a wide perspective, describing some of the meanings of the term proof in different contexts, such as Mathematics and mathematical foundations research, sciences, and Mathematics class. The second paper focuses on the domain of Mathematics education research, where different usages of the term proof are identified. While I refer to these papers, together with more recent contributions (Balacheff, 2002/04; Reid, 2005), for an explicit comparison between different perspectives, I will try to make my position explicit through a short introduction that might facilitate understanding of what I am going to present in the following sections.

AN EPISTEMOLOGICAL PERSPECTIVE

Proof in the history of mathematics culture

Taking a biologic metaphor, a historic and epistemological analysis throughout the centuries highlights different "mutations of proof", following the evolution and systematisation of Mathematics knowledge.

Although Mathematics cannot be reduced to theoretical systems, its theoretical nature certainly constitutes a fundamental component. As Hilbert and Cohn Vossen clearly point out in the introduction to their book *Geometry and the Imagination*, Mathematics is characterised by a twofold nature: Intuitive understanding on the one hand and a systematic order within logical relations on the other hand.

> In Mathematics ... we find two tendencies present.
> On the one hand, the tendency towards abstraction seeks to crystallise the logical relations inherent in the maze of material that is being studied, and to correlate the material in a systematic and orderly manner.
> On the other hand, the tendency towards intuitive understanding fosters a more immediate grasp of the objects one studies, a live rapport with them, so to speak, which stresses the correct meaning of their relations. (Hilbert & Cohn-Vossen, 1932)

Actually a theoretical perspective of Mathematics has historic roots that lead us to the ancient book of Euclid's *Elements* and its particular way of presenting the "corpus" of knowledge, which since then has become a paradigm of scientific discourse. Euclid's exposition was characterised by a particular modality, which appeared as a brilliant solution to a delicate problem, as Proclo expressed it:

> Now it is difficult, in each science, both to select and arrange in due order the elements from which all the rest proceeds, and into which all the rest is resolved. (...) In all these ways Euclid 's system of elements will be found to be superior to the rest. (Heath, 1956, vol. I, pp. 115-116)

The crucial point seems to be a suitable order in which a corpus of knowledge may be expressed and communicated. The problem of the transmission of knowledge was solved by Euclid in a very peculiar way: Rather than in terms of "revelation", the elements were transmitted according to "logic arguments", that is through what has been called a "proof". As already mentioned, since then the need for particular arguments in communicating mathematical knowledge became a shared practice and a relevant part of the Mathematics culture.

This basic reference to Euclid is not sufficient and it can be even misleading when used to outline the complex nature of what is and has been called proof in past centuries. Nevertheless, it is interesting to remember that, although crucial contributions were possible, mostly neglecting requirements of rigour, the need for validation within the frame of an acceptable script of arguments appeared recurrently. An interesting example is offered by the case of Thabit ibn Qurra (826-900) who, in his book entitled *Correction of problems of algebra by geometric proofs* aims to provide acceptable, i.e. geometrical, justifications of the algorithms previously given by qu'al-Kawarizmi (Abdeljaouad, 2002).

In the history of Mathematics it is possible to observe a regularity in the successive phases of development in a given area: After an initial flourishing of ideas and methods a second phase occurs (sometimes separated from the first by a long gap) in which systematisation and reorganization is accomplished, aimed at making the corpus of knowledge acceptable and usable within the community of mathematicians. This social dimension, after the individual creative part of Mathematics development, has a crucial role, which has often been stressed and cannot be forgotten. The standards of acceptability are changeable and subject to different constraints which vary according to different variables, the first being the different areas of the discipline.

Focussing on Geometry, one of the salient features of the structure of Euclid's *Elements* is certainly its logical structure –the hypothetical / deductive structure– although this definitely differs from the "deductive structure of logic derivation within a formal theory" (Rav, 1999, p. 29). The main difference lies in the fact that, contrary to what happens within a formal theory, in the practice of Mathematics deduction depends on understanding and on prior assimilation of the meaning of the concepts from which certain properties are to follow logically. This is the sense in which Euclid's work must be interpreted: Deductive arguments are to be considered as means of fostering understanding of the whole Geometry and relating new properties to indubitable facts.

The style of rationality introduced by Euclid has become a prototype for all kinds of science, and the power of this method may be related to its treatment of truth.

A twofold criterion of truth characterises the structure of Euclid's *Elements*: Evidence, on which principles are assumed, and consistency, on which the truth of derived knowledge is based. In this framework a deep unity relates organisation of knowledge to understanding: Organisation becomes functional to understanding, which consequently becomes strictly tied to the constraints of acceptability and validation shared within a given community that will become a scientific community.

A crucial point that I like to stress is that Euclid's *Elements* accomplish a twofold aim: On the one hand the need for understanding and on the other hand the need for validity, i.e. to be accepted by a community. These two main aspects seem to be recognised as being characteristic of a theoretical corpus and can be found in most of the discussions about the nature and the function of proof. Let us take for instance the following quotation from the classic paper Hanna (1989a):

> Mathematicians accept a new theorem only when some combination of the following holds:
> They understand the theorem (that is, the concepts embodied in it, its logical antecedents, and its implications) and there is nothing to suggest it is not true;
> The theorem is significant enough to have implication in one or more branches of mathematics, and thus to warrant detailed study and analysis;
> The theorem is consistent with the body of accepted results;
> The author has an unimpeachable reputation as an expert in the subject of the theorem.
> There is a convincing mathematical argument for it, rigorous or otherwise, of a type they have encountered before. (p. 21-22)

Despite the crucial change of perspective that led mathematicians at the beginning of the last century to a radical revision of the idea of truth, the relationship between understanding and acceptability of mathematical statements has not dramatically changed in the centuries and still constitutes a characterising element of this discipline.

The slow elaboration of the idea of rigour, which had its climax at the end of the nineteenth century, has a counterpart in the development of the ever more complex relationship between two fundamental moments of the production of mathematical knowledge: The formulation of a conjecture, as the core of the production of knowledge, and the systematisation of such knowledge within a theoretical corpus (Mariotti, 2001b). This leads one to recognise a deep continuity between the development of knowledge and its systematisation within a theoretical "corpus"; between aspects relevant in the communication process, such as the need for understanding, and aspects related to the fact that knowledge is a shared cultural product, such as the need for acceptability.

Certainly the issue of understanding, and in particular the issue of the relationship between proof as a hypothetical-deductive argument and its explaining function, is crucial. Different opinions are possible, according to the relevance given to the distance between the semantic level, where the truth (the epistemic value) of a statement is fundamental, and the formal / logical level, where only the logical validity of an argument is concerned.

Although the logical dependence of a statement in respect to axioms and theorems of the theory is considered, the issue of understanding arises inasmuch as it refers to the links between the meanings involved in both the statement and the arguments. On the one hand, these links may not necessarily be expressed through the structure of logic consequence; on the other hand, when required, it is impossible to formulate and prove the logical link between two statements without any reference to meanings.

In other terms, in spite of the fact that the epistemic value has no relevance at the theoretical level, it is impossible to conceive a practice of mathematical proof without any reference to the semantic level. From both an epistemological and a cognitive point of view, it seems impossible to make a clear separation between the semantic and the theoretical level, as required by a purely formal perspective.

> To expose, or to find, a proof people certainly argue, in various ways, discursive or pictorial, possibly resorting to rhetorical expedients, with all the resources of conversation, but with a special aim ... that of letting the interlocutor see a certain pattern, a series of links connecting chunks of knowledge. (Lolli, 1999)

As a consequence, from the cognitive point of view, in spite of the fact of its theoretical autonomy, proof is strictly related to semantics. The explanation function of proof is fundamental, because it provides the support needed for understanding, but this function depends on the semantics of the statements and the truth value attributed to them.

The two basic elements of proof, arising from this short discussion, the explanation function and the need for acceptability, are expressed very effectively by Maturana, as quoted by Reid (2005):

> [...] the observer accepts or rejects a reformulation [...] as an explanation according to whether or not it satisfies an implicit or explicit criterion of acceptability [...]. If the criterion of acceptability applies, the reformulation [...] is accepted and becomes an explanation, the emotion or mood of the observer shifts from doubt to contentment, and he or she stops asking over and over again the same question. As a result, each [...] criterion for accepting explanatory reformulations [...] defines a domain of explanations, [...]. (Maturana, 1988, p. 28)

The discussion so far aimed to share with the reader the deep sense of complexity and, to some extent, the fleetingness of the idea of proof, when thought of as a living phenomenon. Such complexity, together with its centrality in mathematics practice, has fuelled a passionate debate, but has also generated a rich and varied collection of research studies. As anticipated in the introduction, the following discussion is divided into three directions, which I'd like to propose as different paths by which to enter the domain of research on proof and proving.

PROOF IN THE CURRICULUM

The first direction concerns contributions that aim to provide a description of the status of proof at school and in relation to the curriculum. These contributions are integrated and sometimes intermingled with those concerning students' conceptions of proof, but they seem to be born of the urgency to capture and describe the relevance of particular phenomena in terms of frequency or diffusion across different contexts.

Although there are few studies concerning teachers and these are very often limited to prospective teachers, currently most of the studies in this area report on students' responses to proof tasks. Some of them are more oriented towards giving a general picture of students' views on proof, through large-scale nationwide investigations (see for instance the seminal work of Hoyles, 1997 and Healy & Hoyles, 1998), followed by a number of successive research projects (Küchemann & Hoyles, 2001, 2002; Hoyles, Healy, Küchemann, 1995-2003). The main results of these studies highlight the recurrent difficulty that students face with proof: The difficulty emerges of controlling the complex relationship between mathematical validation, rooted in the frame of a theoretical system, and common sense validation, rooted in empirical verification (facts versus logical implications). Not only young pupils, but also high school and university students do not seem able to give mathematically adequate answers. In describing and classifying the answers, the effect of schooling has been investigated, and interesting aspects concerning the influence of the curriculum emerged (Hoyles, 1997).

The case of the research projects carried out in the UK represents a paradigm, but also an exception; only a few examples exist of large-scale nationwide studies of such a kind. Investigations in this direction are highly demanding due to the huge amount of data to be processed, but also due to the intrinsic complexity of their design, which needs to express both the specificity of a given country and the generality of comparable questions.

A recent effort in this direction was presented at PME29 Conference (Lin, 2005). Generally speaking, studies aimed at accomplishing cross-cultural comparison in my opinion constitute a promising direction of investigation. In this respect, other interesting approaches have been proposed (Knipping, 2001) that are complementary to large scale investigations and focalised on comparing specific teaching cultures regarding proof, for further discussion see (Mariotti, in press).

Aimed at sketching a global picture, large-scale studies have been profoundly inspired by previous studies on students' conceptions of proof and at the same time provide new and rich data on this issue. In this sense, these studies can be considered strictly related to more analytic investigations aimed at obtaining a better insight into cognitive processes related to "proof" and "proving". The following section is devoted to this theme.

PROOF IS DIFFICULT: DIFFERENT APPROACHES TO STUDENTS' CONCEPTION OF PROVING

As it is not possible to give a comprehensive account of the different contributions, what I will try to do is discuss two main perspectives that generate different directions of research. In so doing it is my intention to offer a possible framework for a virtual debate with the reader.

- On the one hand, the researcher takes a broad perspective, according to which different ways of thinking are described and classified as "proof". The main source is the analysis of students' production in solving problems where recurrent behaviours can be identified.
- On the other hand, starting from an explicitly epistemological perspective which recognizes a specific status of a *mathematical formal proof*, the researcher describes and explains difficulties and obstacles encountered by students in relation to this specific idea of proof.

Analysis and classification of students' reasoning: The proof schemes

A paradigmatic example of the first type of analysis is provided by the research studies carried out by Harel and Sowder and based on the notion of a "proof scheme", first presented in a research report at PME20 (Harel & Sowder, 1996).

The individual's perspective is taken and the researchers finally outline a comprehensive map summarizing the full description of the taxonomy (see Harel & Sowder, 1998, and Harel, 1999, 2001, for further explanations). In the last elaborations of the model the categories emerging from the interpretation of empirical data have been supported by historical and epistemological analysis[2].

The interesting characteristic of this kind of investigation is the combination of a detailed analysis of students' production with the need to maintain the unity of the issue in focus. The successive elaborations of this model describe students' ways of reasoning, mainly in the solution of given problems, thus providing a highly refined classification of what are called "proof schemes". The authors formulate an explicit definition of the process of proving (of which a proof can be considered a product) (Harel & Sowder, 1998):

> Proving is the process employed by an individual [...] to remove or create doubts about the truth of an assertion.
> The process of proving includes two sub-processes: *Ascertaining* and *persuading*. (p. 241)

As the authors explain, ascertaining is the process an individual employs to remove her or his own doubts, whilst persuading is the process employed to remove others' doubts.

According to this definition, different types of reasoning are described. A proof might analyse a single case, establish the formal truth of a theorem, explain a statement, test a problematic hypothesis or be purely a ritual procedure devoid of any sense except maybe its status of expected answer.

Different observable phenomena are related to each other, so that different students' answers are interpreted as sharing common features, leading the authors to define them as different ways of thinking, each of which is referred to a proving process. As pointed out by Harel, the term *proof* is largely referred to any kind of argument, and "need not connote mathematical proof" (Harel & Sowder, 1996, p. 60). Thus, different kinds of arguments are all recognized as strictly related so as to be classified as products of particular *proof schemes*.

Classic epistemological perspective

In contrast to what I have just presented, other studies originate in the epistemological distinction between mathematical proof and other forms of proving processes. As already mentioned, one of the classic contributions on this theme

2 It is important to remind that, starting from this model and according to general pedagogical assumptions, a complex teaching project was set up, aiming to make students' proof schemes evolve (PUPA - Proof Understanding, Production and Appreciation).

was by Fischbein and Kedem (1982). In the same vein as other studies investigating the tension between intuitive and mathematical thinking (Fischbein, 1987), the issue of proof was addressed in the general perspective, concerning the potential conflict between an *empirical approach* and a *formal approach*.

Besides direct acquisition of information that is mostly related to factual evidence and attained through experience, human culture has developed a complex way of obtaining information and knowledge, which is not direct, but is rather mediated by means such as language, logic and reasoning. As a consequence of this mediation, the structural unity between cognition and adaptive reactions has been broken:

> Knowledge through reasoning becomes a relatively autonomous kind of activity, not directly subordinated to the adaptive constraints of the behaviour of human beings. (Fischbein, 1987, p. 15)

In particular, as claimed by the authors (Fischbein & Kedem, 1982; Fischbein, 1982), crucial differentiation occurs between empirical verification and logical deduction, so that their relationship becomes very problematic.

The comparison between truth evaluation in terms of factual verification and logical validity in terms of deductive inferences leads one to consider the effect of a factual confirmation of the validity of a statement; of course different attitudes can be described according to an empirical approach and to the theoretical approach: Despite the fact that a formal proof confers a general validity to a mathematical statement, further checks seem to be desirable, in order to confirm that validity (Fischbein, 1982). The reasonable conclusion is that the discrepancy between empirical verification (typical of common behaviour) and deductive reasoning (typical of theoretical behaviour) is recognized as a source of difficulties. These findings have been confirmed by other studies (for instance, Vinner, 1983) and the tension between empirical and theoretical ways of supporting or rejecting the truth of a statement have been investigated further. The issue of generality clearly emerged from these studies in its twofold complexity: Not only do students seem not to realize that empirical verifications (measures, for instance) cannot be directly generalized, but conversely they may not grasp the generality of a deductive argument, strictly related to the use of a single drawing. A first discussion on the potentialities of a Dynamic Geometry Environment in respect to these issues can be found in (Chazan, 1988); as we will see in a later section, this theme has been further elaborated and discussed in the subsequent years.

Argumentation versus proof

The possible discrepancy, described above, between the empirical and the theoretical point of view has been developed and radicalised by Duval (1989, 1992/93), who stresses the distinction between different approaches to proof, outlining an opposition between *argumentation* and *proof*.

In one of his classic papers (Duval, 1992/93), the author carries out an accurate analysis of the nature and the status of the discourse that people use to support the truth or the falsehood of a particular statement; the comparison between discourses in different domains, and in particular in mathematics practice. The author claims a neat distinction between what is commonly referred to as *argumentation* and what is referred to as *mathematical proof*. Argumentation may be regarded as a process in which the discourse is developed with the specific aim of making an interlocutor change the epistemic value given to a particular statement; in short, argumentation consists in whatever rhetoric means are employed in order to convince somebody of the truth or the falsehood of a particular statement. On the contrary, proof consists in a logical sequence of implications that derive the theoretical validity of a statement.

> Une argumentation ne fonctionne pas d'abord sur le statut des propositions mais sur leur contenu. [An argumentation does not firstly function on the status of the propositions, rather on their content]. (Duval, 1989, p. 234)

Duval certainly holds a very radical position, nonetheless he focuses on a crucial point: The difference between the semantic level, where the epistemic value of a statement is fundamental, and the theoretical level where, in principle, only the validity of a statement is concerned. The assumption that at the theoretical level the logical dependence of a statement in respect to axioms and theorems of the theory is independent from the epistemic value that one attributes to the propositions in play leads Duval to recognize a cognitive rupture between *argumentation* and *proof*. Coherently, Duval stresses the relevance of this issue from an educational point of view, both in explaining difficulties met by students and inspiring the organization of a coherent educational activity (Duval, 1991).

According to Duval, the rupture between the two levels (the semantic and the theoretical) may be irretrievable, so that the conception of proof as a process that aims to convince the interlocutor (as the author says, "to affect the epistemic value of a statement") may conflict with the requirements of a mathematical proof.

As clearly discussed in Balacheff (1999), such a conflict may become an epistemological obstacle (Brousseau, 1997) that students have to overcome in order to grasp the very idea of proof in mathematics. In fact, the learner has to make sense of the difference between argumentation and proof, without rejecting one for the other. Argumentation as experienced in everyday practice has to be consciously brought back into the mathematical classroom; but achieving a theoretical perspective means becoming aware of the particular nature of mathematics validation, so that particular argumentative competencies that naturally emerge in social interaction might appear inadequate and, for this reason, are likely to be overcome.

Overcoming the dichotomy: The notion of Cognitive Unity

The main point that emerges from the previous discussion seems to be how to manage the possible rupture and the consequent possible conflict between argumentation and proof.

Of course a preliminary question arises: Is it possible to overcome this rupture?

A critical reflection is needed to at least understand, if not conciliate, different epistemologies.

In this perspective, interesting studies have been carried out with the aim of clarifying the relationship between mathematical proofs and the process of producing arguments. These studies do not deny the distinction between argumentation and mathematical proof, but are centred on the idea of a possible continuity rather than a rupture between them. This idea has subsequently been elaborated into the notion of Cognitive Unity, which seems to present great potentialities and which I'd like to discuss below.

In the context of a long term teaching experiment that exploited the semantically rich field of experience (Boero, Dapueto, Ferrari, Ferrero, Garuti, Lemut, Parenti, Scali, 1995) of sun shadows, interesting results came to light concerning students' production of conjectures (Boero, 1994; Boero et al., 1995) and the argumentation accompanying it. The teaching experiments were part of a long-term experiment aiming to introduce pupils to Geometry and were based on the solution of an open-ended problem, requiring both a conjecture and its proof. Clear evidence was found of different kinds of argumentative processes appearing in the solution. Further investigations demonstrated that when the phase of producing a conjecture had shown a rich production of arguments that aimed to support or reject a specific statement, it was possible to recognize an essential continuity between these arguments and the final proof; such continuity was referred to as Cognitive Unity:

> - during the production of the conjecture, the student progressively works out his/her statement through an intense argumentative activity functionally intermingling with the justification of the plausibility of his/her choices;
> - during the subsequent statement proving stage, the student links up with this process in a coherent way, organizing some of the justifications ("arguments") produced during the construction of the statement according to a logical chain. (Boero, Garuti, Lemut & Mariotti, 1996, p. 113)

Although the notion of Cognitive Unity emerged within the limits of a very particular teaching experiment and as part of a specific teaching project, it immediately showed its potential, suggesting new directions of investigation. If the first results supported a sort of "continuity" (as the authors called it), further investigation brought evidence of a possible gap between the arguments supporting the production of a conjecture and the proof validating it.

> We defined as *gap between the exploration of the statement and the proving process* the distance between the arguments for the plausibility of the conjecture, produced during the exploration of the statement, and the arguments, which can be exploited during the proving process. (Garuti, Boero & Lemut, 1998, p. 347)

The term Cognitive Unity, firstly coined to express a hypothesis of continuity, was later redefined to express the possible congruence between the argumentation phase and the subsequent proof produced, clearly assuming that congruence may or may not occur.

The main strength of this construct is that of providing a way to escape the rigid dichotomy setting argumentation against proof: The possible distance between argumentation and proof is not denied but also not definitely assumed to be an obstacle; in this perspective, the essential irretrievable distinction between argumentation and proof is substituted by focussing on analogies, without forgetting the differences. This position opened the way to a new approach where the complex relationship between argumentation and proof is taken as an object of research and the notion of Cognitive Unity can be used as a means to structure the investigation.

Proof and theory

A further element aimed at clarifying the status of proof in relation to argumentation has been elaborated (Mariotti, Bartolini Bussi, Boero, Ferri & Garuti, 1997). Proof is traditionally considered in itself, as if it were possible to isolate a proof from the statement to which it provides support, and from the theoretical frame within which this support makes sense. When one speaks of proof, all these elements, although not always mentioned, are actually involved at the same time, and it is not possible to grasp the sense of a *mathematical proof* without linking it to the other two elements: A *statement* and overall a *theory*.

In their practice, mathematicians prove what they call "true" statements, but "truth" is always meant in relation to a specific theory. From a theoretical perspective, the truth of a valid statement is drawn from accepting both the hypothetical truth of the stated axioms and the fact that the stated rules of inference "transform truth into truth".

> A statement B can be a theorem only relatively to some theory; it is senseless to say that it is a theorem (or a truth) in itself: Even a proposition like '2+2=4' is a theorem in a theory A (e.g., some fragment of Arithmetic). (Arzarello, in press)

Generally speaking, for students it does not seem spontaneous to reach such a theoretical perspective on truth, which on the contrary becomes automatic and unconscious for the expert. For a mathematician, the existence and the reliability of a theoretical framework within which the proof of a statement is situated is unquestionable and tacitly assumed, even when it is not made explicit. On the contrary, for novices, the idea of a truth as *theoretically situated* may be difficult to grasp; however, this way of thinking cannot be taken for granted and its complexity cannot be ignored. In particular, the confusion between an *absolute* and a *theoretically situated* truth, corresponding to the two main functions of proof – explication and validation– may have serious consequences.

> In my eyes it would even be an error of epistemological character to let students believe, by a sort of Jourdain effect, that they are capable of producing a mathematical proof when all they have done is argue. (Balacheff, 1999)

Thus, in order to remember the contribution given by each of the different components involved in producing a theorem, the following characterization of Mathematical Theorem was introduced, where a proof is conceived as part of a system of elements:

> The existence of a reference theory as a system of shared principles and deduction rules is needed if we are to speak of proof in a mathematical sense. Principles and deduction rules are so intimately interrelated so that what characterises a Mathematical Theorem is the system of statement, proof and theory. (Mariotti et al., 1997, p. 182)

Balacheff clearly indicated a possible articulation between the notion of Cognitive Unity and that of Mathematical Theorem, recently introduced, proposing an audacious parallel in the study of proof, which has become a plan of investigation:

> I will give a capsule description of the place I think possible for argumentation in mathematics, using the sense of the concept of Cognitive Unity of theorems coined by our Italian colleagues:
> Argumentation is to a conjecture what mathematical proof is to a theorem. (Balacheff, 1999)

Following this parallel, Pedemonte (2001, 2002) carried out a systematic investigation that aimed to study the relationship between the process of producing a conjecture and the related proof.

According to the first studies, Cognitive Unity was mainly discussed considering the "referential system"[3] of argumentation and proof. There is Cognitive Unity if it is possible to recognize elements which students used during the argumentation activity in the proof, i.e. in the chain of theorems and definitions used. It is usually possible to identify expressions or particular words that refer to the objects and the properties expressed by theorems and definitions.

Cognitive Unity and structural continuity

Taking into account the definition of Mathematical Theorem introduced above, it is possible to outline a correspondence between the reference system, i.e. the system of conceptions from which a conjecture emerges and within which it is formulated and supported by more or less explicit arguments, and the theory, i.e. available theorems and definitions within which the proof is produced. As a consequence, Cognitive Unity is recognizable when there is congruence between the system of conceptions on which the conjecture and its supporting arguments are constructed and the theory within which the proof is produced.

---

[3] The use of the term "referential system" may require some clarification. It generally refers to the knowledge system available to the subjects and used during the construction of a conjecture and the consequent proof (Pedemonte, 2002). Sometimes, mainly when the representational system (such as language, drawings, etc) is in focus, one can refer to the notion of *cadres* (Douady, 1986), and other times to the notion of *in act concept* (Vergnaud, 1990).

Nevertheless, although continuity in content is often recognizable, it sometimes happens that the construction of a deductive chain that correctly relates the theoretical elements involved may be difficult to achieve. In fact, differently from what happens in the case of content, continuity between the structure of the argumentation and that of the proof may be problematic, leading to errors or inconsistencies.

For example, abduction is a very common structure in argumentation, but in order to construct a proof, students must change the abductive structure into a deductive structure. In this case, continuity would lead the student to fail, while the construction of a correct mathematical proof has to overcome a structural distance.

For this reason, it becomes useful to introduce a distinction between *referential* and *structural* Cognitive Unity (Pedemonte, 2002).

Structural cognitive unity is the cognitive unity derived from a structural continuity, i.e. the continuity between the structure of the argumentation and the structure of the proof.

The examples discussed by Pedemonte (2002) are very interesting, as is the theoretical tool used to accomplish this analysis. The ternary model introduced by Toulmin (1958) allows the author to interpret the argumentation supporting a conjecture and to outline its whole structure.

On the base of such a structural analysis, the author can compare an argumentation, supporting the statement of a conjecture, and its final proof; as far as argumentation is concerned, different structures can be recognized, such as deduction, abduction, induction. Not all of them are consistent with a mathematically acceptable logical structure, thus the transposition of a given argumentation into a mathematical proof cannot always be accomplished straightforwardly. As previously mentioned, transforming an abductive argument into a deductive proof requires its structure to be reversed, so that "the transition from argumentation to proof may demand relevant (and sometimes difficult to perform) changes concerning structures" (Toulmin, 1958, p. 35).

The interest in the case of abduction lies in the fact that, according to experimental evidence, exploration supporting a conjecture is very often accompanied by arguments showing this structure, so that passing from conjecturing to proving would require transformation from an abductive into a deductive structure. This passage presents difficulties that seem to require specific didactical treatment to overcome (Mariotti & Maracci, 1999).

The inductive type of argumentation is also quite common. There are different kinds of arguments that can be generally classified as 'inductive' but that actually present essential differences. Mathematicians have come to an agreement about the acceptability of a particular type of inductive argument, commonly called *Mathematical Induction*. The development of this type of proof has been difficult and not free from debate[4], however, nowadays the Principle of Mathematical Induction is commonly used and taught in advanced mathematics courses.

---

4 Though the utilization of this kind of reasoning may be dated earlier, it was Dedekind (1870) who explicitly formalized it, introducing the Induction Axiom.

This type of proof is recognized as difficult; let us see for instance what can be read on the web, on one of the many sites offering explanations on Mathematical Induction:

> First off, don't get mad at your instructor. Induction makes perfect sense to him, and he honestly thinks he's explained it clearly. When I took this stuff, I know I had a good professor, so I know I got a "good" lesson. But I still didn't trust induction. So I'll try to pick up where your instructor left off. (retrieved March 27, 2005, from http://www.purplemath.com/modules/inductn.htm)

I'd like to present a brief discussion on this type of proof because it offers a good opportunity to coordinate different research studies, one shedding light on the other.

The case of Mathematical Induction

According to Harel and Sowder's classification of proof schemes, two different types of arguments can be recognized as referring to "induction" and can be explained as follows:

- Generalization is achieved by recognizing a general pattern in the result itself (*result pattern generalisation*). For instance, after a series of calculations, the subject observes the regularity of the result of a calculation.
- Generalization is derived from the process *(process pattern generalisation)* that leads to the results. For instance, after a series of calculations, the subject observes the regularity of the process used to get the result, i.e. one may observe a particular chain of steps interrelating the results.

From the point of view of Harel and Sowder's classification, the former argument is a case of an *empirical* proof scheme, whilst the latter is a *transformational* proof scheme. The analogy between the arguments consists in the fact that, in both cases, the support of the general statement is obtained from an *inductive* process, i.e. from the verification of a limited number of particular cases. What makes the arguments different is the fact that the elaboration of the particular cases is different. In the first case, the examples function as generic elements on which the proving arguments can be applied; in the second case, the passage from one case to the following is focused on and generalization applies to this passage.

In spite of the apparent analogy, the two types of inductive argumentations have quite different relationships with the type of proof by Mathematical Induction.

Using the principle of Mathematical Induction requires a shift of attention from proving the general statement P(n) to proving the inference [P(n-1)→P(n)], conceived as a generic step in a chain of inferences. This difference is certainly crucial, and leads to difficulties that cannot be underestimated.

Such difficulties become even more evident if described in terms of Cognitive Unity. In fact, when a conjecture is generated by *result pattern generalization*, producing a proof by Mathematical Induction requires shifting from one type of argument to the other, meaning that the student has to control the gap between the two types of arguments, but this is not all. If a student has never experienced the production of arguments of a *process pattern generalisation* type, it might be difficult for him/her to grasp the sense of a proof by Mathematical Induction. Thus, looking at it from a pedagogical perspective, one can assume that promoting process pattern generalization could facilitate students' introduction to Mathematical Induction and consequently design a didactic intervention.

The brief discussion on the case of Mathematical Induction can be enlarged and adapted to other cases (interesting examples in the case of abduction are given by Arzarello, Micheletti, Olivero & Robutti, 1998), where it is possible to identify a gap between arguments produced by the students –in particular, supporting their production of a conjecture– and arguments used by and acceptable to experts, in mathematics practice.

In this same vein, the possible discrepancy between the individual/private and the social/public perspectives is highlighted by the results presented in the doctoral dissertation by Raman (2002). The examples discussed in the dissertation are interesting and deeper insight could come from a more detailed analysis; the use of the Toulmin's model, for instance, could reveal the potential continuity between the private and public aspects of proof, as well the potential gap between them.

Social versus individual perspective

The distance between different types of arguments exists and is certainly stressed by the fact that, in the case of mathematical proof, the standards of acceptability for an argument limit them to a well defined and clearly stated set of paradigms: Some of them are commonly used, some of them are not very frequent, and some of them are definitely extraneous to the common practice of argumentation. A detailed analysis of the types of arguments ("proof schemes" in the terminology of Harel and Sowder) and a critical comparison with mathematical proofs brings a crucial aspect to light: Consciousness required to manage the distance between argumentation and proof belongs to a meta-level where arguments in themselves become an issue to inspect.

In fact, in order to decide about the acceptability of a proof rather than its content –for instance whether to accept an argument by mathematical induction or reject an argument by abduction– the proof method itself becomes the subject of discussion, in order to decide on its acceptability.

Generally speaking, this corresponds to taking the fundamental characteristic of proof into account, namely its social dimension, meaning that proof makes sense in respect to a community that shares (more or less implicitly) the criteria of acceptability of the arguments in play.

At school, the social dimension related to the community of mathematicians must be coordinated with the social dimension related to the classroom community: The crucial role of the teacher comes to the forefront, representing contemporaneously the guarantor of the mathematics community and the guarantor of the classroom community. In short, the teacher has to become a cultural mediator and introduce students to the standards of mathematical validation.

It is important to remark the fact that the tasks proposed in the experimental investigation are often of the "proof that" type, meaning that students are asked to prove the validity of a given statement. This kind of task does not seem to be as effective in triggering the production of arguments as the task requiring the production of a conjecture. In the latter case it is plausible to expect that arguments arise to fuel the reasoning and this type of situation was often suggested as useful to approach the theme of proof at school for this reason (Balacheff, 1987; Boero, Garuti & Mariotti, 1996).

This remark leads us to the third direction of research, concerning didactic proposals for introducing pupils to proof.

PROPOSALS FOR INTRODUCING PUPILS TO PROOF

Different research projects at different age levels in different countries have designed and implemented possible approaches to proof. Naturally, this has been done assuming different epistemological perspectives and different cultural contexts in respect to proof.

Results of survey studies and research work focused on students' conceptions of proof often motivated and, at the same time, inspired the development of innovation projects aimed more or less directly at introducing pupils to proof. A clear indication from the research studies focused on the need for an early start in proving practice and, consistently with this indication, seminal work can be found at the primary school level, dating back to a long time ago. A common feature that characterizes most of these innovation projects is immediately recognizable: Attempts to foster the development of mathematical meaning are widely based on thoughtful mathematical activities investigated by children. In this case one of the basic aims is very often that of establishing a "mathematical community in the classroom" (Bartolini Bussi, 1991, 1998; Arsac, 1992; Maher & Martino, 1996; Yackel & Cobb, 1996).

Arguments and proof in the construction of knowledge

According to a widely shared point of view in mathematics education research, different approaches express the need to coordinate psychological and sociological perspectives, coherently with the interpretation of education as a way to encourage students participate in a culture rather than a way to transmit a piece of knowledge. Although not always made explicit, there seems to be a widely shared assumption (Boero et al., 1995) that reasoning and argumentation contribute to knowledge construction.

In the theory of didactical situations (Brousseau, 1997) this assumption is recognizable in the coordination between the three main types of situations, related respectively to action, formulation and validation. From this perspective, validation actually represents the key issue of learning, whose goal is envisaged as making the subject place action (eventually involving manipulations of representation systems) under the control of his/her mathematical knowledge. The functioning of the didactical system is accurately described and the metaphor of the *game* used by the author (Brousseau, 1997) clearly expresses the functioning of validation in relation to a system of rules.

The metaphor of game

When the pupil is playing, s/he develops strategies; this means that actions are selected from a set of potentialities according to intuitive or rational reasons; the feedback produced by the environment allows the subject to check the effectiveness of her choice and may consequently lead her to accept or reject it. The sequence of interactions between the student and the environment (*milieu*) constitutes what is called the "dialectic of action". Continuing in the game and the student passes through what is called the "dialectic of formulation" that consists in "progressively establishing a shared language", making "possible the explanation of actions and modes of action". During this phase, according to Brousseau's (1997) model,

> [...] it can happen that one student's propositions are discussed by another student, not from the point of view of the language [...] but from the point of view of the content (that is to say, its truth or its efficacy). [...] these spontaneous discussions about the validity of strategies are usually referred to as "validation phases". (p. 12)

The means of convincing the interlocutor may vary widely and they may remain beyond the student's control.

It is only by entering what the author calls the *dialectic of validation* that the student is motivated to discuss a situation and encouraged to express his/her reasons, which might previously have remained implicit. Although the reasoning may be insufficient or incorrect and adopt false theories (ibid., p. 17), the features of the milieu[5] should prevent "illegitimate" means from being used to obtain the agreement of the other, such as authority, force, seduction (ibid., p. 70) and favour students to use mathematical knowledge, and in any case to root it in rational thought. The dialectics of contradiction and the role counter-examples can be interpreted in this sense, as introduced and successively elaborated by Balacheff (1985, 1987, 1991).

Stating and developing socio-mathematical norms

Though related to the individual and to his/her personal relationship with the specific context, the effectiveness of the chosen strategy can be established depending on its intrinsic functioning: Social interaction constitutes a basic factor that affects, motivates and fuels a dialectic of validation. Collaborative work, amongst peers or in small groups, seems to be a favourable social context in which

[5] In particular, if the characteristic of the milieu is *being a-didactical*, that is not directly controlled by a didactic goal, it becomes possible for the student to enter a correct dialectic of validation.

to make cognitive conflicts arise as they are naturally brought to students' consciousness in confronting answers and arguments. Nonetheless, the emerging knowledge still needs to be related to the mathematical domain. In other words, in order to enter a mathematical perspective, students have to share a system of social norms (Yackel & Cobb, 1996) that state what is considered acceptable and, in particular, mathematically acceptable. The introduction of young children to the practice of "mathematical argumentation" has been the key objective of a number of research projects (Maher & Martino, 1996; Zack, 1997) designed to create classroom environments within which teachers can develop cultural norms, favouring the emergence of argumentation and proof making in children's discourse.

This issue becomes even more crucial when young children are involved. In fact, at the primary school level it seems difficult for a child to recognize something as a mathematical "object" if nobody tells the child what "mathematical" might mean. As Yackel and Cobb (1996) clearly point out, it is necessary to establish what makes certain arguments less mathematical than others. Thus, beyond the social norms controlling what students are expected to do, it becomes crucial to establish *socio-mathematical* norms in the classroom: Not only the practice of supporting one's own statements is introduced, but the criteria for acceptability of mathematical arguments are also negotiated in the classroom:

> [...] the understanding that students are expected to explain their solutions is a social norm, whereas the understanding of what counts as an acceptable mathematical explanation is a socio-mathematical norm. (Yackel, 2001, p. 12)

> The school and classroom learning site is a community of practice which Richards (1991) has called inquiry math; it is one in which the children are expected to publicly express their thinking, and engage in mathematical practice characterized by conjecture, argument, and justification (Cobb, Wood & Yackel, 1993, p. 98). (Graves & Zack, 1996, p. 28)

The introduction of the mathematical perspective is clearly a responsibility of the teacher, as described in the following passage:

> [...] the teacher initiated both the diagram and the verbal elaboration of Louis' solution. Her actions accomplished several goals. One was to call attention to the argumentative support for the conclusion. Second, she contributed to the class' understanding of what is taken as argumentative support. (Yackel, 2001, p. 16)

The experiences carried out and discussed by Bartolini Bussi (1996) and Bartolini Bussi, Boni, Ferri & Garuti (1999) are consistent with this perspective but more explicitly oriented not only towards introducing pupils to mathematical arguments, but also towards framing mathematical arguments within a theoretical system. In the frame of long term teaching experiments, young pupils are introduced to what the authors call "germ theories", meaning that, starting from a set of explicit assumptions, arguments are produced to support specific statements. A basic characteristic is that assumptions[6] are collectively negotiated in the modelling process and triggered by a problem solving activity.

Analogously, the field of experience of shadows has functioned to foster a rich context in which the need for explanation leads to modelling and conceptualizing (Boero et al., 1995; Boero et al., 1996). As mentioned above, the cognitive analysis of students' arguments has highlighted interesting aspects concerning the process of producing conditional statements and complex arguments.

The relationship between empirical evidence and theoretical perspective has been a longstanding issue in the field of math education, which has mainly stressed the contraposition between them; however, a new approach to empirical evidence and its link with the mathematical validity emerged from these projects.

In the same vein the empirical, or rather the *pragmatic* perspective, as the authors call it, is widely discussed by Hanna and Jahnke (1993). The authors propose a distinction between the *pre-formation* and the *established* phase of a theory, and stress the need to let pupils have their own experience with the process of establishing a theoretical perspective. The need to state assumptions in relation to answering the question "why?", and the need for a reasonable empirical base for these assumptions is part of the "theoretical physicist" approach, that Hanna and Jahnke (2002) promote and hold to be indispensable in the development of a sense of proof.

The distance between the established and the pre-formation phase of a theory should not be ignored. In fact, the inability to realise that student and teacher are arguing from completely different points of view may be the origin of serious misunderstandings about the sense of proof, and the sense of mathematics in general.

In summary, different studies have supported the proposal that proof might be rooted in a "culture of why questions" (Jahnke, 2005) and students might be introduced to a theoretical perspective that emerges as a way of describing and explaining experienced phenomena through a modelling process.

These kinds of modelling contexts reveal their power, in fact in that case the need to share assumptions springs out of the modelling process, as accomplished in classroom activities, while the specific status of such assumptions in respect to possible consequences requires a clear definition of their mutual relationships. In this sense, the coordination between constructing a model and reflecting on this construction offers the opportunity to make sense of a theoretical environment. In such a context, arguments are elaborated to explain what is observed, as well to foresee new properties, so that the rigour of a hypothetical –deductive system can be assured, without loosing the connection with the original meaning.

Taking this approach, the choice of an experiential context within which the modelling process can be realized may become crucial, and therefore research studies aimed at exploring the potential of particular contexts are needed in order to shed light on the general characteristics required.

---

[6] Although they are not explicitly called Axioms, these assumptions have the theoretical status of Axioms.

Specific contexts related to the use of new technologies, among others, have been at the core of a number of studies; in particular, the development of Dynamic Geometry Environments has brought new life to Geometry classes and revitalized classic mathematical activities that had nearly disappeared from the classroom. The following section will provide a brief discussion on some aspects concerning proof within a Dynamic Geometry Environment.

PROVING IN A DYNAMIC GEOMETRY ENVIRONMENT

In spite of the doubts arising at the very beginning and concerning the new relationship between students, experience and mathematics, it has emerged from computational environments that a number of studies consider specific computer-integrated contexts as very promising[7]. Within the limits of this chapter, only the contribution of a very specific context has been considered –that of Dynamic Geometry Environments (DGEs). In particular, it is a widely shared opinion that DGEs have opened new frontiers, linking informal argumentation with formal proof (Hadas & Hershkowitz, 1998, 1999; Hoyles & Healy, 1999; Olivero & Robutti, 2001).

> Our results show that the computer-integrated teaching experiments were largely successful in helping students widen their view of proof and in particular link informal argumentation to formal proof [...]. (Hoyles & Healy, 1999, p. 112)

The contribution of DGEs

In the last years a number of different contributions on the theme of proof shared the choice of a DGE as context. The joint efforts of some members of the PME community resulted in a set of papers published in a special issue of the international journal *Educational Studies in Mathematics* (Jones, Gutiérrez & Mariotti, 2000).

While it was immediately clear that a DGE could contribute in developing geometrical reasoning, particularly in supporting the solution of geometrical problems, the contribution that such a context could provide to fostering a culture of proof appeared to be more questionable.

Certainly, the availability of graphing capabilities "has given a new impetus to mathematical exploration, and has brought a welcome new interest in the teaching of Geometry", but also "Dynamic software has the potential to encourage both exploration and proof, because it makes it so easy to pose and test conjectures" (Hanna, 2000).

It seems clear that within a DGE, dragging provides the students with strong perceptual evidence that a certain property is true. Nevertheless, the contribution

---

[7] Other chapters in this volume are devoted to discussing the general issues concerning the impact of new technologies in mathematics education.

provided to finding a proof does not seem as clear (Mason, 1991), although the possible contribution to the main problem seems even more critical, i.e. that of introducing students to a theoretical perspective. In pragmatic terms, can DGE provide a context for a culture of why questions?

As often stressed, it may be natural and reasonable for the student to jump to the conclusion that exploration via dragging is sufficient to guarantee the truth of what can be observed (Mason, 1991), thus preventing the emergence of any "why questions" and as a consequence, a possibility of access to a proof sense. Thus the critical point, concerning the relationship between empirical evidence and theoretical reasons returns, in the new context, in the case of a DGE.

Using the notion of milieu (Brousseau, 1997), Laborde (2000) clearly explained the didactic complexity of the organization of a learning context:

> [...] a DGE itself without an adequately organized milieu would not prompt the need of proof. It is a common feature [...] to have constructed a rich milieu with which the student is interacting during the solving process and the elaboration of a proof. (p. 154)

In this respect, an interesting issue concerns the comparison between different possible contexts. For instance, the comparison between physical experience with concrete linkages and virtual experience with simulations in the Cabri environment was explicitly addressed in Vincent & McCrae (2001) and Vincent, Chick & McCrae (2002). Referring to the work of Bartolini Bussi (1993), the authors investigate the potentialities of virtual models of mechanical linkages as a context for the emergence of the need of proof. The realization of the linkages in a Cabri figure constitutes a first model of the concrete apparatus within a very particular representation context which, differently from a paper and pencil context, may offer a support orientated towards geometric reasoning. Cabri can offer accurate measurements, the possibility of tracing the trajectory of a point, and thus the possibility of obtaining a precise representation of the locus to be studied. In short, Cabri may support that modelling process which can prelude, as the author claims, the emergence of "why questions". As suggested by De Villiers (1991, 1998), by overcoming the verification function, that is the use of DGE for verifying the truth of a statement, a new specific function of a DGE emerges.

A large number of contributions have been presented at the successive PME Conferences, focussing on different aspects and contributing to clarifying the potentialities and limits of DGEs in relation to proof. It is not possible and may be not worthwhile to give a full account of the single contributions here; I would rather focus on a specific but in my view crucial point, namely the relationship between dragging tool and theoretical control and, more generally, the dialectics between action and proof in the very specific context of a DGE.

Dragging tool and logical control

DGEs contain within them the seeds for a Geometry of relations. In this sense there is an opposition between a DGE and the paper and pencil environment, where

Geometry may emerge from the experience of the evidence of unrelated facts; in fact, entering a DGE offers the opportunity to experience the break between these two worlds and to experience this break at the level of actions (Laborde 2000). But I'd like to go further and remember the fact that actions are mediated by tools which, according to vygotskian perspectives, can become "semiotic tools" (Vygotsky, 1978), meaning that actions with tools may contribute to knowledge construction inasmuch as tools themselves may become semiotic mediators.

The use of computational tools –such as primitives, macro, or dragging– may be exploited by the teacher with the aim of developing students' personal meanings towards mathematical meanings, according to specific didactic objectives.

In particular, a semiotic analysis concerning the "dragging" tool highlights the link between this tool and the meaning of "theoretical control", thus opening an interesting perspective on the potentialities of this tool as an "instrument of semiotic mediation" (Mariotti, 2002). In fact, the test consisting in the dragging mode, by which a construction is validated, may be used as an instrument of semiotic mediation to introduce the meaning of theoretical control within a Geometry theory (Mariotti & Bartolini Bussi, 1998). In other terms, in the field of experience of geometrical constructions in the Cabri environment, the coordinated use of the different tools offered by the microworld make them function as instruments of semiotic mediation to make the meaning of "Mathematical Theorem" evolve (Mariotti, 2000, 2001a, 2002).

In this case, personal meanings concern the idea of dependent movement as it emerges from pupils' own experience in the Cabri environment; general mathematical meanings concern the mathematical ideas of logical dependence between hypothesis and thesis, as expressed in a Mathematical Theorem (that is the system of mutual relationships among the three main components: A statement, its proof and the theory within which the proof makes sense).

It is interesting to remark that in a recent project, based on the notion of semiotic mediation, a similar approach has been used to promote a theoretical perspective in a completely different mathematical field, namely Algebra. Inspired by the case of the DGE Cabri, a microworld was designed and experimented with the aim of providing a suitable experiential context to mediate and develop the meaning of proving within an Algebra Theory (Mariotti & Cerulli, 2001).

Dragging and theorems

Let us focus on the case of a DGE. Evidence from different studies indicates that using DGE tools does foster students' access to the world of Geometry theory, for instance by giving sense to inclusive definitions and consequently to explanations based on the logical relationships between properties (see for instance Jones, 2000). In particular, the dialectics of conjecture and empirical findings may lead students to experience contradiction and uncertainty, opening the way to the need for explanations and overcoming the strength of empirical evidence (Hadas, Hershkowitz & Schwarz, 2000). Functional dependency related to the functioning of the DGE constitutes a key element: Conditional motion is certainly one of the main features of DGEs. In fact, the sequential organization of tools used to produce any dynamic figure (Cabri figure) states a dependency between different elements of the figure: Such a dependency may not be immediately grasped, but it becomes evident to a user as soon as the dragging tool is activated. In fact, two main kinds of motions are possible using the mouse: Direct and indirect motion.

The direct motion of a basic element (for instance, a point) is related to the direct action on a particular point (or other Cabri object). It represents the variation of this element in the plane; this is the way of representing a generic element[8] in Cabri. The indirect motion of an element occurs when a *construction* has been accomplished; in this case, dragging the basic points from which the construction originates will determine the motion of the new elements obtained through the construction. According to the basic semiotic relation, constraints stated by the tools used in the construction correspond to geometrical properties relating to the geometrical objects involved, so that motion dependency corresponds to logical dependency between properties.

Actually, the use of dragging allows one to experience *motion dependency* that can be interpreted in terms of *logical dependency* within the DGE, but also interpreted in terms of logical dependency within the geometrical context (i.e. logical dependency between geometrical relationships within a Geometry Theory).

The difficulty of establishing a correct and effective interpretation of different kinds of movements is well documented (Hölzl, Hoyles & Noss, 1994; Jones, 2000; Talmon & Yerushalmy, 2004), nevertheless, such a "correct" interpretation constitutes the basic element for effective use of the dragging tool for both conjecturing and proving, i.e. for producing conjectures and their mathematical proofs.

Consider the Cabri microworld[9]: Any Cabri figure may be related to a Mathematical Theorem, as defined above. The correspondence is not unique, but can be identified as follows: A *statement* can be reconstructed considering the construction process, performed to obtain the Cabri figure; the relationships stated by the construction constitute the *hypothesis*, while the properties derived from them and appearing as invariants in the dragging mode constitute a possible *thesis*. Thus, when an open problem is given, constructing a figure and dragging points represents a way to make relationships between properties appear. In other words, conjectures may emerge from the coordination between properties used in the construction and properties highlighted as invariant by dragging mode. Such a coordination is easy to state but not easy to realize. Nevertheless, the observation of students using the mouse while solving open problems in the Cabri environment

---

8 Different movements are possible, realizing different kinds of variation. The tool "point on an object" represents the variation of a point within a specific geometrical domain, a line, a segment, a circle, and the like. This is a way to represent the relationship " ... belongs to ...", and consequently the general statement "For all points, P belonging to a line r" may find a counterpart in the construction of a point P on a generic line r.

9 In the following discussion, I will take the example of Cabri, although with slight differences the discussion can be transferred to other DGEs.

has shown the appearance of different dragging modalities, as described in (Arzarello et al., 1998; Olivero, 2003).

Beside the basic mode that the authors call *Wandering dragging* –moving the basic points on the screen randomly without a plan– other modes are described.

- *Bound dragging*: Moving a semi-draggable[10] point (already linked to an object).
- *Guided dragging*: Dragging the basic points of a figure in order to give it a particular shape.
- *"Dummy locus"*[11] *dragging*: Moving a basic point so that the figure keeps a discovered property, meaning that you are following a hidden path (the *dummy locus*) even without being aware of this.
- *Line dragging*: Drawing new points on the ones that keep the regularity of the figure.
- *Linked dragging*: Linking a point to an object and moving it onto that object.
- *Dragging test*: Moving draggable or semi-draggable points in order to see whether the figure keeps its initial properties. If so, then the figure passes the test; if not, then the figure was not constructed according to the geometric properties you wanted it to have.

According to the experimental data reported by the authors, these dragging modalities can be successfully exploited during the exploration phase, leading to the formulation of a conjecture. Taking a perspective coherent with the notion of Cognitive Unity, it seems reasonable to hypothesize a link between the dragging modalities used by the solver in the exploration and the subsequent proof of the conjecture. The dragging modalities used by the subject may correspond to a sort of *instrumented arguments* supporting the conjecture produced, which can be compared with formal arguments that can be used in constituting a mathematical proof.

This hypothesis opens a new direction of investigation, raising a number of complex but fascinating research questions concerning the correspondence between motion dependency and logical dependency. In particular, the basic hypothesis can be further elaborated as follows:

Is it possible to foster cognitive continuity in students' performances, provided the teacher supplies students dragging modes as mediators?

CONCLUSIONS

As mentioned at the beginning, a general consensus has been achieved on the fact that the development of a sense of proof constitutes an important objective of mathematical education, and there seems to be a general trend towards including proof in the curriculum[12]: This objective is strictly linked to other objectives concerning the development of other mathematical competencies.

---

[10] A semi-draggable point is a point on an object that can be moved but only on the object it belongs to.

[11] In French: *lieu muet.*

[12] We like to think, with Hoyles (1997), that this trend emerged under the pressure of educational research.

Besides the importance of proof and the need to include it in the mathematics curriculum, current research has shown the complexity of the idea of proof and the difficulties that teachers and students face when proof becomes part of classroom mathematical activities.

Proof clearly has the purpose of validation –confirming the truth of an assertion by checking the logical correctness of mathematical arguments– however, at the same time, proof has to contribute more widely to knowledge construction. If this is not the case, proof is likely to remain meaningless and purposeless in the eyes of students. Alternative approaches have been proposed for a long time and the crucial point that has emerged from different research contributions concerns the need for proof to be acceptable from a mathematical point of view but also to make sense for students. For instance, when Hanna (1989b) spoke of explanatory proofs (p. 12), the main goal was that of achieving flexible thinking, moving from different functions of proof, and in particular from validating to explaining and vice versa.

Encouraging student engagement and ownership of the proving activity has to be integrated into explanatory proving in a social dimension, where students explain their arguments to a peer or to the whole class, including the teacher, also to convince themselves of their truth. It is in this vein that a number of teaching experiments and research projects have been taken up. Suggestions coming from these studies have highlighted key elements, mainly concerning how to choose and organize meaningful contexts within which the different components of the sense of proof can be developed. Among others, DGEs have opened new perspectives, which appear very promising. Nevertheless, further investigation is needed concerning students' active production of proofs in order to design appropriate contexts; in particular, analysis of the cognitive processes involved in producing and proving conjectures seems to shed new light on students' difficulties as well on the possible source of these difficulties. The notion of cognitive unity, which addresses the link between spontaneous arguments and mathematically acceptable arguments, may provide a powerful tool of investigation and is open to further elaboration (a recent example in this direction can be found in Vincent, Chick & McCrae, 2005).

The need to develop mathematical ideas in relation to arguments and provide effective argumentation that can become mathematical proof is strictly related to the potential congruence between conceptions and theorems: Arguments produced to support one's own conjecture must be compared with arguments that are acceptable, i.e. that are already stated and shared in the mathematics community that the individual has to participate in, as Harel and Sowder say, arguments must be recognized as acceptable at the same time for both ascertaining and persuading.

Consistency between these two facets of the problem of proof may be considered a main educational objective. Nevertheless, there is an even more basic issue: To become aware of the existence of different points of view and the need to negotiate the relevance and the acceptability of the mathematical perspective in respect to other forms of argumentation requires a complex and delicate teaching intervention. The perspective of *cognitive unity* makes it clear why, in the relation between argumentation and mathematical proof, there must not be a mere rejection of the first in favour of the second. Meanwhile, as discussed above, the existence of an *epistemological obstacle* explains why the tension cannot disappear completely, and students can only be made aware of it.

All this corresponds to quite a demanding objective from the educational point of view, requiring the teacher to bring about development both at a cognitive and meta-cognitive level. In particular, students' attitude to proof is strictly and more generally related to their beliefs about mathematics. Thus, the horizon of the field of research has to be expanded to embrace the cognitive and the meta-cognitive perspectives; in particular, the teacher's role as a cultural mediator comes to the forefront. Further investigation is required in this direction, concerning both practice at school and the training of teachers. On the one hand more has to be known mainly about the potentialities of contexts to introduce students to the practice of proof. On the other hand, the delicate and complex role of cultural mediator to which the teacher is called requires careful preparation involving both the cognitive and the meta-cognitive level.

The evolution of a mathematical culture in the classroom is a long-term process, requiring specific strategies of intervention that begin very early and develop over a long period. In this respect, investigation cannot be detached from classroom reality and, generally speaking, from the school environment: Classroom investigations are of great value, and, although they raise difficult methodological problems, they should be promoted both in the form of comparison between different cultural experiences and in the form of teaching experiments.

REFERENCES

Abdeljaouad, M. (2002). Proof in Arabian algebra. *Newsletter on Proof, Hive 2002r.* Retrieved from http://www.lettredelapreuve.it/

Arsac, G. (1992). *Initiation au raisonnement au college.* Lyon, France: Presse Universitaire de Lyon.

Arzarello, F. (in press). The proof in the 20th century: from Hilbert to automatic theorem proving. In P. Boero (Ed.), *Theorems in school from history and epistemology to cognitive and educational issues.*

Arzarello, F., Micheletti, C., Olivero, F., & Robutti, O. (1998). A model for analysing the transition to formal proofs in geometry. In A. Olivier & K. Newstead (Eds.), *Proceedings of the 22nd PME International Conference, 2,* 24–31.

Balacheff, N. (1985). Experimental study of pupils' treatment of refutation in a geometrical context. In L. Streefland (Ed.), *Proceedings of the 9th PME International Conference,* 223–229.

Balacheff, N. (1987). Processus de preuve et situations de validation. *Educational Studies in Mathematics, 18*(2), 147–76.

Balacheff, N. (1991). Treatment of refutations: aspects of the complexity of a constructivist approach to mathematical learning. In E. von Glasersfeld (Ed.), *Radical constructivism in mathematics education* (pp. 89–110). Dordrecht, The Netherlands: Kluwer.

Balacheff, N. (1999). Is argumentation an obstacle? Invitation to a debate ... *Newsletter on Proof, Mai/Juin 1999.* Retrieved from http://www.lettredelapreuve.it/

Balacheff, N. (2002/2004). The researcher epistemology: a deadlock from educational research on proof. In F.-L. Lin (Ed.), *2002 International Conference on Mathematics – "Understanding proving and proving to understand"* (pp. 23–44). Taipei, Taiwan: NSC and NTNU. Reprinted in *Les Cahiers du Laboratoire Leibniz, 109.* Retrieved from http://www.leibniz.imag.fr/NEWLEIBNIZ/Les Cahiers/index.xhtml

Bartolini Bussi, M. G. (1991). Social interaction and mathematical knowledge. In F. Furinghetti (Ed.), *Proceedings of the 15th PME International Conference*, *1*, 1–16.

Bartolini Bussi, M. G. (1993). Geometrical proof and mathematical machines: an exploratory study. In I. Hirabayashi, N. Nohda, K. Shigematsu, & F.-L. Lin (Eds.), *Proceedings of the 17th PME International Conference*, *2*, 97–104.

Bartolini Bussi, M. G. (1996). Mathematical discussion and perspective drawings in primary school, *Educational Studies in Mathematics*, *31*, 11–41.

Bartolini Bussi, M. G. (1998). Verbal interaction in mathematics classroom: A Vygotskian analysis. In H. Steinbring, M. G. Bartolini Bussi, & A. Sierpinska (Eds.), *Language and Communication in the Mathematics Classroom* (pp. 65–84). Reston, VA, USA: NCTM.

Bartolini Bussi, M. G., Boni, M., Ferri, F., & Garuti, R. (1999). Early approach to theoretical thinking: Gears in primary school, *Educational Studies in Mathematics*, 39(1–3), 67–87.

Boero, P. (1994). Approaching rational geometry: From physical relationships to conditional statements, In J. P. Ponte & J. F. Matos (Eds.), *Proceedings of the 18th PME International Conference*, *2*, 96–105.

Boero, P., Dapueto, C., Ferrari, P., Ferrero, E., Garuti, R., Lemut, E., et al. (1995). Aspects of the mathematics-culture relationship in mathematics teaching-learning in compulsory school. In L. Meira & D. Carraher (Eds.), *Proceedings of the 19th PME International Conference*, *1*, 151–166.

Boero, P., Garuti, R., Lemut, E., & Mariotti, M. A. (1996). Challenging the traditional school approach to theorems: A hypothesis about the cognitive unity of theorems. In L. Meira & D. Carraher (Eds.), *Proceedings of the 19th PME International Conference*, *2*, 113–120.

Boero, P., Garuti, R., & Mariotti, M. A. (1996). Some dynamic mental processes underlying producing and proving conjectures. In L. Puig & A. Gutiérrez (Eds.), *Proceedings of the 20th PME International Conference*, *2*, 121-–128.

Brousseau, G. (1997). *Theory of didactical situations in mathematics*. Dordrecht, The Netherlands: Kluwer.

Chazan, D. (1988). Proof and measurement: an unexpected misconception. *Proceedings of the 12th PME Conference*, Veszprem, Hungary,*1*, 207–214.

Cobb, P., Wood, T., & Yackel, E. (1993). Discourse, mathematical thinking and classroom practice. In E. Forman, N. Minick, & C. A. Stone (Eds.), *Context for learning: sociocultural dynamics in children's development* (pp. 91–119). New York, USA: Oxford University Press.

De Villiers, M. (1991). Pupils' needs for conviction and explanation within the context of geometry. In G. Vergnaud, J. Rogalski, & M. Artigue (Eds.), *Proceedings of the 13th PME International Conference*, *1*, 255–262.

De Villiers, M. (1998). An alternative approach to proof in dynamic geometry. In R. Lehrer & D. Chazan (Eds.), *Designing learning environments for developing understanding of geometry and space* (pp. 369–393). Hillsdale, NJ, USA: Lawrence Erlbaum.

Douady, R. (1986). Jeux de cadres et dialectique outil-objet, *Recherches en Didactique des Mathématiques*, 7(2), 5–31.

Duval, R. (1989). Langage et representation dans l'apprentissage d'une demarche deductive. In G. Vergnaud, J. Rogalski, & M. Artigue (Eds.), *Proceedings of the 13th PME International Conference*, *1*, 228–235.

Duval, R. (1991). Structure du raisonnement déductif et apprentissage de la démonstration. *Educational Studies in Mathematics*, *22*(3), 233–263.

Duval, R. (1992-93). Argumenter, demontrer, expliquer: Continuité ou rupture cognitive? *Petit x*, *31*, 37–61.

Fischbein, E. (1982). Intuition and proof. *For the Learning of Mathematics*, *3*(2), 9–18.

Fischbein E. (1987). *Intuition in science and mathematics*. Dordrecht, The Netherlands: Kluwer.

Fischbein, E., & Kedem, I. (1982). Proof and certitude in the development of mathematical thinking. In A. Vermandel (Ed.), *Proceedings of the 6th PME International Conference*, 128–131.

Garuti, R., Boero, P., & Lemut, E. (1998). Cognitive unity of theorems and difficulty of proof. In A. Olivier & K. Newstead (Eds.), *Proceedings of the 22nd PME International Conference*, *2*, 345–352.

Godino, J. D., & Recio, A. M. (1997). Meaning of proofs in mathematics education. In E. Pehkonen (Ed.), *Proceedings of the 21st PME International Conference*, *2*, 313–320.

Graves, B., & Zack, V. (1996). Discourse in an inquiry math elementary classroom and the collaborative construction of an elegant algebraic expression. In L. Puig & A. Gutiérrez (Eds.), *Proceedings of the 20th PME International Conference*, *3*, 25–32.

Hadas, N., & Hershkowitz, R. (1998). Proof in geometry as an explanatory and convincing tool. In A. Olivier & K. Newstead (Eds.), *Proceedings of the 22nd PME International Conference*, *3*, 25–32.

Hadas, N., & Hershkowitz, R. (1999). The role of uncertainty in constructing and proving in computerized environment. In O. Zaslavsky (Ed.), *Proceedings of the 23rd PME International Conference*, Haifa, Israel, *3*, 57–64.

Hadas, N., Hershkowitz, R., & Schwarz, B. (2000). The role of contradiction and uncertainty in promoting the need to prove in dynamic geometry environments. *Educational Studies in Mathematics*, *44*(1-2), 127–150.

Hanna, G. (1989a). More than formal proof. *For the Learning of Mathematics*, *9*(1), 20–25.

Hanna, G. (1989b). Proofs that prove and proofs that explain. *Proceedings of the 13th PME Conference*, Paris, France, *2*, 45–51.

Hanna, G. (1996). The ongoing value of proof. In L. Puig & A. Gutiérrez (Eds.), *Proceedings of the 20th PME International Conference*, *1*, 21–34.

Hanna, G. (2000). Proof, Explanation and Exploration: An Overview. *Educational Studies in Mathematics*, *44*(1-2), 5–23.

Hanna, G., & Jahnke, H. N. (1993). Proof and Application. *Educational Studies in Mathematics*, *24*(4), 421–438.

Hanna, G., & Jahnke, H. N. (2002). Arguments from physics in mathematical proofs: An educational perspective. *For the Learning of Mathematics*, *22*(3), 38–45.

Harel, G. (1999). Students' understanding of proof: A historical analysis and implications for the teaching of Geometry and linear algebra. *Linear Algebra and its Applications*, *302–303*, 601–613.

Harel, G. (2001). The development of mathematical induction as a proof scheme: A model for DNR-based instruction. In S. Campbell & R. Zazkis (Eds.), *Learning and teaching number theory* (pp. 185–212). New Jersey, USA: Ablex Publishing Corporation.

Harel, G., & Sowder, L. (1996). Classifying processes of proving. In L. Puig & A. Gutiérrez (Eds.), *Proceedings of the 20th PME International Conference*, *3*, 59–65.

Harel, G., & Sowder, L. (1998). Students' proof schemes: Results from exploratory studies. In A. Schoenfeld, J. Kaput, & E. Dubinsky (Eds.), *Research in collegiate mathematics education III* (pp. 234–282). Providence, RI, USA: American Mathematical Society.

Healy, L., & Hoyles, C. (1998). *Justifying and proving in school mathematics. Summary of the results from a survey of the proof conceptions of students in the UK* (Research Report) (pp. 601–613). London, UK: London Institute of Education, University of London.

Heath, T. (1956). *The thirteen books of Euclid's Elements*. New York, USA: Dover.

Hilbert, D., & Cohn-Vossen, S. (1932). *Anschauliche geometrie*, Berlin, Germany: Springer. (English translation: *Geometry and the imagination*. New York, USA: Chelsea, 1952)

Hölzl, R., Hoyles, C., & Noss, R. (1994). Geometrical relationships and dependencies in Cabri, *Micromath, 10*(3), 8–11.

Hoyles, C. (1997). The curricular shaping of students' approaches to proof. *For the Learning of Mathematics*, *17*(1), 7–16.

Hoyles, C., & Healy, L. (1999). Linking informal argumentation with formal proof through computer-integrated teaching experiments. In O. Zaslavsky (Ed.), *Proceedings of the 23rd PME International Conference*, *3*, 105–112.

Hoyles, C., Healy, L., & Küchemann, D. (1995-2003). *Justifying and proving in school mathematics project* and *Longitudinal proof project.* Description and list of publications retrieved from http://www.ioe.ac.uk/proof/index.html

Jahnke, H. N. (2005). *A genetic approach to proof.* Paper presented at CERME4, Sant Feliu de Guixols, Spain.

Jones, K. (2000). Providing a foundation for a deductive reasoning: students' interpretation when using dynamic geometry software and their evolving mathematical explanations. *Educational Studies in Mathematics*, *44*(1–2), 55–85.

Jones, K., Gutiérrez, A., & Mariotti, M. A. (Guest Eds.). (2000). Proof in dynamic geometry environments [special issue]. *Educational Studies in Mathematics*, *44*(1–2).

Knipping, C. (2001). Towards a comparative analysis of proof teaching. In M. van den Heuvel-Panhuizen (Ed.), *Proceedings of the 25th PME International Conference*, *3*, 249–256.

Küchemann, D., & Hoyles, C. (2001). Investigating factors that influence students' mathematical reasoning. In M. van den Heuvel-Panhuizen (Ed.), *Proceedings of the 25th PME International Conference*, *3*, 257–264.

Küchemann, D., & Hoyles, C. (2002). Students' understanding of a logical implication and its converse. In A. D. Cockburn & E. Nardi (Eds.), *Proceedings of the 26th PME International Conference*, *3*, 241–248.

Laborde, C. (2000). Dynamic geometry environment as a source of rich learning context for the complex activity of proving. *Educational Studies in Mathematics*, *44*(1–2), 151–61.

Lin, F.-L. (2005). Modeling students' learning on mathematical proof and refutation. In H. L. Chick & J. L. Vincent (Eds.), *Proceedings of the 29th PME International Conference*, *1*, 3–18.

Lolli, G. (1999). Truth and proofs, a short course in the epistemology of mathematics. In F. Arzarello & P. L. Ferrari (Eds.), *Proceedings of the School on Epistemology of Mathematics and Didactics*, Levico Terme, 8–12 February 1999.

Maher, C., & Martino, M. A. (1996). The development of the idea of mathematical proof: A 5-year case study. *Journal for Research in Mathematics Education*, *27*(2), 194–214.

Mariotti, M. A. (2000). Introduction to proof: the mediation of a dynamic software environment. *Educational Studies in Mathematics*, *44*(1–2), 25–53.

Mariotti, M. A. (2001a). Justifying and proving in the Cabri environment. *International Journal of Computer for Mathematical Learning*, *6*(3), 257–281.

Mariotti, M. A. (2001b). La preuve en mathématique. *Canadian Journal of Science, Mathematics and Technology Education*, *1*(4), 437–458.

Mariotti, M. A. (2002). Influence of technologies advances on students' math learning. In L. English (Ed.), *Handbook of international research in mathematics* (pp. 695–724). Mahwah, NJ, USA: Lawrence Erlbaum.

Mariotti, M. A. (in press). Reasoning, proof and proving in mathematics education. In *Proceedings of ICME10*, Copenhagen, Denmark.

Mariotti, M. A., & Bartolini Bussi, M. G. (1998). From drawing to construction: teachers mediation within the Cabri environment. In A. Olivier & K. Newstead (Eds.), *Proceedings of the 22nd PME International Conference*, *1*, 180–95.

Mariotti, M. A., Bartolini Bussi, M. G., Boero, P., Ferri, F., & Garuti, R. (1997). Approaching geometry theorems in contexts: from history and epistemology to cognition. In E. Pehkonen (Ed.), *Proceedings of the 21st PME International Conference*, *1*, 180–95.

Mariotti, M. A., & Cerulli, M. (2001). Semiotic mediation for algebra teaching and learning. In M. van den Heuvel-Panhuizen (Ed.), *Proceedings of the 25th PME International Conference*, *3*, 343–350.

Mariotti, M. A., & Maracci, M. (1999). Conjecturing and proving in problem-solving. In O. Zaslavsky (Ed.), *Proceedings of the 23rd PME International Conference*, *3*, 265–272.

Mason, J. (1991). Questions about geometry. In D. Pimm & E. Love (Eds.), *Teaching and learning mathematics: a reader* (pp. 77–99). London, UK: Holder and Stoughton.

Maturana, H. (1988). Reality: The search for objectivity or the quest for a compelling argument. *The Irish Journal of Psychology*, *9*(1), 25–82.

National Council of Teachers of Mathematics (NCTM). (2000). *Principles and standards for school mathematics*. Reston, USA: NCTM.

Olivero, F. (2003). *The proving process within a dynamic geometry environment.* Unpublished PhD dissertation, University of Bristol, UK.

Olivero, F., & Robutti, O. (2001). Measure in Cabri as bridge between perception and theory. In M. van den Heuvel-Panhuizen (Ed.), *Proceedings of the 25th PME International Conference, 4*, 9–16.

Pedemonte, B. (2001). Some cognitive aspects of the relationship between argumentation and proof in mathematics. In M. van den Heuvel-Panhuizen (Ed.), *Proceedings of the 25th PME International Conference, 44*, 33–40.

Pedemonte, B. (2002). *Etude didactique et cognitive des rapports de l'argumentation et de la démonstration*. Unpublished PhD dissertation, Università di Genova, Genova, Italy, and Université Joseph Fourier, Grenobre, France.

Raman, M. J. (2002). *Proof and justification in collegiate calculus*. PhD dissertation, University of California, Berkeley, CA, USA. Retrieved from http://www.lettredelapreuve.it/Newsletter/03Automne/ManyaThesis.pdf

Rav, Y. (1999). Why do we prove theorems?. *Philosophia Mathematica, 7*(3), 5–41.

Reid, D. (2001). *Proof, proofs, proving and probing: Research related to proof*. Paper based on a Short Oral Presentation at the 25th PME International Conference, Utrecht, The Netherlands. Retrieved from http://ace.acadiau.ca/~dreid/publications/proof/proof.htm

Reid, D. (2005). *The meaning of proof in mathematics education*. Paper presented at CERME4, Sant Feliu de Guixols, Spain.

Richards, J. (1991). Mathematical discussion. In E. von Glasersfeld (Ed.), *Radical constructivism in mathematics education* (pp. 13–52). Dordrecht, The Netherlands: Kluwer.

Steffe, L. P., & Thomson, P. (2000). Teaching experiments methodology: Underlying principles and essential characteristics. In E. Kelly & R. Lesh (Eds.), *Research design in mathematics and science education*. Hillsdale, NJ, USA: Laurence Erlbaum.

Talmon, V., & Yerushalmy, M. (2004). Understanding dynamic behavior: Parent-child relations in dynamic geometry environments. *Educational Studies in Mathematics, 57*(1), 91–119.

Toulmin, S. E. (1958). *The use of arguments*. Cambridge, UK: Cambridge University Press.

Vergnaud, G. (1990). La théorie des champs conceptuels. *Recherches en Didactique des Mathématiques, 10*(2–3), 133–170.

Vincent, J., Chick, H., & McCrae, B. (2002). Mechanical linkages as bridges to deductive reasoning: a comparison of two environments. In A. D. Cockburn & E. Nardi (Eds.), *Proceedings of the 26th PME International Conference, 4*, 313–320.

Vincent, J., Chick, H., & McCrae, B. (2005). Argumentation profile charts as tools for analysing students' argumentations. In H. L. Chick & J. L. Vincent (Eds.), *Proceedings of the 29th PME International Conference, 4*, 281–288.

Vincent, J., & McCrae, B. (2001). Mechanical linkages and the need for proof in secondary school. In M. van den Heuvel-Panhuizen (Ed.), *Proceedings of the 25th PME International Conference, 4*, 367–384.

Vinner, S. (1983). The notion of proof: Some aspects of students' views at the senior high level. In R. Hershkowitz (Ed.), *Proceedings of the 7th PME International Conference*, 289–294.

Vygotsky, L. S. (1978). *Mind in society. The development of higher psychological processes*. Cambridge, MA, USA: Harvard University Press.

Yackel, E. (2001). Explanation, justification and argumentation in mathematics classrooms. In M. van den Heuvel-Panhuizen (Ed.), *Proceedings of the 25th PME International Conference, 1*, 9–24.

Yackel, E., & Cobb, P. (1996). Socio-mathematical norms, argumentation, and autonomy in mathematics. *Journal for Research in Mathematics Education, 27*(4), 458–477.

Zack, V. (1997). "You have to prove us wrong": Proof at the elementary school level. In E. Pehkonen (Ed.), *Proceedings of the 21st PME International Conference, 4*, 291–298.

AFFILIATION

Maria Alessandra Mariotti
Dipartimento di Scienze Matematiche ed Informatiche
Università di Siena
Piano dei Mantellini, 44
53100 Siena (Italy)
mariotti.ale@unisi.it

NORMA PRESMEG

RESEARCH ON VISUALIZATION IN LEARNING AND TEACHING MATHEMATICS

Emergence from Psychology

INTRODUCTION

In 1988, at the 12th Annual Conference of the International Group for the Psychology of Mathematics Education (PME-12), in Veszprem, Hungary, Alan Bishop introduced his review of research on visualization in mathematics education as follows:

> This review builds on and extends from earlier reviews written either by the author or by others (Bishop, 1980; Bishop, 1983; Bishop, 1986; Clements, 1982; Presmeg, 1986b; Mitchelmore, 1976) but will be restricted to the notion of 'visualisation'. This construct interacts in the research literature with the ideas of imagery, spatial ability, and intuition, but it is certainly *not* the case that visualisation has been felt to be a significant research area in mathematics education in the recent past. Whilst searching the literature in preparation for this review, it was surprising to discover that in the JRME listing of 223 research articles in 1985 only 8 were remotely connected with the topic, that in the same listing for 1986 only 7 out of the 236 articles were related and at PME XI *no* papers were specifically focused on visualisation in mathematics education. (Bishop, 1988, p. 170, his emphasis)

Research on mental imagery in all of the sense modalities (sight, hearing, smell, taste, touch) and their interconnections –as in synaesthesia– was prevalent in psychology already in the 19th century. However, with the rise of behaviorism in the 20th century, such research was largely discontinued in mainstream psychology for the first half of that century (Richardson, 1969). It is noteworthy that visual imagery research was still conducted during this 'dormant' period, in the fields of psychotherapy and behavior modification (Singer, 1974). In mathematics education research, Bishop (1973) engaged in important early studies on visualization and spatial ability. Apart from Bishop's research, in 1982 when Presmeg (1985) started her doctoral investigation of the role of visually mediated processes in high school mathematics, there were only a few reported studies in this field that were specific to mathematics education (Clements, 1982; Krutetskii, 1976; Lean & Clements, 1981; Moses, 1977; Suwarsono, 1982).

A. Gutiérrez, P. Boero (eds.), Handbook of Research on the Psychology of Mathematics Education: Past, Present and Future, 205–235.

The decade of the 1980s was an important watershed: Constructivism was on the rise, countering the influence of behaviorism; and qualitative research methodologies were beginning to be accepted as valuable for addressing complex questions in mathematics education. The period was ripe for a renewed interest in the role of visual thinking in the teaching and learning of mathematics, and qualitative research was a suitable vehicle for investigating the otherwise inaccessible thought processes associated with the use of mental imagery and associated forms of expression in learning mathematics. The importance of visual processing and external manifestations of this cognition in mathematics was increasingly recognized. After all, mathematics is a subject that has diagrams, tables, spatial arrangements of signifiers such as symbols, and other inscriptions as essential components. As reflected in PME conference proceedings, this renewed interest in the topic of visualization research in mathematics education started to become apparent from 1988 onwards. In the PME-12 proceedings, Bishop's (1988) paper is the only one that is specifically about visualization, although there are a few papers that are tangentially related to the topic (Cooper, 1988; Fry, 1988; Goldin, 1988).

TERMINOLOGY

Because the term *visualization* has been used in various ways in the research literature of the past two decades, it is necessary to clarify how it is used in this review. Following Piaget and Inhelder (1971), the position is taken that when a person creates a spatial arrangement (including a mathematical inscription) there is a visual image in the person's mind, guiding this creation. Thus visualization is taken to include processes of constructing and transforming both visual mental imagery and all of the inscriptions of a spatial nature that may be implicated in doing mathematics (Presmeg, 1997b). This characterization is broad enough to include two aspects of spatial thinking elaborated by Bishop (1983), namely, *interpreting figural information* (IFI) and *visual processing* (VP).

Note that following the usage of Roth (2004), the term *inscriptions* is preferred to that of *representations* in this chapter, because the latter became imbued with various meanings and connotations in the changing paradigms of the last two decades. The difficulty in articulating an accurate definition for the term representation is worth stressing. An indication of this difficulty is that definitions for the term "representation" in the literature often include the word "represent" (Kaput, 1987). Kaput maintained that the concept of representation involved the following components: A representational entity; the entity that it represents; particular aspects of the representational entity; the particular aspects of the entity it represents that form the representation; and finally, the correspondence between the two entities. This level of detail is unnecessary for the purposes of the present chapter. Thus the term *inscriptions* will be employed, characterized by Roth (2004) as follows: "Graphical representations, which in the sociology of science and in post-modern discourse have come to be known as *inscriptions,* are central to scientific practice" (p. 2). Roth viewed these inscriptions as essential to the rhetoric of scientific communication. Nevertheless, the term *representations* is maintained in this chapter when it is used by the authors cited.

Following the usage of Presmeg (1985, 1986a, 1986b), a *visual image* is taken to be a mental construct depicting visual or spatial information, and a *visualizer* is a person who prefers to use visual methods when there is a choice. (Rationales for the use of these terms and their definitions may be found in Presmeg, 1997b.)

GATHERING MOMENTUM

At PME-13 in Paris (1989), there was one paper that was specifically devoted to research on visual imagery (Mariotti, 1989), and at least one other that might be overlooked because *visualization* does not appear in its title, although it deals with visual inscriptions in its substance (Arcavi & Nachmias, 1989). In research involving images of geometric solids and their nets, Mariotti (1989) identified two levels of complexity in the intuitive visual thinking of ten 11-year-olds and twelve 13-year-olds. It is noteworthy that the methodology of this investigation included clinical interviews with the 22 participants, resonating with the qualitative methodologies that were increasingly gaining acceptance. The study by Arcavi and Nachmias (1989) reported on the use by adults in a computer environment of a novel *parallel axes representation* for linear functions, and the effect of these inscriptions on the thinking of the adults, enabling them to visualize the notion of slope. Reported at the same conference, two studies that were peripherally related to visualization (Nadot, 1989; Yerushalmy, 1989) also used qualitative methods, and one (Pesci, 1989) compared the performance of a control group and an experimental group of 11-12 year-olds on inverse procedures, following a didactic treatment presented to the experimental group, with mixed results. Methodologically and theoretically, these studies are a foretaste of research in future years, in which issues of quality in methodologies and careful attention to theoretical constructs gradually became more robust. The research reports of Nadot and of Yerushalmy also hint at the influence of computer technology on conceptions of the nature of visualization in mathematics in future years (Zimmermann & Cunningham, 1991) –a theme that will emerge later in this chapter.

The following year, at PME-14 in Mexico (1990), one important paper introduced a theme that would recur, suggesting that students are reluctant to use visual processing in college level mathematics (Dreyfus & Eisenberg, 1990). This theme is also treated in more detail in a later section of this chapter. At PME-14 there was a poster (Brown & Wheatley, 1990) expounding on the significant role of imagery in the mathematical reasoning of grade 5 students in Florida, USA. Brown and Wheatley's work combined quantitative research using the Wheatley Spatial Ability Test (WSAT) with four classes of students, and qualitative interpretation of interviews with four of those learners. One issue that their research raised is the question of time taken to form and work with images. The WSAT is a timed test of mental rotations, allocating higher scores to students who can work quickly. However, Presmeg's (1985) extensive review of the psychological literature in this field suggested that construction and work with mental images may take more time than do analytic methods –a point that was not resolved in the WSAT. At PME-14, there were also three peripherally-related research reports (Farfán & Hitt, 1990; Hitt, 1990; Lea, 1990), two of which gave a foretaste of Fernando Hitt's interest in and important later role in promulgating the significance of visualization in mathematics education, as he organized the Working Group on Representations and Mathematical Visualization (1998-2002) at the annual meetings of the North American Chapter of PME, and edited a published volume on the work of this group (Hitt, 2002).

It was in 1991, at PME-15 in Assisi, Italy, that visualization in mathematics education came to fruition as a research field. This was the first year that Imagery and Visualization was presented as a separate category in the list of topics in the proceedings, with ten research reports listed in this category (Antonietti & Angelini; Bakar & Tall; Bodner & Goldin; Hershkowitz, Friedlander & Dreyfus; Lopez-Real; Mariotti; O'Brien; Presmeg; Shama & Dreyfus; Yerushalmy & Gafni; all 1991), as well as three posters. Further, two of the three plenary addresses were directed specifically to this topic (Dörfler, 1991; Dreyfus, 1991). "Meaning: Image schemata and protocols" was the title of Dörfler's plenary, in which he took the approach that "Meaning is viewed here to be induced by concrete 'mental images' as opposed to propositional approaches" (p. 17). His theory involved mental image schemata with their "concrete carriers" (e.g., diagrams) as well as protocols of action. Of particular relevance for visualization were the four kinds of image schemata that he propounded.

Table 1. Comparison of Dörfler's image schemata and Presmeg's types of imagery

Dörfler's kinds of image schemata	*Presmeg's types of imagery used by high school learners*
Figurative (purely perceptive)	Concrete imagery ("picture in the mind")
Operative (operates on/with the carrier)	Kinaesthetic imagery (of physical movement, e.g., "walking" several vectors head to tail with fingers)
Relational (transformation of concrete carrier)	Dynamic imagery (the image itself is moved or transformed)
Symbolic image schemata (e.g., formulas with symbols and spatial relations)	Memory images of formulae
- - -	Pattern imagery (pure relationships stripped of concrete details)

Although Dörfler did not make the connection, his categories of image schemata could be considered to correspond roughly to four of the five types of imagery identified by Presmeg (1985, 1986a, 1986b, 1997b) in empirical research with 54 high school students, as outlined in table 1. In Presmeg's research, concrete imagery was the most prevalent (used by 52 of the 54 visualizers in her study), followed by memory images of formulae (32), pattern imagery (18), and kinaesthetic imagery (16). Dynamic imagery was used effectively but rarely (by only two students). The comparisons in table 1 are not intended to imply exact matches between the respective categories in Dörfler's and Presmeg's formulations. For instance, pattern imagery, which was a strong source of generalization for the learners who used it in Presmeg's research, might also involve elements of Dörfler's figurative image schemata because it is perceptual, without transformations. However, pattern imagery by its nature is capable of depicting relations (e.g., in the "lines of force" described by master chess players in describing a game on the board), thus it also incorporates elements of relational image schemata. Further, the categories may overlap, e.g., pattern imagery may also be dynamic. An important result of Presmeg's research was that all of the mathematical difficulties encountered by the 54 visualizers in her study related in one way or another to problems with generalization. Pattern imagery, and use of metaphor via an image, are two significant ways by means of which a static image may become the bearer of generalized mathematical information for a visualizer. Presmeg (1986a; 1997b) pointed out that concrete imagery needs to be coupled with rigorous analytical thought processes to be effectively used in mathematics, a result that was highlighted by Dreyfus (1991) in the second plenary of PME-15 that addressed visualization, as described next.

The title of Dreyfus's (1991) plenary paper at PME-15, "On the status of visual reasoning in mathematics and mathematics education", hinted at the kernel of his thrust in this presentation: "It is therefore argued that the status of visualization in mathematics education should and can be upgraded from that of a helpful learning aid to that of a fully recognized tool for learning and proof" (p. 33). A second central point (addressed in a later section of this chapter) was that the basic reluctance of students to use visualization in mathematics is the result of the low status accorded to visual aspects of mathematics in the classroom. However, he also gave many effective examples demonstrating the power of visualization in mathematical reasoning. Some of these examples were of the nature of the "proofs without words" that have since become a regular feature in publications of the Mathematical Association of America. His enthusiasm for visualization was however tempered with the knowledge that there are difficulties associated with students' use of visual reasoning, which because it operates holistically, in his opinion creates a greater cognitive load than more sequential modes of reasoning. He also claimed that "Since pattern and dynamic imagery is more apt to be coupled with rigorous analytical thought processes, this means that students are likely to generate visual images but they are unlikely to use them for analytical reasoning" (p. 34). This claim, as it was stated by Dreyfus at this time, is too strong and was not borne out in Presmeg's (1985) research, in which it could not be claimed that rigorous analytical thought processes were more apt to be coupled with pattern imagery or dynamic imagery than with other types. All of her classified types of imagery were coupled on occasion with rigorous analytical thought processes, to good effect. However, the effectiveness of pattern imagery and dynamic imagery was evident on the relatively rare occasions when they were used. One final point (again foreshadowing future developments) in Dreyfus's plenary was that computers impart the advantage of flexibility to visual reasoning.

Relatively few of the PME papers up to this point (1991), even in the greater pool of those peripherally addressing visual thinking in learning mathematics, had provided empirical evidence to suggest what aspects of instruction might encourage learners to use visualization, and what aspects might help them to overcome the difficulties and make optimal use of the strengths of visual processing. Presmeg's (1985) research had investigated these issues at the high school level, with surprising results, and in view of the lacuna in this area her results reported at PME-15 in 1991 are presented in some detail in the next section.

TEACHING THAT PROMOTES EFFECTIVE USE OF VISUALIZATION IN MATHEMATICS CLASSROOMS

The title of Presmeg's (1991) research report was "Classroom aspects which[1] influence use of visual imagery in high school mathematics". The aim of the complete three-year study (Presmeg, 1985) was to understand more about the circumstances that affect the visual pupil's operating in his of her preferred mode, and how the teacher facilitates this or otherwise. She had chosen 13 high school mathematics teachers for her research, based on their mathematical visuality scores from a "preference for visuality" instrument she had designed and field tested for reliability and validity (with parts A, B, and C reflecting increasing difficulty). The teachers' scores (on parts B and C) reflected the full range of cognitive preferences, from highly visual to highly nonvisual. Subsequently, 54 visualizers (who scored above the mean on parts A and B of this instrument) were chosen from the mathematics classes of these teachers to participate in the research. Lessons of these teachers were observed over a complete school year, and 108 of these audio taped lessons were transcribed. The teachers were also interviewed, and so were the visualizers, their students, on a regular basis (188 transcribed clinical interviews, apart from the interviews with the teachers). Teaching visuality (TV) of the 13 teachers was judged using 12 refined classroom aspects (CAs) taken from the literature to be supportive of visual thinking. (For an account of the refinement process and the triangulation involved in obtaining this teaching visuality score for each teacher, see Presmeg, 1991.) These classroom aspects included a non-essential pictorial presentation by the teacher, use of the teacher's own imagery as indicated by gesture (a powerful indicator) or by spatial inscriptions such as arrows in algebraic work, conscious attempts by the teacher to facilitate students' construction and use of imagery (either stationary or dynamic), teacher's requesting students to use the motor component of imagery in arm, finger, or body movements, teaching with manipulatives, teacher use of color, and

[1] This usage of "which" without a preceding comma was grammatical in 1991, before Microsoft in its spellchecker designated "that" as the correct usage here.

finally, teaching that is not rule-bound, including use of pattern-seeking methods, encouragement of students' use of intuition, delayed use of symbolism, and deliberate creation of cognitive conflict in learners (Presmeg, 1991, p. 192).

The first major surprise relating to the teachers was that their teaching visuality (TV) was only weakly correlated with their mathematical visuality (Spearman's rho = 0.404, not significant). This result was understandable in the light of the common sense notion that an effective teacher adapts to the needs of the students: For instance, Mr. Blue (pseudonym) felt almost no need for visual thinking in his mathematical problem solving, but he nevertheless used many visual aspects in his mathematics classroom as evidenced by his TV score of 7 out of a possible 12. The TV scores divided the teachers neatly into three groups, namely, a visual group (5 teachers), a middle group (4 teachers), and a nonvisual group (4 teachers), as shown in table 2.

Table 2. Teaching visuality scores of 13 teachers

Nonvisual Group		Middle group		Visual Group	
Teacher	*Score*	*Teacher*	*Score*	*Teacher*	*Score*
Mrs Crimson	2	Mr Blue	7	Mr Red	9
Mr Black	3	Mrs Turquoise	7	Mrs Gold	9
Mr Brown	4	Mrs Green	7	Mrs Silver	10
Mr White	3	Mr Grey	6	Mrs Pink	9
				Miss Mauve	10

Based on field notes of observations in the classes of these teachers, and on transcripts of 108 audio-recorded lessons, further classroom aspects that characterized the practices of teachers in each group were identified in four areas, namely, relating to teaching, students, mathematics, and visual methods. In a nutshell, the visual group of teachers, while sometimes using the lecturing style and other aspects characteristic of the nonvisual group, in addition manifested a myriad of additional aspects:

> The essence of the teaching of those in the visual group is captured in the word *connections*. The visual teachers constantly made connections between the subject matter and other areas of thought, such as other sections of the syllabus, other subjects, work done previously, aspects of the subject matter beyond the syllabus, and above all, the real world. ... It was a totally unexpected finding that visual and nonvisual teachers were distinguishable in terms of certain characteristics associated with creativity ... such as openness to external and internal experience, self-awareness, humour and playfulness. (Presmeg, 1991, p. 194)

Teachers in the middle group used many of the visual methods characteristic of the visual teachers. However, whereas the visual teachers were unanimously positive about these aspects, the middle group of teachers entertained beliefs and attitudes that suggested to their students that the visual mode was not really necessary or important –that generalization was the goal, and that visual thinking could be dispensed with after it had served its initial purpose. (See Presmeg, 1991, pp. 95-96 for examples.) Thus the middle group of teachers inadvertently helped their visualizers to overcome the generalization problem, while allowing them to use their preferred visual mode for initial mathematical processing. The result was that visualizers were most successful with teachers in the middle group –a counterintuitive and unexpected result! However, it was suggested that if teachers in the visual group had been more aware of the potential pitfalls relating to visualization and generalization, they might have been more successful in helping visualizers to overcome these difficulties. Visualizers in the classes of the nonvisual group of teachers tried to dispense with their preferred visual methods in favor of the nonvisual modes used by their teachers. Rote memorization and little success were the unfortunate consequences in most cases (Presmeg, 1986b, 1991).

With the exception of Presmeg's (1991) paper on teaching and classroom aspects of visualization, most of the PME research reports related to visualization at this period had a distinct psychological flavor (appropriate for PME, although interest in social and cultural aspects of learning mathematics was already growing in this association). Many of these studies involved structured or semi-structures clinical interviews with individual students for the purpose of investigating aspects of their use of visualization in the service of learning mathematics, a theme that is continued in the next section.

VISUALIZATION RESEARCH CONTINUES IN A PSYCHOLOGICAL FORMAT

At PME-16 in 1992 in Portsmouth, New Hampshire, USA, a Discussion Group organized by M. A. Mariotti and A. Pesci on *Visualization in problem solving and learning*, which had started in 1991, was continued. The discussions in this group explored in some detail various aspects of individual children's mathematical visualization, thus continuing the psychological focus of research reported. This focus is also reflected in the titles of some of the Research Reports: *Children's concepts of perpendiculars* (Mitchelmore, 1992), *Representation of areas: A pictorial perspective* (Outhred & Mitchelmore, 1992), *Spatial thinking takes shape through primary school experiences* (Owens, 1992), and *The elaboration of images in the process of mathematics meaning making* (Reynolds & Wheatley, 1992). Four Short Oral reports (arranged in a Featured Discussion Group) and two Posters continued the trend. Visualization also featured in Goldin's (1992) plenary presentation, *On developing a unified model for the psychology of mathematics education and problem solving*, through his construct of "imagistic systems", which was one of his five categories of cognition and affect involved in mathematics education. Further, a Plenary Panel devoted to *Visualization and imagistic thinking* (Clements, Dreyfus [organizer and chair], Mason, Parzysz & Presmeg) captured some aspects of the "state of the art" of visualization research at that time, including both the interpreting of figural information (IFI) and visual processing (VP) in its public and personal aspects, and in its relation to both cognition and affect.

Still strong at PME-17 in 1993 in Tsukuba City, Japan, the psychological treatment of visualization entered into some aspects of two Working Groups, namely, one on representations (organized by G. Goldin) and one on geometry (organized by A. Gutiérrez). Section 8 in the Proceedings, *Geometrical and Spatial Thinking*, contained 5 relevant Research Reports. More specifically, Section 9 was devoted to the topic of *Imagery and Visualization*. The six papers in this section (Brown & Presmeg; Dörfler; Gutiérrez & Jaime; Hazama & Akai; Lopez-Real & Veloo; Mariotti; all 1993) addressed the use of visual imagery in the full range of ages, showing clearly not only that imagery is used in mathematical processing by learners from elementary school right up to high school, and also in collegiate mathematics, but also the wide range of individual differences and effectiveness in this imagistic processing. One other paper, categorized under *Problem Solving* in Section 13, documented the interplay of high school students' beliefs about the nature of mathematics, and their problem solving styles using visualization in clinical interviews (Presmeg, 1993).

MOVING TOWARDS VISUALIZATION AS AN ASPECT OF CURRICULUM DEVELOPMENT

From the strong emphasis on psychological aspects of understanding the uses and difficulties of visualization by individual learners that characterized the previous two years, in 1994 at PME-18 in Lisbon the trend reflected in papers was for visualization research to move towards aspects of curriculum development. The *Visualization* Discussion Group was in its fourth year (Mariotti & Pesci), and the *Geometry* (Gutiérrez) and *Representations* (Goldin) Working Groups continued from the previous year. There were 16 Research Reports categorized as *Geometrical and Spatial Thinking*, and some of these reports were also concerned with aspects of curriculum development, but I want to concentrate on five papers that were placed specifically under the category of *Imagery and Visualization*. All five of these papers described the use of research on visualization in the development of mathematics curriculum, at levels ranging from grade 4 (Ainley, 1994; Arnon, Dubinsky & Nesher 1994), through an Algebra I course in the USA (Chazan & Bethel, 1994) and a non-matriculation track of low-ability 10th, 11th, and 12th graders in Israel (Arcavi, Hadas & Dreyfus, 1994), to a survey inquiry into the concept images of the continuum, of non-experts using mathematics (Romero & Azcárate, 1994). The research of Ainley, and also that of Chazan and Bethel, involved students drawing and understanding graphs, interpreting figural information and using visual processing (IFI and VP). The influence of computer technology was a continuing trend, reflected in Ainley's research, in which learners who were accustomed to drawing graphs using spreadsheets were asked to draw similar types of graphs by hand. The grade four students' intuitions and imagery helped them to complete the tasks successfully. The research methodologies in both of these projects incorporated mildly numerical comparisons of interview transcripts with two different treatment groups of students. The curriculum development of Arcavi et al. (1994) of a unit for studying line graphs in the

Cartesian coordinate plane, in the cyclical nature of its methodology, foreshadowed the developmental research and multi-tiered teaching experiments described in Kelly and Lesh's (2000) handbook.

The Research Reports at PME-19 (1995) and PME-20 (1996) continued the trends both of attention to curriculum or implications for curriculum (e.g., Solano & Presmeg, 1995), and of individual clinical interviews as data collection methods (e.g., Irwin, 1995). Attention to curriculum was taken to a new level later by Kidman (2002), who used seven criteria to analyze curriculum materials from the Australian Integrated Learning Systems. Returning to Irwin's (1995) research, her empirical investigation of the images of rational numbers between zero and one held by learners of 10–12 years of age revealed some interesting metaphors: When the interviewer asked, in the context of these rational numbers, "Tell me what your picture is like", an interviewee replied, "A baby that's not quite one, not newly born, it's about three months old". Also in connection with rational numbers, Herman, Ilucova, Kremsova, Pribyl, Ruppeldtova, Simpson, et al. (2004) reported that a 6th grader in their study invoked the metaphor of time; the improper fraction $\frac{7}{6}$ was described as "one hour and ten minutes", accompanied by an image of a clock face. The research of Presmeg (1985, 1992, 1997a, 1997b) also illustrated the importance of such personal metaphors, encapsulated in imagery, not only for individual meaning making and retention, but also in the service of mathematical generalization.

The Working Group on *Geometrical and Spatial Thinking* continued in both those years (1995 and 1996), without a separate Working Group on *Visualization*. At first glance there seemed to be a large discrepancy in the numbers of papers on *Imagery and Visualization* presented at these two conferences: Only three were listed in this category at PME-19 (Irwin; Presmeg & Bergsten; Solano & Presmeg; all 1995) but 16 were reported at PME-20. However, closer examination revealed that unlike PME-19 where only Research Reports were listed in this category, the PME-20 categorization included a plenary, five Short Orals, and five papers that overlapped with *Geometrical and Spatial Thinking*. When these were omitted and papers in the category *Problem Solving* were also taken into account, there were seven Research Reports directly concerning visualization at PME-20 (Gorgorió; Gray & Pitta; Healy & Hoyles; McClain & Cobb; Pitta & Gray; Thomas, Mulligan & Goldin; Trouche & Guin; all 1996). An important Plenary Paper directly concerning visualization, *Visualization in 3-dimensional geometry: In search of a framework* (Gutiérrez, 1996) surveyed definitions of imagery and visualization presented in the literature, carefully defined those used in the empirical investigation that was reported, and attempted to unify theoretical developments up to that point, taking into account the work of Bishop (1983), Kosslyn (1980), Krutetskii (1976), Presmeg (1986b), and others in the psychological community during that period. Gutiérrez described empirical work that started in 1989 (see also Gutiérrez & Jaime, 1993), which involved an investigation of visualization of 3-dimensional solids rotated by learners ranging from 7 to 17 years of age in a dynamic computer environment in Spain. The topic of computer rotation of images of solids was also addressed in interesting unpublished research by Solano in the USA. However, at PME-19 Solano and Presmeg (1995) reported on a different facet of Solano's work, namely, university students' visualization while working with a series of two-dimensional geometrical tasks.

As Mogens Niss reported in his Presidential Address at the 8th International Congress on Mathematical Education, in 1996 "images and visualization" were topics that were continuing to increase in significance: Research in this area was alive and well!

ON THE RELUCTANCE TO VISUALIZE IN MATHEMATICS

Two papers, Presmeg & Bergsten (1995) at PME-19 and Healy & Hoyles (1996) at PME-20, directly addressed the topic, which had been raised in Dreyfus's (1991) plenary address at PME-15, of students' reluctance to visualize in their learning of mathematics. Healy and Hoyles (1996) effectively summarized the issue, as follows:

> It is generally reported that students of mathematics, unlike mathematicians, rarely exploit the considerable potential of visual approaches to support meaningful learning. ... Where the mathematical agenda is identified with symbolic representation, students are reluctant to engage with visual modes of reasoning. (p. 67)

Healy and Hoyles continued by stressing the advantages, also noted by others (e.g., Presmeg, 1985, 1997b), of being able to use particular images or diagrams in the service of mathematical generalization, and of *connections* between modes of thinking. Healy and Hoyles elaborated as follows:

> In many ways, these findings are unsurprising. Mathematicians know what to look for in a diagram, know what can be generalized from a particular figure and so are able to employ a particular case or geometrical image to stand for a more general observation. Our question is, how can students best be encouraged to share in these ways of thinking –what systems of support can we offer which will encourage them to make connections between visual and symbolic representations of the same mathematical notions[?] (Op. cit.)

Their question remains an important one, which will be revisited later in this chapter.

The research of Presmeg and Bergsten (1995) on high school students' preference for visualization in three countries (South Africa, Sweden, and Florida in the USA) suggested that the claim that students are reluctant to visualize was complex and should not be interpreted simplistically to mean that students do not use this mode of mathematical thinking. On the contrary, the frequency distribution graphs based on Presmeg's (1985) instrument for measuring preference for visualization in mathematics suggested that preference for mathematical visualization follows a standard Gaussian distribution in most populations. For most people, the task itself, instructions to do the task a certain way (Paivio, 1991), and sociocultural factors including teaching situations (Dreyfus, 1991) influence the use of visual thinking in mathematics. However, there are a few people for whom visualization is not an option –they *always* feel the need for this mode of cognition in mathematics– whereas some others do not feel this need at all (Presmeg, 1985; Presmeg & Bergsten, 1995).

Eisenberg (1994) had claimed that "A vast majority of students do not like thinking in terms of pictures –and their dislike is well documented in the literature" (p. 110). He invoked, *inter alia,* Clements' (1984) study of the gifted mathematician Terence Tao –a nonvisualizer– in support of this claim. However, Krutetskii's (1976) extensive case studies showed clearly that amongst gifted, or even merely "capable" students in mathematics, there is no dearth of visualizers in addition to nonvisualizers such as Terence Tao. Krutetskii described representatives of each of his categories or types of mathematical giftedness, which were based on students' ability to use visual methods as well as their preferences. Presmeg's (1985) research bore out Krutetskii's claim that students who have the ability to use visual methods may on occasion prefer not to do so. However, it is too sweeping a claim that "students are reluctant to visualize in mathematics". Krutetskii identified "geometric" as well as "analytic" types, and two subtypes of "harmonic" thinkers. Some researchers have even taken the position, and provided evidence for their claim, that imagistic processing is central to mathematical reasoning (Wheatley, 1997; Wheatley & Brown, 1994). At PME-25 in Utrecht, Stylianou (2001) suggested that even in the learning of collegiate mathematics the picture of "reluctance to visualize" had changed in the decade since Dreyfus's (1991) plenary address. She reported evidence from her study of the perceptions and use of visualization by mathematicians and undergraduate students, and concluded as follows.

> The results of this study gave prevalent evidence that both experts and novices perceive visual representations as a useful tool and frequently attempt to use them when solving problems, suggesting that the "picture" in advanced mathematics instruction may be changing. However, further analysis clearly showed that the changes may only be covering the surface; students may be willing to use visual representations but have little training associated with this skill. Recognition of the willingness and at the same time difficulties identified in this study can lead mathematics educators to make more explicit and informed decisions about visual representation use in curricular materials and instruction, providing opportunities for students to become more successful problem solvers. (p. 232)

Stylianou's call for mathematics educators to become more knowledgeable about the difficulties and strengths associated with visual processing resonates with Presmeg's (1985, 1986a, 1997b) suggestion that the 13 teachers in her study would have been better able to help the visualizers in their classes to overcome the difficulties and exploit the strengths if they had been more explicitly aware of these issues.

Broadening the scope of this discussion of "reluctance to visualize" at PME-21 in Lahti, and referring to Hilbert's two tendencies purported to illuminate the dual nature of mathematics, Breen (1997) described these two types of mathematical thinking as follows.

> The one was the tendency towards abstraction ... The other was the tendency towards intuitive understanding which stresses processes of visualization and imagery. Generally schools have mainly concentrated on the former and a consequence of this has led to the claim that 'a vast majority of students do not like thinking in terms of pictures' (Eisenberg, 1994). This view has been challenged ... My own experience has been that images provide an important tool for learning. (p. 97)

Breen proceeded to give vignettes illustrating the effective use with pre-service mathematics education students of dynamic imagery of two kinds, namely, mathematical images and those of a more personal "educational" nature. His important paper stressed the affect often associated with imagery, which was also noted in Presmeg's (1985) research. However, he went further and added another dimension in illustrating the possible therapeutic use of imagery of both types – mathematical and educational, in his terms– but especially the second (as in psychotherapy: Singer, 1974), in the pre-service education of mathematics teachers. The "canonical" nature of some mathematical imagery, noted in Breen's paper, will be revisited in a later section on the advantages and disadvantages of prototypical imagery in the learning of mathematics. The importance of the connection between personal imagery and emotional aspects of learning mathematics was reflected later in a PME Discussion Group on *Imagery and Affect in Mathematical Learning* (organized by L. English and G. Goldin) that ran for three years (2000-2002).

DIVERSIFICATION OF INTEREST IN MATHEMATICAL VISUALIZATION

Two other papers in the proceedings of PME-21 were concerned with imagery and visualization. In a computer environment, Gomes Ferreira and Hoyles (1997) used the methodology of "blob diagrams" to illustrate the results of their longitudinal study of students learning mathematics using two software programs. A blob diagram "served two purposes: It was a tool for analysis and helped to identify points of development as well as a means of presentation of the longitudinal analysis of students' interactions with different microworlds" (p. 327). Another paper, under the classification heading of *Measurement*, described the use of visualization by young children in tiling tasks (Owens & Outhred, 1997). The diversity of researchers' interests regarding visualization, captured in the contrast between these two papers, was even more striking in the papers presented at PME-22 in 1998, where visualization was subsumed under the heading *Geometrical thinking, imagery and visualization* in the research domain classification. Table 3 illustrates the predominant focal areas, and the numbers of presentations of various kinds under this general heading, which included a total of 42 presentations of various types.

Table 3. Diversity of presentations in the visualization category at PME-22

Focus	*Research Reports*	*Short Orals*	*Posters*
Geometry	11	10	2
Representation	3	3	1
Computers	3	2	-
Problem solving	1	-	-
Measurement	-	2	-
Spatial thinking and visualization	1	2	1
Total	19	19	4

Visualization was anything but a dominant category at PME-22. Even the one Research Report that I have placed under the focus on *Spatial thinking and visualization* could have been classified in the *Representation* category: The title was *On the difficulties of visualization and representation of 3-D objects in middle school teachers* (Malara, 1998). The trend was apparently for the initial focused interest in visualization as a research area to be diffused and included under broader fields, e.g., representation. Interest in theories of semiotics –which includes visual signs– was also growing, although not all papers using semiotics as a theoretical lens had a focus on visualization (e.g., Godino & Recio, 1998). Later, a Discussion Group on semiotics (organized by A. Sáenz-Ludlow and N. Presmeg) ran for four years at PME (2001-2004) and included aspects of visual inscriptions.

The trend for mathematics education visualization research to diversify was continued at PME-23 (Haifa, 1999) and PME-24 (Hiroshima, 2000). The research in this area was also prolific: Of the 20 presentations in the category *Imagery and Visualization* at PME-23, 4 were included in a Research Forum on this topic, 9 were Research Reports, 3 were Short Orals, and 4 were Posters. Of the 16 papers placed in this category at PME-24, 6 were Research Reports, 4 were Short Orals, 4 were Posters, and 2 appeared to be misclassified under this heading. Some of the topics of Short Orals and Posters pertained to limits of functions, models of mathematical understanding, solutions of quadratic equations, manipulatives, calculators, texts, various aspects of geometry including geometrical constructions and work with solids, probability, and complex numbers. The diverse nature of this research can be gleaned from this list of topics. Research Forum papers and Research Reports at these two conferences are treated in the following sections, along with relevant papers from later PME and PME-NA conferences.

THE INFLUENCE OF COMPUTERS

Reinforcing the widening effects of computer technology in mathematical visualization (Zimmermann & Cunningham, 1991), at PME-23 in Haifa an important Research Forum report described *Visualization as a vehicle for meaningful problem solving in algebra* (Yerushalmy, Shternberg & Gilead, 1999). This presentation and the reaction by Parzysz (1999) emphasized that visualization can be powerful not only in apparently visual mathematical topics such as geometry and trigonometry but also in algebra. Further, Yerushalmy et al. made plain some of the special advantages of computer software that encourages dynamic visualization. Introducing the topic by describing the "oven problem", presented in words but without any numerical data, Yerushalmy et al. described approaches by two learners (Ella and Yoni) to the modeling of this unusual problem, in which a cook has to decide whether switching between two ovens (microwave and conventional) can shorten the cooking time. As Parzysz pointed out, some characteristic aspects of mathematical modeling are implicit in this problem: It is highly unlikely that a microwave oven has a constant rate of heating (as given in the problem), thus the presentation of the problem is already one step removed from the real situation. Thus such problems belong to "a kind of 'idealized reality', in Plato's sense" (Parzysz, 1999, p. 213). He characterized the modeling process as follows:

Real situation ⟶ Pseudo-concrete model ⟶ Mathematical model

The pseudo-concrete model represents the 'realistic' situation; the first arrow depicts an idealization process, whereas the second depicts mathematization.

Regarding this mathematization process, the powerful contribution of Yerushalmy et al. (1999) was to describe their process of classifying what became, eventually, 96 different types of algebraic word problems. They started by classifying such problems in terms of their graphs, using slopes, domains, and ranges as foci for analysis. Continuing the process, their classification involved combinations of givens and constraints. They exemplified a major distinction in types by means of two distance-rate-time problems that despite having the same organizing table for the given information, were essentially very different. In the first, it was possible to draw a specific distance-time graph; in the second, only a family of line segments governed by a parameter could be directly inferred. It is in this second case that the visualization capacities of their dynamic software program were shown to be especially useful. The advantages of being able to move flexibly amongst multiple registers (Duval, 1999) are also powerfully illustrated in their research. The visual depiction clearly manifests the difference between various types of algebraic word problems, and this visual process is encouraged and enhanced by the dynamic software. In an intriguing response, Parzysz (1999) demonstrated how similar situations are also prevalent in geometric problems: For example, in inscribing a square inside a triangle (with their bases collinear) it is useful to consider a family of squares in working out the solution –in a manner comparable to the parametric second case of Yerushalmy et al.'s (1999) distance-rate-time algebraic problems.

Further research reported at PME conferences has also addressed learners' use of visualization through dynamic geometry software (e.g., Markopoulos & Potari, 1999; Hadas & Arcavi, 2001; Arcavi & Hadas, 2002; Pratt & Davison, 2003; Sinclair, 2003). Arcavi and his associates have also investigated the use of spreadsheets in mathematical tasks (Friedlander & Arcavi, 2005). It should be noted that all of the advocates of dynamic computer software cited do not consider the use of this software as replacing the need for proof and rigorous analytical thought processes in mathematics: The software facilitates visualization processes (both IFI and VP) which may clarify and further the solution to a mathematical problem by providing insight, thus suggesting productive paths for reason and logic. Sinclair (2003) reported that students in her study involving "pre-constructed, web-based, dynamic geometry sketches in activities related to proof at the secondary school level" (p. 191) manifested a "diagram bias". They were accustomed to being presented with diagrams that were inaccurate in the sense that they merely represented the given information and were not drawn to scale, thus they mistrusted the accuracy of the Cabri or Sketchpad diagrams in their dynamic geometry programs. Sinclair reported as follows.

> Extensive studies of Cabri have shown that a geometry problem cannot be solved simply by perceiving the onscreen images, even if these are animated. The student must bring some explicit mathematical knowledge to the process. ... That is, an intuition about a generalization involves more than observed evidence. (p. 192)

Also using Cabri, Pratt and Davison (2003) reported on the affordances, but also the constraints, of using interactive whiteboards in the construction of definitions of a kite by two 11-year-old girls in England. The affordances were both visual and kinaesthetic; the constraints were related to prototypical images held by the girls, of a rhombus with a horizontal base, which they could not reconcile with their views of an interactive Cabri kite. Pratt and Davison concluded that "Their prototypes are useful resources for simple manipulations of orientation but do not support hierarchical inclusive definitions" (p. 37). These results are confirmed in other studies reporting constraints of prototypes –but also some mnemonic advantages– discussed in a later section.

FURTHERANCE OF THEORY AND LINKS WITH TEACHING

Drawing on Owens' extensive research with young children and adults, the second presentation in the Research Forum on visualization at PME-23 (Owens, 1999) furthered the systematization of a theoretical framework, *Framework for imagery for space mathematics* (p. 225). Owens' framework has two purposes, as summarized by the reactor, Gray (1999), as follows.

> Within her paper, Owens considers two features designed to inform readers about young children's early spatio-mathematical development. The first is a framework that provides a basis for teachers to assess children's thinking and build a teaching programme. The second is a mechanism for assessing the children against the framework. It is claimed that an important aspect of the two is the relationship between spatial understanding and visualization. Indeed, some of the tasks are 'specifically designed to encourage

visualization' and the framework itself is associated with a 'hierarchical' list of imagery strategies. (p. 235.)

In his thoughtful reaction paper, informed by his research in collaboration with Demetra Pitta, Gray made further distinctions, e.g., that between the use of imagery that is essential to thought and the use of imagery that generates thought. He also pointed out –and this is an issue that should be kept in mind by all researchers in this field– that "The study of imagery in any context is fraught with difficulty. We make an assumption that report, description and external representation in the form of words, drawings and actions provide an indication of the nature of the mental image" (p. 241). There is no guarantee that the researcher's construction of the nature of this imagery is accurate, nor that the thoughts of the individual were uninfluenced by the research process. The difficulties associated with research on mathematical imagery have been noted by others (e.g., DeWindt-King & Goldin, 2001; Presmeg, 1985). However, the papers by Owens (1999) and by Gray (1999) suggest that research in this area is nevertheless informative and that it can be insightful.

Several of the Research Reports at both PME-23 and PME-24, as well as plenaries and other presentations at the 21st Annual Meeting of PME-NA, brought out the power of mathematical visualization when it is connected with logical reasoning and symbolic inscriptions, as addressed in the next section.

CONNECTIONS BETWEEN VISUAL AND SYMBOLIC INSCRIPTIONS

In the North American Chapter of PME, the 21st Annual meeting in Cuernavaca, Mexico, in 1999, was particularly rich in papers with a focus on visualization in mathematics education. Seven of the ten plenary and reaction papers were on topics concerning representation and visualization, and this focus was also apparent in several Research Reports and in papers presented in a Working Group on *Representations and Mathematics Visualization*, whose papers were published in revised and extended form (Hitt, 2002). The first plenary paper at PME-NA 21 (Duval, 1999) was titled *Representation, vision and visualization: Cognitive functions in mathematical thinking. Basic issues for learning.* This paper was especially important for English-speaking researchers because Duval's extensive research had been previously published largely in French. His theoretical framework posits the connections both within and amongst different representational registers as absolutely fundamental to deep understanding of mathematics. His conceptual framework has been used extensively by other researchers (e.g., Acuña, 2001, 2002). In another thoughtful plenary that linked visual and symbolic inscriptions, Arcavi (1999) spoke on *The role of visual representations in the learning of mathematics.* In several interesting examples, he championed the cause of seeing what was formerly unseen in data by means of inscriptions. In many cases, the accompanying insight provides an "aha!" experience for the perceiver. Arcavi and Hadas also contributed a chapter for the Working Group publication (Hitt, 2002), extending their ideas on computer mediated learning (Arcavi & Hadas, 2002), which was also a theme in their presentation at PME-25 (Hadas & Arcavi, 2001). As noted in the prior section on the influence of computers in visual learning of mathematics, such learning is not exempt from the difficulties resulting from prototypical mental images and inscriptions. These prototypes are the focus of the next section.

CANONICAL OR PROTOTYPICAL MATHEMATICAL IMAGES, DIVERSITY, AND GENERALIZATION

Prototypical visual images may have mnemonic advantages (Presmeg, 1986a, 1986b, 1992), but they may also bring attendant difficulties to learners (Aspinwall, Shaw & Presmeg, 1997; Presmeg, 1986a, 1992, 1997b). In an interesting study, Mourão (2002) analyzed the visual imagery of a 15-year-old learner, Alice, as she considered graphs associated with various quadratic and cubic functions. Using Dörfler's (1991) theoretical framework, Mourão identified episodes in which the concrete carriers of the graphs were at odds with Alicia's schema that a quadratic function must have two roots, or a double root. Alice went so far as to want to translate a parabola that did not cut the x-axis so that is was in line with her visual prototype: "We can adjust here the graph ... we make a translation ... if we put the vertex here [on the x-axis] it'll have a double root" (p. 381). This study of a high school student's imagery, as in Presmeg's (1997b) research, highlights issues of the difficulties associated with generalization in prototypical imagery. The research of Bills and Gray (1999) investigated issues of generalization in elementary school learners, as summarized next.

In a naturalistic exploratory study using phenomenography as a conceptual framework, Bills and Gray (1999) described the specific and general images of children aged 5–11 years in an English school. As noted also by other researchers working with learners in both elementary and high schools (e.g., Brown & Presmeg, 1993), they described the variety of individual constructions, and the "medium-term proto-typical representations that are formed by the pupils" (Bills & Gray, 1999, p. 116). They further examined their data in terms of Kosslyn's (1980) representational-development hypothesis, conjecturing that a longitudinal study would be required to ascertain whether the imagery of individuals changes over time in the manner suggested by Kosslyn. Presmeg (1985) found no evidence for Kosslyn's hypothesis in her research with high school students, but the one-and-a half years of her data collection gave account of a relatively limited time period in the lives of her 54 visualizers, although they described earlier formative experiences in retrospect. Bills and Gray (2000) continued their research with 7–9 year olds in the first year of a longitudinal study exploring individual differences in visual processing. Neither the quantity nor the quality of the learners' imagery correlated with their accuracy in mental calculations; they found marked diversity in this regard (as also reported in the research of Gray & Pitta, 1999), but no evidence to support a developmental model for mathematical images. In a similar vein, in carefully scripted clinical interviews 16 months apart, DeWindt-King and Goldin (2001) found no evidence for Kosslyn's hypothesis. The imagery of the elementary school children they interviewed was consistent from the first interview to the second.

From the foregoing, it seems clear that individual differences in types of imagery, quality and quantity, preference for and skill in using, persist through the school years and possibly through lifetimes, without evidence of general developmental trends in forms of imagery or in their personal use. Bruner's (1964) well known *enactive, iconic,* and *symbolic* modes of cognition should therefore be taken as metaphors for types of thinking rather than as a developmental hierarchy.

SPECIFIC MATHEMATICAL CONTENT AREAS

In the years 1999 and 2000, visualization research continued in the PME community to address the learning of specific mathematical topics, e.g., "calculus in context" (Kent & Stevenson, 1999), gender differences in use of visual representations in calculus (George, 1999), trigonometry (Pritchard & Simpson, 1999), and statistics (Shaw & Outhred, 1999, Aharoni, 2000). Visualization in early algebra was also addressed (Warren, 2000). Problem solving at all levels continued to be a theme of visualization research (Pehkonen & Vaulamo, 1999; Stylianou, Leikin & Silver, 1999). Stylianou et al.'s research also falls into the category of solid geometry: Building on the work of Mariotti (1989, 1991) and others, they investigated American 8th grade students' imagery in a problem involving nets of solids, a topic in common with the research of Lawrie, Pegg, and Gutiérrez (2000) in Australia with a similar age group but using different theoretical lenses (SOLO taxonomy and Van Hiele levels). The well known and oft-cited distinction between concept definition and concept image developed by Tall and Vinner (Vinner & Tall, 1981; Vinner, 1983) was used as a lens in the geometric visualization research of Matsuo (2000), and also later in Thomas's (2003) study of the role of representations in the understanding of function by prospective high school teachers, for many of whom the graphical perspective had a strong dominance. Finally, in an unusual and interesting comparison of grade 5 students matching melodies with their visual representations in line graphs and in musical notation, Nisbet and Bain (2000) reported that it was the global shape of the inscription rather than interval sizes that caught the attention of the learners, in a simultaneous mode of processing. Success in matching the melodies with their line graphs correlated with mathematical ability of the students.

RECENT TRENDS

Because no classification index of research domains was provided in the proceedings of PME-27 in Hawai'i (2003), it was necessary to examine all of the Research Reports published that year, 19 of which (and two Short Orals) had titles suggesting visualization. Of these 19, nine turned out to be directly concerned with the topic (Cohen; Nardi & Iannone; Hewitt; Owens, Reddacliff & McPhail; Pratt & Davison; Safuanov & Gusev; Sinclair; Thomas; White & Mitchelmore, all 2003) and three were indirectly related to it (Oehrtman; Radford, Demers, Guzman &

Cerulli; Sekiguchi, all 2003); the remaining seven mentioned visualization incidentally. In the 12 papers cited, visualization in mathematics education was investigated in the following areas: Computer technology (Pratt & Davison; Sinclair –discussed in an earlier section); geometric solids (Cohen), notations and representation (Hewitt; Thomas), use by mathematicians (Nardi & Iannone), theoretical development of models for cognition (Safnanov & Gusev; Sekiguchi), metaphors (Oehrtman), gestures (Radford et al.), and finally, teaching and curriculum development (Owens et al.; White & Michelmore).

At PME-28 in Bergen, Norway (2004), the research domain index listed seven Research Reports (and no Short Orals) classified under the heading *Imagery and Visualization.* Three of the research studies reported (all conducted in Cyprus) addressed a family of topics involving the role of pictures and other representations in problem solving, the number line, fractions and decimals, with children in grades ranging from 1 to 6 (Elia & Philippou; Gagatsis & Elia; Michaelidou, Gagatsis & Pitta-Pantazi, all 2004). The results of these studies stressed the need for multiple representations of fractions and decimals, and led to further theory construction in this content area. The Cyprus researchers, under the direction of Athanasios Gagatsis, have been prolific not only in their research output, but also in addressing the need for an overarching theory with regard to the role of visual representation in mathematics education (Marcou & Gagatsis, 2003). The need for theory building is addressed again at the end of this chapter.

One other Research Report at PME-28 investigated fractions and developed theory (Herman et al., 2004). The results of this study suggested that the process-object duality of notation for a fraction results in images for fraction as a product that are problematic in the sense that they cannot easily be converted into images of the process required in addition of fractions. Their research suggested "the routes to seeing the fraction symbol as process and as object may be cognitively separate" (p. 249). This result led Herman et al. to conclude that the difficulty experienced by students in their study "may just be because (in the domain of fractions at least) objects are not the encapsulation or reification of processes after all" (p. 255). This rather startling conclusion seems to call for further research, and if confirmed in related studies, may have implications both for the teaching of fraction concepts and processes, and also for avenues of further investigation of how use of imagery may facilitate or hinder reification.

PME-29 in Melbourne, Australia (2005) witnessed the consolidation of a trend that had been gaining momentum in the last few years, namely, *Gesture and the construction of mathematical meaning*, which was the title of a Research Forum organized by F. Arzarello and L. Edwards. The connection of gesture and visual imagery was noted already by Presmeg (1985); use of gesture by her teachers and their students was one of the surest indicators of the presence of visual thinking in teaching and learning mathematics. However, the recent trend of conducting systematic research on the use of gesture links these indicators to "the birth of new perceivable signs" (Arzarello, Ferrara, Robutti & Paola, 2005, p. 73), thus focusing particularly on this mode of semiotic mediation. The connection of gestures with semiotic theories, and also with theories of embodiment, is further epitomized in the research of Maschietto and Bartolini Bussi (2005), and that of Radford and his collaborators (Radford, Bardini, Sabena, Diallo & Simbagoye, 2005; Sabena, Radford & Bardini, 2005). This development marks the genesis of a typology of kinds of gestures and their uses in mathematics education. The visual nature of this research endeavor is illustrated by the inclusion of photographic evidence in many of these research reports.

On a different topic, also at PME-29, Diezmann (2005) reported on research with students in grades 3 and 5, concluding "that it is fallacious to assume that students' knowledge of the properties of diagrams will increase substantially with age" (p. 281). This result not only provides further refutation of Kosslyn's representational development hypothesis, but also hints at the importance of teaching in the development of visual facility in mathematics, as implicit also in the following research report at PME-29. Imagery is one of the categories posited by Pirie and Kieren (1994) in their nested model of the mathematical learning process. This framework was used by Martin, LaCroix, and Fownes (2005) in their investigation of the images held by an apprentice plumber in attempting to solve a pipefitting problem. They concluded that "it cannot be assumed that the images held by adult apprentices for basic mathematical concepts are flexible or deep" (p. 305) and they pointed to the need for education that causes these images to be revised through *folding back* (Pirie & Kieren, 1994). Thus for young children and adults alike, the quality of mathematical visualization may be improved by education (see also Oikonomou & Tzekaki, 2005; Owens, 2005).

FUTURE DIRECTIONS AND BIG RESEARCH QUESTIONS

Where have we been and where are we going? At this point the diffused nature of the continuing research on visualization would seem to be a disadvantage –but it is probably necessary, as puzzle pieces are necessary in the completion of a whole picture. After a brief summary of trends in the last two decades, as reflected in PME proceedings, I highlight some themes in recent papers that point to the need for further research on topics related to visualization in mathematics education. Finally, based on these themes, I attempt to generate what I see as the *big research questions* in need of investigation at this time.

Summary of trends

This chapter started with a short account of the re-emergence of imagery research in psychology after the hiatus caused by the dominance of behaviorism in the first half of the 20th century. Visualization research in mathematics education started slowly, growing from this psychological basis in the late 1970s and early 1980s. Early studies used both quantitative and qualitative methodologies, but particularly the latter because it was conducive to gaining insights into the visual mathematical thinking of human beings. Both difficulties and strengths associated with this mode of processing, as well as its cognitive and affective aspects, were investigated. During the 1990s, when visualization research came to be recognized as a significant field for mathematics education, some studies incorporated aspects of curriculum development, and particular content areas were investigated. Some early research had been conducted (starting in the 1980s) into teaching that promotes effective mathematical visualization, but there is still a lacuna in this area. The influence of technology, particularly in dynamic computer environments, was explored and continues to be a significant focus. Gender differences in use of mathematical visualization, and mathematicians' uses of imagery in their work, were also topics of interest. Important questions were investigated, including the seeming reluctance of students to visualize in mathematics, and whether representational means followed a genetic developmental path (the answer to the latter query being negative in all studies that investigated this aspect). The 2000s saw a broadening of the focus on visualization to include semiotic aspects and theories. Research on the use of gesture in meaningful learning of mathematics began to take on a significant role, linked with aspects of the embodied nature of mathematics. Connections between different inscriptions or mathematical registers were acknowledged as important, and began to receive more research attention. Finally, the need for overarching theories that could unify the whole field of visualization in mathematics education was recognized and was receiving ongoing attention, as summarized in the next paragraph.

Already in 1992, in his plenary address at PME-16, Goldin outlined a unified model for the psychology of mathematics learning, which incorporated cognitive and affective attributes of visualization as essential components in systems of representation in mathematical problem solving processes. More specifically, also in a plenary address, Gutiérrez (1996) posited a framework for visualization in the learning of 3-dimensional geometry. More recently, from a review of the extant literature, Marcou and Gagatsis (2003) developed a first approach to a taxonomy of mathematical inscriptions based on distinctions between external and internal, descriptive and depictive, polysemic and monosemic, autonomous and auxiliary representations as used in mathematical problem solving. This work is not yet fully available in English but gives promise of valuable theory development. I see some aspects of their taxonomy relating to the triadic semiotics of Peirce (1998): Descriptive and depictive systems are reminiscent of symbolic and iconic signs respectively. Peirce's indexical signs, with their emphasis on context and metaphor, might add an element to the taxonomy of these authors, who did not make a connection with semiotics. The further development of theory concerning the use of visualization in mathematics was also suggested by Kadunz and Strässer (2004), and this development could include connections with semiotics regarding gestures and other signs (Radford et al., 2003, 2005). The need for ongoing theory development is clear.

Some of the themes in recent papers point to further directions in which research is needed. For instance, Nardi and Ionnone's (2003) important study of the perceptions of mathematicians concerning the role of concept images in their work highlights the need to link mathematical imagery with "the whole landscape" (p. 369), i.e., with conventionally accepted inscriptions as well as the bigger picture. The image (of a mathematician) "emerges from his desire for simplicity" (ibid.).

Exactly what makes imagery effective in mathematics (as it is for these mathematicians) remains a significant research topic, linking also with the need for abstraction and generalization noted again in recent papers (White & Mitchelmore, 2003; Pitta-Pantazi, Gray & Christou, 2004), and linking with ways in which imagery helps or hinders the processes of reification of mathematical objects (Hewitt, 2003; Herman et al., 2004).

An ongoing and important theme is the hitherto neglected area of how visualization interacts with the didactics of mathematics. Effective pedagogy that can enhance the use and power of visualization in mathematics education (Woolner, 2004) is perhaps the most pressing research concern at this period: Very few studies have addressed this topic since Presmeg (1991) reported the results of her study of classroom aspects that facilitate visualization.

Big research questions

In the spirit of Freudenthal's thirteen questions for mathematics education research (Adda, 1998), I here propose a list of questions that appear to be of major significance for research on visualization in mathematics education.

1. What aspects of pedagogy are significant in promoting the strengths and obviating the difficulties of use of visualization in learning mathematics?
2. What aspects of classroom cultures promote the active use of effective visual thinking in mathematics?
3. What aspects of the use of different types of imagery and visualization are effective in mathematical problem solving at various levels?
4. What are the roles of gestures in mathematical visualization?
5. What conversion processes are involved in moving flexibly amongst various mathematical registers, including those of a visual nature, thus combating the phenomenon of compartmentalization?
6. What is the role of metaphors in connecting different registers of mathematical inscriptions, including those of a visual nature?
7. How can teachers help learners to make connections between visual and symbolic inscriptions of the same mathematical notions?
8. How can teachers help learners to make connections between idiosyncratic visual imagery and inscriptions, and conventional mathematical processes and notations?
9. How may the use of imagery and visual inscriptions facilitate or hinder the reification of processes as mathematical objects?
10. How may visualization be harnessed to promote mathematical abstraction and generalization?
11. How may the affect generated by personal imagery be harnessed by teachers to increase the enjoyment of learning and doing mathematics?
12. How do visual aspects of computer technology change the dynamics of the learning of mathematics?
13. What is the structure and what are the components of an overarching theory of visualization for mathematics education?

Addressing questions such as these will entail careful examination of research methodologies. There is still scope for the qualitative methodologies that include clinical interviewing and classroom observation, which are powerful in yielding the opportunity for depth of insight. However, in order to ascertain how widespread a phenomenon is, or how generalizable the results are, it is necessary to investigate the use of appropriate statistical tools and quantitative designs.

"The role of visual imagery in mathematical problem solving remains an active question in educational research" (Stylianou, 2001, p. 232). And not only in mathematical problem solving, but in the interactional sphere of classroom teaching and learning of mathematics at all levels, the need for research on visualization remains strong.

ACKNOWLEDGEMENT

The author wishes to thank Athanasios Gagatsis and Abraham Arcavi for helpful comments on an earlier version of this chapter.

REFERENCES

Acuña, C. (2001). High school students' conceptions of graphic representations associated to the construction of a straight line of positive abscissas. In M. van den Heuvel-Panhuizen (Ed.), *Proceedings of the 25th PME International Conference, 2*, 1–8.

Acuña, C. (2002). High school students' identification of equal slope and y-intercept in different straight lines. In A. D. Cockburn & E. Nardi (Eds.), *Proceedings of the 26th PME International Conference, 2*, 1–8.

Adda, J. (1998). A glance over the evolution of research in mathematics education. In A. Sierpinska & J. Kilpatrick (Eds.), *Mathematics education as a research domain: A search for identity* (pp. 49–56). Dordrecht, The Netherlands: Kluwer.

Aharoni, D. (2000). What you see is what you get – the influence of visualization on the perception of data structures. In T. Nakahara & M. Koyama (Eds.), *Proceedings of the 24th PME International Conference, 2*, 1–8.

Ainley, J. (1994). Building on children's intuitions about line graphs. In J. P. Ponte & J. F. Matos (Eds.), *Proceedings of the 18th PME International Conference, 2*, 1–8.

Antonietti, A., & Angelini, A. (1991). Effects of diagrams on the solution of problems concerning the estimation of differences. In F. Furinghetti (Ed.), *Proceedings of the 15th PME International Conference, 1*, 65–71.

Arcavi, A. (1999). The role of visual representations in the learning of mathematics. In F. Hitt & M. Santos (Eds.), *Proceedings of the 21st North American PME Conference, 1*, 55–80.

Arcavi, A., & Hadas, N. (2002). Computer mediated learning: An example of an approach. In F. Hitt (Ed.), *Representations and mathematical visualization*. Mexico D.F.: Cinvestav – IPN.

Arcavi, A., Hadas, N., & Dreyfus, T. (1994). Engineering curriculum tasks on the basis of theoretical and empirical findings. In J. P. Ponte & J. F. Matos (Eds.), *Proceedings of the 18th PME International Conference, 2*, 280–287.

Arcavi, A., & Nachmias, R. (1989). Re-exploring familiar concepts with a new representation. In G. Vergnaud (Ed.), *Proceedings of the 13th PME International Conference, 1*, 77–84.

Arnon, I., Dubinsky, E., & Nesher, P. (1994). Actions which can be performed in the learner's imagination: The case of multiplication of a fraction by an integer. In J. P. Ponte & J. F. Matos (Eds.), *Proceedings of the 18th PME International Conference, 2*, 32–39.

Arzarello, F., Ferrara, F., Robutti, O., & Paola, D. (2005). The genesis of signs by gestures: The case of Gustavo. In H. L. Chick & J. L. Vincent (Eds.), *Proceedings of the 29th PME International Conference, 2*, 73–80.

Aspinwall, L., Shaw, K., & Presmeg, N. (1997). Uncontrollable mental imagery: Graphical connections between a function and its derivative. *Educational Studies in Mathematics, 33*, 301–317.

Bakar, M., & Tall, D. (1991). Students' mental prototypes for functions and graphs. In F. Furinghetti (Ed.), *Proceedings of the 15th PME International Conference, 1*, 104–111.

Bills, C., & Gray, E. (1999). Pupils' images of teachers' representations. In O. Zaslavsky (Ed.), *Proceedings of the 23rd PME International Conference, 2*, 113–120.

Bills, C., & Gray, E. (2000). The use of mental imagery in mental calculation. In T. Nakahara & M. Koyama (Eds.), *Proceedings of the 24th PME International Conference, 2*, 81–88.

Bishop, A. J. (1973). Use of structural apparatus and spatial ability: A possible relationship. *Research in Education, 9*, 43–49.

Bishop, A. J. (1980). Spatial abilities and mathematics education: A review. *Educational Studies in Mathematics, 11*, 257–269.

Bishop, A. J. (1983). Space and geometry. In R. Lesh & M. Landau (Eds.), *Acquisition of mathematics concepts and processes* (pp. 175–203). New York, USA: Academic Press.

Bishop, A. J. (1986). What are some obstacles to learning geometry? *UNESCO Studies in Mathematics Education, 5*, 141–159.

Bishop, A. J. (1988). A review of research on visualization in mathematics education. In A. Borbás (Ed.), *Proceedings of the 12th PME International Conference, 1*, 170–176.

Bodner, B. L., & Goldin, G. A. (1991). Drawing a diagram: Observing a partially-developed heuristic process in college students. In F. Furinghetti (Ed.), *Proceedings of the 15th PME International Conference, 1*, 160–167.

Breen, C. (1997). Exploring imagery in P, M and E. In E. Pehkonen (Ed.), *Proceedings of the 21st PME International Conference, 2*, 97–104.

Brown, D. L., & Presmeg, N. C. (1993). Types if imagery used by elementary and secondary school students in mathematical reasoning. In I. Hirabayashi, N. Nohda, K. Shigematsu, & F.-L. Lin (Eds.), *Proceedings of the 17th PME International Conference, 2*, 137–144.

Brown, D., & Wheatley, G. (1990). The role of imagery in mathematical reasoning. In G. Booker, P. Cobb, & T. N. Mendicuti (Eds.), *Proceedings of the 14th PME International Conference, 1*, 217.

Bruner, J. S. (1964). The course of cognitive growth. *American psychologist, 19*, 1–15.

Chazan, D., & Bethel, S. (1994). Sketching graphs of an independent and a dependent quantity: Difficulties in learning to make stylized conventional "pictures". In J. P. Ponte & J. F. Matos (Eds.), *Proceedings of the 18th PME International Conference, 2*, 176–184.

Clements, M. A. (1982). Visual imagery and school mathematics. *For the Learning of Mathematics, 2*, 2–9, & *3*, 33–39.

Clements, M. A. (1984). Terence Tao. *Educational Studies in Mathematics, 15*, 213–238.

Cohen, N. (2003). Curved solids nets. In N. Pateman, B. J. Dougherty, & J. Zillox (Eds.), *Proceedings of the 27th PME International Conference, 2*, 229–236.

Cooper, M. (1988). The effect of order-coding and shading of graphical instructions on the speed of construction of a three-dimensional object. In A. Borbás (Ed.), *Proceedings of the 12th PME International Conference, 1*, 231–238.

DeWindt-King, A., & Goldin, G. A. (2001). A study of children's visual imagery in solving problems with fractions. In M. van den Heuvel-Panhuizen (Ed.), *Proceedings of the 25th PME International Conference, 2*, 345–352.

Diezmann, C. M. (2005). Primary students' knowledge of the properties of spatially-oriented diagrams. In H. L. Chick & J. L. Vincent (Eds.), *Proceedings of the 29th PME International Conference, 2*, 281–288.

Dörfler, W. (1991). Meaning: Image schemata and protocols. In F. Furinghetti (Ed.), *Proceedings of the 15th PME International Conference, 1*, 17–32.

Dörfler, W. (1993). Fluency in a discourse or manipulation of mathematical objects? In I. Hirabayashi, N. Nohda, K. Shigematsu, & F.-L. Lin (Eds.), *Proceedings of the 17th PME International Conference, 2*, 145–152.

Dreyfus, T. (1991). On the status of visual reasoning in mathematics and mathematics education. In F. Furinghetti (Ed.), *Proceedings of the 15th PME International Conference, 1*, 33–48.

Dreyfus, T., & Eisenberg, T. (1990). On difficulties with diagrams: Theoretical issues. In G. Booker, P. Cobb, & T. N. Mendicuti (Eds.), *Proceedings of the 14th PME International Conference, 1*, 27–36.

Duval, R. (1999). Representation, vision and visualization: Cognitive functions in mathematical thinking. Basic issues for learning. In F. Hitt & M. Santos (Eds.), *Proceedings of the 21st North American PME Conference, 1*, 3–26.

Eisenberg, T. (1994). On understanding the reluctance to visualize. *Zentralblatt für Didaktik der Mathematik, 26*(4), 109–113.

Elia, I., & Philippou, G. (2004). The function of pictures in problem solving. In M. J. Høines & A. B. Fuglestad (Eds.), *Proceedings of the 28th PME International Conference, 2*, 327–334.

Farfán, R. M., & Hitt, F. (1990). Intuitive processes, mental image and analytical and graphic representations of the stationary state (a case study). In G. Booker, P. Cobb, & T. N. Mendicuti (Eds.), *Proceedings of the 14th PME International Conference, 1*, 45–52.

Friedlander, A., & Arcavi, A. (2005). Folding perimeters: Designer concerns and student solutions. In H. L. Chick & J. L. Vincent (Eds.), *Proceedings of the 29th PME International Conference, 1*, 108–114.

Fry, C. (1988). Eye fixation during the reading and solution of word problems containing extraneous information: Relation to spatial visualization ability. In A. Borbás (Ed.), *Proceedings of the 12th PME International Conference, 1*, 326–333.

Gagatsis, A., & Elia, I. (2004). The effects of different modes of representation on mathematical problem solving. In M. J. Høines & A. B. Fuglestad (Eds.), *Proceedings of the 28th PME International Conference, 2*, 447–454.

George, E. A. (1999). Male and female calculus students' use of visual representations. In O. Zaslavsky (Ed.), *Proceedings of the 23rd PME International Conference, 3*, 17–24.

Godino, J. D., & Recio, A. M. (1998). A semiotic model for analyzing the relationships between thought, language and context in mathematics education. In A. Olivier & K. Newstead (Eds.), *Proceedings of the 22nd PME International Conference, 3*, 1–8.

Goldin, G. A. (1988). The development of a model for competence in mathematical problem solving based on systems of cognitive representation. In A. Borbás (Ed.), *Proceedings of the 12th PME International Conference, 2*, 358–365.

Goldin, G. A. (1992). On the developing of a unified model for the psychology of mathematics learning and problem solving. In W. Geeslin & K. Graham (Eds.), *Proceedings of the 16th PME International Conference, 3*, 235–261.

Gomes Ferreira, V., & Hoyles, C. (1997). A visual presentation of a longitudinal study: Design and analysis. In E. Pehkonen (Ed.), *Proceedings of the 21st PME International Conference, 2*, 321–328.

Gorgorió, N. (1996). Choosing a visual strategy: The influence of gender on the solution process of rotation problems. In L. Puig & A. Gutiérrez (Eds.), *Proceedings of the 20th PME International Conference, 3*, 19–26.

Gray, E. (1999): Spatial strategies and visualization, In O. Zaslavsky (Ed.), *Proceedings of the 23rd PME International Conference, 1*, 235–242.

Gray, E., & Pitta, D. (1996). Number processing: Qualitative differences in thinking and the role of imagery. In L. Puig & A. Gutiérrez (Eds.), *Proceedings of the 20th PME International Conference, 3*, 35–42.

Gray, E., & Pitta, D. (1999). Images and their frames of reference: A perspective on cognitive development in elementary arithmetic. In O. Zaslavsky (Ed.), *Proceedings of the 23rd PME International Conference, 3*, 49–56.

Gutiérrez, A. (1996). Visualization in 3-dimensional geometry: In search of a framework. In L. Puig & A. Gutiérrez (Eds.), *Proceedings of the 20th PME International Conference, 1*, 3–19.

Gutiérrez, A., & Jaime, A. (1993). An analysis of the students' use of mental images when making or imagining movements of polyhedra. In I. Hirabayashi, N. Nohda, K. Shigematsu, & F.-L. Lin (Eds.), *Proceedings of the 17th PME International Conference, 2*, 153–160.

Hadas, N., & Arcavi, A. (2001). Relearning mathematics – the case of dynamic geometrical phenomena and their unexpected Cartesian representations. In M. van den Heuvel-Panhuizen (Ed.), *Proceedings of the 25th PME International Conference, 3*, 81–88.

Hazama, S., & Akai, T. (1993). Pupil's development of graphical representations of 3-dimensional figures: On technical difficulties, conflicts or dilemmas, and controls in the drawing process. In I. Hirabayashi, N. Nohda, K. Shigematsu, & F.-L. Lin (Eds.), *Proceedings of the 17th PME International Conference, 2*, 161–168.

Healy, L., & Hoyles, C. (1996). Seeing, doing and expressing: An evaluation of task sequences for supporting algebraic thinking. In L. Puig & A. Gutiérrez (Eds.), *Proceedings of the 20th PME International Conference, 3*, 67–74.

Herman, J., Ilucova, L., Kremsova, V., Pribyl, J., Ruppeldtova, J., Simpson, A., et al. (2004). Images of fractions *as* processes and images of fractions *in* processes. In M. J. Høines & A. B. Fuglestad (Eds.), *Proceedings of the 28th PME International Conference, 4*, 249–256.

Hershkowitz, R., Friedlander, A., & Dreyfus, T. (1991). Loci and visual thinking. In F. Furinghetti (Ed.), *Proceedings of the 15th PME International Conference, 2*, 181–188.

Hewitt, D. (2003). Notation issues: Visual effects and ordering operations. In N. Pateman, B. J. Dougherty, & J. Zillox (Eds.), *Proceedings of the 27th PME International Conference, 3*, 63–69.

Hitt, F. (1990). The concept of function: Continuity image versus discontinuity image (computer experience). In G. Booker, P. Cobb, & T. N. Mendicuti (Eds.), *Proceedings of the 14th PME International Conference, 2*, 67–74.

Hitt, F. (Ed.). (2002). *Representations and mathematics visualization*. (Papers presented in this Working Group of PME–NA, 1998–2002). Mexico D.F.: Cinvestav - IPN.

Irwin, K. (1995). Students' images of decimal fractions. In L. Meira & D. Carraher (Eds.), *Proceedings of the 19th PME International Conference, 3*, 50–57.

Kadunz, G., & Strässer, R. (2004). Image – metaphor – diagram: Visualization in learning mathematics. In M. J. Høines & A. B. Fuglestad (Eds.), *Proceedings of the 28th PME International Conference, 4*, 241–248.

Kaput, J. J. (1987). Representational systems and mathematics. In C. Janvier (Ed.), *Problems of representation in the teaching and learning of mathematics* (pp. 19–26). Hillsdale, NJ, USA: Lawrence Erlbaum.

Kelly, A., & Lesh, R. (Eds.). (2000). *Handbook of research design in mathematics education*. Mahwah, NJ, USA: Lawrence Erlbaum.

Kent, P., & Stevenson, I. (1999). "Calculus in context": A study of undergraduate chemistry students' perceptions of integration. In O. Zaslavsky (Ed.), *Proceedings of the 23rd PME International Conference, 3*, 137–144.

Kidman, G. C. (2002). The accuracy of mathematical diagrams in curriculum materials. In A. D. Cockburn & E. Nardi (Eds.), *Proceedings of the 26th PME International Conference, 3*, 201–208.

Kosslyn, S. M. (1980). *Image and mind*. London: Harvard University Press.

Krutetskii, V. A. (1976). *The psychology of mathematical abilities in schoolchildren*. Chicago, USA: University of Chicago Press.

Lawrie, C., Pegg, J., & Gutiérrez, A. (2000). Coding the nature of thinking displayed in responses on nets of solids. In T. Nakahara & M. Koyama (Eds.), *Proceedings of the 24th PME International Conference, 3*, 215–222.

Lea, H. (1990). Spatial concepts in the Kalahari. In G. Booker, P. Cobb, & T. N. Mendicuti (Eds.), *Proceedings of the 14th PME International Conference, 2*, 259–266.

Lean, G. A., & Clements, M. A. (1981). Spatial ability, visual imagery and mathematical performance. *Educational Studies in Mathematics, 12*, 1–33.

Lopez-Real, F. (1991). Describing geometric diagrams as a stimulus for group discussion. In F. Furinghetti (Ed.), *Proceedings of the 15th PME International Conference, 2*, 342–349.

Lopez-Real, F., & Veloo, P. K. (1993). Children's use of diagrams as a problem solving strategy. In I. Hirabayashi, N. Nohda, K. Shigematsu, & F.-L. Lin (Eds.), *Proceedings of the 17th PME International Conference, 2*, 169–176.

Malara, N. (1998). On the difficulties of visualization and representation of 3D objects in middle school teachers. In A. Olivier & K. Newstead (Eds.), *Proceedings of the 22nd PME International Conference, 3*, 239–246.

Marcou, A., & Gagatsis, A. (2003). A theoretical taxonomy of external systems of representation in the learning and understanding of mathematics. In A. Gagatsis & I. Elia (Eds.), *Representations and geometrical models in the learning of mathematics* (1, pp. 171–178). Nicosia, Cyprus: Intercollege Press (in Greek).

Mariotti, M. A. (1989). Mental images: Some problems related to the development of solids. In G. Vergnaud (Ed.), *Proceedings of the 13th PME International Conference, 2*, 258–265.

Mariotti, M. A. (1991). Age variant and invariant elements in the solution of unfolding problems. In F. Furinghetti (Ed.), *Proceedings of the 15th PME International Conference, 2*, 389–396.

Mariotti, M. A. (1993). The influence of standard images in geometrical reasoning. In I. Hirabayashi, N. Nohda, K. Shigematsu, & F.-L. Lin (Eds.), *Proceedings of the 17th PME International Conference, 2*, 177–182.

Markopoulos, C., & Potari, D. (1999). Forming relationships in three dimensional geometry through dynamic environments. In O. Zaslavsky (Ed.), *Proceedings of the 23rd PME International Conference, 3*, 273–280.

Martin, L. C., LaCroix, L., & Fownes, L. (2005). Fractions in the workplace: Folding back and the growth of mathematical understanding. In H. L. Chick & J. L. Vincent (Eds.), *Proceedings of the 29th PME International Conference, 3*, 305–312.

Maschietto, M., & Bartolini Bussi, M. G. (2005). Meaning construction through semiotic means: The case of the visual pyramid. In H. L. Chick & J. L. Vincent (Eds.), *Proceedings of the 29th PME International Conference, 3*, 313–320.

Matsuo, N. (2000). States of understanding relations among concepts of geometric figures: Considered from the aspect of concept definition and concept image. In T. Nakahara & M. Koyama (Eds.), *Proceedings of the 24th PME International Conference, 3*, 271–278.

McClain, K., & Cobb, P. (1996). The role of imagery and discourse in supporting the development of mathematical meaning. In L. Puig & A. Gutiérrez (Eds.), *Proceedings of the 20th PME International Conference, 3*, 353–360.

Michaelidou, N., Gagatsis, A., & Pitta-Pantazi, D. (2004). The number line as a representation of decimal numbers: A research with sixth grade students. In M. J. Høines & A. B. Fuglestad (Eds.), *Proceedings of the 28th PME International Conference, 3*, 305–312.

Mitchelmore, M. C. (1976). Cross-cultural research on concepts of space and geometry. In J. L. Martin (Ed.), *Space and geometry*. Columbus, Ohio, USA: ERIC/SMEAC.

Mitchelmore, M. C. (1992). Children's concepts of perpendiculars. In W. Geeslin & K. Graham (Eds.), *Proceedings of the 16th PME International Conference, 2*, 120–127.

Moses, B. E. (1977). *The nature of spatial ability and its relationship to mathematical problem solving*. Unpublished PhD dissertation, Indiana University, USA.

Mourão, A. P. (2002). Quadratic function and imagery: Alice's case. In A. D. Cockburn & E. Nardi (Eds.), *Proceedings of the 26th PME International Conference, 3*, 377–384.

Nadot, S. (1989). The computer produces a special graphic situation of learning the change of coordinate systems. In G. Vergnaud (Ed.), *Proceedings of the 13th PME International Conference, 3*, 11–17.

Nardi, E., & Iannone, P. (2003). Mathematicians on concept image construction: Single 'landscape' vs 'your own tailor-made brain version'. In N. Pateman, B. J. Dougherty, & J. Zillox (Eds.), *Proceedings of the 27th PME International Conference, 3*, 365–372.

Nisbet, S., & Bain, J. (2000). Listen to the graph: Children's matching of melodies with their visual representations. In T. Nakahara & M. Koyama (Eds.), *Proceedings of the 24th PME International Conference, 4*, 49–56.

O'Brien, T. C. (1991). The status of children's construction of relationships. In F. Furinghetti (Ed.), *Proceedings of the 15th PME International Conference, 3*, 117–120.

Oehrtman, M. C. (2003). Strong and weak metaphors for limits. In N. Pateman, B. J. Dougherty, & J. Zillox (Eds.), *Proceedings of the 27th PME International Conference, 3*, 397–404.

Oikonomou, A., & Tzekaki, M. (2005). Improving spatial representations in early childhood. In H. L. Chick & J. L. Vincent (Eds.), *Proceedings of the 29th PME International Conference, 1*, 268.

Outhred, L., & Mitchelmore, M. C. (1992). Representation of area: A pictorial perspective. In W. Geeslin & K. Graham (Eds.), *Proceedings of the 16th PME International Conference, 2*, 194–201.

Owens, K. (1992). Spatial thinking takes shape through primary school experiences. In W. Geeslin & K. Graham (Eds.), *Proceedings of the 16th PME International Conference, 2*, 202–209.

Owens, K. (1999): The role of visualization in young students' learning, In O. Zaslavsky (Ed.), *Proceedings of the 23rd PME International Conference, 1*, 220–234.

Owens, K. (2005). Substantive communication of space mathematics in upper primary school. In H. L. Chick & J. L. Vincent (Eds.), *Proceedings of the 29th[th] PME International Conference, 4*, 33–40.

Owens, K., & Outhred, L. (1997). Early representations of tiling areas. In E. Pehkonen (Ed.), *Proceedings of the 21st PME International Conference, 3*, 312–319.

Owens, K., Reddacliff, C., & McPhail, D. (2003). Facilitating the teaching of space mathematics: An evaluation. In N. Pateman, B. J. Dougherty, & J. Zillox (Eds.), *Proceedings of the 27th PME International Conference, 1*, 339–345.

Paivio, A. (1991). *Imagery and verbal processes*. New York, USA: Holt, Rinehart & Winston.

Parzysz, B. (1999). Visualization and modeling in problem solving: From algebra to geometry and back. In O. Zaslavsky (Ed.), *Proceedings of the 23rd PME International Conference, 1*, 212–219.

Pehkonen, E., & Vaulamo, J. (1999). Pupils in lower secondary school solving open-ended problems in mathematics. In O. Zaslavsky (Ed.), *Proceedings of the 23rd PME International Conference, 4*, 33–40.

Peirce, C. S. (1998). *The essential Peirce: Selected philosophical writings, Vol. 2 (1893–1913)*. The Peirce Edition Project. Bloomington, IN, USA: Indiana University Press.

Pesci, A. (1989). Inverse procedures: The influence of a didactic proposal on students' strategies. In G. Vergnaud (Ed.), *Proceedings of the 13th PME International Conference, 3*, 111–118.

Piaget, J., & Inhelder, B. (1971). *Mental imagery and the child*. London: Routledge & Kegan Paul.

Pirie, S., & Kieren, T. (1994). Growth in mathematical understanding: How can we characterize it and how can we represent it? *Educational Studies in Mathematics, 26*, 165–190.

Pitta, D., & Gray, E. (1996). Nouns, adjectives and images in elementary mathematics: Low and high achievers compared. In L. Puig & A. Gutiérrez (Eds.), *Proceedings of the 20th PME International Conference, 4*, 155–162.

Pitta-Pantazi, D., Gray, E., & Christou, C. (2004). Elementary school students mental representations of fractions. In M. J. Høines & A. B. Fuglestad (Eds.), *Proceedings of the 28th PME International Conference, 4*, 41–48.

Pratt, D., & Davison, I. (2003). Interactive whiteboards and the construction of definitions for the kite. In N. Pateman, B. J. Dougherty, & J. Zillox (Eds.), *Proceedings of the 27th PME International Conference, 4*, 31–38.

Presmeg, N. C. (1985). *The role of visually mediated processes in high school mathematics: A classroom investigation*. Unpublished PhD dissertation, Cambridge University, Cambridge, UK.

Presmeg, N. C. (1986a). Visualization and mathematical giftedness. *Educational Studies in Mathematics, 17*, 297–311.

Presmeg, N. C. (1986b). Visualization in high school mathematics. *For the Learning of Mathematics, 6*(3), 42–46.

Presmeg, N. C. (1991). Classroom aspects which influence use of visual imagery in high school mathematics. In F. Furinghetti (Ed.), *Proceedings of the 15th PME International Conference, 3*, 191–198.

Presmeg, N. C. (1992). Prototypes, metaphors, metonymies, and imaginative rationality in high school mathematics. *Educational Studies in Mathematics, 23*, 595–610.

Presmeg, N. C. (1993). Mathematics – 'A bunch of formulas'? Interplay of beliefs and problem solving styles. In I. Hirabayashi, N. Nohda, K. Shigematsu, & F.-L. Lin (Eds.), *Proceedings of the 17th PME International Conference*, *3*, 57–64.

Presmeg, N. C. (1997a). Reasoning with metaphors and metonymies in mathematics learning. In L. D. English (Ed.), *Mathematical reasoning: Analogies, metaphors and images* (pp. 267–279). Mahwah, NJ, USA: Lawrence Erlbaum.

Presmeg, N. C. (1997b). Generalization using imagery in mathematics. In L. D. English (Ed.), *Mathematical reasoning: Analogies, metaphors and images* (pp. 299–312). Mahwah, NJ, USA: Lawrence Erlbaum.

Presmeg, N. C., & Bergsten, C. (1995). Preference for visual methods: An international study. In L. Meira & D. Carraher (Eds.), *Proceedings of the 19th PME International Conference*, *3*, 58–65.

Pritchard, L., & Simpson, A. (1999). The role of pictorial images in trigonometry problems. In O. Zaslavsky (Ed.), *Proceedings of the 23rd PME International Conference*, *4*, 81–88.

Radford, L., Bardini, C., Sabena, C., Diallo, P., & Simbagoye, A. (2005). On embodiment, artifacts, and signs: A semiotic-cultural perspective on mathematical thinking. In H. L. Chick & J. L. Vincent (Eds.), *Proceedings of the 29th PME International Conference*, *4*, 113–120.

Radford, L., Demers, S., Guzman, J., & Cerulli, M. (2003). Calculators, graphs, gestures and the production of meaning. In N. Pateman, B. J. Dougherty, & J. Zillox (Eds.), *Proceedings of the 27th PME International Conference*, *4*, 56–62.

Reynolds, A., & Wheatley, G. (1992). The elaboration of images in the process of mathematics meaning making. In W. Geeslin & K. Graham (Eds.), *Proceedings of the 16th PME International Conference*, *2*, 242–249.

Richardson, A. (1969). *Mental imagery*. London: Routledge & Kegan Paul.

Romero, C., & Azcárate, C. (1994). An inquiry into the concept images of the continuum: Trying a research tool. In J. P. Ponte & J. F. Matos (Eds.), *Proceedings of the 18th PME International Conference*, *2*, 185–192.

Roth, W.-M. (2004). *Towards an anthropology of graphing: Semiotic and activity-theoretic perspectives*. Dordrecht, The Netherlands: Kluwer.

Sabena, C., Radford, L., & Bardini, C. (2005). Synchronizing gestures, words and actions in pattern generalization. In H. L. Chick & J. L. Vincent (Eds.), *Proceedings of the 29thth PME International Conference*, *4*, 129–136.

Safuanov, I. S., & Gusev, V. A. (2003). Thinking in images and its role in learning mathematics. In N. Pateman, B. J. Dougherty, & J. Zillox (Eds.), *Proceedings of the 27th PME International Conference*, *4*, 87–94.

Sekiguchi, Y. (2003). An analysis of mental space construction in teaching linear equation word problems. In N. Pateman, B. J. Dougherty, & J. Zillox (Eds.), *Proceedings of the 27th PME International Conference*, *4*, 143–150.

Shama, G., & Dreyfus, T. (1991). Spontaneous strategies for visually presented linear programming problems. In F. Furinghetti (Ed.), *Proceedings of the 15th PME International Conference*, *3*, 262–269.

Shaw, P., & Outhred, L. (1999). Students' use of diagrams in statistics. In O. Zaslavsky (Ed.), *Proceedings of the 23rd PME International Conference*, *4*, 185–192.

Sinclair, M. P. (2003). The provision of accurate images with dynamic geometry. In N. Pateman, B. J. Dougherty, & J. Zillox (Eds.), *Proceedings of the 27th PME International Conference*, *4*, 191–198.

Singer, J. L. (1974). *Imagery and daydream methods in psychotherapy and behavior modification*. New York, USA: Academic Press.

Solano, A., & Presmeg, N. C. (1995). Visualization as a relation of images. In L. Meira & D. Carraher (Eds.), *Proceedings of the 19th PME International Conference*, *3*, 66–73.

Suwarsono, S. (1982). *Visual imagery in the mathematical thinking of seventh grade students*. Unpublished PhD dissertation, Monash University, Australia.

Stylianou, D. (2001). On the reluctance to visualize in mathematics: Is the picture changing? In M. van den Heuvel-Panhuizen (Ed.), *Proceedings of the 25th PME International Conference*, *4*, 225–232.

Stylianou, D. A., Leikin, R., & Silver, E. A. (1999). Exploring students' solution strategies in solving a spatial visualization problem involving nets. In O. Zaslavsky (Ed.), *Proceedings of the 23rd PME International Conference, 4*, 241–248.

Thomas, M. (2003). The role of representations in teacher understanding of function. In N. Pateman, B. J. Dougherty, & J. Zillox (Eds.), *Proceedings of the 27th PME International Conference, 4*, 291–298.

Thomas, N., Mulligan, J., & Goldin, G. (1996). Children's representation of the counting sequence 1–100: Cognitive structural development. In L. Puig & A. Gutiérrez (Eds.), *Proceedings of the 20th PME International Conference, 4*, 307–314.

Trouche, L., & Guin, D. (1996). Seeing is reality: How graphic calculators may influence the conceptualization of limits. In L. Puig & A. Gutiérrez (Eds.), *Proceedings of the 20th PME International Conference, 4*, 323–330.

Vinner, S. (1983). Concept definition, concept image and the notion of function. *International Journal for Mathematical Education in Science and Technology, 14*(3), 293–305.

Vinner, S., & Tall, D. (1981). Concept image and concept definition in mathematics with particular reference to limits and continuity. *Educational Studies in Mathematics, 12*, 151–169.

Warren, E. (2000). Visualisation and the development of early understanding of algebra. In T. Nakahara & M. Koyama (Eds.), *Proceedings of the 24th PME International Conference, 4*, 273–280.

Wheatley, G. H. (1997). Reasoning with images in mathematical activity. In L. D. English (Ed.), *Mathematical reasoning: Analogies, metaphors and images* (pp. 281–297). Mahwah, NJ, USA: Lawrence Erlbaum.

Wheatley G. H., & Brown, D. (1994). The construction and representation of images in mathematical activity. In J. P. Ponte & J. F. Matos (Eds.), *Proceedings of the 18th PME International Conference, 1*, 81.

White, P., & Mitchelmore, M. (2003). Teaching angles by abstraction from physical activities with concrete materials. In N. Pateman, B. J. Dougherty, & J. Zillox (Eds.), *Proceedings of the 27th PME International Conference, 4*, 403–410.

Woolner, P. (2004). A comparison of a visual-spatial approach and a verbal approach to teaching mathematics. In M. J. Høines & A. B. Fuglestad (Eds.), *Proceedings of the 28th PME International Conference, 4*, 449–456.

Yerushalmy, M. (1989). The use of graphs as visual interactive feedback while carrying out algebraic transformations. In G. Vergnaud (Ed.), *Proceedings of the 13th[th] PME International Conference, 3*, 252–260.

Yerushalmy, M., & Gafni, R. (1991). The effect of graphic representation: An experiment involving algebraic transformations. In F. Furinghetti (Ed.), *Proceedings of the 15th PME International Conference, 3*, 372–377.

Yerushalmy, M., Shternberg, G., & Gilead, S. (1999). Visualization as a vehicle for meaningful problem solving in algebra. In O. Zaslavsky (Ed.), *Proceedings of the 23rd PME International Conference, 1*, 197–211.

Zimmermann, W., & Cunningham, S. (1991). *Visualization in teaching and learning mathematics.* Washington, DC, USA: Mathematical Association of America.

AFFILIATION

Norma Presmeg
Mathematics Department
Illinois State University
313 Stevenson Hall
Normal, IL 61790-4520 (USA)
npresmeg@ilstu.edu

FRANCESCA FERRARA, DAVE PRATT, AND ORNELLA ROBUTTI

THE ROLE AND USES OF TECHNOLOGIES FOR THE TEACHING OF ALGEBRA AND CALCULUS

Ideas Discussed at PME over the Last 30 Years

INTRODUCTION

In the history of humankind, many "representational infrastructures" (Kaput, Noss & Hoyles, 2002) were introduced, as written language, number systems, computation systems, algebraic notations, which gave the possibility to register, transfer and record various kinds of information, and also to support the capacities of the human brain. The notion of an automatic computing machine that precedes the modern computer is not new: Leibniz was searching for such a kind of tool, being aware of the fact that "not only that choice of notation system was critically important to what one could achieve with the system, but also and more specifically, that a well-chosen syntax for operations on the notation system could support ease of symbolic computation" (Kaput et al., 2002). Technology can be seen not only as the last powerful representational infrastructure introduced by humankind to present thoughts, to communicate and to support reasoning and computation, but it can also be seen as an infrastructure that supports at least two developments: Human participation is no longer required for the execution of a process, and the access to the symbolism is no longer restricted to a privileged minority of people, as it was in the past. The first development caused the incoming of new kinds of employment, and the death of others. The second is responsible for a general democratisation of access to knowledge, particularly in the mathematics and science disciplines.

Following Kaput et al. (2002), we can say: "The extent to which a medium becomes infrastructural is the extent to which it passes as unnoticed". Representational forms are often transparent to the expert user: Musicians do not think about musical notation when they play an instrument, any more than expert mathematicians do. Transparency can be reached through using the instrument, but also the evolution of technology can help this process. Since the first technological instruments were introduced at school (more or less thirty years ago), more and more people have gained access to them, because of the creation of new interfaces that mediate our knowledge in using them (in terms of operating systems, programming languages, and so on). So, not only the new technologies can be seen

A. Gutiérrez, P. Boero (eds.), Handbook of Research on the Psychology of Mathematics Education: Past, Present and Future, 237–273.

as a more democratic representational infrastructure, with respect to the old ones, but within the new technologies themselves. In their evolution in the last thirty years, we have seen a democratisation process in the sense of an increasing number of users. On the one hand, there has been a reduction of the competencies needed to use technologies; on the other it has also reduced the need to make sense of how computational systems do what they do.

So if the machines can perform calculations, what is left of mathematics? Almost everything. Machines cannot do argumentations, reasoning, conjectures, proofs (not in the sense of automatic proof, but justifying the passages) and so on. These are peculiar to the human capacity of reasoning: "The devolution of processing power to the computer has generated the need for a new intellectual infrastructure; people need to represent for themselves how thinks work, what makes systems fail and what would be needed to correct them" (Kaput et al., 2002).

Over the last thirty years, technology has shaped the way algebra is perceived. Algebra continues to be seen as an extension to arithmetic but technology is allowing students to explore the symbolic language as a computational tool and as an entry point to the major concepts in calculus. At the same time, algebra's symbol system is being linked more powerfully to the tabular, geometric and graphical contexts. Central concepts in algebra, like those of variable and function, can be treated dynamically in contrast to conventional paper and pencil technology where they are constrained to a static existence. Similarly, key ideas in calculus, such as limit, derivative and integral, benefit from dynamic representation that digital technology affords. Allied to the provision of a more dynamic representation, new technology promises the potential for a more interactive experience. Perhaps as a consequence, research interest and teaching focus have begun to emphasise the construction of meanings more than symbolic manipulation.

How technology is used inevitably depends upon the task. For example, to solve mathematical problems, technology is often used to take care of the calculations to simplify or verify the activities. In a more complex task, where the pedagogic aspiration may be turned more towards sense-making activity, technology may be used to explore, to conjecture, and to test conjectures, to validate a statement just found and to express the mathematical idea in a formal manner.

In fact the reader at this stage may begin to glimpse the complexity of issues that will pervade our review of the impact of technology on algebraic and analytical thinking. The complexity is not simple to deal with. In fact, as Hershkowitz and Kieran (2001) point out: "In designing as well as in studying a classroom learning activity in a computerized mathematics learning environment, one should consider contextual factors of various origins, like: (a) The mathematical content to be learned and its epistemological structure; (b) The learners, their mathematical knowledge culture, and the history with which they started the researched activity; (c) The classroom culture and norms, the role of the teacher, the learning organization –in small groups or individually–, etc.; and (d) The potential 'contribution' of the computerized tool".

Technology re-awakens us to the complexity that fundamentally underlies the teaching and learning of mathematics; in effect age-old questions are re-energised: "Regarding educational goals, appropriate pedagogical strategies, and underlying beliefs about the nature of the subject matter, the nature of learners and learning, and the relation between knowledge and knower", and their implementation "also forces reconsideration of traditional questions about control and the social structure of classrooms and organizational structure of schools" (Kaput, 1992).

In this chapter, we have decided to map out this complexity by focussing in turn on each of three domains. In the next section, we consider how PME researchers have studied the use of technology with respect to expressions and variables. In the second section, we set out the research on the algebraic notion of function. The third of these sections considers technology with respect to calculus concepts.

TECHNOLOGY IN THE TEACHING AND LEARNING OF EXPRESSIONS AND VARIABLES

As we trace the history of PME research on the teaching and learning of expressions and variables with technologies over the past thirty years, we note different kinds of uses or supports as offered by different tools. Using technology to support the teaching of a mathematical topic demands a transformation, sometimes in the mathematics itself but often in the pedagogic stance of the teacher. The mathematical notations traditionally evolved in the context of static, inert media, whereas the advent of technology brought changes in the perspectives from which a concept can be seen, progressively introducing interactivity and dynamicity. In this respect, the introduction of technology to the teaching of expressions and variables has been linked to reforms in the teaching of the subject generally. The nature of the transformation will depend upon the topic and so we find a connection between the topic and the type of tool used. As a consequence, "the question of whether a child can learn and do more mathematics with a computer (or other forms of electronic technology, including calculators and various video systems) versus traditional media is moot, not worth proving"; and "the real questions needing investigation concern the circumstances where each is appropriate" (Kaput, 1992).

From this historical review, we note a significant change occurring at the end of the '80s, when research started to pay attention to the relevance of multiple representations to the teaching of algebra. Prior to that there had been a major interest in the use of programming to approach specific contextual knowledge, for example that related to the concept of variable. During those years a flourishing use of languages such as Logo, Pascal, Basic, and others in teaching expressions and variables influenced research in the field. Towards the end of the decade, research interest in programming as a medium for learning about expressions and variables waned. It is not clear whether this is mostly a matter of fashion or whether somehow the complexity of learning the particulars of the language was seen as counter-productive to the intended development of general cognitive and thinking skills through the programming activity. This feature of 'less or non-immediacy' is one of the major difference between programming and microworlds, where the students' actions on objects is more direct than in a programming environment. The increasing development and experimentation of these kind of microworld supported the bridge of the gap between manipulation skills and abstract reasoning with algebraic symbols.

The previous perspective has strongly characterised research on the teaching and learning of expressions and variables over the last decade, when new technology (as for example computer algebra systems, and symbolic-graphic calculators) entered the scene. Studies have mainly focused on investigating students' appreciation of formal algebraic notations, generalisation and abstraction processes, and meaningful construction of symbolic language for expressing mathematical ideas. The uses of technology varied from graphing calculators supporting only formal algebraic notations, to non-standard algebraic notations of spreadsheets, and to microworlds specifically designed to learn different aspects of algebra.

Programming and the concept of variable

Toward the end of '80s the first investigations of the use of *programming* in teaching and learning began. Languages, such as Logo, Pascal, and LSE became popular in educational research as a means to analyse the difficulties encountered and approaches used by students in acquiring the concept of *variable*. In fact, the solution of a programming problem is not a result but a procedure to be represented by the subject as a function operating on data; this representation entails a consideration of the data as variable. However, the use of programming languages is not an easy matter and needs some further reflection. First, it is not possible to study the concept of variable independently from the programming languages and the domain of problems to solve; for example, operating on numbers or characters or graphical objects has not the same meaning for the subjects (Samurçay, 1985). In addition, variables can have different functional status in that their values can be in users' or in programmer's control (as explicit inputs and outputs of a problem or as variables only necessary for its solution). Two consequential effects have to do with the design of classroom activities: On the one hand, the need for a definition of the conceptual field about which the didactic experiences are to be organised; on the other, an attention to the nature of objects that can be manipulated with a given language. Samurçay (ibid.) set out the main aspects related to a teaching approach using programming. 8-9 year-old children who used Logo appeared confused between objects and the procedures defining them, which seemed to be a specificity of learning programming. For 16-17 year-old college students using Pascal and LSE, troubles were in conversion of their algebraic description into a procedural description.

Regarding students already used to programming in Logo, a strong hypothesis was that certain programming experiences could provide students with a conceptual basis for variable, enhancing their work with paper and pencil algebra (Sutherland, 1987). The relevance of integrating different learning environments (paper and pencil, and technology), rather than abandoning one in favour of the other, appeared. Sutherland (ibid.) tested the hypothesis analysing the activity of pairs of students playing a game. The game involved one pupil defining a function and the other pupil predicting the function by trying out a range of inputs. The latter had to define the same function when he/she was convinced that his/her prediction was correct. The pupils then had to establish that both functions were identical in structure although the function and variable names used might be different. Later individual structured interviews showed that students were able to use their Logo derived understanding in an algebra context.

Structures in expressions and equations

The importance of *structure* was also the focus of research in mathematics education concerned with the study of *expressions and equations*. Many of the errors in manipulating an algebraic expression seemed to be due to students' inattention to the expression's structure: Parentheses or conventions for the order of operations (Thompson & Thompson, 1987). A special computer program, called Expression, was developed in order to enable students to manipulate expressions with the constraint that they could act on an expression only through its structure. The program showed both the sequential format of expressions and the form of an expression tree. The statistical analysis of 7th graders' responses to some numeric-transformation and identity derivation problems suggested that when the students internalised the structural constraints they were less likely to commit errors and were more efficient in their solution strategies. This behaviour arose from the fact that pupils could attempt a lot of incorrect transformations of expressions by using the computer, but the program would not carry them out. Even experimentation became natural and beneficial thanks to the availability of different representational systems of an expression.

Concerned with solving equations or producing *equivalent* equations, a real problem for students is recognising and understanding even a simple case of equivalent equations. Recent studies have tried to elaborate on ways in which technology might be helpfully used to overcome such an obstacle. For example, Aczel (1998) claims that the use of a simulation of a balance could improve children's knowledge of equation solving. Other researchers consider the effectiveness of the use of an Interactive Learning package, called The Learning Equation (Norton & Cooper, 2001). They describe students' views about working with the software, concluding that it provides cognitive scaffolding.

Multiple representations

The significance of *multiple representations* and their mutual links rose in the late '80s, when research was beginning to identify specific reasons why algebra is so hard to learn and what the appropriate curricular and pedagogical responses might be (Kaput, 1987). Of course, it is not an easy task since algebra is complex both in its structure and in the multiplicity of its representations. But the representational aspects are essential. Mathematical meaning can be naturally grasped by: Transformations within a particular representation system without reference to another representation; translation across mathematical representation systems; translations between mathematical and non-mathematical representations (e.g. natural language, visual images, etc.); consolidation and reification of actions, procedures and concepts into phenomenological objects, which can serve later as the basis of new actions, procedures and concepts (Kaput, ibid.). As a consequence, meanings are developed within or relative to particular representations. Take the mathematical word "function" as an example. There is no an absolute meaning for it; there is, however, a whole range of meanings depending on the many available representations of functions and correspondences. Think of a function as a transformer of numbers (that is a typical instance of procedural meaning), or as a relation between numbers (which instead is a case of relational meaning). Each of these meanings is then associated to some specific representation, such as: "f(x)=..." for the first example above, and "y=..." for the second example. Furthermore, individuals use representation systems to structure the creation and elaboration of their own mental representations. In light of these perspectives, a central goal of algebra research became to determine how those representational forms are learned and applied by individuals to produce useful mental representations. For what explicitly concerns technology, computer-based models came to make multiple representations available, with the additional feature of serving not simply to display representations but especially to allow for *actions* on those representations (Kaput, ibid.). Here is one of the reasons that the idea of variable had been so difficult to learn: The static nature of the media in which everybody had historically been forced to represent it.

A dynamic view of algebra

Within the previous perspective, a dynamic view of algebra flourished; a lot of software and games were designed to favour it. The dynamicity is a fundamental feature of the new developing media. In fact, as Kaput (1992) stresses "one very important aspect of mathematical thinking is the abstraction of invariance. But, of course, to recognize invariance –to see what stays the same– one must have variation. *Dynamic media inherently make variation easier to achieve*" (emphasis in the original). A particular case was the attempt to improve the conceptual understanding of the *use of letters* in algebraic expressions and equations. For example, software conceived as generic organisers had a wide diffusion. A generic organiser is a "microworld which enables the learner to manipulate examples of a concept. The term "generic" means that the learner's attention is directed at certain aspects of the examples which embody a more abstract concept." (Tall, 1985). It provides an environment, which enables the users to manipulate examples of a specific mathematical concept or a related system of concepts, to aid the learners in the abstraction of the more general concept embodied by the examples (Thomas & Tall, 1988). The software gives an external representation of the abstract concepts and acts in a cybernetic manner, responding in a pre-programmed way to any input by the users. In this way, it enables both teacher and pupil to conjecture what will happen if a certain sequence of operations is set in motion, and then carry out the sequence to see if the prediction is correct. As a result of a long-term study with 11 and 12 year-old algebra novices, Thomas and Tall (1988) outlined that the generic organiser allows for an ideal medium to manipulate visual images. In so doing, it acts as a model for the mental manipulation of mathematical concepts, entailing emphasis on conceptual understanding and use of mental images rather than skill acquisition. Long-term conceptual benefits and a more versatile form of thinking related to the experiences with the computer were evident by the study.

Algebra as a symbol system

Taking into account the difficulty in bridging the gap between algebra as an extended arithmetic and algebra as a formal system of symbols, some researchers began to design novel activities through the use of fresh microworlds that provide access to multiple representations. In Israel, grade 8 students were involved in an experimental work with a computer package, which combines *skill-drills and logical reasoning* by competitive games relative to *substitution in algebraic expressions* (Zehavi, 1988). The positive effects coming from the use of the software were clear thanks to the comparison with a control group and discussion with the teacher in cognitive workshops.

Robust mathematical meaning can also be supported by the relations of the mathematics in a problem with the *relevant situational knowledge* of the problem. Around this belief, some research in mathematics education built up computer animation-based tutors to enhance students' mental representations. One tutoring system, called Animate, was specifically developed to provide students with an improved ability to generate a formal set of algebraic expressions or equations from problems presented in story form (Nathan, 1992). A positive effect of such a tutor came from its interpretive feedback to the students: In fact, they could continue to develop expressions containing conceptual errors, learning to detect and repair them in the process. As a result, students refined the solutions in an iterative way until the situation and the mathematics were seen as mutually consistent. Their competency in interpreting abstract expressions in a situational way improved. On the basis of this analysis, Nathan (ibid.) highlighted that the coupling of the mathematical expressions to a concrete depiction of the situation is necessary.

Meaningful symbolic syntax

Algebra as a symbol system entails a meaningful view of variables, unknowns, and parameters in formulas as well as in expressions and equations. Some recent studies have looked at the cognitive aspects of the abstraction and generalisation processes in learning environments supporting different types of *algebraic notations*. For example, Yerushalmy and Shternberg (1994) compare generalisations of number patterns found by students with a microworld, called

Algebraic Patterns, and with paper and pencil. Algebraic Patterns displays a dynamic numbers' lattice, and provides tools to describe local relations either by one or by many variables, and by functional notations. Arzarello, Bazzini and Chiappini (1995) sketch a theoretical model for analysing students' activities of production and manipulation of algebraic *formulas* using a spreadsheet. They examine iteratively and with increasing detail the relationships between the model and the learning environments. In so doing, they generate a fine-grained description of the features of school activities that support a meaningful learning of algebra. On the other hand, Ainley (1995) addresses the early stages of children's introduction to the use of variables in formal algebraic notation. Her conjecture is that some of the difficulties encountered by children in this area may be accentuated by their lack of appreciation of the purpose, or power, of *formal notation*. Ainley (ibid.) aims at situating the use of formal notation in meaningful contexts. She invoked case study evidence from children working with this approach, using spreadsheet and graphical feedback in problem solutions to suggest links to other areas of cognitive research.

The implementation of tools as media to give powerful visual insights supporting the generation of algebraic meaning, and to bridge the gap between action and expression, is the focus of research by Healy and Hoyles (1996). They studied 12 year-old students' use of spreadsheets and the Mathsticks microworld to examine their visual and symbolic strategies while interacting with these software environments.

A wide study on the teaching and learning of Algebra as a theory has been carried out more recently by some Italian researchers (Mariotti & Cerulli, 2001). They focused on the idea that a technological tool is seen as an instrument of semiotic mediation the teacher can use in order to introduce pupils to a theoretical perspective. The didactic problem considered concerns the ways of realising a theoretical approach to symbolic manipulation. A key-point of the research:

> Is that of stating the 'system of manipulation rules' as a system of axioms of a theory. The nature of the particular environment may foster the evolution of the theoretical meaning of symbolic manipulation. This is not really the approach pupils are accustomed to, on the contrary, Algebra, and in particular symbolic manipulation, are conceived as sets of unrelated 'computing rules', to be memorized and applied. (Mariotti & Cerulli, ibid.)

Within this perspective, a microworld, L'Algebrista, was designed, incorporating the basic theory of algebraic expressions. Algebra theory, as far as it is imbedded in the microworld, is evoked by the expressions and the commands available in L'Algebrista. A significant point of the activity is the fact that L'Algebrista is a symbolic manipulator totally under the user's control: The user can transform expressions on the basis of the commands available; these commands correspond to the fundamental properties of operations, which stand for the axioms of a local theory. As a consequence, the activities in the microworld, which produce a chain of transformations of one expression into another, correspond to a proof of the equivalence of two expressions in that theory. A further issue, which is not explicitly discussed in the research but it is worthy of attention, is that concerning the role of the teacher in the process of evolution of meanings. The researchers assert that the role of the teacher "becomes determinant in a process of de-contextualisation required in order to redefine the role of "buttons", and "new buttons", outside the microworld. In fact, commands must be detached from their context and explicitly referred to mathematical theory. Further investigations into the delicate role played be the teacher are required for a better and clearer description" (Mariotti & Cerulli, ibid.).

CAS and symbolic-graphic calculators

The introduction and diffusion of CAS (Computer Algebra System) and symbolic and graphic calculators to teach elementary algebra mainly occurred over the last decade. As a consequence, research work on their use and implementation at school is still little and can be considered at its early stages. One of the studies carried out with algebra beginners (11-year old Mexican students) investigates the extent to which the use of a graphing calculator can help as a tool (Cedillo, 1997). The study points out that the language of the calculator turns out to be means of expressing general rules governing number patterns, helping children grasp the algebraic code.

Looking specifically at the use of CAS, Drijvers (2001) studied how they can contribute to a higher level of understanding of parameters in algebra. Throughout the analysis of a classroom episode, the research discusses the relationship between machine techniques and mathematical conceptions. The use of CAS appears helpful to clarify problem solving strategies, but the adoption of higher order mathematical conceptions behind procedures seems to be limited. The impact of using CAS for students' mastery of algebraic equivalence has been explored by Ball, Pierce and Stacey (2003). The research pointed out that, in the context of solving equations, recognising equivalence, even in simple cases, is a significant obstacle for students.

One important and general issue related to calculators which is not considered in PME research is that stated by Kissane (2001):

> The development of the graphics calculator demands that we take a fresh look at the existing algebra curriculum, how it is taught and how it is learned, under an assumption of continuing and self-directed personal access to technology. Similarly, the development of the algebraic calculator suggests that we look closely at the content of our algebra curriculum and consider carefully a new role for symbolic manipulation, both by hand and by machine.

Concluding remarks on expressions and variables

From the review of research on teaching expressions and variables with technology, many issues and questions are to be faced or solved. Trends in emphasising students' learning and multiple views of concepts through multiple representations clearly appear, but so little, if not any, attention has been paid to curricular aspects and teachers' knowledge or teaching practice up to now. However, it is clear that the introduction of any kind of technology at school affects not only learning processes but even the conception and the control of the teaching situations, as outlined by Guin and Trouche (2000). For example, it requires efforts and time to be spent in the designing of suitable activities with technology and in instruction on the technology itself. This lack in research on school algebra was already stressed at the beginning of the '90s: "Unfortunately, there is a grave scarcity not only of models of the teaching of algebra but also of literature dealing with the beliefs and attitudes of algebra teachers" (Kieran, 1992). At that time the investigation was concerned with the learning and teaching of algebra without any specificity on the use of technology, but nowadays even considering the advent of technological tools the situation yet remains the same as then. As a matter of fact, some recent research also investigates curricular aspects, not in relation to an implementation of technology in the didactical practice. For example, Tsamir and Bazzini (2001) analysed the similar difficulties Israeli and Italian students had in solving standard and non-standard inequalities. The study was designed in order to extend the existing body of knowledge regarding students' ways of thinking and their difficulties when solving various types of algebraic inequalities. It was a result of the fact that in both Italy and Israel, algebraic inequalities receive relatively little attention and are usually discussed only with mathematics majors in the upper grades of secondary school. An open hypothesis is then that studies concerning curricular aspects do not generally pay attention to the use of technology.

From the viewpoint of educational research, an overarching question is how can we direct our use of the computer in mathematics education to the algebra of the future in addition to the algebra of the past and present (Tall, 1987a). Some related research questions we can raise here are the following:

- In which ways does the use of technology tend to re-define the school subject of expressions and variables?
- Is the curricular role of elementary algebra changing as a result of the availability of new technologies?
- How could research of expressions and variables with technology inform the design of technology?
- What are the most urgent areas in research of expressions and variables with technology that can support teaching of school algebra?

TECHNOLOGY IN THE TEACHING AND LEARNING OF FUNCTIONS

In the conventional curriculum, early algebraic work tends to focus on the solution of simple equations in which a single unknown value is given a symbolic representation. This strand of work develops through increasingly complex situations, where nevertheless the aim is to find the value of one or more unknowns (for example in quadratic and simultaneous equations).

However, a parallel strand emerges from the early algebraic work in which the symbolization encapsulates not a single value but a variable or parameter, which represents a set of values in a domain or co-domain. This strand leads to the study of functions and graphs and is seen by many as the forerunner to the study of calculus. In this section, we review PME research on technology and functions.

We can appreciate functions through three dynamic representational systems:

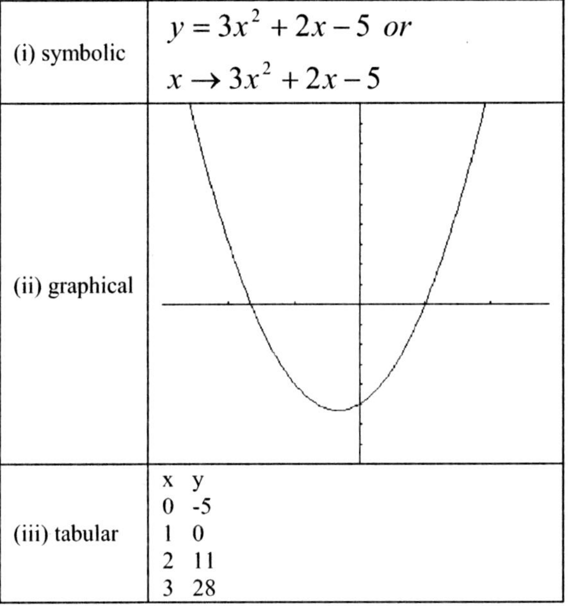

(i) symbolic	$y = 3x^2 + 2x - 5$ *or* $x \to 3x^2 + 2x - 5$
(ii) graphical	
(iii) tabular	x y 0 -5 1 0 2 11 3 28

Much of the learning effort seems to involve assimilating these three types of representation into a meaningful and coherent whole. There is of course a fourth *verbal* representation, more often associated with older technologies, such as paper and pencil, than digital technology, which is our focus here.

We can now look back over the research in PME over the last three decades and identify three different approaches to the task of understanding how technology impacts upon this process of assimilation. One strategy has been to investigate the use of technology as a means of placing emphasis on one type of representation, perhaps simplifying others. The initial emphasis on one representation may be seen as a means of giving access to the notion of function before other types of representation are introduced. A second approach is diametrically opposite in that it has attempted to use the technology to support simultaneous connections between the various systems of representation. Finally a third approach has sought to consider how the learner uses the tool itself sometimes taking into account the broader setting. We will consider each of these approaches in turn.

Technology as simplifier

One clear affordance of technology is that it can reduce the demands of handling difficult numbers in a task. One such demand challenges confidence in calculations. Technology can be used to carry out or check calculations or graphs of functions. Mesa and Gómez (1996) presented a study based on the methodology of two groups of students: One experimental and one control. This study focused on students' responses to problems given in the classroom using graphic calculators. The authors analysed the different strategies applied by the students in the solutions and classified them on the basis of students' understanding and findings. It seems that technology was used more to verify strategies of calculations than to make conjectures and test them.

An analogous outcome was presented by Moreira (2002), who described the activities of a small group of students in a curriculum project, aimed at developing "democratic competence" in the context of mathematics education. The students were in the first year of a degree course in Management. They used Excel to work on problems about functions (graphs and calculations). The use of this technology was mainly oriented in two directions: The creation of a clear and well-presented graph of the function and the avoidance of fastidious calculations. The students verified claims about the size of the whale population involved in the problem. The potential of the computer was shown in the work of these students, who were able to verify claims about the whale population problem.

The above research shows how verification of calculations and graphs can be used in the graphing and tabular representation of functions, though it is not difficult to imagine symbolic manipulators being used to verify functions in the third type of representation. However, apart from simplifying the problem by easing the verification process, we are also able to simplify through the elimination of the need for symbols. How though do we input functions without the use of symbols or a symbolic language? We found in the research two main methods; one approach has been to use a device through which data is captured directly and transferred automatically to the computer. The other approach is to allow data entry by the student when that data has been generated during experimentation. In both cases, the aim is to study variation as a precursor perhaps to formal work on functions or statistics.

Data capture through the use of devices. Recent work includes an innovative type of experimentation with situations and representations, using Microcomputer-based Laboratories (MBLs) to allow students to represent situations with devices that gather data in real time and present the data graphically. These technologies eliminate algebraic symbols as the sole channel into mathematical representation and motivate students to experiment with the situation –to analyse and reflect upon it– even when the situation is too complicated for them to approach it symbolically. Compared to working with visual representations of algebraic or numeric symbols, the visual analysis that is enabled by working with MBL tools is quite distinctive.

For example, Yerushalmy, Shternberg and Gilead (1999) used the mouse to draw trajectories of a "body" in motion so that the activities' focus is on the transition from the drawing action to an analysis of graphs of the mathematical functions. Other technologies that support links between body activity and "official" representations were studied by Nemirovsky, Kaput & Rochelle (1998) and Borba & Scheffer (2003). They suggested that it is possible to deepen students' connection with everyday experience through environments, which combine phenomena and their modelling. The interplay between notations, simulations and physical phenomena can be expanded by incorporating kinaesthetic activity, by empowering notations as controls over the creation of phenomena, and by comparing the physical with the virtual. In this sense we should consider the introduction of another type of representation, the kinaesthetic sense of function. The research of Nemirovsky and others proposes that the kinaesthetic representation might be a particularly facilitating starting point.

Nemirovsky (1995) reported a study of 10-year-old students who created "motion trips" on a meter tape by walking, running and stopping. They were then asked to represent these trips using tables and graphs. They were also able to use a program to invent such trips and then view them in various representational forms. More recently, 14 year-old students used a motion sensor in a similar way (Robutti & Ferrara, 2002) and were then set an interpretation task of a space-time graph. In this latter study however, the performance of the students was compared to that of a control group on the same task. The researchers concluded that the technology facilitated transitions between static and dynamic interpretations of the space-time graphs, leading to normalised meanings for the graph.

Two studies of the second type suggest that this facilitating effect of the technology is also apparent when the independent variable is not time. In one study (Nemirovsky, 1994), a high school student used a so-called "contour analyser" to trace a surface along a certain plane. The device generated a computer-based graph of height or slope versus position. The student learned about slope by striving to grasp what the tool does. This sense-making activity drew on previous knowledge, which had to be re-assessed. Noble and Nemirovsky (1995) used a motion detector as above but focussed on non-temporal graphs of velocity v position. The report describes the evolution of a high school student's thinking through his articulations in his attempts to match the graph with the motion of his car.

Kaput and Hegedus (2002) provided examples of classroom connectivity in which students discussed representations of families of functions with TI-83 calculators. They examined how the technological connectivity generated a personal identity as a resource for focusing attention and generating engagement with the tasks. A firm connection between this work and formal algebra was reported by Hegedus and Kaput (2003). Using a pre-test/post-test approach, they reported gains in learning through SimCalc, software which enables initial access to functions through virtual simulations of everyday situations, typically of time dependent phenomena. Their central claim was that combining the dynamic of SimCalc environment with classroom connectivity made possible significant improvements in students' performance on 10th grade MCAS algebra-related questions in a short period of time. The use of kinaesthetic approaches leads to a modelling perspective on functions in the sense that functions are seen as a means of exploring or analysing real world or simulated behaviour.

Data capture through experiments. One strand of research (Ainley, 1994; Pratt, 1994; Pratt, 1995; Ainley, Nardi & Pratt, 1998; Ainley, 2000) involved children carrying out an experiment that generated bivariate data and iteratively using scatter graphs to make sense of the emerging data. The kinaesthetic involvement of the children in the experiment supported their emergent appreciation of the analytic use of the graphs. In some cases, these experiments could be algebraically modelled. In such cases, the children were challenged to teach the formula to the spreadsheet. The approach then was to begin with kinaesthetic, tabular and graphical types of representation in order to open up the possibility of a symbolic representation. These papers report on how this approach allows the children to draw on a range of intuitions for interpreting scatter graphs, based on an intimate knowledge of their own experiment and spatial skills presumably drawn from other mathematical or everyday experiences. The students began to correct irregularities in the graphs (*normalising*) and construct meanings for trend. Connections between this and Nemirovsky's work have been made (Nemirovsky, 1998) indicating the value in paying close attention to students' ideas in the contexts within which they arose.

How are we to interpret the success of these technology-based studies in comparison to a range of prior studies that have shown graphing, and in particular the interpretation of graphs, as immensely challenging for young students? First it is worth noting that all of these studies involve experimentation. Whether the student is controlling the independent variable directly or indirectly, they do have a sense of active engagement with the technology. In some cases, the student is led towards trying to make sense of the technology itself. In other cases, it provides a tool to allow the student to pursue a more purposeful agenda by focussing on interpretation rather than on the technical skills of drawing a graph. Indeed, drawing on their work on graphing, Ainley and Pratt (2002) have discussed two constructs, *Purpose* and *Utility*, as providing a way of thinking about the design of pedagogic tasks.

The experimentation appears then to be allied to a greater sense of involvement in the sense of motivation, but also in the sense of bodily participation. In a PME Research Forum, Nemirovsky (2003) conjectured that perceptuo-motor activity (PCM) might be the root of mathematical abstraction, and that thinking might be PCM distributed across different areas of perception and motor action as shaped by early experiences with the subject. As evidence towards the substantiation of these conjectures, Borba and Scheffer (2003) reported on students using sensors attached to mini-cars to argue that technologies of information can create links between body activity and official representations. As further evidence, Rasmussen and Nemirovsky (2003) reported on students using a water wheel connected to real-time graphing software to conclude that knowing acceleration through a tool like the water wheel is something that grows and emerges in students across a range of representational systems.

Although there is a need for further research in this area, there seems reason to believe that, perhaps not only in the domain of graphing, we might design effective tasks that connect purpose to significant elements of mathematics by drawing upon perceptuo-motor activity.

This "function as simplifier" strand of PME research appears to have made considerable progress from a narrow perspective in which technology was essentially used to verify procedures to a proposal that we approach the teaching of functions through a further type of representation, that of the kinaesthetic, by using the technology to model behaviour in which we are personally and directly engaged.

Technology as integrator

Functions are often introduced in school textbooks through a static definition (static in the sense that this approach emerges from pencil and paper technology in which the definition can not be seen directly as having dynamic computational potential). Confrey and Smith (1992), illustrating their argument through the work of one imaginary student, claimed that it was important to build an understanding of functions through multiple representations and contextual problems before emphasis was placed on static definitions. An affordance of technology is to offer access to the various types of representation of function. This affordance has been widely exploited in PME research over the last three decades.

Excited by the possibilities inherent in the notion of multiple representations, researchers have developed distinctions around the notion of function. For example, some researchers have focused on the classes of translations between representational systems. Other researchers have focussed on the new ways that technology allows students to manipulate functions –mainly as graphical objects.

Translations between representational systems. Schwarz and Bruckheimer (1988) considered the transfer of knowledge between representations in a computerised TRM (Triple Representational Model: Algebraic, graphical and tabular) environment. Grade 9 children in junior high school were asked to use TRM to search for solutions. One group began by searching through the graphing representation before using the algebraic type of representation. Another group was asked to approach the problem in the reverse order. The authors concluded that they could sketch three cognitive levels of functional thinking: The numerical level where searching for a solution was systematic, the functional reasoning level where the search was systematic but logical sequences of computations were not used, and the dynamic functional reasoning level where the richness of the concept of function was understood and searching was efficient. They also concluded that focusing on graphing before algebra led to a higher level of functional reasoning as accuracy and convergence procedures transferred from graphing to algebra but not vice versa.

The research of Schwarz and Bruckenheimer leant towards a prescription favouring an introduction to graphing representations prior to algebraic (and note that in the previous section, there was some evidence to suggest the introduction of kinaesthetic aspects even earlier than this). However, as the power of technology has increased, software design has moved to a point where there can be increased fluidity between representations. Indeed, when representations are "hot-wired", it is impossible to detect any delay when one representation synchronises to reflect a change in another. A series of studies have found benefits in exploiting the connectivity between representational systems.

Resnick, Schwartz and Hershkowitz (1994) discussed how 9th graders, using graphic calculators to solve problems relating perimeter and area of a rectangle, found different ways to articulate arguments by shifting from one representation to another and noticing local and global properties. The authors proposed that there is a radical difference between paper and pencil representations, which are passive descriptions, and computer-based representations that are driven by actions. Schwarz and Hershkowitz (1996) reported a comparative study to probe into these differences. The control group used only linear functions and resisted using others, even when they were mentioned. The experimental group used a technology-intensive curriculum and developed a much richer variety of prototype functions to support reasoning and to exemplify strategies and properties. In 1997, Hershkowitz and Schwarz presented two studies on learning the function concept. In the first study, which was based on a questionnaire, the authors characterized the concept image of 9th graders after they had learned in an interactive environment, based on multi-representational tools and open ended activities. They found that these students, (a) used many examples, (b) provided rich justifications to answers, (c) showed flexibility within and among representations, (d) considered the acceptability of answers in light of the context, and (e) integrated prototypic examples with other examples. The second study was classroom-based with the same children. The focus now was on interactions between individuals, the problem situation, tools, and the community. Although the role of the computer might be seen as minor in this study. In fact the researchers claim that the internalised representations of manipulations aided the construction of hypotheses about the behaviour of the functions. Tabach and Hershkowitz (2002) traced how their students attempted to construct generalizations of growth patterns and used them to represent phenomena numerically and graphically, all through the use of spreadsheets. The report claimed that students constructed new knowledge and subsequently consolidated it. Smart (1995) reported a study in which girls had open access to graphic calculators during their mathematics lessons. The girls started to develop a robust visual image of many algebraic functions. Sutherland and Rojano (1996) looked at the impact of a modelling approach to understanding science concepts using spreadsheets. Students of two courses, one in Mexico and another in the UK, submitted pre-evaluation and post interview data. The authors claimed that spreadsheets helped students relate graphical and numerical representations, and make sense of the algebraic models of the physical phenomena. We have already discussed other aspects of the modelling perspective of functions.

Other studies though have alerted educationalists to some problems in using technology. Goldenberg (1997) illustrated a range of illusions inherent in the way that graphs could be presented. Perceptual strategies that were sufficient for interpreting scale and relative position in real world spaces were inappropriate when dealing with the infinite and relatively featureless objects in coordinate graphs. In fact the prevalence of illusions appeared to be an issue for the reading of graphs in conventional settings as well as computer-based ones. However, as is so often the case, it was the use of technology that triggered awareness of the problem and arguably illusions may have been accentuated by the technology. Cavanagh and Mitchelmore (2000) investigated how students interpreted linear and quadratic graphs on a graphics calculator screen. They identified three common misconceptions: A tendency to (a) Accept the graphic image uncritically, without attempting to relate it to other symbolic or numerical information, (b) A poor understanding of the concept of scale, and (c) An inadequate grasp of accuracy and approximation.

Actions on graphs. When using conventional pencil and paper and technology, graphs are essentially an output resulting from the calculation and plotting of points. In that sense, they are an end point, offering no further actions that can be carried out on the graphs, without starting a new and lengthy procedure. Manipulations in algebra are reserved for symbolic manipulations, and the graphs are driven by them. Technology allows students and teachers to directly manipulate graphs of functions.

Confrey (1994) examined six different approaches to transformation (translations and dilations) of functions. She based her analysis on several years of experience using *Function Probe* (FP) in a variety of settings. Confrey constructed a schedule of transformations as defined by a set of parameters, for example A, B, C, and D. The paper presented this schedule as a framework for thinking about the teaching of transformation of functions and how the students might approach these problems. She claims that these six approaches are distinctive, each offering its own advantages and disadvantages. Borba (1994, 1995) studied the roles of visualization and direct actions on graphs in the FP environment. Borba's findings cover a wide range of aspects of multiple representation software, and in particular the study of manipulations of graphs. Borba's (1994) analysis was based on an episode with one student who predicted how the operation of "stretching" would change the graph. This episode served as an illustration of the different elements of the model. In the 1995 article, Borba described how a student, using multi-representational software, resolved a discrepancy in results by mentally adding features to the software design. Indeed, Borba refined a model for understanding in multi-representational environments and argued that students' reasoning can inspire software design.

Technology as instrument or mediator

Some research has looked broadly at the value added of using a piece of technology compared to conventional approaches. Thus, Guttenberger (1992) compared the performance of 31 Grade 11 students with access to a computer-based function plotter to those without. The post-test showed that these students performed at a higher level. Comparing students who used graphic calculators in activities on functions with others who did not, Gómez and Fernández (1997) found no differences between the two groups at the adaptation phase but significant differences were found at the consolidation phase. However, such research is limited in its ability to explain, either from the design or cognitive perspectives, how or why such improvements happened. For example, Dagher and Artigue (1993) studied 33 students, aged 16-18 years, working on second degree polynomials, and 21 students, aged 14 to 15 years, working on linear functions. These students were given a game, consisting of a curve that had to be represented algebraically. Points were awarded according to how little assistance was needed. Post test success on paper and pencil test about functions was much higher than on the pre-test. The authors noticed sudden crystallisations of thinking after which a clear game strategy emerged. By looking closely at the learning process in relation to the structuring resources in the game, the researchers were able to identify certain catalysts for the crystallisations. They noticed the importance of (i) meeting a particular parabola, (ii) changing one representation to a different form and (iii) locating specific points. This detailed analysis promotes a focus on aspects of the design of the game as well as how the resource mediated learning, in this case in the form of the breakthrough insights.

There has been little research on the design of tools to support the teaching and learning of functions. In an early theoretical paper, Lesh and Herre (1987) applied Dienes principles to the use of virtual instantiations of polynomials to propose that Dienes ideas, developed originally in the context of designing material manipulatives, have explanatory power even in the virtual setting. It is perhaps disappointing that this work has not been picked up by subsequent PME researchers in the field.

Rather more studies have focussed on mediating aspects. Lagrange (1999) reported on a study about the schemes of use introduced by students of the 11th grade, learning about functions with complex calculators (TI92). From the perspective of instrumental genesis (Verillon & Rabardel, 1995), the author's analysis of the development of the students' schemes of use in a pre-calculus course emphasized the role of calculators in terms of the mediation they offered to the learning process. He noticed, as others have done (see in § *Limits*), that students using symbolic manipulations saw the limit as an object but that they lost the sense of the process. He pointed out that the symbolic-graphic calculator could enhance the understanding of calculus concepts in terms of numerical and graphical representations before their symbolic form. The calculator acted as a mediator in the learning process and in this mediation it is by no means neutral. Meeting new potentialities and constraints, the students have to elaborate schemes of use potentially rich in mathematical meanings, a process that requires support and encouragement from the teacher.

A few studies looked specifically at general aspects of the tool reflected throughout the learning processes. Gitirana (1998) reported on students who interacted with three microworlds, all focusing on the learning of functions. The students' explanations suggested different conceptualizations of function according to the pedagogical and technical aspects of the microworlds and according to their interactions during the activities, thus highlighting a sensitivity of learning to the structuring resources in the setting.

Hershkowitz and Kieran (2001) focused on two different ways in which students used tool-based representatives: A mechanistic and a meaningful way. A case study with three Canadian students who worked on growth patterns of rectangle areas was compared with a prior study with Israeli students. The Canadian students applied a recursive expression technique and generalized it with the help of the tool. The authors questioned whether this may have hindered them from mathematizing the problem and from thinking in terms of an exponential function. Friedlander and Stein (2001) studied Israeli students' choices among tools (e.g. spreadsheets, symbolic calculators, graphic calculators) to solve equations. The results showed that students not only employed a variety of solution methods to solving equations but, more importantly, made connections between the representations afforded by different tools.

Concluding remarks on functions

In summary, there appears to be some consensus that technology can be exploited to privilege certain types of representation over others, focussing attention in specific aspects of function. Of the three standard types of representation (graphing, the use of symbolic algebra and tabularisation), there appears to be some evidence that students can use intuitive knowledge of the graphing aspect of functions to make sense of symbolisation more easily than vice versa. However, there also seems to be some evidence to suggest that a kinaesthetic approach may offer access at an intuitive level that can be utilised by allowing that type of representation to drive experience of the three standard representational systems. There has been considerable research effort to exploit the potential of technology to offer multiply-linked representations and some results seem to suggest that the linking of representations on screen may support such mental connections being constructed. However, too little is understood about this process. Some approaches have allowed these connections to be hot-wired, running the risk that the child may simply not attend to the changes being made. Others have tried to put the child in situations where they have to make the connections in order to pursue some broader objective. We need to know more about typical ways in which children make these connections. What are the critical parameters in enabling such learning and what is the range of learning outcomes in such circumstances? There has been little PME research on the design of the tools. Given the wide interest in the situatedness of learning, it seems odd that there is little research into the relationship between design and learning about functions. Instead we have a set of interesting examples of how innovative tools have been used without sufficient analysis of how the design intentions played out in practice. We argue that research of learning with tools cannot ignore the design of those tools.

Although we have, for the purposes of this review, treated the solving of equations as a separate activity from that of working with functions, clearly the broader pedagogic aim is to help children connect these two domains. In fact, the technology-based work on functions promises to have pay-offs for the understanding of equations. Yerushalmy (1997) and Yerushalmy & Bohr (1995) reported two studies, which were part of a three-year longitudinal investigation based on VisualMath, a functions-based approach to algebra. The former article reported significant changes in students' thinking about symbols, equations, and problems in context. This study included an analysis of common models of problem solvers, who were mainly low attaining students. The enhanced performance and thinking processes of students, who had previously been unsuccessful with algebra in general and with solving contextual problems in particular, has recently emerged from studies on the integration of graphing technology and contextual problem solving. Because students of VisualMath learned to view any equation in a single variable as a comparison between two functions, the second article posed the question of what the mental image for equations in two variables would be for these students. We therefore look forward to research which links the themes of expression, variable, function and calculus to inform our understanding of the longer term development of thinking about functions and its relationship to the affordances in the setting.

TECHNOLOGY IN THE TEACHING AND LEARNING OF CALCULUS

Looking back historically, there are three root aspects of calculus as a discipline (Kaput, 1994): One concerns the computations of areas, volumes and tangent, and first of all it was practical, as in the work of Archimedes. The second was a blend of practical and theoretical interest, involving the study of physical quantities variation. It began in ancient Greece with the mathematization of change and had a golden period with Newton's study of motion, with the application of new mathematical tools for calculation. While the third was inherently theoretical, beginning with Zeno's ancient motion paradoxes and continuing with the complete formalization of analysis in the 19th century, and has been recently completed with the non-standard analysis. These three roots, as Kaput (1994) wrote, "interweave complexly, and the story of their interweaving is still being written".

The introduction of technology in calculus in recent years touches these three roots, exploring the potentialities of them with different supporting contexts, as for example: The numerical calculation of areas, volumes and tangents (with programming languages, spreadsheet or software); the elaboration of data taken from measures of quantities (by sensors connected on-line with calculators), for investigating the relations and the variations of these quantities, and the approach to continuous and to infinitesimal analysis, through functions and variables managed in a symbolic way (CAS).

We develop at least three elements of analysis: Epistemological, cognitive and curricular. In calculus, the power of technology is particularly important to facilitate students' work with numerous epistemological discontinuities such as discrete/continuum, finite/infinite, determinate/indeterminate, and so on which also relate to other subjects (e.g. arithmetic, algebra, analytical geometry) previously learned by students. These discontinuities can remain epistemological obstacles not understood by the students or may be overcome on the road towards the construction of concepts. "The construction of pedagogical strategies for teaching students must then take such obstacles into account. It is not a question of avoiding them but, on the contrary, to lead the student to meet them and to overcome them" (Cornu, 1991, p. 162). The obstacles create the cognitive demand for an overcoming, and only with deep research in mathematics education can we understand them and try to find some solution. The same solutions can then be used to plan curricular projects: In this way, research can be useful to teaching practice.

Our analysis focuses on the mediation of technology and the role of the teacher about these epistemological obstacles: Limits, derivatives, infinite sums, integrals.

The approaches to calculus in the past three decades, according to the parallel introduction of technology at school, have been different: First of all, numerical investigations could be possible, due to the programming languages used to solve problems relative to functions in a numerical way. Then graphical environments rendered possible the investigations on the shape of functions, both at a global and at a local level. Finally, symbolic performances became possible, for the introduction of Computer Algebra Systems in computers and calculators. These environments were used in an independent way from each other, and also simultaneously. But the big revolution in teaching mathematics with technologies was the introduction of dynamicity in software: A dynamic way to control and master the virtual objects on the computer let the student explore many situations and notice what changes and what does not. And the mathematics of change is the first step on the road to calculus. We can intend change at a numerical level, as well as the graphical or symbolic level. If some researchers concentrated their attention on one of these levels, others were more interested in the simultaneous use of them in order to integrate their potentialities.

In using technology at school there was the necessity to adapt the mathematical activities to the potentialities offered by the software in use, and sometimes the limitations of this software could influence the construction of a concept (as mentioned by Magidson, 1992) referring to slope, conceptualised by the students as a value not more than 8. This necessity, over the years, has been decreasing and the idea of a generic organiser entered the scene (see § *A dynamic view of Algebra*). It embodies a theoretical structure and the user may come to understand it using the generic organiser in specific examples. The existence of such a structure absolutely does not guarantee that the user will abstract the general concept. So technology can never guarantee learning or take the place of the teacher. Surely it can help students to overcome certain difficulties, but research shows that it will be effective only within a coherent teaching-learning context. Better if this is done in a social way, working in small groups and then sharing the ideas in a class discussion, guided by the teacher, as reported in many articles.

Limits

Traditionally, limits are often introduced through the epsilon-delta definition, which compels the students to reason without the consideration of functions as maps between x and y values in the Cartesian plane, and, on the contrary, fixes their attention on intervals on the y axis, and finding a corresponding interval on the x axis. This way of reasoning is different from previous algebraic thinking, and breaks a balance about functions, often causing cognitive difficulties, as witnessed in literature. For students it is very difficult to reverse the order (Kidron, Zehavi & Openhaim, 2001). There can be considered three paradigms for teaching limits: A (formula-bound) dynamic limit paradigm, a functional/numeric computer paradigm and the formal epsilon-delta paradigm (Li & Tall, 1993). The first is based on arithmetic and geometric progressions and convergence of the latter. This approach emphasises the potential infinity of a process that cannot be completed in a finite time. The second is based on programs written in Basic that give as output a certain value of a sequence. They support a numerical exploration of sequences, and ground limit as a procept in the sense of Cauchy, being the terms indistinguishable at a certain step, instead of evaluating the limit value. The third is the traditional approach, based on formal definition. The authors use the second paradigm for experimentation and finally recognise that difficulties in passing to the formal definition remain for the epistemological discontinuities in the concept definition itself.

As in the previous case, where alternatives routes to traditional teaching are used in calculus with the integration of technology, many other studies have been carried out in this direction. They outline that technology by itself does not promote change (Valero & Gómez, 1996). What promotes change is the curricular project in which technology is inserted, and in particular, the didactic sequences planned by the teachers in order to introduce calculus concepts, which use technology as a support. Planning these sequences involves re-considering activities, methodologies, lessons, learning contexts and all aspects of teaching, integrating the “old” and the “new”. So, it means that we have to make important choices about technology: How, when, why, and what kind of technology we must use.

According to the kind of technology used, and, more importantly, the type of use of it, a teacher may convey a given meaning in a particular way. For example, as said before, it is possible to teach the concept of limit centring on the idea of “getting closer”, or on the “limit value” as the object that constitutes the limit. Students are usually familiar with the former, which is more intuitive than the latter. Using Derive to calculate limits, it is possible to orientate students with the latter meaning, because they are able, with this software, to see the numerical value of the limit. On the other hand, this approach leads students to consider limit as a static value, losing the sense of the approaching process. They acquire the advantage of seeing the limit as an object, but they miss the sense of the process that lies beneath the object itself (Monaghan, Sun & Tall, 1994). In other approaches, the conceptualisation of limits may pass through a discrete process (e.g. using graphic calculators), that here have the role of reinforcing former limit conceptions based on the process of "getting closer" to something. Conversely this line of teaching seems to make more difficult the construction of the meaning of limit as a concept of "limit value", as it follows from the formal definition (Trouche & Guin, 1996).

Between these two ways of conceiving the limit (namely, process of getting closer to something or limit value), there seems to be a gap, which is difficult to bridge. It corresponds to an epistemological discontinuity, which is also present in the history of calculus, in which the static epsilon-delta definition of the object limit was only the last step of this history, which started with the intuitive process of getting closer. Calculus is difficult for our students, because it reflects the great difficulties faced in the history of mathematics.

What is the role of technology in these different approaches to limits? There have been cases put forward for using Derive to calculate limits (Monaghan et al., 1994) and exploring functions by conjecturing, solving and checking (Trouche & Guin, 1996).

A possible choice for teachers at secondary school level, where calculus is only partially taught, is to support the conceptualisation of limits with intuitive basic ideas about infinitesimals, together with a brief history of them and without a strong and abstract formalisation. Infinitesimal conceptions have been used to teach limits (Cornu, 1991). Adding to the mathematical legitimacy of infinitesimals, recent research (Milani & Baldino, 2002) offers a challenge to mathematics education: "What if, instead of waiting for the infinitesimal conceptions to emerge, we stimulated them? What if the students became aware of the abyss between mathematics and its applications produced by the, now unfounded, discrimination of infinitesimals? Will such an awareness stimulate the transposition of the obstacle towards the understanding of limits or will it create new obstacles?" (Milani & Baldino, 2002, p. 346). With the technological support of CorelDraw zoom, four freshmen in a calculus course for physics students first were introduced to the basic ideas of infinitesimals and their use in calculus, then they demonstrated such ideas to the whole class. For example, the zoom function of CorelDraw has been used to visualise the merging together of a curve and its tangent line at the point P, showing that curve and tangent appear as parallel straight lines at $P+dP$, and so on. Not only was an instrument introduced in order to use infinitesimals, but also a sign: $\approx$, to indicate "infinitely close to". These are the words of a student after this experience: "In physics we have to imagine the situation, we have to imagine what happens in a very small space, with tiny dimensions. The zoom helps. In the physics class the teacher also spoke about the zoom, taking an infinitely close view, but it was not clear for all the students." This research shows the mingling of mathematical, continuous, infinitesimal conceptions with the physical, discrete, subatomic reality. The authors come to the conclusion that "the whole research process led the students to spontaneously enlarge their concept images so as to incorporate elements from the microscopic physical world among infinitesimals." (Milani & Baldino, 2002, p. 346).

At a higher level of content, a remarkable example is offered by Kidron et al. (2001), who studied the possibility to enhance students' ability for passing from visual interpretation of the limit concept to formal reasoning; they used symbolic computation and graphics. The task consists in approximating functions by Taylor polynomials. The students used two methods to approximate a given function by polynomials: Analytical and algebraic. In the analytical method they approach the notion of *order of contact* with Mathematica. In the algebraic one they *follow the original text of Euler* (1988), applying his approach to represent infinite sums with Mathematica. Both methods lead to the coefficients of the Taylor series but with different features: The analytical one describes the *process* of the different polynomials approaching a given function; the other represents the polynomials with "an infinite number of terms" as an *object*.

The Mathematica software was useful both in the calculations of the algebraic approach and in the analytical method; for example, a sequence of plots helped illustrate the fact that, in a given interval, the higher the degree of the approximating polynomials the closer the function $\sin(x)$ and the polynomial are. This animation generated by the software helps students in the conceptualisation of limit because it permits them to see the dynamic process in one picture.

The static object introduced by Euler becomes a dynamic process of convergence to a function: In these activities, the students used Mathematica to visualise functions and to construct animations, but this was not enough in order to transform a process into the concept of limit. So the students "had to *interact* with the dynamic graphics, to *have control over the dynamic representations*" (Kidron et al., 2001). In this article the process of instrumentation (Verillon & Rabardel, 1995) is described, by the schemes of use activated by the students, who transformed the artefact Mathematica into an instrument for conceptualisation.

One year later one of the authors (Kidron, 2002) continues the investigation of this problem, adding a new element to her previous theoretical framework: The embodied cognition analysis of infinity (Lakoff & Núñez, 2000). The analytical approach is seen as a way to represent *potentially infinite* processes, while the algebraic one as a way to represent *actual infinite* sums as objects in the author's mind: "The illusion that the infinite calculations are performed at once might facilitate the transition from symbolic manipulation to a symbolic object" (Kidron, 2002). The researchers' aim is to examine to what extent the interrelationship between the two approaches and the different uses of the software helped the students to perceive an infinite sum as the limit of an infinite process. It seems that using different approaches the students were able to understand that an infinite sum is not necessarily an expression that tends to infinite, that it could be equal to a given number; that it can be conceived as an object; and that it might be rendered easier if we apply an algebraic approach to it, as Euler said. Particularly, a sort of balance between the conception of an infinite sum as a process and as an object seems to be supported by the use of the software, together with the didactical methodology applied.

With regards to the other themes related to the limit of functions, namely the problem of continuity, we do not yet have studies, apart from Vinner (1987), on students' competencies about continuous and discontinuous functions, investigated through a questionnaire. It turns out that, although they succeed in the identification task in the common cases, they fail very often to justify their answers. Moreover, their use of the limit concept is quite fuzzy and they often rely on irrelevant argument. As a result, the level of their mathematical reasoning is quite inadequate.

Derivative and integral

Teaching derivatives and integrals raises issues analogous to the ones on teaching limits: The intuitive approach versus the formal one. It can be seen as a part of the theme of functions, as it is often so presented in the literature. The studies of Tall (1989) grounded these contents on the cognitive roots of local straightness of a function and area under a graph, for derivative and integral respectively. Ensuing literature followed these studies. The use of new technologies demonstrates the possibility of grounding the concepts of derivative and integral on simpler ones, implemented through various environments such as the numerical one, the graphical one, and, last but not least, the symbolic one. The suggestion for mathematics education research is a progressive conceptualisation toward the abstract definition and use of these concepts, passing through activities of exploring, conjecturing and testing conjectures. The use of software such as Graphic Calculus can be done at different levels, as Tall shows in his articles. In general, it can be used in a rich way employing the dynamic images in a fruitful cognitive way. For example, a function and its gradient function can be plotted together on the same screen, and moving a chord on the first renders possible the generation of the second. As one student put it: "I never understood what it meant to say that the derivative of $\sin x$ was $\cos x$ until I saw it grow on the computer". The verb "grow" really embodies the dynamic nature of the gradient function, as seen on the screen. As students explore and enrich their concept images in a more personal way, they seem to regard the computer as an authority that does not present the same threat as the teacher. They seem far more willing to discuss conceptual difficulties thrown up by the computer than they would difficulties in understanding a teacher's explanation (Tall & Sheath, 1983).

Another study at secondary school level over several years shows that Graphic Calculus can be used as a generic organiser in different ways. In order to introduce derivative, it can be used to magnify graphs, allowing the student to see what happens to functions when their graphs are magnified. Many graphs look "less curved" under higher magnification. After using this organiser (with the guidance of the teacher in order to explore different functions, with or without the property to become straight when magnified), the student can look along a graph, "magnifying it in his mind's eye, and seeing the gradient vary" (Tall, 1985). The use of the same software as another organiser is to observe the variation of the gradient of a graph, moving the chord through two near points along the curve, changing the x of the first point but not the proximity of the two. In this way, the notion of gradient can be constructed in a dynamic and a global way, even if the final construction, the curve of the gradient, is a static picture on the screen. Thus the concept image of gradient can be created both as a process and as a concept, and therefore as a procept.

Linked to the derivative and the slope of a function, we have the concept of tangent to a graph at a certain point. As pointed out by Artigue (1991) there are many ways to conceive the tangent to a curve. For example: As a line passing through a point but not crossing the curve in a neighbourhood of it, as a line having a double intersection with the curve at a certain point, as a line passing through two points infinitely close to a point on the curve, and so on. If these different points of view can coexist in the mind of a mathematician, it may not be the same for a student, because their contemporary presence can be a source for misconceptions, obstacles and conflicts. Mathematicians analyse a concept in a formal manner, producing a hierarchical development and linking different concept definitions in a proper way. But this way may be inappropriate for the developing learner. The computer can help to overcome such difficulties, by giving the possibility of introducing new concepts that had previously seemed extremely abstract to pupils, or by offering them the opportunity to coordinate different perspectives on the same concept. A study carried out in three experimental classes (Tall, 1987b), aimed at the construction of the concept image of a tangent made use of the computer to draw a line through two very close points on the graph of a function as part of a broader introduction to the idea of gradient. The students experienced the presence of a tangent in some situation and the absence of it in others, such as the case of the absolute value of sin$x$, which has "corners". The study emphasised the difficulties embodied in the tangent concept, but suggests that the experiences of the experimental groups helped them to develop a more coherent concept image, with an enhanced ability to transfer this knowledge to a new context.

The use of graphic calculators opens up the possibility to represent functions and to pass gradually from functions to their derivatives. A research report on first year Biology students focused on functions and derivatives with graphic calculators, Borba and Villareal (1998) point out that the calculators were always present conceptually, if not physically, and did not bar other media from being used. The evidence suggests that the technology does not merely supplement but actually acts as a reorganiser of cognition.

Exploiting multiple representations offered by TI92 calculators, Kendal and Stacey (2000) report on an introductory program of differential calculus at grade 11. The aim of the teaching sequence was the introduction of competencies on derivative and proficiency with various representations. The paper reports on the conceptual understanding of differentiation by two different classes of students. The competencies were tested by a set of items designed to measure levels of understanding with respect to the numerical, graphical and symbolic environments of the calculator. To this aim, different types of questions have been developed, as for example: "Find a rate of change" in the numerical case, "Find a gradient" in the graphical case, and "Find the derivative" in the symbolic case. They were based on the fact that: A numerical representation of derivative (derivative calculated at a point) is approximated by a difference quotient; a graphical representation is given by the gradient of the tangent to the curve at a point; a symbolic derivative is determined as a function manipulating formulas or as the limit of a function.

In a study presented by Ubuz and Kirkpinar (2000), first year undergraduate students were engaged in learning the concepts of calculus, particularly derivative. The authors analyse the factors contributing to learning calculus in a computer-based learning environment (Interactive Set Language ISETL and Derive). The outcome shows that there was a significant improvement in learning derivative in general in the graphical interpretation and in the use of the definition.

Integration is usually the last element in the curricular sequence of calculus, after limit and derivative, but with the use of technology a didactic inversion may offer an appropriate and attractive cognitive approach. In this case, as in the case of derivative, research demonstrates that introducing limits in a formal way only at the end of calculus, after derivative and integral, can be the better choice from a cognitive point of view (Tall, 1986a). The differentiation-integration concept takes place first at the numerical and graphical level, exploiting the computer, starting from physical or mathematical situations, than can be managed at the symbolic level. The area under a simple graph such as $f(x) = x^2$ may be approximated by dividing the interval into n equal width strips and adding together the "upper" and "lower" rectangular approximation in each strip. Knowing the formula to simplify the sums, it is possible to see what happens as n gets very large. In 1635 the Italian mathematician Cavalieri demonstrated his computational facility by performing the calculations for all powers of x up to 9. It was excellent and hard work, but today this can be done with the help of computers. With an algorithm in a programming language it is possible to see the results of these sums, but with this method the process of calculation of intermediate sums will be lost. Another way to approach the problem could be to use Graphic Calculus (the environment Area). In order to follow the process in each step: Drawing the graph of a function, calculating the area under a function. Students may explore many possibilities in a short time, choosing the function, the interval where to determine the area and the strip. Then some intriguing explorations can take place, as for example what about inverting the two extremes of the interval? The software dynamically shows a negative step and the picture of the area approximations builds up from right to left (Tall, 1986b). Another dynamic feature of the software permits observation of the generation of the integral function in real time, having fixed the interval of integration and the step. Another stage of the exploration can be the change of the number of steps, and one more could be the discovery of the addition property for integrals, starting from particular cases. This path tends to the fundamental theorem, as a final aim of a sequence of meaningful activities that can prepare students to the more formal approach to theory.

A paper by Hong and Thomas (1997) focuses on a significant improvement of conceptual thinking in integration through the use of computers and curricular modules of work in classroom. The use of these environments favoured an enhanced proceptual understanding with a tendency to understand in a concept-oriented manner, rather than as rote processes. In contrast, the control group of students with their traditional learning of calculus often experienced no change showing the same misconceptions in both pre- and post-test.

Implications for teaching and curriculum

The role of technology in supporting students engaged in mathematical activities may differ according to many variables: The students themselves and their background, the task, the mathematical context, the class context, the kind of technology used, the teacher's use of technology, etc. Given this complexity it is difficult to find patterns of use. For instance, students might sometimes use technology in a certain way because of certain teacher's beliefs. Let us review the role of the teacher in introducing technology in a classroom.

A case study in which three teachers were involved is described by Kendal and Stacey in order to find differences in the approach to calculus by students who had full access to calculators with CAS in the classroom, at home, and during tests (Kendal & Stacey, 1999). The study shows that each of the three classes obtains similar average scores of the test. However, they made very different use of the CAS environment and performed differently on the items of the test. The authors pointed their attention on "privileging", as the act that reflects the teacher's underlying beliefs about the nature of mathematics and how it should be taught. Privileging is derived from the interplay of teachers' beliefs and interrelated knowledge sources (i.e. content, content pedagogical, pedagogical); it is moderated by institutional knowledge about students and school constraints; it is shown through teachers' practice and attitudes and it is highly influential in students' learning. The study demonstrates how teachers' privileging can have an impact on students' learning and influence it. The great potential of CAS in providing multiple representations of mathematical concepts has been differently implemented by the three teachers. These differences have been translated into substantial differences in how their students solved problems and what they understood. For example, the students of class C understood what to do in algebraic contexts so they could compensate for poor algebraic skills by appropriate use of the calculator and by substituting algebraic with graphical procedures.

The same authors present a case study in which two teachers were involved (Kendal & Stacey, 2001): They discuss the classroom process data, referring to a 25 lesson course on introductory differential calculus to 16-17 year old students.. Analysis shows two distinct teaching styles, methods, representation preferences, functional and pedagogical uses of technology (the environment CAS in TI92 calculators). In their study, the authors concentrate on three components of privileging: Teaching approach; calculus content; use of technology (evidenced by the nature of use of the CAS calculator). Analysing the three aspects of each teacher's privileging during the teaching of an introductory calculus unit, the study monitors the changes that occurred over two years and explores the impact of new knowledge and a new situation on the changes in technology privileging, linking them to each teacher's beliefs and pedagogy. The results are that the two teachers changed technological privileging according to their prior beliefs and knowledge.

Other studies (Valero & Gómez, 1996) about teacher's beliefs in classrooms that used graphic calculators for functions, pointed out that there are real modifications in actions and expressed opinions on the role of technology in teaching mathematics but not in thoughts. The methodology for collecting data, based on interviews aimed at identifying the teacher's position on it, showed that some destabilisation in the belief system may occur, but that no significant change arises. The authors remarked the conclusion that technology itself does not promote change, neither in learning, nor in teaching.

The use of the same technology in a pre-calculus course is presented by Doerr and Zangor (1999), who analyse the role and beliefs of the teacher related to the patterns and modes of students' use of graphic calculators in supporting their mathematical activities. They found a set of ways in which the tool is used by the students and related mathematical norms. The teacher's confidence, flexibility of use, and her awareness of the limitations of technology itself, led to the establishment of: A norm that required results to be justified on mathematical grounds; multiple ways for visually checking hypothesised relationships between variables, a shifting role for the calculator from graphing to checking, and the use of non-calculator strategies for periodic transformations.

Pre-service mathematics teachers, most of who were concurrently engaged in their student teaching experience, were observed in order to study the impact of a multimedia teaching case on their professional development (Doerr, McClain & Bowers, 1997). The study presents the benefits and the limitations of the multimedia case.

Another important level of implications deals with curriculum design. In a period such as the last decade, when all over the world there have been new curricular projects in mathematics (see for example NCTM, 2000; Anichini, Arzarello, Ciarrapico & Robutti, 2004), it is important to reflect on the use of old and new symbols by students in order to support their construction of meaning. "How much and what kind of actions on formal symbol systems are needed to support the mental construction of objects that can in turn serve as referents for new symbols and systems of reasoning?" (Kaput, 1994). The passage from process conception to conceptual entity is difficult (see § *Limits*), and it is traversable with appropriate forms of deliberately designed experiences, as defining and manipulating wide varieties of function in a computer environment, possibly starting from perceptuo-motor activities, as shown in many cases (Arzarello & Robutti, 2003; Nemirovsky, 2003; Rasmussen & Nemirovsky, 2003). The problem of studying students' conceptualisation in terms of a semiotic approach has particularly pointed out by Radford (Radford, Demers, Guzmán & Cerulli, 2003; Radford, Cerulli, Demers & Guzmán, 2004) and by Arzarello (2005), and their studies converge on the kind of activities where students are involved and on the theoretical analysis, based on the objectification of knowledge, as making something apparent in a social way. These experimental and theoretical studies show their power in the didactical implication on the mathematics curriculum. As an example, the very recent curriculum proposal made by UMI in Italy (Anichini et al., 2004) realises the findings from these studies and points out the importance of the mathematics laboratory, intended as a methodology based on activities with materials and artefacts, where students are actively engaged in social work.

Concluding remarks on calculus

> "As for the precise contents envisaged by the research, even where the works concern different levels, one finds again common preoccupations:
>
> - Concern with developing a functional approach,
>
> - Concern to focus the notion of derivative on the existence of a good approximation of the first order, the computer allowing exact visualization of this property by magnification of the graph, even before the notion of limit is mastered." (Artigue, 1991)

Calculus needs to be studied across many years of school, from early grades onward, much as a subject like geometry should be studied. Hence its many purposes should be examined, not merely its refined methods. But most especially, its root problems should take precedence as the organizing force for curriculum design.

The power of new dynamic interactive technologies should be exploited in ways that reach beyond facilitating the use of traditional symbol systems (algebraic, numeric, and graphical), and especially in ways that allow controllable linkages between measurable events that are experienced as real by students and more formal mathematical representations of those events. (Kaput, 1994).

To educate students to observe numerical sequences, to see a graph and to read through symbols seems to identify the most common feature of the articles in this review.

FINAL REMARKS

The three main sections above have raised questions or drawn conclusions in relation to research on the use of technology in expressions and variables, functions and calculus. We do not therefore intend to summarise or repeat those conclusions here. In this short section, we constrain ourselves to a few overarching comments.

From the technology perspective

We can outline general trends relative to the implementation of technology for the teaching and learning of all the subject matters considered in this review. In fact, we have seen that new technology allows for dynamical approaches to the major concepts in algebra as well as in calculus, contrasting the static existence of traditional paper and pencil practices. Equally, the power of linking multiple representations, rich in terms of interactivity, is made explicit through the use of digital technology. As a consequence, interactivity and dynamicity are two features for which technology promises a wide potential, providing attention to the construction of meanings more than to the manipulative aspects.

We have also seen changes in the kinds of technologies used over time: Programming languages, such as Logo, Pascal and Basic, flourished toward the end of '80s as an approach to addressing specific contextual knowledge, such as that of variable, or function. But, at the end of the decade research interest in programming, at least as a medium for learning concepts, has all but vanished.

An open issue is then whether this trend is mostly a matter of fashion, or whether somehow the complexity of learning the particulars of the language was seen as counter-productive to the development of general cognitive and thinking skills through programming. Furthermore, software in which particular commands allow students to operate directly on mathematical objects and to see changes as results of their actions offer an immediate perception that can support the construction of those specific concepts, though, arguably, may be more constrained in terms of rich extensions.

From those years on, research increasingly focused on the development and the experimentation of new packages, games and tutorials, with the aim of improving the learning of mathematics, with specific didactical aims. Such programs are centred on the construction of meanings for circumscribed mathematical objects (for example, geometric figures, functions and their transformations, vectors, ...). But they can also be oriented to the construction of a 'piece' of theory, around the notion of theorem, for example, or proof, or deductive system. These programs are generally more 'mathematics-oriented', than open spaces where many different kinds of operations (related to more than one subject matter) are possible, such as a spreadsheet can be. We are referring in the first case, to L'Algebrista for example, and in the second case to CAS environments, which are paradigmatic cases of the introduction and diffusion of new technology over the last decade.

Implications for teaching practice and research

The review raises a number of issues, often with no answers at present, and indeed these issues often raise further questions. Indeed, Hershkowitz and Kieran (2001), set out the contextual factors of various origins that one should consider in the design as well as in the study of a classroom learning activity in a computerized mathematics learning environment: "(a) The mathematical content to be learned and its epistemological structure; (b) The learners, their mathematical knowledge culture, and the history with which they started the researched activity; (c) The classroom culture and norms, the role of the teacher, the learning organization –in small groups or individually–, etc.; and (d) The potential 'contribution' of the computerized tool" (ibid.). We have seen in this review that it is quite complex, even from the research point of view, to analyse an integration of all the variables, in order that they can be fit together in a harmonic whole. In the practice of teaching, the implementation of technology "forces reconsideration of traditional questions about control and the social structure of classrooms and organizational structure of schools" (Kaput, 1992). The curricular choices and beliefs of teachers acquire great relevance in these terms. Substantially, technology re-awakens us to the complexity underlying the teaching and learning of mathematics, re-posing age-old questions that regard: "Educational goals, appropriate pedagogical strategies, and underlying beliefs about the nature of the subject matter, the nature of learners and learning, and the relation between knowledge and knower" (ibid.).

REFERENCES

Aczel, J. (1998). Learning algebraic strategies using a computerised balance model. In A. Olivier & K. Newstead (Eds.), *Proceedings of the 22nd PME International Conference, 2*, 1–8.

Ainley, J. (1994). Building on children's intuitions about line graphs. In J. P. Ponte & J. F. Matos (Eds.), *Proceedings of the 18th PME International Conference, 2*, 1–8.

Ainley, J. (1995). Reasons to be formal: Contextualising formal notation in a spreadsheet environment. In L. Meira & D. Carraher (Eds.), *Proceedings of the 19th PME International Conference, 2*, 26–33.

Ainley, J. (2000). Exploring the transparency of graphs and graphing. In T. Nakahara & M. Koyama (Eds.), *Proceedings of the 24th PME International Conference, 2*, 9–17.

Ainley, J., Nardi, E., & Pratt, D. (1998). Graphing as a computer-mediated tool. In A. Olivier & K. Newstead (Eds.), *Proceedings of the 22nd PME International Conference, 1*, 243–250.

Ainley, J., & Pratt, D. (2002). Purpose and utility in pedagogic task design. In A. D. Cockburn & E. Nardi (Eds.), *Proceedings of the 26th PME International Conference, 2*, 17–24.

Anichini, G., Arzarello, F., Ciarrapico, L., & Robutti, O. (Eds.). (2004). *New mathematical standards for the school from 5 through 18 years* (Edition for ICME 10, on behalf of UMI-CIIM, MIUR). Bologna, Italy: Unione Matematica Italiana.

Artigue, M. (1991). Analysis. In D. Tall (Ed.), *Advanced mathematical thinking* (pp. 167–198). Dordrecht, The Netherlands: Kluwer.

Arzarello, F. (2005). Mathematical landscapes and their inhabitants: Perceptions, languages, theories (Plenary lecture). In M. Niss et al. (Eds.), *Proceedings of the 10th International Congress of Mathematics Education.*

Arzarello, F., Bazzini, L., & Chiappini, G. (1995). The construction of algebraic knowledge: Towards a socio-cultural theory and practice. In L. Meira & D. Carraher (Eds.), *Proceedings of the 19th PME International Conference, 1*, 199–206.

Arzarello, F., & Robutti, O. (2003). Approaching algebra through motion experiences. In N. A. Pateman, B. J. Dougherty, & J. T. Zilliox (Eds.), *Proceedings of the 27th PME International Conference, 1*, 111–115.

Ball, L., Pierce, R., & Stacey, K. (2003). Recognising equivalent algebraic expressions: An important component of algebraic expectation for working with CAS. In N. A. Pateman, B. J. Dougherty, & J. T. Zilliox (Eds.), *Proceedings of the 27th PME International Conference, 4*, 15–22.

Borba, M. (1994). A model for students' understanding in a multi-representational environment. In J. P. Ponte & J. F. Matos (Eds.), Proceedings *of the 18th PME International Conference, 2*, 104–111.

Borba, M. C. (1995). Overcoming limits of software tools: A student's solution for a problem involving transformation of functions. In L. Meira & D. Carraher (Eds.), *Proceedings of the 19th PME International Conference, 2*, 248–255.

Borba, M., & Scheffer, N. (2003). Sensors, body, technology and multiple representations. In N. A. Pateman, B. J. Dougherty, & J. T. Zilliox (Eds.), *Proceedings of the 27th PME International Conference, 1*, 121–128.

Borba, M. C., & Villareal, M. E. (1998). Graphing calculators and the reorganisation of thinking: The transition from functions to derivative. In A. Olivier & K. Newstead (Eds.), *Proceedings of the 22nd PME International Conference, 2*, 136–143.

Cavanagh, M., & Mitchelmore, M. (2000). Student misconceptions in interpreting basic graphic calculator displays. In T. Nakahara & M. Koyama (Eds.), *Proceedings of the 24th PME International Conference*, *2*, 161–168.

Cedillo, T. E. A. (1997). Algebra as a language in use: A study with 11–12 year olds using graphing calculators. In E. Pehkonen (Ed.), *Proceedings of the 21st PME International Conference*, *2*, 137–144.

Confrey, J. (1994) Six approaches to transformation of functions using multi-representational software. In J. P. Ponte & J. F. Matos (Eds.), *Proceedings of the 18th PME International Conference*, *2*, 217–224.

Confrey, J., & Smith, E. (1992). Revised accounts of the function concept using multi-representational software, contextual problems and student paths. In W. Geeslin & K. Graham (Eds.), *Proceedings of the 16th PME International Conference*, *1*, 153–160.

Cornu, B. (1991). Limits. In D. Tall (Ed.), *Advanced mathematical thinking* (pp. 153–166). Dortrecht, The Netherlands: Kluwer.

Dagher, A., & Artigue, M. (1993). The use of computers in learning to correlate algebraic and graphic representation of functions. In I. Hirabayashi, N. Nohda, K. Shigematsu, & F.-L. Lin (Eds.), *Proceedings of the 17th PME International Conference*, *2*, 1–8.

Doerr, H. M., McClain, K., & Bowers, J. (1997). Creating a shared context: The use of a multimedia case in a teacher development course. In E. Pehkonen (Ed.), *Proceedings of the 21st PME International Conference*, *2*, 217–224.

Doerr, H. M., & Zangor, R. (1999). Creating a tool: An analysis of the role of the graphing calculator in a pre calculus classroom. In O. Zaslavsky (Ed.), *Proceedings of the 23rd PME International Conference*, *2*, 265–272.

Drijvers, P. (2001). Reaction to "A meta study on IC technologies in education. Towards a multidimensional framework to tackle their integration". In M. van den Heuvel-Panhuizen (Ed.), *Proceedings of the 25th PME International Conference*, *1*, 123–130.

Euler, L. (1988), *Introduction to Analysis of the Infinite* (1, pp. 50–55). New York, USA: Springer Verlag. (translated by John Blanton)

Friedlander, A., & Stein, H. (2001). Students' choice of tools in solving equations in a technological learning environment. In M. van den Heuvel-Panhuizen (Ed.), Proceedings *of the 25th PME International Conference*, *2*, 441–448.

Gitirana, V. (1998). Conceptions as articulated in different microworlds exploring functions. In A. Olivier & K. Newstead (Eds.), *Proceedings of the 22nd PME International Conference*, *3*, 9–16.

Goldenberg, P. (1997). Believing is seeing: How preconceptions influence the perception of graphs. In J. C. Bergeron, N. Herscovics, & C. Kieran (Eds.), *Proceedings of the 11th PME International Conference*, *1*, 197–203.

Gómez, P., & Fernández, F. (1997). Graphing calculators use in pre-calculus and achievement in calculus. In E. Pehkonen (Ed.), *Proceedings of the 21st PME International Conference*, *3*, 1–8.

Guin, D., & Trouche, L. (2000). Thinking of new devices to make viable symbolic calculators in the classroom. In T. Nakahara & M. Koyama (Eds.), *Proceedings of the 24th[th] PME International Conference*, *3*, 9–16.

Guttenberger, E. W. (1992) The learning of trigonometric functions in a graphical computer environment. In W. Geeslin & K. Graham (Eds.), *Proceedings of the 16th PME International Conference*, *3*, 106–113.

Healy, L., & Hoyles, C. (1996). Seeing, doing and expressing: An evaluation of task sequences for supporting algebraic thinking. In L. Puig & A. Gutiérrez (Eds.), *Proceedings of the 20th PME International Conference*, *3*, 67–74.

Hegedus, S. J., & Kaput, J. (2003). The effect of SimCalc connected classrooms on students' algebraic thinking. In N. A. Pateman, B. J. Dougherty, & J. Zilliox (Eds.), *Proceedings of the 27th PME International Conference*, *3*, 47–54.

Hershkowitz, R., & Kieran, C. (2001). Algorithmic and meaningful ways of joining together representatives within the same mathematical activity: An experience with graphing calculators. In

M. van den Heuvel-Panhuizen (Ed.), Proceedings *of the 25th PME International Conference*, *1*, 96–107.

Hong, Y. Y., & Thomas, M. (1997). Using the computer improve conceptual thinking integration. In E. Pehkonen (Ed.), *Proceedings of the 21st PME International Conference*, *3*, 81–88.

Kaput, J. (1987). PME XI algebra papers: A representational framework. In J. C. Bergeron, N. Herscovics, & C. Kieran (Eds.), *Proceedings of the 11th PME International Conference*, *1*, 345–354.

Kaput, J. (1992). Technology and mathematics education. In D. Grouws (Ed.), *Handbook of research on mathematics teaching and learning* (pp. 515–556). New York, USA: Macmillan.

Kaput, J. (1994). Democratizing access to calculus: New routes to old roots. In A. Schoenfeld (Ed.), *Mathematical thinking and problem solving* (pp. 77–156). Hillsdale, NJ, USA: Lawrence Erlbaum.

Kaput, J., & Hegedus, S. J. (2002). Exploiting classroom connectivity by aggregating student constructions to create new learning opportunities. In A. D. Cockburn & E. Nardi (Eds.), *Proceedings of the 26th PME International Conference*, *3*, 177–184.

Kaput, J., Noss, R., & Hoyles, C. (2002). Developing new notations for a learnable mathematics in the computational era. In L. English (Ed.), *Handbook of international research in mathematics education* (pp. 51–75). Hillsdale, NJ, USA: Lawrence Erlbaum.

Kendal, M., & Stacey, K. (1999). CAS, calculus and classrooms. In O. Zaslavsky (Ed.), *Proceedings of the 23rd PME International Conference*, *3*, 129–136.

Kendal, M., & Stacey, K. (2000). Acquiring the concept of derivative: Teaching and learning with multiple representations and CAS. In T. Nakahara & M. Koyama (Eds.), *Proceedings of the 24th PME International Conference*, *3*, 127–134.

Kendal, M., & Stacey, K. (2001). Influences on and factors changing technology privileging. In M. van den Heuvel-Panhuizen (Ed.), *Proceedings of the 25th PME International Conference*, *3*, 217–224.

Kidron, I. (2002). Concept definition, concept image, and the notion of infinite sum in old and new environments. In A. D. Cockburn & E. Nardi (Eds.), *Proceedings of the 26th[th] PME International Conference*, *3*, 209–216.

Kidron, I., Zehavi, N., & Openhaim, E. (2001). Teaching the limit concept in a CAS environment: Students' dynamic perceptions and reasoning. In M. van den Heuvel-Panhuizen (Ed.), *Proceedings of the 25th PME International Conference*, *3*, 241–248.

Kieran, C. (1992). The learning and teaching of school algebra. In D. Grouws (Ed.), *Handbook of research on mathematics teaching and learning* (pp. 390–419). New York, USA: Macmillan.

Kissane, B. (2001). *Algebra and technology: Emerging issues*. Presentation at the Biennial Conference of the Australian Association of Mathematics Teachers, Canberra, Australia.

Lagrange, J. B. (1999). Learning pre-calculus with complex calculators: Mediation and instrumental genesis. In O. Zaslavsky (Ed.), *Proceedings of the 23rd PME International Conference*, *3*, 193–200.

Lakoff, G., & Núñez, R. (2000). *Where mathematics comes from: How the embodied mind brings mathematics into being*. New York, USA: Basic Books.

Lesh, R., & Herre, J. (1987). Dienes revisited: Multiple embodiments in computer environments. In J. C. Bergeron, N. Herscovics, & C. Kieran (Eds.), *Proceedings of the 11th PME International Conference*, *1*, 211–220.

Li, L., & Tall, D. (1993). Constructing different concept images of sequences & limits by programming. In I. Hirabayashi, N. Nohda, K. Shigematsu, & F.-L. Lin (Eds.), *Proceedings of the 17th PME International Conference*, *2*, 41–48.

Magidson, S. (1992). What's in a problem? Exploring slope using computer graphing software. In W. Geeslin & K. Graham (Eds.), *Proceedings of the 16th PME International Conference*, *2*, 64–71.

Mariotti, M. A., & Cerulli, M. (2001). Semiotic mediation for algebra teaching and learning. In M. van den Heuvel-Panhuizen (Ed.), *Proceedings of the 25th PME International Conference*, *3*, 343–349.

Mesa, V. M., & Gómez, P. (1996). Graphing calculators and pre-calculus: An exploration of some aspects of students' understanding. In L. Puig & A. Gutiérrez (Eds.), *Proceedings of the 20th PME International Conference*, *3*, 391–398.

Milani, R., & Baldino, R. (2002). The theory of limits as an obstacle to infinitesimal analysis. In A. D. Cockburn & E. Nardi (Eds.), *Proceedings of the 26th PME International Conference, 3*, 345–352.

Monaghan, J., Sun, S., & Tall, D. (1994). Construction of the limit concept with a computer algebra system. In J. P. Ponte & J. F. Matos (Eds.), *Proceedings of the 18th PME International Conference, 3*, 279–286.

Moreira, L. (2002). Mathematics education and critical consciousness. In A. D. Cockburn & E. Nardi (Eds.), *Proceedings of the 26th PME International Conference, 3*, 369–376.

Nathan, M. J. (1992). Interactive depictions of mathematical constraints can increase students' levels of competence for word algebra problem solving. In W. Geeslin & K. Graham (Eds.), *Proceedings of the 16th PME International Conference, 2*, 160–169.

National Council of Teachers of Mathematics (NCTM). (2000). *Principles and standards for school mathematics*. Reston, VA, USA: NCTM.

Nemirovsky, R. (1994). Slope, steepness, and school math. In J. P. Ponte & J. F. Matos (Eds.), *Proceedings of the 18th PME International Conference, 3*, 344–351.

Nemirovsky, R. (1995). Panel Presentation. In L. Meira & D. Carraher (Eds.), *Proceedings of the 19th PME International Conference, 1*, 79–86.

Nemirovsky, R. (1998). Symbol-Use, fusion and logical necessity: On the significance of children's graphing: A reaction paper to Ainley et al. In A. Olivier & K. Newstead (Eds.), *Proceedings of the 22nd PME International Conference, 1*, 259–267.

Nemirovsky, R. (2003). Three conjectures concerning the relationship between body activity and understanding mathematics. In N. A. Pateman, B. J. Dougherty, & J. T. Zilliox (Eds.), *Proceedings of the 27th PME International Conference, 1*, 105–113.

Nemirovsky, R., Kaput, J., & Roschelle, J. (1998). Enlarging mathematical activity from modelling phenomena to generating phenomena. In A. Olivier & K. Newstead (Eds.), *Proceedings of the 22nd PME International Conference, 3*, 287–294.

Noble, T., & Nemirovsky, R. (1995). Graphs that go backwards. In L. Meira & D. Carraher (Eds.), *Proceedings of the 19th PME International Conference, 2*, 256–265

Norton, S., & Cooper, T. J. (2001). Students' responses to a new generation ILS algebra tutor. In M. van den Heuvel-Panhuizen (Ed.), Proceedings *of the 25th PME International Conference, 3*, 439–446.

Pratt, D. (1994). Active graphing in a computer-rich environment. In J. P. Ponte & J. F. Matos (Eds.), *Proceedings of the 18th PME International Conference, 4*, 57–64.

Pratt, D. (1995). Passive and active graphing: A study of two learning sequences. In L. Meira. & D. Carraher (Eds.), *Proceedings of the 19th PME International Conference, 2*, 210–217.

Radford, L., Cerulli, M., Demers, S., & Guzmán, J. (2004). The sensual and the conceptual: Artefact-mediated kinesthetic actions and semiotic activity. In M. J. Høines & A. B. Fuglestad (Eds.), *Proceedings of the 28th PME International Conference, 4*, 73–80.

Radford, L., Demers, S., Guzmán, J., & Cerulli, M. (2003). Calculators, graphs, gestures, and the production meaning. In N. A. Pateman, B. J. Dougherty, & J. T. Zilliox (Eds.), *Proceedings of the 27th PME International Conference, 4*, 55–62.

Rasmussen, C., & Nemirovsky, R. (2003). Becoming friends with acceleration: The role of tools and bodily activity in mathematical learning. In N. A. Pateman, B. J. Dougherty, & J. T. Zilliox (Eds.), *Proceedings of the 27th PME International Conference, 1*, 127–134.

Reid, D. A. (2002). Describing young children's deductive reasoning. In A. D. Cockburn & E. Nardi (Eds.), *Proceedings of the 26th PME International Conference, 4*, 105–112.

Resnick, Z., Schwarz, B., & Hershkowitz, R. (1994). Global thinking "between and within" function representations in a dynamic interactive medium. In J. P. Ponte & J. F. Matos (Eds.), *Proceedings of the 18th PME International Conference, 4*, 225–232.

Robutti, O., & Ferrara, F. (2002). Approaching algebra through motion experiences. In A. D. Cockburn & E. Nardi (Eds.), *Proceedings of the 26th PME International Conference, 1*, 111–118.

Samurçay, R. (1985). Learning programming: Constructing the concept of variable by beginning students. In L. Streefland (Ed.), *Proceedings of the 9th PME International Conference, 1*, 77–82.

Schwarz, B., & Bruckheimer, M. (1988). Representations of functions and analogies, In A. Borbás (Ed.), *Proceedings of the 12th PME International Conference, 2*, 552–559.

Schwarz, B. B., & Hershkowitz, R. (1996). Effects of computerized tools on prototypes of the function concept. In L. Puig & A. Gutiérrez (Eds.), *Proceedings of the 20th PME International Conference, 4*, 259–266.

Smart, T. (1995). Visualising quadratic functions: A study of thirteen-year-old girls learning mathematics with graphic calculators. In L. Meira & D. Carraher (Eds.), *Proceedings of the 19th PME International Conference, 2*, 272–279.

Sutherland, R. (1987). A study of the use and understanding of algebra related concepts within a Logo environment. In J. C. Bergeron, N. Herscovics, & C. Kieran (Eds.), *Proceedings of the 11th PME International Conference, 1*, 241–247.

Sutherland, R., & Rojano, T. (1996). Mathematical modelling in the sciences through the eyes of Marina and Adam. In L. Puig & A. Gutiérrez (Eds.), *Proceedings of the 20th PME International Conference, 4*, 291–298.

Tabach, M., & Hershkowitz, R. (2002). Construction of knowledge and its consolidation: A case study from the early-algebra classroom. In A. D. Cockburn & E. Nardi (Eds.), *Proceedings of the 26th PME International Conference, 4*, 265–272.

Tall, D. (1985). Using computer graphics programs as generic organisers for the concept image of differentiation. In L. Streefland (Ed.), *Proceedings of the 9th PME International Conference, 1*, 105–110.

Tall, D. (1986a). *Building and testing a cognitive approach to the calculus using interactive computer graphics*. Unpublished PhD. dissertation, University of Warwick, UK.

Tall, D. (1986b). A graphical approach to integration and the Fundamental Theorem. *Mathematics Teaching, 113*, 48–51.

Tall, D. (1987a). Algebra in a computer environment. In J. C. Bergeron, N. Herscovics, & C. Kieran (Eds.), *Proceedings of the 11th PME International Conference, 1*, 262–271.

Tall, D. (1987b). Constructing the concept image of a tangent. In J. C. Bergeron, N. Herscovics, & C. Kieran (Eds.), *Proceedings of the 11th PME International,* 3, 69–75.

Tall, D. (1989). Concept images, generic organizers, computers & curriculum change. *For the Learning of Mathematics*, *9*(3), 37–42.

Tall, D., & Sheath, G. (1983). Visualizing higher level mathematical concepts using computer graphics. In R. Hershkowitz (Ed.), *Proceedings of the 7th PME International Conference,* 357–362.

Thomas, M., & Tall, D. (1988). Longer-term conceptual benefits from using a computer in algebra teaching. In A. Borbás (Ed.), *Proceedings of the 12th PME International Conference, 2*, 601–608.

Thompson, P. W., & Thompson, A. G. (1987). Computer presentations of structure in algebra. In J. C. Bergeron, N. Herscovics, & C. Kieran (Eds.), *Proceedings of the 11th PME International Conference, 1*, 248–254.

Trouche, L., & Guin, D. (1996). Seeing is reality: How graphing calculators may influence the conceptualisation of limits. In L. Puig & A. Gutiérrez (Eds.), *Proceedings of the 20th PME International Conference, 4*, 323–330.

Tsamir, P., & Bazzini, L. (2001). Can x=3 be the solution of an inequality? A study of Italian and Israeli students. In M. van den Heuvel-Panhuizen (Ed.), *Proceedings of the 25th PME International Conference, 4*, 303–310.

Ubuz, B., & Kirkpinar, B. (2000). Factors contributing to learning of calculus. In T. Nakahara & M. Koyama (Eds.), *Proceedings of the 24th PME International Conference, 4*, 241–248.

Valero, P., & Gómez, P. (1996). Precalculus and graphic calculators: The influence on teacher's beliefs. In L. Puig & A. Gutiérrez (Eds.), *Proceedings of the 20th PME International Conference, 4*, 363–370.

Verillon, P., & Rabarbel, P. (1995). Cognition and artifacts: A contribution to the study of thought in relation to instrumented activity. *European Journal of Psychology of Education*, *X* (1), 77–101.

Vinner, S. (1987): Continuous functions – Images and reasoning in college students, In J. C. Bergeron, N. Herscovics, & C. Kieran (Eds.), *Proceedings of the 11th PME International Conference*, *3*, 177–183.

Yerushalmy, M. (1997). Emergence for new schemes for solving algebra word problems: The impact of technology and the function approach. In E. Pehkonen (Ed.), *Proceedings of the 21st PME International Conference*, *1*, 165–172.

Yerushalmy, M., & Bohr, M. (1995). Between equations and solutions: An odyssey in 3D. In L. Meira & D. Carraher (Eds.), *Proceedings of the 19th PME International Conference*, *2*, 218–225.

Yerushalmy, M., & Shternberg, B. (1994). Symbolic awareness of algebra beginners. In J. P. Ponte & J. F. Matos (Eds.), *Proceedings of the 18th PME International Conference*, *4*, 393–400.

Yerushalmy, M., Shternberg, B., & Gilead, S. (1999). Visualisation as a vehicle for meaning of problem solving in algebra. In O. Zaslavsky (Ed.), *Proceedings of the 2nd PME International Conference*, *1*, 197–206.

Zehavi, N. (1988). Substitutions leading to reasoning. In A. Borbás (Ed.), *Proceedings of the 12th PME International Conference*, *2*, 665–672.

AFFILIATIONS

Francesca Ferrara
Dipartimento di Matematica
Università di Torino
10123 Torino (Italy)
ferrara@dm.unito.it

Dave Pratt
Centre for New Technologies Research in Education
University of Warwick
Coventry CV4 7AL (UK)
dave.pratt@warwick.ac.uk

Ornella Robutti
Dipartimento di Matematica
Università di Torino
10123 Torino (Italy)
robutti@unito.it

COLETTE LABORDE, CHRONIS KYNIGOS,
KAREN HOLLEBRANDS, AND RUDOLF STRÄSSER

TEACHING AND LEARNING GEOMETRY WITH TECHNOLOGY

INTRODUCTION

In the past three decades, technological environments have been created that offer novel ways of carrying out geometrical activities in mathematics education. This chapter reviews research investigating the impact of these various technologies on the learning and teaching of geometry. The chapter begins by providing a general overview of the various theoretical approaches, on which such research is based. The second section focuses on specific technologies. The third section synthesizes results from research and organizes them within four categories: The nature of geometry mediated by technology, technology and the learning of geometry, the design of tasks, the use of geometry technology by teachers. The final section concludes the chapter by linking the results of past research to perspectives for the future. This review of research is based on research that developed in the International Group for the Psychology of Mathematics Education (PME) and/or was published in international journals on mathematics education or on computers in mathematics education.

GENERAL THEORETICAL ISSUES

This section addresses the theoretical approaches underlying various research studies on technology for the teaching and learning of geometry. It attempts to explain the development of technology by analyzing the background of this development: The epistemological nature of geometry, the problems with which the teaching of geometry was faced in the past decades, and the cognitive processes involved in geometry problem solving. We present various theoretical approaches that have been used in research for analyzing the impact of technology on learning and the interactions between students and technology. More recently, researchers have paid greater attention to the integration of technology into teaching and consequently different theoretical approaches have been employed.

A. Gutiérrez, P. Boero (eds.), Handbook of Research on the Psychology of Mathematics Education: Past, Present and Future, 275–304.

Epistemological perspective

The teaching of geometry can be understood only if geometry is considered as an activity with at least two aspects: On the one hand, it is the study of concepts and logical relations, which historically came from an extensive analysis of space, but later became a field of investigation and discussion of axiomatic foundations detached from any spatial experience. On the other hand, geometry refers to spatial concepts, procedures and relations used within society for various purposes, such as architecture, building, structuring settlements, villages, cities, designing packages of goods for storage and other purposes and activities (Strässer, 1996). Since ancient Greece, the dual nature of geometry has often been claimed and discussed: Was and is geometry dealing with what our senses perceive or with intellectual ideas? It was also stressed even by one of the founders of an axiomatic approach of geometry, namely Hilbert who claimed the coexistence of two tendencies, one toward abstraction and another toward intuitive understanding (Hilbert & Cohn Vossen, 1952, in the Preface).

Teaching and learning geometry

The teaching of geometry has always been an object of discussion in the past forty years and susceptible to dramatic changes with respect to the place given to the duality of empirical/theoretical. Particularly in several countries, it was deeply affected by the so-called reform of Modern Mathematics that mainly emphasized the formal part of geometry while avoiding recourse to diagrams. The argument was that geometry was especially difficult for students because of the use of diagrams; the combination of empirical evidence provided by diagrams and the teachers' demand to resort only to deductive thinking confused students.

The empirical/theoretical duality led to a problematic role of geometry in compulsory education curricula. Some educational researchers nevertheless viewed the origin of the problem in the absence of exploiting graphical representational registers associated with Geometry as part of the repertoire for expressing mathematical meanings, a shortcoming especially significant in geometry where they could be uniquely relevant. Freudenthal (1973) was one of the first researchers to raise the problem. He was followed by a growing number of voices, which pled for reintroducing diagrams in geometry teaching that eventually took place in the end of the seventies and beginning of the eighties. Even with this important role of graphical representations in the teaching of geometry, a conceptual analysis of this role was not yet carried out at that time. It is only at the end of the eighties and beginning of the nineties, that several theoretical approaches merged.

Duval (1988, 1998, 2000) distinguished three kinds of cognitive processes involved in a geometric activity: Visualization processes, construction processes by tools, and reasoning. Each of these processes fulfils a specific epistemological function but they are closely connected and "their synergy is cognitively necessary for proficiency in geometry" (Duval, 1998, p. 38). Duval also analyzed the role of visualization in the solution processes of a geometry problem and distinguished several approaches to a diagram in geometry: An immediate perceptual approach that may be an obstacle for the geometric interpretation of the diagram, an operative approach that is used for identifying sub-configurations useful for solving the problem and a discursive approach that is related to the statement describing the givens of the problem.

Another psychological approach that was almost simultaneously developed by Fischbein (1993; see also Mariotti, 1995), considers geometrical concepts as made of two components that cannot be dissociated: The figural one and the conceptual one, similar to two sides of a coin. This intrinsic link between figural and conceptual is not at all spontaneous and must be grounded in a long construction process by students.

The teaching of geometry is based on the use of two registers, the register of diagrams and the register of language. Language is a means of describing geometrical objects and relations using specific terminology while diagrams in 2D geometry play an ambiguous role. On the one hand they refer to theoretical objects whereas on the other hand they offer graphical –spatial properties, which can give rise to a perceptual activity from the individual (Parzysz, 1988; Strässer, 1991; Laborde, 1998). This ambiguous role of diagrams is completely implicit in the traditional teaching of geometry in which theoretical properties are assimilated into graphical ones (Berthelot & Salin, 1998). It is as if it were possible to read the properties of the theoretical object, which is represented by the diagram, by only looking at the diagram. One of the consequences is that students often assume that it is possible to construct a geometrical diagram using only visual cues, or to deduce a property empirically by checking on the diagram, as shown by several researchers (Chazan, 1993). When students are asked by the teacher to construct a diagram, the teacher expects them to use theoretical knowledge whereas students very often stay at the graphical level and try to satisfy only visual constraints.

The construction of the dual nature of geometrical concepts may be ignored by the teaching of geometry. This type of teaching obscures the distinction between the spatial and theoretical. Contrasting with this teaching practice, on the basis of their investigations, researchers and educators stressed the importance of the role of visualization in a geometry activity: Solving a geometry problem goes beyond the visual recognition of spatial relations. It is commonly assumed that the teaching of geometry should contribute to the learning of: (1) The distinction between spatial graphical relations and theoretical geometrical relations, (2) The movement between theoretical objects and their spatial representation, (3) The recognition of geometrical relations in a diagram, (4) The ability to imagine all possible diagrams attached to a geometrical object. The second kind of ability is particularly critical in the solving processes of students faced with geometry problems requiring exploration in which a cycle of interpreting, conjecturing, and proving may take place because of this flexibility between spatial representations and theoretical knowledge. Such assumptions about the teaching and learning of geometry have led some researchers to focus on the role of graphical representations provided by computer environments.

Use and role of technology for learning geometry

The contribution of technology in the teaching and learning of geometry is now mainly perceived as strongly linked with dynamically manipulable interactive graphical representations. However, the first appearance of digital media for the learning of Geometry, the Logo-based Turtle Geometry (Abelson & diSessa, 1981) came at a time when this functionality was not yet available. In the absence of dynamic manipulation, the graphical representational register was not given central attention. The main priority was the newly realized potential affordances of dynamic text editing, programming, and constructionism for mathematical meaning making (Papert, 1980; Noss & Hoyles, 1996). Graphical representations were part of the picture but appeared to be third in line of importance, after symbolic and turtle–associated, body-syntonic representations (Papert, 1980). In the mid-nineties, Papert and his team put forward the notion of constructionism in mathematical learning to signify that special aspect of constructivist learning which involved the activity of dynamic construction (Kafai & Resnick, 1996).

In the last thirty years, research has been mainly devoted to two kinds of technology providing graphical representations:

- Logo driven Turtle Geometry (TG) and its intrinsically linked philosophy of microworld,
- Dynamic geometry environments ("DGE" –with varying and generally growing degrees of interactivity and direct manipulation).

Both kinds of technology are attached to a theoretical perspective on learning. Logo TG and its decedents were clearly answering to a precise view of the nature of learning attached to the idea of a microworld. The main underlying principle was to provide programmability as a means for expressing and exploring mathematical ideas and the joint use of three representational registers: Symbolic programming, graphics, and a notional connection with body movement. Taking advantage of the huge progress of the graphic interface of computers, dynamic geometry environments arrived later on the scene; the first DGEs appeared in the eighties. The main underlying learning principle was to provide a family of diagrams as representing a set of geometrical objects and relations instead of a single static diagram. One of the motivations was to help students see the general aspects of a static diagram.

A constructivist perspective in a broad sense is generally adopted in research on the role and use of technology in the teaching of geometry: Learning is not taken as a simple process of the incorporation of prescribed and given knowledge, but rather as the individual's (re)construction of geometry. The interactions taking place between the learner and the machine are viewed as impacting this reconstruction. However, it is important to mention that additional theoretical perspectives have been used and/or developed taking into account: The structure of knowledge to be (re)constructed, and the environment of the learner –in particular, the social interactions in which learning takes place as well as institutional constraints coming from the institution "responsible" for learning (e.g. the school embedded within the larger school system).

Growing attention to the epistemology of the mathematical content whose learning is at stake has also developed over time. In the first years of technology in school, learning was mainly considered as emerging only from the interactions between the student and the machine, rather than between the students and appropriate tasks to be done with the machine. The focus moved onto the teaching environment, and in particular to the role of the teacher and the social interactions he/she could organize in the classroom as well as the social norms developing in the context of the classroom. The following paragraphs present the general theories underpinning this move.

According to an important hypothesis generally shared among researchers in particular in PME, when interacting with technology for solving mathematical tasks, students' actions and strategies are shaped by technology. Noss and Hoyles proposed the Using, Discriminating, Generalizing and Synthesizing (U.D.G.S.) model to describe the conceptualization process of students interacting with technology (Hoyles & Noss, 1987). Students start by using the technology and progressively discriminate the mathematical relations and concepts underpinning the behaviour of the tools. This is followed by generalizations, which are local to the situations from which they emerged. Finally they move on to synthesizing their generalizations with different contexts and representational registers outside the specific technology used. Noss and Hoyles introduced the concept of "situated abstraction" to account for the constructions of the learner. Situated abstractions are invariants that are shaped by the specific situation in which the learner forges them. Although these invariants are situated, they simultaneously contain the seed of the general that could be valid in other contexts.

The instrumental perspective, developed independently by psychologists in the mid-nineties (Vérillon & Rabardel, 1995) shares the same idea of the role of the tool on the constructs of the user. It was also recently adopted by researchers in mathematics education to understand the strategies used by students when beginning to use software programs for solving mathematical tasks. A tool is not transparent. It affects the way the user solves the tasks and thinks. The instrument, according to the terms of Vérillon and Rabardel, denotes this psychological construct of the user:

> The instrument does not exist in itself, it becomes an instrument when the subject has been able to appropriate it for himself and has integrated it with his activity.

The subject develops procedures and rules of actions when using the artefact and so constructs instrumentation schemes and simultaneously a representation of the properties of the tool (according to what Vérillon and Rabardel call instrumentalisation schemes). The first studies about instrumentation processes addressed the use of the CAS by students (Guin & Trouche, 1999). They were mainly focusing on the difficulties of students using technology and on the detours they sometimes follow in order to perform an activity with technology (Artigue, 2002). Today, research pays more attention to the mathematical knowledge involved in instrumental knowledge. Because technology used in mathematics embarks mathematics, mathematical knowledge is intrinsically linked to the knowledge about how to use the tool. Developing instrumental knowledge may also involve developing mathematical knowledge (Artigue, 2002; Lagrange, 1999; Laborde, 2003).

Two theoretical approaches were developed according to which learning with the use of technology develops. In the first one, tools, and in particular technologies, offer opportunities for learning. The subject is faced with constraints imposed by the artefact and new possibilities of actions, to identify, to understand and with which to cope. In terms of the theory of didactic situations (Brousseau, 1997), the tool is part of the "milieu". In the second approach, following a Vygotskian perspective, operations carried out with technology may be subject to an internalization process with the guidance of the teacher and interpersonal exchanges within the class in the form of collective discussions (Bartolini Bussi, 1998; Mariotti & Bartolini Bussi, 1998). The interventions of the teacher are essential for making possible the construction of a correspondence between mathematical knowledge and knowledge constructed from the interactions with the computer environment. According to the instrumentation theory, the meaning constructed by the student when using the artifact may differ from what is intended by the teacher. Consequently, the interventions of the teacher are critical to let the meanings evolve towards culturally shared meanings of mathematical knowledge.

The page limitation of a chapter does not offer the opportunity of doing justice to all theoretical approaches underpinning research studies. In particular, the Van Hiele theory dedicated to geometry learning was not mentioned although it has been used in a small number of studies, essentially as a tool for assessing the impact of technology on the possible progress in the hierarchy of levels according to which students conceptualize geometrical figures.

RESEARCH ON SPECIFIC TECHNOLOGIES

This section emphasizes aspects of research related to specific features of various technologies. Two main kinds of technology are distinguished: The Logo-driven Turtle Geometry technology and related microworlds and the Dynamic Geometry environments. Students' learning of particular geometry topics, use of diagrams in problem solving, proving, and justifying were investigated by taking into account the role of technology in those processes.

Research on logo-driven turtle geometry

Logo is a programming language intended to bring to the field of mathematics education the philosophy of programming to express meaning and to tinker with difficult problems which characterized its older sister, the LISP AI language (Sinclair & Moon, 1991). This intention was part of a broader, powerful and forerunning idea at the time, to make this kind of activity with technology accessible to young children. It originated from Papert in the late 1960s and became well known in the mathematics education community as a result of his

'Mindstorms' book (Papert, 1980). From a mathematical learning theory point of view, Papert's main intention was to move beyond Piaget's paradigm, which focused on the shortcomings of children's thinking in relation to adult formal thinking, by asking the question of what mathematical thinking children can do in situations where they can explore with mathematically rich computational tools such as Logo.

The connection between Logo and Geometry is through a specific subset of the former, which was termed "Turtle Geometry" (TG). TG is a computational environment where the user gives commands to a computational entity called 'the turtle' which has a position and a heading. Position changes create a linear graphical output on the screen and the turtle icon changes its position and heading as an immediate result of such commands. Turtle commands are Logo primitives and consequently, Logo programs can be written which drive the turtle to construct geometrical figures. Abelson and diSessa (1981) gave the mathematical foundations of Turtle Geometry and agreed with Papert that its geometrical nature was based on a different geometrical system to those usually associated with the learning of geometry in school curricula, i.e. the Euclidean or analytic (e.g. Cartesian): TG is based on differential (intrinsic) Geometry. Most TG related research, however, is based on the figural products created by the turtle, on the connections students make between the formal programming/mathematical code and the graphical output and on how children link experiences of their body movements to the behaviour of the turtle, termed 'body-syntonicity' by Papert in 1980.

Various Logo TG have been developed across the world and one can say that there are presently more than 100 such digital environments. The ones which gave rise to investigations in mathematics education including those in the PME group, listed alphabetically, include: Boxer (a programmable computational medium with the Logo-like language 'Boxer' including TG, diSessa & Lay, 1986), Elica Logo (including 3d TG, Boychev, 1999), Imagine Logo (Kalas, 2001), Microworlds Pro (Silverman, 1999), NetLogo (a parallel Logo programming language with a very large number of turtles, Wilensky, 1999), E-slate-based Turtleworlds (based on USB Logo but including dynamic variation tools offering dynamic manipulation of procedure variable values, Kynigos, 2001) and USB Berkeley Logo (Harvey, 2005).

Logo based microworlds. A central aspect of learning with Logo is the activity of mathematical exploration with microworlds. The term was originally borrowed from artificial intelligence (A.I.). Its meaning evolved within the mathematics education community and was shaped by Papert. He described it as a self-contained world where students can "learn to transfer habits of exploration from their personal lives to the formal domain of scientific construction" (Papert, 1980, p. 177).

Microworlds are computational environments embedding a coherent set of mathematical concepts and relations designed so that with an appropriate set of tasks and pedagogy, students can engage in exploration and construction activity rich in the generation of mathematical meaning. TG itself has been considered as a microworld within Logo but later research involved learning with the use of microworlds embedding a much narrower set of mathematical concepts, escorted by more focused theories on learning and pedagogy (Noss & Hoyles, 1996; Edwards, 1988; Clements & Sarama, 1997; Sarama & Clements, 2002).

In PME research, a number of studies involved the design and use of geometrical microworlds. Hoyles and Noss (1987) used a parallelogram microworld in developing their U.D.G.S. theory. This consisted of permutations of specially designed Logo procedures with independent variable values for turns and position changes, so that students would investigate relations between angular and linear features so that the procedure would construct a parallelogram. Their focus was on the process of students' formalization of intuitive descriptions (Hoyles & Noss, 1988). Edwards built a transformation geometry microworld addressing the issue of the representational aspect of microworlds (Edwards, 1988, 1990) and then later used a microworld generating star figures to study the process by which the students discriminated the underlying mathematical properties (Edwards, 1994). Kynigos took a more transversal approach by building a series of microworlds to study how students make links between Differential (intrinsic), Euclidean and Cartesian systems (Kynigos, 1988, 1989, 1991). Hoyles, Noss and Sutherland (1989) studied how students come up against pre-conceptions of additive or doubling strategies when working with a ratio and proportion microworld and were then joined by Sutherland in evaluating what students gained with respect to the strategies they applied in their investigations (Hoyles, Noss & Sutherland, 1991).

Learning processes at the core of research. TG appeared at a time when the 'problem solving' movement was thriving, at least in the U.S., and its exploratory nature along with the somewhat obscure connection with school curricula facilitated the views that TG was a tool for building learning strategies. In particular, learning how to learn. The geometrical concepts were there, but in the background of many researchers' attention.

In PME research, there was thus an emphasis on generative, focused theory-building methodologies. Many researchers perceived learning with Logo as a new kind of learning process, with the consequence that the paradigm of qualitative, illuminative research methods (i.e. adopting the role of 'naïve observer' for the researcher) seemed appropriate (Hoyles & Noss, 1987). The main research emphasis seemed to be 'what kind of learning goes on' rather than 'what kind of geometrical learning'. The focus was on student learning processes and some aspects of this process emerging from Logo geometry environments were recorded. Such aspects included:

- 12 year old students' use of a drawing cognitive scheme and their resistance to dissociate from the procedural visible aspects of their Logo work (Hillel, Kieran & Gurtner, 1989);
- 12 year old students' initial use of an intrinsic schema and their progressive dissociation to a composite schema including the use of absolute positioning on the plane (Kynigos, 1989);

- Students' process of using geometrical ideas, then discriminating the ones that matter for the task at hand, followed by generalization and then synthesis with other contexts (U.D.G.S., Hoyles & Noss, 1987);
- Students' situated abstractions, i.e. abstractions derived directly from the specific context of defining and changing geometrical figures and objects (Hoyles & Noss, 1988 –the construct was rigorously elaborated later in Noss & Hoyles, 1996).

In other studies, the focus was on the nature of interactions between students and the computer that included the use of: Multiple representations, feedback, and editing and constructing (Hoyles et al., 1991; Edwards, 1990; Kynigos & Psycharis, 2003). Also, in a number of studies the focus was on the issues related to the design of mathematically focused computational environments (microworlds) and discussion on their affordances (Hoyles et al., 1989; Edwards, 1988; Kynigos & Psycharis, 2003; Sacristán, 2001). Finally, there were some studies adopting a different strand which at the time was considered as a more mainstream approach to research, using standardized tests or experimental methods. In two cases for example, the focus was on using the Van Hiele levels to test students' abilities to identify geometrical figures (Olive & Lankenau, 1987; Scally, 1987). For a much larger study in this framework, see also Clements & Battista (1992).

Research on geometrical thinking with TG was highly influenced by two phenomena which were related to the time in which the technology appeared. One was the power of the newly-born idea of deep structural access of ordinary people (even children) to a technology which was up to that point only used by computer scientists (see diSessa, 2000; Eisenberg, 1995 for an elaboration of the idea in later times, and Kynigos, 2004; diSessa, 1997 for this idea applied to teachers). This led to an emphasis on the learning process which was perceived as new in nature and was enhanced by the problem solving movement which focused on learning strategies rather than mathematical content at hand. It also led to a connection between research on geometrical learning with technology and the itinerary of Logo related learning research in general which in itself has been subject to big changes in different parts of the world (Kynigos, 2002; Papert, 2002). The second influence came from the constructivist learning movement, which in the mathematics education community appeared in the early eighties and initially adopted a rather individualist perspective on learning. Research on geometrical learning with TG did address geometrical concepts, communication between students, the design of tasks and the influence of the teacher. However, although these aspects were part of several research studies including PME research, they were not in focus, nor were they part of a more general research attention to these issues which came later along with the advent of DGE. technology.

Moreover, TG research focused on the idea of meaningful formalism (diSessa, 2000; Kynigos & Psycharis, 2003; Hoyles & Noss, 1988). With respect to mathematical formalism there is a strong view that, although it may be a powerful representational register for mathematicians, it can be rather meaningless for students (Dubinsky, 2000), i.e. an imposed code to tackle meaningless routines.

Furthermore, the advent of DGE has provided access to mathematical ideas by allowing the bypassing of formal representation and access to dynamic graphing which is particularly important for the learning of geometry. This does not however necessarily mean that formalism can only be useful to established mathematicians who can convey abstract mathematical meaning through its use. Just as digital technology provides means to by-pass formalism, it may also provide the means to transform the way formalism is put to use by students. Technologies affording programmability and symbolic expression in conjunction with the representational repertoires of DGE could thus be considered in geometrical learning research set within developing theoretical frameworks (Clements & Sarama, 1995; Clements & Battista 1994; Sherin, 2002; Kynigos & Psycharis, 2003; Kynigos & Argyris, 2004).

Research on Dynamic Geometry Environments (DGE)

In DGE, diagrams result from sequences of primitives expressed in geometrical terms chosen by the user. When an element of such a diagram is dragged with the mouse, the diagram is modified while all the geometric relations used in its construction are preserved. These artificial realities can be compared to entities of the real world. It is as if diagrams react to the manipulations of the user by following the laws of geometry, just like material objects react by following the laws of physics. A crucial feature of these realities is their quasi-independence from the user once they have been created. When the user drags one element of the diagram, it is modified according to the geometry of its constructions rather than according to the wishes of the user. This is not the case in paper-and-pencil diagrams that can be slightly distorted by students in order to meet their expectations. In addition to the drag mode, dynamic geometry environments offer specific features such as macro-constructions, trace, and locus, which differ from paper and pencil tools (Strässer, 2002).

Computer diagrams are also external objects whose behaviour and feedback require interpretation by the students. Geometry is one means, among others, of interpreting this behaviour. In the design of DGE, spatial invariants in the moving diagrams represent geometrical invariants and these geometry microworlds may offer a strong link between spatial graphical and geometrical aspects. Inspired by the theory of variation in the tradition of phenomenographic research approach, Leung (2003) suggests the idea of simultaneity is a promising agent to help bridge the gap between experimental and theoretical Mathematics, or the transition between the processes of conjecturing and formalizing. Simultaneity is intrinsically related to discernment in the theory of variation:

> In DGE, it is possible to define a way of seeing (discernment) in terms of actually seeing invariant critical features (a visual demarcation or focusing) under a continuous variation of certain components of a configuration.

Various DGEs have been developed across the world and one can say that there are presently around 70 such environments. However most of them are clones of original DGEs, which are no more than ten. The DGEs which gave rise to investigations in mathematics education and especially in the PME group, listed alphabetically, include: Cabri-Géomètre (Laborde, Baulac & Bellemain, 1988; Laborde & Bellemain, 1995; Laborde, 1999), GEOLOG (Holland, 2002), Geometer's Sketchpad (Jackiw, 1991), Geometry Inventor (Brock, Cappo, Carmon, Erdös, Kamay, Kaplan & Rosi, 2003), Geometric Supposer (Schwartz, Yerushalmy & Shternberg, 1985, 2000), and Thales (Kadunz & Kautschitsch, 1993).

Dynamic Geometry Environments and the move from the spatial to the theoretical.

Construction tasks. Several researchers investigated how students solve construction tasks in DGEs. Since the construction must be preserved by the drag mode, a construction by eye or by manual adjustment fails. Students must do the construction by using geometrical objects and relations offered by the environment (perpendicular, parallel, circle, ...). It has often been reported that beginners have difficulty in constructing diagrams in a DGE that is resistant to the drag mode (i.e. preserves relationships upon dragging) and resort to construction strategies by eye (e.g., Noss, Hoyles, Healy & Hoelzl, 1994). An indicator of the difficulty students experience in relating the spatial to the theoretical is also given by their difficulties in interpreting the behaviours of a diagram or of elements of a diagram under the drag mode. Soury-Lavergne (1998) shows how the immobility of a point in Cabri was not related to its geometrical independence from the dragged points. For the student there were two separate worlds, the mechanical world of the computer diagram (in our terms, the spatial) and the theoretical (or geometrical).

The distinction that we made between spatial-graphical and geometrical is expressed in various terms in several papers: For example, in Noss et al. (1994) this distinction is called empirical/theoretical.

The notion of dependency and functional relationship. Geometrical objects, which are linked by geometrical relationships, can be viewed as dependent. The drag mode can be used to externalize this theoretical dependency in the diagram. If students have not constructed a relation between the spatial-graphical level and the theoretical level, they may not recognize or understand the dependency relationship in a DGE. As a consequence, it is not surprising that several papers (mainly from the United Kingdom) focus on the construction of this notion of dependency by students interacting with a DGE (Hoyles, 1998; Jones, 1996; Pratt & Ainley, 1996). Several functionalities in a DGE (Jones, 1996) can serve as tools for externalizing the notion of dependency. Among these functionalities are the following: The drag mode, in which a dependent point cannot be dragged directly; the delete function (when an object is deleted all dependent objects are also deleted and a warning message is displayed), and the redefinition of an object (redefining an object in Cabri is changing its dependency relations with other objects).

All papers mention that the notion of dependency is difficult for students and not understood initially. By interacting with a DGE and a teacher students may construct this notion of dependency, as expressed by two pairs of pupils in Pratt and Ainley (1996): "They are all real shapes because you can move them without deforming the shape", and "The initial objects are the ones on which everything else depends". It is also clear from these papers that such a constructed notion of dependency is situated in the context of the DGE. It contains some generality but in terms of the context or of the tool (an example of what Hoyles and Noss call "situated abstraction"). "So because it depends on it, it moves" (a student in Jones, 1996). However simply considering that two objects are dependent because one moves when the other one moves does not mean that students are able to analyze the dependency existing among objects.

The use of drag mode. Certainly, the drag mode is a key element of DGEs. The mathematical counterpart of the drag mode is variation. Experts can immediately recognize variation in the dragging of elements of a diagram. But the learners being more at a spatial graphical level may just view the drag mode as a mode moving and changing the shape of a diagram, or as a mechanical motion of solid objects.

From the beginning of the use of Dynamic Geometry Environments, it has been observed that the students did not spontaneously use the drag mode. Bellemain and Capponi (1992) claim that a new contract must be negotiated in the classroom and that it takes time for students to enter this contract. They mention that all but one pair of students called the teacher to check that their diagram was correct. It has also been observed that when students use the drag mode, they do not use it on a wide zone but on a small surface as if they were afraid to destroy their construction (Rolet, 1996). Sinclair (2003) observed that 12th graders, although initially intrigued by the ability to drag points, usually stopped dragging after a short time and concentrated on interpreting a static figure. Some of them inadvertently created a special case by dragging, then generalized from this static but unsuitable figure. Talmon and Yerushalmy (2004) asked ninth grade students and mathematics education graduate students to predict the dynamic behaviour of points that were part of a geometric construction they had executed using a DGE (The Geometer's Sketchpad 3 and The Geometric Supposer for Windows) according to a given procedure, and to explain their predictions. The study reveals that users often grasp a reverse hierarchy in which dragging an object affects its parent. The authors suggest that this reversed hierarchy may be caused by terms and knowledge built into paper-and-pencil geometry. All these observations can be interpreted in terms of instrumentation theory: The instrumental genesis of the drag mode is a long process, and students construct several schemes of utilization that are influenced by former tools and may differ from the expected use by the designers of the environments. As already claimed by Strässer (1992), dragging offers a mediation between drawing and figure and can only be used as such at the cost of an explicit introduction and analysis organized by the teacher.

Dragging for conjecturing in an exploratory approach. Investigations about the way dragging is used by students in solving problems was carried out by Italian researchers (Arzarello, Micheletti, Olivero & Robutti, 1998; Arzarello, 2000; Olivero, 2002). By means of a very fine analysis of the use of dragging, these researchers established a categorization of different kinds of dragging, in particular (Olivero, 2002, p.98):

- *Wandering dragging* is moving the points on the screen randomly in order to discover configurations,
- *Guided dragging* is done with the intention to obtain a particular shape,
- *Lieu muet dragging* is moving a point with the constraint of keeping a particular property satisfied at the initial state, the variable point follows a hidden path even without being aware of this.

Olivero observed that "wandering dragging" and especially "guided dragging" were mainly used by students whereas "lieu muet dragging" was only sometimes used and not by all students. An example of "lieu muet dragging" is provided by a girl, Tiziana, investigating at what conditions the quadrilateral HKLM built by the perpendicular bisectors of the sides of a quadrilateral ABCD is a point (Figure 1).

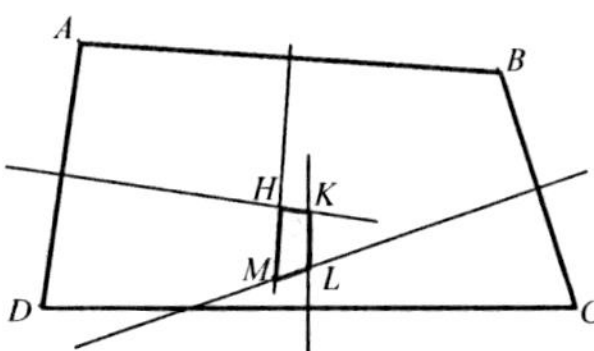

Figure 1. Quadrilateral HKML.

Working together, Tiziana and Bartolomeo used wandering dragging to discover that HKLM is a point when ABCD is a rectangle (Figure 2). Bartolomeo wanted to drag the vertices of ABCD in order to obtain a specific quadrilateral HKLM, a parallelogram, a rhombus, a trapezium (guided dragging). Tiziana did not share this approach and tried to drag point B of the rectangle in order to keep HKLM as a point (an example of lieu muet dragging).

Other researchers stressed the key role of dragging in forming a mathematical conjecture (Healy, 2000; Hölzl, 2001; Hollebrands, 2002; Leung & Lopez-Real, 2000) and even proving by contradiction (Leung & Lopez-Real, 2002). Hölzl (2001) distinguished two ways of using the mediating functions of the drag mode, a test mode on the one hand, and a search mode on the other. All his observations led him to conclude that the second use of the drag mode is not a short term affair but results from a "learning process that is characterized by different layers of conceptions".

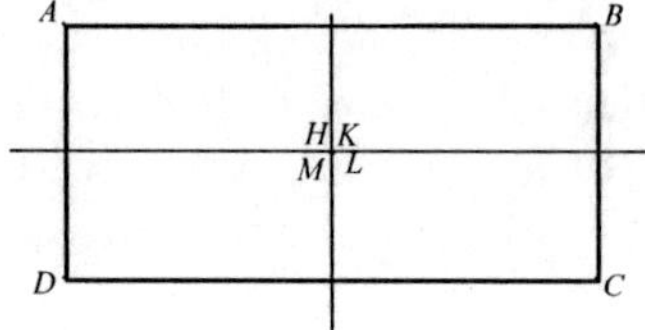

Figure 2. HKML reduced to a point.

Dragging for adjusting in construction tasks. As mentioned above, students encounter difficulties in using DGE to construct "robust" diagrams, which keep their properties in the drag mode. However it was observed that students refined their successive constructions partly made by adjusting (see for instance Jones, 1998, pp. 79-82). Students elaborate a sequence of successive constructions involving more and more geometrical properties. A construction obtained by adjustment enables the students to recognize properties and to mobilize them in a further construction giving less room to visual adjusting. Constructions done by adjusting are not only part of the solving process but they scaffold the path to a definite robust construction. They play an important role in moving from a purely visual solution using adjustments to a solution entirely based on theoretical solutions but achieved by dragging. These constructions are culturally not accepted. Since the time of the Greeks, geometry rejected constructions based on motion and restricted the allowed constructions to those created with straight edge and compass. Hölzl (1996) also observed what he called a "drag and link approach" in students' strategies for solving construction tasks in Cabri. Students relax one condition to do the construction and then drag to satisfy the last condition. They obtain a diagram visually correct and want to secure it by using the redefinition facility of Cabri. However most of the time it does not work because of hidden dependencies.

Robust versus soft constructions. Later Healy (2000) introduced the distinction 'soft versus robust constructions' to give account of constructions that students could change by dragging in order to satisfy a condition. She discovered through observation that, rather than constructions preserved under dragging, students preferred to investigate constructions, "in which one of the chosen properties is purposely constructed by eye, allowing the locus of permissible figures to be built up in an empirical manner under the control of the student". Healy introduced in that paper the distinction "soft/robust" and decided to call the latter constructions soft constructions and the former ones robust constructions. She illustrated the distinction between robust and soft approaches by means of the example of two pairs of students investigating whether the conditions, two congruent sides and a congruent angle, determined one triangle or not. Students using a soft construction immediately found a point for which the third side was not congruent and rejected the condition Side-Side-Angle. Healy (2000) comments how the two kinds of construction are complementary: The general emerges in the exploration of soft constructions and can be checked by using robust constructions as in the case of Tiziana reported above. The cycle 'soft then robust' seems to be a driving force behind students' generalization processes.

Proving and justifying processes. There is a continuing discussion about the question whether the "authority" of the computer leads to a greater resistance to proving on the part of the learner or if adequately chosen and presented proof problems within a computer "milieu" further the need for proofs by the learner (not only) of geometry. Among arguments in favour of the use of DGE, the need in DGE to carry out explicit construction methods based on theoretical properties could lead to consider them as good environments for introducing formal proof. Among arguments given about students' not seeing the need to construct proofs due to the authority of the computer, the facility of computer programs to provide measurements is often mentioned. The role of measurement in DGE was investigated in proving activities (Kakihana, Shimizu & Nohda, 1996; Vadcard, 1999; Flanagan, 2001; Hollebrands, 2002). Studies generally conclude that measurement is not restricted to empirical arguments but is also used in deductive arguments. The study of proving processes carried out in DGE shed light on the explanatory power of proof. Whereas proof is often considered as a means of deciding about the truth of statements, it becomes a means of explanation of phenomena observed on the computer screen that are striking or surprising (De Villiers, 1991; Chazan, 1993; Hanna, 1998). The greater integration of DGE into teaching allows for opportunities to design instructional activities, even sometimes over a long-term period aimed at introducing or fostering deductive reasoning and proof (Sánchez & Sacristán, 2003). Four papers show the diversity and novelty of ways offered by DGE to promote understanding of the need for and the roles of proof:

- Students must give explanations for the fact that a drawing remains a specified quadrilateral in the drag mode (Jones, 2000),
- A teaching experiment is designed to enable students to produce deductive justifications of the correctness of their constructions. In a fine analysis the growing of the quality of the justifications is documented. The teacher plays a critical role in guiding the discussion and ensuring that the justification rules are correct (Marrades & Gutiérrez, 2000),
- By means of an adequate sequence of tasks in a DGE, the need for proof is created through a cognitive conflict that generates in students an intellectual curiosity about why an unexpected property is true (Hadas, Hershkowitz & Schwarz, 2000)
- A system of axioms and theorems is constructed by students themselves as a system of commands introduced in the software, which has no geometric

relations implemented at the beginning of the teaching sequence. Proof is the means for justifying that the new command will provide the expected outcome (Mariotti, 2000).

In two papers (Marrades & Gutiérrez, and Mariotti) proof fulfils a twofold role: Establishing the validity of a construction for each individual and convincing the other students to accept the construction process.

GENERAL TRENDS OF RESEARCH ON THE USE OF TECHNOLOGY FOR TEACHING AND LEARNING GEOMETRY

Research on the use of technology in geometry learning and teaching is multifaceted and based on several theoretical frameworks presented earlier in this chapter. The geometrical topics studied by researchers are very heterogeneous. Topics include basic traditional Euclidean concepts such as triangles, quadrilaterals (in particular parallelograms Hoyles and Noss, 1987, 1988), geometric transformations (Edwards, 1988, 1990; Gallou-Dumiel, 1989; Jahn, 2000; Bellemain & Capponi, 1992; Hollebrands, 2003), polyhedra (Pallascio, 1987), angles (Zack, 1988; Parmentier, 1989; Magina & Hoyles, 1991; Kieran, 1986) measurements of areas, and ratio and proportion (Hoyles et al., 1989; Hoyles et al., 1991). Other topics are less typical like fractals as chaos-game investigation (Sereno, 1994), as a context to study infinity (Sacristán, 2001), curvature (Kynigos & Psycharis, 2003), inscribed star figures (Edwards, 1994), or in precalculus the variations of functions (Arcavi & Hadas, 2000; Falcade, Laborde & Mariotti, 2004; Furinghetti, Morselli & Paola, 2005). Some transversal topics were also addressed like construction activity and of course proof that is a recurring theme in research. Traditional Euclidean concepts have received more attention by researchers than other concepts such as geometric transformations. There is a scarcity of research on using technology in the teaching and learning of loci (Jahn, 2002) and little on students' use of the macro facility available with many DGE (Jones, 2002; Kadunz, 2002). Research on multiple linked representations often mentioned in algebra or calculus have appeared only recently, even though several DGE offer the possibility of constructing graphical representations dynamically linked with geometric diagrams.

In most countries technology is not yet fully adopted by teachers. As a consequence there is very little research that has been done on geometry curricula that start from scratch with technology. Pratt and Ainley (1996) investigated how primary school children in England without explicit geometric teaching create their own geometric constructions with Logo and Cabri. Most research investigated the impact of technology on geometry learning for students already introduced to geometrical concepts. An example of introducing a formal approach by means of a DGE is given in Mariotti (2001) who reports on a long term teaching which taking advantage of the flexibility of Cabri started the teaching with an empty menu and introduced a command only after it was discussed, according to specific statements selected as axioms. Then, in the sequence of the activities, the other elements of the microworld were added, according to new constructions and in parallel with corresponding theorems.

Inspired by the multidimensional analysis of Lagrange, Artigue, Laborde and Trouche (2003), the research trends are presented below according to the following four dimensions: (1) Epistemological and semiotic dimension: The nature of geometry mediated by technology, (2) Cognitive dimension: Technology supporting learning, (3) Situational dimension: The role of the design of the tasks on learning, and (4) Teacher dimension: The role of the teacher.

Nature of geometry mediated by technology

The objects offered by technology on the computer or calculator screen are representations of theoretical objects, which behave by following a computerized (hopefully mathematical) model underlying the software program. The representation process may introduce some differences between the theoretical behaviour and the actual behaviour on the computer screen. Based on the analogy with the process of didactical transposition, this transformation of knowledge due to its technological mediation is called "computational transposition" (Balacheff, 1993, in French: "transposition informatique"). For example, drawing a "circle" in Logo involves a differential (intrinsic) perception of curve, i.e. the construction of a polygon with a large number of sides (more than 30) and a small (e.g. 1 degree) constant turtle turn from side to side. Goldenberg and Cuoco (1998) have pointed to some differences between Euclidean Geometry and DGE Geometry. For example, the behaviour of a point on a segment is a direct result of a design decision and is taken as a postulate upon which other DGE theorems are based. Such a postulate does not exist in Euclidean Geometry. Do students make distinctions between behaviour that results as a consequence of the tool design and behaviour that is a direct result of mathematics? Scher (2001) found that students in fact did not make those types of distinctions and rather they considered the behaviours of each type to be of equal importance. Ways to address this dilemma include the careful design of tasks and the milieu that is not restricted to technology and a focus on the critical role of the teacher (§3.4).

Technology and the learning of geometry

Software environments like Logo TG or DGE are considered as favouring learning as they require actions from the students to achieve a goal and in the process, students "learn by coordinating and reflecting upon the form of their interactions" (Hoyles, 1995, p. 202). Hoyles and Noss developed the concept of "situated abstraction" to account for the development of the conceptual framework developed by students in such interactions with a computer environment: Situated abstractions are both general and situated in the environment in which they develop. The development of situated abstractions in the eyes of Noss and Hoyles is certainly related to the exploratory nature of the environments. Logo TG or DGE allow students to explore screen constructions and offer a way of accessing the mathematical characteristics of the underlying geometry. In such processes, software tools become extensions of the own thinking of the students (Mason, 1992). The 'computational scaffolding' (i.e. the support system available in the setting (Hoyles *ibid.*)) contributes to the process of constructing situated abstractions.

> The software tools exploited by the students provide them with the hooks they need on which to hang their developing ideas.

The examples given above on the use of the drag mode and on soft constructions illustrate very well the idea of 'computational scaffolding' (see §2.2.2). The concept of situated abstraction nevertheless also points to the importance of the necessity of a transfer from the computer environment to the world outside the computer (Olive & Lankenau, 1987; Zack, 1988; Parmentier, 1989; Scally, 1987).

The exploratory nature of these environments amplifies the search processes of students solving a task and brings under a spotlight their understandings. Hoyles contends that the software constrains students' actions in novel ways and forces the researcher or the teacher to notice a student's point of view, which could have not been noticed in a paper and pencil environment. It offers a "window" on the students' conceptions and learning (Noss & Hoyles, 1996). The constraints and new possibilities with regard to paper and pencil technology are often considered as shaping the students' strategies and thus their ways of thinking. They can encourage new ways of conceptualizing mathematical ideas. By means of several examples, Resnick (1995) shows how Star Logo used with 5000 turtles leads to solving classical geometric problems with a statistical approach, giving a new meaning to geometrical configurations.

The design of tasks

Some researchers also stress that the choice of the tasks in relation to the affordances of the technological geometry environment may be critical for the development of the students' understandings. A relevant combination of tools made available to students and of problem situations is generally considered as a good "milieu" (in the sense of the theory of didactic situations) for the emergence of new knowledge (see for example Kordaki & Potari, 2002 about the use of a microworld for area measurement offering several tools and feedback).

Arzarello, Olivero, Paola and Robutti (2002) argue that task design and teacher moderation play very important parts in encouraging students to press on beyond perceptual impression and empirical verification in DGE. Pratt and Davison (2003) conclude from an investigation on the use of the Interactive White Board (IWB) with a dynamic geometry software that the visual and kinaesthetic affordances of the IWB are insufficient to encourage the fusion of conceptual and visual aspects of children's figural concepts when these affordances are embodied in tasks that simply focus on the visual transformation of geometric figures. They claim that the kinaesthetic affordances of the IWB need to be embodied in tasks based on the utilities of contrasting definitions that draw attention to the conceptual aspect.

Sinclair (2003) draws the same type of conclusion about the use of pre-constructed dynamic diagrams: The design of the accompanying material has the potential to support or impede the development of exploration strategies and geometric thinking skills.

The role of technology in students' solving processes is multiple: The tools offered by the environment allow students' strategies that are not possible in paper and pencil environment, the meaning of the task is provided by the environment, the environment offers feedback to the students' actions.

Laborde (2001) distinguishes four kinds of tasks used by teachers with DGE:

- Tasks in which the environment facilitates the material actions but does not change the task for the students, for example, producing figures and measuring their elements.
- Tasks in which the environment facilitates students' exploration and analysis, for example, identifying relations within a figure through dragging
- Tasks that have a paper and pencil counterpart but can be solved differently in the environment, for example a construction task may be solved in DGE by using a geometric transformation or the sum of vectors.
- Tasks that cannot be posed without the mediation of the environment, for example, reconstructing a dynamic diagram through experimenting with it to identify its properties.

In the first two types, tasks are facilitated, rather than changed, by the mediation of DGE. In the last two types, tasks are changed in some way by the mediation of DGE, either because the solving strategies differ from what they usually were, or because they simply are not possible outside DGE. In the example of the last type, the meaning of the task comes from the possibility of dragging.

The second type of task may be used as a research tool for investigating students' ideas. It acts as a window on students' conceptions and understandings, as visible in Arzarello et al.'s (2002) research reported above. The last two types may be used in teaching as a tool for fostering learning. For example, DGE may foster the use of geometric transformations as construction tools for providing geometric relationships between objects (third type of tasks). The last type may also be the source of a different perspective on mathematics. The task of identifying properties in a dynamic diagram requires a back-and-forth process made of guesses based on visualization and checks on the diagram possibly involving deductions drawn from what has been observed. The nature of mathematical activity is changed and becomes a modelling activity –what may deeply differ from the kind of mathematics the teacher wants to develop.

The role of feedback

Technology offers feedback to the actions of the user. The role of feedback was stressed by research on microworlds. It was also stressed by research on DGE, when students check their constructions through the drag mode or check their conjectures using various tools (e.g., measuring and constructing). Such feedback can be used to create the need for searching for another solution in case provided feedback gives evidence of the incorrectness or inadequacy of the solution. In the sequence of tasks (mentioned above; designed by Hadas et al., 2000), a cognitive conflict was created because students developed expectations, which turned out to be wrong when they checked them in the dynamic geometry environment. This interplay of conjectures and checks, of certainty and uncertainty was made possible by the explorative power and checking facilities offered by the DG environment.

Feedback can be the source of refinements in students' answers. Leron and Hazzan (1998) describe a strategy by successive refinements provoked by feedback generated by the software. Hillel, Kieran and Gurtner (1989) reported similar results with middle-school students working in a Logo computer environment. Within a Logo programming environment, students enter commands and then they can visually observe and interpret the results of the code and make modifications to their commands. Edwards (1992) found students working with a computer microworld for geometric transformations, who refined their understanding of transformations based on the visual feedback they received from the computer as they engaged in a matching game. The software incorporating knowledge and reacting in a way consistent with theory impacts on the student's learning trajectory in the solving process. Here, one can recognize the philosophy underpinning the notion of microworld discussed in §2.1.1.

The use of geometry technology by teachers

Since the very beginning, research carried out on the use of technology focused on the students and their solving processes in technology based tasks. Some researchers pointed out, that interactions with technology, even in carefully designed tasks, could not lead to learning by themselves and stressed the need for teacher interventions (about the notion of angle in Hoyles & Sutherland, 1990, about the notion of reflection in Gallou-Dumiel, 1989). In the mid-nineties, the way teachers integrated technology into their teaching practice started to become an object of investigation. Noss and Hoyles (1996, ch. 8) related the teacher practice to their attitude with regard to technology and learning in a case study of some teachers following a university case about the use of microworlds in mathematics.

After several years, it appeared that an analysis of the use of technology in classrooms cannot be carried out without taking into account the complexity of teaching and learning situations and the multiplicity of factors related to the use of technology in the classrooms. Teachers are key elements in this complexity. What changed in recent years is the focus on the teacher practice in ordinary classrooms using technology.

Ruthven, Hennessy and Deaney (2005) report on a multiple-case study of "archetypical current practice" in using DGE in secondary mathematics education in England. The authors (p. 155) found that

> the prime purpose of DGE use by teachers was evidencing geometric properties through dragging figures. Most commonly, this involved dragging to examine multiple examples or special cases.

But teachers very seldom used dragging to analyze dynamic variation. The authors also found most striking, "the common emphasis on mediating geometrical properties through numerical measures, with little direct geometrical analysis of situations in order to explain numerical patterns and theorize geometrical properties". This probably results from (a long before DGE prevailing) didactical norm anchored in the teacher practice in the UK. The teachers adapt the available tools to this norm. The authors also report how teachers may reduce the exploratory dimension of DGE in order to control students' exploration and to avoid students meeting situations that could obscure the underlying rule or could require explanations going beyond the narrow scope of the lesson, like for example explanations about rounding measurements in a lesson about inscribed angle in a circle.

The study of teacher practice when using technology revealed that teachers must cope with all the complexity of the management of a classroom: Instead of following textbooks the teacher must design worksheets (Monaghan, 2004), they must adapt the management of several kinds of time in their classroom and the relationship between, on the one hand old and new knowledge, and on the other hand paper and pencil techniques and Cabri techniques (Assude, 2005). Monaghan (*ibid.*) also showed how technology could affect the emergent goals of the teacher during the lesson.

According to a Vygotskian approach, some researchers investigated semiotic mediation processes organized by teachers making use of technology for mediating mathematical knowledge through the use of DGE. External operations are carried out by students faced with tasks completed in the environment and the teacher contributes to an internalization process by organizing social interactions and collective discussions in the classroom in which s/he intervenes in order to transform the meaning of what has been done on the computer into a meaning that could be related to the "official" mathematical meaning (see Mariotti, 2000, about the notion of geometric construction, and Mariotti, Laborde & Falcade, 2003, about the notion of graph of function with a DGE).

FROM THE PAST TOWARDS THE FUTURE

Geometry is often characterized by its recourse to diagrams and its special relationship with reasoning and proof, a specificity that we interpreted at the beginning of this chapter as due to the two-folded nature of geometry: Geometry resorts both to visualization and theory. The introduction of technology for the teaching and learning of geometry influenced both aspects of geometry in different ways, somehow complementing each other. According to the classification proposed by Hoyles and Noss (2003), Logo and microworlds belong to the "programming and microworlds" category whereas DGE belong to the "expressive tools" category. Logo somehow introduced the idea of microworld and exploratory environment that goes beyond only geometry. Several researchers also consider Logo as a tool to forge links between students' actions and the corresponding symbolic representations they develop. Students must express actions in a symbolic language to produce diagrams on the computer screen. In dynamic geometry, students' actions deal directly with tools producing geometric objects and relations or consist in manipulating dynamic diagrams: Students move from action and visualization to a theoretical analysis of diagrams and possibly to the expression of conjectures and reasoning. It must be mentioned that some dynamic geometry environments may also be considered as microworlds. Conversely, TG microworlds can be used as expressive tools.

Research on the use of technology in geometry not only offered a window on students' mathematical conceptions of notions such as angle, quadrilaterals, transformations, but also showed that technology contributes to the construction of other views of these concepts. Research gave evidence of changes and progress in students conceptualization due to geometrical activities (such as construction activities or proof activities) making use of technology with the design of adequate tasks and pedagogical organization. Technology revealed how much the tools shape the mathematical activity and led researchers to revisit the epistemology of geometry.

Even if the various technologies differ in the access to geometrical concepts, some invariants can be drawn from the research studies and their development over time. The focus initially was on the learner and his/her interactions with technology, giving rise to theoretical reflections about learning processes in mathematics by means of technology. The focus moved to the design of adequate tasks in order to meet some learning aims and then to the role of the teacher. The integration of technology into the everyday teacher practice became the object of investigation. Finally, the role of the features of software and technology design were also questioned and investigated in order to better understand how the appropriation of the technological environment by students could interfere with the learning of mathematics and how the teacher organizes students' work for managing this interaction between appropriation of the tool and learning. By focusing on everyday teacher practice, the constraints of the teaching institutions come to the foreground in the analysis of the integration of technology: How does the teacher manage the use of technology in taking into account the curriculum, and the time constraints? Technology is also still developing at a high pace: At the moment, the integration of symbolic programming with DGE, the development of special software for spatial Geometry software in the sense of 3D-software and the integration of Geometry software (especially DGE) with Computer Algebra Systems (CAS) seem to be most noteworthy. Additional research issues could deal with the integration of algebra and geometry allowed by technology. The fast evolution of interfaces calls for two main research strands:

- From the perspective of learning how do the students' instrumentation processes develop and what are their links with growth of mathematical knowledge? An object of investigation could especially be the impact of the novel kind of 3D dynamic and direct manipulation, in particular from an embodied cognition approach focusing, for example, on the role of gestures in mathematical construction of knowledge. One can incidentally wonder why the impact of technology extensively used outside school (such as the gaming technology) has only very recently started to become an object of investigation in the research in mathematic education community;

- From the perspective of teaching, the integration processes of technologies by teachers into their everyday practice could be extended to new technologies. Such studies seem to be particularly relevant in this time of massive entry of a new generation of teachers. Teacher preparation offers a research domain on such issues of high social importance.

Since geometry teaching has been changing so frequently in most countries in the past decades and differs from one country to another one, future research could address the question whether technology would lead to the tendency of smoothing the differences among geometry curricula across the world.

Studying the role of technology in the teaching and learning geometry led research in mathematics education to take into account and question all the complexity of teaching and learning processes. There is a dialectical link between the development of theories and research on the use of technology in geometry and generally speaking in mathematics teaching. Technology gave the opportunity of making use of available theoretical approaches, but also acted as a catalyst for the growth of new theoretical approaches and concepts in research in mathematics education. This is why we believe that research on the use of technology in geometry teaching needs more contributors.

REFERENCES

Abelson, H., & DiSessa, A. (1981). *Turtle geometry: The computer as a medium for exploring mathematics*. Cambridge, MA, USA: MIT Press.

Arcavi, A., & Hadas, N. (2000). Computer mediated learning. An example of an approach. *International Journal of Computer for Mathematical Learning*, *5*(1), 25–45.

Artigue, M. (2002). Learning mathematics in a CAS environment: The genesis of a reflection about instrumentation and the dialectics between technical and conceptual work. *International Journal of Computers for Mathematical Learning, 7*(3), 245–274.

Arzarello, F. (2000). Inside and outside: Spaces, times and language in proof production. In T. Nakahara & M. Koyama (Eds.), *Proceedings of the 24th PME International Conference, 1*, 23–38.

Arzarello, F., Micheletti, C., Olivero, F., & Robutti, O. (1998). Dragging in Cabri and modalities of transition from conjectures to proofs in geometry. In A. Olivier & K. Newstead (Eds.), *Proceedings of the 22nd PME International Conference, 2*, 32–39.

Arzarello, F., Olivero, F., Paola, D., & Robutti, O. (2002). A cognitive analysis of dragging practices in Cabri environments. *Zentralblatt für Didaktik der Mathematik, 34*(3), 66–72.

Assude, T. (2005). Time management in the work economy of a class: A case study: Integration of Cabri in primary school mathematics teaching. *Educational Studies in Mathematics, 59*(1–3), 183–203.

Balacheff, N. (1993). Artificial intelligence and real teaching. In C. Keitel & K. Ruthven (Eds.), *Learning through computers: Mathematics education and technology* (pp. 131–158). Berlin, Germany: Springer Verlag.

Bartolini Bussi, M. G. (1998). Verbal interaction in mathematics classroom: A Vygotskian analysis. In H. Steinbring et al. (Eds.), *Language and communication in mathematics classroom.* (pp. 65–84). Reston, USA: NCTM.

Bellemain, F., & Capponi, B. (1992). Spécificité de l'organisation d'une séquence d'enseignement lors de l'utilisation de l'ordinateur. *Educational Studies in Mathematics, 23*(1), 59–97.

Berthelot, R., & Salin, M.-H. (1998). The role of pupils' spatial knowledge in the elementary teaching of geometry. In C. Mammana & V. Villani (Eds.), *Perspectives on the teaching of geometry for the 21st century* (pp. 71–77). Dordrecht, The Netherlands: Kluwer.

Boychev, P. (1999). *Elica* [Computer program]. Sofia, Bulgaria: University of Sofia.

Brock, C., Cappo, M., Carmon, N., Erdös, A., Kamay, Y., Kaplan, D., et al. (2003). *Geometry Inventor* (v. 3.04) [Computer Program]. San Francisco, CA, USA: Riverdeep.

Brousseau, G. (1997). *Theory of didactical situations in mathematics*. Dordrecht, The Netherlands: Kluwer.

Chazan, D. (1993). High school geometry students' justifications for their views of empirical evidence and mathematical proof. *Educational Studies in Mathematics*, *24*(4), 359–387.

Clements, D., & Battista, M. (1992). Geometry and spatial reasoning. In D. A. Grouws (Ed.), *Handbook of research on mathematics teaching and learning* (pp. 420–464). New York, USA: MacMillan.

Clements, D., & Battista, M. (1994). Computer environments for learning geometry. *Journal of Educational Computing Research*, *10*(2), 173–197.

Clements, D. H., & Sarama, J. (1995). Design of a Logo environment for elementary geometry. *Journal of Mathematical Behavior*, *14*, 381–398.

Clements, D., & Sarama, J. (1997). Research on Logo: A decade of progress. *Computers in the Schools*, *14*(1–2), 9–46.

De Villiers, M. (1991). Pupils' needs for conviction and explanation within the context of geometry. In F. Furinghetti (Ed.), *Proceedings of the 15th PME International Conference*, *1*, 255–262.

diSessa, A. (1997). Open toolsets: New ends and new means in learning mathematics and science with computers. In E. Pehkonen (Ed.), *Proceedings of the 21st PME International Conference*, *1*, 47–62.

diSessa, A. (2000). *Changing minds, computers, learning and literacy*. Cambridge, MA, USA: MIT Press.

diSessa, A., & Lay, E. (1986). *Boxer* [Computer program]. Berkeley, CA, USA: University of Berkeley.

Dubinsky, E. (2000). Meaning and formalism in mathematics. *International Journal of Computers for Mathematical Learning*, *5*, 211–240.

Duval, R. (1988). Pour une approche cognitive des problèmes de géométrie en termes de congruences. *Annales de Didactique et de Sciences Cognitives*, *1*, 57–74. Strasbourg, France: IREM et Université Louis Pasteur.

Duval, R. (1998). Geometry from a cognitive point of view. In C. Mammana & V. Villani (Eds.), *Perspectives on the teaching of geometry for the 21st century* (pp. 37–52). Dordrecht, The Netherlands: Kluwer.

Duval, R. (2000). Basic issues for research in mathematics education. In T. Nakahara & M. Koyama (Eds.), *Procedings of the 24th PME International Conference*, *1*, 55–69.

Edwards, L. D. (1988). Children's learning in a transformation geometry microworld. In A. Borbás (Ed.), *Proceedings of the 12th PME International Conference*, *1*, 263–269.

Edwards, L. D. (1990). The role of microworlds in the contruction of conceptual entities. In G. Booker, P. Cobb, & T. N. Mendicuti (Eds.), *Proceedings of the 14th PME International Conference*, *2*, 235–242.

Edwards, L. (1992). A comparison of children's learning in two interactive computer environments. *Journal of Mathematical Behavior*, *11*, 73–81.

Edwards, L. D. (1994). Making sense of a mathematical microworld: A pilot study from a Logo project in Costa Rica. In J. P. Ponte & J. F. Matos (Eds.), *Proceedings of the 18th PME International Conference*, *2*, 296–303.

Eisenberg, M. (1995). Creating software applications for children: Some thoughts about design. In A. diSessa, C. Hoyles, & R. Noss (Eds.), *Computers and exploratory learning* (pp. 175–196). Heidelberg, Germany: Springer Verlag.

Falcade, R., Laborde, C., & Mariotti, M. A. (2004). Towards a definition of function. In M. J. Høines & A. B. Fuglestad (Eds.), *Proceedings of the 28th PME International Conference*, *2*, 367–374.

Fischbein, E. (1993). The theory of figural concepts. *Educational Studies in Mathematics*, *24*(2), 139–162.

Flanagan, K. (2001). *High school students' understandings of geometric transformations in the context of a technological environment*. Unpublished PhD dissertation, Pennsylvania State University, USA.

Freudenthal, H. (1973). *Mathematics as an educational task*. Dordrecht, The Netherlands: Reidel.

Furinghetti, F., Morselli, F., & Paola, D. (2005). Interaction of modalities in Cabri. In H. L. Chick & J. L. Vincent (Eds.), *Proceedings of the 29th PME International Conference, 3*, 9–16.

Gallou-Dumiel, E. (1989). Logo et symétrie centrale. In G. Vergnaud, J. Rogalski, & M. Artigue (Eds.), *Proceedings of the 13th PME International Conference, 2*, 3–10.

Goldenberg, E. P., & Cuoco, A. (1998). What is dynamic geometry? In R. Lehrer & D. Chazan (Eds.), *Designing learning environments for developing understanding of geometry and space* (pp. 351–368). Mahwah, NJ, USA: Lawrence Erlbaum.

Guin, D., & Trouche, L. (1999). The complex process of converting tools into mathematical instruments: The case of calculators. *International Journal of Computers for Mathematical Learning, 3*(3), 195–227.

Hadas, N., Hershkowitz, R., & Schwarz, B. (2000). The role of contradiction and uncertainty in promoting the need to prove in dynamic geometry environments. *Educational Studies in Mathematics, 44*(1–3), 127–150.

Hanna, G. (1998). Proof as explanation in geometry. *Focus on Learning Problems in Mathematics, 20*(2–3), 4–13.

Harvey, B. (2005). *USB Logo* [Computer program]. Berkeley, CA, USA: University of California at Berkeley.

Healy, L. (2000). Identifying and explaining geometrical relationship: Interactions with robust and soft Cabri constructions. In T. Nakahara & M. Koyama (Eds.), *Proceedings of the 24th PME International Conference*, 1, 103–117.

Hilbert, D., & Cohn Vossen, S. (1952). *Geometry and the imagination*. New York, USA: Chelsea Publishing. (translation by P. Nemenyi of *Anschauliche Geometrie*. Berlin, Germany: Springer-Verlag, 1932).

Hillel, J., Kieran, C., & Gurtner, J. (1989). Solving structured geometric tasks on the computer: The role of feedback in generating strategies. *Educational Studies in Mathematics, 20*, 1–39.

Holland, G. (2002). *GEOLOG* [Computer program]. Giessen, Germany: University of Giessen.

Hollebrands, K. (2002). The role of a dynamic software program for geometry in high school students developing understandings of geometric transformations. In D. Mewborn (Ed.), *Proceedings of the 24th PME–NA Annual Meeting*, 695–706.

Hollebrands, K. (2003). High school students' understandings of geometric transformations in the context of a technological environment. *Journal of Mathematical Behavior, 22*(1), 55–72.

Hölzl, R. (1996). How does 'dragging' affect the learning of geometry. *International Journal of Computers for Mathematical Learning, 1*, 169–187.

Hölzl, R. (2001). Using dynamic geometry software to add contrast to geometric situations – A case study. *International Journal of Computers for Mathematical Learning, 6*(1), 63–86.

Hoyles, C. (1995). Exploratory software, exploratory cultures? In A. di Sessa, C. Hoyles, R. Noss, & L. Edwards (Eds.), *Computers and exploratory learning* (pp. 199–219). Berlin, Germany: Springer Verlag.

Hoyles, C. (1998). A culture of proving in school mathematics. In D. Tinsley & D. Johnson (Eds.), *Information and communication technologies in school mathematics* (pp. 169–181). London, UK: Chapman and Hall.

Hoyles, C., & Noss, R. (1987). Seeing what matters: Developing an understanding of the concept of parallelogram through a Logo microworld. In J. Bergeron, N. Herscovics, & C. Kieran (Eds.), *Proceedings of the 11th PME International Conference, 2*, 17–24.

Hoyles, C., & Noss, R. (1988). Formalising intuitive descriptions in a parallelogram microworld. In A. Borbás (Ed.), *Proceedings of the 12th PME International Conference, 2*, 449–456.

Hoyles, C., & Noss, R. (2003). Digital technologies in mathematics education In A. Bishop, M. A. Clements, C. Keitel, J. Kilpatrick, & F. Leung (Eds.), *Second international handbook of mathematics education* (1, pp. 323–350). Dordrecht, The Netherlands: Kluwer.

Hoyles, C., Noss, R., & Sutherland, R. (1989). A Logo-based microworld for ratio and proportion. In G. Vergnaud, J. Rogalski, & M. Artigue (Eds.), *Proceedings of the 13th[th] PME International Conference, 2*, 115–122.

Hoyles, C., Noss, R., & Sutherland, R. (1991). Evaluating a computer based microworld: What do pupils learn and why? In F. Furinghetti (Ed.), *Proceedings of the 15th PME International Conference, 2*, 197–204.

Hoyles, C., & Sutherland, R. (1990). Pupil collaboration and teaching interventions in the Logo environment. *Journal für Mathematik-Didaktik, 4*, 324–343.

Jackiw, N. (1991). *The Geometer's Sketchpad* [Computer program]. Berkeley, CA, USA: Key Curriculum Press.

Jahn, A.-P. (2000). New tools, new attitudes to knowledge: The case of geometric loci and transformations in dynamic geometry environment. In T. Nakahara & M. Koyama (Eds.), *Proceedings of the 24th PME International Conference, 1*, 91–102.

Jahn, A.-P. (2002). "Locus" and "Trace" in Cabri-géomètre: Relationships between geometric and functional aspects in a study of transformations. *Zentralblatt für Didaktik der Mathematik, 34*(3), 78–84.

Jones, K. (1996). Coming to know about dependency within a dynamic geometry environment. In L. Puig & A. Gutiérrez (Eds.), *Proceedings of the 20th PME International Conference, 3*, 145–151.

Jones, K. (1998). Deductive and intuitive approaches to solving geometrical problems. In C. Mammana & V. Villani (Eds.), *Perspectives on the teaching of geometry for the 21st century* (pp. 78–83). Dordrecht, The Netherlands: Kluwer.

Jones, K. (2000). Providing a foundation for deductive reasoning: Students' interpretations when using dynamic geometry software and their evolving mathematical explanations. *Educational Studies in Mathematics, 44*(1–2), 55–85.

Jones, K. (2002). Research on the use of dynamic geometry software: Implications for the classroom. *MicroMath, 18*(3).

Kadunz, G. (2002). Macros and modules in geometry. *Zentralblatt für Didaktik der Mathematik, 34*(3), 73–77.

Kadunz, G., Kautschitsch, H. (1993). *THALES - Software zur experimentellen Geometrie* [Computer program]. Stuttgart, Germany: Ernst Klett Schulbuchverlag.

Kafai, Y., & Resnick, M. (Eds.). (1996). *Constructionism in practice. Designing, thinking and learning in a digital world.* Mahwah, NJ, USA: Lawrence Erlbaum.

Kakihana, K., Shimizu, K., & Nohda, N. (1996). From measurement to conjecture and proof in geometry problem. In L. Puig & A. Gutiérrez (Eds.), *Proceedings of the 20th PME International Conference, 3*, 161–168.

Kalas, I. (2001). *Imagine Logo* [Computer program]. Cambridge, UK: Logotron.

Kieran, C. (1986). Logo and the notion of angle among fourth and sixth grade children. In C. Hoyles & L. Burton (Eds.), *Proceedings of the 10th PME International Conference*, 99–104.

Kordaki, M., & Potari, D. (2002). The effect on area measurement tools on students' strategies: The role of a computer microworld. *International Journal of Computers for Mathematical Learning, 7*(1), 65–100.

Kynigos, C. (1988). Constructing bridges from intrinsic to cartesian geometry. In A. Borbás (Ed.), *Proceedings of the 12th PME International Conference, 2*, 449–456.

Kynigos, C. (1989). Intrinsic versus Euclidean geometry: Is the distinction important to children learning with the turtle? In G. Vergnaud, J. Rogalski, & M. Artigue (Eds.), *Proceedings of the 13th PME International Conference, 2*, 194–201.

Kynigos, C. (1991). Can children use the turtle metaphor to extend their learning to non-intrinsic geometry? In F. Furinghetti (Ed.), *Proceedings of the 15th PME International Conference, 2*, 269–276.

Kynigos, C. (2001). *E-slate turtleworlds* [Computer program]. Athens, Greece: Educational Technology Lab, School of Philosophy, PPP Faculty, Department of Education, University of Athens and Patra, Greece: Research Academic Computer Technology Institute.

Kynigos, C. (2002). Generating cultures for mathematical microworld development in a multi-organisational context. *Journal of Educational Computing Research, 27*(1–2), 185–211.

Kynigos, C. (2004). Black and white box approach to user empowerment with component computing. *Interactive Learning Environments, 12*(1–2), 27–71.

Kynigos, C., & Argyris, M. (2004). Teacher beliefs and practices formed during an innovation with computer-based exploratory mathematics in the classroom. *Teachers and Teaching: Theory and Practice, 10*(3), 247–273.

Kynigos, C., & Psycharis, G. (2003). 13 year olds' meanings around intrinsic curves with a medium for symbolic expression and dynamic manipulation. In N. Paterman, B. Dougherty, & J. Zilliox (Eds.), *Proceedings of the 27th PME International Conference, 3*, 165–172.

Laborde, C. (1998). Relationship between the spatial and the theoretical in geometry: The role of computer dynamic representations in problem solving. In D. Tinsley & D. Johnson (Eds.), *Information and communication technologies in school mathematics* (pp. 183–194). London, UK: Chapman & Hall.

Laborde C. (2001). Integration of technology in the design of geometry tasks with Cabri-geometry. *International Journal of Computers for Mathematical Learning, 6*, 283–317.

Laborde, C. (2003). Technology used as a tool for mediating knowledge in the teaching of mathematics: The case of Cabri-geometry. In W.-C. Yang, S. C. Chu, T. de Alwis, & M. G. Lee (Eds.), *Proceedings of the 8th Asian Technology Conference in Mathematics* (1, pp. 23–38). Hsinchu, Taiwan ROC: Chung Hua University.

Laborde, J.-M. (1999). Some issues raised by the development of implemented dynamic geometry as with Cabri-geometry. In H. Brönnimann (Ed.), *Proceedings of the 15th European Workshop on Computational Geometry* (pp. 7–19). Sophia Antipolis, France: INRIA.

Laborde, J.-M., Baulac Y., & Bellemain, F. (1988). *Cabri-géomètre I* [Computer program]. Grenoble, France: University Joseph Fourier.

Laborde J.-M., & Bellemain, F. (1995) *Cabri-géomètre II* and *Cabri-géomètre II plus* [Computer programs]. Dallas, USA: Texas Instruments and Grenoble, France: Cabrilog.

Lagrange, J.-B. (1999). Complex calculators in the classroom: Theoretical and practical reflections on teaching pre-calculus. *International Journal of Computers for Mathematical Learning, 4*, 51–81.

Lagrange, J.-B., Artigue, M., Laborde, C., & Trouche, L. (2003). Technology and math education: A multidimensional overview of recent research and innovation. In J. Bishop, K. Clements, C. Keitel, J. Kilpatrick, & F. Leung (Eds.), *Second international handbook of mathematics education* (pp. 237–270). Dordrecht, The Netherlands: Kluwer.

Leron, U., & Hazzan, O. (1998). Computers and applied constructivism. In D. Tinsley & D. C. Johnson (Eds.), *Information and communications technologies in school mathematics* (pp. 195–203). IFIP, London, UK: Chapman and Hall.

Leung, A. (2003). Dynamic geometry and the theory of variation. In N. A. Pateman, B. J. Dougherty, & J. T. Zilliox (Eds.), *Proceedings of the 27th PME International Conference, 3*, 197–204.

Leung, A., & Lopez-Real, F. (2000). An analysis of students' explorations and constructions using Cabri geometry. In M. A. Clements, H. Tairab, & W. K. Yoong (Eds.), *Science, mathematics and technical education in the 20th and 21st centuries* (pp. 144–154). Brunei: Universiti Brunei Darussalam.

Leung, A., & Lopez-Real, F. (2002). Theorem justification and acquisition in dynamic geometry: A case of proof by contradiction. *International Journal of Computers for Mathematical Learning, 7*, 145–165.

Magina, S., & Hoyles, C. (1991). Developing a map of children's conception of angle. In F. Furinghetti (Ed.), *Proceedings of the 15th PME International Conference, 2*, 358–465.

Mariotti, M. A. (1995). Images and concepts in geometrical reasoning. In R. Sutherland & J. Mason (Eds.), *Exploiting mental imagery with computers in mathematics education* (pp. 97–116). Berlin, Germany: Springer Verlag.

Mariotti, M. A. (2000). Introduction to proof: The mediation of a dynamic software environment. *Educational Studies in Mathematics, 44*(1–2), 25–53.

Mariotti, M. A. (2001). Influence of technologies advances on students' mathematics learning. In L. English, M. G. Bartolini Bussi, G. Jones, R. Lesh, & D. Tirosh (Eds.), *Handbook of international research in mathematics education* (pp. 695–723). Mahwah, NJ, USA: Lawrence Erlbaum.

Mariotti, M. A., & Bartolini Bussi, M. G. (1998). From drawing to construction: Teachers mediation within the Cabri environment. In A. Olivier and K. Newstead (Eds.), *Proceedings of the 22nd PME International Conference, 1*, 180–95.

Mariotti, M. A., Laborde, C., & Falcade, R., (2003). Function and graph in a DGS environment. In N. A. Pateman, B. J. Dougherty, & J. T. Zilliox (Eds.), *Proceedings of the 27th PME International Conference, 3*, 237–244.

Marrades, R., & Gutiérrez, A. (2000). Proofs produced by secondary school students learning geometry in a dynamic computer environment. *Educational Studies in Mathematics, 44*(1–2), 87–125.

Mason, J. (1992). Geometric tools. *Micromath, 8*(3), 24–27.

Monaghan, J. (2004). Teachers' activities in technology-based lessons. *International Journal of Computers for Mathematical Learning, 9*(3), 327–357.

Noss, R., & Hoyles, C. (1996). *Windows on mathematical meanings*. Dordrecht, The Netherlands: Kluwer.

Noss, R., Hoyles, C., Healy, L., & Hoelzl, R. (1994). Constructing meanings for constructing: An exploratory study with Cabri-geometry. In J. P. Ponte & J. F. Matos (Eds.), *Proceedings of the 18th PME International Conference, 3*, 360–367.

Olive, J., & Lankenau, C. (1987). The effects of Logo-based learning experiences on students' non-verbal cognitive abilities. In J. Bergeron, N. Herscovics, & C. Kieran (Eds.), *Proceedings of the 11th PME International Conference, 2*, 24–31.

Olivero, F. (2002). *The proving process within a dynamic geometry environment*. Unpublished PhD dissertation, University of Bristol, Graduate School of Education, Bristol, UK.

Pallascio, R. (1987). Les habiletés perspectives d'objets polyhédriques. In J. Bergeron, N. Herscovics, & K. Kieran (Eds.), *Proceedings of the 11th PME International Conference, 2*, 39–46.

Papert, S. (1980). *Mindstorms. Children, computers and powerful ideas*. Brighton, UK: Harvester Press.

Papert, S. (2002). The turtle's long slow trip: Macro-educological perspectives on microworlds. *Journal of Educational Computing Research, 27*(1), 7–28.

Parmentier, C. (1989). Angles et pixels – Quelle synergie à 9 ans? In G. Vergnaud, J. Rogalski, & M. Artigue (Eds.), *Proceedings of the 13th PME International Conference, 3*, 90–97.

Parzysz, B. (1988). Knowing vs seeing: Problems of the plane representation of space geometry figures. *Educational Studies in Mathematics, 19*(1), 79–92.

Pratt, D., & Ainley, J. (1996). Construction of meanings for geometric construction: Two contrasting cases. *International Journal of Computers for Mathematical Learning, 1*(3), 293–322.

Pratt, D., & Davison, I. (2003). Interactive whiteboards and the construction of definitions for the kite. In N. A. Pateman, B. J. Dougherty, & J. T. Zilliox (Eds.), *Proceedings of the 27th PME International Conference, 4*, 31–38.

Resnick, M. (1995). New paradigms for computing, new paradigms for thinking. In A. di Sessa, C. Hoyles, R. Noss, & L. Edwards (Eds.), *Computers and exploratory learning* (pp. 31–44). Berlin, Germany: Springer Verlag.

Rolet, C. (1996). *Dessin et figure en géométrie: Analyse et conceptions de futurs enseignants dans le contexte Cabri-géomètre*. Unpublished PhD dissertation, University of Lyon 1, Lyon, France.

Ruthven, K., Hennessy, S., & Deaney, R. (2005). Incorporating dynamic geometry systems into secondary mathematics education: Didactical perspectives and practices of teachers. In The Association of Mathematics Teachers (Ed.), *Moving on with dynamic geometry* (pp. 138–158). Derby, UK: The Association of Mathematics Teachers.

Sacristán, A. I. (2001). Students' shifting conceptions of the infinite through computer explorations of fractals and other visual models. In M. van den Heuvel-Panhuizen (Ed.), *Proceedings of the 25th PME International Conference, 4*, 129–136.

Sánchez, E., & Sacristán, A. I. (2003). Influential aspects of dynamic geometry activities in the construction of proofs. In N. A. Pateman, B. J. Dougherty, & J. T. Zilliox (Eds.), *Proceedings of the 27th PME International Conference, 4*, 111–118.

Sarama, J., & Clements, D. (2002). Design of microworlds in mathematics and science education. *Journal of Educational Computing Research, 27*(1), 1–3.

Scally, S. P. (1987). The effects of learning Logo on ninth grade students' understanding of geometric relations. In J. Bergeron, N. Herscovics, & C. Kieran (Eds.), *Proceedings of the 11th PME International Conference, 2*, 46–53.

Scher, D. (2001). *Students' conceptions of geometry in a dynamic geometry software environment.* Unpublished PhD dissertation, New York University, New York, USA.

Schwartz, J., Yerushalmy, M., & Shternberg, B. (1985). *The Geometric Supposer* [Computer program]. Pleasantville, NY, USA: Sunburst Communication.

Schwartz, J., Yerushalmy, M., & Shternberg, B. (2000). *The Geometric Supposer-3* [Computer program]. Israel: The Center for Educational Technology.

Sereno, F. (1994). A perspective on fractals for the classroom. In J. P. Ponte & J. F. Matos (Eds.), *Proceedings of the 18th PME International Conference, 4*, 249–256.

Sherin, B. (2002). Representing geometric constructions as programs: A brief exploration. *International Journal of Computers for Mathematical Learning, 7*, 101–115.

Sinclair, K., & Moon, D. (1991). The philosophy of Lisp. *Communications of the ACM, 34*(9), 40–47.

Sinclair, M. (2003). Some implications of the results of a case study for the design of pre-constructed, dynamic geometry sketches and accompanying materials. *Educational Studies in Mathematics, 52*(3), 289–317.

Silverman, B. (1999). *MicroworldsPro* [Computer program]. Highgate Springs, Vermont, USA: LCSI.

Soury-Lavergne, S. (1998). *Étayage et explication dans le préceptorat distant, le cas de TéléCabri.* Unpublished PhD dissertation, University Joseph Fourier, Grenoble, France.

Strässer, R. (1991). *Dessin et figure - Géométrie et dessin technique à l'aide de l'ordinateur* (Occasional paper No. 128). Bielefeld, Germany: Universität Bielefeld, Institut für Didaktik der Mathematik.

Strässer, R. (1992). Didaktische Perspektiven auf Werkzeug-software im Geometrie-Unterricht der Sekundarstufe I. *Zentralblatt für Didaktik der Mathematik, 24*(5), 197–201.

Strässer, R. (1996). Students' constructions and proofs in a computer environment – Problems and potentials of a modelling experience. In J.-M. Laborde (Ed.), *Intelligent learning environments: The case of geometry* (pp. 203–217). Berlin, Germany: Springer Verlag.

Strässer, R. (2002). Research on dynamic geometry software (DGS) – An introduction. *Zentralblatt für Didaktik der Mathematik, 34*(3), 65.

Talmon, V., & Yerushalmy, M. (2004). Understanding dynamic behavior: Parent–child relations in dynamic geometry environments. *Educational Studies in Mathematics, 57*(1), 91–119.

Vadcard, L. (1999). La validation en géométrie au collège avec Cabri-géomètre: Mesures exploratoires et mesures probatoires. *Petit x, 50*, 5–21.

Vérillon, P., & Rabardel, P. (1995). Cognition and artifacts: A contribution to the study of thought in relation to instrumented activity. *European Journal of Psychology in Education, 9*(3), 77–101.

Wilensky, U. (1999). *NetLogo* [Computer program]. Evanston, IL, USA: Center for Connected Learning and Computer-Based Modeling, Northwestern University.

Zack, V. (1988). Say it's perfect then pray it's perfect: The early strategies of learning about Logo angle. In A. Borbás (Ed.), *Proceedings of the 12th PME International Conference, 2*, 657–664.

AFFILIATIONS

Colette Laborde
Université Joseph Fourier & Institut Universitaire de Formation des Maitres
46 Avenue Felix Viallet
38000 Grenoble (France)
colette.laborde@imag.fr

Chronis Kynigos
Educational Technology Lab
Dept of Education
P.P.P. Faculty, School of Philosophy
University of Athens
Athens (Greece)
kynigos@ppp.uoa.gr

Karen F. Hollebrands
Mathematics Education
North Carolina State University
326K Poe Hall, Box 7801
Raleigh, NC 27695 (USA)
karen_hollebrands@ncsu.edu

Rudolf Strässer
Justus-Liebig-Universitaet
Giessen (Germany)
and
Lulea University of Technology
Lulea (Sweden)
rudolf.straesser@math.uni-giessen.de

JERE CONFREY AND SIBEL KAZAK

A THIRTY-YEAR REFLECTION ON CONSTRUCTIVISM IN MATHEMATICS EDUCATION IN PME

INTRODUCTION

As the International Group for the Psychology of Mathematics Education (IG PME) grew up, so did constructivism. Reflecting over the role of constructivism in the history of mathematics education is a daunting task, but one which provides an opportunity to reflect on what has been accomplished, honor the contributions of scholars around the world, and identify what remains unfinished or unexplained. In undertaking this task, we divide our treatment into five major sections: (1) The historical precedents of constructivism during the first ten years (1976-85); (2) The debates surrounding the ascendancy of constructivism during the next ten years (1986-95); (3) Our own articulation of key principles of constructivism; (4) Thematic developments over the last ten years (1996-present); and (5) An assessment of and projection towards future work. Looking back, we hope we can share the excitement of this epoch period in mathematics education and the contributions to it which came from across the globe.

Since its inception at the 1976 International Congress on Mathematical Education (ICME) in Karlsruhe, PME has addressed three major goals all addressing the need to integrate mathematics education and psychology. While PME clearly has welcomed and thrived on multiple theories of psychology, beginning with Skemp's (1978) *The Psychology of Learning Mathematics,* it has preferred those with a cognitive, and to some extent, an affective orientation. Two major theories of intellectual development have been dominant, namely constructivism and socio-cultural perspectives. In recent years, these two theories have intermingled, but in this volume, they are separated as we trace their paths, overlapping and distinctive. We will not give in to the frequent temptation to cast constructivism and socio-cultural perspectives as a diametrically opposed where one is personal/individual and the other social; but rather track the evolution of the theory via the theorists and the perspectives that they assign to their work.

A. Gutiérrez, P. Boero (eds.), Handbook of Research on the Psychology of Mathematics Education: Past, Present and Future, 305–345.

PART 1: THE HISTORICAL PRECEDENTS FOR CONSTRUCTIVISM (1976-1985)

We would classify constructivism as a "grand theory" in the typology offered by diSessa and Cobb (2004), in that it was paradigmatic for mathematics education, though as they put it, grand theories are often "too high-level to inform the vast majority of consequential decisions" (p. 80), at least at a level of specificity to guide instructional practice (also see Ernest, 1991b, and Thompson, 2002). To specify practice, constructivism relied on partner instructional theories, such as "Realistic Mathematics Education (RME)" (De Lange, 1987; Freudenthal, 1991; Gravemeijer, 1994), "didactical engineering" (Artigue, 1990; Balacheff, 1990), "cognitively guided instruction" (Carpenter, Fennema, Franke, Levi & Empson, 1999) or "constructionism" (Harel & Papert, 1991), all of which were compatible with the grand theory and were a part of PME deliberations.

As a grand theory, constructivism served as a means of prying mathematics education from its sole identification with the formal structure of mathematics as the sole guide to curricular scope and sequence. It created a means to examine that mathematics from a new perspective, the eyes, mind and hands of the child. Constructivism developed in mathematics education to counter the effects of behaviorism (Gagné, 1965; Thorndike, 1922), which had focused on measurement and the production of patterns and levels of outcomes by stimuli. Constructivism evolved as researchers' interests in the child's reasoning went beyond a simple diagnostic view of errors to understanding the richness of student strategy and approach. It took hold in practice, because it addressed the two primary concerns of teachers: (1) Students' weak conceptual understanding with over-developed procedures (relational vs. instrumental in Skemp's, 1978, language), and (2) Students demonstrated difficulties with recall and transfer to new tasks. Constructivism did so by focusing the strengths and resources children brought to the tasks, and by making their active involvement and participation central to the theoretical framework.

Understanding how the constructivist movement swept through mathematics education requires one to take an evolutionary look at its inception and development. Some argued that its quick ascension demonstrated the tendency of the field to respond too quickly to fashions (Wheeler, 1987), or even reflected zealotry of the part of its proponents (Kilpatrick, 1987). With time, we can ask what propelled it to such notoriety, looking critically, why was it so often it was the trappings of constructivism, and not the solid conceptual basis that was practiced? Further, it will be helpful to consider if the overall research programme[1] of constructivism is still progressive, static or degenerating in the Lakatosian sense (Lakatos, 1976).

---

[1] Lakatos (1976) argued that the best way to describe a paradigm was to identify it as a research programme which consisted of a theoretical hardcore of ideas, core commitments surrounded by a protective belt of theories and finally surrounded by empirical studies. Challenges to the programme such as anomalies would cause changes in the empirical studies first and if necessary to the protective belt of bridging theories. The hardcore could not be directly challenged; although depending on the success of the adjustments, the programme could be cast as progressive (gaining power) or degenerating (losing power).

We locate the roots of constructivism in three traditions, very much a part of the tradition of PME: (1) Problem solving (Garofalo & Lester, 1985; Goldin & Gennain, 1983; Polya, 1957; Schoenfeld, 1985), (2) Misconceptions, critical barriers, and epistemological obstacles (Brousseau, 1983; Confrey, 1990; Driver & Easley, 1978; Hawkins, 1978), and (3) Theories of cognitive development (Krutetskii, 1976; Piaget, 1954; Sinclair, 1987; Van Hiele & Van Hiele-Geldof, 1958). All of these traditions impregnated mathematics education with the view that something more than the logic of mathematics was necessary to explain, predict, and facilitate mathematics learning. They all recognized that the difficulty or ease of learning could not be explained simply by looking at the complexity of the material, but rather that other factors were needed to account for the path learning traversed and levels of success or failure. While behaviorism had presented the simplest account from an external viewer's perspective (a set of stimulus-response connections), a more complex psychological theory was needed to capture not only the behaviors but the experience of learning. Also, a black box approach (one which lacks constructs to explain non-observable processes) to the mind left one unable to gain explanation, much less prediction, over students' thinking and reasoning, both alone and within interactions.

The first tradition of problem solving provided a number of key elements for constructivist thought. Polya's (1957) four stages (understanding, devising a plan, carrying out the plan, and looking back) emphasized that mathematics was more than a set of formal definitions, theorems, and proofs and acknowledged the central role of problems in generating new solutions, propelling the field forward. Research on heuristics (Goldin & Gennain, 1983) demonstrated the power of examining the problem solver's strategies. And the need to be aware of the problem solving process itself promoted increased emphasis on meta-cognition's role in thinking (Garofalo & Lester, 1985). In problem solving theories, there was always a philosophical sense that the problems existed independent of the solver, and by learning a fruitful set of techniques, solutions could be more easily and effectively be sought. Polanyi (1958), in *Personal Knowledge,* described it as "looking for it [the solution] as if it were there, pre-existent." As a result, problem solving was viewed as an acceptable extension to mathematics, not challenging in any fundamental way the epistemological character of the enterprise, but only extending and enhancing it. Debates focused typically only how much time should be devoted to it.

The second major tradition was that of systematic errors and misconceptions. In this, the concept of errors had ripened to include the idea of epistemological obstacles (Bachelard, 1938; Brousseau, 1983; Sierpinska, 1992), misconceptions (Bachelard, 1938; Confrey, 1990), critical barriers (Hawkins, 1978), and alternative conceptions (Driver & Easley, 1978). Typically, practitioners assumed that errors could be eradicated by drawing students' attention to them and providing them the correct procedures. In contrast, misconceptions seemed to pop back up like weeds, and their attraction to students suggesting some deeper compelling quality. Three examples have been extensively discussed at PME: (1) "Multiplication makes bigger, division makes smaller (MMBDMS)" (Greer, 1987);

(2) "The graph as a picture of the path of an object" (Monk & Nemirovsky, 1994); and (3) "Additive equal amounts to numerators and denominators preserves proportionality" (Hart, 1984). Other examples also abound in the literature such as longer numbers are bigger so 1. 217 > 1.3 (Resnick, Nesher, Leonard, Magone, Omanson & Peled, 1989). Explanations for misconceptions required one to find ways to identify cases in which the formation of the generality made sense, and to recognize where an extension of the idea would produce errors. Thus, MMBDMS works for positive rational numbers greater than one, but fails as one extends the meaning of multiplication and division to rational numbers between 0 and 1. In other cases, misconceptions revealed competing ideas and led to a recognition of the need to know more about the context of a concept's use in order to select the correct alternative (i.e., for rational numbers, we recognized that there are multiple legitimate meanings, and the context often is needed to determine the appropriate selection). And finally, research on misconceptions often led us to examine the historical development of an idea, only to discover that many of the competing ideas retained a worthy and still debatable co-existence (alternative conceptions), establishing that an enduring concept's victory could be the result of culture, convention or logical primacy (e.g., Shapin and Schaffer's, 1989, *Leviathan and the Air Pump*). Overall, misconceptions established clearly that learning was not a simple and direct accumulation of ideas and beliefs, with simple correction and replacement, but that its course would be circuitous, demanding revisiting and revising ideas as they gained intellectual breadth and power, and requiring careful attention to learners' thoughts and perceptions. It further signaled that one's view of epistemology and one's philosophy of intellectual development in mathematics could be seen as relevant to an understanding of learning. Within the tradition of misconceptions, one critique which developed was that use of the term, misconceptions, focused too exclusively on the way in which student ideas deviated from traditional ones; and hence some researchers preferred the term, alternative conceptions, to signal the potential viability of their ideas (Driver & Easley, 1978). This emphasis on understanding the potential in student reasoning foreshadowed some of the developments of constructivism.

The third, and surely the most influential, tradition shaping the development of constructivism was the work of Piaget on theories of cognitive development. Whether Piaget's work belonged to constructivism, agreed with constructivism, or defined constructivism is a matter of some debate (Ernest, 1991a; Von Glasersfeld, 1982). His prodigious writings and research production make it inevitable that he changed over the course of his lifetime that his co-workers and disciples often expressed varying perspectives, and thus individuals each interpret the work of Piaget. In our review of Piaget's work, we recognize seven major contributions: (1) A child's view is different qualitatively from an adult's, (2) General stages of development viewed as likely intellectual resources for building ideas occur sequentially and provide important background information for studying children, (3) The development of an idea determines its meaning, rather than a simple statement of a formal definition and set of relationships, known as *genetic epistemology*, (4) Because of the first three premises, one can witness two major kinds of encounters and responses to new ideas and information which are *assimilation* and *accommodation*, and (5) The process of moving from action, to operation, to mathematical object, required a level of consciousness that he labeled *reflective abstraction, (6)* The patterns of thought available for reuse and modification were cast as *schemes*, and (7) Describing foundational ideas often involved a search for *conservation* and invariance. These contributions due to their theoretical force and their connections to many replicable results through relatively simple experimentation stimulated the field to pay close attention to how fundamental concepts could be viewed as developmental and children could be rich resources of information. Added to the way it made one wonder about alternative ideas and ways children were not just incomplete mathematicians, the work of Piaget undergirded many of the constructivist activities.

PART 2: THE ASCENDANCY OF CONSTRUCTIVISM (1986-1995)

If constructivism was forged out of these three elements, problem solving, misconceptions literature and Piagetian thought, one might ask, what catalyzed the movement as a whole, how was the whole greater than the parts, and what progress and/or limitations followed from the reformation of elements? In answering these questions, we will engage in our own form of "genetic epistemology" applying it to constructivism itself in relation to mathematics education over the last thirty years. We ask the question, what did the theory permit us to do, and where were its resistances, in the sense of the idea of viability or fit, rather than match, as proposed by Von Glasersfeld (1982)? Further, in the tradition of Lakatos, what we will be telling is a form of a "rational reconstruction" over the thirty-year history of PME, not a straight bibliographical retelling, but a re-positioning of the role of constructivism in the history of mathematics education as a response to a problematic. Further, we will ask the question of whether at the current time, it constitutes a progressive, degenerating, or static research programme.

The problematic that constructivism sought to address was described at the sixth PME-NA meeting by Confrey (1984) as (1) Rigidity and limited student knowledge, (2) Excessively formal knowledge, isolated from experience and sense-making, (3) Dependence on external sources for evaluation rather than self-regulation; and (4) Emotionally intimidating and alienating. There was a clear focus on students and their perceptions of mathematics. In our approach then we will first outline the critical issues which emerged from the seminal meeting of PME in which constructivism was the theme. Then we propose our own framework of ten principles which we believe more completely captures the key elements of the theory. Our work on this can be viewed as a form of rational reconstruction in that we have selected these ten for their explanatory value in describing what is common and what is variable among the various interpretations of the theory. Because we cast constructivism as a grand theory, we see these ten principles as the hardcore and then suggest that one way to view the development of constructivism in PME is to report on the various bridging theories which linked constructivism into the practice of schools. These theories varied by region, by content area and level, and by the aspect of educational practice selected. We present examples of these bridging theories in order to do some modest amount of justice to the breadth of work undertaken in the field. Finally, we discuss the overall directions in which constructivism has progressed and those in which more emphasis is needed.

In our reconstruction, we took a close look particularly at the watershed meeting in Montréal in 1987, as a means to consider what was attractive, what was controversial and disputed, and what was consensual. While the theme of the conference was constructivism, two of the plenary sessions were given by constructivist scholars Sinclair (1987) and Vergnaud (1987) whilst two were devoted to critiques (Kilpatrick, 1987; Wheeler, 1987). It was notable that two of the scholars whose works were continuously referenced and critiqued, Ernest von Glasersfeld and Leslie Steffe, were not provided an opportunity at the podium. We summarize their contributions as part of this section, recognizing them for their seminal work articulating clear, albeit controversial, versions of the theory. Their students, Cobb, P. Thompson, and A. Thompson among others, became some of the most influential scholars in developing the subsequent theoretical work.

Hermine Sinclair, a lifelong colleague of Piaget, gave the opening plenary, in which she expressed the view that the central tenet to Piaget's work was "the essential way of knowing the real world is not directly through our senses, but first and foremost through our actions" (Sinclair, 1987, p. 28). Actions were defined as "behavior by which we bring about a change in the world around us or by which we change our own situation in relation to the world" (ibid, p. 28). She proceeded to describe how this constituted not just a learning stance, but an epistemological stance, in which one builds the cognitive structures that are needed to "make sense of experience." In order to do so, she stressed the importance of the learner's theories and successive models, that seek to know an object "which continues to possess unknown properties" (ibid, p. 29). She pointed out that constructivism represented a challenge to the Platonist view, noting that "to many adults, scientists as well as laymen, mathematical 'truths' appear to be a priori, Platonic ideas, that emerge at some point in development, whereas physical 'truths' are rooted in learning through experience, and thus fit into empiricist theories of knowledge" (ibid, p. 33). However, she also acknowledged that while rejecting Platonism, Piaget argued that logico-mathematical knowledge still differed from scientific knowledge. She discussed the importance of correspondences (and comparison) and transformation as the two primary instruments or processes linking the human subject and the objects of his knowledge. The starting point is through actions that become transformed into operations and processes. Then she emphasized that the construction of schemes from these interactions is a slow and gradual process, one which is "deeply rooted in all human endeavors to make sense of the world" (ibid, p. 35). She ended with a challenge to the audience to consider what other intellectual resources might explain the construction of mathematics beyond counting and possibly measuring.

In contrast, Jeremy Kilpatrick's plenary also identified reasons for the constructivist movement in mathematics education and harshly attacked against aspects of it. He cited Von Glasersfeld's description of radical constructivism as entailing two principles: (1) "Knowledge is actively constructed by the cognizing subject, not passively received from the environment", and (2) "Coming to know is an adaptive process that organizes one's experiential world; it does not discover an independent, pre-existing world outside the mind of the knower" (Kilpatrick, 1987, p. 7). In the next section, we discuss why this synopsis of constructivism left the field open to the debates that followed.

Constructivism was, for Kilpatrick, relegated to a metaphor, which responded to the question of whether mathematics is discovered or created (constructed). He suggested that the term 'construct' finds a particular resonance in mathematics where, in contrast to physical science concepts, one sees mental constructions as necessary for abstractions which eventually lack a material referent. If the metaphor of construction is solely to apply to a means to maximize students' involvement, engagement in mathematical activities, then he found it palatable. If, instead, it entailed a rejection of an external, knowable reality, objective truth or Platonist views of mathematics, he opposed it. He claimed that one could take a step into a development perspective and the evolution of child thought, without stepping into epistemology, which entailed redefining or reconstituting mathematics itself. Two imperatives of some versions of constructivism were objected to are: (1) The description of humans as self-organizing, based on their responses to perturbations (which he described as based on "negative feedback or blind" and "closed" (Kilpatrick, 1987, p. 9), (2) The limitation of knowledge to issues of epistemology rather than ontology, the study of what is in the sense of "being" or "reality". Finally, he required that constructivism pertain only to learning, hence rejecting Von Glasersfeld's described consequences of constructivism for educational practice. Furthermore, he argued what constructivism needed to do was to accept the views of mathematics provided by mathematicians, such as Ruben and Hersch, accepting math as a Platonist enterprise, only explaining the behavior of mathematicians as a socio-cultural artifact. Kilpatrik's concerns were subsequently shared or discussed by others (Ernest, 1991a; Goldin, 1989), hence our careful treatment of it is included.

The pressure on the two discussants, Vergnaud and Wheeler, was palatable for those at the meeting. Gerard Vergnaud began with a clear challenge, stating "As a matter of fact, our job, as researchers, is to understand better the processes by which students learn, construct or discover mathematics and to help teachers, curriculum and test devisers, and other actors in mathematics education, to make better decisions. This is our practical burden" (Vergnaud, 1987, p. 43). Vergnaud recognized that epistemology was a key part of Piaget's work, and pointed out that for Piaget, "constructivism contradicts both empiricism and a priori rationalism" (ibid, p. 44). He reminded the audience that Piaget's work on space and time rejected Kant's claim that these two constructs transcended human knowledge. Piaget rejected Hume as well, based on the view that it could not be assumed that knowledge comes directly from sensory perception. Vergnaud attributed Piaget's brilliance to finding a way to weave together empiricism and rationalism, which

Vergnaud argued "must be probably traced in his background as a biologist and an evolutionist" (ibid, p. 44).

This emphasis on adaptation was key for Vergnaud (1987) as children ...

> ... have schemes and categories to interpret experience, and that these schemes and categories are not a priori schemes and categories but derive from inborn schemes and experience. Action is essential as children accommodate their schemes through action upon the physical (and social) world, in order to assimilate new situations, nearly in the same way as scientists develop new procedures and concepts from former knowledge to understand and master new phenomena. (p. 44)

Vergnaud then carefully distinguished his position from radical constructivism, premised on his view that radical constructivism entails a "denial of an independent pre-existing world" and "fails to provide a theory of objective knowledge" (ibid, p. 46). He simply stated that "Piaget was not interested in this metaphysical question" (ibid, p. 45). While we would argue that both of these attributions to radical constructivism are incorrect in our understanding of it, his clear negotiation of the disputes on both sides was a feat of diplomacy and scholarship.

The final section of Vergnaud's talk concentrated on mathematics, which he emphasized, had not been sufficiently addressed in the previous talks. He questioned the cogency of Piaget's distinction between empirical abstraction and reflective abstraction, offering instead his concept of "theorems in action" (Vergnaud, 1987, p. 47) which he claimed must precede the development of formal theorems. By arguing that in the beginning, for children, physics and mathematics are indistinguishable, as quantity and measure both require ideas of space and time, he suggested that this level of challenge of the distinction was needed to overcome the view that mathematics was about "additive rules, symbolic calculus and static structures" (ibid, p. 47). At the same time, he acknowledged that the development of the irrational number and the need to move towards an understanding of "pure numbers" symbolized places where mathematics would depart from its physical roots.

Wheeler's final plenary veered back towards the critical. Renouncing constructivism as a theory, he wrote, "It is not a theory because it is not formulated in terms that could lead to refutation. At the heart of discussions about constructivism is the difficulty that its espousal and its rejection are more products of taste than of evidence" (Wheeler, 1987, p. 56). What Wheeler did was to suggest that constructivists were mixing together uncritically a number of elements: (1) Constructivism as practiced in mathematics (of which he wrote, "The platonist-constructivist dichotomy puts us in the position of either denying that we have any choice in the directions in which mathematics develops or deny that the inner coherence of mathematics ever takes us in directions different from those we intended to follow" (ibid, p. 57)); (2) Constructivism and psychology (where he cited Blakemore, 1973, who stated, "our seemingly unified view of the world around us is really only a plausible hypothesis on the basis of fragmentary evidence" (ibid, p. 57) and stressed the impact of "a priori powers of the mind or the brain that enable us to select invariants form the flux of sensory data" (ibid, p. 57)); (3) Constructivism and philosophy (he noted Piaget's contribution to the philosophy of mathematics by stating "Piaget's constructivism, meaning is cumulative and the evolution of mathematical structures is towards increasing comprehensiveness and rigor. Logico-mathematics structures build on those that came before, integrating them while overcoming their inadequacies. Mathematics therefore moves towards increasing objectivity –which Piaget understands as a process and not as a state" (ibid, p. 59)); and, finally, (4) Constructivism and education where he acknowledged the importance of linking knowledge to the intentions of the learner while respecting the context of school's need for organized and generalized knowledge. He too acknowledged a place for students "to see themselves as originators and modifiers of knowledge" (ibid, p. 59).

As indicated previously, the contributions of Ernst von Glasersfeld and Leslie Steffe to constructivism were of considerable theoretical importance. Von Glasersfeld generally took a philosophical approach he termed "radical constructivism" which he linked to Aristotle, Vico, Dewey, and James which classifies "knowledge is the result of a learner's activity rather than of passive reception of information or instruction" (Von Glasersfeld, 1991, p. xiv) and that therefore he argued that knowledge should be conceived of as an "*adaptive function* [which] ... means that the results of our cognitive efforts have the purpose of helping us to cope in the world of our experience, rather than the traditional goal of furnishing "objective" representation of the world as it might "exist" apart from us and our experience" (ibid, p. xv). This position led him to articulate a fundamental distinction between "fit" and "match" where he drew an analogy to a lock. He pointed out that many keys could potentially fit a lock and hence knowledge was more akin to devising a possible key than creating a mirror image of the lock itself or "matching it" (Von Glasersfeld, 1982). Steffe's contributions were both theoretical and methodological. Besides the careful analysis and set of distinctions Steffe, Von Glasersfeld, Richards and Cobb (1983) offered on how children developed counting and operations, Steffe and his colleagues also wrote numerous articles concerning the methodologies of teaching experiments and clinical interviews which describe how to build a model of children's mathematics (Cobb & Steffe, 1983; Steffe & Thompson, 2000).

Steffe's subsequent distinction between first- and second-order models provides a way to consider the role of social interactions explicitly both by the interviewer and when observing students' and teachers' interactions (Steffe, 1995). His critical contribution was his articulation and illustrations that knowing how other's conceive of mathematics is a challenging enterprise and must be based on extensive observations with carefully sequenced tasks: "As a teacher, one must intensively interact with students to learn what their numerical concepts and operations might be like, and how they might modify them as they interact in situations of learning" (ibid, p. 495). He suggested that the first-order models were a means to describe subjective mathematical experience. To build on an issue raised by Thompson who argued, "One notion that I resist is the notion of *social cognition* ... it is only in the mind of an observer that socially constructed knowledge is 'out there' ... and ... as a consensual domain" (ibid, p. 496), Steffe proposed the idea of a second-order models. These were used to explain social interactions which are "necessarily constructed through social interaction because they are the models that the observer constructs of the observed." (ibid, p. 496).

Looking back, we are struck by the sense of incompleteness of the session, and suggest that the field was not yet ready to negotiate a way to settle the disputes. In our rational reconstruction, we locate the heart of the problem in the statement of constructivism's two principles, which led to a view that if one accepted only the first, one was cast as a trivial constructivist and if one accepted the second together with the first statement, one was a radical constructivist (Von Glasersfeld, 1995). Many mathematics educators faced with a choice steered clear of the controversy and hence never confronted the subtler implications of the constructivist theory. As a result, we would argue that this debate distracted from the essential point in constructivism which is to recognize the profound impact of theories of evolution on intellectual work. It turns out that all three major theorists, Piaget, Dewey, and Vygotsky were addressing these implications to various degrees. As Dewey recognized in *The Influence of Darwin on Philosophy* (McDermott, 1981),

> That the combination of the very words *origin* and *species* embodied an intellectual revolt and introduced a new intellectual temper is easily overlooked by the expert. The conceptions that had reigned in the philosophy of nature and knowledge for two thousand years, the conceptions that had become the familiar furniture of the mind, rested on the assumption of the superiority of the fixed and final; they rested upon treating change and origin as signs of defect and unreality. In laying hands upon the sacred ark of absolute permanency, in treating the forms that had been regards as types of fixity and perfection as originating and passing away, the *Origin of the Species*, introduced a mode of thinking that in the end was bound to transform the logic of knowledge, and hence the treatment of morals, politics and religion. (p. 32)

PART 3: TEN PRINCIPLES OF CONSTRUCTIVISM

As we reflected back over the 1987 Montréal meeting and subsequent work, we conjectured that the concise and elegant two-principle statement may have contributed to perpetuating and polarizing the debate. It reduced the complexity of the epistemological import of constructivism to a single statement too easily misunderstood. Partly as a result of this and as a result of the lack of precise specification of the mathematical implications of the theories, constructivism was frequently associated with excessive student-centeredness, lacking deep enough attention to the role and value of established mathematical accomplishments and proficiencies.

This analysis led us to restate the theory in terms of ten principles selected for their explanatory potential to help to highlight the characteristics of the subsequent work on constructivism by the international PME community. As a "rational reconstruction" of the thirty years, one seeks to explain both the commonalities and variations in the theory as it evolved in a variety of locations, with concentrations of different age groups, topics, and forms of instructional practice. This articulation is also intended as our own contribution to subsequent work in the area. Thus, we are suggesting that a more complete and satisfactory articulation of the principles of constructivism might be stated as including the following:

1. An *explanatory* model for development is necessary to guide educational practice. A descriptive model of stages is insufficient as it will only tell one what behaviors to look for, and not how to achieve them. An explanatory model is needed identifying processes for change as well as likely paths of change over the course of learning.

2. Since evolution and adaptation provide a convincing model for conceptual-historical evolution of ideas (phylogeny), a strong candidate for articulating an explanatory model and underlying mechanism for development (ontogeny) is likely to reside in identifying parallel constructs. Likewise, it would need to explain variation, similarity, change over time, and selection. *Genetic epistemology* is such a theory as it seeks to explain the ontogeny of intellectual development in terms of an individual's interactions, both social and environmental. It changes our focus from classical epistemology where we concentrate solely on the products of knowledge and their justification abbreviated in the phrase "justified true belief" (or what we know and why we believe it). In addition, it focuses our attention on how we come to know it (processes) and how we communicate that knowledge with others (social interaction). This principle of constructivism does not require one to reject ontology, or an external reality or existence, but only to recognize and focus on our ongoing active participation, by means of tradition, practice, and physiology, in the process of knowing. Accepting that as an organism, our ways of interacting shape what we claim as knowledge, does not obligate one to reject the view that things independent of us shape those possibilities and action. The debate concerning the relationship between reality and knowledge still flourishes in some circles, especially concerning what legitimate appeals are for warrant and the meaning of truth. However, our treatment of constructivism emphasizes the ideas of viability and fit (Von Glasersfeld, 1982) rather than of permanent truth and assured objective properties. Fallibilism in epistemology (Ernest, 1991b) was mistaken for solipsism in ontology by many critics of constructivism. Rather, constructivism seeks to steer a course between positivism and solipsism. As stated by Larochelle and Bednarz (1998), "Escaping the dictatorship of the object –the position of naive empirico-realism– only to come under the rule of the subject is not a particularly innovative solution" (p. 5). Genetic epistemology focuses our attention on creating an explanatory theory which elaborates "a theory of the organism who creates for him- or her-self a theory of the world" (Von Glasersfeld, 1987, cited in Larochelle & Bednarz, 1998, p. 5). It concerns how and by what means an individual determines what theories of the world "fit" his/her experience writ large (including social and environmental factors) rather than to decide to what extent these theories "match" an external reality, hence the stress is on

epistemology. Emphasizing adaptive fit requires a rejection of a correspondence theory of truth, which then needs to be replaced by alternative ways of linking human activity and the world to produce and explain forms of warranted knowledge. Two such approaches are described in principles 3 and 4.

3. Truth can be obtained in relation to a *coherence* theory of knowledge within the mathematical practice of building axiomatic systems, if it serves the role of establishing consistency within a limited system. That is, one accepts the "truth" of statements that are derived deductively from axioms taken as starting points. While some may prefer to call it truth, others may prefer the term "certainty" (Von Glasersfeld, 1990) in recognition of the fact that even rules produce ambiguity and the need for further refinement of the terms, definitions and scope of applicability. Coherence alone, however, is not sufficient as a lone explanation of truth because of the incompleteness of axiomatic systems to describe all of mathematics and hence even with coherence, one still needs to also consider other sources of warrant. Furthermore, one will need to consider the balance of attention to be paid to these multiple sources of warrant and how an understanding of coherence is developed.

4. In mathematics, *warrant* also derives from the careful development of conjecture, argument and justification concerning the study of number, space, pattern, change, chance and data. We refer to these processes as chains of reasoning which are the hallmark of mathematical thought, and they include intuition, visualization, generalization, problem solving, symbolizing, representing, demonstrating and proving etc. In these areas, constructivism attends to how actions, observations, patterns, and informal experiences can be transformed into stronger and more predictive explanatory ideas through encounters with challenging tasks. These ideas or concepts can then become tools for building new concepts within each of these subfields. While deductive reasoning is certainly one important aspect of this (discussed in principle 3 with coherence), constructivism recognizes the value of other forms of securing mathematical certainty such as the coordination of representations, the identification of patterns, the recognition of similar ideas in apparently dissimilar settings (connections), the development and refinement of conjectures, and the applications of the ideas to other fields. This myriad of mathematical concepts and processes retain their connections to everyday experience, hence replacing the need for correspondence with the satisfaction of purposeful activity to resolve outstanding problematics.

5. We select the individual as the primary *unit of analysis* for assessing and evaluating cognitive achievements in acknowledgement of the need to ensure that the complete patterns of reasoning associated with key ideas are understood at the individual level with associated coherence, adaptive fit and continuity. This is akin to Steffe's first-order models, and does not imply neglect of the ways in which those experiences are nested and shaped within patterns of participation in larger collective membership units (dyads, classes etc.). It is further a practical decision based on typical schooling, which treats students as individuals as they move across grades, across locations, at the level of assignment, in relation to future studies and work, and in relation to the basic accountability systems. We recognize

the importance and viability of also including other units of analysis, such as dyads, groups, classes, schools etc., as a second-order model in relation to the assessment of an individual's developmental path. The distinction between first- and second-order models will prove useful to the observer/researcher, but should not lead one to assume that the individual student experiences them as separate. We liken this decision to place the individual as the first-order model to Vygotsky's choice of the word as the fundamental unit of analysis which did not preclude his theorizing about sentences or complex social interactions, but it guided his empirical designs and permitted him to identify the building block of his theory. Likewise, constructivist scholars investigate collective social interactions, purposes, and forms of engagement, and coordinate these with students' interactions with various physical devices and tools, but our claim is that collective social interactions should be linked with its effects on individual student's intellectual growth. Further this should not be construed to mean that personal identities are considered only as individually constituted, nor does it imply that membership in multiple groups is neglected or ignored.

6. To explain sources of *variation for individuals* and avoid a standardized or uniform theory of knowledge, one needs to consider three broad and interacting factors: The individual's current state of development, social and cultural influence as members of a tribe (group), and environmental/physical factors in relation to the task at hand. While in evolution, mutation is the primary source of variation, we rather ascribe unique arrangements of the three interacting factors as the means of producing the essential diversity that spawns invention and serves as a source of variation. One of the most compelling contributions of constructivism is the documentation of rich and interesting ways that children express about ideas. We see it in the form of inventive representations, language, forms of reasoning, alternative pathways, and explanations. Many of these expressions are regularly overlooked in traditional classrooms. This can result in missed opportunities for interesting connections among ideas, can undermine children confidence in their own emerging reasoning, and result in proposals which are labeled as erroneous that may support alternative paths.

7. To explain *selection*, one must consider how the same three forces act to define criteria for viability for cognitive ideas, (as mortality vs. survival would not serve this purpose). First, we point out that selection depends on processes of change and adaptation. We propose that pragmatism, in relation to functional fitness, provides the means for this; that a difference is viable when it makes a difference (James, 1907). This conception then invites one to propose sets of processes that instigate, regulate, and evaluate change in terms of functional fitness. For Piaget, these were assimilation and accommodation. For Dewey, it was the process of inquiry, wherein the indeterminate situation is transformed to a determinant situation. For Peirce, the stress was placed on the importance of doubt in securing deep understanding (see Peirce, 1877, 1878). In constructivism, compatible with both of these philosophers, cognitive change, or intellectual growth, begins with a perturbation, or a problematic, which is a perceived roadblock to where one wants to be (Confrey, 1991). It is followed by an action, to

attempt to eliminate that perturbation or to satisfy the felt-disequilibration. As emphasized in Sinclair (1987), the action of the individual is key in that the degree of active participation often determines the success of the action in resolving the problematic. Also as she emphasized that action often involves comparison or transformation of the original situation. In most school-related settings, as well as many others, a representation is produced to record, signify or communicate the results of that action. This leads to and supports an act of reflection, to assess whether the original perturbation or felt-need was satisfied, or whether more action is required. The cycle repeats itself, continuing to transform the problematic hopefully towards resolution. This *cycle of constructive activity* represents the activity of selection for viability of ideas. In all steps, to varying degrees, the influence of social and environmental factors are at play –sometimes with more or less emphasis on one or the other. Summarizing this process, Larochelle and Bednarz (1998) wrote,

> Drawing on a range of fields including second order cybernetics and contemporary linguistics and epistemology, constructivism centers of the development of a "rational" model of cognitive activity of either an individual or collective variety, including the narratives which are devised to give shape and meaning to our actions ... Or, to take Korzbsky's metaphor, a map can never be said to "be" the territory –all the more so in that the territory is a question of representation as well. What the map refers to inevitably an affair of not only the particularities decided on by its maker but also the distinctions he or she chooses to make in accordance with his or her project and the success with which his or her cognitive and deliberative experiences have met. (p. 6)

8. In learning, there is an unavoidable element of *recursiveness* in the process. One recognizes multiple forms of awareness of oneself as a learner –as one: (a) Determines if the goal, purpose or problematic has been satisfied; (b) Creates records and representations to communicate with others and/or to assist in reflection and evaluation, and (c) Remembers successful and viable methods for future use (schemes). In addition, in the description of learning, the levels of recursiveness accumulate further. As stated by Von Foerster (1984), "it takes a brain to write a theory of the brain; now, for this theory to be complete, it should also be able to explain the fact of its own elaboration, and what is more, the writer of this theory ought to be able to account for his or her writing" (p. 11). Properties of the observer must be part of the description of what is observed (Larochelle & Bednarz, 1998). That is, our explanations must serve to both describe what we observe and to explain our own experience, at the level of mechanism. It is this recursiveness that produces in humans the particular ability to abstract, a key element of mathematics.

9. Because in constructivism, the focus is on genetic epistemology, *objectivity* must be redefined as the result of a consensus among a group of qualified individuals to authorize a particular description or explanation as viable and as shared among them. According to the standards of any particular set of knowledge

games (discipline), the standards for authorizing knowledge differ, and as a theory about functional fitness, objectivity represents a perceived stability in ideas, not a permanent state of being. This is more akin intersubjectivity as discussed in Thompson (2002). It can be a case of a symmetric assumed tacit understanding by all parties as Cobb's "taken-as-shared" (Cobb, Yackel & Wood, 1990), or a case of a stated and negotiated understanding or asymmetric but uncontested recognized difference by one or more parties, as Confrey's "agreeing to agree" (Confrey, 1995). How these bear upon and are used in the development of an individuals' independent reasoning in mathematics or science is a source of valuable investigation and has led to the development of socio-constructivism as a distinct subset of constructivism. Within such an approach, one can examine the development of "knowledge communities" as a larger unit of analysis, provided it is connected to its effects on independent reasoning patterns for individual students, as also a target unit of analysis.

10. An understanding of the first ideas will lead people to more viable and effective models of knowledge and will engender more productive knowledge acts as one recognizes the observer-observed interactions not as limitations but as accomplishments and agreements, and not simply received knowledge, but as active choices and selections by reflective knowers or *consciousness*. This treatment of consciousness should be a primary outcome of learning in science or math. Désautels (1998) recognized the need for a broader level of awareness than what is obtained by reflective abstraction in terms of understanding by jumping to a recognition of how these chains of reasoning are embedded in a larger framework of knowledge construction and debate:

> One is justified in thinking that ignorance of the relative, discontinuous, and historically located character of the development of scientific knowledge (Serres, 1989) will leave this student quite unprepared to gauge the limits of this type of knowledge and to appreciate the real worth of other knowledge forms and knowledge games. (p. 124)

> Whence the necessity, if one wishes to participate in the conversation of scientists, of understanding how the latter impart meaning to the notions and concepts they use; whence also the importance of epistemological reflexivity. Only when knowing subjects become aware of the postulates which underlie their usual ways of knowing, and when they place their own knowledge, they will become able to open themselves to other potentialities. Although the intellectual process of reflexivity is often associated with metacognition, it is distinct from the latter in that it does not involve the intellectual operations or strategies in developing this or that bit of knowledge. Instead, reflexivity draws attention to "that which goes without saying" –that is, the unspoken assumptions or the un-reflected aspects of thought which lead one to be referred to metaphorically as the blind spot of a conceptual structure which is a condition necessary for beginning that process whereby thought is complexified and autonomized (Varela, 1989). (p. 128)

This restatement and elaboration of the premises of constructivism into ten principles simultaneously accomplishes two goals. First, it rejects the dichotomy between radical and trivial constructivism, arguing instead for a more nuanced set of distinctions. Secondly, it draws upon the contributions of each of the scholars cited previously. It is consistent with the statements by Sinclair (1987) about the centrality of action and the multiple roles of reflection. It responds to the criticisms of Kilpatrick (1987) by clarifying the atheoretical position of constructivism on ontology and by redefining objectivity within a social constructivist perspective. It links constructivism to its philosophical basis as demanded by Wheeler (1987), and demands that the psychological view of constructivism recognize the epistemological central hardcore of the theory. And finally it avoids the criticisms of creating an overly individualistic or solipsistic theory.

While this revised statement is consistent with the arguments by Vergnaud (1987) and his criticisms of his interpretation of constructivism, it does not accomplish his primary challenge, which is to use constructivism to explain mathematical knowledge and instructional practice. Nonetheless in our rational reconstruction of the constructivist research programme, we believe it prepares the way more adequately for doing so, as it restricts the theory's scope of application to reasoned knowledge and locates the coherence of evolution in the individual's students' minds, while recognizing the significant forces exerted by other types of knowledge and other units of analysis. Thus, in the remainder of the paper, we address how constructivism has affected our understanding of how children learn the concepts of numeration, quantification, space, logic, chance, change, and data.

PART 4: MAJOR ENDURING LEGACIES OF THE CONSTRUCTIVIST RESEARCH PROGRAMME (1996-PRESENT)

Because we do not see the contributions of constructivism as only theoretical, but also specific and practical, we have identified nine major enduring legacies of the constructivist research programme. We select a few examples from each to illustrate how these provide the "protective belt" around the constructivist core principles and support the empirical evidence to link it with practice. One possible exercise, beyond the scope of this paper would be to consider how each of these bridging theories draws upon or modifies the ten fundamental principles of constructivism as previously outlined.

Bridging theories

As a grand theory, or perhaps a paradigmatic theory, constructivism is too general to reach to the classroom directly. This gap is accounted for in different ways by different people. Some say it is because it is a theory of learning rather than of teaching (Simon, 1995). Others say that it is not specific enough to mathematics, or perhaps particular subfields (geometry, multiplicative structures, etc.). For others, the missing elements are the artifacts of practice –curricula, technologies or assessments. In this first section, we describe how members of PME brought to our community means of linking constructivist theories into practice.

Examples of bridging theories in PME are numerous. We would point to examples in the work at the Freudenthal Institute on Realistic Mathematic Education (RME) (De Lange, 1987, 2001; Gravemeijer, 1994, 2002), the work on additive and multiplicative conceptual fields (Harel & Confrey, 1994; Steffe, 1994; Vergnaud, 1996), theories of advanced mathematical thought (Sfard, 1991; Sierpinska, 1990; Tall, 1991), didactical engineering (Artigue, 1987; Brousseau, 1997), modeling and applications (Blum, 1993; Burkhardt, 1981; Niss, 1992), the theoretical work of Pirie and Kieran (1994) (descriptions of stages of concept development), and cognitively guided instruction (CGI) (Carpenter et al., 1999) to name only a few.

RME was both an approach and a set of curricular materials. Freudenthal, beginning in the 1960s, had invented the idea of mathematization with two components: Horizontal and vertical. Horizontal mathematization was "where students come up with mathematics tools that can help to organize and solve a problem set in a real-life situation" and vertical mathematization "is the process of reorganization within the mathematical system itself" (Van der Heuvel-Panhuizen, 1999, p. 4 cited in Perry & Dockett, 2002, p. 89). These initial distinctions led to the development of design heuristics that included "guided reinvention" and "didactical phenomenology", both of which provided a genetic aspect to the instructional approaches and worked to capture the need for students to strengthen their understanding of abstract ideas while linking them to practices involving the application of quantifiable knowledge. De Lange (1987) followed with the development of a new curriculum focusing on applications and assessment for upper secondary mathematics. In recent times, Gravemeijer (1999) has further extended the work to include the ideas of "emergent modeling". In all of these efforts, we see clear links to the constructivist principles including an explanatory theory of what mathematics represents, how students' move towards increasing proficient uses of symbolization, the importance of reflection in that process, within social and interactional settings, and the importance of distinguishing teacher and student perspectives and make the observer's position one of problematizing and gathering evidence on students' perspective.

The area of advanced mathematical thought demonstrates another example of a bridging theory between constructivism and classroom practice. The theories in this arena arose from the recognition that many students demonstrate a gap between their informal and formal knowledge, having learned to correctly reproduce the formal definitions, but retaining contradictory commitments in their informal knowledge. Beginning with the work of Tall and Vinner (1981) distinguishing concept image and concept definition, researchers in this tradition tried to reestablish the roots of complex ideas in constructivist beginnings. For instance, Vinner's work on concept images in functions demonstrated that while students could recite the formal definition of functions with some accuracy, they still reasoned with specific cases in ways that were not consistent with that definition (Vinner & Hershkowitz, 1980). For instance, when presented with a graph in pieces, students reasoned that it could not be a function, though it met the formal criteria. Ascertaining what students think and reasoning what the implications of those responses are critical element of constructivist perspective.

This research evolved into producing Advanced Mathematical Thinking (Tall, 1991) and a PME working group that continues to the present. It included Douady's dialectique outil-object (Douady, 1986), Sfard's dual nature of conceptions (Sfard, 1991), Gray and Tall's procept (Gray & Tall, 1994), and Dubinsky's APOS (action, process, object and schema) (Dubinsky & McDonald, 2001). All sought to explain how to move from contextually situated, action-oriented ideas to increasing levels of abstraction. They sought to explain the development of reification, where in mathematics, an idea used at one level, becomes an object on which to act at the next. While some criticized the linearity of the approach (Tall, 1991) and the narrow focus on abstraction as the absence of context (Confrey & Costa, 1996), the research had strong ties to constructivism, particularly in its use of reflective abstraction as a means to bootstrap into advanced thinking, and it helped instructors to learn to pay closer attention to students' thinking in the building of mathematical ideas. To a degree, it broadened the views of mathematics, emphasizing the need at all levels to consider the role of student conjecture, reflection, and development. These major contributions of bridging theories by scholars typically entailed most of the ten principles as they worked out extensive ways to create curricula or to influence instructional programmes at various levels.

Grounding in action, activity and tools

A second common element of most of the constructivist initiatives in mathematics came from the claim that mathematical ideas are fundamentally rooted in action and situated in activity. During the thirty years of PME, we witnessed researchers from around the world prospecting the sources of mathematics ideas, in a variety of ways. One generative route came from the ways in which performance on everyday tasks contrasted with performance on school-based or more formal tasks. While this research tradition evolved into situated learning (Brown, Collins & Duguid, 1989; Greeno, 1989) and ethno-mathematics (Carraher & Schliemann, 1988; D'Ambrosio, 1985), and typically attached themselves to socio-cultural perspectives as the "grand theory", many of the ideas served as the basis for conceptual development within the constructivist tradition as well. For example, research on candy sellers revealed a different form of primary units that base 10, which at 35 cents a candy bar, tended to group to $1.05 as a unit. Besides demonstrating again the differences in character of formal and informal knowledge, it taught researchers to look for competence in formally less educated clients, rather than to assume only formal knowledge was productive and accurate. We still see this heritage in developmentally early curricular tasks focusing on situational units (silhouettes of footprints, handprints) as measurement units.

This research led researchers to explore and validate student strategies and approaches (Ginsburg, 1989; Kamii, 1985). Ginsburg began his work with the observation from extensive clinical interviews that children's thinking is seldom capricious. Kamii used the Piagetian approaches to develop a variety of ways to use manipulatives and related materials to build young students' understanding of arithmetic; and she paid careful attention to how to transition from the material actions and operation to notational and symbolic use.

The focus on action as the source of mathematical ideas spread throughout mathematics education beyond the use of manipulatives and everyday objects to consider the potential generativeness of a variety of tools. One potent source of this was by researchers interested in the development of algebra and the concept of function, who located this work in the curve drawing devices of the seventeenth century (Bartolini Bussi, 1993; Dennis, 1995; Taimina, 2005). Their work illustrated the potential of historical investigations that showed that algebraic descriptions of curves did not come in an f(x) format, where independent variable produced dependent variables. Even the Cartesian plane, as constructed by Descartes, was not dependent on perpendicular axes, but located them for convenience in describing the curve (Smith, Dennis & Confrey, 1992). Demonstrating the links between algebra and geometry through similarity and proportional reasoning, these scholars (Bartolini Bussi, 1993; Dennis, 1995) showed that the development of algebraic expressions for functions had their roots in a variety of tools for constructing different curves, well-beyond the traditional constructions with straight edge and compass to hinged devices. Later as dynamic geometry became available, it was used as a powerful representational media for exploring these ideas further. In it, students could experience how it was invariant properties of a class of curves, and not scale, that was the defining feature of families of functions.

Others extended this type of work to create new devices for exploring the sources of student reasoning (like Meira's, 1995, gears, and Nemirovsky's, 2002, trains), and motion detectors, and other devices provided potent sources of mathematical explorations.

More recently, a research forum, titled "Perceptuo-Motor Activity and Imagination in Mathematics Learning," was organized at PME-27 by Nemirovsky and Borba in 2003 just to discuss how the devices such as water wheel, sensors together with graphing calculators and software such as LBM connected to mini-cars brought different experience students have outside the classroom into the teaching and learning of themes, such as middle school algebra, introduction to functions, calculus, and dynamical systems. This forum became recently a special issue of *Educational Studies in Mathematics* (Nemirovsky & Borba, 2004) which was published in a format of a video-paper, a multimedia artifact brings voice of students in a new way to mathematics education research. Not only the voice of students can be literally heard, but body language related to their interaction with standard mathematics representations (e.g. graphs) and to the artifact can be differently experienced by the reader-viewer.

We can definitely see the roots of constructivism in the examples presented in this section. They emphasize the notion of voice of the students and how it affects the perspectives of the teachers/researchers and how their thoughts are modeled by the others (Confrey, 1998). Differences in understanding of a given concept in differing contexts and situations has been a hallmark in this kind of research, as well as careful documentation of how different students develop and contribute diverse ideas as they interact.

It was a small but profound step from these physical environments to the application of new technologies as surrogates for concrete grounded activities. Best known was Logo (Papert, 1993), with its successor in Star Logo (Resnick, 1994) and Lego/Logo (Resnick & Ocko, 1991), which led to a closely related branch of theory called constructionism based on the concept of microworlds. In 1988, we saw the maturation of such research in the work of Hoyles and Noss (1988) on Logo programming environment. Nesher (1988b) tackled directly the issues of truth in mathematics when she developed the concept of learning systems suggesting that one can find "microworlds" that are nearly isomorphic to the axiomatic systems but which are held together by a more experiential glue that formal deductive reasoning and cites Logo microworlds as such an example. She argues that these provide a means of giving children the experience of the coherence view of truth.

Other environments that profoundly affected PME were Cabri-Géomètre (Baulac, Bellemain & Laborde, 1988), the Function Supposer (Schwartz & Yerushalmy, 1988) and Function Probe (Confrey & Maloney, 1991) and spreadsheets (Sutherland & Rojano, 1993), SimCalc Math Worlds (Kaput, 2001), and quantification of motion in Thompson (2002). In all of these, we watched as physical actions on objects were transformed into machine-driven actions in which students became active investigators of the properties illustrated in the technologies and software. These software tools permitted students to link their opportunities for conjecture and exploration to the new century's tools of mathematics.

We would suggest that these efforts constitute means to strengthen the meaningfulness of mathematics. In relation to our framework, we emphasize that the approaches provide examples of genetic epistemology, that they provide a means to see how correspondences between symbolic activity and everyday activity could be fostered within mathematical activity.

Alternative perspectives, student reasoning patterns and developmental sequences

One characteristic of constructivism is to offer adaptation as mechanism to explain the transformation of human thinking over time. Research in this area has included work on counting, ratio, statistics, probability, limits, functions, and geometric proofs.

This has led mathematics educators to identify critical moments in learning where an earlier way of thinking fails to account sufficiently for new ideas and where an invention is needed to account for those examples, extensions or phenomena (Nakahara, 1997). A number of these ideas are found in mathematics: Perhaps the best known is multiplication makes bigger, division makes smaller. Researchers recognized that extending multiplication and division to these values must be accompanied by encountering directly this conflict in expectations. Such an encountering is not simply a matter of seeing the result, but often of reexamining one's underlying models. For instance, if multiplication is based in arrays, then multiplication by a fractional part will require a transition to area models. Further, if the problem of a x b for $a>1$ and $0<b<1$ is managed by using commutativity and repeated addition of the fractional unit, the next case where both $0<a<1$ and $0<b<1$ must still be managed instructionally. As this research evolved, we learned that even when the issue is "resolved" for multiplying a/b x c/d, it resurfaces when students are faced with multiplying 3.45 x 0.56. Here, Greer (1987) examined what students predicted when asked to calculate prices of gasoline where flaps over the values obscured the numbers and how they changed operations when revealing the numbers faced this with values like those given previously. He argued that students should not be inclined to change their predictions if they possessed what he labeled "conservation of number" (Greer, 1987). This research tradition suggested that certain beliefs of children develop in limited settings, and that extending them in ways that conflict with those original predictions one not only to provide them with the new procedures, but to get them to think through why there is a need to revise their ideas.

This work has evolved into current research on students' computational strategies and understanding where one considers the interplay among their understanding of number types and magnitude, operations, situations, units, and complexity of operations (number of steps; order of operations) (Verschaffel, De Corte & Vierstraete, 1999).

Similar work has been conducted in two areas: (1) Counting, addition, and subtraction, and (2) Fractions, ratio, and multiplicative structures. Research on counting and the development of adding units (Carpenter, Moser & Romberg, 1982; Steffe et al., 1983) commenced a string of work which culminated revisions to curricula around the world. Here, Vergnaud first presented his work on "theorems in action" and conceptual fields (Vergnaud, 1982). In the beginning, Noelting (1980) developed insight into a set of stages he observed in students learning ratio and proportion reasoning. Others (Hart, 1984; Streefland, 1991) extended this work to document the types of common errors made by students in rational number reasoning. One set of researchers then recognized that the student difficulty with these ideas was at least as likely to be a product of competing conceptions of rational number and identified six major parts. The Rational Number Project group (Behr, Lesh, Post & Silver, 1983), Nesher (1988a), Kieren, (1992) and Vergnaud (1996) discovered that it was not just an issue of the numbers but of the interplay between the numbers, their representation, the situation and operations, and properties that created a network of relations that one must move among to operate correctly, referred as a multiplicative conceptual field. It was in this context that Vergnaud developed further his observation that students were in fact drawing on implicit "theorems in action" (p. 225). By setting the work on multiplication and division in the context of exponential functions, Confrey and Smith (1989) argued that there were multiple legitimate concepts of rate. It can be seen that this research programme had a clear constructivist tenor--- it recognized the pragmatist roots of different conceptions and the lack of distinction inherent in the symbolic form of a/b. It began with an expectation of a single conceptual development trajectory and quickly found that in fact, a number of different concepts are in conflict with each other and that while a single consistent formal structure can be imposed on these, the need for distinctions continues as students work in context.

The work on developmental sequences, undertaken in many areas of mathematics, geometry, statistics as well as those outlined above, have contributed key insights into student reasoning. Over the years of constructivist research, we have come to realize that the success of learning depends on a careful but flexible sequence of activities which adapt to student ideas while encountering critical barriers. Much productive work needs to be undertaken to test these sequences at large scales with more carefully designed experimental and comparative studies.

Student invented representations, and multiple representations

These had constructivist roots in that they were used as evidence of students' active participation and their ability to compare and transform their basic ideas, building more and more abstract ones.

Another shift that accrued due to the constructivist research programme was in the exploration of role of representations in mathematics. At the younger levels, researcher explored the ways in which children would build their own representations of ideas with increasing sophistication. Maher, Speiser, Friel and Konold (1998) demonstrated repeated instances in which children's reasoning about probability was affected by the ways in which they recorded their results and communicated those with peers and teachers. Likewise, Fuson (1988) explored how children generated algorithms often revealed a spatial orientation on the page that made the possibilities of success more or less likely, and hence how restricting students' use of format prematurely could frustrate the expression of their competence.

At the more advanced levels of mathematics, the focus was on the use of multiple representations. Instead of assigning the most prestige to the most symbolic of representations, researchers discovered that different representations afforded students differing insights into the mathematical ideas (Artigue, 1992; Confrey & Smith, 1989; Dreyfus, 1993; Janvier, 1987; Kaput, 1987).

An excellent example of the use of multiple representations came with the movement for algebra to emphasize not only the development of symbolic manipulation skills but to act as a means to understand families of functions. Families of functions were characterized in two ways: (1) A particular family (linear, quadratic, exponential, and trigonometric) was related by their individual familial bonds (rates of change, curve shapes, algebraic form) and (2) The families shared certain general traits as demonstrated in transformations (actions on the classes of functions that provided a measure of generalizability across the families). In the area of transformations, students formed deeper generalizations when they were able to make explanations and predictions in multiple representations (graphs, tables, equations) and this process of explaining the impact of various parameters, often required them to work in dynamic environments across these representations (Borba, 1993; Dreyfus, 1993).

For example, at PME-18, Borba (1994) discussed how students used a given software, Function Probe (Confrey & Maloney, 1991), as they struggled to coordinate of different representations. A model is presented to show how knowledge can be constructed by such coordination. Borba (1995) illustrated how in such a process of coordinating representations, students may transform the software adding features that were not thought of by the designers (Borba & Confrey, 1996). More recently, Borba & Villarreal (2005) and Borba & Scheffer (2004) have extended the notion of multiple representations and demonstrated the need to extend it to coordination across different media, including graphing calculators, computers, sensors, and paper. Moreover, they claim that this coordination has also to be integrated with a very basic activity within humans' body motion.

Socio-constructivist norms

These were produced as researchers took constructivism into the classroom. As stated in the principles, in order to participate successfully in a constructivist environment, classrooms must shift from a passive to an active role. Some explored how these shifts disrupted normal assumptions under the "didactical contract" (Brousseau, 1984; Chevallard, 1988), and discussed the need for changing the expectations of the students. In 1986, Cobb, Yackel and Wood found that they needed to shift the behaviors of the students as early as first to third grades, to encourage them to listen to other students and to talk about their solutions (diSessa & Cobb, 2004). Drawing on the work of Bauersfeld (1998) and Voigt (1985) and symbolic interactionism, Cobb and his colleagues established that if a teacher were to successfully develop a constructivist orientation among students, s/he would need to "renegotiate classroom social norms." For example, they explain that constructivist classrooms tend to count as "different" solutions that while producing the same result, represent different cognitive processes. This shift is what is seen as different, changes what is learned in two ways: (1) Different ideas are foregrounded, and (2) Students' reflections on their own thinking are strengthened. Finally, teacher learning from students is often reported. Other norms explored included what is a clear, acceptable, or sophisticated explanation. In diSessa and Cobb (2004), this area of research was considered to be an "ontological innovation" and led to the identification of this approach as a distinct branch of constructivism, socio-constructivism. Wood, Cobb and Yackel (1995) wrote, "It is useful to see mathematics as both cognitive activity constrained by social and cultural processes, and as a social and cultural phenomenon that is constituted by a community of actively cognizing individuals" (p. 402).

New Topics

The introduction of the technological learning environments in various topics in school mathematics curriculum, such as geometry and statistics, provided new insights into how students learn these topics and how we teach them. For example, dynamic geometry computer environments, such as the Geometer's SketchPad [GSP] (Jackiw, 1991), Cabri-Géomètre (Baulac et al., 1988), the Geometric Supposer (Schwartz & Yerushalmy, 1985), and 3-D dynamic images (Gutiérrez & Jaime, 1993) provided students with different tools for exploring and understanding geometric concepts, and thus offered alternative ways to learning geometry, reasoning about geometry, and constructing proofs (Arzarello, Micheletti, Olivero, Robutti, Paola & Gallino, 1998; Gutiérrez, 1995; Hollebrands, 2002; Laborde, 1993; Marrades & Gutiérrez, 2000). The constructivist perspective of Piaget and the theory of Van Hiele on geometric thinking and proofs are key to the theoretical foundation for use of such computer environments in learning geometry (Clements & Battista, 1992). Furthermore, there is a key issue in considering how mathematics must be reframed when placed into electronic media such as when Balacheff introduced the ideas of computational transposition (Balacheff, 1993) in which he recognized the need in technology for the coordination of mathematical screen representation with the underlying computational models.

Furthermore, using statistics as an example, one can see how constructivism has spawned inventive and original ideas with mathematical import as well as identifying key landmarks in learning. As statistics and data analysis are becoming focal areas of mainstream school curricula in many countries, attention on research in statistics education is paid to the students' development in statistical thinking and reasoning, students' understanding of statistical topics, and the use of dynamic statistical computer software, such as Fathom (Finzer, 2001), TinkerPlots (Konold & Miller, 2005), and Minitools (Cobb, Gravemeijer, Bower & McClain, 2001). Although mathematics provides the theoretical foundations for statistical procedures, statistics education does not necessarily conform the traditional approaches to teaching and learning mathematics. For instance, statistics is a relatively new curricular area in which the new content and approaches to data analysis in statistics education develop as the field of statistics changes with the new techniques of data exploration and data analysis tools (Ben-Zvi & Garfield, 2004; Biehler, 2001). Moreover, the use of technological tools clearly offers new ways to support the development of students' statistical reasoning through providing students with dynamic construction of statistical concepts (Bakker & Gravemeijer, 2004; Ben-Zvi, 2000). Furthermore, in the field of statistics education research, one can trace the shift in emphasis on statistical topics and ideas in instruction: From a focus solely on measures of central tendency to the idea of variation in reasoning about data (Shaughnessy, 2004); focus on the big ideas, such as the notion of distribution, rather than a collection of loosely related topics (McClain, Cobb & Gravemeijer, 2000); and linking probability and statistics through the topics of variation on probability sample space (Reading &

Shaughnessy, 2000) and statistical inference (Pfannkuch, Budgett, Parsonage & Horring, 2004; Watson & Moritz, 1999).

Assessment

One major effect of constructivism was that it opened up the topic of assessment. Assessment was viewed as a means to support constructivist practices in a variety of ways. First, concerns were raised that the traditional testing approaches failed to evaluate students' knowledge sufficiently with their focus on multiple-choice format or solely on the production of answers. Secondly, assessments were viewed as key contributors to students' awareness of their own learning and to increasing their ability towards reflective abstraction (Bell, Swan, Onslow, Pratt, Purdy, et al., 1985; Simon, Tzur, Heinz & Kinzel, 2004). Thirdly, researchers focused on using richer tasks to give teachers increased understanding of student reasoning, and as a means to support constructivist curricular changes, and to strengthen teachers' diagnostic teaching (Schoenfeld, 1998). The Shell Centre in Nottingham linked up to researchers in the United States (Berkeley, Michigan State) to form MARS as web-based resource for the development of these initiatives (http://www.nottingham.ac.uk/education/MARS) and Balanced Assessment (http://www.nottingham.ac.uk/education/MARS/services/ba.htm). Given the importance of assessment in instruction, a number of researchers have realized that providing teachers direct access to artifacts of student work proves to be an excellent means to engage them in examining their own beliefs and in looking more deeply into student thinking and reasoning.

Teaching and teacher education

Constructivist theory has had a dramatic effect on teacher education. It has been repeatedly debated whether constructivism entails a theory of teaching (Bauersfeld, 1995; Kilpatrick, 1987; Simon, 1995; Steffe & Gale, 1995). The argument is a critical and complex one. It derives from the question "what is constructivism a theory of?" If it is an explanatory model of how learning occurs, then it is not clear that it can be directly transformed into a normative theory of what teachers ought to do? If it is a theory of "good learning", then what a teacher should do is to promote constructivist learning. Or possibly, constructivism itself is not sufficient to produce a theory of teaching; an additional theoretical framework for mathematics pedagogy are needed (Simon, 1995, p. 117).

To resolve this dilemma, a number of researchers have been engaged in developing pedagogical frameworks that focus on the design of tasks, planning of lessons, stimulating, guiding and supporting students' discourse and activities, creating a learning environment and analyzing and assessing student work and progress. Brousseau's work on the didactical contract and how to devise tasks that leads students to take responsibility for the problem, devolution is one such example (Balacheff, 1990). Douady (1986) discussed how this becomes "situations for institutionalization". Confrey (1998) discussed the dialectic of voice and perspective, where the voice of the student is interpreted through the teachers' perspective and likewise, the perspective of the teacher is transformed as she views her on knowledge through the voice of the student. Similarly, Ball (1993) refers to the "bifocal perspective" (p. 159). Ball described teaching as "essentially an ongoing inquiry into content and learners and into ways that contexts can be structured to facilitate the development of learner's understanding" (p. 166). And researchers examine how teachers negotiate student trajectories of learning (Confrey, 1998; Simon, 1995).

These initial work on teaching has been complemented by the profound influence of constructivism on teacher education around the world. Much of this has been stimulated through an ongoing series of working groups by PME members and the products of scholarship produced by them. They recognize that teachers need to both learn about constructivist learning, and experience mathematics from a constructivist perspective. Researchers in PME have thus conducted studies of teacher education (Ball, 1993; Bauersfeld, 1995; Jaworski, 1991, 1994; Ma, 1999; Simon, 1988) and at least three volumes of studies (Jaworski, Wood & Dawson, 1999; Ellerton, 1999; Zack, Mousley & Breen, 1997). In most cases, they have determined that teachers need time to both engage with the material as learners within a constructivist paradigm and to consider what this implies for their practice. At the current time, there is particular interest in three arenas: How to describe the nature of teachers' knowledge as illustrated in Ma's (1999) "profound understanding of fundamental mathematics", in Ball's current characterizations of teacher knowledge (Bass & Ball, 2005), and in Japanese professional development process "Lesson Study" (Yoshida, 1999).

Methodology

Over the course of the past thirty years, there have been a number of developments in the methods of conducting research. Piaget was the inventor of the "clinical method" (Piaget, 1976), which led to extensive use of clinical interviews by scholars in PME. Writings on the conduct of the interview were presented by Ginsburg (1997), Opper (1977) and Steffe, Cobb & Von Glasersfeld (1988). One major shift in that work was the recognition that the purpose of the interview is for the interviewer to build a model of the student's evolving conceptions. The role of the interviewer became clearer, the interviews extended over longer periods of time, and interviews were described by learners as learning experiences, the clinical interview began to be replaced by teaching experiments (Cobb, 2000; Confrey & Lachance, 2000; Lesh & Kelly, 2000; Simon, 2000). These were repurposed from the Russian didactical community and led to extended studies of student and student-teacher interactions. Simultaneously, the learning sciences evolved as a sub-field (Sawyer, in press) and as it did, design experiments were added to the repertoire of constructivist methodologies. In "Design Experiments in Educational Research", Cobb, Confrey, diSessa, Lehrer and Schauble (2003) identified five cross-cutting features of design experimentation towards "develop[ing] a class of theories about both the process of learning and the means that are designed to support that learning, be it the learning of individual students, of a classroom community, of a professional teaching community, or of a school or school district viewed as an organization" (p. 10). These five features of design research indicated that they were: (1) Highly interventionist in vision, (2) Design-based, (3) Theory generative, (4) Built and revised based on iterative revisions and feedback, (5) Ecologically valid- and practice oriented. More recently, Confrey (in press) wrote a chapter on the evolution of design studies and in it, she described the goal of design studies to provide a perspective on conceptual corridors in which one creates a set of constraints for development within a broad web of relations and then conducts design experiments to identify likely landmarks and obstacles along that corridor. The expectation is not to reproduce a learning trajectory to be increase the likelihood of successful learning by defining a corridor of possible opportunities and constraints and recognizable typical patterns for use by teachers in conducting practice.

In reviewing these nine areas of constructivist practice (bridging theories, grounding in activity and tools, alternative perspectives and developmental sequences, multiple representations, socio-constructivist norms, new content topics, assessment, teaching and teacher education and methodology), we have sought to acknowledge that constructivism has had a profound impact on the field. Further, we have identified a set of key themes that provide critical links between the ten principles and the ongoing practices of schools.

PART 5: IS CONSTRUCTIVISM PROGRESSING, DEGENERATING, OR STATIC?

Constructivism's influence on mathematics education is, in our opinion, unfortunately, waning while simultaneously being welcomed anew in places where it has not been yet, such as Singapore and Turkey. One wonders if this is because some of its key ideas have been "taken for granted" so completely they bear little explicit reference or constructivism's potential was exhausted, other ideas are proving more compelling, or because the field tends to be fickle, changing theories too frequently. We suspect that two influences account for the shift: (1) The field lacks maturity in how to use theory and systematically accumulate findings and results; and (2) The understanding of the social-cultural, political and economic forces that influence mathematics learning has drawn attention away. While we acknowledge the value of situating constructivism in relation to broader patterns and trends, we warn that attention to issues of content must be maintained if the work is to adequately serve mathematics education. Even as we offer these observations, we see areas in which progress continues and thus we end the chapter with a discussion of these topics as particularly worthy projections of the constructivist research programme.

We suggest that constructivism has not been adequately understood as a grand theory. Drawing on Lakatos (1976), we would argue that constructivism constitutes a research programme, with a theoretical hardcore, that does not directly predict empirical data, but is protected by a belt of bridging theories. At its core, we are arguing that the ten principles outlined in the second section provide a description of the theoretical hardcore of constructivist theory and avoid the polarization into trivial and radical constructivism generated by the two-principle summary. We see the epistemological dimension of the framework, as captured in genetic epistemology as central to the theory and as holding further potential for investigations. Thus, we reject statements which suggest that constructivism is solely individualistic, solipsistic, or lacking a view of objectivity (Goldin, 1989, 2002).

In order to address our concerns about the use of theory to inform practice and the means to evaluate the quality of empirical data, we argue for the need for more specific and elaborated bridging theories. These theories do more than to restate the principles, as they should spell out how the theory translates into practice and yield testable and refutable hypotheses and conjectures. A challenge presented by this approach is that bridging theories are often curricular specific, and the generalizability of the research for international consumption may become restricted and difficult to share at that level. This may force us to articulate new ways of conducting and reporting research. We see three kinds of theories that provide the kinds of theory-driven empirical work we have in mind.

One set of bridging theories has an explicit design or engineering orientation and presents an overall theory of instructional approach. The design orientation embraces the novelty associated with design propelling it beyond what has been established in research and yet addressing all the elements of instructional practice, in an ongoing way through design studies or teaching experiments conducted over long periods of time. The goal is document the effects of the theoretical work on students' reasoning across a variety of topics, and should lead to clear forms of prediction based on the continuity and duration of the studies. Instructional design theories, such as RME, or didactical engineering, represent such examples.

Curricular innovations with subsequent evaluation represent another type of bridging theory (Mathematical Sciences Education Board, 2004). In these, a full curriculum is developed meeting the needs of the particular context in which it is implemented (e.g., Singapore Math, Connected Math, etc.). Studies on the effectiveness of these curricula report on the intended, enacted and achieved curricula, and link these with a variety of measures of student performance.

A third approach is to articulate clear and explicit views of the structure of particular sub-domain, such as statistics, rational number, or class of algebraic functions and to treat them as a conceptual field (Vergnaud, 1996). In these studies, the emphasis is on how students' thinking evolves as they are provided sequences of tasks designed to highlight what is possible and likely in students' approaches and in hypothesizing about their conceptual structures. In all such initiatives, we would expect to see explicit attention to the concepts, situations, properties, proof forms, representations, algorithms and structures. Some kind of genetic-epistemological analysis would accompany the articulation of these constructs of mathematics over time. The empirical work could be comparative, or it could be a documentation what was learned, how and when over what particular students. As stated in Confrey and Lachance (2000), the development of a conjecture followed by clear, measurement-based indicators of student work (i.e., test results, scoring by rubric, and other means to dimensionalizing and categorizing student accomplishments) and thinking would have to accompany the research analysis. The work would be expected to be followed by the development of a stable, repeatable and well-defined product or process that could be tested in a more scaled and systematic way and would depend on the creation of shared outcome measures for use across research initiatives focused on similar or related content. While the product of the design experiments can support multiple realizations and elaborations as stated in the corridor concept (Confrey, in press), key indicators would be held stable to permit comparative analysis within the class over time.

It is easy to become distracted from the central effort of articulating, developing, refining and evaluating conceptual corridors for all of the major strands of mathematics, and to date, attention to some has overwhelmed attention to the other key topics. In reviewing the past thirty years, we see significant amounts of repetition and rediscovery of ideas, a proliferation of new terms for similar occurrences, an absence of negotiation and agreement on controversies, and a paucity of careful empirical study beyond initial experimentation. We further see a dearth of synthesis of prior work with identification of key topics for extensions. We find ourselves guilty of these same sins, and we propose that part of the reason for it is that too often, we have worked with a grand theory at a cost to the specificity of a bridging theory. Bridging theories are more likely to be subject to falsifiability if they fail to achieve improved student performance on valid assessments. The field needs to work to reduce its advocacy and strengthen its reliance on evidence that can be understood and accepted by experienced practitioners. This is in part due to the small number of us in the field, and the multiple demands on our time (research, teaching teachers, conducting in-service, preparing materials, etc.), but it has contributed to our tendency to be cavalier about our uses of theory, dismissive of others, and imprecise about our own. Perhaps some of the reason that theories have such short lives is due to this lack of deeper analysis and negotiation of resolutions to controversies. The maturity of the field will be evident when these changes decelerate.

We further believe that socio-cultural perspectives have gained in stature in the field which has diverted attention to constructivist research. While we believe that strengthening students' agency, their beliefs in their rights, claims and abilities to learn mathematics is a critical element of change, making the subject compelling, organizing for successful and deep learning, and ensuring that teachers know the content in a substantive way are also imperative. We raise the concern that as socio-cultural perspectives have gained force, less and less attention is being paid to the environmental/contextual/physical issues raised by constructivist scholars. As a result, less emphasis is being paid to the mathematics itself, how it is learned and how to communicate that to teachers. We reject the view that this can be cast as simply individualistic vs. cultural or social; we further reject the view that knowledge in the two views should be cast as cognitive vs. culturally distributed. Rather, we prefer the view that mathematics learning entails critical elements of grounded activity and socio-cultural communication and that these components interact in important and interesting ways. Constructivism, more than any other theory to date, has emphasized the importance of development and growth, in understanding learning. It clearly recognized that both biological-physical-environmental forces and social-cultural-political forces affect that process. What constructivism did is to locate the primary source of mathematical knowledge in patterns that can be generated in relation to biological/physical/environmental surroundings, and to recognize how the socio-cultural context signifies, facilitates/retards, and shapes that learning, while keeping the individual as the primary unit of analysis embedded in groups, classes, schools, communities and cultures. Neither influence is viewed as primary, nor can either instance be in fact separated due to our membership as observers and participants in all these enterprises, at all times.

A revised grand theory that draws upon constructivism and socio-cultural perspectives fully enough to satisfy the proponents of each is likely to emerge. This theory will need to address both theoretical and methodological elements and is likely to propose a mixed method approach that is staged over time. It will need to address in a broader way than constructivism how to engage students in the reasons for the pursuit of mathematical or scientific proficiency, and pay careful attention to the larger social and cultural issues surrounding such decisions. In addition, it will recognize the acculturation involved in engaging in the practice of mathematizing, while ensuring careful attention to the development of independent thought and precise patterns of reasoning. To do this, multiple units of analysis will be precisely and carefully linked.

In projecting forward the future development of constructivism, we see the need to continue to recognize the changes in a technological society and their impact on schooling. Research on how professionals and experts work effectively (Greeno & Hall, 1997; Hall, 1995, 1998) provide insight into the real ways in which the socio-cultural and the environmental/physical/tool-based, media-based business of technological work is conducted, and too few students in schools have knowledge of how mathematics is embedded in these diverse settings, much less what kinds of work are available and needed. These environments/working circumstances have potential to both attract students into quantitative disciplines and compel them to work hard to be successful. What then remains is to consider how such connections are linked to the constructivist research programme.

We predict, with others, that research on modeling in mathematics represents a key bridge and is likely to be one rightful successor to constructivism (Confrey & Maloney, 2005; Gravemeijer & Stephan, 2002; Lehrer & Pritchard, 2002; Lesh & Doerr, 2003). Within such a perspective, one views knowledge construction as the mapping of and exploration of the systematicity of relations between a base and a target domain. The reason we make a claim of succession is epistemological, as modeling can address the dual challenges of providing a focus on coherence views of truth, while replacing the correspondence theory with a viable alternative. Correspondence is cast as the relationship between two domains of understanding, one secure and then other more uncertain, rather than between an individual and an external reality. However, those two domains can be of varied levels of abstraction. Moreover, one can compare and contrast a variety of types of models, and hence produce a more nuanced continuum for guiding students' mathematical development. Lehrer and Schauble (2000) provided a four-part taxonomy of modeling designed to move from literal resemblance to relational structure: Physical microcosms (e.g. a physical model of an elbow), representational systems (e.g. a map), syntactical models (e.g. modeling phenomena as a coin toss) and hypothetical-deductive models (e.g. modeling gas as collisions of billiard balls). As students move increasingly towards the hypothetical-deductive models, one expects significant use of coherence as a means of deciphering relationships and producing predictions beyond the physical correspondences, obtaining the mathematics of axiomatic systems. At the other end of the spectrum, children are confronted with the challenge of understanding how one explains the source of mathematical ideas can be rooted physical settings. Representational systems begin to reveal the potential insights obtained by comparing and contrasting multiple representations, in which consistency is sought, while differences are used to highlight new features and assist in establishing warrant for various conjectures. Across the spectrum, Lehrer and Schauble emphasize the mathematical underpinnings of the effort in the acts of quantification, the creation of measure, the understanding of data and probability, and/or the development of a spatial form of reference. A modeling approach brings together mathematics with other disciplines, while also reserving significant time for developing its internal relations and meanings. Much more work remains on how the development of model-based reasoning emerges, but we see significant promise in this area as the epistemological successor to constructivist epistemology.

Overall, constructivism has had an impressive impact on mathematics education, in that it has propelled the children into the forefront of activity and asked genuine questions about how to make effective use of the resources, language, inscriptions, and ideas they bring to the enterprise of learning. It has produced many practical accomplishments from curricula to new technological tools, as well as documented a number of substantial considerations of student thinking about which all teachers need to know. Because of the theory, we have realized that careful attention must be paid to how students become increasing aware of what they believe and know, and how this is refined and developed in the company of others. Our views of the role of teachers has been transformed to recognize their critical contributions as stimulators, guides, facilitators and critics – assisting students in developing the fundamental reasoning abilities that are the hallmark of mathematics as students complete a tour of the rich variety of topics in the fields. We end our chapter with the humble recognition that the task we undertook, to summarize thirty years of scholarship across the globe, was impossible; and that we have been able only to identify some critical moments, to summarize some key principles, and to reflect on some of the major legacies of constructivism. We have not recognized all the contributions adequately and apologize in advance to those whose ideas were not selected to illustrate the key points. Our examples were no doubt influenced by our own context and experience of the field, though we worked diligently to recognize contributions across the world. With these limitations in mind, we can say without a doubt, that PME has played a most substantial role in the development of constructivist theory, critical in making the theory an international effort. It is our hope, then, that the synthesis offered here can assist in guiding us to continued productivity and significant and compelling advances over the next thirty years.

ACKNOWLEDGMENT

The authors acknowledge Marcelo de Carvalho Borba for his careful review of the article and his contributions to multiple sections. We also acknowledge the helpful reviews by Barbara Jaworski and Pearla Nesher. The final opinions in the article are those of the authors, who benefited significantly from the thoughtful comments and insights of the reviewers.

REFERENCES

Artigue, M. (1987). Ingénierie didactique à propos d'équations differentielles. In J. C. Bergeron, N. Herscovics, & C. Kieran (Eds.), *Proceedings of the 11th PME International Conference*, *3*, 236–242.

Artigue, M. (1990). Ingénierie didactique. *Recherches en Didactique des Mathématiques*, *9*, 283–307.

Artigue, M. (1992). The importance and limits of epistemological work in didactics. In W. Geeslin & K. Graham (Eds.), *Proceedings of the 16th PME International Conference*, *3*, 195–216.

Arzarello, F., Micheletti, C., Olivero, F., Robutti, O., Paola, D., & Gallino, G. (1998). Dragging in cabri and modalities of transition from conjectures to proofs in geometry. In A. Olivier & K. Newstead (Eds.), *Proceedings of the 22nd PME International Conference*, *2*, pp. 32–39.

Bachelard, G. (1938). *La formation de l'esprit scientifique*. Paris, France: Vrin.

Bakker, A., & Gravemeijer, K. (2004). Learning to reason about distribution. In D. Ben-Zvi & J. Garfield (Eds.), *The challenge of developing statistical literacy, reasoning and thinking* (pp. 147–168). Dordrecht, The Netherlands: Kluwer.

Balacheff, N. (1990). Towards a problematique for research on mathematics teaching. *Journal for Research in Mathematics Education, 21*(4), 258–272.

Balacheff, N. (1993). Artificial intelligence and real teaching. In C. Keitel & K. Ruthven (Eds.), *Learning from computers: Mathematics education and technology* (pp. 131–158). Berlin, Germany: Springer.

Ball, D. L. (1993). Halves, pieces, and twoths: Constructing representational contexts in teaching fractions. In T. P. Carpenter, E. Fennema, & T. A. Romberg (Eds.), *Rational numbers: An integration of research* (pp. 157–196). Hillsdale, NJ, USA: Lawrence Erlbaum.

Bartolini Bussi, M. (1993). Geometrical proofs and mathematical machines: An exploratory study. In I. Hirabayashi, N. Nohda, K. Shigematsu, & F.-L. Lin (Eds.), *Proceedings of the 17th PME International Conference*, *2*, pp. 97–104.

Bass, H., & Ball, D. L. (2005). *Mathematical knowledge for teaching*. Presentation at the MET Summit II Follow-up Conference, Atlanta, GA, USA.

Bauersfeld, H. (1995). The structuring of the structures: Development and function of mathematizing as a social practice. In L. P. Steffe & G. Gale (Eds.), *Constructivism in education* (pp. 137–158). Hillsdale, NJ, USA: Lawrence Erlbaum.

Bauersfeld, H. (1998). Remarks on the education of elementray teachers. In M. Larochelle, N. Bednarz, & J. Garrison (Eds.), *Constructivism and education* (pp. 195–212). New York, NY, USA: Cambridge University Press.

Baulac, Y., Bellemain, F., & Laborde, J. M. (1988). Cabri-géomètre (v. 1.7) [Computer program]. Paris, France: Cedic-Nathan.

Behr, M., Lesh, R., Post, T., & Silver, E. (1983). Rational number concepts. In R. Lesh & M. Landau (Eds.), *Acquisition of mathematics concepts and processes* (pp. 9–61). New York, USA: Academic Press.

Bell, A., Swan, M., Onslow, B., Pratt, K., Purdy, D., et al. (1985). *Diagnostic teaching for long term learning* (ESRC Project No. HR8491/1). Nottingham, UK : Shell Centre for Mathematical Education, University of Nottingham.

Ben-Zvi, D. (2000). Toward understanding the role of technological tools in statistical learning. *Mathematical Thinking and Learning, 2*, 127–155.

Ben-Zvi, D., & Garfield, J. (2004). Statistical literacy, reasoning, and thinking: Goals, definitions, and challenges. In D. Ben-Zvi & J. Garfield (Eds.), *Challenges in developing statistical reasoning, thinking, and literacy* (pp. 3–16). Dordrecht, The Netherlands: Kluwer.

Biehler, R. (2001). Developing and assessing students' reasoning in comparing statistical distributions in computer-supported statistics courses. In C. Reading (Ed.), *Proceedings of the 2nd International Research Forum on Statistical Reasoning, Thinking, and Literacy (SRLT-2)*. Armidale, Australia: University of New England.

Blakemore, C. (1973). Environmental constraints on development in the visual system. In R. A. Hinde & J. Stevenson-Hinde (Eds.), *Constraints on learning*. New York, USA: Academic Press.

Blum, W. (1993). Mathematical modelling in mathematics education and instruction. In T. Breiteig, I. Huntley, & G. Kaiser-Messmer (Eds.), *Teaching and learning mathematics in context* (pp. 3–14). New York, USA: Ellis Horwood.

Borba, M. (1993). *Students' understanding of transformations of functions using multi-representational software*. Unpublished PhD dissertation, Cornell University, Ithaca, NY, USA.

Borba, M. (1994). A model for students' understanding in a multi-representational environment. In J. P. Ponte & J. F. Matos (Eds.), *Proceedings of the 18th PME International Conference, 2*, pp. 104–111.

Borba, M. (1995). Overcoming limits of software tools: A student's solution for a problem involving transformation of functions. In L. Meira & D. Carraher (Eds.), *Proceedings of the 19th PME International Conference, 2*, 248–255.

Borba, M., & Confrey, J. (1996). A student's construction of transformations of functions in a multiple representational environment. *Educational Studies in Mathematics, 31*, 319–337.

Borba, M., & Scheffer, N. (2004). Coordination of multiple representations and body awareness [videopaper]. *Educational Studies in Mathematics, 57*(3) [on CD-ROM], 16 min. video (132 Kb), 126 text pages, 118 images (1156 Kb).

Borba, M. C., & Villarreal, M. E. (2005). *Humans-with-media and the reorganization of mathematical thinking information and communication technologies, modeling, experimentation and visualization*. New York, USA: Springer.

Brousseau, G. (1983). Les obstacles épistémologique et les problèmes en mathématiques. *Revue Internationale de Philosophie Recherches en Didactique des Mathématiques, 4*, 165–198.

Brousseau, G. (1984). The crucial role of the didactical contract in the analysis and construction of situations in teaching and learning mathematics. In H. G. Steiner (Ed.), *Theory of mathematics education* (ICME-5 Topic Area and miniconference) (pp. 110–119). Bielefeld, Germany: Institut für Didaktik der Mathematik, Universität Bielefeld.

Brousseau, G. (1997). *Theory of didactical situations in mathematics*. Dordrecht, The Netherlands: Kluwer.

Brown, J. S., Collins, A., & Duguid, P. (1989). Situated cognition and the culture of learning. *Educational Research, 18*, 32–42.

Burkhardt, H. (1981). *The real world and mathematics*. Glasgow, UK: Blackie and Son.

Carpenter, T. P., Fennema, E., Franke, M. L., Levi, L., & Empson, S. (1999). *Children's mathematics: Cognitively guided instruction*. Portsmouth, NH, USA: Heinemann.

Carpenter, T. P., Moser, J. M., & Romberg, T. (1982). *Addition and subtraction: A cognitive approach*. Hillsdale, NJ, USA: Lawrence Erlbaum.

Carraher, T. N., & Schliemann, A. D. (1988). Culture, arithmetic and mathematical models. *Cultural Dynamics, 1*, 180–194.

Chevallard, Y. (1988). *Sur l'analyse didactique: Deux études sur els notions de contrat et de situation*. Marseille, France: IREM 14.

Clements, D. H., & Battista, M. T. (1992). Geometry and spatial reasoning. In D. A. Grouws (Ed.), *Handbook of research on mathematics teaching and learning* (pp. 420–464). New York, USA: Macmillan.

Cobb, P. (2000). Conducting teaching experiments in collaboration with teachers. In A. E. Kelly & R. Lesh (Eds.), *Handbook of research design in mathematics and science education* (pp. 307–333). Mahwah, NJ, USA: Lawrence Erlbaum.

Cobb, P., Confrey, J., diSessa, A., Lehrer, R., & Shauble, L. (2003). Design experiments in educational research. *Educational Researcher, 32*, 9–13.

Cobb, P., Gravemeijer, K. P. E., Bowers, J., & McClain, K. (2001). Statistical minitools (Version Revised). Utrecht, The Netherlands: The Freudenthal Institute, Utrecht University.

Cobb, P., & Steffe, L. P. (1983). The constructivist researcher as teacher and model builder. *Joumal for Research in Mathematics Education, 14*, 83–94.

Cobb, P., Yackel, E., & Wood, T. (1990). Classrooms as learning environments for teachers and researchers. In R. B. Davis, C. A. Maher, & N. Noddings (Eds.), *Constructivist views on the teaching and learning of mathematics* (pp. 125–146). Reston, VA: NCTM.

Confrey, J. (1984). Towards a framework for constructivist instruction. In J. M. Moser (Ed.), *Proceedings of the 6th PME–NA Annual Meeting, 1*, 477–483.

Confrey, J. (1990). A review of the research on student conceptions in mathematics, science, and programming. In C. Cazden (Ed.), *Review of research in education* (16, pp. 3–56). Washington, DC, USA: American Educational Research Association (AERA).

Confrey, J. (1991). Learning to listen: A student's understanding of powers of ten. In E. von Glasersfeld (Ed.), *Radical constructivism in mathematics education* (pp. 111–138). Dordrecht, The Netherlands: Kluwer.

Confrey, J. (1995). How compatible are radical constructivism, sociocultural approaches, and social constructivism? In L. P. Steffe & G. Gale (Eds.), *Constructivism in education* (pp. 185–225). Hillsdale, NJ, USA: Lawrence Erlbaum.

Confrey, J. (1998). Voice and perspective: Hearing epistemological innovation in students' words. In M. Larochelle, N. Bednarz, & J. Garrison (Eds.), *Constructivism and education* (pp. 104–120). New York, NY, USA: Cambridge University Press.

Confrey, J. (in press). The evolution of design studies as methodology. In K. Sawyer (Ed.), *Cambridge handbook of the learning sciences*.

Confrey, J., & Costa, S. (1996). A critique of the selection of "mathematical objects" as a central metaphor for advanced mathematical thinking. *International Journal of Computers for Mathematical Learning, 2*, 139–168.

Confrey, J., & Lachance, A. (2000). Transformative teaching experiments through conjecture-driven research design. In A. Kelly & R. Lesh (Eds.), *Handbook of research design in mathematics and science education* (pp. 231–266). Mahwah, NJ, USA: Lawrence Erlbaum.

Confrey, J., & Maloney, A. (1991). Function Probe [Computer program]. Santa Barbara, CA, USA

Confrey, J., & Maloney, A. (2005). A theory of mathematical modeling in technological settings. In ICMI (Ed.), *Applications and modelling in mathematics education*. Berlin, Germany: Springer.

Confrey, J., & Smith, E. (1989). Alternative representations of ratio: The Greek concept of anthyphairesis and modern decimal notation. In D. E. Herget (Ed.), *The history and philosophy of science in science education: Proceedings of the 1st International Conference* (pp. 71–82). Tallahassee, FL, USA: Science Education & Department of Philosophy, Florida State University.

D'Ambrosio, U. (1985). Ethnomathematics and its place in the history and pedagogy of mathematics. *For the Learning of Mathematics, 5*, 44–48.

De Lange, J. (1987). *Mathematics, insight, and meaning*. Utrecht, The Netherlands: OW & OC.

De Lange, J. (2001). The P in PME : Progress and problems in mathematics education, In M. van den Heuvel-Panhuizen (Ed.), *Proceedings of the 25th PME International Conference, 1*, 3–4.

Dennis, D. (1995). *Historical perspectives for the reform of mathematics curriculum: Geometric curve drawing devices and their role in the transition to an algebraic description of functions.* Unpublished PhD dissertation, Cornell University, Ithaca, NY, USA.

Désautels, J. (1998). Constructivism-in-action: students examine their idea of science. In M. Larochelle, N. Bednarz, & J. Garrison (Eds.), *Constructivism and education* (pp. 121–138). New York, USA: Cambridge University Press.

diSessa, A., & Cobb, P. (2004). Ontological innovation and the role of theory in design experiments. *The Journal of the Learning Sciences, 13*(1), 77–103.

Douady, R. (1986). Jeu des cadres et dialectique outil-objet. *Recherches en Didactiques des Mathématiques, 7*, 5–31.

Dreyfus, T. (1993). Didactic design of computer-based learning environments. In C. Keitel & K. Ruthven (Eds.), *Learning from computers: Mathematics, education, and technology* (pp. 101–130). New York, NY: Springer.

Driver, R., & Easley, J. (1978). Pupils and paradigms: A review of literature related to concept development in adolescent science students. *Studies in Science Education, 5*, 61–84.

Dubinsky, E., & McDonald, M. (2001). Apos: A constructivist theory of learning in undergraduate mathematics education research. In D. Holton (Ed.), *The teaching and learning of mathematics at university level* (pp. 273–280). Dordrecht, The Netherlands: Kluwer.

Ellerton, N. F. (Ed.). (1999). *Mathematics teacher development: International perspectives*. Perth, Australia: Meridian Press.

Ernest, P. (1991a). Constructivism, the psychology of learning, and the nature of mathematics. In F. Furinghetti (Ed.), *Proceedings of the 15th PME International Conference, 2*, pp. 25–32.

Ernest, P. (1991b). *The philosophy of mathematics education.* Bristol, PA, USA: The Falmer Press, Taylor and Francis Inc.

Finzer, W. (2001). *Fathom dynamic statistics* (v. 1.16) [Computer program]. Emeryville, CA, USA: KCP Technologies.

Freudenthal, H. (1991). *Revisiting mathematics education. China lectures.* Dordrecht, The Netherlands: Kluwer.

Fuson, K. C. (1988). *Children's counting and concepts of number.* New York, USA: Springer.

Gagné, R. M. (1965). *The conditions of learning.* New York, USA: Holt, Rinehart & Winston.

Garofalo, J., & Lester, F. K. (1985). Metacognition, cognitive monitoring, and mathematical performance. *Journal for Research in Mathematics Education, 16*, 163–176.

Ginsburg, H. P. (1989). *Children's arithmetic.* Austin, TX, USA: Pro-Ed.

Ginsburg, H. P. (1997). *Entering the child's mind: The clinical interview in psychological research and practice.* New York, USA: Cambridge University Press.

Goldin, G. A. (1989). Constructivist epistemology and discovery learning in mathematics. In G. Vergnaud, J. Rogalski, & M. Artigue (Eds.), *Proceedings of the 13th PME International Conference, 2*, pp. 15–22.

Goldin, G. A. (2002). Representation in mathematical learning and problem solving. In L. D. English (Ed.), *Handbook of international research in mathematics education* (pp. 197–218). Mahwah, NJ, USA: Lawrence Erlbaum.

Goldin, G. A., & Gennain, Y. (1983). The analysis of a heuristic process: "Think of a simpler problem". In J. C. Bergeron & N. Herscovics (Eds.), *Proceedings of the 5th PME–NA Annual Meeting, 2*, 121–128.

Gravemeijer, K. (1994). *Developing realistic mathematics education.* PhD dissertation, CD-ß Press / Freudenthal Institute, Utrecht, The Netherlands.

Gravemeijer, K. (1999). How emergent models may foster the constitution of formal mathematics. *Mathematical Thinking and Learning, 1*, 155–177.

Gravemeijer, K. (2002). Preamble: From models to modeling. In K. Gravemeijer, R. Lehrer, B. van Oers, & L. Verschaffel (Eds.), *Symbolizing, modeling and tool use in mathematics education* (pp. 7–24). Dordrecht, The Netherlands: Kluwer.

Gravemeijer, K., & Stephan, M. (2002). Emergent models as an instructional design heuristic. In K. Gravemeijer, R. Lehrer, B. van Oers, & L. Verschaffel (Eds.), *Symbolizing, modeling and tool use in mathematics education* (pp. 146–169). Dordrecht, The Netherlands: Kluwer.

Gray, E. M., & Tall, D. O. (1994). Duality, ambiguity and flexibility: A proceptual view of simple arithmetic. *Journal for Research in Mathematics Education, 25*, 115–141.

Greeno, J. (1989). Situations, mental models, and generative knowledge. In D. Klahr & K. Kotovsky (Eds.), *Complex information processing*. Hillsdale, NJ, USA: Lawrence Earlbaum.

Greeno, J. G., & Hall, R. P. (1997). Practicing representation: Learning with and about representational forms. *Phi Delta Kappan, 78*, 361–367.

Greer, B. (1987). Nonconservation of multiplication and division involving decimals. *Journal for Research in Mathematics Education, 18*, 37–45.

Gutiérrez, A. (1995). Learning dynamic geometry: Implementing rotations. In A. A. diSessa, C. Hoyles, & R. Noss (Eds.), *Computers and exploratory learning* (pp. 275–288). Berlin, Germany: Springer.

Gutiérrez, A., & Jaime, A. (1993). An analysis of the students' use of mental images when making or imagining movements of polyhedra. In I. Hirabayashi, N. Nohda, K. Shigematsu, & F.-L. Lin (Eds.), *Proceedings of the 17th PME International Conference, 2*, 153–160.

Hall, R. (1995). Exploring design-oriented mathematical practices in school and work settings. *Communications of the ACM*, 62.

Hall, R. (1998). *A case study of making and using representations of quantity in architectural design.* Unpublished manuscript, University of California, Berkeley, USA.

Harel, G., & Confrey, J. (1994). *Development of multiplicative reasoning in the learning of mathematics*. Albany, NY, USA: State University of New York Press.

Harel, I., & Papert, S. (1991). *Constructionism.* Norwood, NJ, USA: Ablex.

Hart, K. A. (1984). *Ratio: Children's strategies and errors*. Windsor, Berkshire, UK: NFER-Nelson.

Hawkins, D. (1978). Critical barriers to science learning. *Outlook, 3*, 3–25.

Hollebrands, K. (2002). The role of a dynamic software program for geometry in high school students' developing understandings of geometric transformations. In D. Mewborn (Ed.), *Proceedings of the 24th PME–NA Annual Meeting*, 695–706.

Hoyles, C., & Noss, R. (1988). Formalising intuitive descriptions in a parallelogram logo microworld. In A. Borbás (Ed.), *Proceedings of the 12th PME International Conference, 2*, 417–424.

Jackiw, N. (1991). The Geometer's Sketchpad [Computer program]. Berkeley, CA, USA: Key Curriculum Press.

James, W. (1907). *Pragmatism: A new name for some old ways of thinking.* New York, USA: Longman Green and Co.

Janvier, C. (1987). *Problems of representation in the learning of mathematics*. Hillsdale, NJ, USA: Lawrence Erlbaum.

Jaworski, B. (1991). Some implications of a constructivist philosophy for the teacher of mathematics. In F. Furinghetti (Ed.), *Proceedings of the 15th PME International Conference, 2*, 213–220.

Jaworski, B. (1994). Investigating mathematics teaching: A constructivist enquiry. London, UK: The Falmer Press.

Jaworski, B., Wood, T., & Dawson, A. J. (1999). *Mathematics teacher wducation: Critical international perspectives*. London: Falmer Press.

Kamii, C. K. (1985). *Young children reinvent arithmetic: Implications of Piaget's theory*. New York, USA: Columbia University, Teachers College Press.

Kaput, J. (1987). Representation and mathematics. In C. Janvier (Ed.), *Problems of representation in the learning of mathematics* (pp. 19–26). Hillsdale, NJ, USA: Lawrence Erlbaum.

Kaput, J. (2001). New activity structures exploiting wirelessly connected graphing calculators. In R. Speiser, C. Maher, & C. Walter (Eds.), *The Proceedings of the 23rd PME–NA Annual Meeting, 2*, 1017–1018.

Kieren, T. E. (1992). Rational and fractional numbers as mathematical and personal knowledge: Implications for curriculum and instruction. In G. Leinhardt, R. Putnam, & R. Hattrup (Eds.),

Analysis of arithmetic for mathematics teaching (pp. 323–372). Hillsdale, NJ, USA: Lawrence Erlbaum.

Kilpatrick, J. (1987). What constructivism might be in mathematics education. In J. C. Bergeron, N. Herscovics, & C. Kieran (Eds.), *Proceedings of the 11th PME International Conference, 1*, pp. 3–27.

Konold, C., & Miller, C. D. (2005). Tinkerplots dynamic data exploration (v. 1.0) [Computer program]. Emeryville, CA, USA: Key Curriculum Press.

Krutetskii, V. A. (1976). *The psychology of mathematical abilities in school children*. Chicago, IL, USA: The University of Chicago Press.

Laborde, C. (1993). The computer as part of the learning environment: The case of geometry. In C. Keitel & K. Ruthven (Eds.), *Learning from computers: Mathematics education and technology* (pp. 48–67). Berlin, Germany: Springer.

Lakatos, I. (1976). *Proofs and refutations*. Cambridge, UK: Cambridge University Press.

Larochelle, M., & Bednarz, N. (1998). Constructivism and education: Beyond epistemological correctness. In M. Larochelle, N. Bednarz, & J. Garrison (Eds.), *Constructivism and education* (pp. 3–20). New York, NY, USA: Cambridge University Press.

Lehrer, R., & Pritchard, C. (2002). Symbolizing space into being. In K. Gravemeijer, R. Lehrer, B. van Oers, & L. Verschaffel (Eds.), *Symbolizing, modeling and tool use in mathematics education* (pp. 59–86). Dordrecht, The Netherlands: Kluwer.

Lehrer, R., & Schauble, L. (2000). Modeling in mathematics and science. In R. Glaser (Ed.), *Advances in instructional psychology, Vol. 5: Educational design and cognitive science* (pp. 101–159). Mahwah, NJ, USA: Lawrence Erlbaum.

Lesh, R., & Doerr, H. (2003). *Beyond constructivism. Models and modeling perspectives on mathematics problem solving, learning, and teaching*. Mahwah, NJ, USA: Lawrence Erlbaum.

Lesh, R., & Kelly, A. E. (2000). Multitiered teaching experiments. In A. E. Kelly & R. Lesh (Eds.), *Handbook of research design in mathematics and science education* (pp. 197–230). Mahwah, NJ, USA: Lawrence Erlbaum.

Ma, L. (1999). *Knowing and teaching mathematics: Teachers understanding of fundamental mathematics in China and the United States*. Mahwah, NJ, USA: Lawrence Eribaum.

Maher, C. A., Speiser, R., Friel, S., & Konold, C. (1998). Learning to reason probabilistically. In S. Berenson, K. Dawkins, M. Blanton, W. Columbe, J. Kolb, & K. Norwood (Eds.), *Proceedings of the 20th PME–NA Annual Meeting, 1*, pp. 82–87.

Marrades, R., & Gutiérrez, A. (2000). Proofs produced by secondary school students learning geometry in a dynamic computer environment. *Educational Studies in Mathematics, 44*, 87–125.

Mathematical Sciences Education Board, N. R. C. (2004). *On evaluating curricular effectiveness: Judging the quality of k-12 mathematics evaluations*. Washington, DC, USA: The National Academies Press.

McClain, K., Cobb, P., & Gravemeijer, K. (2000). Supporting students' ways of reasoning about data. In M. J. Burke & F. R. Curico (Eds.), *Learning mathematics for a new century* (pp. 174–187). Reston, VA, USA: NCTM.

McDermott, J. J. (1981). *The philosophy of John Dewey*. Chicago, IL, USA: University of Chicago Press.

Meira, L. (1995). Mediation by tools in the mathematics classroom. In L. Meira & D. Carraher (Eds.), *Proceedings of the 19th PME International Conference, 1*, 102–111.

Monk, S., & Nemirovsky, R. (1994). The case of Dan: Student construction of a functional situation through visual attributes. In E. Dubinsky, A. H. Schoenfeld, & J. Kaput (Eds.), *Research in collegiate mathematics education. I* (pp. 139–168). Providence, RI, USA: American Mathematical Society.

Nakahara, T. (1997). Study of the constructive approach in mathematics education: Types of constructive interactions and requirements for the realization of effective interactions. In E. Pehkonen (Ed.), *Proceedings of the 21st PME International Conference, 3*, 272–279.

Nemirovsky, R. (2002). On guessing the essential thing. In K. Gravemeijer, R. Lehrer, B. van Oers, & L. Verschaffel (Eds.), *Symbolizing and modeling in mathematics education* (pp. 233–256). Dordrecht, The Netherlands: Kluwer.

Nemirovsky, R., & Borba, M. (2004). Bodily activity and imagination in mathematics learning. *Educational Studies in Mathematics*, *57*(3) [on CD-ROM].

Nesher, P. (1988a). Multiplicative school word problems: Theoretical approaches and empirical findings. In M. Behr & J. Hiebert (Eds.), *Number concepts and operations in the middle grades* (pp. 19–40). Reston, VA, USA: Lawrance Erlbaum and NCTM.

Nesher, P. (1988b). Beyond constructivism: Learning mathematics at school. In A. Borbás (Ed.), *Proceedings of the 12th PME International Conference*, *1*, 54–74.

Niss, M. (1992). Applications and modelling in school mathematics – directions for future development. In I. Wirzup & R. Streit (Eds.), *Development in school mathematics education around the world* (Vol. 31). Reston, VA, USA: NCTM.

Noelting, G. (1980). The development of proportional reasoning and the ratio concept: Part ii – problem structure at successive stages : Problem solving strategies and the mechanism of adaptive restructuring. *Educational Studies in Mathematics*, *11*(3), 331–363.

Opper, S. (1977). Piaget's clinical method. *Journal of Children's Mathematical Behavior*, *5*, 90–107.

Papert, S. (1993). *The children's machine: Rethinking school in the age of the computer*. New York, NY, USA: Basic Books.

Perry, B., & Dockett, S. (2002). Yound children's access to powerful mathematical ideas. In L. D. English (Ed.), *Handbook of international research in mathematics education* (pp. 81–111). Mahwah, NJ, USA: Lawrence Erlbaum.

Pfannkuch, M., Budgett, S., Parsonage, R., & Horring, J. (2004). *Comparison of data plots: Building a pedagogical framework*. Paper presented at ICME-10, Copenhagen, Denmark.

Piaget, J. (1954). *The construction of reality in the child*. New York, USA: Basic Books.

Piaget, J. (1976). *The child's conception of the world*. Totowa, NJ, USA: Littlefield.

Pirie, S., & Kieren, T. (1994). Growth in mathematical understanding: How can we characterise it and how can we represent it? *Educational Studies in Mathematics*, *26*, 165–190.

Polanyi, M. (1958). *Personal knowledge: Towards a post-critical philosophy*. Chicago, IL, USA: University of Chicago Press.

Polya, G. (1957). *How to solve it*. Princeton, NJ, USA: Princeton University Press.

Reading, C., & Shaughnessy, J. M. (2000). Students' perceptions of variation in a sampling situation. In T. Nakahara & M. Koyama (Eds.), *Proceedings of the 24th PME International Conference*, *4*, pp. 89–96.

Resnick, L., Nesher, P., Leonard, F., Magone, M., Omanson, S., & Peled, I. (1989). Conceptual bases of arithmetic errors: The case of decimal fractions. *Journal for Research in Mathematics Education*, *20*, 827.

Resnick, M. (1994). *Turtles, termites, and traffic jams, explorations in massively parallel microworlds*. Cambridge, MA, USA: MIT Press.

Resnick, M., & Ocko, S. (1991). Lego/Logo: Learning through and about design. In I. Harel & S. Papert (Eds.), *Constructionism* (Vol. 2). Norwood, NJ, USA: Ablex Publishing.

Sawyer, K. (in press). *Cambridge handbook of the learning sciences*.

Schoenfeld, A. H. (1985). *Mathematical problem solving*. Orlando, FL, USA: Academic Press.

Schoenfeld, A. H. (1998). Toward a theory of teaching-in-context. *Issues in Educational Research*, *4*, 1–94.

Schwartz, J., & Yerushalmy, M. (1985). *The Geometric Supposer* [Computer program]. Pleasantville, NY, USA: Sunburst Communications.

Schwartz, J. L., & Yerushalmy, M. (1988). *The Function Supposer: Explorations in algebra* [Computer program]. Pleasantville, NY, USA: Sunburst Communications.

Sfard, A. (1991). On the dual nature of mathematical conceptions: Reflections on processes and objects as different sides of the same coin. *Educational Studies in Mathematics*, *22*, 1–36.

Shapin, S., & Schaffer, S. (1989). *Leviathan and the air-pump: Hobbes, Boyle, and the experimental life*. Princeton, USA: Princeton University Press.

Shaughnessy, M. (2004). *Students' attention to variability when comparing distributions*. Paper Presented at the Research Presession of the 82nd Annual Meeting of the NCTM, Philadelphia, PA.

Sierpinska, A. (1990). Some remarks on understanding in mathematics. *For the Learning of Mathematics*, *10*, 24–36.

Sierpinska, A. (1992). On understanding the notion of function. In G. Harel & E. Dubinsky (Eds.), *The concept of function. Aspects of epistemology and pedagogy* (pp. 25–58). Washington, DC, USA: Mathematical Association of America.

Simon, M. A. (1988). Formative evaluation of a constructivist mathematics teacher inservice program. In A. Borbás (Ed.), *Proceedings of the 12th PME International Conference*, *2*, 576–583.

Simon, M. A. (1995). Reconstructing mathematics pedagogy from a constructivist perspective. *Journal for Research in Mathematics Education*, *26*, 114–145.

Simon, M. A. (2000). Research on the development of mathematics teachers: The teacher development experiment. In A. E. Kelly & R. Lesh (Eds.), *Handbook of research design in mathematics and science education* (pp. 335–359). Mahwah, NJ, USA: Lawrence Erlbaum.

Simon, M. A., Tzur, R., Heinz, K., & Kinzel, M. (2004). Explicating a mechanism for conceptual learning: Elaborating the construct of reflective abstraction. *Journal for Research in Mathematics Education*, *35*, 305–329.

Sinclair, H. (1987). Constructivism and the psychology of mathematics. In J. C. Bergeron, N. Herscovics, & C. Kieran (Eds.), *Proceedings of the 11th PME International Conference*, *1*, pp. 28–41.

Skemp, R. (1978). *The psychology of learning mathematics*. Hillsdale, NJ, USA: Lawrence Erlbaum.

Smith, E., Dennis, D., & Confrey, J. (1992). Rethinking functions: Cartesian construction. In S. Hills (Ed.), *Proceedings of the 2nd International Conference on the History and Philosophy of Science in Science Teaching* (2, pp. 449–466). Kingston, Ontario, Canada: Queens University.

Steffe, L. P. (1994). Children's multiplying schemes. In G. Harel & J. Confrey (Eds.), *The development of multiplicative reasoning in the learning of mathematics* (pp. 3–40). Albany, NY, USA: State University of New York Press.

Steffe, L. P. (1995). Alternative epistemologies: An educators' perspective. In L. Steffe & J. Gale (Eds.), *Constructivism in education* (pp. 489–523). Hillsdale, NJ, USA: Lawrence Erlbaum.

Steffe, L. P., Cobb, P., & Von Glasersfeld, E. (1988). *Young children's construction of arithmetical meanings and strategies*. New York, USA: Springer.

Steffe, L., & Gale, J. (1995). *Constructivism in education*. Hillsdale, NJ, USA: Lawrence Erlbaum.

Steffe, L. P., & Thompson, P. W. (2000). Teaching experiment methodology: Underlying principles and essential elements. In R. Lesh & A. E. Kelly (Eds.), *Research design in mathematics and science education* (pp. 267–307). Hillsdale, NJ, USA: Lawrence Erlbaum.

Steffe, L. P., Von Glasersfeld, E., Richards, J., & Cobb, P. (1983). *Children's counting types: Philosophy, theory, and application*. New York, USA: Praeger.

Streefland, L. (1991). *Fractions in realistic mathematics education. A paradigm of developmental research*. Dordrecht, The Netherlands: Kluwer.

Sutherland, R., & Rojano, T. (1993). A spreadsheet approach to solving algebra problems. *Journal of Mathematical Behavior*, *12*, 353–382.

Taimina, D. (2005). *Historical mechanisms for drawing curves*. Retrieved June 3, 2005, from http://techreports.library.cornell.edu:8081/Dienst/UI/1.0/Display/cul.htmm/2004-9

Tall, D. O. (Ed.). (1991). *Advanced mathematical thinking*. Dordrecht, The Netherlands: Kluwer.

Tall, D., & Vinner, S. (1981). Concept image and concept definition in mathematics with particular reference to limits and continuity. *Educational Studies in Mathematics*, *12*, 151–169.

Thompson, P. W. (2002). Didactic objects and didactic models in radical constructivism. In K. Gravemeijer, R. Lehrer, B. van Oers, & L. Verschaffel (Eds.), *Symbolizing and modeling in mathematics education* (pp. 197–220). Dordrechht, The Netherlands: Kluwer.

Thorndike, E. (1922). *The psychology of arithmetic*. New York, USA: Macmillan.

Van Hiele, P. M., & Van Hiele-Geldof, D. (1958). A method of initiation into geometry at secondary schools. In H. Freudenthal (Ed.), *Report on methods of initiation into geometry* (pp. 67–80). Groningen, The Netherlands: J. B. Wolters.

Vergnaud, G. (1982). A classification of cognitive tasks and operations of thought involved in addition and subtraction problems. In T. P. Carpenter, M. J. Moser, & T. A. Romberg (Eds.), *Addition and subtraction: A cognitive perspective* (pp. 39–58). Hillsdale, NJ, USA: Lawrence Erlbaum.

Vergnaud, G. (1987). About constructivism. In J. C. Bergeron, N. Herscovics, & C. Kieran (Eds.), *Proceedings of the 11th PME International Conference*, *1*, 42–54.

Vergnaud, G. (1996). The theory of conceptual fields. In L. Steffe & P. Nesher (Eds.), *Theories of mathematical learning* (pp. 219–239). Mahwah, NJ, USA: Lawrence Erlbaum.

Verschaffel, L., De Corte, E., & Vierstraete, H. (1999). Upper elementary school pupils' difficulties in modeling and solving nonstandard additive word problems involving ordinal numbers. *Journal for Research in Mathematics Education, 30*(3), 265–285.

Vinner, S., & Hershkowitz, R. (1980). Concept images and some common cognitive paths in the development of some simple geometric concepts. In R. Karplus (Ed.), *Proceedings of the 4th PME International Conference*, 177–184.

Voigt, J. (1985). Patterns and routines in classroom interaction. *Researches en Didactique de Mathématiques*, *6*(1), 69–118.

Von Foerster, H. (1984). On constructing a reality. In P. Watzlawick (Ed.), *Invented reality: How do we know what we believe we know?* (pp. 41–61). New York, USA: Norton.

Von Glasersfeld, E. (1982). An interpretation of Piaget's constructivism. *Revue Internationale de Philosophie*, *36*(142–143), 612–635.

Von Glasersfeld, E. (1990). An exposition of constructivism: Why some like it radical. In R. D. Davis, C. A. Maher, & N. Noddings (Eds.), *Constructivist views on the teaching and learning of mathematics* (JRME Monograph 4) (pp. 19–29). Reston, VA, USA: NCTM.

Von Glasersfeld, E. (1991). *Radical constructivism in mathematics education*. Dordrecht, The Netherlands: Kluwer.

Von Glasersfeld, E. (1995). *Radical constructivism: A way of knowing and learning*. London, UK: Falmer Press.

Watson, J. M., & Moritz, J. B. (1999). The beginning of statistical inference: Comparing two data sets. *Educational Studies in Mathematics*, *37*, 145–168.

Wheeler, D. (1987). The world of mathematics: Dream, myth or reality? In J. C. Bergeron, N. Herscovics, & C. Kieran (Eds.), *Proceedings of the 11th PME International Conference*, *1*, pp. 55–66.

Wood, T., Cobb, P., & Yackel, E. (1995). Reflections on learning and teaching mathematics in elementary school. In L. Steffe & J. Gale (Eds.), *Constructivism in education* (pp. 401–422). Hillsdale, NJ, USA: Lawrence Erlbaum.

Yoshida, M. (1999). *Lesson study: A case study of a japanese approach to improving instruction through school-based teacher development*. Unpublished PhD dissertation, University of Chicago, USA.

Zack, V., Mousley, J., & Breen, C. (1997). *Developing practice: Teachers inquiry and educational change*. Melbourne, Australia: Deakin University Press.

AFFILIATIONS

Jere Confrey
Department of Education,
Washington University in Saint Louis
St. Louis (U.S.A.)
jconfrey@artsci.wustl.edu

Sibel Kazak
Department of Education,
Washington University in Saint Louis
St. Louis (U.S.A.)
skazak@wustl.edu

STEPHEN LERMAN

SOCIO-CULTURAL RESEARCH IN PME

The International Group for the Psychology of Mathematics Education (PME) has grown in size, activity and importance within the mathematics education research community as a whole over the years since its first meeting in 1977. It is timely therefore for a review of PME's work and the role of this chapter is to examine particular aspects of the trends in the theoretical resources drawn upon by researchers in PME. In 1992 we can already find recognition of the developing range of theories in use amongst researchers in PME. Hoyles (1992) in a footnote to her plenary address regarding "the multitude of approaches adopted within and outside PME" listed the following: "Vygotsky, metacognition; constructivism; personal construct theory; psychoanalytic theory; social/cultural perspectives" (p. 281). My task is to examine the adoption of socio-cultural theories within and outside PME.

Some comments will be made about the trends in the use of those resources in the wider research community but the scope of forums for publications means that those comments will of necessity be only partial. The importance of PME as the leading international research group in the field has attracted the participation of many excellent mathematics education researchers whose orientation, as they would readily claim, would not come under PME's understanding of the term 'psychology' in the initial stages of the Group. Some of their work has appeared in Proceedings and at meetings either because the review process, inevitably a looser process than for research journals given the sheer size of the review operation, the eight-page limitation on word length, and the lack of opportunity for revision by authors, has allowed them into the Proceedings or because researchers have shaped their writing to fit the criteria. That all Research Reports must address the P (psychology), the M (mathematics) and the E (education) has been a constant concern for the International Committee (IC) and for members at annual general meetings but how to regulate the review process to ensure such compliance is an on-going task for the IC.

In any case, since educational research takes place in a knowledge-producing community, we are examining a field of practice. It is inevitable and, I would argue, healthy that there are disputes about what characterises any sub-group of the field and indeed the field itself. Given that socio-cultural theory is so close to sociology, anthropology and perhaps other fields that are clearly different from psychology, the issue being addressed in this chapter requires some consideration of what psychology is and what it is not, and I will therefore commence with some

A. Gutiérrez, P. Boero (eds.), Handbook of Research on the Psychology of Mathematics Education: Past, Present and Future, 347–366.

remarks on boundaries. I will then review the Proceedings from the first 29 meetings of PME and present an analysis in terms of socio-cultural research. I will be reviewing only Research Reports. The rationale for this is as follows:

- Research Reports represent the on-going work of members of the community
- Plenary speakers are chosen, for the most part, for one of a number of reasons: They are from the local community; they are to be honoured for having made major contributions to mathematics education research; as Presidents they are honoured with an invitation; their work represents an approach or orientation or focus that the Local Organising Committee and the IC wish to see represented in future PME work. It is only in this final case, I would argue, that the theme says something about the theoretical intellectual resources of the PME community. It is not possible, however, to retrace the decisions leading to the invitation of a Plenary speaker, not least of all because several of these reasons for choice of speaker often apply at any one time.
- The nature of Working Groups, Research Forums, Discussion Groups and others have changed substantially over the years, and were not even represented in Proceedings at first.
- Short Orals do not contain enough information, most of the time, to make a firm decision about their theoretical orientation. The same applies to Posters, as they appear in the Proceedings. I recognise that this is a loss to the analysis because posters and short orals are often followed the following year by full papers and therefore perhaps indicate future directions.

Following that analysis of Research Reports, I will relate socio-cultural research in PME to the work of the mathematics education research field as a whole. Finally I will suggest some trends and directions for PME's future research in relation to socio-cultural theories.

BOUNDARIES

Research within PME, and beyond in the wider field of research in mathematics education, draws on a range of theories, often drawing from other intellectual fields. In PME those theories are to support the promotion of studies in the psychology of mathematics education, according to the goals of the Group, whereas the wider community is of course not so restricted. The expansion of what constitutes the psychological theoretical base of PME research has played a major part in the soul-searching that has taken place over some years now (if it can be accepted that an organisation has a soul). Arguments have been made for a change of name and/or focus in an attempt to widen the goals and allow access legitimately to other intellectual fields. In practice, PME has been very accepting of a range of theories, as evidenced in the Proceedings, although some authors will readily admit that, at times, they distort their writing to make it acceptable. However, as is a feature of most intellectual fields, 'psychology' itself incorporates a diversity of theories and engages in disputes about the boundaries that demarcate it from other fields. In a recent discussion with a Professor of Psychology with a special interest in child development (D. Messer, personal communication), it was made clear to me that issues of the philosophy of psychology, of competing paradigms and, in particular, of the extent to which individual consciousness is a process of enculturation, of biology, of individual construction, or a combination of these, are regular features of conferences and other interactions within the psychological research community and in particular within the sub-fields of child and developmental psychology. Just as Margaret Brown suggested at the Hiroshima meeting in 2000 (Brown, 2000) that some in education and elsewhere may have a view of medical research that does not reflect how those within the field perceive it, and hence perpetuate a distorted goal of a medical model for research practice in education, so too we may have a view of psychology that is too narrow.

Thus, socio-cultural theories as they pertain to the development of cognition or of affect, or of the two together as a unit of analysis, are not outside of psychology as evidenced by the practices of that community. Under the umbrella of socio-cultural theories, where researchers have in fact turned to sociology, we may well have been in a position to say this is outside of the field, according to the aims in place until 2005. However, empirically, that is to say arising from an analysis of Proceedings, there will be Research Reports that are classified as drawing on sociology and we must recognise that is just a feature of the PME community. It should be noted that the research that has been carried out to provide this analysis is not psychological, but in that it is a study of the practices of a community it is itself sociology.

In conclusion, I am suggesting that 'psychology' is much broader than many perceive and hence the concerns of many of those who want to present their work at PME meetings but worry that 'psychology' is too narrow and thus excludes them are working under an illusion. It must be said that those who wish to tighten the brief to restrict the definition of 'psychology' are perhaps working under a similar illusion.

At the 29th annual meeting in Melbourne in July 2005 the annual general meeting voted to change the aims of the Group, retaining the psychological focus but widening it also to other theoretical perspectives. Nevertheless, the analysis in this chapter pertains to the research up to and including the 2005 meeting and hence precedes the constitutional change.

Defining the scope of the socio-cultural in PME

I will not go further in defining psychology but in order to set boundaries for the analysis for this chapter I must explain how I will count a Research Report as socio-cultural.

In a Guest Editorial for a special issue of *Educational Studies in Mathematics* in 1996 entitled "Socio-cultural Approaches to Mathematics Teaching and Learning" I defined these approaches as:

> The investigation of frameworks which build on the notion that the individual's cognition originates in social interactions (Harré, Gillett, 1994) and therefore the role of culture, motives, values, and social and discursive

> practices are central, not secondary ... The perspective to which I refer can be distinguished by its insertion of socially-situated meaning as mediating the development of consciousness, making psychology the study of how consciousness comes about. Other psychological theories take human consciousness as an *a priori* assumption and thereby remove it from the domain of study. Perhaps the most elaborated framework, particularly in relation to teaching and learning, is the materialist psychology of Vygotsky, the main elements of which are: That development is led by learning (Vygotsky, 1986); that concepts appear first on the social plane and only subsequently on the individual plane; that the individual plane is formed through the process of internalisation (Leont'ev, 1981, p. 57); that psychological phenomena are social events (Luria, 1973, p. 262); that learning takes place in the zone of proximal development and pulls the child into their tomorrow; and that motives are integral to all actions. Vygotsky's use of the notion of mediation by tools, particularly cultural tools and the semiotic mediation of language, situates people in their time and place ... Other frameworks, such as hermeneutics and post-structuralism, characterise the socio-cultural space in different ways.

In that Editorial (Lerman, 1996a, pp. 4-5) I referred also to socio-linguistics and psychoanalytic perspectives, although they were not represented in the Special Issue.

More recently, in a presentation of the work of PME at the Tenth International Congress on Mathematical Education (ICME10), my colleagues and I analysed PME Proceedings from 1991 to 2003 and drew largely on the same categories of socio-cultural research. The analysis that follows builds on that work[1].

To be more specific, I will begin by establishing what is to be excluded as socio-cultural. Of course the choices are contestable. First, Research Reports that draw on mathematical concepts as the theory will not be counted as socio-cultural. For example, a Report that examines pupils' knowledge or student teachers' knowledge in a particular domain will not be counted as socio-cultural. More controversially, drawing on the distinction I made above, Reports that draw on individualistic psychology will not be counted as socio-cultural. This includes Piagetian research and especially constructivist and radical constructivist research. I am aware that social interactions, together with textual and physical interactions, are the material that can result in disequilibrium in the individual and, indeed, that social interactions are the most frequent and significant. The response to such perturbations is the individual's, however, whether it is ignored, is assimilated into the individual's knowing or the individual's knowledge accommodates the new experience. Thus the study of social interactions *per se* would not lead to the Report being classified as drawing on socio-cultural theory. It would depend on the theory being used.

---

[1] The other members of the team that produced the presentation were Jill Adler, Peter Gates and Robyn Zevenbergen and I acknowledge here their invaluable contribution.

A number of factors play a part in the classification of a Research Report as socio-cultural and, subsequently, to one of the categories. It is most important that the rules a researcher uses to make these decisions are made explicit, both so that others can check and, if they wish, dispute the decisions, but also so that others may apply the same rules to other studies, facilitating comparisons and developments. First, the title and abstract might indicate Reports that need further examination. Next, the references drawn upon by the author(s) are examined in all Reports. Where well-known authors in the field of socio-cultural research are cited, such as Vygotsky, Wertsch, Davydov, Daniels, Lave, Wenger, and so on, there is certainly a case for reading the Report. Where the references are to people in mathematics education research, perhaps members of PME, who often draw on socio-cultural theories, a more detailed check through the Report is required. Where there are no indications from the title, abstract, or references that the orientation is socio-cultural, that Report is, of course, not classified as such. Finally, when there is reason to examine the Report further, I was looking for evidence that the authors base their work on the notion that learning and/or meaning-making originate on the social plane, in social interactions, in language, and/or in enculturation.

The empirical study that was carried out for the PME presentation at ICME10, as well as the categories that emerged in a recent research project (Tsatsaroni, Lerman & Xu, 2003) led to the following categories of socio-cultural theories for the analysis in this chapter:

- Cultural psychology, including work based on Vygotsky, activity theory, situated cognition, communities of practice, social interactions, semiotic mediation
- Ethnomathematics
- Sociology, sociology of education, poststructuralism, hermeneutics, critical theory
- Discourse, to include psychoanalytic perspectives, social linguistics, semiotics.

These categories mirror those we presented in Lerman and Tsatsaroni (1998).

Figure 1: Pedagogic modes

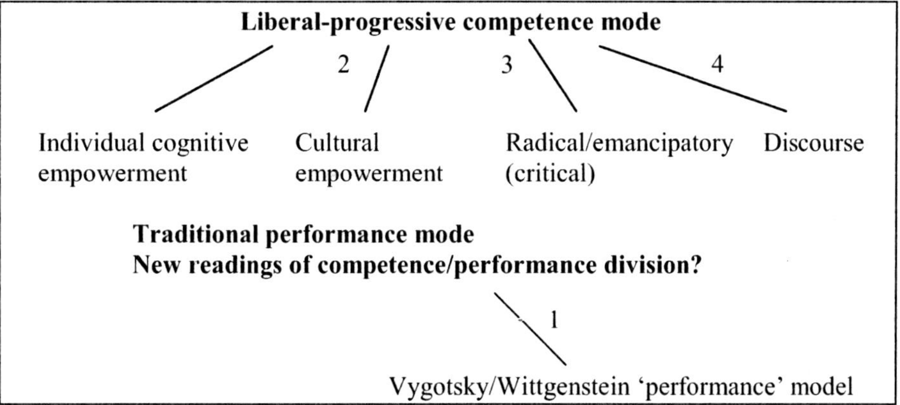

Drawing on Bernstein's description of the turn from traditional performance pedagogy to a liberal-progressive competence pedagogy in the late 1950s, we proposed that this latter could be subdivided into: An individual cognitive focus, that is, Piagetian/reform/constructivism; a social or cultural focus, for example ethnomathematics (as in (2) above); and a critical focus, such as a Freirian approach (as in (3) above). We also suggested that there is evidence of a linguistic turn, to include social linguistics, critical discourse analysis and psychoanalytical approaches (as in (4) above), and, further, an emerging new performance model, quite different from the traditional, based on Vygotskian theories (as in (1) above). If indeed there is a new performance model, we must be conscious of the dangers of the accountability regime in many Western countries. Focusing on performance can be misinterpreted and draw us back into old performance models. This framework formed the basis of our discourse analytic tool (see Tsatsaroni et al., 2003), and these latter four constitute the four sub-sections of what I have called socio-cultural theories in the PME analysis. Of course further fragmentation of theories into sub-sections would, in some sense, give us a finer-grained analysis but would also lose both the theoretical rationale provided here and also the possibility of being able to identify trends over time.

Two categories that required a decision to include or not arose in the analysis we presented at the PME session at ICME10 mentioned above. They were gender studies and social views of mathematics. In the case of gender, the topic forms the focus of Peter Gates' chapter in this volume. In the case of a social view of the nature of mathematical knowledge, I have decided for the purposes of this chapter that it does not of itself constitute a socio-cultural orientation but would call for further examination.

Table 1: Numbers of Research Reports classified as socio-cultural

PME meeting	*Total no. of Research Reports*	*Categories*				*Total*	*Percentage*
		1	*2*	*3*	*4*		
PME2 1978	26						
PME3 1979	49						
PME4 1980	58						
PME5 1981	74						
PME6 1982	60						
PME7 1983	74						
PME8 1984	53						
PME9 1985	76	2				2	3
PME10 1986	82	2				2	2
PME11 1987	153	2				2	1
PME12 1988	73	1				1	1
PME13 1989	102	3				3	3
PME14 1990	111	6	1		2	9	8
PME15 1991	126	7	1	3	2	13	10
PME16 1992	91	10	3	1	2	16	18
PME17 1993	88	9	1	1	2	13	15

PME meeting	*Total no. of Research Reports*	*Categories*				*Total*	*Percentage*
		1	*2*	*3*	*4*		
PME18 1994	157	15	3	3	2	23	15
PME19 1995	77	12	1	1	2	16	21
PME20 1996	160	9			2	11	7
PME21 1997	122	12		1	7	20	16
PME22 1998	119	8	1	5	1	15	13
PME23 1999	136	7	3		4	14	10
PME24 2000	117	4	1		1	6	5
PME25 2001	171	8		1	4	13	8
PME26 2002	165	7		3	1	11	7
PME27 2003	176	6	3	5	1	15	9
PME28 2004	198	23		2	4	29	15
PME29 2005	130	14	1	5	8	28	22

In Table 1 above, the total number of Research Reports published in the Proceedings and the numbers of Reports that fall into the categories above, using the rules I set out, are listed. The total number of Reports is important because increases in quantities of Reports of a particular orientation must be measured against the general increase in the numbers of Reports appearing in Proceedings over the years. PME9 in 1985 was the last meeting to fit all the Research Reports into one volume. PME28 in 2004 required 4 very full volumes, although for many years now Short Orals, Posters, Research Forums, descriptions of Discussion, Working or other groups, and Plenary addresses have also been included whereas this was not always the case in earlier times. Thus percentages of each year are also presented as a ratio of the number of reports classified in one category or another as socio-cultural to the total number of Research Reports in the Proceedings that year.

Comment

There is no doubt that the number of Research Reports classified as socio-cultural has grown substantially from 1990 onwards. However the growth is neither monotonically increasing nor consistent. In addition to other factors the variability may well reflect the effects of the location of the meetings. There is always a major impact of local research in the Reports and that will change around the world. I would conjecture that the high point of 21%, until the 22% at the 2005 meeting, at PME19 in 1995 in Recife, Brazil, was in large part due to the fact that it was attended by a relatively small number of non-Brazilians and that there is a strong influence of situated, ethnomathematical, and cultural psychological theories in Brazilian research, resulting in that high percentage. Similarly the subsequent low point of 5% at PME24 in 2000 possibly reflects the character of research orientations in Japan. However the three years following the Hiroshima meeting are also quite low, although there is a jump in 2004 and a further jump in 2005. The jump of 2004 might have been stimulated by the conference theme of diversity, an issue that attracts a range of research methods and ones that focus on social contexts in particular.

The majority of Reports that fall into the socio-cultural categories are developments of cultural psychology, and that is the case in 2004 and 2005 in particular. This is unsurprising perhaps, since Vygotsky was undoubtedly a psychologist, and PME members have found his theories and those of followers and of what have been called neo-Vygotskian scholars of increasing use and applicability in their work.

SOME KEY RESEARCH RESULTS

Given that I have listed 262 Research Reports as within the socio-cultural domain of mathematics education research as presented in PME, any account of the main findings will of necessity be partial and certainly subjectively selective.

Semiotic mediation

A key contribution by Vygotsky to psychology was the notion of mediation. His move away from associationism, one of the two dominant psychological theories in Russia at the time of the revolution (the other being introspection), and towards a Marxist psychology was made by recognising that the simple stimulus-response process is replaced by a complex, mediated act. Vygotsky's theory of mediation provides an historical socio-cultural account of the development of human consciousness and the process of meaning-making. By analogy with physical tools Vygotsky argued that tools, predominantly the psychological tool of language but also different kinds of artefacts (the number line, historical artefacts such as geometrical tools, technology), through internalisation, function to change consciousness internally and change what becomes possible to act upon the world externally, a reflexive process. Vygotsky's contribution has been developed substantially by some PME researchers to demonstrate how classroom interactions can be seen as students aligning their subjective interpretations with the cultural-historical meanings that precede them as they come to understand established mathematical meanings. I will give two examples. These are chosen because, in both cases, they represent examples of an on-going substantial body of work well represented in PME Proceedings. There are other examples that could have appeared here, both of these authors' work and that of others, but for the necessity of choice.

Radford, Bardini, Sabena, Diallo and Simbagoye (2005) discuss texts from students working on interpreting graphs of movement towards and away from a door as recorded electronically by a Ranger. Radford and his colleagues set these classrooms interactions in the context of an examination of the claims of embodied cognition in an attempt to indicate how that theory needs to engage with culture if it is to avoid the 'transcendental "I" of idealism' (p. 114). They show the reflexive process involved in the students aligning their reading of the graphical representation with the mathematical meaning.

> The alignment of subjective and cultural meanings involved a profound active re-interpretation of signs by the students, framed by the teacher and the particular context of the classroom, leading to a progressive awareness of significations and conceptual relations ... (p. 120)

Boero, Pedemonte and Robotti (1997) examine students' work on falling bodies in which they contrasted voices from the past (Aristotle and Galilei) with their own subjective experiences, in this case for the researchers to engage with the gap between spontaneous and scientific, or theoretical knowledge. Although the authors here do not refer directly to mediation this is precisely the function of the students' engagement with the range of voices in the teaching experiment.

> We believe that the 'multiple echo' and the production of 'classroom voices' are the conditions which allowed some meaningful experiences of true scientific debate to take place during our teaching experiment. (p. 87)

Key to these and a growing number of other studies with the same orientation is that the setting, including the teacher, texts and artefacts play essential roles in the development of cognition in that they mediate the meanings developed by students, established meanings that precede the students' entry into mathematical activity. Many researchers will argue that the internalisation process is best studied over a long term (Bartolini Bussi, 1991). Short-term studies of teaching and learning have also proved fruitful, however.

Short term studies of mediation and the zone of proximal development

Here I will mention, in brief, a selection of papers and their findings that, according to the authors (and in all cases I concur) are informed by aspects of Vygotsky's work.

Arzarello, Bazzini and Chiappini (1994) investigated the difficulties pre-university and first year university students face in acquiring the mathematical register and, drawing on Vygotsky's theory of concept development, they carried out a study of 137 students, proposing that "a long cognitive apprenticeship" is required "during which the student learns to separate the representative function of the algebraic code from the purely instrumental function" (p. 47).

Ohtani (1994) studied a seventh-grade classroom over the course of a year. Analysing one typical episode for the 'voices' that are speaking out and through the students he writes, "Vygotsky-Bakhtin's perspective suggests that what comes to be incorporated into an utterance are voices that were formerly represented explicitly in intermental functioning" (p. 391).

Zack (1994) studied her own classroom and, in this paper she explains the effects of peer interactions in terms of Vygotsky's ZPD. In particular she analyses to whom the students turn by asking for their 'votes' and she concludes "The findings seem to indicate that the children do nominate the explanations of the more adept more often than others" (p. 415).

Brodie (1995) studied a classroom in which the pedagogy was motivated by the desire to fulfil post-apartheid goals of a learner-centred, non-authoritarian classroom, in which the active participation of students is to be encouraged. From a detailed study of one particular group, she concludes that collaboration may better be seen from a ZPD perspective rather than the constructivist orientation implied in the goals, which is often interpreted as requiring "a particular approach to teaching, that of facilitating learning with a reluctance to intervene directly" which did not, in this case "enable the pupils to make progress" (p. 222).

Askew (2004) developed a model, based on categorising mediating means: Tasks, artefacts, talk and actions, and personal meanings: Activity, tools and images, in an attempt to study "the dialectic between the processes of participating in mathematics lessons and the process of individual cognition" (p. 71). Askew demonstrates the potential of this model through reporting on one lesson taken from a five-year study.

A number of studies over the years have examined the role of handheld graphing technologies and mathematical software in terms of tool use. For instance, Rivera and Becker (2004) analysed 30 students' work using the TI-89 handheld graphing calculator to work on algebra and precalculus in terms of mediation. They concluded that "Both the TI-89 and other learners mediated in ways that made it difficult to analyze the influence of one apart from the other, which is but an effect of instrumented activity" (p. 87). They also explained aspects of the role played by the technology as mediating through the fact that "the various commands and functions in the TI-89 reflect mainstream mathematical processes" (*op cit*), describing this as an 'intentional experience', quoting Kozulin (1998, p. 65).

Finally, Yoshida (2004) discusses how everyday and mathematical/scientific concepts develop in the context of fractions in a third-grade class. Arguing, with Brushlinski, that scientific concepts subsume the everyday rather than replace them, Yoshida works with the notion of *sublation* in studying how the concepts develop. Yoshida concludes "their everyday concepts are finally subordinated to the view in which fractions themselves can express quantities." (p. 480).

This selection of findings demonstrates applications and developments of socio-cultural theories in PME Research Reports that make significant contributions to studies of mathematics teaching and learning.

Researching equity

Given the key role of the teaching-learning setting, a range of socio-cultural theories have been drawn upon to enable research on equity issues. The problem faced by individualistic psychology, and I include constructivism here, is that failure is the responsibility of the individual set against a psychological norm of development. I would suggest that many forms of social constructivism (Lerman, 1996b) also do not incorporate a strong enough sense of 'social' to be able to account for failure in any other terms. I will take three examples that draw on different theoretical frameworks in researching equity.

Sullivan, Mousley and Zevenbergen (2004) review work that has addressed "aspects of schooling that tend to exacerbate the obvious difficulties that some students experience" (p. 258) and extend that work to look at the use of particular language genres, contexts, teaching strategies and student expectations. Of particular concern to them, drawing on a range of sociologically inspired research, is that teachers should make implicit pedagogies more explicit since this feature of classroom interactions disadvantages students from low socio-economic settings. Setting questions in everyday contexts plays into that disadvantage (Sethole, 2005).

The metaphor of participation has been seen by researchers as fruitful for engaging more students in school mathematics. Adler (1997) discusses teachers' strategies in multilingual classrooms and she proposes, drawing on Lave and Wenger's idea that access to a practice requires its resources to be transparent, that seeing language as a resource "offers possibilities for enhancing access to mathematics, especially in multilingual classrooms" (p. 1). Boylan and Povey (2001) argue similarly that the effects of whole-class interactive teaching can be that of greater student participation.

Gorgorió and Planas (2005), in examining the engagement of new immigrant groups into schools in the Catalan region of Spain, draw on the notion of cultural scripts in re-interpreting the construct of social norms (Cobb, Yackel & Wood, 1992) in order to take account of "the different and multiple cultural and social histories of the individuals" (p. 67). In their re-interpretation, in which norms play a mediational role interposed in processes of change, the analysis of these roles "addresses issues around who (appropriately) participates, whose participation is (not) welcomed, and the different roles played by individuals within the mathematics conversation" (p. 70). Setati (2003) draws on a similar framework, Gee's cultural models (Gee, 1999), in her study of the code switching in multilingual classrooms in South Africa. Her use of that framework enables a deep understanding of the social and political functions of different languages in such classrooms, an analysis which therefore offers the possibility of change.

In the next section I will make some remarks about the presence of socio-cultural research in the mathematics education field in general, and then return to discuss possible future directions within the PME community.

THE GENERAL PICTURE

PME has a specific agenda of course. Nevertheless it is of value to examine how the particular orientations being discussed in each of the chapters in this book are reflected and represented in the wider field of mathematics education research. To do this for socio-cultural research I will report here on the findings of a recent research project, followed by some unsystematic observations of other publications and developments.

In Lerman (2000) I argued that there has been a turn to the social in the mathematics education research community as a whole. I attempted to trace the beginnings of that turn although not in any systematic way. Subsequently I developed a unit of analysis that drew together what I argued are the major insights from theories that constitute the social turn. The extent to which my argument for the social turn was valid called for a more systematic study.

The recent research project to which I referred above, the major findings of which were presented at the American Educational Research Association conference in 2003 and published in ERIC (Tsatsaroni, Lerman & Xu, 2003), looked at a representative selection of research texts in PME Proceedings and the journals *Educational Studies in Mathematics* (ESM) and *Journal for Research in Mathematics Education* (JRME) between 1990 and 2001. The aim of our research project[2] was broader than just to identify the trends in socio-cultural research. We wanted to analyse the processes whereby mathematics educational 'theories' are produced and the circumstances whereby they become current in the mathematics education research field, and the extent to which they are recontextualised and acquired by teacher educators and teachers. We aimed to construct a representation of the field of mathematics education research through which we could explore the reproduction of identities, as positions, of researchers and teacher educators in the field, who produces theories in mathematics education, with what methodologies and to what consequences for research and for school practice and who are the managers of these identities (e.g. the funding agents, journal publishers etc.). Finally, we intended to talk about identities of academics, and changes in those identities over time and place.

To carry out this project we developed a specific tool for textual analysis based largely on the later work of the sociologist of education Basil Bernstein, but also on other sources, including Morgan, Tsatsaroni and Lerman (2002). We used the analysis both to describe those aspects of the research field mentioned above and also to develop an informed characterisation of the field and its agents, a sort of answer to the question "Where are we now?" Although the findings are based on a limited range of texts, in terms of the language in which the research was written, in terms of the number and range of journals, and in terms of the time span, those findings clearly shed some light on the present discussion, offering a perspective, to some extent, of where PME is positioned within the community as a whole.

Although the study had a broader brief, an element of it was certainly to chart the trends in research in general and amongst those trends we identified the socio-cultural theories. In relation to socio-cultural theories, we wrote:

> Table 2 (below) was constructed out of the following categories: Psycho-social studies, sociology/sociology of education/socio-cultural studies and historically orientated studies, linguistics/social linguistics and semiotics, philosophy/philosophy of mathematics, educational theory/educational research/neighbouring fields of mathematics education and curriculum studies. In the Table there is also space to record those cases where no theory has been used. To enhance readability, the data obtained from each type of text were grouped into two time periods (1990-1995 and 1996-2001), though detailed year by year tables are also available. The first interesting point to notice is that, as already said, the predominant fields from which researchers draw in all three journals are traditional psychological & mathematical

[2] See http://www.lsbu.ac.uk/~lermans/ESRCProjectHOMEPAGE.html for publications from the project.

theories, though the percentage in JRME, in the first period, is substantially lower, compared to the other two. Over the two period spans papers drawing on traditional psychology and mathematics have decreased in PME and ESM (from 73.1% to 60.5% for PME; and from 63.4% to 51.6% in ESM), but have increased in the case of JRME (from 54.8% to 57.9%) ... this finding must be linked to the substantially higher percentage of JRME papers which exhibit an 'empiricism', i.e., did not draw on any theory in the first period (24.2%, compared to 6.0% in PME, and 9.8% in ESM), while in the second period there is a substantial drop in the papers that are found not to use theories at all from 24.2% to 10.5%. There is a drop also in ESM papers, but not substantial and a slight increase in PME papers that do not draw on any theory; though the numbers of the papers considered is small to allow any hypotheses. The second point to notice is that a good number of papers in all three types of text draw on psycho-social theories, including re-emerging ones, and that this is on the increase in ESM and JRME over the two time periods (from 9.8% to 20.0% and from 6.5% to 13.2%, respectively), with a very slight decrease in PME texts (from 11.9% to 9.9%). The papers drawing on sociological and socio-cultural theories are also on the increase (from 3.0% to 9.9% in PME, from 3.7 to 11.6% in ESM, and from 1.6 to 7.9 in JRME) but they are all below 12%; and there is a noticeable increase, over the two time periods, in the use of linguistics, social linguistics and semiotics in all three types of text, though the number of papers drawing on these are still very small. (pp. 19-20)

Table 2. Theories in use in mathematics education research

	PME		ESM		JRME	
	90 -95 No. %	96 - 01 No. %	90 - 95 No. %	96 - 01 No. %	90 - 95 No. %	96 - 01 No. %
Traditional psychological and mathematics theories	49 73.1	49 60.5	52 63.4	49 51.6	34 54.8	44 57.9
Psycho-social, including re-emerging ones	8 11.9	8 9.9	8 9.8	19 20.0	4 6.5	10 13.2
Sociology, Sociology of Education, Socio-cultural studies, and Historically orientated studies	2 3.0	8 9.9	3 3.7	11 11.6	1 1.6	6 7.9
Linguistics, social linguistics and semiotics	0 0.0	2 2.5	1 1.2	5 5.3	2 3.2	6 7.9
Neighbouring fields of Maths Educ, Science ed and Curriculum studies	1 1.5	0 0.0	0 0.0	0 0.0	1 1.6	0 0.0

	PME		ESM		JRME	
	90 -95 No. %	96 - 01 No. %	90 - 95 No. %	96 - 01 No. %	90 - 95 No. %	96 - 01 No. %
Recent broader theoretical currents, feminism, post-structuralism and psychoanalysis	1 1.5	0 0.0	8 9.8	1 1.1	0 0.0	1 1.3
Philosophy/philosophy of mathematics	0 0.0	3 3.7	0 0.0	3 3.2	1 1.6	1 1.3
Educational theory and research	2 3.0	0 0.0	1 1.2	1 1.1	2 3.2	0 0.0
Other	0 0.0	0 0.0	1 1.2	1 1.1	2 3.2	0 0.0
No theory used	4 6.0	11 13.6	8 9.8	5 5.3	15 24.2	8 10.5
Total	67 100.0	81 100.0	82 100.0	95 100.0	62 100.0	76 100.0

(Tsatsaroni, Lerman & Xu, 2003, pp. 19-20)

The percentages in Table 2 of theories that fall outside the main category, in the first row, are quite small, thus any claims about trends are to be read with caution. The biggest difference between PME and the two journals is in the percentage of what we called there psycho-social theories, what I have called here category 1, cultural psychology and its developments. In the second period, from 1996 to 2001, just 9% of our PME sample were research texts identified in this category, whereas 20% were so classified in ESM and 13.2% in JRME. Indeed, as we noted, the PME percentage had fallen between the two periods whereas the ESM and JRME percentages had more than doubled. Now that I have extended this study and brought it up to date we can see that there was a dip in the years 2000 to 2003 below double figures but a substantial increase in 2004 and 2005.

Although the figures are small, we can note the similar increase in studies drawing on sociology and sociology of education across all three publications. Taking a total of the second, third and fourth rows, corresponding to the classifications of socio-cultural theories in this chapter, they constitute a little more than a third of all articles in ESM and a little less than a third in JRME during the second period.

Whilst not the subject of this chapter, we can also note the larger percentage of research papers that do not draw on any theory in PME Proceedings as compared to both ESM and JRME. I would suggest that this is a matter for concern for our Group.

One of our major interests in our study was to examine the role of agents such as journal editors and the financial concerns of the publishing houses. PME is not subject to the same influences but there are of course effects of the regulations on acceptance and rejection on the identities of PME researchers and on the kinds of research that appear in the Proceedings. The equivalent of the Senior Editor of a journal is the Programme Committee of PME that meets in March each year to review the review process and make whatever changes and modifications it sees fit. Publication policy is in the hands of the IC, represented by those members of the Programme Committee who are on it. As I mentioned above, the reviewing task for each Programme Committee is huge and must draw on people with less experience than those who review for journals. The Programme Committee works hard to try and ensure some consistency. It usually chooses to accept those Reports receiving 3 (out of 3) acceptances and also those that receive 2. Those receiving 1 acceptance and all those with less than 3 completed reviews are read by the committee, a process that should raise the level of consistency. They will often monitor the review process as a whole by sampling Reports rejected and accepted and not read for other reasons.

The outcome, I would argue, is a much less regulated system in PME than in the journals, which ought to result in a wide diversity of research orientations. In fact there is much more uniformity than might be expected following this analysis, which suggests that the identity of PME is itself a constraint on the breadth of research focuses. Researchers will choose not to attend PME or not to submit their work to PME, in spite of the high international status of the Group, because they do not see their work as fitting under a 'psychology' umbrella. I have suggested, in this chapter, that 'psychology' is a much broader umbrella than is perhaps understood by many people in our community. This is not to suggest that whatever is written can be appropriate. Indeed a paper my colleagues and I submitted in 2003 that reported on the PME aspect of the research study I have been drawing on in this chapter, and was of necessity sociological in that psychology is not a suitable field for a systematic study of research texts, was rejected (of course it may just be that the paper was poorly written!). It will be very interesting to see the effects of the constitutional change in 2005 on the research trends in the coming years.

There have been a number of publications in recent years that draw on socio-cultural theories, such as Atweh, Forgasz & Nebres (2001), Adler (2001), De Abreu, Bishop & Presmeg (2001) and Alrø & Skovsmose (2004) to name just a few. I have not carried out a systematic study of books on research in mathematics education, however. These are, I would suggest, an indication of a growing trend.

Finally, I want to refer to a development in the mathematics education research community that, I believe, supports the argument that there is a growing interest in socio-cultural theories. The international group called Mathematics, Education and Society held its fourth meeting (MES4) in July 2005 in Australia. Its stated focus can be seen in the following extract from the aims of the conference: "There is a need for discussing widely the social, cultural and political dimensions of mathematics education; for disseminating research that explores those dimensions; for addressing methodological issues of that type of research; for planning international co-operation in the area; and for developing a strong research community interested in this view of mathematics education. The MES4 Conference aims to bring together mathematics educators from around the world to provide such a forum, as well as to offer a platform on which to build future collaborative activity." There is an overlap of participation in PME and MES, although the latter does not have a membership as such. Currently at each meeting the next one is proposed. There is no standing committee, only a group of advisers to the local committee.

FUTURE DIRECTIONS

In this final section I will suggest some areas of socio-cultural theory that are developing as key themes in current research and should appear in Research Reports in the future.

The first is work around the notion of identity. In calling for a focus on the practice of teaching, Boaler (2003) referred to the 'dance of agency' that teachers (as well as students) engage in, at the intersection of knowledge and thought. In introducing this notion Boaler was drawing on the main focus of sociology, the tension between structure and agency. As we move into late modernity, social scientists in general are focusing on what happens to identity in a period when the social structures dominated by workplace and social status are in a state of flux. "Modernity replaces the *determination* of social standing with a compulsive and obligatory *self*-determination" (Bauman, 2001, p. 145). In 1996 Stuart Hall said, "there has been a veritable explosion in recent years around the concept of "identity" (Hall & Du Guy, 1996), to which Bauman (2001) added "the explosion has triggered an avalanche."

If one looks at children's lives, whether it be the clothes they wear, the music they listen to, the ways they must speak, move, and behave to be accepted by their peers, their home life, or their race/ethnicity/gender/religion, their construction of 'identity' is paramount. The mathematics teacher's task is to lay yet another identity onto all that, a *mathematical* identity. The notion of identity has been studied in psychology for many years under such headings as self-concept, self-worth, self-efficacy and others. The current notion of identity owes much to Lave and Wenger's "learning involves the construction of identities" (Lave & Wenger, 1991, p. 53).

> Participation in social practice ... suggests a very explicit focus on the person, but as person-in-the-world, as member of a socio-cultural community. This focus in turn promotes a view of knowing as activity by specific people in specific circumstances. (Lave & Wenger, 1991, p. 52)

Their notion of 'person-in-the-world' of course re-voices Vygotsky's *Mind in Society*.

Schooling, and the mathematics classroom in particular, is just such a specific circumstance. Studies of the emergence of a school-mathematical identity, in the midst of the pressures on children to negotiate their lives through many identities, are needed in our community. Sfard's (2005) plenary presented a study of student identity (see also Lerman, 2005) indicating a development already in that direction.

The second area is that of studies of teaching mathematics, as called for directly in Boaler (2003), but already signalled in Hoyles (1992), and in my chapter in a PME-sponsored publication in 1993 (Bishop, Hart, Lerman & Nunes, 1993). One can see a range of current research work around the world focusing on the teaching of mathematics and drawing on a range of theoretical resources. Boaler's plenary address and her work over a number of years (including Boaler, 1997; Boaler & Greeno, 2000) indicate very clearly how different modalities of teaching can effect different identities as mathematics learners. A study by Graven (2004) examined the developing identities of teachers within an in-service course, drawing on theories of situated cognition. Ball and Bass and colleagues (e.g. Ball, Bass & Hill, 2004) are carrying out detailed studies of the teaching of mathematics and, together with Adler and her colleagues (Adler & Davis, in press), are working to elaborate the notion of 'mathematics for teaching'. There are two aspects of this developing work that I want to mention here as important present and future developments. The first is the ever-present issue of teacher learning. For many years we have been aware that teacher education courses, in general, make little difference ultimately to how teachers will teach (Brown, Cooney & Jones, 1990). Socio-cultural theories and indeed sociological theories are well placed to shed light on the problem (Ensor, 1999; Graven, 2004). The second issue is: What are the processes whereby different modalities of teaching determine the school-mathematical identities of students? What are the micro-genetic processes in the learning of mathematics in schools that lead to different ways of perceiving what it means to be school-mathematical?

Finally, related closely to the point above, who fails in school mathematics and how do they fail; that is, what causes them to fail, and why? In many countries around the world particular social groups are associated with failure in school mathematics, determined by social class, ethnicity, poverty, gender and the intersection of some of these identities.

REFERENCES

Adler, J. (1997). The dilemma of transparency: Seeing and seeing through talk in the mathematics classroom. In E. Pehkonen (Ed.), *Proceedings of the 21st PME International Conference, 2*, 1–8.

Adler, J. (2001). *Teaching mathematics in multilingual classrooms*. Dordrecht, The Netherlands: Kluwer.

Adler, J., & Davis, Z. (in press). *Opening another black box: Researching mathematics for teaching in mathematics teacher education.*

Alrø, H., & Skovsmose, O. (2004). *Dialogue and learning in mathematics education: Intention, reflection, critique*. Dordrecht, The Netherlands: Kluwer.

Arzarello, F., Bazzini L., & Chiappini, G. (1994). The process of naming in algebraic problem solving. In J. P. Ponte & J. F. Matos (Eds.), *Proceedings of the 18th PME International Conference, 2*, 40–47.

Askew, M. (2004). Mediation and interpretation: Exploring the interpersonal and the intrapersonal in primary mathematics lessons. In M. J. Høines & A. B. Fuglestad (Eds.), *Proceedings of the 28th PME International Conference, 2*, 71–78.

Atweh, B., Forgasz, H., & Nebres, B. (Eds.). (2001). *Socio-cultural aspects in mathematics education: An international perspective*. Mahwah, NJ, USA: Lawrence Erlbaum.

Ball, D., Bass, H., & Hill, H. (2004). Knowing and using mathematical knowledge in teaching: Learning what matters. In A. Buffgler & R. Lausch (Eds.), *Proceedings of the 12th Annual Conference of the South African Association for Research in Mathematics, Science and Technology Education*. Durban, South Africa: SAARMSTE.

Bartolini Bussi, M. (1991) Social interaction and mathematical knowledge. In F. Furinghetti (Ed.), *Proceedings of the 15th PME International Conference, 1*, 1–16.

Bauman, Z. (2001). *The individualized society*. Cambridge, UK: Polity Press.

Bishop, A., Hart, K., Lerman, S., & Nunes, T. (1993). *Significant influences on children's learning of mathematics*. Paris, France: UNESCO.

Boaler, J. (1997). *Experiencing school mathematics: Teaching styles, sex and setting*. Buckingham, UK: Open University Press.

Boaler, J. (2003). Studying and capturing the complexity of practice: The case of the dance of agency. In N. A. Pateman, B. J. Dougherty, & J. Zilliox (Eds.), *Proceedings of the 27th PME International Conference, 1*, 3–16.

Boaler, J., & Greeno, J. G. (2000). Identity, agency and knowing in mathematical worlds. In J. Boaler (Ed.), *Multiple perspectives on mathematics teaching and learning* (pp. 171–200). Westport, CT, USA: Ablex.

Boero, P., Pedemonte, B, & Robotti, E. (1997). Approaching theoretical knowledge through voices and echoes: A Vygotskian perspective. In E. Pehkonen (Ed.), *Proceedings of the 21st PME International Conference, 2*, 81–88.

Boylan, M., & Povey, H. (2001). "I'd be more likely to talk in class if ...": Some students' ideas about strategies to increase mathematical participation in whole class interactions. In M. van den Heuvel-Panhuizen (Ed.), *Proceedings of the 25th PME International Conference, 2*, 201–208.

Brodie, K. (1995). Peer interaction and the development of mathematical knowledge. In L. Meira & D. Carraher (Eds.), *Proceedings of the 19th PME International Conference, 3*, 217–223.

Brown, M. (2000). Does research make a contribution to teaching and learning in school mathematics? Reflections on an article from Diane Ravich. In T. Nakahara & M. Koyama (Eds.), *Proceedings of the 24th PME International Conference, 1*, 80–83.

Brown, C., Cooney, T. A., & Jones, D. (1990). Mathematics teacher education. In W. R. Houston (Ed.), *Handbook of research on teacher education* (pp. 639–656). New York, USA: Macmillan.

Cobb, P., Yackel, E., & Wood, T. (1992). A constructivist alternative to the representational view of mind. *Journal for Research in Mathematics Education, 23*, 2–33.

De Abreu, G., Bishop, A., & Presmeg, N. C. (Eds.). (2001). *Transitions between contexts of mathematical practices*. Dordrecht, The Netherlands: Kluwer.

Ensor, P. (1999). *A study of the recontextualising of pedagogic practices from a South African University preservice mathematics teacher education course by seven beginning secondary mathematics teachers*. Unpublished PhD dissertation, University of London, London, UK.

Gee, J. (1999). *An introduction to discourse analysis: Theory and method*. London, UK: Routledge.

Gorgorió, N., & Planas, N. (2005). Reconstructing norms. In H. L. Chick & J. L. Vincent (Eds.), *Proceedings of the 29th PME International Conference, 3*, 65–72.

Graven, M. (2004). Investigating mathematics teacher learning within an in-service community of practice: The centrality of confidence. *Educational Studies in Mathematics, 57*(2), 177–211.

Hall, S., & Du Guy, P. (Eds.). (1996). *Questions of cultural identity*. London, UK: Sage.

Harré R., & Gillett, G. (1994). *The discursive mind*. London, UK: Sage.

Hoyles, C. (1992). Illuminations and reflections – teachers, methodologies, and mathematics. In W. Geeslin & K. Graham (Eds.), *Proceedings of the 16th PME International Conference, 3*, 263–286.

Kozulin, A. (1998). *Psychological tools*. Cambridge, MA, USA: Harvard Educational Press.

Lave, J., & Wenger, E. (1991). *Situated learning: Legitimate peripheral participation*. New York, USA: Cambridge University Press.

Leont'ev, A. N. (1981). The problem of activity in psychology. In J. V. Wertsch (Ed.), *The concept of activity in Soviet psychology* (pp. 37–71). Armonk, NY, USA: Sharpe.

Lerman, S. (1996a). Socio-cultural approaches to mathematics teaching and learning. *Educational Studies in Mathematics, 31*(1–2), 1–9.

Lerman, S. (1996b). Intersubjectivity in mathematics learning: A challenge to the radical constructivist paradigm? *Journal for Research in Mathematics Education, 27*(2), 133–150.

Lerman, S. (2000). The social turn in mathematics education research. In J. Boaler (Ed.), *Multiple perspectives on mathematics teaching and learning* (pp. 19–44). Westport, CT, USA: Ablex.

Lerman, S. (2005). *Learning mathematics as developing identity in the classroom.* Keynote lecture to the Annual Meeting of the Canadian Mathematics Education Study Group, University of Ottawa, Canada (to be published in Proceedings, 2006).

Lerman, S., & Tsatsaroni, A. (1998). Why children fail and what mathematics education studies can do about it: The role of sociology. In P. Gates (Ed.), *Proceedings of the 1st International Conference on Mathematics, Education and Society* (MEAS1) (pp. 26–33). Nottingham, UK: Centre for the Study of Mathematics Education, University of Nottingham.

Luria, A. R. (1973). *The working brain.* Harmondsworth, UK: Penguin Books.

Morgan, C., Tsatsaroni, A., & Lerman, S. (2002). Mathematics teachers' positions and practices in discourses of assessment. *British Journal of Sociology of Education, 23*(3), 445–461.

Ohtani, M. (1994). Socio-cultural mediateness of mathematical activity: Analysis of "voices" in seventh-grade mathematics classroom. In J. P. Ponte & J. F. Matos (Eds.), *Proceedings of the 18th PME International Conference, 3,* 384–391.

Radford, L., Bardini, C., Sabena, C., Diallo, P., & Simbagoye, A. (2005). On embodiment, artefacts, and signs: A semiotic-cultural perspective on mathematical thinking. In H. L. Chick & J. L. Vincent (Eds.), *Proceedings of the 29th PME International Conference, 4,* 113–120.

Rivera, F., & Becker, J. R. (2004). A socio-cultural account of students' collective mathematical understanding of polynomial inequalities in instrumented activity. In M. J. Høines & A. B. Fuglestad (Eds.), *Proceedings of the 28th PME International Conference, 4,* 81–88.

Setati, M. (2003). Language use in a multilingual mathematics classroom in South Africa: A different perspective. In N. A. Pateman, B. J. Dougherty, & J. Zilliox (Eds.), *Proceedings of the 27th PME International Conference, 4,* 151–158.

Sethole, G. (2005). From the everyday, through the inauthentic, to mathematics: Reflection on the process of teaching from contexts. In H. L. Chick & J. L. Vincent (Eds.), *Proceedings of the 29th PME International Conference, 4,* 169–175.

Sfard, A. (2005). Identity that makes a difference: Substantial learning as closing the gap between actual and designated identities. In H. L. Chick & J. L. Vincent (Eds.), *Proceedings of the 29th PME International Conference, 1,* 37–52.

Sullivan, P., Mousley, J., & Zevenbergen, R. (2004). Describing elements of mathematical lessons that accommodate diversity in student background. In M. J. Høines & A. B. Fuglestad (Eds.), *Proceedings of the 28th PME International Conference, 4,* 257–264.

Tsatsaroni, A,; Lerman, S., & Xu, G. (2003). *A sociological description of changes in the intellectual field of mathematics education research: Implications for the identities of academics.* Paper presented at Annual Meeting of the American Educational Research Association, Chicago. (ERIC# ED482512)

Vygotsky, L. (1986). *Thought and language* (revised edition, A. Kozulin (Ed.)). Cambridge, MA, USA: MIT Press.

Yoshida, K. (2004). Understanding how the concept of fractions develops: A Vygotskian perspective. In M. J. Høines & A. B. Fuglestad (Eds.), *Proceedings of the 28th PME International Conference, 4,* 473–480.

Zack, V. (1994). Vygotskian applications in the elementary mathematics classroom: Looking to one's peers for helpful explanations. In J. P. Ponte & J. F. Matos (Eds.), *Proceedings of the 18th PME International Conference, 4,* 409–416.

AFFILIATION

Stephen Lerman
Department of Education
London South Bank University
103 Borough Road
London SE1 0AA (UK)
lermans@lsbu.ac.uk
http://www.lsbu.ac.uk/~lermans

PETER GATES

THE PLACE OF EQUITY AND SOCIAL JUSTICE IN THE HISTORY OF PME

INTRODUCTION

While thinking about how to start this chapter, I visited a newly qualified teacher of mathematics in a local high school, who said to me:

> You know, a lot of my bottom group really struggle with maths –and I've noticed they all come from the same part of town, and they have got similar family backgrounds. Surely that can't be a coincidence?

Of course it is no coincidence that children from low socioeconomic backgrounds do less well at mathematics than children from more privileged homes –and the literature shows that sufficiently convincingly as an international trend. The fact that this is not a coincidence, and that it is internationally relevant, has to make it of central concern to all those engaged in mathematics education. It therefore seemed an appropriate place to start this chapter about the position of equity and social justice in the history of PME.

Elsewhere in this book, Lerman takes a slightly different perspective to understanding "the social" in PME through an examination of the adoption of sociocultural theories within and outside the PME community. He makes it clear how important PME is:

> The importance of PME as the leading international research group in the field has attracted the participation of many excellent mathematics education researchers whose orientation, as they would readily claim, would not come under PME's understanding of the term 'psychology' in the initial stages of the Group. (Lerman, this volume, p. 347)

In saying this Lerman raises the fundamental question that regularly appears within PME community –the appropriateness or otherwise of the focus on psychology within the aims of the organisation, and on the effect that has had upon the "PME research"– by which I mean the research presented at conferences and reported in the proceedings. I do not want here to take a simplistic approach to understanding "psychology". As I will go on to describe, the birth of PME came from a cognitive orientation which led to PME having an orientation toward the cognitive and psychological aspects of learning. In recent years psychology itself

A. Gutiérrez, P. Boero (eds.), Handbook of Research on the Psychology of Mathematics Education: Past, Present and Future, 367–402.

has developed into cultural and social directions and these are now powerful trends within psychology that could help us understand inequitable situations linked to the context of mathematics education. However, the initial orientation of PME would appear to have been responsible for directing the shape of current PME research into a cognitive orientation. I argue in this chapter that this has had important implications, but also that it is a changing and developing situation.

So let us look at the major goals of PME between PME1 and PME29:

(i) To promote international contacts and exchange of scientific information in the **psychology** of mathematical education;
(ii) To promote and stimulate interdisciplinary research in the aforesaid area with the cooperation of **psychologists**, mathematicians and mathematics teachers;
(iii) To further a deeper and more correct understanding of the **psychological** aspects of teaching and learning mathematics and the implications thereof.

Clearly each major goal privileges a psychological outlook (*my emphasis*). It is important to have these in our mind as we travel through the history of PME research, because a key moment in this story is the change of these at PME29 – which I will refer to at the end of this chapter.

When discussing the structure of this chapter with the Editors, I suggested it was rather a wide brief to include gender, social class, ethnicity, diversity etc. The editors were unequivocal –there was very little attention to equity and social justice issues in PME proceedings. Having now worked on this chapter– I agree with them. Neither equity nor social justice (nor gender either!) play a particularly significant role in PME research. I do not want to fall into the trap of assuming that PME has some objective existence; it is an annual conference with published proceedings. PME members do not only present and publish through PME; yet I will argue that PME is significant in the discipline because of the dominant position it has.

So what I do in this chapter is present a developmental history of the place of equity issues in PME and to locate that within the discipline itself. It is not my place here to present a review of the discipline of mathematics education; that has been presented adequately and thoroughly elsewhere (Tsatsaroni, Lerman & Xu, 2003a, b; Hanna & Sidoli, 2002; Kieran 1994; Kilpatrick, 1992) and I will briefly draw on this work. As Tsatsaroni et al., I will compare a limited subset –the *PME Proceedings* (1-29), the published articles in *Educational Studies in Mathematics* and *Journal for Research in Mathematics Education.* Yet unlike Tsatsaroni et al., who only looked at 1990-2001, I will look over the whole 30 years of PME. My reason for selecting these sources is largely pragmatic; they all span the years 1976-2005 and were immediately available to me. (Interestingly a paper on the development of theories in mathematics education research in PME proceedings by Lerman, Tsatsaroni and Xu submitted for PME27 (2003), was rejected for falling outside the aims of PME (Stephen Lerman, personal communication) (See Lerman, Xu & Tsatsaroni, 2003).

I will start with what I do *not* focus on in this chapter. I do not look at sociocultural theory, because that appears elsewhere in this volume (see Lerman's chapter, nor, for the same reason, do I touch on affect –because that too has a chapter in this volume (see Gilah Leder's chapter). Neither of these, however are fully embedded in an *equity* framework and so do not explore the part played by mathematics education in social exclusion or in the differential appropriation of power. Similarly I do not look into classroom social interaction where that is not predicated upon an examination of those social categories which lead to differential treatment; the missing dimension being an explicit focus upon broader social variables, such as social class, gender, ethnicity, etc. I recognise however that some might argue that it is exactly in classroom interactions that social injustice and inequity are evident and therefore can be challenged (Nuria Gorgorió, personal communication). I do not disagree with that, but these aspects are not evident in PME research. I also do not look into the writing of those who work principally within an equity framework (e.g. Michael Apple, Walter Secada, Ole Skovsmose, Paola Valero, Renuka Vithal, etc.) because they are not closely associated with PME. A thorough study of the place of equity and social justice within mathematics education research requires a book in itself.

FROM WHENCE WE CAME

I want to begin by giving a small sense of history of PME –and this will be relevant to the central themes of this chapter. To understand who we are, we need to understand where we came from. At ICME1 (1969), Hans Freudenthal proposed an *ad hoc* round table devoted to the "psychological aspects of mathematics education". The success of this round table discussion lead, at ICME2 (1972), to the setting up of a workshop which was reconvened at ICME3 in Karlsruhe in 1976. This again proved so successful that ...

> it was decided to form PME. Hans Freudenthal convened the first meeting at Utrecht in 1977. The meeting lasted 2 or 3 days and there were 70 participants. Proceedings were not published formally, but copies of the talks were circulated to all members. I was secretary to a small committee formed to establish the group. The next meeting was in 1978 at Osnabruck; this produced the first bound proceedings. The 1979 meeting was organized by Richard Skemp and David Tall in Warwick, and the 1980 meeting, held in conjunction with ICME4, was hosted by Karplus and others in Berkeley. At this meeting, Vergnaud, Meissner and I were appointed to write a constitution, and this was adopted in the following year. (Alan Bell, personal communication)
>
> I attended PME1 in Utrecht and it was a memorable event. It was chaired by Hans Freudenthal speaking simultaneously English and French and sometimes German, organized by IOWO (free of charge, even the lunch!). There were no proceedings. The participants only sent abstracts when applying for presenting. (Colette Laborde, personal communication)

Nine of those attending PME1 were still registered as members in 2005 (Bell, Van Dormolen, Hart, Laborde, Nesher, Tall, Verhoef, Vinner, Zimmermann). There were 85 members in 1977 –97% from just 7 countries and 86% from Europe. By 2004, membership had risen to 822. In PME28 (Bergen), 485 attended from 42 countries (though only 21 countries had more than 6 participants); in PME29 (Melbourne), 359 attended from 71 countries (with only 10 countries sending more than 6), with 50% from just three countries (Australia, New Zealand, USA). PME is clearly a success in human capital terms. Yet, it remains dominated by predominantly rich northern (plus Australia), white countries. Even combining PME28 and PME29 together, 80% of the attendees came from Europe (including Israel), North America or Australia/New Zealand. In geographical terms this shows how little has changed in 29 years. Of course, this represents a vicious cycle, because only those countries with the resources can host a PME conference and these tend to be located away from those countries (mainly in Africa and Asia) traditionally marginalised.

I believe the form of this now huge organisation, rested with the interests of that particular group of people who were there at the time of its genesis –largely white, northern and cognitivist. That is not a criticism –one can hardly be criticised for being any of those– but PME is now into its second or even third generation of researchers, few of whom were there at the start and so intergenerational shifts are bound to occur. Surprisingly, up until PME29, the major goals of PME had not changed since they were originally written, and this does seem to have affected the research that PME has privileged and disseminated. Yet we must see this in context. PME merely reflects the broad focus on the cognitive domain that existed and persisted at the time is was becoming established. It is only relatively recently that sociology has established itself more broadly within educational theory and research. Hence we need to see PME as a growing organism reflecting the environment into which it is developing and responding.

In this celebration of 30 years of PME –I want to ask what or who is PME and how do I give a survey of the contribution to equity. This has to be a pragmatic decision and my focus will be upon the published proceedings rather than the output of its members –although one issue that will be relevant is to consider the PME contributions made in contrast with the broader work by mathematics education researchers. A problem with this approach is a result of the limitations upon the length and therefore the scope of PME Research Reports –a mere 8 pages. We have all experienced the need to cut extraneous material from our papers for this purpose.

In a broad and all encompassing survey of the field of mathematics education research, Kilpatrick (1992) identified its heritage –"Two disciplines have had a seminal influence on research in mathematics education. The first is mathematics itself. [...] The second major influence is psychology" (p. 5) and nowhere is this disciplinary heritage more apparent that in PME and it helps to give us some insight into the genesis of the organisation. What I found particularity astonishing, is that in this 30 page chapter with 271 references, there was **not one** reference to PME or to any single PME research report. This may be partly because research reports are really "work in progress" and the real work is published elsewhere, but it is surprising nevertheless.

GESTATING THE PME IDENTITY

The struggle in writing this chapter is not only in being clear on what research within an equity framework would look like and what focus it might have, but it is the realisation that, whatever it was likely to be, there was not a lot of it in PME research. Given the change of aims at PME29, moving the organisation beyond the psychological to the broader areas of research; there are bound to be implications for the areas of research I focus on in this chapter.

Should everyone be interested in equity and if so, should it permeate their professional academic work? I think this is a complex question bound to raise temperatures –because it is a *political* question. I suspect no-one is going to say they do not agree with equity, but it is how equity is constructed and operationalised which gives it significance. A different, professional and intellectual question is, should PME as an (the?) international research organisation in mathematics education be interested in equity issues? It is clear, that at its establishment, PME had a cognitive orientation and purpose which derives from the state of the discipline in the late 1960's, yet the question remains, is this orientation now sufficiently broad to support research even in those areas that PME has traditionally seen as its domain.

I want to argue that PME has suffered by focusing only weakly on equity issues. By ignoring attributes such as social class, culture, gender, race, ethnicity and so on does not make them go away or reduce the effect they have upon learning and teaching mathematics. Rather, it makes the research less powerful by ignoring the very real contexts which could give us a better understanding of theory.

The problem comes in just how to determine or measure the contribution to knowledge that PME had made –is it through the research reports in proceedings, or the broader activity of its members; do we need to consider the whole research output of PME members or just that presented at PME Conferences. This is a problematic issue –not only for the writing of this chapter, but also in the development of PME. I have taken the decision here to focus upon research reports and plenaries, but have cast an eye toward Discussion Groups and Working Groups. Since the printed outputs of these groups are very limited, I have seen these as indicative of trends within PME. As interest groups, they do after all represent a broader involvement than a single paper presentation. I have then contrasted this with research outside PME.

Research reports from PME1 have proved difficult to find, as they do not exist! However by PME2 a public stance of the position and role of the organisation can already be seen in the preface to the first published proceedings:

> Mathematics seems to the psychologist as a particularly concentrated example of the functioning of human intelligence, hardly concealed by falsifying effects. (Cohors-Fresenborg & Wachsmuth, 1978, p. 4)

This seems to be a very clear articulation of the issue; however, the "falsifying effects" of race, class, and gender do seem to have been concealed quite well. Yet there was already recognition of some controversy over this tension:

> A concern with central concept building and scientific methods of mathematics for the improvement of mathematics teaching cannot be separated from a consideration of the social structures and the interactions in the classroom. In particular in these problems it can be seen that psycho-social phenomena can be, independent of the context of the instruction, causes of difficulty for the schoolchildren in understanding and of obstacles to learning. Psychologists as well as mathematicians appear to be aware of this problem, but as yet few papers have been presented. (Cohors-Fresenborg & Wachsmuth, 1978, p. 4-5)

Although there has been clear movement here –classroom interactions is a strong theme in PME research– almost 30 years later, we can still say "but as yet few papers have been presented" which address the separation of learning obstacles from social structures. Yet we must not lose sight of the intention of the founders of the organisation to focus on the psychology of learning:

> During the ICME of 1976 in Karlsruhe a group including Freudenthal, Fischbein, Skemp and others agreed there did not exist at that time an organization that concentrated on research on the cognitive aspects of mathematics education in particular. It was argued, that 'cognitive aspects' might be too narrow a description and therefore the current name of PME was decided on and PME was conceived. (Joop Van Dormolen, personal communication)

It is interesting that "psychology" was adopted as a broader description than "cognitive aspects", especially given the arguments between PME27 and PME29 over the need to broaden the psychological focus still further. The cognitive and psychological orientation of PME then is no accident or mere short-sightedness; but might be considered an aspect of history. The stunning growth of PME shows the idea was of its time and it captured the spirit of the times and captured imaginations.

This historical interlude then forms the background for this chapter, in which I examine PME research in each of its three decades. Notwithstanding the attractions such a base-10 division must have for mathematicians, I believe we can see such a division in the growth of PME. Table 1 in Lerman's chapter, shows one can see how just the number of research reports increases exponentially. Even looking at three cycles of 10 years (if we ignore the odd outlier connected to conference location effects) we can see clear increases in the growth of the conference.

Table 1. Number of PME Research Reports

	PME 1-10	*PME 11-20*	*PME 21-29*
No. of research reports	50-80	80-150	120-200

I will look in this chapter at the genesis of issues that are related to social structures –to social power, social class, gender, and exclusion by language and ethnicity, and so on. Such terminology might be construed as strange in PME– but they are not peripheral issues. There is a considerable literature located within these fields, and the NCTM articulates a very clear position on this:

> Every student should have equitable and optimal opportunities to learn mathematics free from bias—intentional or unintentional—based on race, gender, socioeconomic status, or language. In order to close the achievement gap, all students need the opportunity to learn challenging mathematics from a well-qualified teacher who will make connections to the background, needs, and cultures of all learners. (NCTM, 2005a)

The "achievement gap" here surely needs to be of concern to PME, because learning mathematics is at the heart of the *raison d'etre* for the organisation. If so, where do we need to be looking?

> Convincing evidence suggests that teachers can play a significant role in closing the achievement gap. Unfortunately, students who have the greatest needs often have the least qualified teachers. Key decision makers in government, industry, community leadership, and education must fully understand the issues related to equity in mathematics education so that they can carry a strong, consistent message. Finally, educators at the local, state, and federal levels should be knowledgeable about equity issues and communicate with their legislative representatives about the current inequities in education. (NCTM, 2005a)

Given that this achievement gap results in large part from issues related to equity and social justice, we might therefore expect such issues to be of central concern to PME and therefore have a high profile in PME conferences. But, do they?

PME – THE EARLY YEARS (PME1-PME10)

Looking over the first ten years of PME, one can begin to see the genesis of some focus on the social context –though this needs exploring to see just what definition we might use. Initially, Fischbein discusses *Intuition and Mathematical Education* and Bauersfeld, *Interpersonal Aspects of Classroom Communication* both in PME2 and both these strands have continued to be explored to the present day, yet, have a particular way of seeing the individual as located within social interaction between other persons and broader social forces are not explored.

Possibly the first entry into the social domain that transcended the individual as key cognising agent followed in PME3 by Lesh (1979) who considered *Social/Affective Factors Influencing Problem Solving Capabilities*. At this stage, his interest is within the social organisation and interactions within the classroom –

namely group problem solving, and interpersonal meta-activity– and so still retaining the person-centred approach.

PME4 produced little in the way of research specifically focussing on the social dimension of learning, but at PME5 Alan Bishop introduced "*Affective factors influencing mathematical involvement*" (Bishop, 1981). However, his treatment at this stage is more "cognitive" than "social" and there is little further discussion of social context until PME6 where "*cultural*" appears in a research report title for the first time in "*A cross cultural study of problem solving*" (Burton, Balachef, Bauersfeld, Branca & Pimm, 1982) which looks at different strategies used by learners in several different countries. It is also in PME6 that "Social Aspects" appears as part of the programme structure and this is quite a significant move. Until this point, there were somewhat isolated contributions activated by a few individuals –in which Alan Bishop appears to have been particularly active.

A challenging paper by Josette Adda argues that the teaching of mathematics is not neutral (Adda, 1982), by presenting the portrayal of French social life in mathematics textbooks as depicting a life alien to many pupils. Adda gets the prize for the first mention of Pierre Bourdieu in PME proceedings; it is only a mention and we have to wait several years for his re-emergence as a significant influence. A study of anxiety suggests girls suffer more than boys (Hutton, 1982), but that is the extent of reports on gender issues.

Hidden away in PME8 we find the following, which throws some light on some potentially significant social implications for teaching mathematics.

> Teachers appeared to value cheerful unquestioning compliance along with demonstrated success in a relatively narrow band of convergent activities. Consequently many individualistic non-conforming pupils were eliminated from the reckoning by their teachers, whereas other pupils who could operate successfully in the class framework but who lacked true talent were included. (Endean & Carss, 1984, p. 198)

This seems a powerful suggestion, because much work at PME reports research into achievement in mathematics, but here is a suggestion that talent at mathematics is not the key indicator of being identified by a teacher as a successful learner –one has also to be compliant and fit into a picture of an ideal pupil held by the teacher– already known as an issue for 30 years in the sociology of education. Becker (1952) suggested teachers have particular images of their "ideal pupil" which are by no mean objective or equitable; the likelihood is that an "ideal pupil" is likely to be white, conforming, and similar in background and values to the teacher. This issue however does not get taken up and reported within PME to any significant degree and is a good example how a blind spot can be caused by looking in one direction and not being eclectic.

Phillip Clarkson introduces us to language and mathematics in Papua New Guinea (Clarkson, 1984) and brings the issue of "indigenous" languages onto the stage for the first time at PME. Clarkson takes a position that language learning and concept formation have always been of interest to educational psychologists

(p. 331) and sows a seed for future research into language related issues – something which does get taken up as we shall see.

Gender issues only begin to be treated in earnest in 1984 at PME8 with its own section in the proceedings –with papers on affective variables (Barboza, 1984) and sex differences in performance (Collis & Taplin, 1984). It is clear by then that the relative lack of participation of girls in mathematics was seen as a concern (p. 399) and it is here we see a suggestion (p. 429) that boys put their errors down to someone else for not teaching them correctly, but girls put their errors down to their own deficiencies. Such features are however not new in the field, yet are "new" to the PME *oeuvre* and still relatively undeveloped therein. PME research on gender thus becomes relatively unsophisticated and undeveloped due to its disconnection with research outside the narrow confines allowed by the aims of PME. This is not just true of gender, but is true of equity issues more broadly.

PME9 shows no attention to the social context of mathematics education at all in the 500 pages of its proceedings –yet interestingly we begin to see the use of the plenary lecture to raise issues which might be broader than research reports offer. (Plenary lectures after all are not refereed!) In his plenary lecture, Bishop (1985) raised some of these issues of social context. In "*The Social Psychology of Mathematics Education*" he raises questions about the ways the social environment influences children, and how consequently it affects teachers' judgements. This seems to be a key paper for identifying future directions PME might take up because Bishop encourages more research at the societal level which

> concerns the various institutions in society and the political and ideological influences which they bring to bear on the mathematics education of our children. (Bishop, 1985, p. 3)

Bishop raised the existence of role stereotyping as a particularly dangerous strategy used by teachers and examines not just ability stereotyping, in which mathematics teachers favour the more able, but also gender stereotyping, class and race stereotyping as well as handicap stereotyping (p. 7-8). A mathematical activity is as much a social activity as it is an intellectual one (p. 10) and the context and the situation are all important. The problem therefore of focussing on the classroom is that key features are not visible –the level of education of the parents, the income and social background of the family, etc.

In PME10 we see a discussion of the effect of culture upon children's cognitive styles by contrasting German and Indonesia children (Cohors-Fresenborg & Marpung, 1986). Sadly the results reported seemed to be rather inconclusive and again rather isolated in PME research. Certainly here the line between the social and the psychological becomes so blurred as to be meaningless.

So after 10 years of PME we have an example of some slight attention to issues that relate to the social context in which learners and teachers live and work. This work is relatively minor and peripheral when compared to the majority of research reported at PME (and which you can read of in this book). In contrast, much of the early focus of PME research was upon children and children's learning of specific mathematical ideas again a reflection of the original cognitive orientation. Celia Hoyles has described this period of PME as concentrating on

> student ability, student understanding, and representation of specific mathematical concepts and "attributes", "attitudes" and "processes" of students in the mathematics classroom. (Hoyles, 1992, p. 32)

In these early days the role of the teacher also was relatively minor:

> The 10th anniversary conference in 1986 appeared to relegate the teacher once again to the position of passive conveyor of facts and information albeit using a variety of diagnostic methods and teaching tools. (Hoyles, 1992, p. 33)

Now of course if we look at this period (1976-1986) with the lenses of today it looks quite limited. However, this needs to be seen as an early stage of a recognisable development. What does become clear is the issue of teacher education, once seen as not the domain of PME begins to emerge after PME10 as at least one strand of research activity for improving learning and teaching. Prior to PME11 papers on teacher development had been rejected as not within the domain of PME, something which is unimaginable now as teacher education, and the teachers themselves have come under greater scrutiny (Janet Ainley, personal communication).

Of course one has to look at the initial setting up of the organisation and the intentionality of that group. A cursory glance at the people who took the initiative suggests the purpose was to come together to explore the cognitive and psychological domain because of the exciting challenges that perspective offered for the development of a new field in research –mathematics education.

I will finish this section with a final extract from PME10 –this time from a plenary lecture by Christine Keitel titled "*Cultural premises and presuppositions in psychology of mathematics education*":

> [It is a] Fiction that education is not pervaded by the social political, economical conflicts in our societies, and that it could comply with its mission in keeping above reality. (Keitel, 1986, p. 48)

Systems of education around the world, and in which mathematics is always central, are all situated within political systems –something which makes that quote significant.

THE DISCIPLINE IN THE FIRST PHASE OF PME

Educational Studies in Mathematics (ESM) itself began in 1968 –at about the same time as PME, and has come to be seen as the most significant journal representing the field (see Hanna & Sidoli, 2002, for a history of *Educational Studies in Mathematics*). What it publishes can therefore reasonably (I claim) be seen as indicating the dominant themes and discourses in the field. Early work in ESM reflected the same cognitive orientation of PME, but there were examples of broader themes relating to equity which were largely of an anthropological nature and largely explored language and learning (Zepp, 1981, 1982; Jones, 1982; Clarkson, 1983). Between 1970 and 1984 the *Journal for Research in Mathematics Education* has a similar cognitive orientation –with interspersions of broader issues– especially issues related to the position of blacks, Native Americans and minority groups and the learning of mathematics.

In terms of gender research, ESM was similarly indicating relatively little attention up to 1985, but prioritized gender-related differences. Leder (1980) and Fennema (1979) looked at gender related differences in learning and intimated that these might be more related to the school system than any more deeply humanistic characteristics.

The practice of ability grouping becomes examined in ESM (Brassell, Pity & Brook, 1980) as a practice requiring greater understanding. This research presents an interest in pupil self-concept and anxiety –both issues related to reducing the learning opportunities for low ranked students. Here the theoretical positioning fails to challenge the practice and is weakly related to the existence of a broader sociological literature already in the public domain.

A first openly political paper (Skovsmose, 1985) argued that if we were to avoid mathematics becoming just a way of socialising children into a technological society, it needed to encompass critical educational theory. This is the first attempt to relate mathematics education to broader social and political issues –and signals a trend resulting in the later publication of Skovsmose's own book (1994) and Steig Mellin-Olsen's "*Politics of Mathematics Education*" (Mellin-Olsen, 1987) –both overtly placing mathematics education within a political framework.

By 1985 therefore we see that PME research interests reflect quite closely the disciplinary traditions more widely with a broadly cognitive orientation –focussing on domain specific learning but with somewhat peripheral attempts to introduce work that locates mathematics education into a broader field of study.

PME – ESTABLISHING AN IDENTITY (PME11-PME20)

The middle years of PME (1987-1996) can be seen as one of distinct changes in key focuses and activity in PME –and in the discipline itself. The 9 volumes of proceedings between 1976 and 1986 contrast starkly with 31 volumes between 1987 and 1996. Discussion of constructivism activated and energised much debate during these years and social constructivism becomes a key focus. It is debatable however whether the "social" in social constructivism is the same as the "social" in social justice –indeed I would maintain they are quite distinct. But in the face of considerable cognitive orientated research there is a clear emergence of a broader set of issues. These issues seem to me to be broadly classifiable under the headings of language and communication, gender and learning, social and cultural context of learning, vocational contents of learning and the rest of this section will be structured around those themes.

Language and communication

It was in 1990 that papers were grouped into a category "social interaction, communication and language" and the emergence of this category of research indicates a broader focus than a cognitive orientation into exploring the contexts in which that cognition takes place; pupil collaboration in classroom tasks, scaffolding classroom discussions, language structure and cognitive appropriation etc. Language here however is related to intra-personal communication and almost exclusively focuses upon language as a means of communication rather than a means of exclusion and injustice. One's language is central to one's social being and the experience of many children is to be located in minority communities where the language of learning is the language of the majority. Khisty, McLeod and Bertilson looked at Hispanic classrooms in the USA and in particular at the positions of children's language and the communication of mathematical ideas (Khisty, McLeod & Bertilson, 1990). This paper is significant for research into bilingualism because it is one of the first that looks at bilingual classrooms in a developed country. The paper also brings an ethnographic perspective that Khisty has been using ever since. The ethnographic approach is important for research into language issues, and arguably equity issues more generally, since it is interested in practices and meanings, rather than in individual cognition; practices and meanings are the link between social structure and individual learning, although how that link functions is incredibly complex (Richard Barwell, personal communication).

Gender and learning mathematics

An overarching focus between PME11 and PME20 is on exploring differences between male and female learners in the classroom and upon strategies for amelioration, yet as of yet, not upon the causes for differences or on broader implications. Over this period, research is still limited in scope, with the Gender and Mathematics section in PME11 for example containing only one six-page research report (Amit & Movshovitz-Hadar, 1987). Research reports tend to focus upon explorations of women's problem solving (Amit & Movshovitz-Hadar, 1987; Evans, 1988; Gentry & Underhill, 1988; Lea, 1988), attitudes toward mathematics, differential choices to study mathematics (Otten & Kuyper, 1988) and the self perception of women (Leder, 1989).

Studies of the choices women make to study mathematics appear to show girls favouring mathematics for different reasons than boys –but there is no clear cut evidence of greater success (Otten & Kuyper, 1988). This seems to indicate thinking has moved on from deficit models to more cultural models –and indeed the research literature outside of PME between 1987 and 1996, supports this. Many of the approaches and pedagogical models were often not working, and new approaches were required, as Leder (1989) pointed out:

> Despite the considerable number of programmes mounted to promote equity in mathematics learning, girls and boys with comparable achievement in

mathematics perceived themselves and were perceived by their teachers differently in a number of subtle ways. (p. 225)

Further research in Holland (Kuyper & Van der Werf, 1990) still focuses upon differential achievement –but in this case identifies a more significant effect– that of attitude –concluding– "the gender differences in maths are not the teachers' fault" (p. 150) –which is nice to know– but still leaves unanswered the question of whose fault it might be? Attribution of "fault" in this sense is hugely problematic though, because schools and mathematics become constitutive of the individual and Underwood (1992) presents PME16 with evidence of gender differentials in classroom interactions resulting in boys being positioned to take advantages of opportunities offered to them more so than girls.

We really need to see this work within the context of work undertaken outside of PME, and there is by 1996 already a considerable literature, attesting to the need to shift a focus away from "girls and mathematics" to "gender and mathematics" (Leder, 1992) and some of the undesirable influences that mathematics has upon the construction of identities in the young (Atweh & Cooper, 1995). The PME preoccupation with exploring *girls* and mathematics from a cognitive perspective rather than by exploring *gender* and identity from a broader social perspective does seem to have reduced the intellectual boundaries upon PME research and positions PME research outside the changing perspectives taking place outside the organisation.

Social and cultural context of learning

Whereas the social context has a relatively low focus in research reports at least up to now, it would appear that social issues appear at PME through both Working Groups and Discussion Groups (in particular Alan Bishop's Social Aspects Group that ran from PME10 to PME16). By the end of this second decade, there were two Working/Discussion Groups focussing on *cultural* and on *social* aspects of learning of mathematics (PME16-23). These groups do not produce PME research reports such, but do provide a clear opportunity for PME members to share related issues –and possibly research activity that is subsequently not presented at PME.

PME members engage intellectually also through plenary lectures, and this second decade provides us with several examples of plenary lectures addressing this issue (Nunes, 1988; Boero, 1989; Bartolini Bussi, 1991; Schliemann, 1995). These plenary lectures have in common a desire to bring in the outside world to our understanding of learning mathematics, yet (or because of this) one might question their being included in a survey of PME research. They are however in the proceedings and have a more public face than research reports at least in the number of attendees and the opportunity for present work with a broader remit; they probably do need to be dealt with slightly differently in considering the development of some cannon of PME.

Nunes's (1988) PME12 plenary lecture on "*Street mathematics and school mathematics*" raised the following issue

> Closely associated with the class structure is the phenomenon of school failure. Children from the dominant classes by and large are successful in school. In contrast children form the working class fail in mathematics in school in high proportions. (p. 1)

What she goes onto say is that thc usual explanation for the failure of large numbers of working class children is seen to lie within their own lack of competence, yet her research (see Nunes, Schliemann & Carraher, 1993) indicates some children's lack of ability in mathematics was not the correct explanation for children failure in school mathematics (Nunes, 1988, p. 7).

Now this direction does appear to identify equity and social justice as key issues –but this research was not reported at PME– although Nunes has presented work on context, culture and cognition to PME conferences illustrating that learning is culturally situated, and takes place outside of school (e.g. Nunes, 1989). This illustrates a further feature of these plenary lectures –they provide an overview of research– much of which lies outside that presented as PME research reports.

In a PME13 plenary lecture, Boero (1989) discussed the issue of mathematical literacy through an understanding of the importance of context and suggested we need to "insert the learning aims into contexts rich in meaning and motivation" (p. 62). Such approaches need to make explicit and link the cultural and didactical choices made by teachers many of whom are identified by Boero as directing the work of pupils with leaning difficulties toward activities having little mathematical value. Studies continue to illustrate that teachers still make such decisions –and restrict the thinking of pupils from poorer social-economic backgrounds. (We need to remember that in 1989 ethno-mathematics had still to reach PME.) In someway this mirrors Ole Skovsmose's approach to using mathematics to develop critical literacy (Skovsmose, 1994) –I understand however, that Skovsmose has never attended a PME conference.

Again in PME15, Bartolini Bussi's (1991) plenary lecture focused upon *Social Interaction and Mathematical Knowledge*. Here she makes a strong case that research into the social construction of knowledge was far from established in the early 90s "because of a lack of worldwide, accepted theoretical and methodological tools" (p. 2). A theoretical approach which might be helpful in developing such an approach –activity theory– is suggested by Bartolini Bussi. Although it is "not very popular" in PME, "it could be very useful in framing research on social interaction in mathematics education research" (p. 3). "The analysis of the process of internalisation of collective activity and of the conditions of its functioning within the zone [of proximal development] are still open problems in activity theory" (Bartolini Bussi, 1991, p. 3) and therefore might be directions for PME research – something which has been taken up by a small number of research reports more recently.

An issue of interest in PME research has been the influence of pupils' background and everyday knowledge in their learning and attainment. For example, Lindenskov (1991) considers the importance of out of school knowledge in the formation of mathematical concepts. Again this is a potentially fruitful avenue –and it draws on previous cognitive studies in PME and begins to relate this to wider elements of the formation of knowledge. It links this also to: Harris' (1987) study of how work traditionally regarded as women's work can be seen as having deeply embedded mathematics; with Mellin-Olsen's (1987) work on the political basis of mathematics education; and to Lave's (1988) work on how mundane daily activities can be explored for their mathematical significance – though these are not embedded within the paper itself. This would seem intellectually to provide a strong stimulus for further research, yet such work might extend significantly outside that more usually presented in PME proceedings.

Bishop and De Abreu (1991) take this issue further drawing on the social cognition tradition (Lave, 1988; Saxe, 1990; D'Ambrosio, 1985). Here again we see attempts to investigate the relationship between school mathematics and out of school experiences and competence of Brazilian children. School mathematics is different to that used in out of school contexts, and this can cause problems on both sides of the school gates. Children fail to use their school mathematics out of school, but in the cane fields, Brazilian sugar farmers appear to calculate the areas of the field "wrongly". I find this a lovely account of children's experiences and the place of mathematics in their lives. It appears that whereas children did demonstrate capacities to work across the boundaries of both in- and out-of-school contexts, the problem remains "to what extent can pupils be enabled to make this link between outside and in school mathematics and will this improve their learning in school" (p. 135).

This theme of where mathematical knowledge is located is taken up again by Analúcia Schliemann in a PME19 plenary lecture "*Some Concerns about Bringing Everyday Mathematics in Mathematics Education*" (Schliemann, 1995). Here she raises concern over the issue of transfer between school mathematics and out of school activities. Students learn algorithms in school mathematics which are "efficient and quick this reducing the mental load involved in working out problems" (p. 47) Such a "focus on rules to be learned without considering the implicit mathematical relations that allow their construction usually leads to wrong steps when memory fails" (p. 48). In contrast, strategies used in the real world context of a problem are characterised by constant reference to the context itself. In a pointer to ethnomathematical tradition, Schliemann closes with the proposal that to develop advanced mathematical ideas one needs a synthesis of all knowledge and tools one has access to (p. 58) something that is developed later in a study of the position of the commutative law (Schliemann, Araujo, Cassundé, Macedo & Nicéas, 1994).

Guida de Abreu takes this further in PME16 (De Abreu, 1992) and takes the approach "where culture and cognition are constitutive of one another" (p. 25). In particular looking at how children experience the clash of cultural practices in a school setting "where the school mathematics culture is markedly different from that demonstrated outside school" (p. 25) –either in home cultures, street cultures or work cultures. The perspective here is that mathematics learning is culturally specific –and therefore socially located. This paper is perhaps one of the earliest attempts to open up ethnomathematics within the PME community –the previous appearance being Bishop and Pompeu (1991). A further study that draws on the work of Bishop, and locates itself within the situated cognition, is a study of Somali children leaning mathematics in the UK (Jones, 1996) –which is yet again an isolated paper whose work or theme in never carried over in PME. These issues are clearly being discussed on the periphery of PME research, but there is a significant item lag between its PME appearance, and the initiation of significant work outside PME.

In PME18-20 there is some emergence of broader social concerns. Khisty introduces us to those groups who predominantly underachieve in mathematics – those from poor backgrounds or ethnic minority groups (Khisty, 1994, p. 89). She claims, quite controversially, that the prevailing paradigm in mathematics education has placed the responsibility for failure on the student (p. 90) –arguing that poor or minority children suffer from poor learning styles, unsupportive families low self-esteem etc. (p. 91). Yet there is an alternative interpretation –that there is a systemic problem of identification and marginalisation of minority students. To some extent PME itself appears to marginalise the problems of minority and poor students –something proposed by Tony Cotton and myself (Cotton & Gates, 1996) in a paper arguing a focus on a psychological perspective without a broader social awareness is unable to support the development of equity and social justice.

Khisty argues that proposals for collaborative, groupwork in mathematics need to take into account –but rarely do– the issue of status, either social or linguistic. Whilst work in PME has looked into the influence of culture, this, according to Khisty, addresses "surface culture" (dress, styles, habits etc) and not "deep culture" (consciousness, identity). Such ignoring of deep culture (possibly related to what Pierre Bourdieu refers to as habitus) results in "a gap between home and school, that increases the chance of alienation and lack of engagement" (Khisty, 1994, p. 94).

> For too long we have held to a mythology that the leaning of mathematics is language, culture, and politically free. One result of this thinking has been that we can assume that "good teaching" is simply good teaching; that we can ignore the unique social-psychological and linguistic needs of minority students. (p. 95)

Understanding pupils' home backgrounds hardly figures in PME research reports between 1987 and 1996, yet Morgan and Merttens (1994) reported a major study involving some 3000 schools in which parents were engaged with the mathematical learning activities with their children. Their work starts from the established principle that "the socio-economic background of the home is the largest single factor in determining children's educational attainment" (p. 303). What their research highlights is the strength of differential power relationships, where parental involvement is limited to doing what the school thinks is appropriate (p. 310). It would seem valuable to connect this research to that looking at home-school cultures, learning in and out of school, and in this way develop an accumulated knowledge base. Schools make decisions on curriculum, on teaching and upon pupil organisation with little involvement or deferral to parents thereby exacerbating the separation of cultures. This however, is never reported again at PME, and no PME research is drawn upon either in the research report, or in the book that came out of this project (Merttens & Vass, 1990).

One issue centrally related to pupil organisation, is one that has received considerable attention recently –that of ability grouping or tracking– the process of placing children into teaching groups based upon some measure of ability. The literature on this is now considerable and shows this practice to be at least questionable (Slavin, 1996). Yet it figures as an almost universal practice in the UK even having Government prescription. It is an aspect of practice in many countries, yet this system received no attention in PME until 1995 in a report by Linchevski (1995). On surveying the research on grouping she concludes:

> It is therefore questionable whether ability grouping advances us toward the goal for which it was designed or whether it actually defeats this purpose. (p. 241)

Interestingly, in spite of having significant research literature to draw on, Linchevski is not able to draw on previous PME published research. What she finds is that the act of placement itself brings about higher achievement in mathematics; if two pupils otherwise equal were placed in different groups, the achievement of the pupil placed in the higher groups would be higher (p. 246). What this paper does not draw on, because the research had not been widely published for mathematics, is the *social* stratification that ability grouping brings about –that pupils from lower social classes are more likely to be placed in lower ability groups– and therefore their attainment would subsequently be lower –a clear equity issue. Mathematics thus serves to alienate and demotivate children form poorer socio-economic backgrounds, and some would argue, that this is one of its key functions –"The function of school mathematics in Western culture as a badge of eligibility for the privileges of society has often been noted" (Atweh, Bleicher & Cooper, 1998, p. 63)– but this function is not often recognised in PME research.

Vocational contexts of learning

An issue which might not be immediately recognised as an equity issue is that of a study of vocational training and the place of mathematics in the workplace. I think it is usefully thought of within an equity framework because of the patterns of employment and its relations to social mobility. Pupils are segregated worldwide through the school system into future vocational trajectories, sometimes at a very early age, as national systems direct young people, often as young as 14 or earlier, into vocational or academic schools or tracks. In this process, mathematics is not a mere bystander acting as a service subject but a tool for social division.

Research into this area first appears in a report by Strässer and Bromme (1989). This research explored teachers' conceptions of mathematics in vocational schools and in particular the use of mathematics. An interesting issue here is on the very strongly utilitarian, "mathematics-as-tool" nature of perceptions, and the relatively undeveloped notions of mathematics; mathematics is seen as purely as an operative tool rather that a way of understanding the contexts in workplace settings. Again here the focus moves beyond the purely cognitive and opens up a more social function that mathematics courses have.

Another strand in this theme is the mathematical demands of the workplace – and an early paper by Masingila (1992) looks at the mathematics in carpet laying. This is clearly part of the trend to look at the place of mathematics in everyday situations but has more than a romantic attachment to valuing the working class. As pointed out by Masingila, mathematics in school can be so sanitised and artificial as to make it virtually worthless as a set of social skills (Masingila, 1992, p. 86). Schoenfeld (1987) blamed the failure of many curriculum reforms upon this cultural conflict for "each of these curriculum reforms reflects an attempt to embed a selected aspect of mathematical thinking into what is essentially an alien culture, the traditional classroom" (p. 214). Here then is a further good reason why this has broad implications for PME research. PME has a tradition of interest and engagement in curriculum reform, but both curriculum, and reform are political entities reflection the priorities and values of the usually dominant social classes (Apple, 1979).

Overview

What is clear is that during the second decade of PME from 1886 to 1996, the "social turn" in mathematics education research (Lerman, 2000) has become manifest in the research literature (Bartolini Bussi, 1991, p. 1). This is true at a number of levels, the individual cognitive level, the classroom level and the social systemic level. The *raison d'etre* for PME appears to have focussed attention very much in the first decade upon the individual level, whereas the second decade has opened this up to consider a more interactionist approach –and a strand of work within the social factors in PME has taken this direction toward studies of culture, cognition and affect (see Evans & Tsatsaroni, 1993, and other chapters in this volume). This however has not yet reached the sophistication that theories have reached outside the PME research literature –the social systemic level. At this level we can begin to look at the influences upon mathematics attainment which are often invisible at the classroom level if one has a focus on the classroom as the system. We have a position where the bulk of PME research takes a distanced position from this –a stance critiqued by one teacher in De Abreu's study:

> What a big mistake it was to think initially that the "cultural and social" basis of mathematics has so little importance. Mathematics is basically a product of the culture of each race. It grows from the needs of each society, and the experiences of each one. These are the bases of its truth. (De Abreu, 1992, p. 31)

However, PME has given considerable attention to the notion of culture, and to understand the work of PME, one has to understand the work of individuals within that. So far the work of Alan Bishop is significantly dominant and influential, not just in presenting the results of research but also in offering new models and strategies (Bishop, 1993).

At the end of the second decade, PME research into equity, gender and ethnomathematics was clearly emerging as was attention to equity and social justice. The influence of the cognitive orientation would appear to mean that in some areas of mathematical learning, PME research had an established tradition (see most chapters in this book for example), yet issues of equity and the social implications of the culture of mathematics teaching were less developed within PME than outside of PME. Consequently such research would appear to be denied to PME participants and the restriction of the aim poses researchers is to force us to adopt strategies for privileging the cognitive at the expense of the social. This is bought home by the question posed by Khisty –"do our reforms actively and fully capitalise upon the working-class and minority students' home, culture and language, or are they excluded through lack of thought" (Khisty, 1994, p. 95). One has to look hard to find research on minority and working class cultures in PME proceedings.

THE DISCIPLINE IN THE SECOND PHASE

During the second phase of PME, we have seen themes beginning to shift to ask broader research questions and look outside of cognitive psychology for solutions. Outside of PME similar trends are apparent. In an article in ESM on ability grouping, Ruthven (1986) suggested teachers' judgements are influenced by the way pupils approach learning. Dominant perspectives on mathematics preference a hierarchical structuring with associated learning strategies; pupils who fit this model are stereotyped as "able". This is an important perspective, but is not one that features in PME research. Ruthven draws on appropriate sociological literature, but stops short of introducing social class as a key classification. At the time, contemporary sociological work had already identified the teacher expectation effect and models of the ideal pupil and made connections with the class nature of society, yet it seems such a connection fails to enter mathematics education literature. It is almost as if there is a semi permeable membrane between the two disciplinary traditions. There are pointers in the mathematics education literature into the related social structural issues, by Popkewitz (1988) for example:

> Mathematics cannot be treated solely as a logical construction or a matter of psychological interpretation. What is defined as school mathematics is shaped and fashioned by social and historical conditions that have little to do with the meaning of mathematics as a discipline of knowledge. (p. 221)

But he goes even further claming "what is transmitted as mathematical knowledge may have little to do with the disciplinary standards, expectations and understandings associated with the field of mathematics" (p. 245) –but at the time these were exactly the dominant interests of PME.

We can see the social context of learning coming more to the fore in mathematics education research during this period especially through the widely published work Nunes and Schliemann (1985). In this *Journal for Research in Mathematics Education* paper they suggest that schools cause disruption in children's learning by privileging certain mathematical routines over others In this paper we see the introduction of a strand of research which to be fully understood requires greater theoretical resources, which as I have argued was only marginally touched upon in PME research and then only in Nunes's (1988) PME12 plenary lecture. This groundbreaking research led to the publication of their seminal work in the field that has spawned much research since (Nunes, Schliemann & Carraher, 1993).

Finally, attention is also given to mathematics teaching as a system of tradition, challenging the view of traditional cognitive orientation. Gregg (1995) for example argues that

> teachers are not funneled into traditional practices ... teachers, student and administrators actively particulate in the production and reproduction of these practices. (p. 461)

According to this position, mathematics teaching is a game played with emphasis on rules, procedure and conventions in order to achieve social stratification, rather than an academic discipline with widely accepted socially neutral principles.

PME – QUESTIONING OUR IDENTITY (21-29)

Part of the difficulty in looking at the third phase of PME is the sheer volume of the research. The printed proceedings for PME21-29 (36 volumes) just about matches that of all that went before in PME1-20 (40 volumes). It was a decade of development and shifts. It was also more difficult finding the boundary between equity and other focuses upon culture, communication etc. all of which become blurred. When does a study of patterns of classroom interaction become an issue of equity? There will be some who might take a different position upon defining "equity". I have not considered studies of classroom communities of practice, as an issue of "equity" unless there are issues of differential power resulting from social-economic factors, or language, minority or ethnicity issues. The result is there are really no more than 10 research reports that come into my remit for this chapter.

In a paper I presented to PME21, I argued that social structure needs to be a central consideration in developing a critical social psychology (Gates, 1997). I am sure there are some who would claim that this paper has nothing to do with what PME stands for, because it has no psychology in it at all, and very little mathematics, yet it was accepted.

Language, discourse and critical consciousness

A thought provoking strand of attention in PME in the third age is a greater focus upon language and the politics of discourse, and more broadly upon critical studies.

Work on multilingual classrooms and pupil cultural background has a considerable airing through the work of Khisty in particular, and has been taken on by the work of Barwell (2001) and Setati (2003) –this broadening continuing with the establishment by Barwell, Setati and Halai in 2003 of the Working Group on Teaching and Learning Mathematics in Multilingual Classrooms. Also, since 2002, PME conferences have also been preceded by a two-day working group meeting of the Multilingual Mathematics Group organised by Barwell. These elements suggest we are seeing a possible theme in the work of PME –which developed in 2004 into a Research Forum (Barwell & Clarkson, 2004). This forum explored the role of theory, and the social and political contexts in which diversity in language is seen as a political force and a potential exclusionary mechanism. The work of Barwell (2001) here is particularly interesting because he offers a methodology drawing on discursive psychology, and draws on significant PME prior research, yet the forum begins to move us into new ground. I believe we are seeing here shifts in the paradigms that define PME research –and consequently define PME as an organisation.

In the real world, multilingualism is closer to the norm than monolingualism. However much research reported at PME conferences is conducted in classrooms where many (or all) the students are multilingual and learning in a second or additional language, but usually no mention is ever made of this. Of course, this argument can be extended to other social categories such as social class, gender, ethnicity etc. (Barwell & Clarkson, 2004, p. 252).

Moschkovich (1996) made a number of contributions to PME research and in an early contribution challenges the deficit view of bilingualism. Setati (2003) further argued that language use "is as much a function of politics as it is of cognition and communication" (p. 151). Whilst Setati argues this is particularly true in countries such as South Africa, I think the argument travels much further –"where English and mathematics both have symbolic power and where procedural discourse dominates over conceptual discourse in school mathematics teaching and learning" (p. 157). Sadly perhaps, this is as true in Nottingham as it is in Johannesburg, though maybe not as visible. Khisty sees language as capital (Khisty, 1998, p. 98), and her work has increasingly focussed on understanding the complexity of the linguistic context in classrooms, and upon the qualities and interventions teachers can implement in order to redress some of the inequity caused by overlooking the political role of language (Khisty, 2001; Morales, Khisty & Chval, 2003).

Gender and learning mathematics

Studies of gender remains an interest to some PME researchers –yet still the emphasis is upon the interplay between the cognitive and the effective, and upon observed differences between boys and girls on different types of mathematics, in spite of the theoretical development outside PME. The approach stops short of asking deeper questions –why these differences come about? How girls and boys become constructed? Is mathematics in some way implicated in their positioning? But the notion of "positioning" is largely a social notion –because it metaphorically contrasts different social positions and as such does not easily fit into the aims of PME.

So we find girls have less confidence on open, applied problems and they rate themselves as lower than boys, and that performance does not account for these differences (Vermeer, Boekaerts & Seegers, 1997) but we do not know why. A consistent finding was that "boys were more inclined to be overconfident, whereas girls were more inclined to be under confident" (p. 268). This is itself is a finding consistent with much gender orientated research outside of PME –but it raises more questions than it solves. Other research identifies changes in relative performance as pupils reach and navigate their way though adolescence (Kota & Thomas, 1997). This would seem to be important –because if the physical, emotional and hormonal changes that take place affect learners differently, maybe we need to take that into account, not only in teaching, but also in research. This is not merely in classroom interaction, but in their interface between cognition and mathematics –for example in the way boys and girls use visual representations when solving more complex problems (George, 1999). However, there is evidence that such differences are not (just) a result of differential maturation, because differences in mathematical argumentation have been found in younger school children (Pehkonen, 1999). There are two strands of questions that may be asked of this research: Where do the differences emanate, and what is to be done about it. Is it a cognitive problem? Is it an equity problem? What is the influence of the teacher and the school? These issues are regularly discussed in the wider research literature.

A paper at PME21 by Hannula and Malmivuori substantiates the existence of differential confidence, but takes the consideration of influences further.

> These factors can be traced back to the learning processes and environmental features operating in mathematics learning situations ... much responsibility for these features may be assigned to mathematics teachers and their actions. [*However*] the teachers' actions may not arise from their personal views, characteristics or experiences as mathematics teachers, but also from the features and lives of schools. (Hannula & Malmivuori, 1997, p. 39)

Now this seems to be to be a nice example of a flow from the cognitive to the social; from the thinking and learning of children, to the functioning of schools, possibly as an unintended consequence of the larger organising features of schools and education systems. This is taken up again by Zevenbergen in a study of boys' learning mathematics (Zevenbergen, 1999). This remains an isolated piece of work within PME, but it seems to me at least to raise some fundamental questions about how mathematics classrooms are. In this paper, Zevenbergen argues that boys' behaviour needs to be seen as a part of the construction of their masculine identity, which is organised according to their social class background. As such, the interactions that result "offer restricted outcomes for learning mathematics" (p. 353) particularly for working class boys. It is not a giant leap to conclude that the social class and gender background of pupils is potentially central to their engagement in and with mathematics. This is a less than astounding finding, consistent (but with a focus on mathematics) with the findings of Willis (1977) in his research on working class boys in the 70s. Zevenbergen's article contains no single reference to PME research.

In a plenary at PME25, Leder (2001) discussed the place of gender research in PME and her response is challenging and quite unequivocal:

> To judge from the contents of the Research Reports included in Conference Proceedings, would those hoping to hear cutting edge research –whether experimental or theoretical, qualitative or quantitative– be more likely to be satisfied or disappointed by the fare at PME conferences? Where are the reports of research studies detailed in other venues? In which more radical feminist perspectives are being adopted, females are less frequently considered a homogenous group, and fine grained rather than collective data are presented? Where are the reports of scholarly evaluations of large scale interventions? Or detailed case studies which focus on individual rather than group differences? Or reflective accounts of the impact of the personal beliefs and theoretical orientation or the researchers undertaking the research on the design of the study, dates gathering decisions, choice of instrumentation? (p. 52)

Although some attention to Gender issues continues through to PME29 with, for example, work on gender differences in younger children (Horne, 2003, 2004) and the role of IT in constructing gendered mathematical identities (Forgasz, 2002, 2003, 2004; Kaino & Salani, 2004) little has changed in the way Leder seeks. The study by Forgasz and her colleagues –which also sparked off a Research Forum in PME27 on equity and ICT (Vale, Leder & Forgasz, 2003) presents us with some thought provoking ideas about the impact of differential access, ownership and interaction with computers in school and the home. Forgasz concludes, "issues of equity cannot be ignored if students' opportunities to learn mathematics are to be optimised" (Forgasz, 2004, p. 406).

In this search for the PME contribution to research on Gender, I experienced the same reaction as Leder (2001) –it has been a "provocative exercise" (p. 53). The contribution to scholarly study on gender and mathematics has been less than one might have hoped for –much of the "cutting edge" work on gender and mathematics takes place outside of PME– often by those researchers attending PME conferences. Yet PME is not the place for presenting and critiquing such research.

Social and cultural context of learning

The recognition of the importance of the pupils' cultural context remains. In particular, studies of the social mathematical norms in the classroom continue to be addressed (Hodge & Stephan, 1998). It is by now well established that 'culture' is a factor and the work of Yackel and Cobb (1996) explored this ground –though this is not always related to issues of equity, diversity and social exclusion.

By the third phase of PME, interest in the compatibility between home and school cultures and context had grown in the literature. A report of a large study in the UK (Baker & Street, 2000) introduced this into PME and began to theorise the boundaries children face between home and school numeracy practices. This can be seen as a continuation, yet extension, of the "street mathematics" and work-related mathematics research previously discussed. Yet this research foregrounds much more strongly the social role of mathematics in potentially being about causing differential underachievement in school compared to the home.

Yet what is very clear between PME22 and PME29 is the increase number of researchers looking toward critical theory and attempts to understand pupils' social background as factors illuminating key features of their learning. Povey and Boylan (1998) explicitly addressed working class students who outside a normal classroom environment were quite capable of being self regulating and with greater engagement in their learning. This contrasts quite starkly with the authority and discipline issues seen as major concerns for school mathematics teachers when working with working class pupils. We might ask here what it is about school mathematics pedagogy and curriculum which alienates significant proportions of pupils.

Frempong (1998) highlights how "research has increased our understanding on how schools and classrooms affect children from diverse backgrounds by addressing two major questions: (1) to what extent do schools and classrooms vary in their outcomes for students of different status? And (2) what school and classroom practices improve levels of schooling outcomes and reduce inequalities between high and low status groups?" (p. 304). In addition, "successful schools tend to be those which have relatively high achievement levels for students from low socio-economic backgrounds" (Frempong, 2005, p. 343). Frempong's research indicates, consistently with Povey and Boylan, that the "general attitude of students towards mathematics rather than individual student attitudes is more important in reducing social class inequalities and levels of mathematics achievement" (p. 304). Hence it is the social level of engagement with mathematics, rather than the individual, which has greater influence –and therefore needs to be the focus of strategies for change. If PME is about producing cutting edge research for change and improvement, it therefore needs a greater focus on the social forces at work.

This social level of engagement again brings us back to how the school organises pupils, and whether we see this as merely a bureaucratic arrangement for organising pedagogy, or a critical strategy for social stratification. Kutscher and Linchevski (2000) presented research which identifies the different ways in which pupils respond to placement in teaching groups. Kutscher and Linchevski found that only high attaining pupils preferred working in tracks, with low and middle attaining students preferring to work in mixed ability groups. Lower and middle attaining students object to tracking because of the shame and failure related to bring assigned to the lower tracks (Kutscher & Linchevski, 2000, p. 204) and the lack of working with stronger students from whom they could learn. There are very consistent finding here with work reported elsewhere by Boaler and others (see

Boaler, 1997a, b), and it would seem to raise very pertinent questions we could explore as part of a cumulative development of PME research.

Of course by recognising differences in pupils, we come then to need to ask the nature of that difference, and notions of identity become useful. Sfard and Prusak (2005) discussed in a plenary lecture to PME29 such differences by exploring notions of identity for immigrant children and in particular how people become positioned as learners by the cultural practices they live in. This look like being a useful approach in our search for answers to many of the endearing problems of learning mathematics.

Over the lifetime of PME, the world has changed, and so have schools and classrooms. In many parts of the world, teachers –mathematics teachers– are facing the challenges of teaching in multiethnic and multilingual classrooms containing, immigrant, indigenous, migrant, and refugee children, and if research is to be useful it has to address and help us understand such challenges. In a paper to PME29, Gorgorió and Planas (2005a) addressed this very issue claiming "immigrant students, most of them socially at risk, tend to be stereotyped as less competent and their mathematical abilities have traditionally been considered from a deficit model approach" (p. 71; see also Gorgorió & Planas, 2005b). I think this represents an encouraging development for PME research, and does indeed indicate that already PME provides a forum for such socially relevant research.

Vocational contexts of learning

Interestingly, studies of work related mathematics appears to have received very little attention this decade. Magajna and Monaghan (1998) address this in a study of computer aided design and the role of school geometry in Slovenia, concluding that the technology governed the mathematics the workers employed. This raises some interesting and very important questions –because work contexts are significantly different from school or home contexts.

The greatest influence on thinking in this area in recent years has been the work of Richard Noss, Celia Hoyles and their colleagues at the London Knowledge Lab, Institute of Education. Their reports of a long term study have been producing cutting-edge research into the very nature of mathematics in use (see http://www.lkl.ac.uk/research/technomaths.html). Their work suggests that understandings – including misconceptions, estimates, errors, etc.– all have different complexities in workplace settings, than we usually expect from classroom knowledge. Mathematics becomes embedded in tools and purpose (Noss, Hoyles & Pozzi, 1999). These ideas have been developed and presented in a plenary by Noss in PME26 in which he describes in some detail, with several case studies, of how

> the analysis of mathematics in work concerns the transformation of knowledge as it is recognised across settings. We have seen how a person's mathematical knowledge is not invariant across time and space; it is transformed into different guises, different epistemologies, more or less visible as mathematics. (Noss, 2002, p. 59)

This work can be seen to fit within the situated learning tradition –one which as we have seen has been explored in PME research. Yet somehow, this work takes the conceptual frameworks into new territory where the boundary between the cognitive and the social become less clear.

THE DISCIPLINE IN THE THIRD PHASE

In the third phase of PME we see traditions in the discipline developing yet further toward broader perspectives. *Educational Studies in Mathematics* for example has three special issues on "Mathematics and Gender" (Vol 28, No 3, Editor Gilah Leder), "Socio-Cultural Approaches" (Vol 31, 1-2, Editor Stephen Lerman) and "Bridging the Individual and the Social: Discursive Approaches to Research in Mathematics Education" (Vol 46, 1-3, Editors Carolyn Kieran, Ellice Foreman and Anna Sfard) –three of whom (Leder, Lerman, Kieran) are past PME Presidents. These issues (amongst many other books and publications) represent the evident social turn, but also the gradual emergence of equity and social justice, with papers on feminism (Burton, 1995; Solar, 1995), social class (Atweh & Cooper, 1995; Zevenbergen, 1995) and school cultures (Taylor 1995; Masingila, Davidenko & Prus-Wisniosa, 1995). What is also evident is the central involvement of core PME members in this turning away from the cognitive.

The mathematics outside of school becomes a greater influence which not only introduces the differing contexts in which mathematics is carried out and learned, but introduces different theoretical approaches (Jurdak & Shanin, 1999; Pozzi, Noss & Hoyles, 1998). What is clear, both in PME and *Educational Studies in Mathematics* is the percentage of psychological papers is high but reducing over time (see also Tsatsaroni, Lerman & Xu, 2003a, p. 20).

A major study of the development of mathematics education research between 1990 and 2000 by Tsatsaroni, Lerman and Xu tells us that "attention to psycho-social theories is slightly higher in *Educational Studies in Mathematics* and *Journal for Research in Mathematics Education* than in PME and papers drawing on sociological and socio-cultural theories, whilst on the increase are all below 12%", that there is "a noticeable increase in the use of linguistics, social linguistics and semiotics, though the number of papers drawing on these are still very small". Importantly, "very few papers draw on the broader field of educational theory and research, and on neighbouring fields of science education and curriculum studies, and if anything percentages are falling" (Tsatsaroni, Lerman & Xu, 2003b, p. 6).

This last issue is a significant observation –again demonstrating the reluctance of mathematics education to feel comfortable adopting the mindset of the sociologist. It could be of course that mathematics education research journals act through reviewers to police the discipline by rejecting papers which place sociology before mathematics.

SUMMARY – THE FUTURE OF PME

I am not arguing here that somehow everyone should be interested in equity, social justice, gender or ethnomathematics –though I do believe it demands greater attention and respect. My intention in this chapter was to track the development of research within PME. Naturally there is much to say about the orientation of PME –and Lerman has made this point very well in his chapter in this volume. But I am arguing that an organisation, such as that which PME has become, can not ignore significant developments in theory in order to remain conservatively within a cognitive domain. Researchers on curriculum for example, might gain by considering equity issues; in a similar way that equity researchers might develop the field by looking closely at curriculum matters. Such micro studies relating learning, curriculum and identity could be very important in working for a programme of mathematics for all.

In undertaking this review, I poured over all proceedings from PME –but did not read all papers in minute detail. It is quite possible I might have missed something– and in such cases I apologise to the authors who feel their work has been overlooked. However if I did, it was more likely an isolated piece of work within PME and would not have had a clear structured theme in PME research. The question those of us who consider ourselves as PME members need to ask is this – is PME a collection of colleagues or a respectable international research organisation. Can it continue to be a respectable cutting edge world-class research organisation with such a blind spot?

What is clear is that the mainstream literature in mathematics education is becoming more culturally sensitive, more discursively orientated, more aware of the nature of identity and more interested in the embodiment of mathematics. We are becoming more aware of social class, of social divisions and the exercising of power. We have new approaches which allow us to explore the way in which communities in mathematics classrooms influence learning in the classroom (Boaler, 1999), and beyond school into the workplace (Nichol, 2002; Zevenbergen, 2004). We have research methodologies and theoretical resources which allow us to understand the nature of linguistic power (Setati & Adler, 2001), and how traditional Mathematics disadvantages children from working class backgrounds (Cooper & Dunne, 2000). The challenge now for PME –and for research in mathematics more generally– is to take the opportunity to bring together the theoretical resources and draw them closer to the theoretical ideas being developed within mathematics education, including mainstream sociology. Signs from PME29 are positive with Research Forums, Discussion and Working Groups and research reports covering gender, indigenous communities, learning in multilingual contexts, embodiment and gesture.

We might want to ask why there is an issue over the conceptualization of mathematics education in relation to other major disciplines. Drawing on Bernstein, Lerman, Tsatsaroni and Xu argue we have a discipline exhibiting a "weak grammar" (Lerman, Tsatsaroni & Xu, 2003). I will stretch this linguistic metaphor a little. Explanatory discourses are introduced and adopted in mathematics education but these do not exhibit the sophistication that would require the adopting of broader theoretical resources. So we develop a language to talk about an interpretation of the world –such as drawing on some sociological ideas which we incorporate into mathematics education. Yet although this language exhibits surface features of a communicative language, vocabulary, syntax, etc. it actually has a weak "grammar" –a weak deep unifying structure which would allow us to construct more complex interpretations. This happens because we do not become sociologists as such and talk sociology, but we dabble as amateur sociologists because we are different and because we lack the disciplinary tradition; we are reluctant to use a deep sociological grammar because we are mathematics educators not sociologists and our disciplinary identity is important to us.

This chapter is not an argument for a move away from the psychological focus of PME attention. It is an argument for a broadening, because broadening the fields of study that inform our work, informs us all, and means we can produce the research, celebrated in this book, with confidence that our work is not isolated, limited or outmoded, but can relate to and understand the real lives of children and adults. Not all children benefit or suffer in the same way by being exposed to mathematics and that is a stark reality for many. It remains yet to become a stark reality for PME. In an organisation such as PME, which surely considers itself a community of researchers, what is important is that we rely upon and build upon each others' work –and this has to be true where our work has bridges to much work already published. Indeed drawing upon work previously reported is one of the guidelines for submitting research reports.

A number of papers in PME have asked the question: What is the role of the teacher in pupils' attainment, self image, problem solving, etc.? A further question we might ask, is what is the role of PME in the understanding of equity and the eradication of social exclusion, which mathematics educating still bears some culpability. This book goes to press in the year PME changes. At PME29 the International Committee proposed a significant change in the major goals of PME which were accepted by the conference. The major goals of PME now read:

> (i) To promote international contacts and exchange of scientific information in the field of mathematical education;
> (ii) To promote and stimulate interdisciplinary research in the aforesaid area;
> (iii) To further a deeper and more correct understanding of the psychological and other aspects of teaching and learning mathematics and the implications thereof.

These clearly do broaden the focus of PME, such that the exclusive focus on psychology has been shifted. The time was right for change –and I think we can see why in this chapter. Changes in theoretical frameworks, methodologies and research questions have slowly influenced those who come together to debate at PME conferences. This has taken PME away from the area of the cognitive into new ground. We can hope this brings about, in time, changes in the overall shape of PME research such that those who have left PME behind might return to the fold. Mathematics can be used as a vehicle for good rather than harm (Boaler,

2002; Gutstein, 2003) and equity and social justice has a clear and central place in the mathematics education research community.

Finally, how might PME research develop a greater focus on equity and social justice? I offer some suggestions (for which I acknowledge the contribution of Nuria Gorgorió):

- Develop more research whose focus of study are non-prototypical classrooms and non-equitable situations;
- Focus more explicitly on the way mathematics as a discipline acts against the interests of certain groups of pupils;
- Explore learning obstacles that go beyond the cognitive or epistemological obstacles to consider cultural and social obstacles;
- Move beyond cognitive psychology, and beyond the individual as a cognitive and affective individual to study mathematics education from a cultural and social psychology perspectives that considers individual pupils interacting within the classrooms as having cultural and social identities as well as identities as mathematics teachers or mathematics learners;
- Explore the idea of classroom culture understood on its connection with a broad idea of the diverse cultures to which the individuals belong to and its connection with the dominant culture of the school, the educational institution and of the social group at large;
- Broaden the idea of social interactions within the mathematics classroom to take into account how these are mediated by social representations and values about teaching and learning mathematics.

I started with a quote, and I will finish with a quote, this time from the NCTM Research Committee:

> Each of us has a responsibility to both think about and act on issues of equity ... An equity focus for research is responsive to practitioners' needs, reflective of NCTM's longstanding commitment, ideal as a site for linking research and practice, *and* the right thing to do. (NCTM, 2005b, p. 99)

I hope as we move into a new phase of a more eclectic PME, *we* will think it is the right thing for *us* to do too.

ACKNOWLEDGEMENTS

I would like to thank Richard Barwell, Gilah Leder, Stephen Lerman, Robyn Zevenbergen, Nuria Gorgorió and Angel Gutiérrez for their useful comments on an earlier draft of this chapter. In addition I would like especially to thank Chris Breen for his encouragement to produce this chapter and for the many conversations on the issues within it.

REFERENCES

Adda, J. (1982). L'enseignement des mathematiques n'est pas neutre. In A. Vermandel (Ed.), *Proceedings of the 6th PME International Conference*, 294–300.

Amit, M., & Movshovitz-Hadar, N. (1987). Gender difference in achievements and in causal attributes of performance in high school mathematics. In J. C. Bergeron, N. Herscovics, & C. Kieran (Eds.), *Proceedings of the 11th PME International Conference, 3*, 101–106.

Apple, M. (1979). *Ideology and the curriculum*. London, UK: Routledge.

Atweh, B., Bleicher, R., & Cooper, T. (1998). The construction of social context of mathematics classrooms. A sociolinguistic analysis. *Journal for Research in Mathematics Education, 2*(1), 63–82.

Atweh, B., & Cooper, T. (1995). The construction of gender, social class and mathematics in the classroom. *Educational Studies in Mathematics, 28*(2), 293–310.

Baker, D., & Street, B. (2000). Maths as social and explanations for 'underachievement' in numeracy. In T. Nakahara & M. Koyama (Eds.), *Proceedings of the 24th PME International Conference, 2*, 49–56.

Barboza, E. (1984). Girls and mathematics: Affective variables associated with the selection of courses in senior school. In B. Southwell, R. Eyland, M. Cooper, J. Conroy, & K. Collis (Eds.), *Proceedings of the 8th PME International Conference*, 399–411.

Bartolini Bussi, M. (1991). Social interaction and mathematical knowledge. In F. Furinghetti (Ed.), *Proceedings of the 15th PME International Conference, 1*, 1–16.

Barwell, R. (2001). Investigating mathematical interaction a multilingual primary school: Finding a way of working. In M. van den Heuvel-Panhuizen (Ed.), *Proceedings of the 25th PME International Conference, 2*, 97–104.

Barwell, R., & Clarkson, P. (2004). Researching mathematics education in multilingual classrooms; Theory methodology and the teaching of mathematics. In M. J. Høines & A. B. Fuglestad (Eds.), *Proceedings of the 28th PME International Conference, 1*, 227–256.

Becker, H. (1952). Social-class variations in the teacher-pupil relationship. *Journal of Educational Sociology, 25*, 451–465.

Bishop, A. (1981). Affective factors influencing mathematical involvement. In Equipe de Recherche Pédagogique (Eds.), *Proceedings of the 5th PME International Conference*, 351–355.

Bishop, A. (1985). The social psychology of mathematics education. In L. Streefland (Ed.), *Proceedings of the 9th PME International Conference, 2*, 1–13.

Bishop, A. (1993). Cultural conflicts in mathematics learning. Developing a research agenda for linking cognitive and affective issues. In I. Hirabayashi, N. Nohda, K. Shigematsu, & F.-L. Lin (Eds.), *Proceedings of the 17th PME International Conference, 3*, 203–209.

Bishop, A., & De Abreu, G. (1991). Children's use of outside school knowledge to solve mathematics problems in school. In F. Furinghetti (Ed.), *Proceedings of the 15th PME International Conference, 1*, 128–135.

Bishop, A., & Pompeu, G. (1991). Influence of an ethnomathematical approach on teacher attitudes to mathematics education. In F. Furinghetti (Ed.), *Proceedings of the 15th PME International Conference, 1*, 136–143.

Boaler, J. (1997a). *Experiencing school mathematics. Teaching styles, sex and setting*. Buckingham, UK: Open University Press.

Boaler, J. (1997b). Setting, social class and the survival of the quickest. *British Educational Research Journal, 23*(5), 575–595.

Boaler, J. (1999). Participation, knowledge and beliefs: A community perspective on mathematics learning. *Educational Studies in Mathematics, 40*(3), 259–281.

Boaler, J. (2002). Learning from teaching: Exploring the relationship between reform curriculum and equity. *Journal for Research in Mathematics Education, 33*(4), 239–258.

Boero, P. (1989). Mathematical literacy for all. Experiences and problems. In G. Vergnaud, J. Rogalski, & M. Artigue (Eds.), *Proceedings of the 13th PME International Conference, 1*, 62–76.

Brassell, A., Pity, S., & Brook, D. (1980). Ability grouping, mathematics achievement and pupil attitude toward mathematics. *Journal for Research in Mathematics Education, 11*(1), 22–28.

Burton, L. (1995). Moving towards a feminist epistemology of mathematics. *Educational Studies in Mathematics, 28*(3), 275–310.

Burton, L., Balachef, N., Bauersfeld, H., Branca, N., & Pimm D. (1982). A cross-cultural study of problem solving involving pupils aged 11–13 years. In A. Vermandel (Ed.), *Proceedings of the 6th PME International Conference*, 42–54.

Clarkson, P. (1983). Types of errors made by Papua New Guinea students. *Educational Studies in Mathematics*, *14*(4), 255–368.

Clarkson, P. (1984). Language and mathematics in Papua New Guinea: A land of 720 languages. In B. Southwell, R. Eyland, M. Cooper, J. Conroy, & K. Collis (Eds.), *Proceedings of the 8th PME International Conference*, 331–338.

Cohors-Fresenborg, E., & Marpung, Y. (1986). Intercultural studies between Indonesian and German children on algorithmic thinking. In Univ. of London Institute of Education (Eds.), *Proceedings of the 10th PME International Conference*, 404–409.

Cohors-Fresenborg, E., & Wachsmuth, I. (1978). Preface. In E. Cohors-Fresenborg & I. Wachsmuth (Eds.), *Proceedings of the 2nd PME International Conference*, 3–5.

Collis, K. F., & Taplin, M. (1984). Sex differences in mathematics performance by cognitive level. In B. Southwell, R. Eyland, M. Cooper, J. Conroy, & K. Collis (Eds.), *Proceedings of the 8th PME International Conference*, 412–431.

Cooper, B., & Dunne, M. (2000). *Assessing Children's Mathematical Knowledge: Class, sex and Problem Solving*. Buckingham, UK: Open University Press.

Cotton, T., & Gates, P. (1996). Why the psychological must consider the social in promoting equity and social justice in mathematics education. In L. Puig & A. Gutiérrez (Eds.), *Proceedings of the 20th PME International Conference*, *2*, 249–256.

D'Ambrosio, U. (1985). *Socio-cultural bases for mathematics education*. Sao Paolo, Brazil: Unicamp.

De Abreu, G. (1992). Approaches to research into cultural conflicts in mathematics learning. In W. Geeslin & K. Graham (Eds.), *Proceedings of the 16th PME International Conference*, *1*, 25–32.

Endean, L., & Carss, M. (1984). SoI-LA in the identification of mathematical talent in children. In B. Southwell, R. Eyland, M. Cooper, J. Conroy, & K. Collis (Eds.), *Proceedings of the 8th PME International Conference*, 181–189.

Evans, J. (1988). Anxiety and performance in practical maths at tertiary level: A report of research in progress. In A. Borbás (Ed.), *Proceedings of the 12th PME International Conference*, *3*, 92–98.

Evans, J., & Tsatsaroni, A. (1993). Linking the cognitive and the affective. A comparison of models for research. In I. Hirabayashi, N. Nohda, K. Shigematsu, & F.-L. Lin (Eds.), *Proceedings of the 17th PME International Conference*, *3*, 210–217.

Fennema, E. (1979). Woman, girls and mathematics – equity in mathematics education. *Educational Studies in Mathematics*, *10*(4), 389–401.

Forgasz, H. (2002). Computers for leaning mathematics gendered beliefs. In A. D. Cockburn & E. Nardi (Eds.), *Proceedings of the 26th PME International Conference*, *2*, 368–375.

Forgasz, H. (2003). Equity and beliefs about the efficacy of computers for mathematics learning. In N. A. Pateman, B. J. Dougherty, & J. T. Zilliox (Eds.), *Proceedings of the 27th PME International Conference*, *2*, 381–388.

Forgasz, H. (2004). Equity and computers for mathematics learning: Access and attitudes. In M. J. Høines & A. B. Fuglestad (Eds.), *Proceedings of the 28th PME International Conference*, *2*, 399–406.

Frempong, G. (1998). Social class inequalities in mathematics achievement: A multilevel analysis of TIMMS South Africa data. In A. Olivier & K. Newstead (Eds.), *Proceedings of the 22nd PME International Conference*, *2*, 304–312.

Frempong, G. (2005). Exploring excellence and equity within Canadian mathematics classrooms. In H. L. Chick & J. L. Vincent (Eds.), *Proceedings of the 29th PME International Conference*, *2*, 337–344.

Gates, P. (1997). The importance of social structure in developing a critical social psychology of mathematics education, In E. Pehkonen (Ed.), *Proceedings of the 21st PME International Conference*, *2*, 305–312.

Gentry, M., & Underhill, R. (1988). A comparison of two palliative methods of intervention for the treatment of mathematics anxiety among female college students. In A. Borbás (Ed.), *Proceedings of the 12th PME International Conference, 3*, 99–105.

George, E. (1999). Male and female calculus students' use of visual representations. In O. Zaslavsky (Ed.), *Proceedings of the 23rd PME International Conference, 3*, 17–24.

Gorgorió, N., & Planas, N. (2005a). Reconstructing norms. In H. L. Chick & J. L. Vincent (Eds.), *Proceedings of the 29th PME International Conference, 3*, 65–72.

Gorgorió, N., & Planas, N. (2005b). Cultural distance and identities-in-construction within the multicultural mathematics classroom. In *Zentralblatt für Didaktik der Mathematik, 37*(2), 64–71.

Gregg, J. (1995). Tensions and contradictions of the school mathematics tradition. *Journal for Research in Mathematics Education, 26*(5), 442–460.

Gutstein, E. (2003). Teaching and learning mathematics for social justice in an urban, Latino school. *Journal for Research in Mathematics Education, 34*(1), 37–73.

Hanna, G., & Sidoli, N. (2002). The story of E.S.M. *Educational Studies in Mathematics, 50*(2), 123–156.

Hannula, M., & Malmivuori, M.-L. (1997). Gender differences and their relation to mathematics classroom context. In E. Pehkonen (Ed.), *Proceedings of the 21st PME International Conference, 3*, 33–40.

Harris, M. (1987). An example of traditional women's work as a mathematics resource. *For the Learning of Mathematics, 7*(3), 26–28.

Hodge, L., & Stephan, M. (1998). Relating culture and mathematical activity: An analysis of socio-mathematical norms. In A. Olivier & K. Newstead (Eds.), *Proceedings of the 22nd PME International Conference, 3*, 49–56.

Horne, M. (2003). Gender differences in the early years in addition and subtraction. In N. A. Pateman, B. J. Dougherty, & J. T. Zilliox (Eds.), *Proceedings of the 27th PME International Conference, 3*, 79–86.

Horne, M. (2004). Early gender differences. In M. J. Høines & A. B. Fuglestad (Eds.), *Proceedings of the 28th PME International Conference, 3*, 65–72.

Hoyles, C. (1992). Mathematics teaching and mathematics teachers: A meta-case study. *For the Learning of Mathematics, 12*(3), 23–43.

Hutton, L. (1982). Assessment of mathematical anxiety. In A. Vermandel (Ed.), *Proceedings of the 6th PME International Conference*, 301–305.

Jones, L. (1996). Somali children learning mathematics in Britain: A conflict of cultures. In L. Puig & A. Gutiérrez (Eds.), *Proceedings of the 20th PME International Conference, 3*, 153–160.

Jones, P. (1982). Learning mathematics in a second language. A problem with more or less. *Educational Studies in Mathematics, 13*(3), 269–281.

Jurdak, M., & Shanin, I. (1999). An ethnographic study of the computational strategies of a group of young street vendors in Beirut. *Educational Studies in Mathematics, 40*(2), 155–172.

Kaino, L., & Salani, E. (2004). Students' gender attitudes towards the use of calculators in mathematics instruction. In M. J. Høines & A. B. Fuglestad (Eds.), *Proceedings of the 28th PME International Conference, 3*, 113–120.

Keitel, C. (1986). Cultural premises and presuppositions in psychology of mathematics education. In Univ. of London Institute of Education (Eds.), *Proceedings of the 10th PME International Conference*, 24–50.

Khisty, L. (1994). On the social psychology of mathematics instruction: Critical factors for an equity agenda. In J. P. Ponte & J. F. Matos (Eds.), *Proceedings of the 18th PME International Conference, 3*, 90–96.

Khisty, L. (1998). Talking math: Proposal for school change. In A. Olivier & K. Newstead (Eds.), *Proceedings of the 22nd PME International Conference, 1*, 97–112.

Khisty, L. (2001). Effective teachers of second language learners in mathematics. In M. van den Heuvel-Panhuizen (Ed.), *Proceedings of the 25th PME International Conference, 3*, 225–232.

Khisty, L., McLeod, D., & Bertilson, K. (1990). Speaking mathematically in multilingual classrooms. An exploratory study of mathematics classrooms. In G. Booker, P. Cobb, & T. N. Mendicuti (Eds.), *Proceedings of the 14th PME International Conference, 1*, 105–112.

Kieran, C. (1994). Doing and seeing things differently: A 25-year retrospective of mathematics education research on learning. *Journal for Research in Mathematics Education, 25*(6), 583–607.

Kilpatrick, J. (1992). A history of research in mathematics education. In Grouws, D. (Ed.), *Handbook of research on mathematics teaching and learning* (pp. 3–38). New York, USA: Macmillan.

Kota, S., & Thomas, M. (1997). Gender differences in algebra problems solving: The role of affective factors. In E. Pehkonen (Ed.), *Proceedings of the 21st PME International Conference, 3*, 152–159.

Kutscher, B., & Linchevski, L. (2000). Moving between mixed-ability and same-ability settings: Impact upon learners. In T. Nakahara & M. Koyama (Eds.), *Proceedings of the 24th PME International Conference, 3*, 199–206.

Kuyper, H., & Van der Werf, M. (1990). Math teachers and gender differences in math achievement. Math participation and attitude toward math. In G. Booker, P. Cobb, & T. N. Mendicuti (Eds.), *Proceedings of the 14th PME International Conference, 1*, 143–150.

Lave, J. (1988). *Cognition in practice. Mind, mathematics and culture in everyday life.* Cambridge, UK: Cambridge University Press.

Lea, H. (1988). Concepts in secondary maths in Botswana. In A. Borbás (Ed.), *Proceedings of the 12th PME International Conference, 2*, 457–462.

Leder, G. (1980). Bright girls, mathematics and the fear of success. *Educational Studies in Mathematics, 11*(4), 411–422.

Leder, G. (1989). Gender differences in mathematics revisited. In G. Vergnaud, J. Rogalski, & M. Artigue (Eds.), *Proceedings of the 13th PME International Conference, 2*, 218–225.

Leder, G. (1992). Mathematics and gender: Changing perspectives. In Grouws, D. (Ed.), *Handbook of research in mathematics teaching and learning* (pp. 597–622). New York, USA: MacMillan.

Leder, G. (2001). Pathways in mathematics towards equity: A 25 year Journey. In M. van den Heuvel-Panhuizen (Ed.), *Proceedings of the 25th PME International Conference, 1*, 41–54.

Lerman, S. (2000). The social turn in mathematics education research. In J. Boaler (Ed.), *Multiple perspectives on mathematics teaching and learning* (pp. 19–44). Westport, CT, USA: Ablex.

Lerman, S., Tsatsaroni, A., & Xu, G. (2003). *Developing theories of mathematics education research: The PME story.* Paper submitted to PME27 conference (rejected). Retrieved October 1, 2005, from http://www.lsbu.ac.uk/~lermans/ESRCProjectHOMEPAGE.html

Lerman, S., Xu, G., & Tsatsaroni, A. (2003). Developing theories of mathematics education research: The PME story. *Educational Studies in Mathematics, 51*(1–2), 23–40.

Lesh, R. (1979). Social/affective factors influencing problem solving capabilities. In D. Tall (Ed.), *Proceedings of the 3rd PME International Conference*, 142–147.

Linchevski, L. (1995). Tell me who your classmates are and I'll tell you what you learn. Conflict principles underlying the structuring of the math class. In L. Meira & D. Carraher (Eds.), *Proceedings of the 19th PME International Conference, 3*, 240–247.

Lindenskov, L. (1991). Everyday knowledge in studies of learning and teaching mathematics in school. In F. Furinghetti (Ed.), *Proceedings of the 15th PME International Conference, 2*, 325–333.

Magajna, Z., & Monaghan, J. (1998). Non-elementary mathematics in a work setting. In A. Olivier & K. Newstead (Eds.), *Proceedings of the 22nd PME International Conference, 3*, 231–328.

Masingila, J. (1992). Mathematics practice in carpet laying. In W. Geeslin & K. Graham (Eds.), *Proceedings of the 16th PME International Conference, 2*, 80–87.

Masingila, J., Davidenko, S., & Prus-Wisniosa, E. (1995). Mathematics learning and practice in and out of school: A framework for connecting these experiences. *Educational Studies in Mathematics, 31*(1–2), 175–200.

Mellin-Olsen, S. (1987). *The politics of mathematics education.* Dordrecht, The Netherlands: Reidel.

Merttens, R., & Vass, J. (1990). *Sharing maths cultures.* London, UK: Falmer Press.

Morales, H., Khisty, L., & Chval, K. (2003). Beyond discourse: A multimodal perspective of learning mathematics in a multilingual context. In N. A. Pateman, B. J. Dougherty, & J. T. Zilliox (Eds.), *Proceedings of the 27th PME International Conference*, *3*, 133–140.

Morgan, C., & Merttens, R. (1994). Parental involvement in mathematics: What teachers think is involved. In J. P. Ponte & J. F. Matos (Eds.), *Proceedings of the 18th PME International Conference*, *3*, 303–311.

Moschkovich, J. (1996). Learning math in two languages. In L. Puig & A. Gutiérrez (Eds.), *Proceedings of the 20th PME International Conference*, *4*, 27–34.

National Council of Teachers of Mathematics (NCTM). (2005a). *Closing the achievement gap*. Retrieved June 10, 2005, from http://www.nctm.org/about/position_statements/position_achievementgap.htm

National Council of Teachers of Mathematics (NCTM). (2005b). Equity in school mathematics education: How can research contribute? *Journal for Research in Mathematics Education*, *36*(2), 92–100.

Nichol, C. (2002). Where's the math? Prospective teachers visit the workplace. *Educational Studies in Mathematics*, *50*(3), 289–309.

Noss, R. (2002). Mathematical epistemologies at work. In A. D. Cockburn & E. Nardi (Eds.), *Proceedings of the 26th PME International Conference*, *1*, 47–63.

Noss, R., Hoyles, C., & Pozzi, S. (1999). This patient should be dead! How can the study of mathematics in work advance our understanding of mathematical meaning-making in general? In O. Zaslavsky (Ed.), *Proceedings of the 23rd PME International Conference*, *3*, 353–360.

Nunes, T. (1988). Street mathematics and school mathematics. In A. Borbás (Ed.), *Proceedings of the 12th PME International Conference*, *1*, 1–23.

Nunes, T. (1989). Numeracy without schooling. In G. Vergnaud, J. Rogalski, & M. Artigue (Eds.), *Proceedings of the 13th PME International Conference*, 164–171.

Nunes, T., & Schliemann, A. D. (1985). Computation routines prescribed by schools: Help or hindrance? *Journal for Research in Mathematics Education*, *16*(1), 37–44.

Nunes, T., Schliemann, A., & Carraher, D. (1993). *Street mathematics and school mathematics*. Cambridge, UK: Cambridge University Press.

Otten, W., & Kuyper, H. (1988). Gender and mathematics: The prediction of choice and achievement. In A. Borbás (Ed.), *Proceedings of the 12th PME International Conference*, *2*, 519–529.

Pehkonen, L. (1999). Gender differences in primary pupils mathematical argumentation. In O. Zaslavsky (Ed.), *Proceedings of the 23rd PME International Conference*, *4*, 41–48.

Popkewitz, T. (1988). Institutional issues in the study of school mathematics: Curriculum research. *Educational Studies in Mathematics*, *19*(2), 221–249.

Povey, H., & Boylan, M. (1998). Working class students and the culture of mathematics classrooms in the UK. In A. Olivier & K. Newstead (Eds.), *Proceedings of the 22nd PME International Conference*, *4*, 9–16.

Pozzi, S., Noss, R., & Hoyles, C. (1998). Tools in practice, mathematics in use. *Educational Studies in Mathematics*, *36*(2), 105–122.

Ruthven, K. (1986) Ability stereotyping in mathematics. *Educational Studies in Mathematics*, *18*(3), 243–253.

Saxe, G. (1990). *Culture and cognitive development. Studies in mathematical understanding*. Hillsdale, USA: Lawrence Erlbaum.

Schliemann, A. (1995). Some concerns about bringing everyday mathematics into mathematics education. In L. Meira & D. Carraher (Eds.), *Proceedings of the 19th PME International Conference*, *1*, 45–60.

Schliemann, A., Araujo, C., Cassundé, M. A., Macedo, S., & Nicéas, L. (1994). School children versus street sellers' use of the commutative law for solving multiplicative problems. In J. P. Ponte & J. F. Matos (Eds.), *Proceedings of the 18th PME International Conference*, *4*, 209–216.

Schoenfeld, A. (1987). What's all the fuss about metacognition? In A. Schoenfeld (Ed.), *Cognitive science and mathematics education* (pp. 189–215). Hillsdale, USA: Lawrence Erlbaum.

Setati, M. (2003). Language use in multilingual mathematics classroom in South Africa. A different perspective. In N. A. Pateman, B. J. Dougherty, & J. T. Zilliox (Eds.), *Proceedings of the 27th PME International Conference*, *4*, 151–158.

Setati, M., & Adler, J. (2001). Between languages and discourses: Language practices in primary multilingual mathematics classrooms in South Africa. *Educational Studies in Mathematics*, *43*(3), 243–269.

Sfard, A., & Prusak, A. (2005). Identity that makes a difference: Substantial learning as closing the gap between actual and designated identities. In H. L. Chick & J. L. Vincent (Eds.), *Proceedings of the 29th PME International Conference*, *1*, 37–53.

Skovsmose, O. (1985). Mathematics education versus critical education. *Educational Studies in Mathematics*, *16*(4), 337–354.

Skovsmose, O. (1994). *Towards a philosophy of critical mathematics education*. Dordrecht, The Netherlands: Kluwer.

Slavin, R. (1996). *Education for all*. Amsterdam, The Netherlands: Lisse, Swetts and Zeitlinger.

Solar, C. (1995). An inclusive pedagogy for mathematics education. *Educational Studies in Mathematics*, *28*(3), 311–333.

Strässer, R., & Bromme, R. (1989). Vocational mathematics. Teachers cognition of mathematical and vocational knowledge. In G. Vergnaud, J. Rogalski, & M. Artigue (Eds.), *Proceedings of the 13th PME International Conference*, *3*, 189–196.

Taylor, P. (1995). Mythmaking and mythbreaking in the mathematics classroom. *Educational Studies in Mathematics*, *21*(1–2), 151–173.

Tsatsaroni, A., Lerman, S., & Xu, G. (2003a). *A sociological description of changes in the intellectual field of mathematics education research: Implications for the identities of academics*. Paper presented at the Annual Meeting of the AERA, Chicago, USA. (ERIC ED482512). Retrieved October 1, 2005, from http://www.lsbu.ac.uk/~lermans/ESRCProjectHOMEPAGE.html

Tsatsaroni, A., Lerman, S., & Xu, G. (2003b). *The production and use of theories of teaching and learning mathematics* (Research Report). Retrieved October 1, 2005, from http://www.lsbu.ac.uk/~lermans/ESRCProjectHOMEPAGE.html

Underwood, D. (1992). Mathematics and gender: An interactional approach. In W. Geeslin & K. Graham (Eds.), *Proceedings of the 16th PME International Conference*, *3*, 98–105.

Vale, C., Leder, G., & Forgasz, H. (2003). Equity, mathematics learning and technology. In N. A. Pateman, B. J. Dougherty, & J. T. Zilliox (Eds.), *Proceedings of the 27th PME International Conference*, *1*, 137–165.

Vermeer, H., Boekaerts, M., & Seegers, G. (1997). Gender differences in cognitive and affective variables during two types of mathematical tasks. In E. Pehkonen (Ed.), *Proceedings of the 21st PME International Conference*, *4*, 262–269.

Willis, P. (1977). *Learning to labour. How working class kids get working class jobs*. London, UK: Saxon House.

Yackel, E., & Cobb, P. (1996). Socio-mathematical norms, argumentation and autonomy in mathematics. *Journal for Research in Mathematics Education*, *27*(4), 458–477.

Zepp, R. (1981). Relationship between mathematics achievement and various English language proficiencies. *Educational Studies in Mathematics*, *12*(1), 59–70.

Zepp, R. (1982). Bilinguals' understanding of logical connectives. *Educational Studies in Mathematics*, *13*(2), 205–221.

Zevenbergen, R. (1995). Constructivism as a liberal bourgeois discourse. *Educational Studies in Mathematics*, *31*(1–2), 95–113.

Zevenbergen, R. (1999). Boys, mathematics and classroom interactions: The construction of masculinity in working class mathematics classrooms. In O. Zaslavsky (Ed.), *Proceedings of the 23rd PME International Conference*, *4*, 353–360.

Zevenbergen, R. (2004). Technologizing numeracy: Intergenerational difference in working mathematically in new times. *Educational Studies in Mathematics*, *56*(1), 97–117.

AFFILIATION

Peter Gates
Centre for Research into Equity and Diversity in Education
School of Education
The University of Nottingham
Nottingham NG8 1BB (UK)
peter.gates@nottingham.ac.uk

GILAH C. LEDER AND HELEN J. FORGASZ

AFFECT AND MATHEMATICS EDUCATION

PME Perspectives

Since the founding of the International Group for the Psychology of Mathematics Education [PME] in 1976 (at the third conference of the International Commission on Mathematics Instruction [ICME 3] in Karlsruhe) both the mathematics education research community and the membership of PME have grown considerably. Official records indicate that the first PME conference held in Utrecht in the Netherlands in 1977 attracted 86 participants. Twenty five years later, when Utrecht once again hosted the PME conference, attendance had increased more than six fold to 559.

Over time, the range of topics covered at the annual conferences of PME has multiplied in line with the community's broader range of research interests, the increased appreciation and acceptance of newer research methodologies and paradigms, and the growing acceptance that multiple research methods allow insights into complex issues not readily explored by simplistic means. Throughout this period, as will be shown in this chapter, interest in affect has been maintained, both within the PME and broader research communities.

We start this chapter with an examination and overview of common descriptions of affect and approaches to its measurement. For these sections we draw primarily on research beyond the PME community, or more accurately, on research beyond that presented at PME conferences. Since membership of PME is closely tied to attendance at the annual conference and fluctuates from year to year, it is no simple task retrospectively to describe PME membership accurately. An overview of research concerned with affect in the early years of PME follows next. To conform with space constraints, we rely heavily on Leder's (1993) review of the earlier period. More recent developments within the PME research agenda, as inferred from presentations at the annual conferences over the past decade, are described next and in greater detail. The strengths and limitations of this body of research are also discussed. Finally, we turn to the future, explore innovative approaches to the study of affect, and speculate on the directions that further, constructive work in the area might follow.

A. Gutiérrez, P. Boero (eds.), Handbook of Research on the Psychology of Mathematics Education: Past, Present and Future, 403–427.

AFFECT: A QUESTION OF DEFINITION?

In daily life, many words are used to describe affect. Petty, DeSteno and Rucker (2001, p. 214) used the term "to encompass the broad range of experiences referred to as *emotions* and *moods*, in which emotions are understood as specific and short-lived internal feeling states, and moods are more global and enduring feeling states" (emphasis in the original). According to Corsini (1984, p. 32) affect covers "a wide range of concepts and phenomena including feelings, emotions, moods, motivation, and certain drives and instincts". Both in his seminal chapter on research on affect in mathematics education (McLeod, 1992) and in his overview of such research included in the *Journal for Research in Mathematics Education [JRME]* during its first 25 years of publication, McLeod (1994) clustered his comments under the headings "attitudes", "beliefs", and "emotional responses". Aiken (1996, p. 168) used the words "emotion and motivation" to denote affect and explicitly noted that affect is one of three components associated with attitude: An attitude "consists of cognitive (knowledge of intellect), affect (emotion and motivation), and performance (behavior or action) components". He, like many other psychologists, further noted that descriptors such "as attitudes, interests, opinions, beliefs, and values can all be viewed as personality characteristics or motivators of behavior" (p. 169) and are often used loosely and interchangeably. None can be observed directly; each needs to be inferred from behaviour, speech, or responses to specifically designed instruments. Goldin's (2003) description of affect highlighted a number of subtle operational differences:

> In the individual we can distinguish certain subdomains of affective representation ...: (1) *emotions* (rapidly changing states of feeling, mild to very intense, that are usually local or embedded in context), (2) *attitudes* (moderately stable predispositions toward ways of feeling in classes of situations, involving a balance of affect and cognition), (3) *beliefs* (internal representations to which the holder attributes truth, validity, or applicability, usually stable and highly cognitive, may be highly structured), and (4) *values, ethics, and morals* (deeply-held preferences, possibly characterized as "personal truths", stable, highly affective as well as cognitive, may also be highly structured). (p. 61)

The overlapping and connected nature of concepts such as affect, feelings, emotions, and attitudes and their link to behaviour is reflected in formal definitions connecting these terms as can be seen from the (representative) definitions given below and spanning some 50 years:

- An attitude is "the degree of positive or negative affect associated with some psychological object" (Edwards, 1957, p. 2);
- "Attitudes involve what people *think* about, *feel* about, and how they would like to *behave* toward an attitude object. Behavior is not only determined by what people *would like* to do but also by what they think they should do, that is, social *norms*, by what they have usually done, that is *habits*, and the *expected consequences of behavior*" (Triandis, 1971, p. 14).

- "The term affect has meant many things to many people, acquiring interpretations that range from 'hot' to 'cold'. At the hot end, affect is used coextensively with the word *emotion*, implying an intensity dimension; at the cold end, it is often used without passion, referring to preferences, likes and dislikes, and choices". (Mandler, 1989, p. 3)
- "One's overall evaluation (attitude) is based on some combination of one's affect, cognition, and behavioral tendencies toward the attitude object" (Forgas, 2001, p. 215).

Though not a specific attempt to define affect, also noteworthy is Lubienski's (1999) decision to use 10 different descriptors, including mathematics anxiety, motivation, student attitudes, and self-esteem, to capture work on student affect and beliefs as part of her overview of mathematics education research published in 48 different educational research journals between 1982 and 1998.

In this chapter we are less concerned with defining subtle distinctions between affective factors such as attitudes, beliefs, feelings, emotions, and moods than with ensuring that coverage of these components at PME conferences is captured and traced. Although the former undoubtedly has its place in overviews of research, the approach we have selected is more congruent with the aims of this chapter.

AFFECT: A FORGOTTEN VARIABLE IN RESEARCH?

Psychologists differ on the extent to which affective issues have dominated their field of research. In a recent handbook Forgas (2001) argued that

> scientific psychology had relatively little to say about affective phenomena until quite recently. This was at least partly the consequence of the single-minded pursuit of first the behaviorist and later the cognitivist agenda in our discipline during most of the 20th century. The situation is now rapidly changing. Research on affect has become one of the most rapidly expanding areas in psychology. There is convergent evidence from such disparate fields as social cognition, neuropsychology, and psychophysiology demonstrating that affect is intimately involved in everything we think and do. (pp. xv-xvi)

Yet some 65 years earlier Allport (1935, p. 798) already asserted that the "concept of attitudes is probably the most distinctive and indispensable concept in contemporary American social psychology. No other term appears more frequently in the experimental and theoretical literature." McGuire's (1986, as cited in Hogg & Vaughan, 1995) description of periods of vibrant research activity on attitudes goes some way towards explaining these contradictory views. According to McGuire (1986, p. 109), in the 1920s and 1930s the focus was on "fairly static issues of attitude measurement and how this related to behavior". In the 1950s and 1960s, attention turned to "the dynamics of change in an individual's attitudes" while in the 1980s and 1990s there was a "swing towards unraveling the structure and function of systems of attitudes".

Thus observable facets of human behavior, rather than aspects of affectivity which needed to be inferred, were the focus of research on attitudes during the first phase described by McGuire. During the second phase, research on the role of cognition in the structure and shaping of attitudes dominated. Affective considerations "were considered only as a disruptive influence". With increased "theoretical integration between various branches of psychology such as social, cognitive, personality, and developmental research" (Forgas, 2001, p. 21) the role of affectivity again became a key component of the research agenda, as implied by McGuire's third phase. Glimpses of the various developments discussed by McGuire are also evident in mathematics education research.

AFFECTIVITY AND MATHEMATICS EDUCATION

In the close to three decades since the founding of PME, research on affect has been of considerable interest to the larger mathematics education community. According to McLeod (1994)[1], of the articles published in JRME between 1970 and 1994, some 100 were concerned with affective issues. Of the more than 3000 articles surveyed by Lubienski (1999) using the ERIC data base, some 12% (365 out of 3011 articles) related to student affect –making this, she argued, an area attracting "significant research attention" (p. 19). Contrasting findings emerged from the review of research by Tsatsaroni, Lerman and Xu (2003)[1]. These authors confined their focus to "a representative sample of the papers in the *Proceedings of the International Group for the Psychology of Mathematics Education* ..., and to two journals: *Educational Studies in Mathematics* ... and the *Journal for Research in Mathematics Education*" (p. 6) published over a 12 year period. Of the various groupings they used to describe and characterize this body of research, two are of particular interest for this chapter. When clustered under the *researchers' aim* category, few of the 463 papers they coded were considered to have as an important aim the "study (of) students' beliefs or attitudes": 2% (3 out of 148) for PME, 5.1% (9 out of 177) for ESM and 4.4% (6 out of 138) for JRME. Under the heading of *pedagogical models*, affect, particularly in PME publications, was "promoted only in a few papers in [the] sample (affective: 6.2%, 6.5%, 1.4% ... for ESM, JRME, and PME respectively)" (p. 29).

McLeod (1992, p. 575) maintained that "affect is a central concern of students and teachers, (yet) research on affect in mathematics education continues to reside on the periphery of the field". An exception to this, he added, were researchers with an interest in mathematics and gender who invariably included affectivity in their design of research in which aspects of mathematics learning were explored. Lubienski's (1999) review of mathematics education research, already mentioned earlier in the chapter, offers some confirmation for this assertion. Thirty per cent of the articles she identified as dealing with affect also had a focus on gender issues. Schoenfeld's (1992, p. 358) appraisal of the body of research on affect and mathematics education *per se* was quite positive. According to him there was "a fairly extensive literature on" student beliefs, "a moderate but growing literature

[1] Both Doug McLeod and Steve Lerman have been long standing members of PME. For them, and many other PME members who are active researchers, there are links rather than clear boundaries between work published within and beyond the restricted setting of the annual PME conference.

about teacher beliefs", but relatively little examination of "general societal beliefs about doing mathematics". This assessment of the community's concern with affectivity is in line with Leder's (1993, p. I 48) review of research on affective aspects of mathematics learning. "Research reports on affective issues were presented at each PME conference held between 1983 and 1992", Leder noted. This, she further argued was "no doubt a reflection of the increasingly widespread recognition among mathematics educators that understanding the nature of mathematics learning requires exploration of affective as well as cognitive factors".

It is no coincidence that references to the importance of engaging students, affectively as well as cognitively, are also found in influential curriculum documents. Several such examples, selected from different countries, are presented chronologically in Table 1. Their content is a useful indicator of broad themes explored in much of the research on affect presented at PME conferences.

Table 1. Affect and the mathematics curriculum

Source	*Excerpt*
Cockcroft (1982, p. 61)	It is to be expected that most teachers will attach considerable importance to the development of good attitudes among the pupils whom they teach ... Attitudes are derived from teachers' attitudes... and to an extent from parents' attitudes. ... Attitude to mathematics is correlated ... with the peer-group's attitude.
Australian Education Council (1991, p. 31)	An important aim of mathematics education is to develop in students positive attitudes towards mathematics. ... The notion of having a positive attitude towards mathematics encompasses both liking mathematics and feeling good about one's capacity to deal with situations in which mathematics is involved.
Schmidt, Jorde, Cogan, Barrier, Gonzalo, Moser, et al. (1996, p. 203)	The two curriculum frameworks –one for mathematics and one for the sciences– represent a multi-category, multi-aspect specification of these two subjects that provide a common language system for TIMSS. Both include multiple categories for each of three aspects of subject matter *–content ..., performance expectation ...,* and *perspective* (the attitudes or perspectives encouraged or promoted ...)
NCTM (2000, pp. 16-17)	Students' understanding of mathematics, their ability to use it to solve problems, and their *confidence in,* and *disposition toward,* mathematics are all shaped by the teaching they encounter in school. The improvement of mathematics education for all students requires effective mathematics teaching ... (Emphasis added)
OECD (2004, p. 12) Programme for International Student Assessment [PISA]	Information gathered as part of this large scale study revealed "how motivation, self-related beliefs and emotional factors are linked to the adoption of effective learning strategies, and thus can help students become life long learners." The increased emphasis in this large scale international project on motivation and emotional factors is noteworthy.

Although a functional link between achievement and positive affect is often implied in documents such as those referred to in Table 1, Cockcroft's (1982, p. 61) caution is still relevant. Despite the "perception (of teachers) that more interesting and enjoyable work will lead to greater attainment ... research certainly suggests caution against overoptimism in assuming a very direct relation between attitude and achievement."

AFFECTIVITY AND MATHEMATICS EDUCATION – A QUESTION OF MEASUREMENT

As mentioned earlier, affect can not be measured directly but needs to be inferred from the way an individual behaves or responds to specifically designed instruments, cues or situations. Indicative and representative approaches, particularly for determining attitudes and beliefs, are listed in Table 2.

Table 2. Common measures of attitudes and beliefs: Scales

Thurstone's Equal-Appearing Interval scales (Thurstone, 1967/1928)	Thurstone's method represents the first major approach to the measurement of attitudes. It is based on acceptance or rejection of opinion statements, assumed to lie on an evaluative continuum. Each opinion statement is assigned a scale value determined by its mean judged position. Respondents are asked to select a small number of statements with which they agree most closely. Their attitude score is calculated by averaging the scaled scores for each item selected. This approach to measuring attitudes and beliefs is of doubtful validity and is no longer common.
Likert-scales (Likert, 1967/1932): Summated rating scales	A Likert-scale consists of a series of statements about the attitude object. Divisions commonly range from (a 5-point scale) 'strongly agree' to 'strongly disagree' and are converted to numerical scores. An attitude score is obtained by summing the scores for each item on the scale. Because of the ease of administering and scoring this instrument, using a Likert-scale is a particularly common approach for tapping attitudes and beliefs (within and beyond PME). However, the validity of this method is not clearly established.
Guttman scaling (Guttman, 1967/1944) - scalogram analysis	Respondents are asked to agree or disagree with a number of statements (usually about six according to Triandis, 1971), ordered along a continuum of levels of acceptance. On a 'true' unidimensional Guttman scale agreement with a particular item assumes acceptance of items with a lower scale value. This scale, again of "not clearly established" validity, is regarded as difficult to construct but easy to interpret.
Osgood's Semantic differential scales (Osgood, Suci & Tannenbaum, 1970/1957)	These scales are defined by a series of bipolar adjectives listed with the same number of divisions (usually 7) between each pair. Each division represents a score on a continuum with the most positive response assigned the highest score. The mean score or the item sum can be used as a total scale score. Three factors are typically found. They assess the semantic connotations of

	concepts: Evaluation (good-bad), potency (strong-weak), and activity (active-passive). This approach to the measurement of beliefs and attitudes makes explicit the differentiation between the cognitive, affective, and behavioural components of attitudes enumerated in various definitions proposed in the literature.
The approaches detailed thus far lend themselves more readily to the measurement of "cold" affect as described by Mandler (1989); those that follow as indicators as well of "hot" emotions.	
Projective techniques	An unstructured or ambiguous stimulus (for example: Story, picture) related to the attitude object is presented and respondents are asked to react/explain, e.g., by choosing between alternative stories or explanations, and completing sentences or stories. This technique, or variations of it, is often adopted by those who favour qualitative approaches to the measurement of beliefs and by those concerned that respondents to Likert items may not express the beliefs they actually hold but rather those they consider socially acceptable.
Checklists/ inventories	A checklist of issues, objects, or adjectives related to the attitude object is presented to respondents who indicate their agreement or disagreement with each item. 'Unsure' may be included as a response category. Alternately, respondents can be asked to indicate which adjectives, for example, are considered applicable to themselves or to a specified group. Inventories typically consist of a list of careers or activities with respondents indicating which are of interest to them. Items such as these are often also used in interviews aimed at tapping attitudes, beliefs, and motivation.
Physiological measures	By comparing physiological reactions such as heart beat, pupil dilation, and galvanic skin responses to neutral and attitude objects respondents' attitudes can be inferred. These measures are not considered reliable since they are also sensitive to factors not related to attitudes. It is not yet common to see this approach used outside a laboratory setting.
Repertory grid techniques	The grid consists of relevant elements (often people) and constructs (usually investigator-generated) and is administered on an individual basis. Respondents make connections between the elements and the constructs, typically through an investigator-initiated activity or interview.
Interviews	Some regard interviews, particularly 'structured' interviews which comprise a predetermined list of specific questions to be asked, as little more than orally administered questionnaires. Unstructured interviews, on the other hand, can uncover views not anticipated in advance. A combination of these approaches –the semi-structured interview– is favoured by many engaged in mathematics education research.
Observations	Observations, particularly by expert and objective observers, have been described as an excellent means for determining affect.

	However, as the researcher cannot predict when pertinent behaviours will be observed it is an inefficient and expensive method. Data gathered in this way can range from structured to unstructured observations collected in a setting that can be natural or highly artificial. Mueller (1986, p. 90) argued that "High-quality observational measurement requires an expert and objective observer, careful selection of behavior situations and of specific behaviors to be observed, a systematic procedure for recording behaviors, and an objective interpretation of the recorded behaviors in making inferences about attitude".

(adapted from Hogg & Vaughan, 1995 and Leder & Forgasz, 2003)

Some of these approaches, particularly physiological measures, interviews, and observations have also been used to gauge emotional states and dispositions and their impact on, or response to, mathematics learning. The high level of inference needed to describe these "hot" (Mandler, 1989) components of affectivity continues to be methodologically challenging to researchers (see, e.g., Hannula, Evans, Philippou & Zan, 2004).

As will be seen in later sections, many of the methods included in Table 2 have also been used in research presented at PME conferences. Studies using these methods in the wider mathematics education research community have been summarized by Leder (1985) and by Leder and Forgasz (2003).

The tension between documenting as comprehensively as possible the research reported at PME conferences and the need to comply with reviewing and publication costs and space constraints has led to a severe restriction on the acceptable length of written contributions[2]. This in turn inevitably limits the amount of information and material able to be shared through PME Proceedings and increases the risk of misinterpreting or simplifying aspects of the work reported. McLeod's (1987, p. 170) concern warrants being repeated. "It seems to me", he argued, "that short papers like these may constitute a form of projective test; readers are likely to see in the paper reflections of their own interests".

AFFECTIVITY AND MATHEMATICS EDUCATION: PME PERSPECTIVES – THE EARLY YEARS

In her review of earlier research presented at PME conferences, Leder (1993) singled out several themes as particularly appropriate for summarizing research presented at PME conferences in the decade prior to 1992. These were: "Measurement of affective factors", "descriptive studies", defined as studies in which affective factors were of secondary interest in studies with a strong focus on other issues, "comparisons of affective and cognitive variables", and a small number of theoretical papers in which no experimental data were reported. A more

[2] In recent years PME Conference Proceedings have been published in CD format, largely removing cost considerations. Nevertheless, importance continues to be attached to reporting core elements of research in a limited space and a limited time.

extensive report of the first of these clusters is sufficient to convey the thrust of this earlier body of research.

Operationalizing affective factors – a PME perspective

In the bulk of studies reviewed self report measures –diverse questionnaires, Likert scales, and interviews– predominated, irrespective of the dimension of affectivity investigated, the nature of the sample, or the geographic setting in which the research was carried out. For example, questionnaires were used to probe beliefs and attitudes towards aspects of mathematics, to perceptions of the classroom learning environment, to mathematics anxiety, to aspects of attitudes to computers, and learned helplessness. Likert scales (variably 4, 5, 6, and even 8 point scales) were used to probe attributions for success and failure, various attitudes to mathematics using at times single, at other times multidimensional scales to measure these, attitudes to school, to significant others, liking of mathematics, confidence in mathematics, mathematics anxiety, test anxiety, aspects of academic choice, expectations of mathematics learning, and exploration of belief systems.

In many studies, most often those concerned with exploring beliefs and attitudes towards assorted and multiple aspects of mathematics, affect was further inferred from interview data, from semantic differential scales and from journal entries. As these methods of data gathering were typically used in conjunction with other approaches, the specific affective factors thus probed are not listed again except to note that these measures were typically used in the few studies in which emotions and feelings were explored. Infrequently data gathering relied on methods other than self report measures. These included observational data (the researcher's perspective), used as an additional measure of affect in a small subset of the studies, electromyograph data (to measure mathematics anxiety), and a projective technique such the Rorschach and Thematic Apperception test (again to measure mathematics anxiety). Thus the instruments used in research reported at PME conferences match, but are more limited than, those described in Table 2.

When used, multiple methods were generally seen as an opportunity to optimise data gathering. Yet in some studies different measures yielded different results:

> There was insufficient evidence to indicate that a linear relationship exists between paper-and-pencil (MAI) and (EMG) physiological measures of mathematics anxiety, implying that the two instruments may be tapping different dimensions of the mathematics anxiety construct. (Gentry & Underhill, 1987, p. 104)

Consistent with findings reported elsewhere, the link between affective variables and achievement in mathematics –most frequently described in terms of correlations– was positive but weak. The author of one large scale study concluded:

> Detailed analyses of correlations between students' achievements and their attitudes, beliefs, and opinions have shown that students with positive attitudes (e.g., those responding that mathematics is important, or easy, or

> enjoyable) generally scored 5% to 10% higher than students with negative attitudes. (Schroeder, 1991, p. 244)

The diversity of samples used in the research studies reviewed, including research mathematicians, university undergraduates, high school and young primary students, mathematics educators and mathematics teachers –at elementary, secondary and university level, inevitably added to the diversity of the design and scope of the content of the measures used. So did the geographic locations from which the samples were drawn: Africa, Australia, Canada, Europe, as well as North and South America. Reflecting on this earlier phase of research on affect one is left with the impression of considerable activity –but of operational diversity, of multi-directional rather than focused research; of relatively little sustained interest in aspects of affectivity, such as emotions, which require careful operationalization and particularly high inference for their description; and of disjoint rather than sustained debate. The space constraints imposed on papers included in PME Proceedings, mentioned earlier, may well have contributed to this episodic reporting. However, a broader reading of the mathematics education literature over that period confirms the limited impact on the field of research on affect.

> Research on affect has been voluminous, but not particularly powerful in influencing the field of mathematics education. It seems that research on instruction in most cases goes on without any particular attention to affective issues. (McLeod, 1992, p. 590)

Like McLeod, to whom we already referred earlier in this chapter, we also excluded research concerned with gender equity issues from this summary. This body of work has had a recognized and discernable impact on the development and delivery of mathematics instruction (see e.g., Freeman, 2004; Hannula & Malmivuori, 1997; Leder, 2004; Leder, Forgasz & Solar, 1996; Kerr & Kurpius, 2004, Vale, Forgasz & Horne, 2004). However, Leder (2001) noted that "cutting edge" gender issues explored by PME members were more likely to be reported in settings beyond PME rather than research presentations at the annual conferences of PME. "Where", she asked with reference to PME,

> are the reports of research studies, detailed in other venues, in which more radical feminist perspectives are being adopted, females are less frequently considered as a homogeneous group, and fine grained rather than collective data are presented? Where are the reports of scholarly evaluations of large scale interventions? Or detailed case studies which focus on individual rather than group differences? Or reflective accounts of the impact of the personal beliefs and theoretical orientation of the researchers undertaking the research on design of the study, data gathering decisions, choice of instrumentation? ... The format adopted for PME written Research Reports ... (seems to have favoured) the reporting of studies with certain data and research designs but discourages the reporting of others. (pp. 52-53)

In recent years, there has been increased recognition of changes in gender-linked achievement patterns in mathematics in reports of large scale studies such as the

Programme for International Student Assessment [PISA] (Thomson, Cresswell & De Bortoli, 2004). Indeed, in many quarters it is argued that the education of boys now needs the careful focus given to the delivery of education for girls in recent decades (see, e.g., House of Representatives Standing Committee on Education and Training, 2002; Warrington & Younger, 2000; Kimmel, 2000, for views expressed in Australia, the United Kingdom, and the United States respectively, and the Organisation for Economic Cooperation and Development, 2001, for a more general, international summary). Gallagher's (2000, p. iii) summary that "beliefs about masculinity influence their [i.e., boys'] willingness to participate in the activities of their school and their attitudes to teachers, subjects, and what is considered worth knowing" is a tacit –and representative– acknowledgement of the interaction between affective factors and educational achievement. The extent to which such interactions and their impact on the delivery of mathematics instruction have been examined by the PME community is indirectly traced in the next section, with its more specific focus on research on affect discussed at PME conferences.

AFFECTIVITY AND MATHEMATICS EDUCATION: PME PERSPECTIVES – THE PAST DECADE

In order to explore the patterns of research on affectivity as reflected in research reports at PME conferences over the past decade, the following criteria were adopted:

- Full research papers as well as Plenaries and Research Forums were examined; short communications and poster presentations were omitted due to the limited information included in them and the inconsistencies in the reporting of the details on the research studies.
- Plenaries and Research Forums from each year between 1996 and 2005 were looked at. However, only research papers from every second year were examined: 1996, 1998, 2000, 2002, and 2004. Since regular PME attendees sometimes present research papers in consecutive years in which different data from the same study are reported, it was considered reasonable to examine the Proceedings from every second year to avoid potential duplication without comprising representativeness. It was recognised, however, that there was the likelihood that some unique reports may have been inadvertently omitted in the analysis.
- A difficulty in deciding which research reports to include in the analysis was partially attributable to the range of descriptors provided to authors through the PME reviewing process. We decided to use the author identified index entries, "affective" and "beliefs", listed in the PME Proceedings, as guides to appropriate research reports. Clearly, if authors had not selected these descriptors, some research reports involving affective dimensions may have been missed in our analysis. On the other hand, had we included papers not found under these categories and relied on our own interpretations we could be

seen to be biased, and may also have been giving greater prominence to "affect" than was intended by the authors themselves.

It was disappointing to find that from 1996 to 2005 "affect" did not feature as the focus of any one of the 40 or so conference plenary presentations or in the plenary panel sessions. Vinner's (1997) plenary included a discussion of moral values in the mathematics classroom. In making ties between mathematical behaviours and general human behaviours, Vinner spoke about the moral dilemma in *playing the game* and using *pseudo-knowledge* (undesirable mathematical knowledge) to obtain *credit* within the system. In high stakes situations, the moral issue, "*To pretend* and get some credit or *not to pretend* and get no credit" (p. 68) would be a non-issue for most people, Vinner maintained.

Examining the Research Forums offered over the same period, only two were found that involved dimensions of affect. In 1996, under the title *Research on the mathematics teacher: Development, change and beliefs*, Becker and Pence (1996) discussed findings on teachers' beliefs about the teaching and learning of mathematics that were gathered using various quantitative and qualitative methods including a Likert-type scale and interviews. In 2004, affect was clearly central to the research forum entitled *Affect in mathematics education –exploring theoretical frameworks*, co-ordinated by Hannula et al. (2004). Several areas of study associated with affect were identified in the introduction: "the role of emotions in mathematical thinking generally, and in problem solving in particular"; "the role of affect in learning"; and "the role of affect in the social context of the classroom" (Hannula, 2004, p. 107). Of the four main concepts associated with affect – attitudes, beliefs, emotions, and values– emotions and values were not categorised separately by Leder (1993) in her earlier review of PME research but have been receiving more attention in recent times. An important contribution of this research forum was the discussion of various theoretical frameworks that had been used by the presenters to conceptualise *affect*.

ANALYSES OF THE RESEARCH REPORTS

Following Leder (1993), the research reports were sorted into four themes: Measurement of affective factors (A), descriptive studies (B), comparisons of affective and cognitive variables (C), or theoretical papers (D); they were also categorized by the instruments or ways in which the measures or dimensions of affect (including attitudes, beliefs, emotions, and values) were undertaken in the studies, and by the category of research methods used –quantitative, qualitative, or mixed methods. An overview of the findings for these various categorizations and their frequencies is provided in Table 3 (at the end of the chapter).

As can be seen in Table 3, there were more papers classified in the Proceedings under the research domains "affect" and "beliefs" in 1996 than in the later years. It became apparent that in some years some papers appeared to be have been classified incorrectly by the authors or the conference organizers. In these instances the research studies appeared to have nothing to do with accepted definitions of affect or beliefs. For example, papers on teachers' understandings/conceptions of various areas of mathematical content were sometimes erroneously included in the attitudes/beliefs category. At other times it seemed that some articles concerned with issues that were not considered to be "psychological", and could not be fitted readily under the other PME research domains, may have been categorized under "affect".

The data in Table 3 also reveal that the four most frequently adopted ways of examining or measuring affectivity were: Interviews, Likert-type items or scales, observations, and questionnaires or surveys including various types of items (with scoring formats often not described). Many of the other traditional measures of affectivity summarized in Table 2 were also represented but not in large numbers. With respect to the research methods adopted, there was a near even split of qualitative, quantitative, and mixed methods but there was a clear trend towards increasing use of qualitative-only studies as the decade progressed. In many of the qualitative-only studies the focus was on individuals and the ways that the affective dimensions were explored was not central to the research, and were generally inferred from a combination of observation and interview.

A weakness evident in many papers was the lack of clear definitions for the affective constructs included in the research designs. The affectivity measures of interest to many researchers were often only vaguely described as "attitudes towards..." or "beliefs about..."; in other cases, the more specific attitudes or beliefs examined were also not clearly defined, operationalized, or related to the literature in the field.

A representative sample of the studies involving affect that were found in the PME research reports and summarised in Table 3 was selected to illustrate the diversity of studies identified and the frequencies of their various categorizations. These are presented in Table 4 (at the end of the chapter). The selection made is representative of:

- The year of the PME conference
- The index category under which the report was located in the Proceedings
- Research report authors and their geographic location,
- The four themes into which the research reports had been categorized (A = *measurement of affective factors* to D = *theoretical papers*),
- The various dimensions of affect examined or measured in the studies, and
- The research methods used and the participants.

The selection of studies shown in Table 4 reveals that PME members from around the globe have engaged in research on affect during the decade 1996-2005.

As mentioned before, research reports in alternate years were examined, i.e., reports published in the 1996, 1998, 2000, 2002, and 2004 Proceedings. The participants in the studies reflected the full spectrum of mathematics learners and educators. The range of affective variables measured included attitudes towards or beliefs about mathematics (e.g., liking mathematics, the role of problem-solving), and oneself as a learner of mathematics (e.g., liking mathematics, confidence, interest). Other dimensions of affect examined included anxiety, motivation, and success orientation. Among the means by which data on the affective dimensions were gathered, traditional pen-and-paper instruments and interviews predominated; other data gathering tools included journal entries.

In summary, it is clear that qualitative approaches have become more prevalent in the exploration of affectivity dimensions across the field of mathematics education research. The more traditional conceptions of affect –attitudes and beliefs– were clearly the dominant dimensions of affect that were of direct and indirect interest to PME researchers. In the latter part of the decade, there was evidence of increased interest in the less well-theorised areas of emotions and values with respect to the teaching and learning of mathematics. It is noteworthy that the categories adopted by Leder (1993) sufficed to capture the overall thrust of research on affect in the years since then.

The affective domain is complex and multidimensional. The interaction between affect, behaviours and achievement has been explored in diverse ways in studies reported at PME conferences. Given the perceived stability of some affective subdomains and the volatility of others, the diversity of samples involved in research, the variability of terminology used by different researchers, and the inconsistent categorising over the years of studies as concerned with affect, it is difficult to identify consistent and sustained findings across the various studies reported. Yet collectively the findings reported in the annual Proceedings are tantalizing. There are provocative glimpses of the interaction between affect, teaching, and learning of mathematics, although our understanding of a directional relationship remains elusive.

FUTURE DIRECTIONS

Earlier in this chapter reference was made to the different areas in psychology in which research on affect is now taking place. Practices to date suggest that, of the fields mentioned, mathematics education is more likely to be influenced in the shorter term by new explorations within the realm of social cognition than in neuropsychology or psychophysiology. Mandler's (1989, p. 8) description of the occurrence of "some visceral or gut reaction" as a co-occurrence of affect has had an influence on the measurement of affect in mathematics education research. Codings of facial, affective verbal (e.g., tone of voice, exclamations, pauses in speech), and other non-verbal expressions (e.g., hand and body movements, posture) have been used at various times within and beyond the PME setting (e.g., DeBellis, 1996; DeBellis & Goldin, 1999) but with the caution that "inferences in affect are difficult, and no claim of reliability is made" (p. 2-251). Hannula et al. (2004) and Op 't Eynde (2004) have alluded to other attempts to trace changes in affect through the measurement of physiological parameters but such research is found more frequently outside the mathematics education research community (see e.g., Dillon, Keogh & Freeman, 2002; Ravaja, 2002). Reliance on physiological responses in mathematics education research carried out in a "real world" setting such as a classroom remains limited. Permission to conduct research involving the wearing of heart monitors, for example, is also likely to be difficult in many settings. School bureaucracies, teachers, parents and children as well as university human ethics committees (from whom permission to conduct studies needs to be obtained in many settings) are not likely to be welcoming of such intrusions. Apart from the practical and methodological difficulties of obtaining and coding non verbal measures for larger samples, further obstacles are again likely to be raised by ethics committees because of their unfamiliarity with, and scepticism about, the use of these methods. Balancing the need to obtain richer and more fluid measures of affect beyond those afforded by self-report questionnaires and simple performance tests, and yet ensuring that the behaviours sampled adequately reflect those encountered in a realistic classroom setting, was cited as an urgent challenge well over a decade ago (Leder, 1993) and continues to this day. For research on affect and mathematics learning to remain relevant, mathematics education researchers, like those exploring affect in the wider research community, must be able to draw on "such disparate fields as social cognition, neuropsychology, and psychophysiology, (fields) demonstrating that affect is intimately involved in everything we think and do" (Forgas, 2001, p. xvi).

In the remainder of this chapter we turn to a different direction and explore other methodological and measurement options stimulated by technological advances.

The Experience Sampling Method

The *Experience Sampling Method* [ESM], developed by Mihaly Csikszentmihalyi some 30 years ago, offers a sustained method for capturing individuals' activities over an extended period of time, as well as their reactions to, and beliefs about, those activities. This combination of data allows insights into the motivations, attitudes, and beliefs associated with the behaviours in which they engage. Csikszentmihalyi (1997) described the ESM as being able to provide "a virtual film strip of daily activities and experiences" (p.15). The ESM has the potential to provide richer and more comprehensive data than conventional survey methods and is less intrusive and less resource intensive than shadowing, a technique used to study the typical daily activities of individuals (e.g., Kephart & Schultz, 2001)

The ESM involves participants responding to signals and charting their activities and reactions on specifically designed *Experience Sampling Forms* or ESFs. Signals are typically sent between five and seven times a day over a period of one week. Response rates to signals are typically high, for example, Minor, Glomb and Hulin (2001) reported a 75-85%, and participants themselves consider the technique to provide fairly accurate portrayals of their activities (Mittelstaedt, 1995).

Modern technology can facilitate the means by which signals are sent to participants, thus extending the geographical diversity of participants who can be included in studies, at minimal cost. In the past, for example, signals have been sent to electronic pagers (Csikszentmihalyi, Rathunde & Whalen, 1993) and pre-programmed palmtop computers (Minor, Glomb & Hulin, 2001) carried by participants. In research on university academics (Leder & Forgasz, 2004) and secondary mathematics teachers (Forgasz & Leder, 2005), mobile phone and computer technology were exploited to send simultaneous SMS (text) messages to participants in diverse geographic locations to signal them that it was time to complete ESFs.

On-line surveys and interviews

There are other potential applications of new technologies that could be used to extend potential participant coverage, modify conventional research response rates, provide data in multiple forms, and facilitate data entry. Op 't Eynde (2004) has pointed to on-line questionnaires as an effective measure for tracing the continuous flow of affective dimensions including emotions. There are probably other advantages not yet conceived. In one study included in Table 4 (Jones & Simons, 2000), on-line surveys were used. Yet, the potential of on-line survey techniques for gathering closed and open-ended responses to tap into affectivity measures has not as yet been fully explored or exploited. While telephone and e-mail have been used as a means of conducting interviews and surveys (e.g., Leder & Forgasz, 2004), the conferencing facilities of conventional phones, and the photographic, video and audio recording capabilities of contemporary mobile phones do not appear to have been employed in affectivity research. Similarly, the conferencing facilities, and the audio and video capabilities of the Internet also do not appear to have been used. The possibilities for the simultaneous collection of data in various forms that are offered by these technologies appear to have great potential in the field of affectivity associated with mathematics education.

FINAL WORDS

The research on affectivity reported at PME conferences largely mirrors the endeavours of those in the broader mathematics education research community. Despite the widespread and continuing rhetoric in official documents about the importance of engaging students affectively as well as cognitively, the number of research reports concerned with affectivity presented (or accepted for presentation) at PME conferences appears to have decreased somewhat in recent years. Both within and beyond the PME community those involved in research on affectivity frequently rely on qualitative methods which often attract stringent, and at times unrealistic, requirements from ethics committees at many tertiary institutions. It remains to be seen to what extent possibilities offered by new technologies that might encompass both quantitative measures on, for example, the more stable aspects of affect (e.g., attitudes and beliefs) and qualitative measures on more volatile aspects (e.g., emotions and values) are embraced by those in the field to develop more refined and robust measurement techniques to allow us to understand better the link between affect and cognition across the field of mathematics education.

ACKNOWLEDGEMENTS

We wish to thank Jeff Evans and Markku Hannula for their helpful comments on an earlier draft of this chapter.

REFERENCES

Aiken, L. R. (1996). *Rating scales and checklists: evaluating behaviour, personality, and attitudes*. New York, USA: John Wiley.

Allport, G. W. (1935). Attitudes. In C. M. Murchison (Ed.), *Handbook of social psychology* (pp. 789–844). Reading, MA, USA: Clark University Press.

Australian Education Council (1991). *A national statement on mathematics for Australian schools*. Brunswick, Victoria, Australia: Australian Education Council and Curriculum Corporation.

Becker, J. R., & Pence, B. J. (1996). Mathematics teacher development: Connections to change in teachers' beliefs and practices. In L. Puig and A. Gutiérrez (Eds.), *Proceedings of the 20th PME International Conference*, *1*, 103–117.

Cockcroft, W. H. (1982). *Mathematics counts*. London, UK: Her Majesty's Stationary Office.

Corsini, R. J. (Ed.). (1984). *Encyclopedia of psychology* (Vol. 1). New York, USA: Wiley.

Csikszentmihalyi, M. (1997). *Finding flaws: The psychology of engagement with everyday life*. New York, USA: Basic Books.

Csikszentmihalyi, M., Rathunde, K., & Whalen, S. (1993). *Talented teenagers*. Cambridge, UK: University of Cambridge Press.

DeBellis, V. A. (1996). *Interactions between affect and cognition during mathematical problem solving: A two year case study of four elementary school children*. Unpublished PhD dissertation, Tutgers University USA. (University Microfilms No. 96-30716).

DeBellis, V. A., & Goldin, G. A. (1999). Aspects of affect: Mathematical intimacy, mathematical integrity. In O. Zaslavsky (Ed.), *Proceedings of the 23rd PME International Conference*, 2, 249–256.

Dillon, C., Keogh, E., & Freeman, J. (2002). "It's been emotional": Affect, physiology and presence. In *Proceedings of the 5th International Workshop on Presence*. Porto, Portugal.

Edwards, A. L. (1957). *Techniques of attitude scale construction*. New York, USA: Appleton, Century, Crofts.

Forgas, J. P. (Ed.). (2001). *Handbook of affect and social cognition*. Mahwah, NJ, USA: Lawrence Erlbaum.

Forgasz, H. & Leder, G. (2005). Mathematics teachers: A study of life inside school and beyond. In P. Clarkson, A. Downton, D. Gronn, M. Horne, A. McDonough, R. Pierce, & A. Roche (Eds.), *Building connections: Theory, research and practice* (1, pp. 361–368). Sydney, Australia: MERGA.

Freeman, J. (2004). Cultural influences on gifted gender achievement. *High Abilities Studies*, *15*(1), 7–23.

Gallagher, M. (2000). Overview of symposium. In *Proceedings of the Conference on Educational Aattainment and Labour Market Outcomes. Factors Affecting Boys and Their Status in Relation to Girls* (pp. i–vi). Canberra, Australia: Commonwealth Department of Education, Training & Youth Affairs.

Gentry, W. M., & Underhill, R. (1987). A comparison of two palliative methods of intervention for the treatment of mathematics anxiety among female college students. In J. C. Bergeron, N. Herscovics, & C. Kieran (Eds.), *Proceedings of the 11th PME International Conference*, 1, 99–105.

Goldin, G. (2003). Affect, meta-affect, and mathematical belief structures. In G. C. Leder, E. Pehkonen, & G. Törner (Eds.), *Beliefs: A hidden variable in mathematics education?* (pp. 59–72). Dordrecht, The Netherlands: Kluwer.

Guttman, L. (1967). A basis for scaling qualitative data. In M. Fischbein (Ed.), *Readings in attitude theory and measurement* (pp. 96–107). New York, USA: John Wiley & Sons. (reprinted from *American Sociological Review*, 1944, *9*, 139–150)

Hannula, M. S. (2004). Introduction. In M. J. Høines & A. B. Fuglestad (Eds.), *Proceedings of the 28th PME International Conference, 1*, 107–109.

Hannula, M., Evans, J., Philippou, G., & Zan, R. (2004). Affect in mathematics education – exploring theoretical frameworks. In M. J. Høines & A. B. Fuglestad (Eds.), *Proceedings of the 28th PME International Conference*, 1, 107–136.

Hannula, M., & Malmivuosi, M.-L. (1997). Gender differences and their relation to mathematics classrooms. In E. Pehkonen (Ed.), *Proceedings of the 21st PME International Conference*, 3, 33–40.

Hogg, M. A., & Vaughan, G. M. (1995). *Social psychology. An introduction*. London, UK: Harvester Wheatsheaf.

House of Representatives Standing Committee on Education and Training. (2002). *Boys: Getting it right. Report on the inquiry into the education of boys*. Canberra, Australia: Commonwealth of Australia.

Jones, K., & Simons, H. (2000). The student experience of online mathematics enrichment. In T. Nakahara & M. Koyama (Eds.), *Proceedings of the 24th PME International Conference, 3*, 103–110.

Kephart, K., & Schultz, C. (2001). *Shedding light on shadowing: An examination of the method*. Paper presented at the Annual Meeting of the AERA, Seattle, Washington, USA.

Kerr, B., & Kurpius, S. E. R. (2004) Encouraging talented girls in math and science: Effects of a guidance intervention. *High Abilities Studies, 15*(1), 85–102.

Kimmel, M. (2000). What about the boys? *Research report, The Wellesley Centers for Women, 21*(2), 6–7.

Leder, G. C. (1985). Measurement of attitude to mathematics. *For the Learning of Mathematics, 5*(3), 18–21, 34.

Leder, G. C. (1993). Reconciling affective and cognitive aspects of mathematics learning: Reality or a pious hope? In I. Hirabayasi, N. Nohda, K. Shigematsu, & F.-L. Lin (Eds.), *Proceedings of the 17th PME International Conference*, 1, 46–65.

Leder, G. C. (2001). Pathways in mathematics towards equity: A 25 year journey. In M. van der Heuvel-Panhuizen (Ed.), *Proceedings of the 25th PME International Conference*, 1, 41–54.

Leder, G. C. (2004). Gender differences among gifted students: Contemporary views. *High Abilities Studies, 15*(1), 103–108.

Leder, G. C., & Forgasz, H. J. (2003). Measuring mathematical beliefs and their impact on the learning of mathematics: A new approach. In G. C. Leder, E. Pehkonen, & G. Törner (Eds.), *Beliefs: A hidden variable in mathematics education?* (pp. 95–113). Dordrecht, The Netherlands: Kluwer.

Leder, G. C., & Forgasz, H. J. (2004). Australian and international mature age students: The daily challenges. *Higher Education Research and Development, 23*(2), 183–198.

Leder, G. C., Forgasz, H. J., & Solar, C. (1996). Research and intervention programs in mathematics education: A gendered issue. In A. Bishop, K. Clements, C. Keitel, J. Kilpatrick, & C. Laborde (Eds.), *International handbook of mathematics education* (2, pp. 945–985). Dordrecht, The Netherlands: Kluwer.

Likert, R. (1967). The method of constructing an attitude scale. In M. Fishbein (Ed.), *Readings in attitude theory and measurement* (pp. 90–95). New York, USA: John Wiley & Sons. (Excerpted from the Appendix of 'A technique for the measurement of attitudes', *Archives of Psychology*, 1932, *140*, pp. 44–53)

Lubienski, S. T. (1999). *What's hot? What's not? A survey of mathematics education research 1982–1998.* Paper presented at the annual meeting of the AERA, Montreal, Canada. (ERIC document ED 429487)

Mandler, G. (1989). Affect and learning: Causes and consequences of emotional interactions. In D. B. McLeod & V. M Adams (Eds.), *Affect and mathematical problem solving. A new perspective* (pp. 3–19). New York, USA: Springer-Verlag.

McLeod, D. B. (1987). New approaches to research on attitudes. In T. A. Romberg & D. M. Stewart (Eds.), *The monitoring of school mathematics – Background papers: Implications from psychology, outcomes of instruction* (2, pp. 279–290). Madison, Wisconsin, USA: Wisconsin Center for Education Research.

McLeod, D. B. (1992). Research on affect in mathematics education: A reconceptualization. In D. A. Grouws (Ed.), *Handbook of research in mathematics teaching and learning* (pp. 597–622). New York, USA: MacMillan.

McLeod, D. B. (1994). Research on affect and mathematics learning in the JRME: 1970 to the present. *Journal for Research in Mathematics Education*, *25*(6), 637–647.

Minor, A. G., Glomb, T. M., & Hulin, C. L. (2001). Mood at work: Experience Sampling Method using palmtop computers. In H. Weiss (Chair), *Experience Sampling Methods (ESM) in organizational research*. Symposium conducted at the 16th Annual Conference of the Society for Industrial and Organizational Psychology, San Diego, CA, USA.

Mittelstaedt, R. D. (1995). *Strengths and limitations of the Experience Sampling Method: An innovative technique in leisure research*. Paper presented at the 1995 Leisure Research Symposium, San Antonio, Texas, USA.

Mueller, D. J. (1986). *Measuring social attitudes: A handbook for researchers and practitioners*. New York, USA: Teachers College Press.

National Council of Teachers of Mathematics (NCTM). (2000). *Principles and standards for school mathematics*. Reston, VA, USA: NCTM.

Organisation for Economic Co-operation and Development (OECD). (2001). *Knowledge and skills for life: First results from the OECD Programme for International Student Assessment (PISA) 2000*. Paris, France: OECD.

Organisation for Economic Co-operation and Development (OECD). (2004). *First results from PISA 2003. Executive summary*. Paris, France: OECD.

Op 't Eynde, P. (2004). A socio-constuctivist perspective on the study of affect in mathematics education. In M. J. Høines & A. B. Fuglestad (Eds.), *Proceedings of the 28th PME International Conference*, 1, 118–122.

Osgood, C. E., Suci, G. J., & Tannenbaum, P. H. (1970). Attitude measurement. In G. F. Summers (Ed.), *Attitude measurement* (pp. 227–234). Chicago, USA: Rand McNally. (reprinted from C. E. Osgood, G. J. Suci, & P. H. Tannenbaum (Eds.), *The measurement of meaning*, 1957, (pp. 189–199). University of Illinois Press)

Petty, R. E, DeSteno, D., & Rucker, D. D. (2001). The role of affect in attitude change. In J. P. Forgas (Ed.), *Handbook of affect and social psychology* (pp. 212–233). Mahwah, NJ, USA: Lawrence Erlbaum.

Ravaja, N. (2002). Presence-related influences of a small talking facial image on psychophysiological measures of emotion and attention. In *Proceedings of the 5th International Workshop on Presence*. Porto, Portugal.

Schmidt, W. H., Jorde, D., Cogan, L. S., Barrier, E., Gonzalo, I., Moser, U., et al. (1996). *Characterizing pedagogical flow*. Dorderecht, The Netherlands: Kluwer.

Schoenfeld, A. H. (1992). Learning to think mathematically: Problem solving, meta-cognition, and sense making in mathematics. In D. A. Grouws (Ed.), *Handbook of research in mathematics teaching and learning* (pp. 334–370). New York, USA: MacMillan.

Schroeder, T. L. (1991). Teachers' and students' beliefs and opinions about the teaching and learning of mathematics in grade 4 in British Columbia. In F. Furinghetti (Ed.), *Proceedings of the 15th PME International Conference*, 3, 238–245.

Thomson, S., Cresswell, T., & De Bortoli, L. (2004). *Facing the future*. Camberwell, Victoria: Australian Council for Educational Research.

Thurstone, L. L. (1967). Attitudes can be measured. In M. Fishbein (Ed.), *Readings in attitude theory and measurement* (pp. 77–89). New York, USA: John Wiley & Sons. (reprinted from *Journal of Sociology*, 1928, *33*, 529–554)

Triandis, H. C. (1971). *Attitude and attitude change*. New York, USA: John Wiley & Sons.

Tsatsaroni, A., Lerman, S., & Xu, G. (2003). *A sociological description of changes in the intellectual field of mathematics education research: Implications for the identities of academics*. Paper presented at annual meeting of the AERA, Chicago, IL, USA. (ERIC document ED482512)

Vale, C., Forgasz, H., & Horne, M. (2004). Gender and mathematics. In B. Perry, G. Anthony, & C. Diezmann (Eds.), *Research in mathematics education in Australasia: 2000–2003* (pp. 75–100). Flaxton, Queensland, Australia: Post Pressed.

Vinner, S. (1997). From intuition to inhibition – mathematics, education and other endangered species. In E. Pehkonen (Ed.), *Proceedings of the 21st PME International Conference*, *1*, pp. 63–78.

Warrington, M., & Younger, M. (2000). The other side of the gender gap. *Gender and Education*, *12*(4), 493–508.

AFFILIATIONS

Gilah C. Leder
Institute for Advanced Study
La Trobe University
Bundoora, Victoria 3086 (Australia)
g.leder@latrobe.edu.au

Helen J. Forgasz
Faculty of Education
Monash University
Wellington Road
Victoria 3800 (Australia)
helen.forgasz@education.monash.edu.au
http://www.education.monash.edu.au/profiles/hforgasz

Table 3. Summary - Paper types in PME Proceedings: 1996, 1998, 2000, 2002 & 2004

Year/ Papers	*PME proceedings index category and frequency*		*Theme[1] and frequency.*		*Instruments/ways affect examined and rank frequency of occurrence*		*Research type and frequency*	
1996	Affect	5	A	14	Interviews	1	Quantitative	8
N=25	Beliefs	19	B	8	Likert items/scales	2	Qualitative	8
	Affect & Beliefs	1	C	1	Observations	3	Mixed	7
			D	2 (1: data)	Questionnaire/Survey	4	Theoretical	2
					Others, including: Guttman, repertory grid, and inference from content items			
1998	Affect	4	A	9	Interviews	=1	Quantitative	7
N=17	Beliefs	8	B	2	Likert items/scales	=1	Qualitative	8
	Affect &	5	C	4	Questionnaire/Survey	3	Mixed	1
	Beliefs		D	0	Observations	4	Theoretical	0
			NA	2	Others, including: Thurstone-type, and inference from game playing		NA	1
2000	Affect	1	A	8	Interviews	1	Quantitative	5
N=15	Beliefs	6	B	2	Observations	2	Qualitative	6
	Affect & Beliefs	7	C	3	Likert items/scales	3	Mixed	3
			D	0	Questionnaire/Survey	4	Theoretical	0
			NA	1	Others, including: physiological measure, and journals			

Year/ Papers	*PME proceedings index category and frequency*		*Theme[1] and frequency.*		*Instruments/ways affect examined and rank frequency of occurrence*		*Research type and frequency*	
2002	Affect	5	A	5	Likert items/scales	1	Quantitative	2
N=11	Beliefs	5	B	3	Interviews	2	Qualitative	2
	Affect & Beliefs	0	C	0	Questionnaire/Survey	3	Mixed	4
			D	2	Observations	4	Theoretical	2
					Others, including: inventory			
2004	Affect	7	A	5	Interviews	1	Quantitative	3
N=17	Beliefs	10	B	5	Questionnaire/Survey	2	Qualitative	11
	Affect & Belief	0	C	3	Observations	=3	Mixed	3
			D	0	Likert items/scales	=3	Theoretical	0
			A&D	1	Others, including: repertory grid			
			NA	2				
			?	1				

[1] Themes:

A. measurement of affective factors
B. descriptive studies (those in which affective factors were of secondary interest)
C. comparisons of affective and cognitive variables
D. theoretical papers (no experimental data were reported)

Table 4. Representative papers from PME Proceedings 1996, 1998, 2000, 2002 & 2004

Author/s	*Year*	*PME Proceedings index category*	*Location*	*Theme*[1]	*Instruments or ways affect was examined or measured*	*Dimensions of affect examined or variables measured*	*Research methods & Participants*
Bishop, A., Brew, C. & Leder, G.	1996	Affect	Australia	A	5-point scales Interviews	Perceived mathematics performance	Mixed: ≈ 180 grade 7 & 9 students; 1/50 interviews
Kyriakides, L.	1996	Beliefs	Cyprus	A	Questionnaire Interviews	Perceptions of curriculum reform	Mixed: ≈ 182 primary teachers surveyed; 20 interviews
Malmivuori, M-L. & Pehkonen, E.	1996	Beliefs	Finland	A	Continuous scales from fully disagree to fully agree	Mathematical beliefs: teaching, solving problems, learning, activity, & self-confidence	Quantitative: 453 grade 7 students
Valero, P. & Gómez, C.	1996	Beliefs	Colombia	A	Likert scale Observations	Various –indicators of "type of teacher"	Mixed: 1 teacher (scale and interviews); 58 teachers (to validate scale)
Risnes, M.	1998	Affect & Beliefs	Norway	A	Likert scales (4-point)	Self-efficacy, motivation, perceptions of ability, interest, and anxiety	Quantitative: 266 commencing economics and business administration students

Author/s	*Year*	*PME Proceedings index category*	*Location*	*Theme*[1]	*Instruments or ways affect was examined or measured*	*Dimensions of affect examined or variables measured*	*Research methods & Participants*
Jones, K. & Simons, H.	2000	Beliefs	UK	A	On-line questionnaires, interviews	Appreciation of mathematics	Mixed: 199 students, 20 interviews
Tsamir, P.	2000	Beliefs	Israel	A	Inferred from answers to problems	Beliefs about division by zero	Quantitative: 153 grade 9-11 students
Charalambos, C., Philippou, G. & Kyriakides, L.	2002	Beliefs	Cyprus	A	Questionnaires: 2 constructs - 5-point Likert items, rank-ordering; interviews	Philosophical beliefs, beliefs about teaching and learning mathematics,	Mixed: questionnaires –229 teachers; 5 interviews
Cohen, R. & Green, K.	2002	Affect	Canada	A	Interviews	Mathematics-related anxiety	Qualitative: 6 teachers (part of larger study)
Forgasz, H. J.	2004	Affect	Australia	A	3 x 5-point Likert scales; achievement self-rating	Attitudes to mathematics, computers, and computers for learning mathematics; 5 point scale	Quantitative: 1613 grade 7-10 students
Bottino, R. M. & Furinghetti, F.	1996	Beliefs	Italy	B	Interviews	Attitudes & beliefs about mathematics teaching	Qualitative: 8 upper secondary teachers
Presmeg, N	1996	Affect	USA	B	Interview	Dislike of mathematics	Qualitative: 1 tertiary student (part of larger study)

Author/s	*Year*	*PME Proceedings index category*	*Location*	*Theme*[1]	*Instruments or ways affect was examined or measured*	*Dimensions of affect examined or variables measured*	*Research methods & Participants*
Roddick, C., Becker, J. R. & Pence, B. J.	2000	Beliefs	USA	B	Journal entries, reflections, interviews	Beliefs about role of problem-solving	Qualitative: 3 prospective secondary teachers
Uusimaki, L. & Nason, R.	2004	Beliefs	Australia	B	Interviews	Reasons for mathematics anxiety	Qualitative: 18 pre-service teachers
Briggs, M	1998	Affect	UK	C	Oral history interviews	Attitudes generally – factors influencing	Qualitative: 5 adults with PhDs
Hannula, M., Maijala, H. & Pehkonen, E.	2004	Affect	Finland	C	Questionnaires – measures unclear; interviews, observations	Self-confidence, success orientation, defence orientation	Mixed: 3057 grade 5 & 7 students, 10 classes observed; ? interviews
Cotton, T. & Gates, P.	1996	Beliefs	UK	D			

[1] Themes:

A. measurement of affective factors
B. descriptive studies (those in which affective factors were of secondary interest)
C. comparisons of affective and cognitive variables
D. theoretical papers (no experimental data were reported)

SALVADOR LLINARES AND KONRAD KRAINER

MATHEMATICS (STUDENT) TEACHERS AND TEACHER EDUCATORS AS LEARNERS

INTRODUCTION

In this chapter and in accordance with the goals of this book, we provide information on relevant research on mathematics teachers' learning produced by the PME community. We summarise trends and key issues, contrast or compare perspectives, analyze results, and suggest directions for future research.

We regard mathematics teachers' learning as a lifelong learning process which starts with one's own experiences of mathematics teaching from the perspective of a student, or even with mathematical activities before schooling. Research assumes that these early experiences have a deep and longlasting impact on teachers' careers. "Teachers tend to teach in the way they have been taught", is an often used statement. However, pre- and in-service teacher education are important interventions in supporting teachers' growth. The teachers play the key role in that learning process. They are regarded as active constructors of their knowledge and thus encouraged to reflect on their practice and to change it where it is appropriate. It is a challenge to find answers to the questions of where, how and why teachers learn, taking into account that teachers' learning is a complex process and is to a large extent influenced by personal, social, organisational, cultural, and political factors.

In our chapter we regard three types of teachers: Student teachers, teachers, and also teacher educators. We use this distinction as a way of structuring our chapter. In section 2 we thus focus on student teachers' learning and regard PME papers that investigate student teachers' growth in beliefs and knowledge, including the impact of first experiences in teaching. In section 3 we report about PME papers and activities that put an emphasis on inquiry into practising teachers' growth when participating in teacher education programmes, underlining the increase of a social dimension in framing our understanding of teacher learning. We sift through major goals of these programmes as well as key factors that promote or hinder teachers' learning. Section 4 refers to a domain which needs closer attention in the future, namely our own learning as teacher educators. It is the field where theory and practice of teacher education inevitably melt together and we thus face the challenge of self-applying our demands on teacher education. Finally, in section 5, we aim at working on key issues that we found in analysing PME research on

A. Gutiérrez, P. Boero (eds.), Handbook of Research on the Psychology of Mathematics Education: Past, Present and Future, 429–459.

mathematics teacher education, and we suggest directions for future research in teachers' learning.

MATHEMATICS STUDENT TEACHERS AS LEARNERS

Teacher knowledge and beliefs

Becoming a mathematics teacher is usually supposed to be a learning process. We assume that student teachers' knowledge acquired before they enter a course influences what they learn and how they learn it (Richardson, 1996). This supposition has prompted studies centred on describing student teachers' beliefs and knowledge as determining factors in their learning processes and on identifying changes in these beliefs and knowledge as evidence that learning has taken place. The aim of studies of this type was to describe and explain the influence of student teachers' beliefs and knowledge on their learning. Consequently, research on mathematics teachers' beliefs and knowledge for teaching has provided information used to prepare research-based material for use in teacher education and to develop research-based teacher education programmes.

Beliefs. Describing and understanding the "positions" from which student teachers view aspects of their worlds is a way of understanding their learning process from a developmental perspective. But researchers have used different means to refer to beliefs in a way more or less explicit (Furinghetti & Pehkonen, 2003; Richardson, 1996; Thompson, 1992). Research on beliefs was first carried out from psychological perspectives, and beliefs were treated as cognitive phenomena (Richardson, 1996). Therefore, understanding the influence of professional development programmes on student teachers involved identifying changes in beliefs (see e.g. Bednarz, Gattuso & Mary, 1996). Beliefs and attitudes about mathematics, its teaching and the role of the teacher were regarded as an influence on student teachers' learning processes from constructivist perspectives on learning. For example, the focus was on describing the profiles of teachers' views of the nature of mathematics using questionnaires and cluster analysis (Jurdak, 1991), conceptions about teaching and learning to teach (Meredith, 1995), attitude questionnaires on teaching mathematics (Relich & Way, 1993), comparing conceptions about mathematics teaching by elementary and high school student teachers using a questionnaire (Gattuso & Mailloux, 1994) and the description of significant events in student teachers' mathematical lives that had contributed to their attitudes to mathematics (Doig, 1994). An alternative approach uses repertory grid methodology and Kelly's personal construct theory (Owens, 1987; Lengnink & Prediger, 2003). From this point of view, the student teacher is recognised as a learner and an active processor of knowledge, assimilating and organizing experience through the development of systems of constructs through which interpret their undergraduate experiences.

The results of these studies led researchers to appreciate the complexity of the notion of "beliefs", so that other research methods began to be used as alternatives to questionnaires, such as asking student teachers to interpret teaching situations (e.g. offering video clips of real children doing mathematics) (Ambrose, Philipp, Chauvot & Clement, 2003). For example, Simon (1991) examined prospective elementary teachers' views of mathematics pedagogy to characterise initial development of their ideas in their final year of study. The prospective teachers were enrolled in a mathematics education course on the teaching and learning of mathematics in elementary schools with the aim of challenging their beliefs. The following pedagogical task was used to infer beliefs about learning mathematics:

Imagine that you are teaching multiplication of fractions. One of your students raises his hand and says, "I am very confused. This doesn't make sense. The answers I am getting are smaller than one of the numbers I started with! What am I doing wrong?" He shows you the following example that he has done

$$2\frac{1}{4} \times 2/3 = 1\frac{1}{2}$$

What would you as a teacher do? Identify what you would say/do in response to this question. Include all teaching behaviours that would be stimulated by this interaction.

From the prospective teachers' written responses, Simon inferred their conceptions of mathematics pedagogy and produced two hypotheses, one of which characterised aspects of elementary student teachers' development "beyond a traditional view of mathematics pedagogy" while the other characterised "difficulties in their ability to generate instruction consistent with current visions" (Simon, 1991, p. 272).

Recently, researchers have begun to consider the social origins of beliefs and their contextualised nature (Gates, 2001). Fernandes (1995) used the biographical approach on the development of student teachers' professional identities. Some pre-service education programmes have concentrated on making student teachers aware of their own beliefs and on encouraging change in a certain direction. This perspective is framed in the context of teacher learning based on reflection on action. Reflection is regarded as a way in which teachers construct the meaning and knowledge that guide their actions. For example, Chapman (1998) argued that the use of reflection should be associated with developing student teachers' craft knowledge in relation to mathematical problem solving. In this case, the use of metaphors provided student teachers with a conceptual framework for thinking about problem solving and shaped the way they thought in order to extend and enhance their interpretations of the nature of problem solving and its teaching. These approaches underline the role of writing when investigating student teachers' beliefs. For example, writing about one's own experience or writing down interpretations (e.g. of teaching situations), are both ways of reflection that support a student teacher's learning when this is shared with other partners and provide a means for researchers to gather relevant data about their learning.

The nature of mathematical knowledge for teaching. It is assumed that it is necessary to have a "good" mathematical knowledge and pedagogical content knowledge (Shulman, 1986, 1987) specific to mathematics for teaching. But what is the nature of mathematical knowledge for teaching? Researchers have concentrated on finding out how student teachers "know" the mathematical content they teach, the role of types of representation and the interrelationship between mathematics teachers' knowledge and the understanding of students' conceptions. One focus of research on student teachers' knowledge has been their understanding of learners' mathematical thought processes. This kind of study relies on the principle that to help students to think mathematically the teacher needs to understand student thinking. Educators assume that student teachers' inquiry into children's mathematical thinking is a means towards student teacher's learning. This is an intersection of research about learning and learners and research on teaching and teachers. Research focused on teacher thinking about their students' mathematical thinking allows connections to be made between teachers' knowledge of mathematics and their pedagogical decisions. This type of research depends on the existence of an extensive body of knowledge on student conceptions. One characteristic of this type of study is the use of open-ended questions based on vignettes describing hypothetical classroom situations involving mathematics where students propose alternative solutions to some mathematical problems. Teachers are invited to engage in mathematical thinking through examining how students might have arrived at those different answers. Providing student teachers with opportunities to learn to use the clinical interview method with children makes it possible to generate opportunities for student teachers to construct models of student's mathematical understanding and revise their ideas about teaching and learning mathematics (see e.g. Civil, 1995; Doig & Hunting, 1995; Schorr, 2001).

In addition, research on student teachers' mathematical knowledge has provided information about the relationship between student teachers' conceptual and procedural knowledge; the role played by different representational systems or knowledge as action or process, and has identified student teachers' misconceptions in different branches of school mathematical content: Arithmetic and number theory (Tirosh, Graeber & Glover, 1986; Sánchez & Llinares 1992; Zazkis & Campbell, 1994); geometry (Burton, Cooper & Leder, 1986; Linchevsky, Vinner & Karsenty, 1992); logic and proof (Harel & Martin, 1986; Becker, 1993); functions and calculus (Martin & Wheeler, 1987; Even, 1988; Harel & Dubinsky, 1991); sets theory (Tsamir, 1999); measurement, area (Tierney, Boyd & Davis, 1990); problem posing and problem solving strategies (Leung, 1994; Taplin, 1996); probability (Koirala, 1998); algebra (Vermeulen, 2000; Leikin, Chazan, Yerushalmy, 2001); proportions and ratio (Ben-Chaim, Ilany & Keret, 2002).

This research reveals the complexity of mathematical knowledge for teaching, and indicates a shift away from regarding mathematical knowledge independent of context to regarding teachers' mathematical knowledge situated in the practice of teaching. For example, Rowland, Huckstep and Thwaites (2004) provide a framework to describe student teachers' pedagogical content knowledge and mathematical subject matter knowledge as evidenced in their teaching. From two mathematics lessons taught by each of the student teachers a brief descriptive synopsis of the lesson was generated and aspects of student teachers' actions in the classroom were examined in particular moments or episodes that seemed to be informed by their mathematics knowledge or pedagogical content knowledge (Shulman, 1987). The authors used four units to describe knowledge for teaching: Foundation, transformation, connection, and contingency. Chazan, Larriva and Sandow (1999) argued that terms such as procedural or conceptual knowledge should be refined to describe the kind of mathematical knowledge that supports teaching for "conceptual understanding". They tried to understand how to describe whether a teacher has subject matter knowledge which will support teaching for conceptual understanding. These researchers described qualities of teachers' substantive knowledge of mathematics by exploring connections between the nature of a teacher's own understanding of solving equations and systems of equations and their notions of how to help students understand why single linear equations have no solution or an infinite number of solutions. The difficulties in categorizing student teacher' understanding led them to discuss the categories of teacher knowledge. They argue that

> Discussions of the sorts of understandings useful for supporting teaching for conceptual understanding might be more usefully organized around a set of dimensions, for example: To what degree is the teacher able to articulate the goals of a problem in terms of relevant mathematical object? To what degree is the teacher able to relate situations and the mathematics used to model situations? To what degree is the teacher able to provide justification for why procedures work? ... (p. 199)

Making use of the understanding of student teachers' learning gained from research on beliefs and knowledge in order to improve the practice of teacher education is a characteristic of some of the research undertaken (Llinares, 1996). Research on the effects of the specific interventions sheds new light on the learning-to-teach process. In this sense, some studies on knowledge and beliefs describe changes in student teachers' knowledge and beliefs as a consequence of having participated in a specifically-designed intervention (Stonewater, 1989; Tirosh, 1999; Roddick, Becker & Pence, 2000). For instance, it is assumed that if student teachers learn mathematics through experiences of mathematical inquiry they will be better equipped to use teaching methods of this type and might change their attitudes about what it means to learn mathematics (Schifter, 1990). The goal of these courses is not only to teach mathematics content, but also to educate teachers so that they have more mathematical power and become reflective thinkers about how they learn and teach (Santos & Lamdin, 1992; McClain & Bowers, 2000). In these approaches, questionnaires, video recordings, classwork notes and student teachers' diaries are analysed in order to describe changes in attitudes towards mathematics. The goal of the interventions is to problematise the mathematics for the student teachers and to develop an understanding of mathematical content.

The growing awareness of relations between student teachers' mathematical knowledge and pedagogical content knowledge in teacher empowerment has led to the development and study of research-based teacher education programmes aimed at promoting teacher subject matter knowledge and pedagogical content knowledge, and at preparing research-based materials for use in teacher education (Markovits & Even, 1994; Even, Tirosh & Markovits, 1996). The long-term research and development project of Even et al. (1996) presented an example of the attempts that are being made to relate the practice of teacher education programmes, research about teacher knowledge and theoretical reflections. These researchers looked for the origins of the representations of teacher material (planning, answering questions and student observations) as sources of knowledge about the subject matter and knowledge about the student. The research was focused on the impact of participation in various models of teacher education programmes focused on students' ways of thinking in mathematics and on the growth of teachers' knowledge and their professional development. This research illustrated how teachers' knowledge of mathematics influences their pedagogical decisions and how teachers' knowledge of subject matter influences their ability to focus on the essence of students' questions.

Like research reported in the *Journal of Mathematics Teacher Education* (see e.g. Ambrose, 2004; Krainer, 2004), PME research shows that professional development programmes that involve (student) teachers actively in *reflecting* on students' mathematical learning and in *sharing* their experiences with colleagues have a positive impact on student teachers' knowledge and beliefs. This shows that learners are a rich source for teachers' learning, and also means that student teachers' learning is always a potential learning opportunity for teacher educators, in research contexts as well as in teacher education practice.

Learning from practice: Reflection on practice as context

One way of coordinating messages produced by different contexts in which learning-to-teach takes place is by incorporating teaching analysis in teacher education programmes. The proponents of introducing analysis and reflection on teaching practice suggest that student teachers will have a better opportunity to integrate theory and practice (for example when student teachers investigate questions stemming from their mathematics teaching) (Nicol & Crespo, 2003). Recently, interactive multimedia learning environments (CD ROMs) are being used to support student teachers' learning about teaching mathematics. These media suggest that student teachers can move beyond merely describing teaching events to detailed analysis and explanation that lead to higher levels of cognitive engagement (Mousley & Sullivan, 1996; Sullivan & Mousley, 1996; Goffree & Oonk, 2001; Oonk, 2001). The interactive multimedia learning environments can have the format of teaching-case study, analysis and reflection on particular incidents or examples of teaching, supporting the interaction between student teachers and focusing on relationships between classroom practice and teacher thinking which support autonomous learning and student teachers' own critical reflection. For Sullivan and Mousley (1998) problematic situations lead to the necessity for teachers to be aware of alternative ways of thinking and patterns of behaviour as well as to make informed choices. From this perspective the use of dilemmas provides student teachers with the awareness of different possibilities. Learning in these environments is viewed as expanding student teachers' vocabulary, changing their view on teaching, becoming more sensitive to students, and acknowledging of the legitimacy of competing perspectives. In the same sense, Doerr, McClain and Bowers (1997) indicate that student teachers working in multimedia learning environments were able to gain significant insight into the complexity of the classroom environment and the teacher's role within that environment. All these studies using multimedia learning environments underline the idea that reflexive processes enable student teachers to have a sense of being in control of their learning and a noticeable development in the quality of the language and thinking associated with interpretation of teaching incidents (Sullivan & Mousley, 1998). The use of theory –theoretical information– by student teachers in order to observe, interpret and analyse the teaching of mathematics in a computer-based environment that provides an investigative representation of teaching in an actual classroom setting was studied by Oonk (2001) (see also Goffree & Oonk, 2001). Experience has shown that student teachers are often not only focused on the actual teaching of mathematics when watching the fragments, but also on general didactic and educational issues. However, the ability to articulate observations of and reflections on practical situations in theoretical terms remains largely undeveloped.

From student teacher to beginner teacher

Learning to teach is viewed as a process generated in different contexts which sometimes transmit contradictory messages to student teachers and reveal the difficulties beginning teachers find in making connections with their university experiences. The process of becoming a teacher requires coordination of the different messages that student teachers receive in different learning contexts (Underhill, 1990; Borko, Eisenhart, Brown, Underhill, Jones & Agard, 1992; Eisenhart, Borko, Underhill, Brown, Jones & Agard, 1993) since teachers' thinking about their role in the classroom is influenced by their university programme (Brown, 1986). From this perspective, the change in student teachers' beliefs across different contexts (a mathematics methodology course, student teaching, first year of teaching) recognises the interrelationship of subjectivity and social context and suggests that the student teacher should be viewed as a human subject inserted into a range of different contexts, each of which can define competence differently (Blanton, Wetbrook & Carter, 2001).

Ensor (1998, 2001) argues that recontextualizing from the mathematics methodology course to the first year of teaching by beginning teachers showed that they took advantage in two ways of the methodology course: They reproduced a small number of discrete tasks that had been introduced to them there, and they also deployed a professional discourse –a way of talking about teaching and learning mathematics. This recontextualizing was shaped by the beginning teachers' educational biographies and school contexts, but most particularly by access to recognition and realization rules. The support provided to the student and beginner teachers in the different contexts –university, teaching practice, school– is a key factor in the transition from student teachers to practicing teachers. In order to reach an acceptable level of harmony between their conceptions and their teaching practice, student teachers struggle to achieve compatibility between their conceptions and their teaching-learning process as well as the limitations and conditions imposed by the school context (Georgiadou-Kabouridis & Potari, 2002).

When teaching practice is regarded as a learning context, the events which student teachers find most relevant and the explanations that they give are key factors in understanding their learning processes. Selinger (1994) observed differences between student teachers' and teachers' responses after watching video recordings of mathematics lessons indicating the complexities of interpreting teaching practice and the transition from student teacher to teacher. To analyse this transition, Lenfant (2001) proposed a multidimensional theoretical framework and explored the complexity of relationships between knowledge and competences focused on professional competence in elementary algebra teaching. Lenfant stressed that learning to teach and the transition from student teacher to beginner teacher is a complex process involving three dimensions of knowledge: Epistemological (about epistemological features of algebraic knowledge), cognitive (about learning processes in algebra) and didactical (knowledge of the curriculum, of specific goals of algebraic teaching at a given grade). Questionnaires and interviews were used during initial training, class observation during teaching practice and a follow-up study of a small group of student teachers during their first year of teaching. This type of multidimensional analysis allows the researcher to identify factors which support or inhibit learning, as well as the relationships between knowledge and the development of competencies. Two findings in Lenfant's initial analysis are particularly relevant. Firstly, the difference between the analyses of videotaped mathematics lessons that student teachers produced when working individually and those when working in small groups; secondly, the influence of short didactic training courses offered by teacher education institutions will remain anecdotal if they are not properly echoed by a reflective analysis of student teachers' practice in classes where they have full responsibility.

These studies underline the importance of meaningful actions and joint reflections among teacher students as a way to help the phenomena of recontextualization. In addition, the type of support received by student teachers –e.g. building networks, writing about the practice and sharing with others– is a key element in the learning process. This indicates the important role of organizational aspects –e.g. relationships between the schools where student teachers begin to teach and the course in the university– in the transition from student teachers to beginner teachers.

Conceptualising learning to teach

Student teachers' learning processes have been conceptualised from different perspectives (Llinares, 1996; Lerman, 2001). Constructivist views of learning are the basis of much of the research on learning to teach; however, they remain in many cases implicit. From this perspective, student teachers' learning can be evidenced by changes in their beliefs and knowledge and conceptualised as a dynamic process of constructing beliefs supported by student teachers' reflections during practice. Reflective practice offers a view of how student teachers learn about teaching and provides information about changes in their mathematics teaching. Student teachers' reflection is a key component in this view of learning and it is assumed that one learns through reflecting on one's experience. Cooney and Shealy (1994) argued that

> the very notion of being reflective and its corollary of being adaptive is based on the ability of a person to see themselves operating in a particular context, that is, the ability to 'step outside of themselves' in order to reorient themselves. (p. 226)

These researchers considered the evolution of a teacher's notion of authority from that of being external to that of being internal as an indicator of development of the student teacher using the Perry Development Scheme, which is condensed into four positions on a developmental scale (Copes, 1979, 1982): Dualism, multiplisticism, relativism, and commitment, and can be described by the metaphor of "lenses" through which persons view their experience. Cooney and Shealy (1994) described this way of conceptualising teacher development by studying four student teachers during their mathematics education programme. The four student teachers were confronted with new ideas and incorporated them in different ways into their systems of beliefs, resulting in different forms of development during the programme. For example, as Greg (one of the student teachers) confronted new ideas, he considered and incorporated them into his beliefs through accommodation and by reconceptualizing his beliefs about mathematics and the teaching of mathematics, thus reflecting Perry's relativistic stages. On the other hand, Henry (another student teacher), rejected and refused to consider alternative views, feeling that teacher education was a waste of his time, and so remained steadfastly dualistic; and Nancy (another student teacher) wanted to know "the right way to teach" and was looking for that way from an external authority, so Nancy did not ignore or reject new ideas, but seemed to assimilate ideas without accommodation (dualistic stage). Cooney and Shealy pointed out:

> What we considered important is that we have an orientation that allows us to conceptualise teacher development and provides us with a basis to reconsider and reshape future teacher education activities. (p. 231)

In this sense, learning is sometimes viewed as a process of cognitive perturbation and accommodation (a Piagetian view of development). For example, Mousley and Sullivan (1997) argued that

> thus teacher education programs need to find ways to perturb students' existing conceptions of mathematics teaching and learning, as well as the wider contexts of schooling and society, to create a milieu in which change is a desired state ... one of the roles of teacher education is to create an environment in which challenge of existing thinking and actions is possible. (p. 32)

From this point of view one can assume that different layers of reflection should be related to student teachers' growth of mathematical knowledge and how it is used in practice. In this context, Goffree and Oonk (2001) defined four levels of integration theory in the analysis of practice: Assimilation of practical knowledge, adaptation and accommodation of practice knowledge, integrating theory and theorizing. This view of learning to teach attempts to describe a way of construction of professional knowledge supported in the analysis of practice, reflection and share with partners.

The integration of constructs from social theories in the analysis of student teachers' learning underlines the social dimension of the learning-to-teach process (see e.g. Blanton, Westbrook & Carter, 2001, using Valsiner's zone theory). In this sense, socio-cultural perspectives conceptualise learning to teach as the development of an identity as a teacher in different communities (Lave & Wenger, 1991; Wenger, 1998). Here, learning can be seen as increasing participation in that community. For instance, Nicol and Crespo (2003) examined the learning of five student teachers by investigating a question stemming from their mathematics teaching. The data were analysed considering the connections between knowledge, practice and identity and how student teachers negotiate new identities as (prospective) mathematics teachers. The use of social factors (e.g. building communities, collaboration among student teachers, modes of participation, regimes of accountability) in the description and explanation of student teachers' learning recognised the role played by the different contexts in which learning takes place (Bohl & Van Zoest, 2002, 2003) and the influence of administrative and organizational aspects (Brown, 2003). From these socio-cultural perspectives, the observable evidence regarding student teachers' learning processes lies in the different ways in which they collaborate, build networks and share knowledge, and in the ways in which they use conceptual instruments and the new language to solve professional problems related to their objectives and aims (Llinares, 2003). Student teachers' learning is thus seen as a multidimensional process which integrates social and individual factors.

To sum up, PME research on student teachers' learning indicates the importance of environments and contexts where student teachers actively work on meaningful (mathematical, didactical, educational, ...) problems. Their own critical reflection of practice (e.g. concerning solving mathematical problems, observing other teachers' lessons, analysing their own teaching experiments) is regarded as an essential learning feature. Even when a single student teacher's growth is the focus of study, social and organizational aspects are increasingly being considered. Sharing knowledge, networking, building different kinds of communities are seen as crucial elements in student teachers' learning and as relevant factors in explaining student teachers' learning. In particular in the case of beginning teachers, the question of participation in teacher communities and socialisation in the school context becomes more prominent.

MATHEMATICS TEACHERS AS LEARNERS

Reform movements in mathematics teaching shed light on the vital role played by teachers in educational change. The proposed changes required teachers to develop approaches to the teaching of mathematics based on investigative methods and centred on the learners. This context favoured the implementation and analysis of initiatives in teachers' professional development. The hypothesis on which these initiatives were based was that the professional development of teachers could lead to improvements in teaching and in their pupils' learning. Research by PME members raised questions related to teachers' learning, the effects of professional development programmes and courses on teachers' beliefs, knowledge and practice, and the identification of factors (e.g. specific features of a programme) which might influence teachers' growth. One characteristic is that mathematics teacher education programmes are reported on by those who designed and implemented them. This situation is not a specific PME phenomenon but an international trend (see Adler, Ball, Krainer, Lin & Novotna, 2005). In the research presentations and discussions the meaning given to the idea of professional development and to factors which encourage teacher learning reflect a variety of theoretical perspectives (Jaworski, Wood & Dawson, 1999). One characteristic of the research presented in PME is the cultural diversity of the different programmes and different national characteristics. The question of how to generalise (on) the knowledge generated by each piece of research on in-service teacher education (Adler, 2001) reveals the need to be able to "tell stories" and to draw inferences from them which would enable them to be compared, related and explained.

This section is composed of three parts: It deals with the objectives and aims of the programmes (their focus), with factors which promote teachers' learning and development, and with the understanding gained. The content is mainly centred on research carried out on teachers' professional development as a consequence of having participated in some kind of programme or course. There are other contexts which encourage and study teacher development and the links to their practice (e.g. participation in projects, teachers examining their own practice, lesson study, ...). These investigations are reviewed in the chapter by J. P. Ponte and O. Chapman in this volume.

Aims of the programmes: The focus

Raising teachers' awareness of mathematical process and content. One of the crucial aspects of teachers' development is their understanding of mathematics. Teachers require a strong mathematical background in order to be able to propose powerful mathematical tasks which will enable pupils to learn mathematics in a meaningful way. Many teacher education programmes are based on the assumption that reflection on solving challenging problems influences teachers' beliefs, knowledge and practice. The importance of the type of mathematical tasks which teachers should handle while participating in professional development programmes has been stressed by Zaslavsky, Chapman and Leikin (2003) since this may "enhance the mathematical, pedagogical and educative power of mathematics educators ..." (p. 899).

Initially, research reports described tasks and how they were used. These reports assumed that teacher learning existed, as did changes in beliefs and attitudes regarding mathematics. The objectives of the teacher educators has since shifted from thinking about the nature of the tasks that should be proposed to teachers and an examination of the characteristics of the methodology used, to finding out how to describe and analyse the ways in which the development of participating teachers' mathematical comprehension takes place.

This new shift leads to the assumption that for teachers to become competent in mathematics it was necessary for them to learn mathematics in the same way as they were expected to teach it. These in-service programmes for teachers implemented a problem-centred approach and encouraged reflection on their experiences. The goal was to improve teachers' knowledge of the process of doing mathematics (Murray, Olivier & Human, 1995). Schifter (1990, 1993) described a mathematics course for teachers whose major goal was to enable its participants to become mathematical thinkers, to help teachers to learn to reason mathematically, to lead them to reconsider and broaden their understanding of what mathematics is and to develop their powers of mathematical reasoning. Schifter thus reconceived mathematical content as the active construction of mathematical concepts and reflection on that activity. The mathematics topics were the means through which the goals of the course were pursued. The teachers carried out mathematical explorations working from an activity sheet in small groups and then sharing discoveries, reading assignments, and journal-keeping as a means of reflection and dialogue that provided them with the opportunity to simultaneously step back from mathematical content in order to reflect on their mathematical process. The relevant aspects of this approach consisted of supporting teachers' reflection on their mathematical practice and building networks among partners in order to share knowledge. The effects of the course are described as the increase of teachers' confidence in their mathematical power, and shifts in the teachers' perception of their mathematical understanding, as well as in their attitudes. The findings of the research suggest that supplying teachers with mathematical experience can encourage reflection on the nature of mathematics and on how mathematics-related learning takes place (Murray et al., 1995). This allows teachers to work from personal experiences to self-constructed theories of practices and helps them to construct meanings that reflect theories that made sense to them in the context of their teaching (Chapman, 1996). McClain's (2003a, 2003b) objective was to describe how teachers' understanding of mathematics develops. Teachers participated in monthly work sessions in which the tasks from a seventh-grade instructional sequence were solved with the aid of computer-based tools and in which norms for argumentation were negotiated during the work sessions.

Videorecording of each monthly work session and the weeklong summer work sessions were analyzed together with copies of teachers' work and transcripts of interviews. The focus of analysis was the participation of the teachers in mathematical discussions. Using an emergent perspective that involved coordinating sociological and psychological perspectives, McClain reported on teachers' learning by characterizing changes in collective mathematical activity – pointing to shifts in teachers' mathematical practice– while highlighting the diversity in individual teachers' reasoning.

Raising teachers' awareness of children's mathematical thinking. Some studies provide support for using student thinking as the basis of professional development. These programmes assume that the knowledge of students' mathematical thinking provides teachers with a basis for their instruction and also for their own continued learning. Carpenter and Fennema (1989) developed "Cognitive Guided Instruction" (CGI), as an intervention in in-service teacher education. Their goals were to help teachers to make informed decisions, to provide them with specific knowledge about student thinking, and to provide them with the opportunity to explore how they might use that knowledge for instruction. Carpenter and Fennema reported that changes in the practice of teachers were slow in coming. When the changes occurred, teachers encouraged students to use a variety of problem-solving strategies and listened to their students' views on the processes since they had come to believe that instruction should build upon students' thinking. Recently, Franke, Carpenter, Levi and Fennema (2001) reported on a follow-up study of professional development in mathematics that showed that after several years some CGI teachers were engaged in generative growth (they continued learning). To document teachers' engagement with student mathematical thinking, Franke et al. (2001) integrated beliefs and practice in a classification scheme with different levels of teacher development. These researchers suggest that focusing on student thinking is a means for engaging teachers in generative growth and that supporting teachers' collaboration with their colleagues can support their learning. In this sense, Whitenack, Knipping, Couts and Standifer (1997) suggested that using interactive technologies to provide opportunities for teachers to explore children's arithmetical activity contributed to the teachers' ongoing professional development. The flexibility of access to the information and the cases (excerpts of movies) contributed to teachers' learning. The results show that there was an interdependence between how teachers used the interactive technology package and the teachers' conceptions about teaching and learning.

What promotes or hinders teachers' learning

There is some evidence that the *structure* adopted by programmes (Simon, 1988; Tirosh & Graeber, 2003) and the type of *mathematical tasks* carried out by teachers (Zaslavsky et al., 2003) are important factors in encouraging and promoting teacher learning and changes in mathematics-teaching classroom practice. Becker and

Pence (1996) noted a variety of aspects of programmes related to teacher change: A support network as teachers tried to implement change; the opportunity for teachers to engage in extended conversation about teaching and learning mathematics, and the length of time spent in staff development. Ellerton (1996) suggested that a greater change in teachers' beliefs and practice might have been possible if action research had been incorporated as an integral part of the programmes. Some of these results strongly indicate that the factors that encourage teacher learning form a network of aspects related to the type of support (e.g. coaching) which teachers receive and the duration of each intervention. In recent years, research on teacher development presented in PME has centred on reflective practice as well as on collaboration and community building, thus indicating an increased awareness of the social dimension (we extend this idea later).

Reflection. Reflection is considered a key element in the development of processes required for on-going learning since it is assumed that reflection is a means by which teachers continue learning about teaching and about themselves as teachers. As a consequence, some initiatives are aimed at developing the awareness necessary to becoming reflective practitioners. In this context, the focus of the reflective process is a key element in supporting the generation of reflection and the critical analysis of teachers' beliefs.

Wood (2001) asked "how do we know if teachers *are* learning? To answer this question it is necessary to investigate the *process of reflection* which is thought to be central in teachers' learning" (p. 431). Wood studied the process of reflection of seven beginning elementary teachers, examining what teachers notice when observing their classes, the interpretations they give of events, and the changes they propose in their practice. The findings revealed that differences in the beginning teachers' reflection were linked to changes in practice and teachers who made little change in their teaching only made descriptions of the events in their classroom.

Lerman and Scott-Hodgetts (1991) encourage pre-service and in-service teachers to use critical classroom incidents as starting points for the teachers' development, with positive effects on teaching practice. In this context, sharing ideas with other participants and tutors, and reflection upon their reading develops the interaction between theory and practice. The activity of writing stories about their teaching allowed teachers to increase their awareness of their teaching and to identify the underlying assumptions influencing it.

Some in-service teacher education programmes and research on teacher learning focus their attention on increasing teachers' awareness of the way they teach as a means of improving their teaching. In these initiatives, teachers are involved in reflection and analysis of teaching and learning that sometimes integrate effecting and researching their own professional development as a way of supporting the process of reforming teaching methods. Action research, which is understood as the systematic reflection of practitioners in action (see e.g., Altrichter, Posch & Somekh, 1993), is used as a means to achieve a broader understanding of situations and to improve the quality of teaching. Teachers are regarded as professionals who systematically aim at investigating their own practice. In many cases, teachers work in teams and/or are supported by "critical friends" (e.g. colleagues or teacher educators). Sometimes, a particular aspect links action research to the notion of teachers as researchers and school-based development as presented in PME (see e.g. Krainer, 1994; Zack, Mousley & Breen, 1997). The notion of teachers as researchers challenges the assumption that knowledge is separate from and superior to practice. Mousley (1992) reported a university course that involved teachers working in small groups to research ideas and articulate their own philosophies about what mathematics is and the ways in which school mathematics should be taught. The research design, with different cycles of action research, allowed Mousley to conclude that experience-based research has the power to emancipate some teachers from taken-for-granted classroom routines. In addition, Halai (1999) pointed out that both critical reflection and structural changes in schools are necessary to promote teacher learning in cycles of action research. However, we still need to understand better how school-based development is carried out. Valero and Jess (2000) suggested that the constitution of a community of practice in a school by a professional development initiative articulated by action research was not an easy task. In this sense, the researchers pointed out that it is necessary to design approaches that prioritise the social dimension of in-service teachers' practice.

Teacher collaboration and community building: Professional development as a social process. In order to help us to understand the factors that encourage teacher development as a social process, Peter-Koop, Santos-Wagner, Breen and Begg (2003) focus our attention on the role of collaboration among teachers. The constitution and support of collaboration between and among mathematics educators and teachers is seen as a factor that has a great impact on the success of teacher development initiatives. Collaboration may adopt many forms, none of which is exempt from difficulties, conflicts, tensions and problems due to the asymmetry of the collaborating partnerships. In collaborative processes, context – organizational aspects– and personal and social dimensions must be taken into account (Wenger 1998; Richardson & Placier, 2001; Krainer, 2004). For example, the dialectical relation between what is personal and what is social was examined in research carried out by Lin (2000). Constructing cases co-operatively by teachers and researchers fostered personal reflection and was an effective teaching method for teachers' professional development. In this way, writing and re-writing cases with the help of teacher educators allowed teachers to share perspectives and ways of translating their theories into classroom practice. This way of collaboration between teachers and teacher educators is supported in order to foster reflection and social interaction in a group. Activities that require writing up cases collaboratively and discussing cases in group sessions seem to favour teacher development.

The factors influencing teacher development (reflection and collaboration), are instruments that teacher educators consider when designing teacher education programmes but they are not professional development objectives in themselves. At the present time, we need to understand better the relationship between these instruments and teachers' different levels of development, as well as the changes in teachers' practice. For example, we need to know how the characteristics of the collaboration within a group of teachers, or between teachers and teacher educators (or the characteristics of a teacher's reflections) might influence teachers' professional growth. How can we grasp such developments?

Recently, some researchers have begun to use the idea of Wegner's (1998) "community of practice" in order to understand what encourages or inhibits teacher learning and development. A community of practice is defined by members' joint enterprise or shared sense of purpose as related to mathematics, such as students' mathematical understanding (Gómez, 2002), knowledge of mathematical content (Nickerson & Sowder, 2002; Koellner & Borko, 2004) or the practice of mathematics teaching (McGraw, Arbaugh & Lynch, 2003; Sztajn, Alexsaht-Snider, White & Hackenberg, 2004). From this perspective, learning is conceptualised as changes in participation in socially organised activities, and individuals' use of knowledge as an aspect of their participation in social practices (Lave & Wenger, 1991). This research uses the group as the unit of analysis to examine teachers' participation in activities of professional development and the challenges involved in community formation, and explore changes in the ways of participation in professional activities over time. It is assumed that participation in communities of practice is a factor that encourages teacher development and that activities within a community of practice can improve the teaching of mathematics and pupils' learning. These programmes underscore school communities as units of change in mathematics education and professional development. Some of these initiatives link cycles of research to action on school-based development projects that can be called intervention research (Krainer, 2003).

One field of research carried out in PME has centred its attention on how these communities are formed and how the networks among teachers are built up, how they are supported, and what factors influence or hinder their creation. The constitution and support of communities and networks is a difficult task since individual, social and organisational factors are involved. For example, McGraw et al. (2003) described two types of activities that support the community of practice development in a professional development project with middle and high school mathematics teachers, university mathematicians, university mathematics educators and pre-service secondary mathematics teachers: Firstly, a cycle of lesson development, implementation and revision and secondly, book discussions that occurred in large group meetings. In spite of the creation or appropriation of artefacts, the development of shared knowledge, and the increase over time of the use of shortcuts to communicate support creation of community of practice, the lack of negotiation of meanings in book discussion in order to achieve consensus makes it difficult to create communities. In this sense, the formation of professional communities is influenced by the different manners in which teachers develop a mutual engagement or how well and closely teachers work together to learn about and improve their instructional practices, how they define a joint enterprise or shared sense of purpose as related to mathematics, the sharing of a repertoire, co-ordinated efforts to improve students' mathematical learning, and how well and closely teachers work together (Nickerson & Sowder, 2002; Bairral & Giménez, 2003; Brown, 2003). Nickerson and Sowder identified several factors that seem to account for the formation of communities: The relationship the mathematics teachers had with the school administration and other classroom teachers; the respect for and access to the knowledge of other mathematics teachers; the presence or absence of teacher leaders; the mathematical content knowledge of the teachers and their reported comfort level when teaching mathematics, and the teachers' familiarity with the culture and language of the student body.

Important factor bundles that promote or hinder teachers' learning are the contents, structures and the processes of teacher education contexts. Meaningful contents (e.g. mathematical domains, students' thinking, new technologies, curriculum development) as well as the structures of teacher education initiatives (e.g. traditional courses, supervised practicum at a school, action research projects, etc.) are manifold. As regards the processes, most studies stress not only the importance of autonomous and meaningful activities by the teachers but highlight also the role of reflection on these actions accompanied by contexts where meanings are shared. Increasingly researchers use theoretical constructs from social theories to explain what we observe in teacher learning. However, we have to reflect critically whether an approach like "community of practice" (stemming from organisational development in enterprises) can be applied to learning at schools and universities.

Enhancing our knowledge about teachers' learning

Research on teachers' professional development reveals that teachers' learning is a complex process in which multiple factors intervene, suggesting an interrelation of the individual, the social and the organizational. If we regard a teacher's professional development as a learning process we must create a model of how we understand this learning process and the factors that influence it. This perspective stresses the fact that the analysis of teachers' professional development needs to take into account a wide range of variables which include the teachers, their relations with other teachers, and the context in which they operate, and of course the content. One factor which has been identified as important is the influence of the context in which the teacher attends a course, the school in which that teacher works and the kind of support he or she is likely to receive (see e.g. Peter, 1995). Importance is therefore attached to the support network as teachers try to change their teaching and consider the length of time in development.

Peter (1995) proposed a model to explain teachers' professional growth with two categories of constructs –analytic domains and mediating processes:

- The personal domain –teacher knowledge and beliefs,
- The domain of practice –classroom experimentations,
- The domain of inference –valued outcomes,

– The external domain –sources of information, stimulus or support.

The mediating processes make it possible to transfer growth from one domain into another within a change-orientated community in which the members can be characterised by their roles. For example, Peter suggested different roles within the change community for teacher, students, subject coordinator, school principal, consultant, programme developer, and researcher. This model makes it possible to consider the different kinds of change that a teacher can undergo and to identify factors that may influence his or her growth. For example, classroom experimentation with exploration and implementation of ideas and strategies required by the programme was a stimulus for the change in some teachers' knowledge and beliefs but not in others. Other teachers contrasted new ideas from the programme with their existing beliefs. Yet other teachers changed because of the necessity of adapting to the reformed school mathematics curriculum. The nature of changes undergone by teachers suggests a link between individual change processes and external conditions determined by the school culture. For example, some of these conditioning factors were the nature of cooperation among teachers of the same subjects and year levels in the planning and teaching of their lessons and the role played by the principals and mathematics coordinators.

Krainer (1994, 1998) suggested a holistic and integrated view of teacher development support in four dimensions of mathematics teachers' professional practice:

– Action: The attitude towards, and competence in, experimental, constructive and goal-directed work;
– Reflection: The attitude towards, and competence in, (self-) criticism and one's own actions systematically reflecting work;
– Autonomy: The attitude towards, and competence in, self-initiating, self-organized and self-determined work; and
– Networking: The attitude towards, and competence in, communicative and cooperative work with increasing public relevance.

In a two-year university course ("PFL-mathematics") aimed at special further education of mathematics teachers and the promotion of professional exchanges of experiences, the four dimensions were used to describe teachers' professional practice and mathematics teachers' learning –the mathematics teachers' activities within an in-service course. These dimensions were used to explain the teachers' activities in the in-service courses and explain the teacher's learning in this context. The activities in the course stressed the importance and interconnectedness of pedagogical and didactical aspects of teaching and learning starting with the practical experiences of the participants. The systematic reflection of practitioners on action and communication and cooperation among teachers were used to promote the culture of communication connecting individual and social learning experiences. Krainer (1994) noticed that the activities of selecting an issue in which teachers have interest and of writing a case study on that issue fostered teachers' systematic reflection on their own teaching, thus producing meaningful knowledge and generating a new kind of teachers' practice. In this case, the action-reflection combination was used to explain one aspect of teachers' development.

On the other hand, fostering autonomous and self-initiated work by teachers and professional communication and cooperation among them with the creation of collaborative communities of learners, contributed to pedagogical and didactical innovation in their classrooms. If discussion with other teachers includes the discussion and study of theoretical documents, the development of autonomous and cooperative dimensions may help to facilitate the development of an autonomous teacher (the enactive perspective, Dawson, 1999), by identifying aspects of practice which the teacher wishes to improve by having theoretical referents at his or her disposal (Wood, 1999). Krainer (1998) notices that "each of the pairs, 'action and reflection' and 'autonomy and networking', express both contrast and unity, and can be seen as complimentary dimensions which have to be kept in a certain balance, depending on the context" (p. 308). Krainer's four-dimension model can be used to design in-service courses and explain how the teacher's learning is generated. In this sense, the integration of reflection, action research, collaboration and the development of communities of practice in this model provide a holistic tool to help us enhance our knowledge about teachers' learning.

MATHEMATICS TEACHER EDUCATORS AS LEARNERS

A direction of reflection which has been recently initiated concentrates on the process of becoming a teacher educator. How can we characterise the growth of mathematics teacher educators? How can we characterise a conceptual framework to think about becoming a teacher educator? How is growth evidenced? What factors influence mathematics teacher educators' growth? What are the characteristic aspects of in-service professional development programmes that support mathematics teacher educators' growth? From two different areas, research is trying to provide information regarding these questions: From in-service professional development programmes with a specific focus on the development of mathematics teacher educators, and from self-reflection on one's own professional trajectory as a mathematics teacher educator through in-service activity with practising teachers. These two areas of experience have different research approaches: On the one hand, using a theoretical model built from literature to analysis and the interpretation of evidence, and on the other hand, using practice to abstract notions of general implications (conceptual model). But also, we can identify common characteristics: Mathematics teacher educators' growth is viewed as a learning-through-teaching process supported by reflective practice –growth through practice– and the use of theoretical references generated in the reflection on professional development of mathematics teachers to think and offer explanations on mathematics teacher educators' growth.

Zaslavsky and Leikin (1999, 2004) described, within a framework of in-service professional development, the processes encountered by staff members which contributed to their growth as teacher educators. The evidence of mathematics teacher educators' growth –such as stories relating to the learning of teacher educators within projects– was associated and interpreted through Krainer's (1999) four dimensions of teachers' professional practice: Action, reflection, autonomy and networking, Jaworski's (1999) teaching triad and Steinbring's (1998) teaching-learning process. These dimensions were used as lenses to look at promoting and hindering factors that influence mathematics teacher educators' practice. Using these theoretical references it is possible to identify the components of programmes that contribute to the development of the team members. Krainer (1999) argued that the programme of Zaslavsky and Leikin not only puts an emphasis on mathematics teacher educators' "actions and reflection" when working with mathematics teachers, but also "strongly initiates and promotes joint actions and reflection" among mathematics teacher educators. From this point of view, supporting elements of programmes that strengthen the combination of reflection and networking –e.g. joint activities, reflection on their work as learners– should support teachers' flexibility and transition from dealing with mathematics itself to elevating their experiences to encompass the mathematics teachers' teaching triad. Therefore, the three-layer model by Zaslavsky and Leikin makes it possible to interpret how the ongoing interactions in this community of mathematics teacher educators helped both newcomers and experienced members to grow professionally.

However, the "autonomy" dimension shows the difference between the development of mathematics teachers and that of teacher educators. This difference is determined by the working contexts of the two professions. While teachers experience more limitations when deciding what to teach –limitations imposed by the curriculum and the educational level– teacher educators experience fewer limitations when making decisions about the focus of reflection in their work with teachers (e.g. freedom to define their own ways to grow professionally within their project). Therefore, if we are to understand and compare the growth of teachers and of teacher educators we need to take into consideration that the two groups operate in entirely different working contexts.

Tzur (1999, 2001) provided a four-focus model for the development of mathematics teacher educator through an exercise of self-reflective analysis: Learning mathematics, learning to teach mathematics, learning to teach teachers, and learning to mentor teacher educators. Tzur (1999) argued that

> development from a lower to a higher level is not a simple extension, the development entails a 'conceptual leap' resulting from making one's and other's activities and ways of thinking at a lower level the explicit focus of the reflection. (p. 179)

This aspect of development points to the difference between reflective and anticipatory states of knowing.

Research has been done on teacher educators' growth in connection with reflection on mathematics teachers' growth. At the present time, the theoretical references used to explain and to interpret the development of mathematics teachers are also being used to explain and to interpret the development of teacher educators. Differences exist, however, and are revealed in the idea of autonomy and freedom associated with the context and the conditions in which each group works. If research in mathematics teacher education is responsible for providing new knowledge which is useful in interpreting and enhancing the practice of mathematics teacher education, the influences of the practical settings in which each practice (teaching mathematics and mathematics teacher education) is developed should be considered from theoretical perspectives.

WHAT WE AS A COMMUNITY OF MATHEMATICS TEACHER EDUCATORS AND RESEARCHERS MIGHT LEARN

Teacher preparation programs might differ among countries (see e.g. Comiti & Ball, 1996), but it is necessary to think about the possibility that knowledge claims from research can be made through "fuzzy generalizations" (Adler, 2001) and provide a new understanding that allow us to understand better key issues as we see mathematics (student) teacher and teacher educator's as learners. In this section, we work out key issues that we found in analysing PME research on the learning of student teachers and teachers and suggest directions for future research in teachers' learning.

The relevance of teachers' reflection on practice

PME research shows that teachers' learning is not only promoted by meaningful activities, but also by reflections on these activities. However, teachers' reflections seem to play a double role: They increase teachers' understanding (of mathematics, of students' mathematical thinking, of institutional constraints on teaching, etc.), and at the same time they are used by researchers as means to describe and interpret teachers' learning. Research instruments influence practice, and practice itself is the place where new instruments are generated. In the following, three interesting aspects of promoting and analysing teachers' reflections in PME research are highlighted.

Firstly, there are significant efforts to use video-taped records of practice (Mousley & Sullivan, 1996; Goffree & Oonk, 2001; Oonk, 2001). In contrast to observations with no recording, they allow observers to watch situations (e.g. classroom teaching or teachers' discussions in a series of professional development meetings) several times. In addition, these records of practice can be used to discuss observations and hypotheses in an evidence-based way, thus supporting teachers' sharing of meaning, but also providing researchers with new data and insights into teachers' learning (e.g. focusing on the question of how the quality of teachers' argumentation develops). Records from practice can stem from concrete activities within a teacher education initiative; more recently multimedia learning environments bring external sources (e.g. CD-ROMs with video-clips of authentic teaching and related reflective tasks and material) into teacher education. We need more research about the impact of using records of practice in different contexts.

Secondly, many records of practice are based on written documents (diaries, small case studies, reflective papers, stories, surveys) by (student) teachers. Writing down experiences, observations, views etc. in a systematic way requires a second cycle of reflection and provides the opportunity for more people to learn from those experiences. Written artefacts can be distributed, read, discussed and shared among all participants of teacher education. Researchers can build on that evidence and use relevant data. Student teachers and teachers are supported in developing a sense of research in mathematics education and might increase their interest in research. If teachers are expected to write case studies, reflective knowledge of teachers is made visible and accessible to a wider public and thus contributes to the further development of the teaching profession. Writing –even short reflective papers– is more difficult for teachers than for us who live in a "culture of publishing". Nevertheless, teachers' writing is a means for their learning as well as a powerful contribution to research on teachers' learning. Thus teachers' writing builds bridges between theory and practice, and can be regarded as an indicator for the growing professionalism of teachers and researchers. More research on the benefits and difficulties of teachers' writing is needed.

Thirdly, corresponding with the importance of reflecting (and in particular writing), there is a growing awareness that teachers who reflect and write are a rich source for teacher educators' and researchers' learning. In a more general way we can say that "learners are a rich source for teachers' learning" (Krainer, 2004), indicating that it makes sense that teachers support students' reflections on their actions and use this as an opportunity to learn. This view of teaching as a two-way street for learning fosters curiosity and investigative attitudes in and among teachers. Putting this view into practice in teacher education might help student teachers and teachers as well as teacher educators to understand themselves as a part of one "learning system". We need more evidence about the impact of this systemic view of teaching, in classrooms as well as in teacher education initiatives.

The individual and the social to explain what we observe

Within PME, investigations of teachers' learning increasingly consider social (and organisational) aspects. Some investigators even study teachers while participating in some kind of team, community or network of teachers (see e.g. Krainer, 2003). The focus is on discussing in groups, negotiating meanings and norms, sharing knowledge, collaborative learning, designing didactical contracts, institutional constraints and organizational and systemic aspects that foster or hinder teachers' learning. Theories (e.g. Valsiner, 1987; Wenger, 1998; Van Huizen, Van Oers & Wubbels, 2005) are used that go beyond cognitive views on learning. The increasing focus on sociological and socio-cultural theories is not restricted to PME research in teacher education: For example, Lerman and Tsatsaroni (2004) reported that from the time period 1990-1995 to 1996-2001 the percentage of papers that draw on such theories increased from 3,0% to 9,9% (and observed a similar trend in ESM and JRME). Teachers are seen as active participants in interaction processes, embedded in social, cultural, organizational and political contexts. More and more, the individual and the social dimension are seen as equally important. Learning needs a balance between individuals' autonomy and collective efforts, putting an emphasis on reflecting and networking among those who are concerned. The consequence for future research in mathematics teacher education is to focus more intensively on the learning of teams, communities or networks of teachers. But even in the case of studying individual teachers' learning it is essential to investigate their involvement in different relevant environments in which they work, which environments influence them and which are influenced by them through their learning. Nevertheless, taking more into account social and organizational aspects of learning, the content of learning (mathematics, students' mathematical thinking, etc.) should stay equally important.

The fusion of teacher education and research

Teacher education is an intervention intended to promote (student) teachers' learning. In the case of practicing teachers from one particular school it means influencing a social system from outside (by people who come from another social system). Research on teacher education investigates (student) teachers' learning influenced by a given intervention. In many cases, PME research (like research in other publications, see e.g. Adler et al., 2005) is done by the same people that are co-responsible for the intervention. This kind of "intervention research" (see e.g. Krainer, 2003) has to balance an "interest in development" and an "interest in understanding" (e.g. investigating which factors had an impact on that development). One interesting feature of this kind of research is that it tries to overcome the institutionalised division of labour between science and practice (Cooney, 1994). Through continuous interaction and communication with practice, it generates "local knowledge" that could not be generated outside the practice. The limitation of that kind of research is that it can be understood and carried out in a naive way, for example, by re-interpreting the task of critically and systematically investigating (research) the impacts of the intervention into showing the success of the intervention (biased evaluation). As in other publication media, there is a tendency in PME to overcome such "success stories" and to report interesting "research-oriented stories". In the future, we need more of these "research-oriented stories", putting an emphasis on explaining phenomena by using empirical evidence as well as theoretical considerations. Action research by teachers (investigating their own practice and writing case studies) and corresponding action research by teacher educators (investigating their teacher education practice and writing about that, using teachers' case studies as a basis for a meta-analysis etc.) was an important feature of some research projects in the past, and we need intensified efforts in the future. Here, the fusion of teacher education and research enters into its most intensive relationship.

However, research on teacher education cannot be reduced to intervention research. This kind of research tends to be small-scale (see Adler et al., 2005) and refers to individual and genuine contexts. One explanation is that most teacher education activities deal with a restricted number of participants, in particular those where research is involved (in order to minimize complexity and to go deeply). Thus more than two thirds of PME research papers on teacher education (1998-2003) focus on less than 20 teachers. This kind of research is highly important.

Nevertheless, for the future, this means that we need more comparative and large-scale studies in teacher education, too.

In summary, PME shows that research on mathematics teacher education is a fascinating and developing field. It is at the heart of mathematics teacher education since it bridges practice (teacher education) and theory (explaining what goes on in teacher education). It is a challenge since we have to play two roles, namely trying to improve something (teachers' learning) and to critically investigate and to understand it. We need intelligent strategies to cope with that challenge, for example, consciously combining these roles and/or clearly differentiating between them. Through intervention research we seem to grasp better the particular case, understanding in depth the complexity of teachers' learning on a small-scale basis. Through comparative and large-scale empirical research we seem to grasp better general relationships, understanding from a broad perspective how different contexts influence teachers' learning. The field of research on teacher education is just starting to figure out how these two trajectories might develop and how they might be related to each other.

REFERENCES

Adler, J. (2001). Learner performance and fuzzy generalisations: Key issues in professional development research. In M. van den Heuvel-Panhuizen (Ed.), *Proceedings of the 25th PME International Conference*, *2*, 9–16.

Adler, J., Ball, D., Krainer, K., Lin, F.-L., & Novotna, J. (2005) Reflections on an emerging field: Researching mathematics teacher education. *Educational Studies in Mathematics*, *60*(3), 359–381.

Altrichter, H., Posch P., & Somekh, B. (1993). *Teachers investigate their work. An introduction to the methods of action research*. London, UK: Routledge.

Ambrose, R. (2004). Initiating change in prospective elementary school teachers' orientations to mathematics teaching by building on beliefs. *Journal of Mathematics Teacher Education*, *7*(2), 91–119.

Ambrose, R. C., Philipp, R., Chauvot, J., & Clement, L. (2003). A web-based survey to assess prospective elementary school teachers' beliefs about mathematics and mathematics learning: An alternative to Likert scales. In N. A. Pateman, B. J. Dougherty, & J. T. Zilliox (Eds.), *Proceedings of the 27th PME International Conference*, *2*, 33–40.

Bairral, M., & Giménez, J. (2003). On-line professional community. Development and collaborative discourse in geometry. In N. A. Pateman, B. J. Dougherty, & J. T. Zilliox (Eds.), *Proceedings of the 27th PME International Conference*, *2*, 429–436.

Becker, G. (1993). Teacher students' use of analogy patterns. In I. Hirabayashi, N. Nohda, K. Shigematsu, & F.-L. Lin (Eds.), *Proceedings of the 17th PME International Conference*, *3*, 97–104.

Becker, J. R., & Pence, B. J. (1996). Mathematics teacher development: Connections to change in teachers' beliefs and practices. In L. Puig & A. Gutiérrez (Eds.), *Proceedings of the 20th PME International Conference*, *1*, 103–118.

Bednarz, N., Gattuso, L., & Mary, C. (1996). Changes in student teacher views of the mathematics teaching/learning process at the secondary school level. In L. Puig & A. Gutiérrez (Eds.), *Proceedings of the 20th PME International Conference*, *2*, 59–66.

Ben-Chaim, D., Ilany, B., & Keret, Y. (2002). Mathematical and pedagogical knowledge of pre- and in-service elementary teachers before and after experience in proportional reasoning activities. In A. D. Cockburn & E. Nardi (Eds.), *Proceedings of the 26th PME International Conference*, *2*, 81–88.

Blanton, M., Wetbrook, S., & Carter, G. (2001). Using Valsiner's zone theory to interpret a preservice mathematics teacher's zone of proximal development. In M. van den Heuvel-Panhuizen (Ed.), *Proceedings of the 25th PME International Conference, 2*, 177–184.

Bohl, J., & Van Zoest, L. (2002). Learning through identity: A new unit of analysis for studying teacher development. In A. D. Cockburn & E. Nardi (Eds.), *Proceedings of the 26th PME International Conference, 2*, 137–144.

Bohl, J., & Van Zoest, L. (2003). The value of Wenger's concepts of modes of participation and regimes of accountability in understanding teacher learning. In N. A. Pateman, B. J. Dougherty, & J. T. Zilliox (Eds.), *Proceedings of the 27th PME International Conference, 4*, 339–346.

Borko, H., Eisenhart, M., Brown, C. A., Underhill, R. G., Jones, D., & Agard, P. C. (1992). Learning to teach hard mathematics: Do novice teachers and their instructors give up too easily? *Journal for Research in Mathematics Education, 23*(3), 194–222.

Brown, C. (1986). A study of the socialization to teaching of a beginning secondary mathematics teacher. In Univ. of London Institute of Education (Eds.), *Proceedings of the 10th PME International Conference*, 336–343.

Brown, T. (2003). Mathematical identity in initial teacher training. In N. A. Pateman, B. J. Dougherty, & J. T. Zilliox (Eds.), *Proceedings of the 27th PME International Conference, 2*, 151–158.

Burton, K., Cooper, M., & Leder, G. (1986). Representations of three-dimensional figures by mathematics teachers-in-training. In Univ. of London Institute of Education (Eds.), *Proceedings of the 10th PME International Conference*, 81–86.

Carpenter, T. P., & Fennema, E. (1989). Building on the knowledge of students and teachers. In G. Vergnaud, J. Rogalski, & M. Artigue (Eds.), *Proceedings of the 13th PME International Conference, 1*, 34–45.

Chapman, O. (1996). Reconstructing teachers' thinking in teaching problem solving. In L. Puig & A. Gutiérrez (Eds.), *Proceedings of the 20th PME International Conference, 2*, 193–200.

Chapman, O. (1998). Metaphors as a tool in facilitating preservice teacher development in mathematical problem solving. In A. Olivier & K. Newstead (Eds.), *Proceedings of the 22nd PME International Conference, 2*, 176–183.

Chazan, D., Larriva, C., & Sandow, D. (1999). What kind of mathematical knowledge supports teaching for "conceptual understanding"? Preservice teachers and the solving of equations. In O. Zaslavsky (Ed.), *Proceedings of the 23rd PME International Conference, 2*, 193–200.

Civil, M. (1995). Listening to students' ideas: Teachers interviewing in mathematics. In L. Meira & D. Carraher (Eds.), *Proceedings of the 19th PME International Conference, 2*, 154–161.

Comiti, C., & Ball, D. L. (1996). Preparing teachers to teach mathematics: A comparative perspective. In A. J. Bishop, K. Clements, C. Keitel, J. Kilpatrick, & C. Laborde (Eds.), *International handbook of mathematics education* (2, 1123–1153). Dordrecht, The Netherlands: Kluwer.

Cooney, T. J. (1994). Research and teacher education. In search of common ground. *Journal for Research in Mathematics Education, 25*, 608–636.

Cooney, T. J., & Shealy, B. E. (1994). Conceptualizing teacher education as field of inquiry: Theoretical and practical implications. In J. P. Ponte & J. F. Matos (Eds.), *Proceedings of the 18th PME International Conference, 2*, 225–232.

Copes, L. (1979). The Perry Development Scheme and the teaching of mathematics. In D. Tall (Ed.), *Proceedings of the 3rd PME International Conference, 1*, 53–58.

Copes, L. (1982). The Perry Development Scheme: A metaphor for leaning and teaching mathematics. *For the Learning of Mathematics, 3*(1), 38–44.

Dawson, S. (1999). The enactive perspective on teacher development: 'A path laid while walking'. In B. Jaworski, T. Wood, & S. Dawson (Eds.), *Mathematics teacher education. Critical international perspectives* (pp. 148–162). London, UK: Falmer Press.

Doerr, H., McClain, K., & Bowers, J. (1997). Creating a shared context: The use of multimedia case in a teacher development course. In E. Pehkonen (Ed.), *Proceedings of the 21st PME International Conference, 2*, 217–224.

Doig, B. (1994). Prospective teachers: Significant events in their mathematics live. In J. P. Ponte & J. F. Matos (Eds.), *Proceedings of the 18th PME International Conference, 2*, 272–279.

Doig, B., & Hunting, R. P. (1995). Preparing teacher-clinicians in mathematics. In L. Meira & D. Carraher (Eds.), *Proceedings of the 19th PME International Conference, 3*, 280–287.

Eisenhart, M., Borko, H., Underhill, R., Brown, C., Jones, D., & Agard, P. (1993). Conceptual knowledge falls through the cracks: Complexities of learning to teach mathematics for understanding. *Journal for Research in Mathematics Education, 24*(1), 8–40.

Ellerton, N. (1996). Mathematics teacher development: An alternative scenario. In L. Puig & A. Gutiérrez (Eds.), *Proceedings of the 20th PME International Conference, Addenda*, 13–22.

Ensor, P. (1998). Teachers' beliefs and the 'problem' of the social. In A. Olivier & K. Newstead (Eds.), *Proceedings of the 22nd PME International Conference, 2*, 280–281.

Ensor, P. (2001). From preservice mathematics teacher education to beginning teaching: A study in recontextualizing. *Journal for Research in Mathematics Education, 32*(3), 296–320.

Even, R. (1988). Pre-service teachers' conceptions of the relationships between functions and equations. In A. Borbás (Ed.), *Proceedings of the 12th PME International Conference, 2*, 304–311.

Even, R., Tirosh, D., & Markovits, Z. (1996). Teachers subject matter knowledge and pedagogical content knowledge: Research and development. In L. Puig & A. Gutiérrez (Eds.), *Proceedings of the 20th PME International Conference, 1*, 119–134.

Fernandes, D. (1995). Analyzing four preservice teachers' knowledge and thoughts through their biographical histories. In L. Meira & D. Carraher (Eds.), *Proceedings of the 19th PME International Conference, 2*, 162–169.

Franke, M. L., Carpenter, T. P., Levi, L., & Fennema, E. (2001). Capturing teachers' generative change: A follow-up study of professional development in mathematics. *American Educational Research Journal, 38*(3), 653–689.

Furinghetti, F., & Pehkonen, E. (2003) Rethinking characterizations of beliefs. In G. Leder, E. Pehkonen, & G. Törner, G. (Eds.), *Beliefs: A hidden variable in mathematics Education?* (pp. 39–58). Dordrecht, The Netherlands: Kluwer.

Gates, P. (2001). Mathematics teacher belief systems: Exploring the social foundations. In M. van den Heuvel-Panhuizen (Ed.), *Proceedings of the 25th PME International Conference, 3*, 17–24.

Gattuso, L., & Mailloux, N. (1994). Conceptions about mathematics teaching of preservice elementary and high-school teachers. In J. P. Ponte & J. F. Matos (Eds.), *Proceedings of the 18th PME International Conference, 2*, 392–399.

Georgiadou-Kabouridis, B., & Potari, D. (2002). From university to school: A longitudinal study of a teacher's professional development in mathematics teaching. In A. D. Cockburn & E. Nardi (Eds.), *Proceedings of the 26th PME International Conference, 2*, 422–429.

Goffree, F., & Oonk, W. (2001). Digitizing real teaching practice for teacher education programmes: The MILE approach. In F.-L. Lin & T. Cooney (Eds.), *Making sense of mathematics teacher education* (pp. 111–146). Dordrecht, The Netherlands: Kluwer.

Gómez, C. (2002). The struggle of a community of mathematics teachers: Developing a community of practice. In A. D. Cockburn & E. Nardi (Eds.), *Proceedings of the 26th PME International Conference, 3*, 9–16.

Halai, A. (1999). Mathematics education research project: Researching teacher development through action research. In O. Zaslavsky (Ed.), *Proceedings of the 23rd PME International Conference, 3*, 65–72.

Harel, G., & Dubinsky, E. (1991). The development of the concept of function by preservice secondary teachers: From action conception to process conception. In F. Furinghetti (Ed.), *Proceedings of the 15th PME International Conference, 2*, 133–140.

Harel, G., & Martin, G. (1986). The concept of proof held by pre-service elementary teachers: Aspects of induction and deduction. In Univ. of London Institute of Education (Eds.), *Proceedings of the 10th PME International Conference*, 386–391.

Jaworski, B. (1999). What does it mean to promote development in teaching. A response to Ron Tzur's paper: Becoming a mathematics teacher-educator: Conceptualising the terrain through self-reflective analysis. In O. Zaslavsky (Ed.), *Proceedings of the 23rd PME International Conference*, *1*, 183–193.

Jaworski, B., Wood, T., & Dawson, S. (Eds.). (1999). *Mathematics teacher education. Critical international perspectives*. London, UK: Falmer Press.

Jurdak, M. (1991). Teachers' conceptions of math education and the foundations of mathematics. In F. Furinghetti (Ed.), *Proceedings of the 15th PME International Conference*, *2*, 221–228.

Koellner, K., & Borko, H. (2004). Establishing a professional learning community among middle school mathematics teachers. In M. J. Høines & A. B. Fuglestad (Eds.), *Proceedings of the 28th PME International Conference*, *2*, 223–230.

Koirala, H. (1998). Preservice teachers' conceptions of probability in relation to its history. In A. Olivier & K. Newstead (Eds.), *Proceedings of the 22nd PME International Conference*, *3*, 135–142.

Krainer, K. (1994). PFL-Mathematics: A teacher in-service education course as a contribution to the improvement of professional practice in mathematics instruction. In J. P. Ponte & J. F. Matos (Eds.), *Proceedings of the 18th PME International Conference*, *3*, 104–111.

Krainer, K. (1998). Some considerations on problems and perspectives of inservice mathematics teacher education. In C. Alsina, J. M. Alvarez, B. Hodgson, C. Laborde, & A. Pérez (Eds.), *8th International Congress on Mathematics Education: Selected lectures* (pp. 303–321). Sevilla, Spain: S.A.E.M. Thales.

Krainer, K. (1999). Promoting reflection and networking as an intervention strategy in professional development programs for mathematics teachers and mathematics teacher educators. In O. Zaslavsky (Ed.), *Proceedings of the 23rd PME International Conference*, *1*, 159–168.

Krainer, K. (2003). Teams, communities & networks. *Journal of Mathematics Teacher Education*, *6*, 93–105.

Krainer, K. (2004). On giving priority to learners' prior knowledge and our need to understand their thinking. Editorial. *Journal of Mathematics Teacher Education*, *7*, 87–90.

Lave, J., & Wenger, E. (1991). *Situated learning: Legitimate peripheral participation*. New York, USA: Cambridge University Press.

Leikin, R., Chazan, D., & Yerushalmy, M. (2001). Understanding teachers' changing approaches to school algebra: Contributions of the concept maps as part of clinical interviews. In M. van den Heuvel-Panhuizen (Ed.), *Proceedings of the 25th PME International Conference*, 3, 289–296.

Lenfant, A. (2001). From student institutional position to a teacher one: What changes in the relationship to algebra? In M. van den Heuvel-Panhuizen (Ed.), *Proceedings of the 25th PME International Conference*, *3*, 297–304.

Lengnink, K., & Prediger, S. (2003). Development of personal constructs about mathematical task – a qualitative study using repertory grid methodology. In N. A. Pateman, B. J. Dougherty, & J. T. Zilliox (Eds.), *Proceedings of the 27th PME International Conference*, *4*, 39–46.

Lerman, S. (2001). A review of research perspectives on mathematics teacher education. In F.-L. Lin & T. Cooney (Eds.), *Making sense of mathematics teacher education* (pp. 33–52). Dordrecht, The Netherlands: Kluwer.

Lerman, S., & Scott-Hodgetts, R. (1991). 'Critical incidents' in classroom learning – their role in developing reflective practice. In F. Furinghetti (Ed.), *Proceedings of the 15th PME International Conference*, *2*, 293–300.

Lerman, S., & Tsatsaroni, A. (2004). *Surveying the field of mathematics education research*. Regular lecture at ICME-10, Copenhagen, Denmark. Retrieved from http://www.icme-organisers.dk/dg10/Lermanpaper.pdf

Leung, S. (1994). On analysing problem-posing processes: A study of prospective elementary teacher differing in mathematics knowledge. In J. P. Ponte & J. F. Matos (Eds.), *Proceedings of the 18th PME International Conference*, *3*, 168–175.

Lin, P. J. (2000). On developing teachers knowledge by using cases constructed by researchers and classroom teachers. In T. Nakahara & M. Koyama (Eds.), *Proceedings of the 24th PME International Conference*, *3*, 231–238.

Linchevsky, L., Vinner, S., & Karsenty, R. (1992). To be or not to be minimal? Student teachers' views about definitions in geometry. In W. Geeslin & K. Graham (Eds.), *Proceedings of the 16th PME International Conference, 2*, 48–55.

Llinares, S. (1996). Improving knowledge, professional growth and monitoring the development of mathematics teachers: A necessary integration of theoretical frameworks. In L. Puig & A. Gutiérrez (Eds.), *Proceedings of the 20th PME International Conference, Addenda*, 23–31.

Llinares, S. (2003). Participation and reification in learning to teach. The role of knowledge and beliefs. In G. Leder, E. Pehkonen, & G. Torner (Eds.), *Beliefs: A hidden variable in mathematics Education?* (pp. 195–210). Dordrecht, The Netherlands: Kluwer.

Markovits, Z., & Even, R. (1994). Teaching situations: Elementary teachers' pedagogical content. In J. P. Ponte & J. F. Matos (Eds.), *Proceedings of the 18th PME International Conference, 2*, 225–232.

Martin, W. G., & Wheeler, M. M. (1987). Infinity concepts among preservice elementary school teachers. In J. C. Bergeron, N. Herscovics, & C. Kieran (Eds.), *Proceedings of the 11th PME International Conference, 3*, 362–368.

McClain, K. (2003a). Supporting teacher change: A case from statistics. In N. A. Pateman, B. J. Dougherty, & J. T. Zilliox (Eds.), *Proceedings of the 27th PME International Conference, 3*, 253–260.

McClain, K. (2003b). Supporting preservice teachers' understanding of place value and multidigit arithmetic. *Mathematical Thinking and Learning, 5*(4), 281–306.

McClain, K., & Bowers, J. (2000). Supporting preservice teachers' understanding of place value and multidigit addition and subtraction. In T. Nakahara & M. Koyama (Eds.), *Proceedings of the 24th PME International Conference, 3*, 279–286.

McGraw, R., Arbaugh, F., & Lynch, K. (2003). Mathematics teacher professional development as the development of communities of practice. In N. A. Pateman, B. J. Dougherty, & J. T. Zilliox (Eds.), *Proceedings of the 27th PME International Conference, 3*, 269–276.

Meredith, A. (1995). Learning to teach: Four salient constructs for trainee mathematics teachers. In L. Meira & D. Carraher (Eds.), *Proceedings of the 19th PME International Conference, 3*, 304–311.

Mousley, J. (1992). Teachers as researchers: Dialectics of action and reflection. In W. Geeslin & K. Graham (Eds.), *Proceedings of the 16th PME International Conference, 2*, 136–143.

Mousley, J., & Sullivan, P. (1996). *Learning about teaching. An interactive tutorial program to facilitate the study of teaching.* Adelaide, Australia: AAMT/Centre for Studies in Mathematics, Science and the Environment, and Deakin University/Australian Catholic University.

Mousley, J., & Sullivan, P. (1997). Dilemmas in the professional education of mathematics teachers. In E. Pehkonen (Ed.), *Proceedings of the 21st PME International Conference, 1*, 31–45.

Murray, H., Olivier, A., & Human, P. (1995). Teachers' mathematical experiences as links to children's needs. In L. Meira & D. Carraher (Eds.), *Proceedings of the 19th PME International Conference, 3*, 312–319.

Nickerson, S., & Sowder, J. (2002). What factors influence the formation of teachers' professional communities and why should we care? In A. D. Cockburn & E. Nardi (Eds.), *Proceedings of the 26th PME International Conference, 3*, 401–408.

Nicol, C., & Crespo, S. (2003). Learning in and from practice: Preservice teachers investigate their mathematics teaching. In N. A. Pateman, B. J. Dougherty, & J. T. Zilliox (Eds.), *Proceedings of the 27th PME International Conference, 3*, 373–380.

Oonk, W. (2001). Putting theory into practice. Growth of appreciating theory by student teachers. In M. van den Heuvel-Panhuizen (Ed.), *Proceedings of the 25th PME International Conference, 4*, 17–24.

Owens, J. E. (1987). Personal constructs of mathematics and mathematics teaching. In J. C. Bergeron, N. Herscovics, & C. Kieran (Eds.), *Proceedings of the 11th PME International Conference, 1*, 163–169.

Peter, A. (1995). Teacher professional growth processes and some of their influencing factors. In L. Meira & D. Carraher (Eds.), *Proceedings of the 19th PME International Conference, 3*, 320–327.

Peter-Koop, A., Santos-Wagner, V., Breen, C. J., & Begg, A. J. C. (Eds.). (2003). *Collaboration in teacher education. Examples from the context of mathematics education.* Dordrecht, The Netherlands: Kluwer.

Relich, J., & Way, J. (1993). Attitudes to teaching mathematics: The development of an attitudes questionnaire. In I. Hirabayashi, N. Nohda, K. Shigematsu, & F.-L. Lin (Eds.), *Proceedings of the 17th PME International Conference, 1*, 276–283.

Richardson, V. (1996). The role of attitudes and beliefs in learning to teach. In J. Sikula, T. Buttery, & E. Guyton (Eds.), *Handbook of research on teacher education* (pp. 102–119). New York, USA: Macmillan.

Richardson, V., & Placier, P. (2001). Teacher Change. In V. Richardson (Ed.), *Handbook of research on teaching* (pp. 905–947). Washington, USA: AERA.

Roddick, C., Becker, J. R., & Pence, B. J. (2000). Capstone courses in problem solving for prospective secondary teachers. Effects on beliefs and teaching practices. In T. Nakahara & M. Koyama (Eds.), *Proceedings of the 24th PME International Conference, 4*, 97–104.

Rowland, T., Huckstep, P., & Thwaites, A. (2004). Reflecting on prospective elementary teachers' mathematics content knowledge. In M. J. Høines & A. B. Fuglestad (Eds.), *Proceedings of the 27th PME International Conference, 4*, 121–128.

Sánchez. V., & Llinares, S. (1992). Prospective elementary teachers' pedagogical content knowledge about equivalent fractions. In W. Geeslin & K. Graham (Eds.), *Proceedings of the 16th PME International Conference, 2*, 2-274–281.

Santos, V., & Lambdin, D. (1992). Empowering prospective elementary teachers. Through social interaction, reflection, and communication. In W. Geeslin & K. Graham (Eds.), *Proceedings of the 16th PME International Conference, 2*, 282–289.

Schifter, D. (1990). Mathematics process as mathematics content: A course for teachers. In G. Booker, P. Cobb, & T. N. Mendicuti (Eds.), *Proceedings of the 14th PME International Conference, 1*, 191–198.

Schifter, D. (1993). Mathematics process as mathematic content. A course for teachers. *Journal of Mathematical Behavior, 12*(3), 271–283.

Schorr, R. (2001). A study of the use of clinical interviewing with prospective teachers. In M. van den Heuvel-Panhuizen (Ed.), *Proceedings of the 25th PME International Conference, 4*, 153–160.

Selinger, M. (1994). Responses to video in initial teacher education. In J. P. Ponte & J. F. Matos (Eds.), *Proceedings of the 18th PME International Conference, 4*, 241–248.

Shulman, L. S. (1986). Those who understand: Knowledge growth in teaching. *Educational Researcher, 15*(2), 4–14.

Shulman. L. S. (1987). Knowledge and teaching: Foundations of the new reform. *Harvard Educational Review, 57*(1), 1–22.

Simon, M. A. (1988). Formative evaluation of a constructivist mathematics teacher inservice program. In A. Borbás (Ed.), *Proceedings of the 12th PME International Conference, 2*, 576–583.

Simon, M. A. (1991). Initial development of prospective elementary teachers' conceptions of mathematics pedagogy. In F. Furinghetti (Ed.), *Proceedings of the 15th PME International Conference, 3*, 270–277.

Steinbring, H. (1998). Elements of epistemological knowledge for mathematics teachers. *Journal of Mathematics Teacher Education, 1*(2), 157–189.

Stonewater, J. K. (1989). Training elementary teachers in problem solving strategies: Impact on their students performance. In G. Vergnaud, J. Rogalski, & M. Artigue (Eds.), *Proceedings of the 13th PME International Conference, 3*, 197–204.

Sullivan, P., & Mousley, J. (1996). Learning about teaching: The potential of specific mathematics teaching examples, presented on interactive multimedia. In L. Puig & A. Gutiérrez (Eds.), *Proceedings of the 20th PME International Conference, 4*, 283–291.

Sullivan, P., & Mousley, J. (1998). Conceptualising mathematics teaching: The role of autonomy in stimulating teacher reflection. In A. Olivier & K. Newstead (Eds.), *Proceedings of the 22nd PME International Conference, 4*, 105–112.

Sztajn, P., Alexsaht-Snider, M., White, D. Y., & Hackenberg, A. (2004). School-based community of teachers and outcomes for students. In M. J. Høines & A. B. Fuglestad (Eds.), *Proceedings of the 28th PME International Conference, 4*, 273–280.

Taplin, M. (1996). Pre-service teachers' problem solving strategies. In L. Puig & A. Gutiérrez (Eds.), *Proceedings of the 20th PME International Conference, 4*, 299–306.

Thompson, A. G. (1992). Teachers' beliefs and conceptions: A synthesis of the research. In D. Grouws (Ed.), *Handbook of research on mathematics teaching and learning* (pp. 127–146). New York, USA: Macmillan.

Tierney, C., Boyd, C., & Davis, G. (1990). Prospective primary teachers' conceptions of area. In G. Booker, P. Cobb, & T. N. Mendicuti (Eds.), *Proceedings of the 14th PME International Conference, 2*, 307–314.

Tirosh, D. (1999). Learning to question: A major goal of mathematics teacher education. In O. Zaslavsky (Ed.), *Proceedings of the 23rd PME International Conference, 4*, 265–272.

Tirosh, D., & Graeber, A. (2003). Challenging and changing mathematics teaching classroom practices. In A. J. Bishop, M. A. Clements, C. Keitel, J. Kilpatrick, & F. K. S. Leung (Eds.), *Second international handbook of mathematics education* (2, pp. 643–687). Dordrecht, The Netherlands: Kluwer.

Tirosh, D., Graeber, A., & Glover, R. (1986). Pre-service teachers' choice of operation for multiplication and division word problems. In Univ. of London Institute of Education (Eds.), *Proceedings of the 10th PME International Conference*, 57–62.

Tsamir, P. (1999). Prospective teachers' acceptance of the one-to-one correspondence criterion for comparing infinite sets. In O. Zaslavsky (Ed.), *Proceedings of the 23rd PME International Conference*, 4, 305–312.

Tzur, R. (1999). Becoming a mathematics teacher-educator: Conceptualizing the terrain through self-reflective analysis. In O. Zaslavsky (Ed.), *Proceedings of the 23rd PME International Conference, 1*, 169–182.

Tzur, R. (2001). Becoming a mathematics teacher-educator. Conceptualizing the terrain through self-reflective analysis. *Journal of Mathematics Teacher Education, 4*(4), 259–283.

Underhill, R. (1990). A web of beliefs: Learning to teach in an environment with conflicting messages. In G. Booker, P. Cobb, & T. N. Mendicuti (Eds.), *Proceedings of the 14th PME International Conference, 1*, 207–214.

Valero, P., & Jess, K. (2000). Supporting change through a mathematics team forum for teachers' professional development. In T. Nakahara & M. Koyama (Eds.), *Proceedings of the 24th PME International Conference, 4*, 249–256.

Valsiner, J. (1987). *Culture and the development of children's actions: A cultural-historical theory of development psychology*. New York, USA: John Wiley & Sons.

Van Huizen, P., Van Oers, B., & Wubbels, T. (2005). A Vygotskian perspective on teacher education. *Journal of Curriculum Studies, 37*(3), 267–290.

Vermulen, N. (2000). Student teachers' concept images of algebraic expressions. In T. Nakahara & M. Koyama (Eds.), *Proceedings of the 24th PME International Conference*, 4, 257–264.

Wenger, E. (1998). *Communities of practice*. New York, USA: Cambridge University Press.

Whitenack, J. W., Knipping, N., Couts, L., & Standifer, S. (1997). Supporting elementary teachers' exploration of children's arithmetical understanding: A case for CD-ROM technology. In E. Pehkonen (Ed.), *Proceedings of the 21st PME International Conference, 4*, 278–284.

Wood, T. (1999). Approaching Teacher Development: Practice into Theory. In B. Jaworski, T. Wood, & S. Dawson (Eds.), *Mathematics teacher education. Critical international perspectives* (pp. 163–179). London, UK: Falmer Press.

Wood, T. (2001). Learning to teach mathematics differently: Reflection matters. In M. van den Heuvel-Panhuizen (Ed.), *Proceedings of the 25th PME International Conference, 4*, 431–438.

Zack, V., Mousley, J., & Breen, C. (Eds.). (1997). *Developing practice: Teachers' inquiry and educational change*. Deakin, Australia: Centre for Studies in Mathematics, Science and Environmental Education.

Zaslavsky, O., Chapman, O., & Leikin, R. (2003). Professional development in mathematics education: Trends and tasks. In A. J. Bishop, M. A. Clements, C. Keitel, J. Kilpatrick, & F. K. S. Leung (Eds.), *Second international handbook of mathematics education* (2, pp. 877–915). Dordrecht, The Netherlands: Kluwer.

Zaslavsky, O., & Leikin, R. (1999). Interweaving the training of mathematics teacher-educators and the professional development of mathematics teachers. In O. Zaslavsky (Ed.), *Proceedings of the 23rd PME International Conference*, *1*, 141–158.

Zaslavsky, O., & Leikin, R. (2004). Professional development of mathematics teachers educators: Growth through practice. *Journal of Mathematics Teacher Education*, *7*(1), 5–32.

Zazkis, R., & Campbell, S. (1994). Divisibility and division: Procedural attachments and conceptual understanding. In J. P. Ponte & J. F. Matos (Eds.), *Proceedings of the 18th PME International Conference*, *4*, 423–430.

AFFILIATIONS

Salvador Llinares
Departamento de Innovación y Educación
Didáctica de las Matemáticas
Facultad de Educación
Universidad de Alicante
Campus "San Vicente del Raspeig"
03080 Alicante (Spain)
sllinares@ua.es

Konrad Krainer
IUS (Institute of Instructional and School Development)
Universität Klagenfurt
Sterneckstrasse 15
9020 Klagenfurt (Austria)
konrad.krainer@uni-klu.ac.at
http://www.iff.ac.at/ius/mitarbeiterinnen/konradkrainer.php

JOÃO PEDRO DA PONTE AND OLIVE CHAPMAN

MATHEMATICS TEACHERS' KNOWLEDGE AND PRACTICES

INTRODUCTION

In education, the study of teachers and teaching has been an active field for a long time. In the 1980s, as PME was developing as an organization, new perspectives of teachers' knowledge had become prominent, notably those of Elbaz (1983), Shulman (1986), and Schön (1983), which influenced the direction of research on teachers. Elbaz (1983) focused on identifying what teachers know that others do not, which she called practical knowledge, and how teachers encapsulate that knowledge. She contended that this knowledge is based on first hand experience, covers knowledge of self, milieu, subject matter, curriculum development and instruction, and is represented in practice as rules, practical principles and images.

Shulman (1986) proposed seven categories of knowledge that make it possible for teachers to teach and deal with more than practical knowledge –knowledge of content, general pedagogical knowledge, curriculum knowledge, pedagogical content knowledge (PCK), knowledge of students, knowledge of educational contexts and knowledge of educational ends, purposes and values. He emphasized PCK as a key aspect to address in the study of teaching.

Schön's (1983) work distinguished between reflective practice and technical rationality, attributing the former to practitioners. When action is required, practitioners act on the basis of what they know, without separating the intellectual or formal knowledge from the practical. For a teacher, this means that reflecting-in-practice has to do with content and content-related pedagogical knowledge. It takes place when teachers deal with professional problems and therefore can be seen as a key part of their knowledge. In this sense, the teachers' knowledge is not only "knowing things" (facts, properties, if-then relationships ...), but also knowing how to identify and solve professional problems, and, in more general terms, knowing how to construct knowledge. These perspectives of teachers' knowledge also include notions of teachers' beliefs and conceptions, which we consider to be relevant constructs to understand what teachers know.

The preceding notions of teachers' knowledge formed the theoretical background we considered to define the activity of the teacher, the focus of this chapter. In order to examine such activity, we assume that two main constructs are required: Teacher knowledge and teacher practice. These constructs are not

A. Gutiérrez, P. Boero (eds.), Handbook of Research on the Psychology of Mathematics Education: Past, Present and Future, 461–494.

independent of each other, but we treat them separately to highlight their unique features. Our intent, then, is to identify and discuss studies reported to the PME community that focus on teacher knowledge and practice in terms of issues, perspectives, results and possible directions for future work.

In order to set a boundary on the studies we identified for this chapter, we also considered the different contexts in which the activity of teachers can be situated. These include: (i) *The classroom.* This may be considered as a natural setting, in which the teacher and students interact, when there is no external intervention (e.g., from a research project). It becomes a different setting with external intervention, such as teachers or researchers who act as observers. (ii) *The school.* Teachers are active participants of the school as an institution, which is another natural community setting. Their activities can be based on the school's own in-house projects, or its participation in wider projects that focus on curriculum innovation or action-research. (iii) *Inservice courses and preservice courses.* Teachers participate in formal preservice courses, when preparing to become teachers. Later, they may participate in formal inservice courses, in their schools, in a neighboring school, or in a teacher education institution. (iv) *Other professional settings.* Outside their schools, teachers can participate in formal or informal groups, associations and meetings. In all of these settings, the teacher acts, thinks and reflects. Thus, they offer opportunities to access teachers' knowledge and teachers' practices. But they also embody other elements of the activity of teachers, in particular, teacher development/education, which is outside the scope of this chapter. In this chapter, then, we focus on the activity of the teacher (interpreted in a broad sense to include preservice and inservice) by him/herself or working cooperatively with other teachers or researchers in all of these settings, but will include teacher education settings only when the focus of the study is on the teachers' knowledge or practice and not on the teacher education program.

Our review of research reports produced by the PME community revealed that, in the early years, researchers focused on students' learning with little attention on the teacher; only a few studies related the activity of the teacher to students' learning. However, beginning in the 1980's there was growing attention on the teacher. This provided us with a substantive list of studies on teacher knowledge and practice. Guided by the theoretical background we discussed earlier, we classified the papers based on the objectives of the studies. This produced four major categories: (i) Teachers' mathematics knowledge; (ii) Teachers' knowledge of mathematics teaching; (iii) Teachers' beliefs and conceptions; and (iv) Teachers' practice. Categories (i), (iii) and (iv) each has over 60 papers while category (ii) has 35. We consider categories (i) and (ii) to be significantly different as knowledge of mathematics has a referent in an academic discipline – mathematics, one of the most formalized and sophisticated fields of human though– whereas knowledge of mathematics teaching is in the realm of professional knowledge, being highly dependent of evolving social and educational conditions and values, curriculum orientations and technological resources.

We used three periods –1977-85, 1986-94, and 1995-2005– as a basis to consider possible trends in quantitative terms (number of papers in each period) and qualitative terms (objects of study, theoretical emphases, methodological approaches, other issues). As we expected, in the first period, there are very few papers dealing with teachers' knowledge. In the second period, there are a great number of papers dealing with aspects of teachers' knowledge (mathematical and mathematics teaching), beliefs and conceptions. Studies on teachers' practices first appear in the second period and grew at an amazing rate in the third. Trends involving the qualitative parameters over the three periods will be integrated in the discussion of each of the four categories as appropriate.

For our discussion of the four categories of studies, we consider our guiding questions to be: (i) What do mathematics teachers know, believe, conceptualize, think and do in relation to mathematics and its teaching and learning? (ii) What methods, theoretical perspectives and assumptions about knowledge, mathematics and curriculum did researchers adopt in studying the teachers? These questions will be addressed by identifying themes based on theoretical and methodological foundations and findings of the studies and discussing particular studies in the context of these themes. Thus, while many of the papers presented at PME conferences may appear to be relevant to this chapter, only those that we select to exemplify each theme are included here. The remainder of the chapter discusses the four categories and ends with our reflection of them collectively.

TEACHERS' MATHEMATICS KNOWLEDGE

Mathematics knowledge is widely acknowledged as one of the critical attributes of mathematics teachers, thus, it is not surprising that studies of teachers' mathematics knowledge is a significant focus of the PME community. Beginning in 1980, studies in this area were reported in almost every year. However, there was less focus in the 1980s than later. These studies, directly or indirectly, dealt with a variety of mathematics topics with greater attention to geometry, functions, multiplication and division, fractions, and problem solving. The themes we identified to discuss this category of studies are based on the following questions: What are the deficiencies in teachers' mathematics knowledge? How do teachers hold their knowledge of mathematics? What are the implications for teaching mathematics and mathematics teacher education?

Deficiencies in teachers' mathematics knowledge

Most of the studies over the three decades of PME conferences, directly or indirectly, focused on the difficulties or deficiencies teachers exhibited for particular mathematics concepts or processes. For example, addressing knowledge about numbers and operations, Linchevsky and Vinner (1989) investigated the extent to which inservice and preservice elementary teachers were flexible when the canonical whole was replaced by another whole for fractions of continuous quantities. They found all of the expected misconceptions and confusions associated with canonical representations of fractions and the teachers' visual representations of fractions incomplete, unsatisfactory and not sufficient to form a complete concept of fractions. In a later paper, Llinares and Sánchez (1991) studied preservice elementary teachers' pedagogical content knowledge about fractions and found that many of the participants displayed incapacity to identify the unity, to represent some fractions with chips and to work with fractions bigger than one.

A few of the studies addressed teachers' knowledge in arithmetic in relation to a particular theoretical model. For example, Tirosh, Graeber and Glover (1986) explored preservice elementary teachers' choice of operations for solving multiplication and division word problems based on the notion of primitive models in which multiplication is seen as repeated addition (with a whole number operator) and division as partitive (with the divisor smaller than the dividend). The findings indicated that the teachers were influenced by the primitive, behavioral models for multiplication and division. The teachers' errors increased when faced with problems that did not satisfy these models. Greer and Mangan (1986) used a similar notion of primitive models. Their study included preservice elementary teachers and focused on the results on single-operation verbal problems involving multiplication and division. They also found that primitive operations affected the participants' interpretation of multiplicative situations.

Another theoretical framework used in some of these studies was the distinction between "concept image", the total cognitive structure that is associated with a concept, and "concept definition", the form of words used to specify that concept (Vinner & Hershkowitz, 1980). For example, Pinto and Tall (1996) investigated seven secondary and primary mathematics teachers' conceptions of rational numbers. Findings indicated that three of the teachers gave formal definitions containing implicit distortions, three gave explicit distorted definitions and one was unable to recall a definition. None consistently used the definition as the source of meaning of the concept of rational number; instead they used their concept imagery developed over the years to produce conclusions, which were sometimes in agreement with deductions from the formal definition, but often were not. Whole numbers and fractions were often seen as "real world" concepts, while rationals, if not identified with fractions, were regarded as more technical concepts.

In geometry, Hershkowitz and Vinner (1984) reported on a study that included comparing elementary children's knowledge with that of preservice and inservice elementary teachers. They found that the teachers lacked basic geometrical knowledge, skills and analytical thinking ability. Using the Van Hiele levels as theoretical framework, Braconne and Dionne (1987) investigated secondary school students and their teachers' understanding of proof and demonstration in geometry, and what kind of relationship could exist between the understanding of a demonstration and the Van Hiele levels. Findings indicated that proof and demonstration were not synonymous for the teachers or for the students. Proofs belong to different modes of understanding but demonstration always pertains to the formal one, teachers emphasizing representation and wording. Furthermore, there was no obvious relationship between the understanding of a demonstration and the Van Hiele levels.

Another topic studied extensively was teachers' knowledge about functions. Ponte (1985) investigated preservice elementary and secondary teachers' reasoning processes in handling numerical functions and interpreting Cartesian graphs. Findings indicated that many of the participants did not feel at ease processing geometrical information and had trouble making the connection between graphical and numerical data. Later, Even (1990) studied preservice secondary teachers' knowledge and understanding of inverse function. She found that many of the preservice teachers, when solving problems, ignored or overlooked the meaning of the inverse function. Their "naïve conception" resulted in mathematics difficulties, such as not being able to distinguish between an exponential function and a power function, and claiming that log and root are the same things. Besides, most of teachers did not seem to have a good understanding of the concepts (exponential, logarithmic, power, root functions). In another function study, Harel and Dubinsky (1991) investigated preservice secondary teachers in a discrete mathematics course for how far beyond an action conception and how much into process conceptions of function they were at the end of the instructional treatment framed in constructivism. Findings indicated that the participants had starting points varying from primitive conceptions to action conceptions of function. How far they progressed depended on several factors such as: (i) Manipulation, quantity and continuity of a graph restrictions; (ii) Severity of the restriction; (iii) Ability to construct a process; and (iv) Uniqueness to the right condition. Thomas (2003) investigated preservice secondary teachers' thinking about functions and its relationship to function representations and the formal concept. Findings indicated a wide range of differing perspectives on what constitutes a function, and that these perspectives were often representation dependant, with a strong emphasis in graphs. Similarly, Hansson (2005), in his study of middle school preservice teachers' conceptual understanding of function, found that their views of it contrast with a view where the function concept is a unifying concept in mathematics with a larger network of relations to other concepts.

Other topics and mathematics processes and understandings addressed include the following examples. Van Dooren, Verschaffel and Onghena (2001) investigated the arithmetic and algebraic word-problem-solving skills and strategies of preservice elementary and secondary school teachers both at the beginning and at the end of their teacher training. Results showed that the secondary teachers clearly preferred algebra, even for solving very easy problems for which arithmetic is appropriate. About half of the elementary teachers adaptively switched between arithmetic and algebra, while the other half experienced serious difficulties with algebra. Barkai, Tsamir, Tirosh and Dreyfus (2002) examined inservice elementary teachers' justification in number-theoretical propositions and existence propositions, some of which are true while others are false. Findings indicated that a substantial number of the teachers applied inadequate methods to validate or refute the proposition and many of them were uncertain about the status of the justification they gave. Shriki and David (2001) examined the ability of inservice and preservice high school mathematics teachers to deal with various definitions connected with the concept of parabola. Findings indicated that both groups shared similar difficulties and misconceptions. Only a few participants possessed a full concept image concerning the parabola and were capable of perceiving the parabola in its algebraic as well as in its geometrical contexts or to identify links between them. Finally, Mastorides and Zachariades (2004), in their study of preservice secondary school mathematics teachers aimed to explore their understanding and reasoning about the concepts of limit and continuity, found that the teachers exhibited disturbing gaps in their conceptualization of these concepts. Most had difficulties in understanding multiquantified statements or failed to comprehend the modification of such statements brought about by changes in the order of the quantifiers.

How teachers hold knowledge

A few of the studies explicitly dealt with how the teachers held their knowledge, in particular, in terms of conceptual and procedural knowledge such as defined in Hiebert (1986). For example, Simon (1990) investigated preservice elementary teachers' knowledge of division. Findings indicated that they had adequate procedural knowledge, but inadequate conceptual knowledge and sparse connections between the two. Weak and missing connections were identified as well as aspects of individual conceptual differences. In general, they exhibited serious shortcomings in their knowledge of division, in particular connectedness of that knowledge.

Philippou and Christou (1994) investigated the conceptual and procedural knowledge of fractions of preservice elementary teachers enrolled in first semester of their studies. Findings indicated that they had a narrow understanding of the ideas underlying the conceptual knowledge of fractions. Participants had greater success on addition and subtraction and lesser on multiplication and treated multiplication and division as unrelated operations. The poorer results were on items measuring their ability to connect real world situations and symbolic computation.

In another study, Zazkis and Campbell (1994) investigated preservice elementary teachers' understanding of concepts related to the multiplicative structure of whole numbers: Divisibility, factorisation and prime decomposition. Findings indicated strong dependence upon procedures. Such procedural attachments appeared to compromise and inhibit development of more refined and more meaningful structures of conceptual understanding.

Chazan, Larriva and Sandow (1999) explored a preservice secondary teacher's conceptual and procedural knowledge related to teaching the solving of equation. They found that the participant had a conceptual understanding of the topic, but this was not clear-cut in relation to how it was used to support her teaching. The authors wondered about using descriptions like conceptual and procedural understanding for an examination of teachers' substantive knowledge of mathematics. They explained, "Perhaps the difficulty is that conceptual understanding is not an 'achievement', that is, something that one either has or does not have. Instead, maybe one can have conceptual understandings of different kinds, including partial, or confused, conceptual understanding" (p. 199).

Finally, Presmeg and Nenduradu (2005) conducted a case study of one middle school teacher, investigating his use of, and movement amongst, various modes of representing exponential relationships. They found that his facility in moving amongst representational registers was not matched by conceptual understanding of the underlying mathematical ideas as the teacher attempted to solve algebraic problems involving exponential relationships. They concluded that his case casts doubt on the theoretical assumption that students who can move fluently amongst various inscriptions representing the same concept have of necessity attained conceptual knowledge of the relationships involved.

Implications for teaching and teacher education

Some of the papers mentioned in the preceding sections explicitly point out implications for teaching based on the findings of the studies. For example, comparing teachers' knowledge with students learning, Hershkowitz and Vinner (1984) investigated the processes of concept formation in children and of the factors that affect their acquisition by studying the same concepts in elementary school teachers. Findings indicated that, on the surface, the children's concept reflected the teachers' conception.

In another study, Van Dooren, Verschaffel and Onghena (2001) found that the problem-solving behavior of the preservice teachers was strongly related to their evaluations of students' solutions. They doubted whether the subgroup of primary school teachers experiencing great problems with algebra will have the proper disposition to prepare their students for the transition to algebra, but also whether the future secondary school teachers will be emphatic towards students coming straight from primary school and bringing with them a strong arithmetic background.

Sánchez and Llinares (1992), in their study of fractions, concluded that the elementary teachers' understanding of subject matter influences presentation and formulation as well as the instructional representations that the teacher uses to make it understandable to students. Shriki and David (2001), based on their participants' lack of depth in their understanding of parabola, raised concerns about teachers' ability to implement reform recommendations.

Based on their findings of the studies, a number of papers also explicitly point out implications for teacher education. For example, Tirosh, Graeber and Glover (1986) suggest that efficient strategies must be developed for training teachers to monitor and control the impact that misconception and primitive models of multiplication and division have on their own thinking and their students'. Simon (1990), based on his findings of the teachers' way of holding their knowledge of division, concludes that it is important to facilitate cognitive connections much more than imparting additional information in teacher education. Philippou and Christou (1994) suggest that teachers need to be exposed to connecting conceptual and procedural knowledge of fractions in education programs. Sánchez and

Llinares (1992) suggested that preservice teacher education should concentrate on the prospective teachers' knowledge about the relationship between mathematical processes and modeling such processes as referents. Finally, Barkai et al. (2002), based on their findings of inservice elementary teachers' justification in number-theoretical propositions and existence propositions, called for more attention of this topic in professional development programs.

The preceding account of studies in this category of teachers' knowledge indicates a range of findings based on a range of theoretical perspectives about mathematics and mathematics knowledge. This suggests the need to pursue the theorization of teachers' mathematics knowledge, framing appropriate concepts to describe its features and processes, and to establish clear criteria of levels of proficiency of mathematics teachers and instruments to assess it. We further reflect on this category later in the discussion section of the chapter.

TEACHERS' KNOWLEDGE OF MATHEMATICS TEACHING

In this section we address studies of teachers' knowledge of mathematics teaching. Using the themes of studies in the early years of PME conferences, studies of pedagogical content knowledge, other studies framed in cognitive psychology and studies dealing with theoretical issues of teachers' professional knowledge, we consider issues such as: What are important elements of teachers' knowledge of mathematics teaching? What is the nature of this knowledge and how does it develop?

Early studies

In the 1980s, only a few papers addressed teachers' knowledge of mathematics teaching. For example, Andelfinger (1981) presented a survey method to get information about everyday teaching and gave an extended example of its use in surveying teachers about the role of fractions versus decimals in mathematics teaching. He indicated that teachers regard fractions and decimals as separated topics, with no problems and difficulties in common and little relationship to other topics.

Also using questionnaires, Brissiaud, Moreau, Perrot, Valentin and Vaudy (1982) investigated the relationship between the perceptions of elementary teachers and pupils regarding what is a problem. The results strongly supported the hypothesis that the pupil's perception of problems is modelled on the teacher's perception. In another paper, Rees (1982) reported on several studies using the notion of diagnostic teaching based in two main assumptions: (i) Teachers' awareness of learners' misconceptions is critical for effective and efficient teaching and (ii) For this a general structure as a diagnostic outcome to which teachers can relate to is essential. She indicated that these studies "suggest strongly that explicit teaching of the concepts underlying the diagnostic tasks does result in more effective learning" (p. 96).

Pedagogical content knowledge studies

In the 1990s, the notion of teachers' pedagogical content knowledge (PCK) (Shulman, 1986) was one of the theoretical constructs introduced in studying the teachers' knowledge of mathematics teaching. Based in this notion, Even and Markovits (1991) studied junior high school teachers' PCK regarding teachers' responses to students' questions, remarks, and hypotheses on the topic of functions. They indicated that teachers often are not aware of students' difficulties: "some teachers ignore students' ways of thinking and their sources. Instead, they evaluate students' work only as either right or wrong" (p. 43). The authors stressed what the teachers could have considered but often did not, such as students' misconceptions, ritual versus meaning orientation, teacher versus student centeredness, and richness of responses. They summarized their findings saying that the teachers "recognized the central role (...) of understanding students' thinking" but most of them did not "recognize the importance of teachers' reaction" (p. 46).

In later studies, the notion of PCK was often combined with other theoretical ideas. For example, Klein and Tirosh (1997) evaluated preservice and inservice elementary teachers' knowledge of common difficulties that children's experience with division and multiplication word problems involving rational numbers and their possible sources. The authors indicated that most inservice teachers provided correct expressions for the multiplication and division word problems, what did not happen with prospective teachers. They summarized the findings saying that "most prospective teachers exhibited dull knowledge" of the difficulties that children's experience with word problems involving rational numbers and their possible sources, whereas "most in-service teachers were aware of students incorrect responses, but not of their possible sources" (p. 144). The researchers suggested that direct instruction related to students' common ways of thinking could enhance both preservice and inservice teachers' PCK.

More recent studies involving PCK show an effort to establish a critical perspective regarding it, either by reformulating it or complementing it with other theoretical notions. For example, Rossouw and Smith (1998) reported a study on elementary teachers' PCK in geometry, two years after they completed an in-service course. The authors emphasized the perspective of knowledge in action (Schön, 1983) and discussed the need to enlarge Shulman's (1986) notion of PCK. They presented a model with four categories (knowledge of geometry, learning geometry, teacher representations, and the environmental context of teaching) and identified three main orientations of the teachers, described as "life skills", "investigative" and "mastery". The authors also indicated that even though the teachers had the same learning experience in the inservice course that they attended two years earlier, their PCK of geometry showed marked differences and concluded that "teachers eventually develop their own pedagogical content knowledge which is shaped by their own experiences and perceptions" (p. 64).

Cognitive psychology studies

Some of the studies show a strong influence of information-processing theory, a major strand in cognitive psychology. In the 1990s, many of the studies framed in this paradigm used an expert-novice contrast to identify different ways of teacher thinking and decision-making. For example, Robinson, Even and Tirosh (1992), dealing with junior and high school teachers, examined the differences between two novice teachers and an expert teacher (reputed as an "excellent teacher") in presenting mathematical material in a connected manner. The authors concluded that experts largely differ from novices in the role that connectedness plays in both their planning and teaching of lessons in algebra, as well as in their reflection on their own lessons. The expert teacher considered the issue of connectedness to be very important and used both vertical and horizontal connections to guide her teaching. In contrast, the novice teachers did not emphasize connectedness in their lesson plans and teaching. They also tended to stick to their plans regardless of what happened and drew conclusions that suited their plans but bore little connections with what really went on in the classrooms. In a later study, Robinson, Even and Tirosh (1994) investigated 7th grade teachers' knowledge of issues related to the incomplete nature of algebraic expressions. The authors reported the customary differences that these studies tend to provide: While experienced teachers were aware of the existence of the difficulty and its possible sources, novice teachers attributed difficulties to other reasons, such as notations.

Also in the 1990s, a new construct grounded in cognitive psychology emerged in the PME community: Cognitively Guided Instruction (CGI), based in the work of Carpenter and Fennema (1989). The main idea is that understanding the knowledge of students' cognition in mathematics is one important component of the knowledge of mathematics teachers. In one study, Bright, Bowman and Vacc (1997) sought to identify frameworks in primary teachers' analysis of children's solutions to mathematical problems and monitored changes in the framework use across the first year of implementing CGI. Five frameworks were identified in the findings: Developmental, taxonomic, problem solving, curriculum, and deficiency. The curriculum framework was used most often, followed by the problem solving and deficiency frameworks.

In another study, Gal and Vinner (1997) addressed the difficulties experienced by students in understanding the concept of perpendicular lines and the difficulties shown by teachers when trying to explain it. The authors corroborated the main assumptions of CGI concluding that the teachers' lack of tools which would help them to understand students' difficulties makes them unable of providing adequate teaching. In addition, Gal (1998) addressed aspects of junior high school teachers' knowledge concerning teaching special segments in the triangle. The aim was to draw teachers' attention to the possibility that some difficulty is hidden (or not-hidden) behind the students' answers, to introduce an opening towards understanding the difficulties, and to increase their motivation to look for solutions. Findings showed that the teachers became aware of their cognitive processes and used them as a "didactic lever".

The nature and development of teachers' knowledge

Some papers gave special attention to theoretical issues regarding teachers' knowledge of mathematics teaching. In one, Ponte (1994) presented several cases to illustrate aspects of this knowledge regarding problem solving and to discuss its nature. Based in the ideas of Schön (1983) and Elbaz (1983), he presented the notion of "professional knowledge" as essentially knowing in action, grounded on experience, reflection on experience and theoretical knowledge. In his view, this knowledge is different from academic and common sense knowledge and ought to be studied on its own right, and not just regarded as "deficient" academic knowledge. Discussing the cases of three middle and secondary school teachers, he analysed possible reasons for different views and practices regarding problem solving, suggesting that specific know how and confidence may interfere with general agreements of curriculum priorities and ways of acting in the classroom. He presented four elements of professional knowledge: (i) Teachers' views and personal relationships with mathematics; (ii) Teachers' knowledge and personal relationship to students; (iii) Teachers' knowledge and attitude regarding the curriculum; and (iv) Teachers' way of living the profession. These elements are shaped by past experience and influenced by the social and institutional contexts.

Chapman (2004) used the construct of "practical knowledge" to describe knowledge that guides actual teacher actions. In her perspective, such knowledge "corresponds with positions teachers take" and is "experiential, procedural, situational, particularistic, and implicit" (p. 192). The author emphasized the procedural aspect of practical knowledge and noted that it can be used either for adapting, shaping, or selecting elements in real life situations. Based in this framework, she presented aspects of the practical knowledge of high school teachers who consistently engaged students in peer interactions in their teaching of mathematics, which included teachers' conceptions that support a social perspective of learning, students' behaviours and outcomes in peer interactions, learning activities, and teacher's behaviours that support peer interactions.

Finally, Simon (1991) addressed the initial development of prospective elementary teachers' conceptions of mathematics pedagogy. This study, framed in terms of a constructivist perspective applied to the construction of teachers' knowledge, aimed to describe the conceptions of prospective elementary teachers early in their preparation to teach. The author sought to identify "what ideas are readily developed or changed and which are not developed or are resistant to development" (p. 271). Focusing on one participant, the author argued that prospective teachers do not have a well-developed model of student learning and that teaching strategies such as questioning and the use of manipulatives "are more easily learned than are new models of students' mathematical learning" (p. 275). However, in his view, prospective teachers have difficulty in decentring from their own thinking to focus on student thinking.

The preceding account of studies in this category of teachers' knowledge and practice depicts a picture of both weaknesses and strengths in teachers' knowledge of mathematics teaching. It suggests the need to pursue a global theory about the specific knowledge involved in the teaching of mathematics and how it relates to knowledge about mathematics, learning, curriculum, and the organization of instruction. We further reflect on this category later in the discussion section of the chapter.

TEACHERS' BELIEFS AND CONCEPTIONS

Beliefs and conceptions have played a prominent role as a basis of studying mathematics teachers and their teaching. While there was little attention on these constructs in papers presented at PME conferences in the 1980s (cf. Hoyles, 1992), there has been a significant increase in their use from the early 1990s. Thompson's work (e.g., Thompson, 1992) and Ernest's work (e.g., Ernest, 1991) seem to be important influences in fuelling this and were cited by many of the studies. In this category of studies we consider the following questions: How are beliefs/conceptions defined? What theoretical models or methods are used to access beliefs/conceptions? What aspects of teachers' beliefs are studied and how is the nature of these beliefs regarded? What is the relationship between beliefs/conceptions and practice?

Concept of beliefs/conceptions

For most of the studies, what is meant by beliefs seems to go unnoticed, or considered to not be an issue, by the researchers. The term belief is treated as a taken-for-granted in that an explicit discussion is not provided. In general, terms such as beliefs, conceptions, views, perspectives, perceptions, personal constructs, belief systems, and images are used synonymously or interchangeably. Our category of beliefs and conceptions, then, can be described by the contracted form 'beliefs/conceptions' and should be understood in a broad sense.

Three exceptions to the general trend of not explicitly defining beliefs/conceptions are the papers of Hoyles (1992), Ponte (1994) and Gates (2001). Ponte (1994) drew distinction between knowledge, beliefs and conceptions in his study of teachers' conceptions and practices regarding mathematical problem solving. He explained, "I take *knowledge* to refer to a wide network of concepts, images, and intelligent abilities possessed by human beings. *Beliefs* are the incontrovertible personal 'truths' held by everyone, deriving from experience or from fantasy, having a strong affective and evaluative component. ... *Conceptions* are the underlying organizing frames of concepts, having essentially a cognitive nature. Both beliefs and conceptions are part of knowledge" (p. 199). Based in the perspective of Pajares (1992), the author regards beliefs as a part of relatively less elaborated of knowledge, not confronted with empirical reality, and that does not require internal consistency. Conceptions, on the other hand, are seen as organizing constructs, frame the way we tackle tasks and play an essential role in thinking and acting.

Hoyles (1992), who explained how the contention that teachers reconstruct their beliefs while interacting with an innovation, based on her work involving teachers' interactions with computer activities and the ways they incorporated them into their practice, led her to propose the notion of situated beliefs, i.e., all beliefs are, to a certain extent, constructed in settings. They are "dialectical constructions, products of activity, context and culture" (p. 280). This notion challenges the separation of what is believed from how beliefs emerged. "Once the embedded nature of beliefs is recognized, it is self evident that any individual can hold multiple (even contradictory) beliefs and 'mismatch', 'transfer' and 'inconsistency' are irrelevant considerations and replaced by notions of constraints and scaffolding within settings" (p. 280). This perspective requires focusing on understanding "beliefs-in-practice".

Another paper that deals with conceptual aspects was presented by Gates (2001). He discussed concepts that provide a sociological perspective of how belief systems are constructed upon teachers' ideological foundations. In his view, much of the literature on teachers' beliefs and conceptions and their effect on the teaching of mathematics fails to locate the sources of beliefs in the social world, treating them as if they existed in a social and political vacuum. One of the concepts he offered is *habitus*, the cognitive embodiment of social structure, that form the generative principles that organize our social practices leading to social action and provides systems of dispositions that force us (or allow us) to act characteristically in different situations. The mathematics teacher's *habitus* will be at the root of the way in which teachers conceptualize themselves in relation to others; how they enact and embody dominant social ideas as well as how they transform and adapt them. The other concept offered by Gates is ideology, which addresses the relationships between ideas, society and individuals. It relates to matters of powers and social structure, as well as ideas and activity to the wider socio-cultural context and resides in language forms used and social imagery adopted. Relating this to teachers, ideological underpinnings appear as ideas and assumptions about human nature, about learning and educational difference, the role of education, the role of the teacher and ideas about priorities for teacher professional development.

Theoretical models for accessing beliefs/conceptions

Most of the studies employed conventional qualitative and quantitative methods to access beliefs/conceptions. While many of the studies were case studies and used interviews and classroom observations, some used questionnaires and quantitative analysis. A few studies adopted specific theoretical models, in particular the Perry scheme and Ernest models, as a basis of data collection and/or data analysis as in the following examples.

In the 1980s, Perry's (1981) theory was used in framing two studies. Oprea and Stonewater (1987) explored the relationship between 13 secondary school mathematics teachers' cognitive development and their belief systems. Findings indicated that five teachers rated as relativistic, five as late multiplistic, and three as early multiplistic. The data did not support the authors' hypotheses that there is (i) A positive correlation between the teachers' Perry position and the view that mathematics is useful and (ii) A negative correlation between that position and the view that mathematics is closed. The authors resulting hypothesis is that Perry level might be different with regard to how teachers think about mathematics and its teaching. Owens (1987) reported on two case studies of preservice secondary school teachers' personal constructs of mathematics and its teaching. Perry's ideas provided a framework for the analysis of the experiential, mathematical and pedagogical perspectives through which the participants interpreted their teacher preparation program and anticipated their roles as teachers. Findings indicated that constructs related to teaching roles tended to focus on personal, non-intellectual qualities. Constructs relating to mathematics were affected by prior success with pre-college mathematics and anticipated uses of mathematics in teaching roles and were often discordant with perception of subject matter preparation at the college level.

Beginning in the 1990s, Ernest's work was used to frame many of the studies as in the following examples. Carrillo and Contreras (1994) reported a study that tested a framework for the analysis of the teachers' conceptions of mathematics and its teaching. The framework included a model for conception of mathematics teaching with four "didactic tendencies" –traditional, technological, spontaneous and investigative and six categories of 35 descriptors (many of which coincided with those in Ernest, 1991) for each tendency– methodology, subject significance, learning conception, student's role, teacher's role and assessment. The framework also had a model for conception of mathematics with three tendencies proposed by Ernest –instrumentalist, platonic, and problem solving–, and three categories of 21 descriptors for each tendency –type of knowledge, aims of mathematical knowledge and means of development of mathematics. Case studies for six inservice secondary teachers were conducted illustrating the use of this analytical tool.

Valero and Gómez (1996) explored the effects on the belief system of a university teacher who was involved in a curricular innovation centered on graphic calculators. They considered five elements of teachers' belief systems: View about mathematics, about the aims of mathematics teaching, about learning, about teaching and about role of instructional materials. They also considered Ernest's (1991) categories of teachers. During the first semester, the teacher was identified as "industrial trainer" with beliefs of mathematics as a set of unquestionable, accepted truths and that mathematics education aims at the mechanization of basic skills. In semester 2, her behaviour changed to "public educator" but her belief system still reflected "industrial trainer", i.e., the calculator influenced change in behaviour in interacting with students but not her beliefs in general.

Charalambous, Philippou and Kyriakides (2002) in their study of teachers' philosophical beliefs, adopted Ernest's (1991) model of Platonist, instrumentalist, and experimental-constructivist views of mathematics. Their goal was to collect empirical data to examine the efficiency of this model in describing primary and secondary teachers' beliefs about mathematics, the factors influencing the development of these beliefs, and their relation to teachers' beliefs and practices about teaching and learning mathematics. Findings revealed a five-factor model representing a combination of the dimensions of Ernest's model but the data failed to verify this model.

Finally, two studies focused on alternative research approaches to take context into consideration. Critiquing Likert scales, Ambrose, Philipp, Chauvot and Clement (2003) developed an alternative instrument, intended to capture qualitative data that are quantified to provide a common metric for measuring change in individuals and for comparing individuals to one another in relation to their beliefs, e.g., about mathematics, knowing and/or learning mathematics, and students learning mathematics. The instrument uses video clips and learning episodes to create contexts to which users respond in their own words rather than choose from one of several options. Findings from two administrations of the instruments with preservice elementary teachers suggest that it is an effective tool for assessing belief change. Chapman (1999) discussed a humanistic approach for researching teacher thinking, defined to include beliefs and conceptions. The approach is related to the work of Connelly and Clandinin (1990) that promotes narratives as a way of capturing and studying lived experience, e.g., the teaching of mathematics. Thus, with it, beliefs can be accessed in a situated way in the form of stories of experience. Teachers can be asked to tell stories of their choice, stories prompted by the researcher, and stories to support claims they make during interviews. Case studies of high school mathematics teachers using this approach suggested that it is effective in capturing their thinking about mathematics and its teaching from their perspective.

Aspects of teachers' beliefs/conceptions

As reflected from the sample of studies discussed in the preceding sections, investigating teachers' beliefs or conceptions about the nature of mathematics and the teaching of mathematics was a key focus of many studies. However, some of the studies focused on describing teachers' beliefs or conceptions in relation to a particular aspect of teaching and learning mathematics, e.g., problem solving, students' mathematics errors, technology, and gender differences. Of these, problem solving and technology were dealt with in multiple studies and we highlight some examples here.

Grouws, Good and Dougherty (1990) interviewed junior high teachers to determine their conceptions about problem solving and its instruction. They found four categories of conceptions of problem solving in which the teachers could be grouped: Problem solving is (i) Word problem, i.e., the mode of presentation of the problem situation was the determining factor; (ii) Solving problems, i.e. anytime students found an answer to a mathematical problem they were doing problem solving; (iii) Solving practical problems, i.e., what teachers perceived as real-life situations; and (iv) Solving thinking problems, i.e., need to incorporate *ideas* in the solution process. The first three focus on the nature of a problem and its computational aspects while the last one is primarily concerned with processes involved in finding a solution.

Chapman (1994) reported on a case study of an elementary teacher's perspective of problem solving and its teaching. Findings indicated that the teacher viewed problem solving as both a cognitive and a social endeavour. She made no distinction between problem and problem solving, i.e., the problem solving is the problem, one does not have a problem until one starts to experience and deal with a barrier in a situation one is curious about or has an interest in. She viewed teaching of problem solving in terms of a three-stage process, i.e., preparation, collaboration, and presentation, as a basis to organize her teaching.

For technology, Ponte (1990) investigated the conceptions and attitudes of secondary and middle school mathematics teachers involved in an innovative inservice program. Findings indicated that the participants had a major concern with the dynamics that the computer could bring to their classroom and some of them were also interested in using this instrument for interdisciplinary activities. Bottino and Furinghetti (1994) focused on the reaction of teachers facing curricular innovations involving the use of computers. They reported on five case studies of inservice secondary teachers' beliefs on the use of computers in teaching mathematics. Findings indicated that the teachers' beliefs on the role of computers were mainly a projection of their beliefs on mathematics teaching. If teaching of mathematics was interpreted as a transmission of knowledge, without real participation of students, the use of computers appeared of little relevance. The teachers interested in constructing knowledge found in computers answers to their needs. Beliefs on the nature of mathematics were less influential in the acceptance or refusal of computers but played a role in the choice of the type of software tools used. Kynigos and Argyris (1999) investigated two elementary teachers' practices and beliefs constructed after eight years of innovative practice involving small cooperative groups of students in a computer-based mathematics classroom. Findings focused more on practice and indicated that one teacher had confidence with mathematics and appreciation of encouraging reflection, but interventions were infrequent and often lacking in mathematics content. The other teacher expressed uneasiness with mathematics, but was very directive and mathematically explicit in her interventions. Finally, Valero and Gómez (1996), discussed in a previous section, focused on a teacher who was involved in a curricular innovation centered on graphic calculators and found that technology by itself does not promote change in beliefs but could play a role in destabilization of the teacher's beliefs.

Relationship between beliefs/conceptions and practice

Many of the studies focused on this relationship directly or indirectly. However, overall, the findings were mixed, with a few researchers offering some explanation for reported inconsistencies in the relationship. For example, Hoyles (1992), in her review of research on teacher beliefs, noted that these studies threw up evidence of inconsistencies between beliefs and beliefs-in-practice. She argued that this mismatch was thrown into relief when teachers were faced with an innovation, particularly when the innovation involved computers –a point brought home by the metaphor of the computer as window and a mirror on beliefs. Grouws et al. (1990) found that while some relationships were evident between the conception of problem solving and the reported instructional practices of their sample of junior high school teachers, other aspects of instruction were heavily influenced by external factors such as textbooks, district expectations, and standardized testing and were similar across all teacher responses. Fernandes and Vale (1994) found that their two participants revealed very similar conceptions of mathematics and problem solving as preservice middle school teachers but as beginning teachers their practices differed quite substantially. In one case mathematical problem solving was integrated in the curriculum and there was a consistency between her claimed ideas and intentions and her practice. In the other case contradictions emerged between what the participant claimed to be his ideas and intentions and what actually happened in his classrooms. The authors suggested their teacher education program, official mathematics curriculum, and pedagogic school culture as possible factors to explain their situations, however, given that both teachers encountered these factors but behaved differently leave the issue unanswered. Finally, Beswick (2004) reported on a case study of one secondary school teacher that focused on what specific teacher beliefs are relevant to teachers' classroom practice in various classroom contexts. She found that the teacher held beliefs that were consistent with the aims of the mathematics education reform movement but there were significant differences in his practice in regard to the various classes. For example, his belief in relation to older students of average ability had a significant impact on his practice in their lessons and limited the extent to which some students in this class were likely to engage in mathematical thinking.

One study that focused on explaining the basis of the inconsistencies was reported by Skott (1999) who investigated the relationship between the teacher's images of mathematics and its teaching and learning and his or her classroom practices. Based on a case study of an inservice elementary teacher, the author explained that certain moments of the teacher's decision making are characterized by the simultaneous existence of multiple motives of his/her activity. These motives may be experienced as incompatible and lead the teacher into situations with apparent conflict between beliefs and practice. Rather than examples of inconsistencies these may be conceived as situations in which the teacher's school mathematical priorities are dominated by other motives of his/her educational activity, motives that may not be immediately related to school mathematics. Thus, apparent inconsistencies may be understood as situations in which the teacher's motive of facilitating mathematical learning is dominated by other and equally legitimate motives of, for instance, ensuring the student a space in the classroom community or developing his or her self-confidence.

The preceding account of studies in this category of teachers' knowledge and practice shows that beliefs and conceptions are important to understand what teachers do and why they do it. We further reflect on this category later in the discussion section of the chapter.

TEACHERS' PRACTICES

This section addresses studies of teachers' practices in mathematics teaching. Guiding questions include: What is the nature of this practice? What are important factors that shape and support development of teacher's practices? We organize this section in terms of the following themes: Cognitive psychology studies, classroom interaction studies, socio-cultural studies, curriculum-based studies, teachers' biographical and collaborative studies, and views of practice. Studies carried out in the early years of PME conferences did not directly deal with teachers' practices, which explains their absence in this category.

Cognitive psychology studies

As could be expected in the PME community, some studies were strongly based in psychological frameworks. One of the first such studies was reported by Dougherty (1990) who investigated cognitive levels of eleven elementary teachers and their relationships with their problem solving instructional practices. The indicators of teachers' practices were classroom variables such as "amount of time spent on lesson development, types of problems selected for examples during development, teaching techniques used for problem solving instruction, teacher use and types of questioning, teacher modelling, lesson format, and so on" (p. 121). The results support the theory that cognitive structures are related to instructional practices and conceptions about mathematics and problem solving. That is, teachers at lower cognitive level used teacher-directed lessons, rigidly adhering to lesson objectives and teachers at high cognitive level valued students' opinions, encouraged creativity, and appreciated divergent thoughts and individual differences.

Within the cognitive tradition, another important line of research is information-processing. For example, Escudero and Sánchez (1999) addressed the relationship between professional knowledge and teaching practice for secondary school mathematics teachers, focusing in the teaching of similarity. Schema is a key theoretical concept and practice is (explicitly) regarded as the work that the teacher faces when performing his/her professional tasks. The authors stressed the interrelation between the structure of the lesson and the teachers' understanding of the mathematical content and point that "some characteristics of the integration of the different domains [of teachers' knowledge] are noted in decision making" (p. 311). In a later paper, Escudero and Sánchez (2002) addressed similar issues, now concerning the teaching of Thales theorem. Discussing the cases of two secondary school teachers, they concluded that PCK and subject matter knowledge were integrated in their decisions. They claimed, however, that the two teachers used different structures and that the teachers' initial decisions regarding the structures to adopt were linked to different characteristics of the domains of knowledge, which these teachers integrated in a different way.

Classroom interaction studies

Another line of interest of teachers' practices stems from the work on classroom interactions and focus on classroom discourse. A study by Khisty, McLeod and Bertilson (1990) addressed the linguistic factors involved in the acquisition of mathematical knowledge by elementary school students with limited English proficiency. The teachers' practices included the language used, the nature of the classroom discourse and the tasks proposed to students. Observing four elementary classrooms, the authors found that Spanish was seldom used to develop mathematical understanding, even by bilingual teachers. They also noted that, similarly to what usually happens in mainstream classrooms, students often work individually and in silence, and little contextualized mathematics activity took place.

In another study, Wood (1996) took mathematical argumentation as a fundamental activity in mathematics. She examined the processes of teaching when elementary school students engage in the resolution of disagreement or confusion in their mathematical thinking. The results, the author noted, "reveal the intricate ways the teacher sustains the interaction to allow children's reasoning to prevail, while restricting her own instructive contributions" (p. 427). The author also stressed the central importance that teachers play in classroom discussions, as active listeners as well as in establishing social norms in the classroom. In a later paper, Wood (1998) proposed a framework with descriptive categories that addressed the work of the elementary teacher in "reformed curricula" (teaching in ways that promote students' thinking and reasoning about mathematics), and discussed the challenges that the teachers faced in putting such perspective into practice. A set of patterns of interaction referred to the teachers' activity in interacting with students, asking questions at different levels of demand. Another dimension concerned the norms established regarding teachers' expectations for students' participation, most notable for students as listeners.

In a more recent study, based in the examples of a Year 1 lesson in Japan and a Year 7 lesson in Australia, Groves and Doig (2004) discussed the nature of "progressive discourse" and examined critical features of teacher actions that contribute to mathematics classrooms working as inquiry communities. They concluded that this is promoted when the teacher (i) Focuses on the conceptual elements of the curriculum and uses complex, challenging tasks, (ii) Orchestrates classroom interventions to allow all students to contribute towards solving the problem; and (iii) Focuses on "seeking, recognizing, and drawing attention to mathematical reasoning and justification, and using it as a basis for learning" (p. 501).

Sociocultural studies

In the 1990s, sociocultural theory, based in the work of Vygotsky, became prominent in the PME community and evolved as one of the more productive lines of work regarding teachers' practices. For example, in a theoretical paper, Adler (1996) suggested the combination of Lave and Wenger's (1991) social practice theory with sociocultural theory for a full and effective elaboration of knowing, learning and teaching mathematics in school. In another paper, Adler (1995) applied this framework to the analysis of the complexities of teaching mathematics embracing democratic ideals in multilingual classrooms, focusing on the nature of the teacher intervention. The paper considered events on a 6th grade classroom and discussed whether inquiry participative pedagogy can "turn on itself", reducing the development of mathematical knowledge. The author concluded that in some cases the teacher must withdraw as a reference point for students, enabling a participatory classroom culture, but in other cases the teacher mediation is essential to improve the substance of communication about mathematics; therefore, finding a proper balance is a continuous professional challenge.

In some papers, the notion of "scaffolding", a sociocultural construct, was used to examine teacher intervention. For example, in a theoretical paper, Anghileri (2002) characterised some classroom practices that can be identified as scaffolding, combining original classifications with further strategies that she identified. In her framework, scaffolding can be done at different levels, beginning with the creation of the physical learning environment, interacting at a low level of cognitive demand, and moving forward to more sophisticated forms of interaction such as making connections, developing representational tools, and generating conceptual discourse. This notion of scaffolding was taken up by Tanner and Jones (1999) who identified several styles of teaching metacognitive skills in a project for pupils aged 11 to 13, the two most successful being the dynamic scaffolders and the reflective scaffolders.

Also from a sociocultural perspective, Khisty (2001) conducted a study on the processes of instruction that contribute to positive student achievement in mathematics. She regarded sociocultural activity as the context in which children participate and from which they appropriate tool use and cultural thinking and studied five teachers of elementary and middle schools with Latino second language learners. The author concluded that writing mathematics is a process that can support and advance student thinking and indicated that "effective teachers" share characteristics such as: (i) Encourage mutual support among students; (ii) Formulate high expectations; (iii) Are skilful at conceptualising of mathematical situations; and (iv) Use probing questions and statements, both oral and written, as tools for learning.

Combining a sociocultural orientation with perspectives from situated cognition, post-structuralism and psychoanalysis, Mendick (2002) focused on the practices through which teachers, explicitly and implicitly, answer the students' question, "Why are we doing this?" The author presented a case study of a secondary school class in which preparing for examination, competition among students, and procedural work were prominent features. She argued that the practices in which students and teachers engage, the meanings they give to them, and the possibilities these make available for the development of their identity are critical to understand students' success and failure in mathematics. The paper draws attention to developing a sense of purpose for learning mathematics as a key issue to understand students' achievements. However, one is left with the question of how much of that sense depends on the teacher and how much is framed by the constraints of the social and educational contexts to which teacher and students belong.

Teachers' biographical and collaborative studies

Some studies of teachers' practices involve teachers researching themselves or working in collaboration with researchers. One such study is reported by Tzur (2002), a mathematics educator who taught a 3rd grade classroom for four months. He examined how useful to guide practice is a theoretical model of mathematics teaching and learning, paying special attention to the activities and its effects. He regarded teaching as a cycle of four main activities: (i) Inferring learners' conceptions; (ii) Hypothesizing a learning trajectory; (iii) Designing and engaging learners in activities; and (iv) Orienting learners' reflections and inferring their new conceptions, etc. The author concluded that this general model is useful to orient teaching and can be combined with content-specific models of students' thinking. Working collaboratively, Rota and Leikin (2002) carried out a study in the first author's 1st grade classroom, addressing her development of proficiency in orchestrating discussion in an inquiry-based learning environment. They suggested elements of a structure for leading discussions and indicate a possible evolution of teacher proficiency.

Based in the study of actual secondary teachers' practices, Jaworski (1991) developed a framework, the "teaching triad", to model the role of the teacher, taking into account the complexity of the classroom. The teaching triad encompasses: (i) Management of learning that describes the teacher's role in the constitution of the classroom learning environment by teacher and students and includes the classroom groupings, planning of tasks and activity, establishment of norms. (ii) Sensitivity to students that concerns the teachers' knowledge of students, attention to their needs and the ways in which the teacher interacts with students and guides group interactions. (iii) Mathematical challenge that refers to the challenges offered to students to engender mathematical thinking and activity and includes tasks set, questions posed and emphasis on meta-cognitive processing. Jaworski and Potari (1998), working in partnership with two secondary school mathematics teachers, used the teaching triad as an analytical device. They saw its three domains as closely interlinked and interdependent and conjectured that teaching is most effective when the three categories are most harmonious.

Curriculum-based studies

Other studies of teachers' practices are strongly based in curriculum issues. For example, some are based in a curriculum perspective that emphasizes one or more aspects regarding the aims and processes of mathematics education. One such study was reported by Askew, Brown, Rodhes, Wiliam and Johnson (1997) who studied elementary school teachers' practices in a numeracy framework. They indicated that transmission and discovery-oriented teachers may provide challenge to the higher attaining pupils but structured the mathematics curriculum differently for lower attaining pupils. In contrast, the connectionist-orientated teachers placed strong emphasis on challenging all pupils, did not see that pupils should have learnt a skill in advance of being able to apply it, and considered that the challenge of application could result in learning.

In another paper, McDonough and Clarke (2003) tried to capture main aspects of the practice of effective teachers of mathematics in the very early years of elementary school. Interviews with the teachers revealed that they had a clear vision of the mathematical experiences needed, were able to engage the students, and were prepared to probe students' thinking and understanding. The authors proposed a detailed framework to describe teachers' practices that includes mathematical focus, features of tasks, materials, tools and representations, adaptations/connections/links, organisational style and teaching approaches, learning community and classroom interaction, expectations, reflection, and assessment methods and suggested that many of the 25 teacher behaviours and characteristics in the list are applicable to other grade levels.

Some of the studies on teachers' practices are framed in current mathematics education reform efforts. For example, Manouchehri (2003) investigated mathematics teachers involved in reform mathematics curriculum to identify common traits and factors that could have influenced their positive disposition towards innovation. The findings indicated that the participants had strong confidence in their ability to control student learning and a detailed view of the type of teaching that could promote it. They also had strong philosophic views on the role of education and mathematics education, seeing teaching as moral and ethical act and seeing themselves as social change agents.

Saxe (1999) reported on a study that evaluated the extent to which upper elementary school teaching practices were aligned with reform principles, focusing on "integrated assessment", the degree to which classroom practices elicit and build upon students' thinking, and "conceptual issues", the extent to which conceptual ideas are addressed in problem solving activities involving fractions. Results showed that, in classrooms low on alignment (whether using traditional or reform curricula), students with poor understanding of fractions had little basis on which to structure mathematical goals except using whole number or procedural strategies. However, at higher levels of alignment, students' post-test scores were related to alignment and these scores increased sharply.

Finally, Boaler (2003) discussed three contrasting teaching and learning environments in reform classes. The author framed her discussion in terms of the *locus* of authority. In two cases, there was adherence to reform principles from the teachers but the classroom culture did not provide the kind of learning experiences that these principles suggest. A more productive situation was found in the third teacher's class where students had more authority than those in traditional settings. This teacher deflected her authority to the discipline of mathematics, implicitly saying, "Don't ask me –consider the authority of the discipline– the norms and activities that constitute mathematical work" (p. 8). Boaler proposed that progress in mathematics requires an interchange of human agency and "agency of the discipline", and stressed that the teacher needs to create conditions so that students engage in a "dance of agency" between these two instances.

Views of practice

In early studies of teachers' practices, practice was mostly regarded as "actions", "acts" or "behaviours". But this evolved in interesting ways over the years as suggested by the following examples. Simon and Tzur (1997) discussed practice as including what the teacher does, knows, believes and intends, adding: "we see the teacher's practice as a conglomerate that cannot be understood looking at parts from the whole (i.e., looking only at beliefs, or questioning, or mathematical knowledge, etc.)" (p. 160). Skott (1999) underlined the importance of motives in the study of teachers' practices. Saxe (1999) considered practices as "recurrent socially organized activities that permeate daily life" (p. 25). A key assumption is that there is a reflective relation between individual activities and practices, since the activities of the individual are constitutive of practices and, at the same time, practices give form and social meaning to the activities of the individual. Boaler (2003) described practices as "the recurrent activities and norms that develop in classrooms over time, in which teachers and students engage" (p. 3). Common to Boaler and Saxe is the notion of stability and recurrence of practices. However, Saxe emphasized their socially organized nature and Boaler considered not only activities but also norms.

If we regard the study of the practices of social actors in their natural contexts to be: The activities, the recurrence, the social setting and the knowledge, meanings and motives of the participants, then teachers' practices can be viewed as the activities that they regularly conduct, taking into consideration their working context, and their meanings and intentions. This includes the social structure of the context and its many layers –classroom, school, community, professional structure and educational and social system. But this can be problematic, as noted by Even and Schwarz (2002) who discussed the issue of competing interpretations of teachers' practice and its implications for research. They showed that any given theoretical framework tends to ask its own kind of questions and leads naturally to a different picture of the situation. They suggested that practice is too complex to be understood by only one perspective but pointed out that while combining several theoretical approaches may seem an appealing proposal, it may raise questions of legitimacy that must be addressed by researchers. However, they leave it as an open question to be addressed by researchers.

The preceding account of studies in this category of teachers' knowledge and practice shows the significant growth of research concerning mathematics teachers' practices, which suggests that it is the most salient aspect of research concerning the activity of the teacher in recent years. We further reflect on this category, along with the other three categories, in the next section of the paper.

DISCUSSION AND CONCLUSIONS

In this section we reflect on each category and discuss them in terms of selected issues related to five themes: Categories of studies, findings, theoretical perspectives, methodology and future directions.

Categories of studies

We found the categories that we used helpful to think about the work reported at PME conferences during these 29 years concerning the activity of mathematics teachers. However, the space in this chapter did not allow us to include all aspects of the work that has been done. The large number of studies covered a broad range of variables and constructs, sometimes in multilayered ways that cut across these categories. For example, the category of teachers' knowledge of mathematics teaching has much fewer papers than the other categories, but this does not necessarily imply a lack of interest in this notion as many papers look at it through the lenses of beliefs and conceptions, which are covered in a separate category; in addition, in the last few years, there is a trend to look at teachers' knowledge of mathematics teaching increasingly in conjunction with teachers' practices. However, we noticed very few studies that implied other inter-category relationships, in particular between teachers' mathematics knowledge and teachers' knowledge of mathematics teaching (exceptions are, e.g., Llinares & Sánchez, 1991; Simmt, Davis, Gordon & Towers, 2003; Tzur, Simon, Heinz & Kinzel, 1998). On the other hand, for the categories of teachers' beliefs and conceptions and teachers' practices, from a scarcity of studies, there was a growth of interest in these themes, asking new and more interesting questions, using more elaborated theoretical frameworks and resorting to more diversified methodologies.

We identified other categories regarding the activity of the teacher but did not discuss them separately because of space restrictions and the relatively small number of papers; they were: "teachers' attitude and affective aspects"; "teachers' researching"; "teachers in community"; "university teachers"; "teacher thinking and metacognition"; and "teacher reflection and reflective practice." We were surprised that so few papers seemed to deal with teachers' actual thinking, reflective practice and metacognitive processes, given the attention these had at some point in cognitive psychology and teacher research in general.

Findings

The papers we reviewed offer a wide range of findings that are insightful and meaningful to our understanding of the activity of the mathematics teacher. Many studies show that teachers' mathematics knowledge is generally problematic in terms of what teachers know, and how they hold this knowledge of mathematics concepts or processes, including fundamental concepts from the school mathematics curriculum. They do not always possess a deep, broad, and thorough understanding of the content they are to teach. We do not find it meaningful to provide summaries of these findings because they are based on a variety of theoretical and research perspectives and are not necessarily generalizable. The findings of teachers' knowledge of mathematics teaching also suggest problems with this knowledge. The studies of mathematics teachers' beliefs and conceptions provide evidence that these constructs can be useful to understand the reasons behind teachers' decisions and classroom behaviours, however, how they develop and operate is still an open question. Overall, the findings in the mathematics knowledge and beliefs/conceptions categories tend to be about teachers' knowledge independent of consideration for its situatedness in practice.

Findings of teachers' practices varied depending on theoretical perspectives. For example, studies framed in cognitive psychology, findings tend to emphasize relation between practice and the need for a strong domain of mathematical knowledge and, in some cases, of PCK. These studies provide important information, but vary widely on which external variables (concerning teachers' content knowledge, PCK or cognitive level) could be a key element to understand teachers' practices. For studies framed in the sociocultural perspective, some offer examples of "good practices", others present the teacher with a critical eye, and still others address tensions that underlie the teachers' activity. The most common conclusion is that teachers need further learning to carry out "better" practices, more aligned with the researchers' espoused perspectives.

Theoretical perspectives

The papers cover an interesting set of theoretical perspectives. Cognitive psychology is an important influence in many of the studies, but specific theoretical influences cited in the papers include beliefs/conceptions frameworks, constructivism, classroom interaction models, and activity theory/situated cognition/social practice theory. On the surface, this seems to suggest progress in terms of the growth of new waves of research with new theoretical perspectives/frameworks. However, the lifespan of these frameworks varies and besides interest in new ideas, there is no clear justification for abandoning 'old ideas'. The concern is that in the rush to adopt new ideas we may disregard what we had too quickly, which may not help in increasing our understanding of the problems and issues.

The framework of cognitive psychology has been challenged, in the last few years, regarding their implicit conception of the nature of the knowledge of mathematics teaching, as just a matter of individual cognitive ability, "amount" of knowledge or "level of thinking". Alternative views have developed suggesting it is rather a matter of teachers' activity in professional contexts, schools and professional cultures, and social and contextual factors. However, it is difficult to explain individual agency and individual actions just in terms of social, cultural and contextual aspects. How may we combine the social and the individual levels of analysis? Not many papers have dealt explicitly with this issue. A specific related construct that has been subjected to many criticisms is Shulman's notion of PCK. Shulman himself has become a critic of his model, which, in his view (i) Lacks emphasis in the level of action, (ii) Posits the individual as the unit of analysis and misses the role of the community of teachers, (iii) Does not consider affect, motivation or passion, and (iv) Needs a starting point broader than just content knowledge, and including students, community, curriculum, etc. (See Boaler, 2003). In fact, the notion of PCK suggests a dominant conception of teacher's knowledge as declarative, rather than action-oriented or imbedded in practice. As a consequence, many of the studies that used this notion viewed the mathematics teacher as a "deficient professional", missing "important ideas" essential for their practice.

Other aspects of theoretical influences on the studies reported are the perspectives used for mathematics, curriculum, good teaching, the teacher and practice. In the case of teachers' mathematics knowledge, although not explicitly stated, many papers seem to treat mathematics in a formalistic way and assume that the curriculum is mainly a collection of mathematics topics, concepts and procedures. However, in later studies, there was evidence of reform orientation of mathematics and curriculum being used. Also, in the case of teacher knowledge of mathematics teaching, there is a sharp contrast between the earlier and later studies regarding the curriculum orientation assumed. At first, the curriculum orientations are implicit, but with time, more and more of the studies assume a reform view about the curriculum, in many cases with explicit references to the NCTM documents and to constructivism. The papers framed in the PCK perspective espouse an implicit model of good teaching. In some cases, good teaching takes into account students thinking as modelled by research in the area; in other cases, it focuses on the very specifics of mathematics knowledge, taking into account research on cognitive processes of constructing such knowledge. Finally, in the case of teachers' practices, some studies assume a descriptive view of practice, often regarded as "what teachers do", whereas others undertake a more conceptual approach, problematizing the notion of practice and relating it to a theoretical framework. Most of these papers assume a "reform view" of curriculum, either focusing on a single main idea (such as problem solving or classrooms as inquiry communities) or on a global vision such as proposed by NCTM (1989, 1991). However, some researchers seem to take new curriculum orientations at face value, whereas others tend to problematize them, taking into account the culture and the conditions of the educational setting.

In all of the four categories of teachers' knowledge and practice, the emergent image of the teacher is that of a professional with a deficient knowledge, in particular, of mathematics and mathematics teaching. Such studies stress what the teacher does not know, does not understand or does not do. Some of these studies are still being carried out today, either framed on a reformed curriculum perspective or on a more traditional view. The expert-novice contrast used in a few studies provides a more positive image, at least for experienced teachers. However, if we look at teachers as professionals, emphasizing the notion of professional knowledge, we may signal the complexity of their knowledge and its intimate relation to their practices. We also suggest that to study teachers' professional knowledge we need to take into account the subject matter (mathematics), the participants (teacher and students), the explicit and implicit aims (curriculum, social values) and the working conditions (context, institutions).

Methodology

The papers cover an interesting set of methodologies. In all of the four categories of teachers' knowledge and practice, there was a clear emphasis on questionnaires in the early years, which later moved towards interviews and observations. Some more "intimate" methods of expression and communication also begun to appear, for example, teacher diaries and joint reflections of teachers and researchers. While many of the papers focus on either quantitative or qualitative methods, some researchers are trying to combine the two. Recently, some sophisticated collaborative studies and teacher research studies have been undertaken, combining insider and outsider views and, in some cases, with a heavy use of technology for data gathering. Other innovative ideas for meeting the challenge of studying teachers' knowledge include using concept maps (Leikin, Chazan & Yerushalmy, 2001) and therapy style "focus groups" (Vinner, 1996). Papers by Brown & Coles (1997) and Chapman (1999) also suggest the relevance of narratives in researching teachers. Even though research in this topic seems to have acquired unprecedented power, it still faces the challenge of addressing multisided social and institutional factors and relating them to actual teachers' and students' meanings and experiences.

Future directions

Research reported on mathematics teachers' activities at PME conferences has grown substantively and is likely to continue to have a significant presence in the future. However, although there has been significant progress in terms of the variety of research topics, perspectives and methodology covered in this area, we offer some ideas for consideration in shaping future directions of this work.

Most of the studies on teachers' mathematics knowledge focused on a particular mathematics fact, concept, or procedure in a way that does not give us a sense of the relationship to practice. While some authors made conjectures about the relationship between the teachers' mathematics knowledge and their ability to teach mathematics meaningfully, few addressed such conjectures. There was also no focus on looking at the knowledge of effective teachers to determine the depth of their knowledge in order to understand what this could look like and whether it reflects theory or conjectures of what is adequate knowledge for teaching. It seems, then, that future work should include a focus on understanding the knowledge the teachers hold in terms of their sense making and in relation to practice.

As we previously pointed out, many of the studies on teachers' beliefs and conceptions also tended to focus on describing the nature of these teacher characteristics as an end in itself with no real connections to other aspects of teachers' activities. This leads us to wonder about the meaningfulness of ongoing studies of teachers' mathematics knowledge and teachers' beliefs and conceptions in themselves, without relating them to other aspects of practice. While we feel that such research has passed its apogee point and is now declining, we also recognize the need for researchers who continue to work in this area to start to follow the lead of those who have shifted to combining these constructs with others related to practice in more creative ways.

Regarding teacher practice, there seems to be an increase in awareness that it is important to analyse the conditions that promote "good" practices, aligned with sound curriculum efforts, looking at the social and institutional conditions in which teachers work and paying special attention to exemplary instances of such practices already taking place. Although such awareness is clear in several authors, not many papers report on studies that do full justice to it, which suggests the need to consider the theoretical and methodological implications of such an undertaking. We need a better grasp regarding how educational, professional and institutional factors influence teachers' practices –noting that this may widely vary from country to country and system to system. For example, some studies report on a school with a particular culture (e.g., Chazan, Ben-Chaim & Gormas, 1996), but what can we say about many other kinds of schools in which teachers collaborate at different levels? What factors promote such collaborations or weaken them? Also, professional cultures and other cultural and affective factors may strongly affect the teachers' way of being in the profession and, therefore, teachers' practices. How can such factors be studied? Another issue is that in most of the studies the value of practices has been implicitly or explicitly judged by their alignment with the researchers' values or reform curriculum principles. However, what about students' learning? Is this a secondary criterion to analyse teacher's practices, or, as Saxe (1999) seems to suggest, should be a main concern?

There are several other aspects of teachers' practices that would be worthwhile to study. One is mathematics teachers' practices in higher education, a level of education where there is strong failure in mathematics, but which is possible to study fruitfully (e.g., Jaworski, 2001). There is also a need for long-term studies about teachers' practices that could help to put things in perspective, as Sztajn (2002) suggests.

Our ideas for future directions in researching the activity of the teacher imply the need for reconsidering theoretical and methodological orientations. This, then, is also something that requires future attention, in particular, the development or adaptation of innovative research designs to deal with the complex relationships among various variables, situations or circumstances that define teachers' activities.

To conclude, research of teacher knowledge and practices has made extraordinary progress in these 29 years of PME conferences. We expect this progress to continue, but with some shifts in focus that could take us to new ways or levels of understanding the mathematics teacher and the teaching of mathematics.

REFERENCES

Adler, J. (1995). Participatory inquiry pedagogy, communicative competence and mathematical knowledge in a multilingual classroom: A vignette. In L. Meira & D. Carraher (Eds.), *Proceedings of the 19th[th] PME International Conference, 3*, 208–215.

Adler, J. (1996). Lave and Wenger's social practice theory and teaching and learning school mathematics. In L. Puig & A. Gutiérrez (Eds.), *Proceedings of the 20th PME International Conference, 2*, 3–10.

Ambrose, R. C., Philipp, R., Chauvot, J., & Clement, L. (2003). A web-based survey to assess prospective elementary school teachers' beliefs about mathematics and mathematics learning: An alternative to Likert scales. In N. Pateman, B. J. Dougherty, & J. T. Zilliox (Eds.), *Proceedings of the 27th PME International Conference, 2*, 33–40.

Andelfinger, B. (1981). Provocative texts and spontaneous reactions of teachers:. A method for recognizing teaching and learning of mathematics. In Equipe de Recherche Pédagogique (Eds.), *Proceedings of the 5th PME International Conference, 1*, 381–386.

Anghileri, J. (2002). Scaffolding practices that enhance mathematics learning. In A. D. Cokburn & E. Nardi (Eds.), *Proceedings of the 26th PME International Conference, 2*, 49–56.

Askew, M., Brown, M., Rodhes, V., Wiliam, D., & Johnson, D. (1997). Effective teachers of numeracy in UK primary schools: Teachers' beliefs, practices and pupils' learning. In H. Pekhonen (Ed.), *Proceedings of the 21st PME International Conference, 2*, 25–32.

Barkai, R., Tsamir, P., Tirosh, D., & Dreyfus, T. (2002). Proving or refuting arithmetic claims: The case of elementary school teachers. In A. D. Cokburn & E. Nardi (Eds.), *Proceedings of the 26th PME International Conference, 2*, 57–64.

Beswick, K. (2004). The impact of teachers' perceptions of student characteristics on the enactment of their beliefs. In M. J. Høines & A. B. Fuglestad (Eds.), *Proceedings of the 28th PME International Conference, 2*, 111–118.

Boaler, J. (2003). Studying and capturing the complexity of practice: The case of the dance of agency. In N. Pateman, B. J. Dougherty, & J. T. Zilliox (Eds.), *Proceedings of the 27th PME International Conference, 1*, 3–16.

Bottino, R., & Furinghetti, F. (1994). Teaching mathematics and using computers: Links between teachers beliefs in two different domains. In J. P. Ponte & J. F. Matos (Eds.), *Proceedings of the 18th PME International Conference, 2*, 112–119.

Braconne, A., & Dionne, J. J. (1987). Secondary school students' and teachers' understanding of demonstration in geometry. In J. Bergeron, N. Herscovics, & C. Kieran (Eds.), *Proceedings of the 11th PME International Conference, 3*, 109–116.

Bright, G. W., Bowman, A. H., & Vacc, N. N. (1997). Teachers' frameworks for understanding children's mathematical thinking. In H. Pekhonen (Ed.), *Proceedings of the 21st PME International Conference, 2*, 105–112.

Brissiaud, R., Moreau, J. P., Perrot, G., Valentin, D., & Vaudy, J. (1982). Representation des problèmes par le maître et par l'élève a l'école elementaire. In A. Vermandel (Ed.), *Proceedings of the 6th PME International Conference, 2*, 84–90.

Brown, L., & Coles, A. (1997). The story of Sarah: Seeing the general in the particular? In H. Pekhonen (Ed.), *Proceedings of the 21st PME International Conference, 2*, 113–120.

Carpenter, T. P., & Fennema, E. (1989). Building on the knowledge of students and teachers. In G. Vergnaud, J. Rogalski, & M. Artigue (Eds.), *Proceedings of the 13th PME International Conference, 1*, 34–45.

Carrillo, J., & Contreras, L. C. (1994). The relationship between the teachers' conceptions of mathematics and of mathematics teaching: A model using categories and descriptors for their analysis. In J. P. Ponte & J. F. Matos (Eds.), *Proceedings of the 18th PME International Conference, 2*, 152–159.

Chapman, O. (1994). Teaching problem solving: A teachers' perspective. In J. P. Ponte & J. F. Matos (Eds.), *Proceedings of the 18th PME International Conference, 2*, 168–175.

Chapman, O. (1999). Researching mathematics teacher thinking. In O. Zaslavsky (Ed.), *Proceedings of the 23rd PME International Conference*, *2*, 185–192.

Chapman, O. (2004). Facilitating peer interactions in learning mathematics: Teachers' practical knowledge. In M. J. Høines & A. B. Fuglestad (Eds.), *Proceedings of the 28th PME International Conference*, *2*, 191–198.

Charalambous, C., Philippou, G., & Kyriakides, L. (2002). Towards understanding teachers' philosophical beliefs about mathematics. In A. D. Cokburn & E. Nardi (Eds.), *Proceedings of the 26th PME International Conference*, *2*, 217–224.

Chazan, D., Ben-Chaim, D., Gormas, J. (1996). Overcoming isolation in teaching. In L. Puig & A. Gutiérrez (Eds.), *Proceedings of the 20th PME International Conference*, *2*, 217–224.

Chazan, D., Larriva, C., & Sandow, D. (1999). What kind of mathematical knowledge supports teaching for "conceptual understanding"? Preservice teachers and the solving of equations. In O. Zaslavsky (Ed.), *Proceedings of the 23rd PME International Conference*, *2*, 193–200.

Connelly, F. M., & Clandinin, D. J. (1990). Stories of experience and narrative inquiry. *Educational Researcher*, *14*(5), 2–14.

Dougherty, B. J. (1990). Influences of teacher cognitive/conceptual levels on problem-solving instruction. In G. Booker, P. Cobb, & T. N. Mendicuti (Eds.), *Proceedings of the 14th PME International Conference*, *1*, 119–126.

Elbaz, F. (1983). *Teacher thinking: A study of practical knowledge*. London, UK: Croom Helm.

Ernest, P. (1991). *The philosophy of mathematics education*. London, UK: Falmer Press.

Escudero, I., & Sánchez, V. (1999). The relationship between professional knowledge and teaching practice: The case of similarity. In O. Zaslavsky (Ed.), *Proceedings of the 23rd PME International Conference*, *2*, 305–312.

Escudero, I., & Sánchez, V. (2002). Integration of domains of knowledge in mathematics teachers' practice. In A. D. Cokburn & E. Nardi (Eds.), *Proceedings of the 26th PME International Conference*, *4*, 177–185.

Even, R. (1990). The two faces of the inverse function: Prospective teachers' use of undoing. In G. Booker, P. Cobb, & T. N. Mendicuti (Eds.), *Proceedings of the 14th PME International Conference*, *1*, 37–44.

Even, R., & Markovits, Z. (1991). Teachers' pedagogical knowledge: The case of functions. In F. Furinghetti (Ed.), *Proceedings of the 15th PME International Conference*, *2*, 40–47.

Even, R., & Schwarz, B. B. (2002). Implications of competing interpretations of practice to research and theory in mathematics education. In A. D. Cokburn & E. Nardi (Eds.), *Proceedings of the 26th PME International Conference*, *2*, 337–344.

Fernandes, D., & Vale, I. (1994). Two young teachers' conceptions and practices about problem solving. In J. P. Ponte & J. F. Matos (Eds.), *Proceedings of the 18th PME International Conference*, *2*, 328–335.

Gal, H. (1998). What do they really think? What students think about the median and bisector of an angle in the triangle, what they say and what their teachers know about it. In A. Olivier & K. Newstead (Eds.), *Proceedings of the 22nd PME International Conference*, *2*, 321–328.

Gal, H., & Vinner, S. (1997). Perpendicular lines: What is the problem? Pre-service teachers lack of knowledge on how to cope with students' difficulties. In H. Pekhonen (Ed.), *Proceedings of the 21st PME International Conference*, *2*, 281–288.

Gates, P. (2001). Mathematics teacher belief systems: Exploring the social foundations. In M. van den Heuvel-Panhuizen (Ed.), *Proceedings of the 25th PME International Conference*, *3*, 17–24.

Greer, B., & Mangan, C. (1986). Choice of operations: From 10-year-olds to student teachers. In Univ. of London Institute of Education (Eds.), *Proceedings of the 10th PME International Conference*, *1*, 25–30.

Grouws D. A., Good T. A., & Dougherty, B. J. (1990). Teacher conceptions about problem solving and problem solving instruction. In G. Booker, P. Cobb, & T. N. Mendicuti (Eds.), *Proceedings of the 14th PME International Conference*, *1*, 135–142.

Groves, S., & Doig, B. (2004). Progressive discourse in mathematics classes? The task of the teacher. In M. J. Høines & A. B. Fuglestad (Eds.), *Proceedings of the 28th PME International Conference, 2*, 495–502.

Hansson, O. (2005). Preservice teachers' view on y = x + 5 and y = x² expressed through the utilization of concept maps: A study of the concept of function. In H. L. Chick & J. L. Vincent (Eds.), *Proceedings of the 29th PME International Conference, 3*, 97–104.

Harel, G., & Dubinsky, E. (1991). The development of the concept of function by preservice secondary teachers: From action conception to process conception. In F. Furinghetti (Ed.), *Proceedings of the 15th PME International Conference, 2*, 133–140.

Hershkowitz, R., & Vinner, S. (1984). Children's concepts in elementary geometry. A reflection of teacher's concepts? In B. Southwell (Eds.), *Proceedings of the 8th PME International Conference*, 63–69.

Hiebert, J. (Ed.) (1986). *Conceptual and procedural knowledge: The case of mathematics*. Hillsdale, NJ, USA: Lawrence Erlbaum.

Hiebert, J. (1988). A theory of developing competence with written mathematical symbols. *Educational Studies in Mathematics, 19*, 333–355.

Hoyles, C. (1992). Illuminations and reflections: Teachers, methodologies and mathematics. In W. Geeslin & K. Graham (Eds.), *Proceedings of the 16th PME International Conference, 3*, 263–286.

Jaworski, B. (1991). Some implications of a constructivist philosophy for the teacher of mathematics. In F. Furinghetti (Ed.), *Proceedings of the 15th PME International Conference, 2*, 213–220.

Jaworski, B. (2001). University mathematics teaching: Where is the challenge? In M. van den Heuvel-Panhuizen (Ed.), *Proceedings of the 25th PME International Conference, 3*, 193–200.

Jaworski, B., & Potari, D. (1998). Characterising mathematics teaching using the teaching triad. In A. Olivier & K. Newstead (Eds.), *Proceedings of the 22nd PME International Conference, 3*, 88–95.

Khisty, L. L. (2001). Effective teachers of second language learners in mathematics. In M. van den Heuvel-Panhuizen (Ed.), *Proceedings of the 25th PME International Conference, 3*, 225–232.

Khisty, L. L., McLeod, D., & Bertilson, K. (1990). Speaking mathematically in bilingual classrooms: An exploratory study of teacher discourse. In G. Booker, P. Cobb, & T. N. Mendicuti (Eds.), *Proceedings of the 14th PME International Conference, 3*, 105–112.

Klein, R., & Tirosh, D. (1997). Teachers' pedagogical content knowledge of multiplication and division of rational numbers. In H. Pekhonen (Ed.), *Proceedings of the 21st PME International Conference, 3*, 144–152.

Kynigos, C., & Argyris, M. (1999). Two teachers' beliefs and practices with computer based exploratory mathematics in the classroom. In O. Zaslavsky (Ed.), *Proceedings of the 23rd PME International Conference, 3*, 177–184.

Lave, J., & Wenger, E. (1991). *Situated learning: Legitimate peripheral participation*. Cambridge, UK: Cambridge University Press.

Leikin, R., Chazan, D., & Yerushalmy, M. (2001). Understanding teachers approaches to school algebra: Contributions of concept maps as part of clinical interviews. In M. van den Heuvel-Panhuizen (Ed.), *Proceedings of the 25th PME International Conference, 3*, 289–296.

Linchevsky, L., & Vinner, S. (1989). Canonical representations of fractions as cognitive obstacles in elementary teachers. In G. Vergnaud, J. Rogalski, & M. Artigue (Eds.), *Proceedings of the 13th PME International Conference, 2*, 242–249.

Llinares, S., & Sánchez, M. V. (1991). The knowledge about unity in fractions tasks of prospective elementary teachers. In F. Furinghetti (Ed.), *Proceedings of the 15th PME International Conference, 2*, 334–341.

Manouchehri, A. (2003). Factors motivating reform: Learning from teachers' stories. In N. Pateman, B. J. Dougherty, & J. T. Zilliox (Eds.), *Proceedings of the 27th PME International Conference, 3*, 221–228.

Mastorides, E., & Zachariades, T. (2004). Secondary mathematics teachers' knowledge concerning the concept of limit and continuity. In M. J. Høines & A. B. Fuglestad (Eds.), *Proceedings of the 28th PME International Conference, 4*, 481–488.

McDonough, A., & Clarke, D. (2003). Describing the practice of effective teachers of mathematics in the early years. In N. Pateman, B. J. Dougherty, & J. T. Zilliox (Eds.), *Proceedings of the 27th PME International Conference*, *3*, 261–268.

Mendick, H. (2002). 'Why are we doing this?': A case study of motivational practices in mathematics classes. In A. D. Cokburn & E. Nardi (Eds.), *Proceedings of the 26th PME International Conference*, *3*, 329–336.

National Council of Teachers of Mathematics (NCTM). (1989). *Curriculum and evaluation standards for school mathematics*. Reston, VA, USA: NCTM.

National Council of Teachers of Mathematics (NCTM). (1991). *Professional standards for teaching mathematics*. Reston, VA, USA: NCTM.

Oprea, J. M., & Stonewater, J. (1987). Mathematics teachers' belief systems and teaching styles: Influences on curriculum reform. In J. Bergeron, N. Herscovics, & C. Kieran (Eds.), *Proceedings of the 11th PME International Conference*, *1*, 156–162.

Owens, J. E. (1987). Personal constructs of mathematics and mathematics teaching. In J. Bergeron, N. Herscovics, & C. Kieran (Eds.), *Proceedings of the 11th PME International Conference*, *1*, 163–169.

Pajares, M. F. (1992). Teachers' beliefs and educational research: Cleaning up a messy construct. *Review of Educational Research*, *62*(3), 307–332.

Perry, W. G. (1981). Cognitive and ethical growth: The making of meaning. In A. Chickering (Ed.), *The modern American college* (pp. 76–116). San Francisco, CA, USA: Jossey-Bass.

Philippou, G., & Christou, C. (1994). Prospective elementary teachers' conceptual and procedural knowledge of fractions. In J. P. Ponte & J. F. Matos (Eds.), *Proceedings of the 18th PME International Conference*, *4*, 33–40.

Pinto, M., & Tall, D. (1996). Student teachers' conceptions of the rational number. In L. Puig & A. Gutiérrez (Eds.), *Proceedings of the 20th PME International Conference*, *4*, 139–146.

Ponte, J. P. (1985). Geometrical and numerical strategies in students' functional reasoning. In L. Streefland (Ed.), *Proceedings of the 9th PME International Conference*, *1*, 413–418.

Ponte, J. P. (1990). Teachers' perceived roles of the computer in mathematics education. In G. Booker, P. Cobb, & T. N. Mendicuti (Eds.), *Proceedings of the 14th PME International Conference*, *1*, 183–190.

Ponte, J. P. (1994). Mathematics teachers' professional knowledge. In J. P. Ponte & J. F. Matos (Eds.), *Proceedings of the 18th PME International Conference*, *1*, 195–210.

Presmeg, N., & Nenduradu, R. (2005). An investigation of a preservice teacher's use of representations in solving algebraic problems involving exponential relationships. In H. L. Chick & J. L. Vincent (Eds.), *Proceedings of the 29th PME International Conference*, *4*, 105–112.

Rees, R. (1982). The teacher and diagnosis: Too much Piaget? In A. Vermandel (Ed.). *Proceedings of the 6th PME International Conference*, *2*, 91–96.

Robinson, N., Even, R., & Tirosh, D. (1992). Connectedness in teaching algebra: A novice–expert contrast. In W. Geeslin & K. Graham (Eds.), *Proceedings of the 16th PME International Conference*, *2*, 258–263.

Robinson, N., Even, R., & Tirosh, D. (1994). How teachers deal with their students' conceptions of algebraic expressions as incomplete. In J. P. Ponte & J. F. Matos (Eds.), *Proceedings of the 18th PME International Conference*, *4*, 129–136.

Rossouw, L., & Smith, E. (1998). Teachers' pedagogical content knowledge of geometry. In A. Olivier & K. Newstead (Eds.), *Proceedings of the 22nd PME International Conference*, *4*, 57–63.

Rota, S., & Leikin, R. (2002). Development of mathematics teachers' proficiency in discussion orchestrations. In A. D. Cokburn & E. Nardi (Eds.), *Proceedings of the 26th PME International Conference*, *4*, 137–145.

Sánchez, V., & Llinares, S. (1992). Prospective elementary teachers pedagogical content knowledge about equivalent fractions. In W. Geeslin & K. Graham (Eds.), *Proceedings of the 16th PME International Conference*, 2, 274–275.

Saxe, G. B. (1999). Professional development, classroom practices, and students' mathematics learning: A cultural perspective. In O. Zaslavsky (Ed.), *Proceedings of the 23rd PME International Conference, 1*, 25–39.

Schön, D. A. (1983). *The reflective practitioner: How professionals think in action*. Aldershot Hants: Avebury.

Shriki, A., & David, H. (2001). How do mathematics teachers (inservice and preservice) perceive the concept of parabola? In M. van den Heuvel-Panhuizen (Ed.), *Proceedings of the 25th PME International Conference, 4*, 169–176.

Shulman, L. S. (1986). Those who understand: Knowledge growth in teaching. *Educational Researcher, 15*(2), 4–14.

Simmt, E., Davis, B., Gordon, L., & Towers, J. (2003). Teachers' mathematics: Curious obligations. In N. Pateman, B. J. Dougherty, & J. T. Zilliox (Eds.), *Proceedings of the 27th PME International Conference, 4*, 175–182.

Simon, M. A. (1990). Prospective elementary teachers' knowledge of division. In G. Booker, P. Cobb, & T. N. Mendicuti (Eds.), *Proceedings of the 14th PME International Conference, 3*, 313–320.

Simon, M. A. (1991). Initial development of prospective elementary teachers' conceptions of mathematics pedagogy. In F. Furinghetti (Ed.), *Proceedings of the 15th PME International Conference, 2*, 40–47.

Simon, M., & Tzur, R. (1997). Generalizing theoretical accounts of mathematics teachers' practices. In E. Pehkonen (Ed.), *Proceedings of the 21st PME International Conference, 4*, 160–167.

Skott, J. (1999). The multiple motives of teacher activity and the roles of the teachers school mathematical images. In O. Zaslavsky (Ed.), *Proceedings of the 23rd PME International Conference, 4*, 209–216.

Sztajn, P. (2002). Changes in mathematics teaching: Learning with an experienced elementary teacher. In A. D. Cokburn & E. Nardi (Eds.), *Proceedings of the 26th PME International Conference, 4*, 257–264.

Tanner, H., & Jones, S. (1999). Dynamic scaffolding and reflective discourse: The impact of teaching style on the development of mathematical thinking. In O. Zaslavsky (Ed.), *Proceedings of the 23rd PME International Conference, 4*, 257–264.

Thomas, M. (2003). The role of representation in teacher understanding of function. In N. Pateman, B. J. Dougherty, & J. T. Zilliox (Eds.), *Proceedings of the 27th PME International Conference, 4*, 291–298.

Thompson, A. G. (1992). Teachers' beliefs and conceptions: A synthesis of the research. In D. Grouws (Ed.), *Handbook of research in mathematics teaching and learning* (pp. 127–146). New York, USA: Macmillan.

Tirosh, D., Graeber, A., & Glover, R. (1986). Pre-service teachers' choice of operation for multiplication and division word problems. In Univ. of London Inst. of Educ. (Eds.), *Proceedings of the 10th PME International Conference, 1*, 57–62.

Tzur, R. (2002). From theory to practice: Explaining successful and unsuccessful teaching activities (case of fractions). In A. D. Cokburn & E. Nardi (Eds.), *Proceedings of the 26th PME International Conference, 4*, 297–304.

Tzur, R., Simon, M. A., Heinz, K., & Kinzel, M. (1998). Meaningfully assembling mathematical pieces: An account of a teacher in transition. In A. Olivier & K. Newstead (Eds.), *Proceedings of the 22nd PME International Conference, 4*, 145–152.

Valero, P., & Gómez, C. (1996). Precalculus and graphic calculators: The influence on teacher's beliefs. In L. Puig & A. Gutiérrez (Eds.), *Proceedings of the 20th PME International Conference, 4*, 363–370.

Van Dooren, W., Verschaffel, L., & Onghena, P. (2001). Arithmetic or algebra? Pre-service teachers' preferential strategies for solving arithmetic and algebra word problems. In M. van den Heuvel-Panhuizen (Ed.), *Proceedings of the 25th PME International Conference, 4*, 359–366.

Vinner, S. (1996). Some psychological aspects of professional lives of secondary mathematics teachers: The humiliation, the frustration, the hope. In L. Puig & A. Gutiérrez (Eds.), *Proceedings of the 20th PME International Conference*, *4*, 403–410.

Vinner, S., & Hershkowitz, R. (1980): Concept images and common cognitive paths in the development of some simple geometrical concepts. In R. Karplus (Ed.), *Proceedings of the 4th PME International Conference*, *1*, 177–184.

Wood, T. (1996). Teaching to create discussion as mathematical argumentation. In L. Puig & A. Gutiérrez (Eds.), *Proceedings of the 20th PME International Conference*, *4*, 427–434.

Wood, T. (1998). Differences in teaching for conceptual understanding of mathematics. In A. Olivier & K. Newstead (Eds.), *Proceedings of the 22nd PME International Conference*, *4*, 193–200.

Zazkis, R., & Campbell, S. (1994). Divisibility and division: Procedural attachments and conceptual understanding. In J. P. Ponte & J. F. Matos (Eds.), *Proceedings of the 18th PME International Conference*, *4*, 423–430.

AFFILIATIONS

João Pedro da Ponte
Departamento de Educação
Faculdade de Ciências
Universidade de Lisboa
Edifício C6 - Piso 1 - Campo Grande
1749-016 Lisboa (Portugal)
jponte@fc.ul.pt
http://www.educ.fc.ul.pt/docentes/jponte

Olive Chapman
University of Calgary
Faculty of Education
2500 University Drive NW
Calgary, Alberta T2N1N4 (Canada)
chapman@ucalgary.ca

AUTHORS INDEX

A. Gutiérrez, P. Boero (eds.), Handbook of Research on the Psychology of Mathematics Education: Past, Present and Future, 495–511.

TERMS INDEX

A. Gutiérrez, P. Boero (eds.), Handbook of Research on the Psychology of Mathematics Education: Past, Present and Future, 513–521.

Printed in the United Kingdom
by Lightning Source UK Ltd.
110505UKS00001B/5